"Strength In Service'
724th Ordnance
Battalion

"Voice Of Victory"
24th Signal
Battalion

24th Quartermaster
Company

24th Medical
Battalion

Division
Artillery

11th F A Field Artillery
Battalion

13th Field Artillery
Battalion

26th AAA (AW)
Battalion (SP)

52nd Field Artillery
Battalion

63rd Field Artillery
Battalion

555th Field Artillery
Battalion

COMBAT HONORS

Civil War

World War I

World War II (Europe)

Indian Wars

Pyogntaek

World War II
(Pacific)

Spanish American
War

Defense of Korea

Philippine Insurrection

Belgian
Croix de Guerre

Kuwait Lib. Medal
(Saudi Arabia)

24TH INFANTRY DIVISION

"The Victory Division"

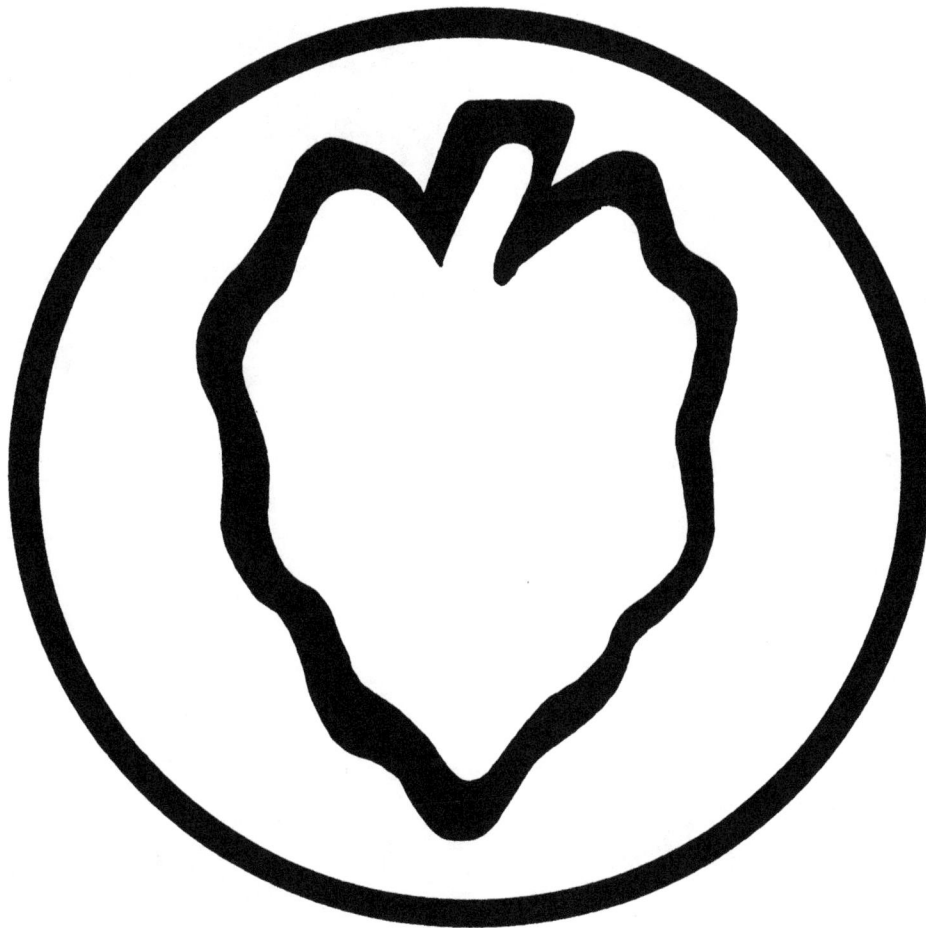

Every combat veteran has memories of the realities of battle, and there is no limit to the variations. This is one of the things that forges the special bond that others, "who were not there," can never comprehend.
Major General Aubrey S. "Red" Newman
Commander 34th Infantry Regiment 1944.

Second Edition

TURNER PUBLISHING COMPANY

Copyright © 1999 Turner Publishing Company.

Turner Publishing Company Staff:
Editor/Designer: Herbert C. Banks II

Library of Congress Card Catalog No: 99-67712

ISBN: 978-1-68162-421-1

First Edition printed
This is a Limited Edition.

LIST OF MAPS

Service Battery 13th F.A. Aritillery, 24th Infantry Division. Saga, Japan - July 1946. (Courtesy of James Danhoff)

Tank Company, 34th Motor Pool at West DMZ. 1955. (Courtesy of Robert F. Stock)

Taking a break after a long road march. 1956 (Courtesy of James C. Bell)

24th Military Police. (Courtesy of Charles Lacroix)

April 1950 at training area at the base of Mt. Fuji outside of Tokyo, Japan. (Courtesy of Joseph Drozd)

TABLE OF CONTENTS

Philippine landing. (Courtesy of Rudy Haukebo)

First rotation to Seattle, Washington late April/early May 1951 aboard the Gen. Leroy Eltgers. (Courtesy of Charley Cole)

INTRODUCTION

Many veterans of the 24th Infantry Division doubted they would ever see a history of the division completed.

The initial idea to create a history of this famed division took root more than 20 years ago in 1975 in Peoria, Illinois. Then the incumbent secretary, treasurer, editor, and historian, Kenwood Ross, embarked on the writing of the history. However, through the years more important matters and a general complacency and lack of interest always seemed to relegate the history project to the "back burner."

Having accumulated much material about the division after the end of World War II and the Korean War, Kenwood made a gallant effort to write the history himself. However, it became evident that Ken could not complete the history on his own or without help.

As late as January 1995, many were inclined to "scrap" the project altogether. Financial complications and lack of subscribers for the book increased the pessimism. The matter surfaced at a mini-reunion in Reno, Nevada, in April 1995. Spearheaded by former association president, Bob Ender, the attendees decided to take advantage of this renewed interest and present the matter to the 24th Division's Executive Board for further review. The President and the board agreed to appoint a committee to obtain proposals from publishing companies for presentation at the annual reunion in Nashville in September 1995. Turner Publishing Company of Paducah, Kentucky, was selected to research, write and publish the history.

Through the dedicated efforts of the committee members listed below and the expertise and experience of Turner Publishing Company, the book was completed two years later. The Association is deeply indebted to Bob Ender for keeping the history project alive. Special thanks also go to Ken Ross for his dedication to the project and for the voluminous amount of information he turned over to the publisher.

We, your committee, together with Turner Publishing Company are proud to be participants in relating the many battles of the 24th Division. It is our hope that these experiences will be an inspiration to our descendants to preserve the peace and the values of our country for which the "Taro Leafers" fought and many gave their lives.

24TH INFANTRY DIVISION HISTORY BOOK COMMITTEE MEMBERS

Mr. B. David Mann, Chairman
Mr. Malcolm D. Aitken
Mr. Eric Diller
Mr. Neil Estes
Dr. Charles R. Lewin
Mr. Harry J. Maihafer
Mr. William J. McKenna
Mr. Kenwood Ross
Mr. Ben H. Wahle, Jr.

안전보장 증명서

북한군 장병들에게

살랴면 지금 넘어오시오

국제련합군 쪽으로 넘어오시오. 우리는 당신을 환영하고 잘대우 하겠읍니다. 좋은 음식도 주고 치료도 하겠읍니다. 이전쟁이 끝 나면 집으로 돌아 갈것입니다. 이 아래 쓴 명문은 맥아더 장군 이 모든 국제련합군과 대한민 국국군은 북한군 포로를 잘 대우하라고 한 명령입니다.

SAFE CONDUCT PASS

ATTENTION ALL SOLDIERS OF THE UNITED NATIONS FORCES:

This certificate guarantees humane treatment to any North Korean desiring to cease fighting.   Take this man to your nearest commissioned officer. Treat him as an honorable prisoner of war.

DOUGLAS MacARTHUR.
General of the Army
Commander in Chief
United Nations Forces

(Courtesy of Ellsworth "Dutch" Nelsen)

PREFACE

Lt. Gen. Joseph E. Defrancisco

No motto has ever rung truer than that ascribed to the famed 24th Infantry Division. From its creation in Hawaii in 1941 to its latest inactivation at Fort Stewart, GA, in 1966, steadfast preparedness, total commitment and unquestionable courage have been the hallmarks of this unit and its brave soldiers. Dubbed "Taro Leafers" because of our Division's Hawaii birthplace, our soldiers were "First to Fight" by being first to record enemy casualties on the infamous 7 December 1941, when Japanese forces attacked Pearl Harbor, Schofield Barracks and other Oahu sites. Those early Taro Leafers then carried the war to Imperial Japan through the treacherous mud and jungles of New Guinea and the bloody beaches of the Philippines. Led by men of great character and courage, such as Col. Red Newman, the Division recorded win after win in tough murderous combat with entrenched Japanese forces. So successful were our operations that we earned another of our cherished nicknames—VICTORY.

Following World War II, the Victory Division settled into occupation duty in Japan. But peace was short-lived. In June 1950, North Korea, backed by Communist China and Russia, brutally attacked its weaker neighbor to the south. Just when it appeared the entire Korean peninsula would be lost to Communism, our nation called on the 24th Division. A small band of Taro Leafers under command of Lt. Col. Brad Smith rushed to Korea to become the first Americans to face the North Korean onslaught. Vastly outnumbered and outgunned, and drained by lack of sleep and inhospitable Korean summer weather, the courageous troops of Task Force Smith fought long enough to allow the deployment of other US forces thus saving the fledgling Republic of Korea. Again First to Fight, again the guarantors of Victory, the storied legend of the 24th continued to grow.

After Korea our Division distinguished itself in Europe as part of the NATO force confronting the Soviet Union and then moved to the continental United States ultimately settling at Fort Stewart, GA. In Georgia, it transitioned from a standard to a mechanized infantry division and became a rapid response force as part of the XVIII Airborne Corps. As the so-called "Iron Fist" of XVIII Airborne Corps, we became leaders in heavy force power projection. Our motto of "First to Fight" took on new meaning as we proved our ability to respond rapidly to crises anywhere in the world. We earned fame for our rapid deployment to Southwest Asia where our soldiers added to our illustrious combat history with their remarkable performance in the Gulf War against Iraq in 1991. Throughout the early 1990s our soldiers never failed to answer our country's call as we responded to a series of crises short of war in places like Somalia, Haiti and Kuwait.

I was privileged to serve in the Division twice - first as Assistant Division Commander from July 1992 to July 1993, then as Division Commander from June 1994 until inactivation in April 1996. Like every other soldier who wore the Taro Leaf, I was strengthened and inspired by the legacy of our great veterans. Their valor under fire, their willingness to sacrifice all for God, country, family and fellow soldier and their indomitable will were a constant source of strength. While assigned to the Division, I enjoyed many proud and happy moments but none were more satisfying than those I spent at Division reunions standing side by side with the brave veterans of World War II, Korea and the Gulf War.

Our Division is again on the inactive roles; our great Taro Leaf banner is folded and cased. But still, our spirit lives on in the hearts and minds of thousands of veterans and in the memories of many more who fought by our side or benefited from our exploits. Read this book with pride and remember fondly what was and what some day may be again.

First to Fight - Victory!

Joseph E. DeFrancisco
Joseph E. DeFrancisco
Lieutenant General, US Army

ORIGINS OF THE DIVISION

1812-1941

The Victory Division, which earned that name for its spearhead role in key Pacific island campaigns, also was literally the "First to Fight" in two major wars, giving rise to its descriptive motto.

The 24th Infantry Division, proud wearers of the Taro Leaf patch, can lay claim as the captor of Hollandia and the principal liberator of Leyte and Mindanao. Before those campaigns, men of the 24th Division were the first American ground troops to fire on the enemy in World War II, and less than nine years later, the division repeated the distinction in Korea.

Through 55 years of history and participation in three wars - the division fought in the Persian Gulf also - the soldiers of the Taro Leaf have compiled a superb combat and peacetime record.

As war clouds were gathering over the Pacific in the fall of 1941, the 24th Infantry Division came into existence, an assembly of elements that individually boasted a rich heritage stretching back through previous conflicts of arms. The 24th Infantry Division's distinguished ancestry gave the unit the fighting pedigree that would prove itself many times.

First the three infantry regiments: The oldest is the 21st, whose lineage dates back to the War of 1812 and the battle of Lundy's Lane near Niagara Falls on the Canadian side. On 25 July 1814, the regiment under the command of Colonel Miller was part of a force that came to the relief of a brigade commanded by General Winfield Scott, which had encountered a superior British artillery force. The 21st Infantry captured the battery in vicious fighting, then held its ground against repeated British counterattacks before and after American reinforcements arrived. The regiment's losses were 126 killed and wounded, 45 percent of the force. General Brown, who had ordered the unit forward, complimented the troops: "You have immortalized yourself," he told Colonel Miller. So they had.

The 19th Regiment traces its origins to the early days of the War between the States, May 1861. The 19th served in the western theatre of operations in the Army of the Cumberland. The regiment, in fact, was given the nickname, "Rock of Chickamauga," indicative of its prominent role in that 1863 north Georgia battle. At the end of the last day's fighting, on 20 September, only four officers and 51 enlisted men remained standing and ready for duty. The regiment at that point was under the momentary command of a second lieutenant. The unit's crest, approved in 1920, includes a rock on which appeared the strap of a second lieutenant, symbolic of the Chickamauga battle and its young commander. The three stars indicate the wars in which the regiment had participated to that time, the War Between the States, the Spanish-American War and the Philippine Insurrection. It was a 19th Regiment officer, Captain Andrew S. Rowan, who carried the famous "Message to Garcia" from President McKinley during the 1898 war with Spain. Garcia was a Cuban revolutionary.

Other campaigning by the "Chicks" took them to New Orleans to quell riots, to Kansas and Nebraska to fight Indians, to the Rio Grande for policing action, and to Vera Cruz, Mexico. The 19th Infantry was ordered to Hawaii in 1922.

The 21st Infantry is listed in some accounts as having been activated for duty in the Civil War on the same day as the 19th, 4 May 1861. Its soldiers, the "Gimlets," as they are nicknamed, first engaged in combat in the War Between the States at Cedar Mountain. The regiment fought in Cuba in the Spanish-American War, participating in the storied capture of San Juan Hill, went to the Philippines later and performed Mexican border patrol duty. The Gimlets' shield features a cedar tree to commemorate its baptism of fire at Cedar Mountain. The regiment was sent to Hawaii in 1921.

The newest regiment of the three, and the last to join the 24th Division in 1941, was the 34th. The outfit was born of World War I preparedness on 3 June 1916, about 10 months before this country entered the war. The unit, then part of the 7th Infantry Division, fought with distinction in Lorraine and was cited by the French government. The 34th Infantry, known as "The Dragons," remained in Germany for occupation duty after the Armistice. On the eve of another world war, the regiment participated in maneuvers in the Carolinas and was named the outstanding unit. On the fateful date of 7 December 1941, the 34th Infantry sailed from the continental United States for the Philippines, but because of the Japanese attack, the regiment landed in Hawaii instead and became part of the new 24th Infantry Division. The regimental motto is "Always in Front," and its crest is a wreath of its colors on a cactus.

Other components of the 24th Division have included four artillery battalions, an antiaircraft battalion, a tank battalion, an engineer battalion, a medical battalion and a special troops unit. Like the regiments, some had their own prior histories independent of the parent division.

The 11th and 13th Field Artillery Battalions were activated not long after the United States entered World War I, and both fought in France. The 11th F.A. Battalion, formed on 3 June 1917, was credited with firing the final artillery round on 11 November 1918, the day the armistice ended the fighting. Its motto is "On Time." The 13th FAB was engaged in some of the heaviest combat of the war and remained in Germany briefly as occupation troops. The 13th had an earlier life as part of Alexander Hamilton's field artillery in the Revolutionary War. Both artillery outfits were sent to Hawaii in 1920 where they first served as coast artillery until World War II began, when they became field artillery battalions.

The other two field artillery battalions, the 52nd and 63rd, came into being on 1 October 1941 simultaneously with the formation of the 24th Division. The 52nd FAB chose "Ready

Company "L", 21st Infantry, Schofield Barracks, Hawaii, November 1941.

and Able" as its motto, and the 63rd FAB, took as its motto, "Born to Battle."

The 11th Field Artillery Battalion was a 155-mm unit; the other three were 105-mm battalions.

The 26th Anti-Aircraft Artillery (Automated Weapons) Battalion (Self-Propelled) was organized on 13 October 1948 and was assigned to the 24th Infantry Division at Camp Hakata, Japan, on 20 March 1949. The outfit can trace its ancestry back to 29 March 1898 as part of the 7th Regiment of Artillery. The regiment was de-activated and re-activated many times over the years before 1948.

The 6th Tank Battalion dates to World War I, 25 April 1918 to be specific, and became part of the 24th Division in Korea on 26 August 1950 under the motto, "We Say, We Do."

The 3rd Engineer Combat Battalion was organized at Fort Totten, N.Y., on 25 March 1901, and later earned the name of "Pacific Engineers" for the many years of service in that theater and adopted the motto, "Let Us Try."

The 24th Medical Battalion was formed out of the 11th Medical Battalion on 1 October 1941, coincidentally with the birth of the 24th Division. The unit's motto is "To Care For."

The 24th Division Special Troops, organized in New Guinea in August 1944, was the umbrella unit for the various administrative and auxiliary functions required to keep an Army division operating. These units originally were as follows: Division Headquarters Company, 724th Ordnance Maintenance Company (later battalion), 24th Quartermaster Company, 24th Signal Company, 24th Military Police Platoon (later company), the Division Band, and the 24th Mechanized Cavalry Reconnaissance Troop (later reconnaissance company)

Thus the modern 24th Infantry Division comprised more than a dozen individual parts pulled together over a period of time. Two other units that were based in Hawaii before becoming part of the 24th Division for a time were the 5th Regimental Combat Team and the 555th Field Artillery Battalion.

The 5th RCT and the Triple Nickel often trained and fought together and enjoyed a close bond of comradeship.. The regiment included many native Hawaiians and Niseis, including, after World War II, some veterans of the famed 442nd Regimental Combat Team and the 100th Battalion Combat Team, which had fought with distinction in Europe. First attached to the 25th Infantry Division in Korea on 30 July 1950, these two units became part of the 24th Infantry Division late in August and fought with the Taro Leafers throughout the rest of that year and 1951 before the division returned to Japan.

The pre-World War II Army occupying the Schofield Barracks base on Hawaii's Oahu island had different contours than the combat outfits that would be formed to fight that war and in Korea. The original regiments, which had been in the islands since the early 1920s, were part of the Hawaiian Division, which was built as an organizational square. Thus the 19th and 21st Regiments formed one of the two division brigades. The other regiments brigaded together, the 27th and 35th, completed the division, which was established in February 1921 to provide land defense of the U.S. territory strategically located at the "crossroads of the Pacific." If the Hawaiian Division was the father of the 24th Infantry Division, the grandfather was the old 11th Infantry Division that fought in World War I.

The Hawaiian Division soldiers wore the Taro Leaf patch that would pass to the 24th Division as its own when that unit was established. The patch consists of the green taro leaf with a yellow border set on a red disk bordered in black. The taro leaf is symbolic of Hawaii, and the plant's root is used to make poi, a basic food in the native diet.

Thus the "Pineapple Army," the old Hawaiian Division, pulled peacetime garrison duty in the idyllic climes of the semi-tropical Pacific islands for more than 20 years. But of course the soldiers did not consider themselves residents of paradise. As in any military outfit, there was plenty to complain about. One strike against Schofield Barracks was its remote location. It was too far for convenience from Honolulu, the only place offering urban diversions the soldier could reach.

The training in the early days was not particularly rigorous. Competitive sports events within and between units were major diversions for the troops and the rivalry was intense. The 21st Infantry Gimlets were especially adept in athletics. Early in the regiment's Schofield Barracks history, a soldier named Private Eugene Riley of Company E formed the Royal Gimlet Clan with the motto "Bore, Brother, Bore," to promote interest in the sports program. The regiment's record speaks for itself: 26 boxing championships and eight individual track champions between 1922 and the outbreak of World War II.

During the summers, the soldiers left Schofield Barracks for encampments elsewhere on the island, exercises one historian indicated were comparatively relaxed.

As the 1920s gave way to the 1930s, the atmosphere in the Hawaiian territory took a turn toward the more serious. The prospect of war began to appear less remote and the identity of the potential enemy was generally recognized. It would be Japan.

The pineapple soldiers' mission – defense of the islands - required a plan with pre-determined positions to repel invaders. Joint exercises with the Navy were carried out with that purpose in mind. The maneuvers became tougher and more frequent as the decade of the '30s wore on.

On virtually the eve of war, the Army undertook some reorganization. The high brass concluded that a divisional structure of three regiments would serve the purposes of modern combat better than the square setup of two brigades of two regiments each, as in the Hawaiian Division. Accordingly, that outfit was broken up, with the 19th and 21st regiments and later the 34th Infantry making up the new 24th Infantry Division, and the 27th and 35th regiments forming the nucleus of the sister division, the 25th.

After the changeover to trimmer new lines, the Pineapple Army had only 68 days of peacetime duty remaining.

President Franklin Delano Roosevelt delivers his now-Famous "Day of Infamy" speech to a captive audience in Congress on December 8. The war against Japan and Germany, which would not end until 1945, had officially started. (Courtesy of the National Archives)

WORLD WAR II
1941-1945

Day of Infamy

The Seventh of December, 1941, is without question the most famous and infamous date in American military history. Nothing that happened that day on the Hawaiian island of Oahu – at Pearl Harbor, Hickam Field, Wheeler Field, Kaneohe Naval Base and Schofield Barracks – could be called a victory for American arms, but in defeat there was no shame for the men who did the fighting that terrible Sunday morning. Any disgrace would be saved for the higher civilian and military authorities responsible for the deplorable state of war readiness.

The attack started at 7:55 local time as waves of Japanese bombers, fighters and torpedo planes swept over the island from the north toward the main target on the south side of the island, Pearl Harbor.

The 24th Division soldiers, those who were on the post and not in Honolulu or some other place of diversion from Army life, were barely stirring at that hour or at best were in the mess hall having breakfast.

The nation being at peace, it took a few moments for the true nature of the huge flight overhead to become known, but once the Rising Sun insignia became discernible on the wings, and bullets from strafing aircraft started tearing into the buildings the reaction on the ground was swift.

The James Jones novel and movie, *From Here to Eternity*, comes to mind at this point. The work of fiction and the actual events of that morning coincided closely as Taro Leafers responded to the situation.

Soldiers broke out weapons, took positions on, in and around the stone Quadrangle buildings and began returning rifle and machine gun fire against the low-flying Zeroes and other attack aircraft. In the war against Japan, still unknown to the civilians on the mainland, the men of the 24th Infantry Division were the first Americans to fight back. It was the factual birth of a motto.

When the shooting ceased and the enemy planes were out of sight, three Taro Leaf soldiers lay dead and eight were wounded.

The division immediately moved out and set up an elaborate system of coastal defenses on the north side of Oahu. From this side of history, that action might seem to have been a mere exercise, but in the hours and days immediately following the 7 December attack, there was ample reason to believe the Japanese might attempt an amphibious landing, and if that had happened, it would have been up to the 24th Division to stop them.

Replacements from stateside feeding into the 24th Division after Pearl Harbor took immediate pride in joining an outfit that already had engaged the enemy and suffered bloodshed. As Malcolm Aitken, then a fresh second lieutenant recently called to active duty (and later a 21st Infantry officer), recalled: "After all, all they had to do was to glance around the barracks in any of the division quadrangles to see

the bomb fragments and .50 caliber bullet holes in the walls to appreciate the prestige of their new assignment."

Besides the defensive work, the division engaged in its own amphibious training, about which the American military had developed only rudimentary tactics and doctrine by 1941. Jungle warfare exercises, drills and marches also helped prepare the men of the 24th Division for the bloody battles that inevitably lay ahead.

Throughout the early stages of the war, the soldiers on Hawaii were quite aware of what was taking place elsewhere. Not far away, U.S. Naval forces scored a decisive victory the first week of June 1942 at Midway, and in August the Marines landed on Guadalcanal. Both actions were major confidence lifts for the men of the 24th Division.

At the same time, the Taro Leafers were suffering the frustration of remaining on the sidelines while other units fought. This was acutely felt late in 1942 when the sister 25th Division shipped out for Guadalcanal and again early in 1943 when the 298th Infantry, the old Hawaiian National Guard and the original Pineapple Army, was broken up into a battalion and went to Italy.

By late spring 1943, training of the division stepped up in intensity and scope. Practice in small-unit tactics gave way to battalion-size maneuvers. Meanwhile, newly arrived units took over the beach and mountain defense as the 24th Division concentrated on combat readiness.

Physical conditioning had high priority. One exercise was forced marches up and down steep slopes the men called "the separator," presumably meaning that is where the men would be separated from the boys.

In mid-summer, the training focus shifted again, away from field exercises and toward orientation and conditioning.

Finally the waiting was over. After 20

Battleship Row, from bottom: Pearl Harbor December 7, 1941, USS Nevada, USS Arizona, USS Vestal, USS Tennessee, USS West Virginia, USS Maryland, USS Oklahoma, USS Neosho, USS California and the USS Avocet. Torpedo wakes are heading for the USS West Virginia already listing to port. (Japanese photo, courtesy of National Archives)

Taken just moments into the attack, this Japanese photo shows ship locations and Japanese planes in the middle and upper right-hand corner of the photo. Hickam Field is burning in the background. (Japanese photo, courtesy of National Archives)

months of wartime duty on Oahu, it was the 24th Division's turn to ship out. In mid-August, the division boarded transports and got under way for an unknown destination. The convoy left Hawaiian waters at 25 knots. "We were on a direct course for somewhere, and hell-bent to get there," Aitken commented.

The 24th Division's destination was Australia's east coast, where the troops were reunited with their equipment arriving from the United States by separate convoy. By September, the division, under the command of Major General Frederick A. Irving, settled in at Camp Caves near the town of Rockhampton. The re-supply of the division on a foreign shore by the independent movement of men and materiel was an Army experiment that worked satisfactorily in this case.

In January, four months after arrival in the theater, the 24th Infantry Division took another step closer to the front line of action when the Army dispatched it to Goodenough Island off the eastern tip of New Guinea, the large and strategic equatorial island that played such a major role of the Pacific land war.

HOLLANDIA

On Goodenough, the Taro Leafers underwent heightened jungle and amphibious training in expectation of an operation at Hansa Bay on the northern coast of Australian New Guinea. Those plans were canceled, however, and in April, the division was alerted to prepare to move against Hollandia to the west in Dutch New Guinea.

This was a campaign of major strategic importance in the Southwest Pacific theater. The area included a plain highly suitable for air strips, and indications were strong that the Japanese, responding to reverses in the Solomons and other points east, were intent on making that region a major base of operations. The enemy already had built three airfields and were constructing a fourth. The mission was to seize the fields and deny the Hollandia area to the Japanese to enable allied forces to establish a stronghold there.

The force, designated Reckless Task Force, comprised the 24th and 41st divisions under the command of Lieutenant General Robert Eichelberger. The units were part of the Sixth Army, commanded by General Walter Krueger.

D-Day was 22 April 1944. A few days before, the troops about to engage in their first combat - at least since Pearl Harbor - sailed to the Admiralty Islands north of New Guinea. The troops thought they were being given one last day of R&R in the Admiralties, but the real reason was to trick the Japanese into thinking the destination of the invasion force was to the north. General Eichelberger attributed the lack of opposition at the beach to this feint to the Admiralties.

The 24th Division drew the assignment to land at Tanahmerah Bay while the 41st was to go ashore farther east at Humboldt Bay. Between the two divisions' landing sites along the northern coast there arose the formidable Cyclops Mountains. Behind that range lay Lake Sentani and the level ground where the airdromes were situated.

According to one account, Irving's assault plan was described by the overall theater commander, General Douglas MacArthur, as not only good but brilliant.

For one thing, the 24th's commanding general insisted - and won Eichelberger to his point of view - that the secondary landing assigned his division not be scrubbed as the Navy was advocating before the invasion.

As commanders drew up the operation, the 24th Division would go ashore at Red Beach 1 and Red Beach 2, the latter being the primary target. Irving's successful contention that his troops hit the beach at both points was later considered one of the most important tactical developments of the Hollandia campaign.

Red Beach 2 was 800 yards long, running north to south in the bay, while Red Beach 1 lay to the south. Four battalions, two each from the 19th and 21st regiments, had the job of securing Red Beach 2. A battalion of the 19th remained in division reserve while Irving assigned the remaining 21st Infantry battalion to

Col Seymour E. Madison BN CMDR; Maj. Francis E. Dice, BN EX O.; 1st Lt. Stanley Lemm S-4; 1st Lt Paul B. Ivey, S-2; Capt John D. Mayer, S-3; Capt James H. Thompson, S-1 and Hq Co C.O. going into New Guinea. 2nd BN Hq. 21st Inf.

Red Beach 1. The 34th Regiment was the task force reserve unit.

The early morning of D-Day was overcast and drizzly. Visibility was poor, which limited the support American aircraft were able to give, but the weather also worked against the Japanese whose inability to see through the mists to seaward helped the invaders achieve local surprise.

American and Australian cruisers and destroyers pounded the beach in preliminary bombardment,and the destroyers later moved in closer to hit targets of opportunity and respond with call-fire missions from the troops after they had reached shore. A single LCI off Red Beach 2 provided rocket and automatic weapons fire until troops were ashore.

The surf was heavy as the assault troops climbed down the netting from the transports to the LCVPs (landing craft, vehicles, personnel), but the men accomplished the maneuver without major trouble. The boats, manned by the 542nd Engineer Boat and Shore Regiment, moved toward shore at H-Hour, 0700. The only resistance came in the form of sporadic small-arms fire from the beach flanks and a harbor island, but the destroyers silenced those guns quickly and the landings at Tanahmerah Bay came off without U.S. casualties.

First to hit Red Beach 2 were the 3rd Battalion, 19th Infantry on the left, and the 2nd Battalion, 21st Infantry on the right. Those troops were about eight minutes late in coming ashore, but after a like adjustment was made for the succeeding waves, the remainder of the invasion proceeded on schedule.

The two assault battalions quickly established their beachhead. As per plan, the 19th Infantry's "Chicks" probed northward as the regiment's 1st Battalion came ashore in the second wave. The 21st Infantry's 3rd Battalion also landed and sent its I Company southward toward Red Beach 1 to try to link up with the invading 1st Battalion.

Lieutenant Aitken described the landing difficulty of his battalion, the 3rd, 21st, through uncharted coral reefs: "LCVPs and tracked amphibious vehicles bottomed out and overturned; those able to make it to shore faced a bottomless swamp."

The swamp caused the first 24th Division casualties. One of the lead soldiers in the assault walked into the swamp by mistake and could not extricate himself. A buddy attempted a rescue by using his rifle. The rifle discharged and killed the rescuer. Before further help arrived, the first soldier drowned.

Led by Company A, 1st Battalion, 21st, hit the shore about 20 minutes after the scheduled 0725 landing because the channel for the LVTs through the reefs was narrower than anticipated.

Contact with the Japanese was light. A patrol led by Lt. Charley Counts captured two prisoners, the division's first. The distinction of making the first kill went to Private Willie Martin who while eating K rations happened to see a Japanese soldier looking at him through the bushes. Without hesitation, the GI shot the enemy.

On Red Beach 1, Company A, after securing the beachhead, explored the maze of

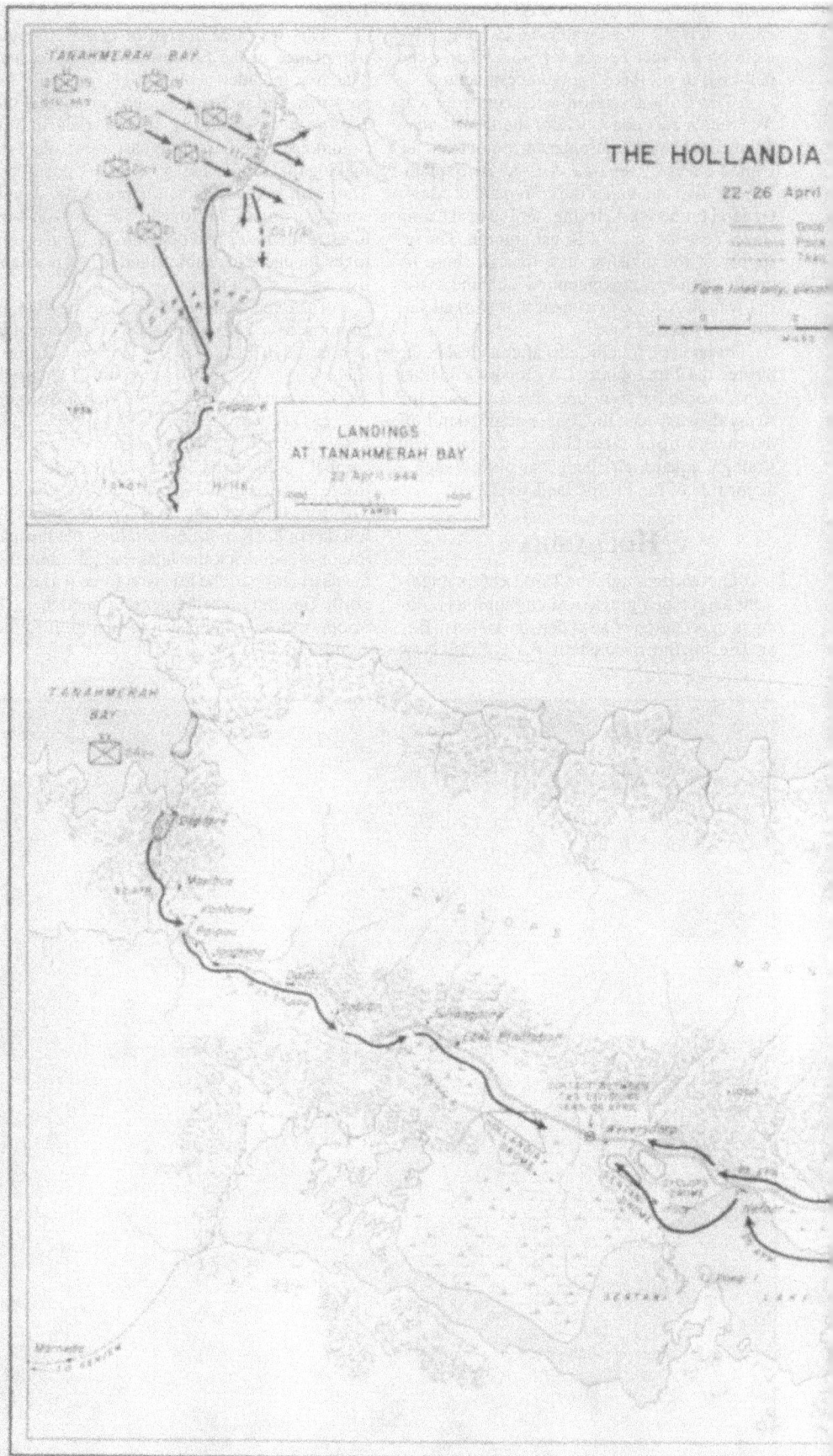

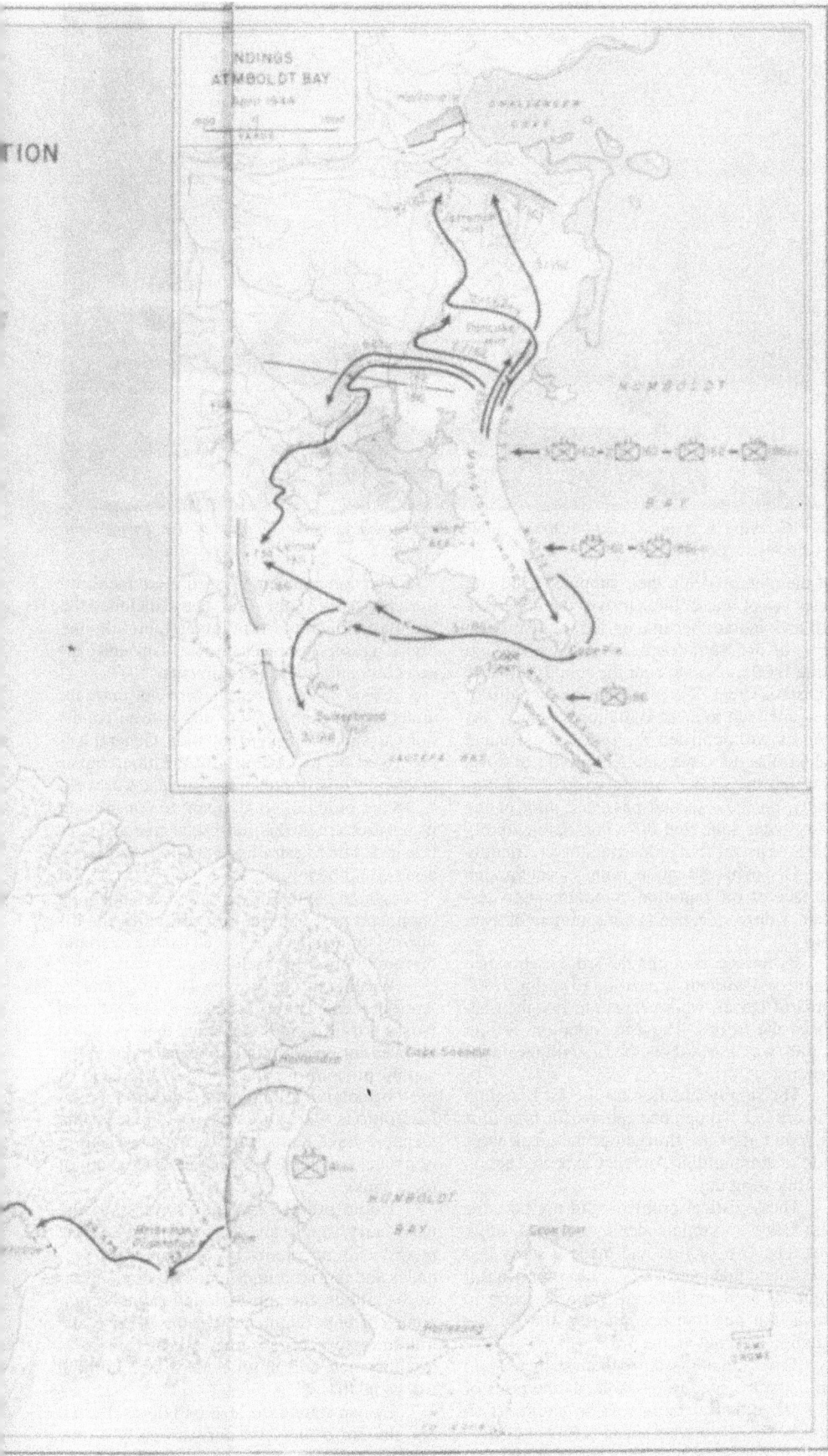

LANDINGS
ATMBOLDT BAY

roads behind the beach, checking huts and other installations left standing from the naval bombardment. The company found and killed a few Japanese stragglers.

When General Irving set up his headquarters on Red Beach 2 at 0930, he discovered that the terrain presented a much more difficult set of problems than planners had anticipated based on earlier aerial photographs.

The beach was only 30 yards deep, backed by a large swamp that was impassable except on foot. In short, the dry dispersal area was too small to accommodate the flood of equipment, supplies and troop reinforcements the invaders expected to arrive throughout that day and those that were to follow. The terrain defied the best efforts of engineers to improve the situation, but they tried. The attempt to hack a road to connect with Red Beach 1 had to be given up, but the effort did create enough space for some 105-mm howitzers.

Nevertheless by the end of D-Day, work crews had completed the unloading of LSTs and Navy cargo ships, jamming the limited space available on Red Beach 2.

It was at this point that the wisdom of Irving's insistence on keeping Red Beach 1 in the landing plans became apparent. As it happened, that area at the south end of Depapre Bay, a smaller inlet in Tanahmerah Bay, provided a larger dry dispersal area. The problem was getting to it. From seaward, the narrow reef opening restricted access and no road had been opened between the two beachheads. The solution was to ferry men and supplies along the shore by shallow-draft boats until Navy demolition men blasted a larger opening through the reef.

The limitations of the Tanahmerah Bay landing beaches caused the Reckless Task Force commander to shift the emphasis from that location to the 41st Division's sector at Humboldt Bay to the east where the terrain lent itself more to the big buildup of supplies necessary to sustain the operation.

Nevertheless, the 24th Division men had been ashore barely an hour before a force started up the Depapre-Lake Sentani trail from Red Beach 1 toward the objective.

The 1st Battalion, 21st Infantry under the command of Lieutenant Colonel Thomas E. Clifford, Jr., was the spearhead outfit for that drive toward the airfields, an operation that would earn the description as a model for a well-coordinated jungle operation.

Clifford left Company A, which had been the first unit ashore, on the beach and headed out with the rest of the battalion over a winding, narrow trail that for the first two to three miles would have presented the Japanese an enormous opportunity to attack, if they had been in position.

All along the trail, the rapid abandonment of positions by the Japanese was evident. Resistance confined itself mostly to light and isolated rifle fire. The vanguard battalion pushed forward through Mariboe, Kantome, and, by nightfall, to Jangkena. The latter location was on flat ground, which provided the Japanese an opportunity to flank the 1st Battalion, so Clifford ordered a withdrawal back to the more defensible Kantome. That turned out to be a good decision, because a small Japanese force did attack that night, but was unable to penetrate the unit's perimeter. The greatest cost was to the GIs' sleep.

The next day, the force moved forward through Dazai, an intermediate objective, and on to the village of Sabron, about 12 miles by trail from the starting point at Depapre.

At 1445, the 1st Battalion, 21st Infantry, encountered the first organized opposition in the Hollandia campaign. Two platoons of Company B had crossed a small stream when they came under sharp rifle and machine-gun fire from a well-hidden Japanese ambush. The two forward platoons withdrew, leaving behind four dead, and Clifford called for air support. Planes from Task Force 58 offshore quickly responded. The battalion's own 81-mm mortars and heavy machine guns also poured fire into the enemy positions, and Clifford tried flanking maneuvers. None of those tactics succeeded in silencing the Japanese or driving them off, and a firefight raged until near dark.

The first 21st Regiment man to fall in the battle was Sgt. Distassi. Thereafter, the nearby creek would be known as Distassi Creek by the American troops.

Clifford pulled his men back to Sabron for the night to give his own ordnance, including 105-mm howitzers of the 52nd Field Artillery Battalion, freedom to saturate the area through the night.

The Japanese responded with their own heavy weapons, including a 90 -mm piece that dropped rounds into the American lines until dawn. The 1st Battalion experienced its second sleepless night.

Back at the beachheads, it did not take senior officers long on D-Day to determine that no Japanese resistance could be expected there, so the decision was made to start moving the entire 21st Infantry to Red Beach 1 and then up the trail toward the lake behind the vanguard companies.

Clifford, whose radio communications with the regimental command post were intermittent at best in the early hours, learned of this maneuver late in the afternoon of 22 April, about 24 hours before the engagement at the creek crossing.

The 3rd Battalion under Lieutenant Colonel Chester A. Dahlen (pronounced DAY-len), originally assigned to the right flank of Red Beach 2, made the first move to Red Beach 1. Except for I Company, which labored overland through rugged terrain and dense vegetation, the movement was by boat along the coast. The next day, the 2nd Battalion followed to Depapre, where the regimental commander, Colonel Charles B. Lyman, set up his headquarters. Thus the 21st Infantry was positioned in full strength to push on toward the airfields, while the 19th Infantry remained to hold Red Beach 2.

The 3rd Battalion, which had moved out in the daylight of D-Day, continued forward even after darkness fell to enable the unit to close up behind the 1st Battalion as much as possible.

The going for the infantrymen was tortuous. The drizzle of D-Day became a downpour on 23 April. The trail was not wide enough for tanks and trucks, and landslides threatened to

Major General F.A. Irving, C.G. 24th Divsion August 1942-November 1944. (Courtesy of Gen. Irving's son, Col. Frederick F. Irving)

cut the men off from their supplies. Mud and water swept one bulldozer over the edge of a cliff and another became buried in the mire.

The 3rd Battalion 21st was close enough to the 1st Battalion to hear the sounds of battle at Distassi Creek. The Navy air support Clifford had called led to a 3rd Battalion casualty. "As soon as we identified the two 'cats (Hellcat fighters) as ours, we crawled out of our holes to watch the show," Aitken wrote. "Unfortunately, on their second pass, the pilot of the lead fighter squeezed off a burst prematurely and gave us our first indoctrination in 'friendly fire.' One of his .50 calibre rounds went through the face of the battalion communication sergeant, side to side, taking out a number of teeth with it."

By the second night, the 3rd Battalion had progressed without opposition to within 1,000 yards of Dazai, where Japanese fire then harassed the troops. The 2nd Battalion, farther behind, was at Mariboe, the first village out of Depapre.

The supply situation for the 1st Battalion was critical. Troops had rations for breakfast only, and after the firefight at the creek were short of ammunition. And they expected action the following day.

The logistical problems did not take the 24th Division commander by surprise, however. The G-4 section had made a study and determined that hand-carry could supply a full regiment well up the trail, from Depapre to Dazai, the position occupied by the middle battalion in echelon, the 3rd.

That estimate assumed that weather would not make the road impassable, as the rains of 23 April did. But there was no choice. Two weeks of hard work lay ahead before engineers could improve the trail even to the extent that Jeeps could move over it. So the 2nd and 3rd battalions carried extra supplies to be passed forward to the advance element. It was not enough.

The commanders pressed more men into the hand-carry supply line. These included the 2nd Battalion of the 19th Infantry, initially the division reserve unit, and the anti-tank and cannon companies of both regiments.

Those resources still were not enough, under the terrible weather and natural conditions, to supply the point battalion. General Irving asked for an airdrop. But the cloud cover and heavy rain limited those prospects as well, so Irving ordered the regiment to consolidate its positions in the Sabron-Dazai area and confine its action to patrolling until the supply situation could be improved.

Lyman having moved up to establish his command post with the forward units, the division commander was forced to slog overland on foot in order to reach him.

Weather throughout the days of 24 and 25 April prevented airdrops, made the muddy and twisting trail more treacherous than ever and allowed for only minimal improvement in the supply problem for the troops at the head of the long column. Ammunition was still low and half-rations were threatened. In places, the Depapre-Lake Sentani trail was knee-deep in rainwater and some of the streams were out of their banks.

Irving pressed still more men into the hand-carry supply chain. Those muscling the boxes of ammo, rations, medical supplies, grenades and mortar rounds included three infantry battalions, the anti-tank and cannon companies of both regiments, various service and headquarters personnel, quartermasters, artillerymen and engineers, 3,500 combat troops in all.

Lyman started his lead battalions, the 1st and the 3rd of the 21st, forward early on the overcast and threatening morning of 25 April. The first objective was wooded hills on either side of the trail about 3,000 yards beyond Sabron. The regimental commander's strategy was to advance on a broad front to prevent Japanese from outflanking his unit and disrupting the supply lines to the rear. But the denseness of the jungle off the trail made that impossible, so the colonel had to settle for driving the main body down the trail in a column and using small patrols to probe outward. Opposition was confined to light small arms fire until the force encountered a small enemy position at a crossing of the next natural barrier, a branch of the Dejaoe River, which the GIs reached about noon.

The Americans flanked the enemy and crossed the stream by mid-afternoon. Next the Gimlets received automatic weapons fire from high ground in the area of Julianadorf east of the river, but mortar fire neutralized that position, and the advance resumed.

Japanese patrols continued to punch at the column. American patrols moved out to counter the enemy, but the process delayed the forward movement for the rest of that day.

The two forward battalions had moved beyond the range of the artillery batteries on

Bulldozer disembarks to lend needed troop support in Hollandia invasion. (Courtesy of J.H. Miller)

Troops use precious available time to attend religious service in Hollandia.

the beach, so Lyman asked for mortars to be transferred inland. The condition of the trail allowed the movement of a single 4.2-inch mortar, and it had top priority. At the same time, a single 105-mm howitzer of Battery A, 52nd Field Artillery Battalion, started over the trail also. But neither piece made it to a position where it could help the infantrymen. The men of Battery C, 11th Field Artillery Battalion, unable to perform their usual gunnery duties, volunteered for the supply chain. Such was the spirit in the 24th Division in those difficult days.

Despite the uncertainty of adequate supply or the strength of Japanese opposition ahead, Irving took the risk of ordering the lead battalions to continue to advance toward the airfields near Hollandia on the 26th.

The troops were on the move by 0830, again encountering only scattered and ineffective opposition, with some exceptions. A patrol from Company G sweeping the jungle ran into a force of about 20 Japanese, and a furious fight ensued. Company L of the 3rd Battalion veered 600 yards off the main trail to drive the Japanese from the Ebeli sawmill. Those troops penetrated to the village of Jenslip where natives greeted them. They were the first white men seen there since the Dutch were driven out in 1942.

The main body of men, meanwhile, continued their push eastward. By noon, they were atop high ground within sight of the airfields and minutes later advance units were at the outer limits of the Hollandia Drome, the westernmost of the air strips on the Lake Sentani plain.

Lyman ordered Clifford's 1st Battalion, which had been on the point throughout the arduous trek from Red Beach 1, to clear out a Japanese encampment north of the Hollandia Drome, while Dahlen's 3rd Battalion drove directly for the airfield itself.

K Company, under command of Captain Tom Suber, took the lead. When the force reached a large level and grassy area, Aitken and Lieutenant Dale Johnson, leader of the point platoon, concluded from the study of maps and terrain features that the unit had reached its objective.

"We reported our findings to Captain Suber and through him to Lieutenant Colonel Dahlen and on to the regimental commander, Colonel Lyman.... He was plainly skeptical but thanked us courteously and dismissed us while he conferred with his staff," Aitken wrote. Lyman ordered his unit to press on to the Hollandia Drome.

However, the 1st Battalion, according to Aitken, could see from a higher vantage point an amazing sight. "Literally hundreds of Japanese planes and vehicles, wrecked, burned, and blown apart (thanks to the U.S. Navy) stretched for miles."

The leading elements of K Company were soon in what Aitken called "a veritable junkyard." The Gimlets had reached their objective. "There could be no question now about our position. And we congratulated each other as we realized that we were the first GIs to set foot on Hollandia Drome since the Japanese occupation two years earlier," he recalled.

Resistance was not appreciable, and by mid-afternoon, the entire Hollandia Drome area had been secured. The 2nd Battalion reached the drome by dark.

General Irving sent his congratulations to the regimental commander, Colonel Lyman, for the successful completion of the mission in five days despite the most adverse weather, terrain and logistics, not to mention the enemy. Though resistance generally was described as light, sporadic and scattered, those are relative terms. The Taro Leafers still suffered 52 casualties in reaching and taking the Hollandia airfields.

Many of the men distinguished themselves in different ways. For instance, Lieutenant Bill Langford, of Valdosta, GA, led his weapons platoon to knock out a Japanese armored vehicle and three machine gun nests. As the American column neared its objective at Hollandia, Private Leo Burkard suffered wounds on two occasions during a Company G encounter. Knocked into a ravine, he urged his fellow GIs to leave him rather than risk a rescue. They ignored their buddy's request and pulled him to safety.

For Lyman, it was a fitting climax as a regimental combat commander. After more than 31 years of active Army service, he was promoted to brigadier general.

With the completion of the mission came improvements in the logistics. An airdrop finally put supplies on the ground and motor transport became available at both ends of the trail. Engineers had succeeded in making the road passable from Depapre eastward for a distance, and 21st Regiment soldiers had captured Japanese trucks at the airfields and driven them as far west as Julianadorf to pick up supplies.

Patrols from the 21st Regiment moved on to a point between the village of Weaversdorp and the eastern end of the airdrome and there linked up with elements of the 41st Division coming west from Humboldt Bay.

The tactical victory for Reckless Task Force in and around Hollandia and the airstrips did not end the operation. The drive inland from the two bays had bypassed many Japanese. Some estimates put the figure at 60,000, and now the dangerous and tedious work of mopping up was in order to cut off escape routes, find large organized enemy units and destroy or capture as much equipment and supplies as possible.

A reinforced company of the 21st Regiment was sent to Marmeda, about five miles southwest of Lake Sentani, to set up a patrol base. Another company held a position at Iris Bay, northwest of Tanahmerah Bay. Patrols from the 19th Infantry probed overland to the coast north of the Cyclops Mountains in order to secure the trails running through the mountains to the airfields and the Depapre-Lake Sentani road. Other units of the 19th Regiment moved by boat to Denta Bay, west of the invasion beaches of Tanahmerah Bay, and established an outpost. Some 24th Division troops scoured the area on the western end of Lake Sentani to Genjem where there ran a major trail over which many Japanese tried to escape the Hollandia area to the west. Company B of the 21st Infantry patrolled the western and southern shores of the big lake.

A 19th Regiment soldier, Private John I. Lowgren, of Torrance, CA, recalls the disease and privations as the principal experience of the New Guinea campaign. His K Company worked the Genjem area.

"We managed to catch some, if not all, of the standard tropical diseases, such as malaria, jungle rot, dengue fever, ringworm, dysentery, etc. When we came out we were in such poor shape that we were not supposed to go on sick call unless our fever was at least 102 degrees," Lowgren wrote.

His company, which went unsupplied for a period of time, was considered "lost", according to the soldier. "We were not at the bug-eating stage yet but were getting there when we spotted a C-46 coming in over the mountain," Lowgren said. "I could read the name of the plane, and it was the 'Wabash Cannon Ball.' It is forever burned into my memory, so I guess I really was hungry."

Lowgren told of a battalion or regimental supply officer who falsified signatures on requisitions in order to obtain the supplies the men needed.

The mop-up work succeeded in eliminating all but a few enemy stragglers by 6 June, the date Reckless Task Force relinquished control over supply and construction in the Hollandia area.

2nd Platoon, Machine Gun "H" Company, 19th Infantry. 1944. (Courtesy of Frank Fantino)

Bringing Japanse prisoners into the compound inland New Guinea. (Courtesy of Rudy Haukebo)

The logistical problems afflicting the ground combat units, incidentally, did not end when the main military objectives were reached on 26 April. The condition of the main trail inland, the limitations of the invasion beaches at Tanahmerah Bay and a disastrous fire at Humboldt Bay shortly after the 41st Division landing all contributed to a continuing supply shortage throughout the operation.

The 34th Regiment of the 24th Division, the task force reserve unit, had shifted positions from Tanahmerah Bay to Humboldt Bay on 24 April and therefore was available to help provide badly needed manpower on White Beach 3 when LSTs beached for off-loading of supplies.

One group of 34th Infantry soldiers participated in the rescue of 120 European nuns and priests, most of whom were German-speaking and had been badly treated by the Japanese. Some were so weak they had to be carried out of a knee-deep bog on stretchers. Fed GI rations, the nuns considered a delicacy what most infantrymen merely tolerated. One member of H Company, the heavy-weapons unit, Eric Diller, was a native of Germany and made good use of his native tongue in communicating with the nuns.

The fighting in and around Hollandia continued to be nasty and dangerous. The Japanese lost about 3,300 killed in the campaign, most of them after 26 April. In fact, 800 of the enemy were killed during the week ending 6 June. U.S. Army casualties in the fight for Hollandia were 124 killed, 1,057 wounded and 28 missing.

Even after 6 June, the 24th Infantry Division continued patrolling in the area until relieved by other units.

The seizing of the Hollandia airfields was a significant victory in which the 24th Division particularly distinguished itself. The American military, as the top brass had anticipated, was able to convert Hollandia to a major air, naval and logistical base for further operations in western New Guinea and for the liberation of the Philippines.

BIAK

As the Hollandia operation was winding down, American military planners were looking toward other objectives north of New Guinea. One of these was Biak, one of the Schouten Islands situated at the mouth of the huge Geelvink Bay off New Guinea's northern coast. This is where the big island narrows down to resemble the head and neck of a bird.

As at Hollandia, the main target was airfields, three of which had been built by the Japanese on Biak's southern coast with room for two more. From east to west, the dromes were Mokmer, Borokoe and Sorido.

The code name for the force that would take Biak was Hurricane Task Force. Getting the leading assignments were the 162nd and 186th regiments of the 41st Infantry Division, fresh from Hollandia. Those troops invaded Biak on 27 May 1944.

The 34th Regiment of the 24th Division, which had been in task force reserve at Hollandia and had gone in on the 41st Division's side of that two-pronged operation, once again was attached to the 41st for the new operation.

Three weeks after the initial landings, hard fighting continued, and the island remained far from secure. So commanders ordered the 34th Infantry to move from Hollandia to Biak to join Hurricane Task Force. The regiment's arrival, 18 June, coincided with Lieutenant General Robert Eichelberger's order for a one-day stand-down for reorganization and redisposition. The general had cancelled the attack plans of Brigadier General Jens Doe, 41st Division commander, and prepared for a coordinated attack on 19 June by the 162nd and 186th regiments against Japanese occupying the terrain from which they could fire on Mokmer Drome.

The 34th Infantry's assignment called for taking positions west of Mokmer that the 186th Infantry had vacated in order to lead the assault. The 34th Regiment was to be ready to seize the westernmost airfields, Borokoe and Sorido.

The next day, 20 June, the 34th Regiment did in fact occupy those airfields as well as the village of Sorido virtually without opposition. Company I then set up a roadblock north of that town to prevent the movement of enemy reinforcements, and the rest of the regiment established outposts on the road to Sorido and various trails along the southeast coast of Biak.

Six days later, the two regiments of the 41st Division plus the 34th Infantry launched another coordinated effort to clean out the enemy west of Mokmer Airdrome. The 2nd and 3rd battalions of the 34th Regiment were to secure the area west of the Borokoe field while the 1st Battalion of the regiment helped the 186th Infantry clear high ground in an area north of Hill 320.

GIs accomplished the latter objective on 26 June, but the 1st Battalion's Company C, having taken a separate route from the rest of the battalion, ran into a Japanese ambush and was forced to fall back to the south. The company rejoined the battalion the next day.

Based on reports from 1st Battalion patrols, headquarters concluded the Japanese might be preparing either for a fierce defensive stand or one of their patented suicidal counterattacks in the area of some sharp cliffs northwest of the battalion's position.

Consequently, General Doe ordered the 1st and 2nd battalions, 34th Infantry, to approach the cliffs from two directions and clear the enemy. On 28 June, the 2nd Battalion

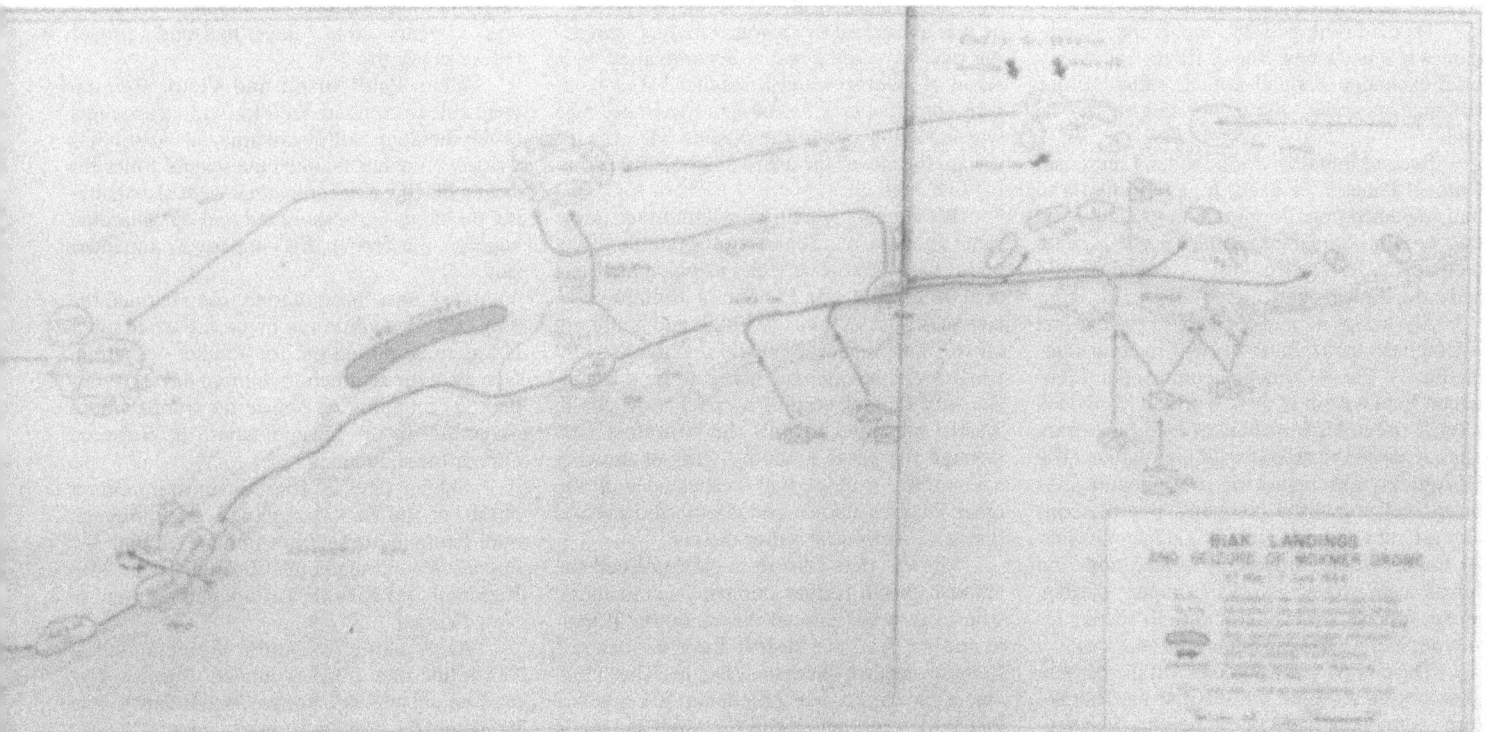

BIAK LANDINGS
AND SEIZURE OF MOKMER DROME

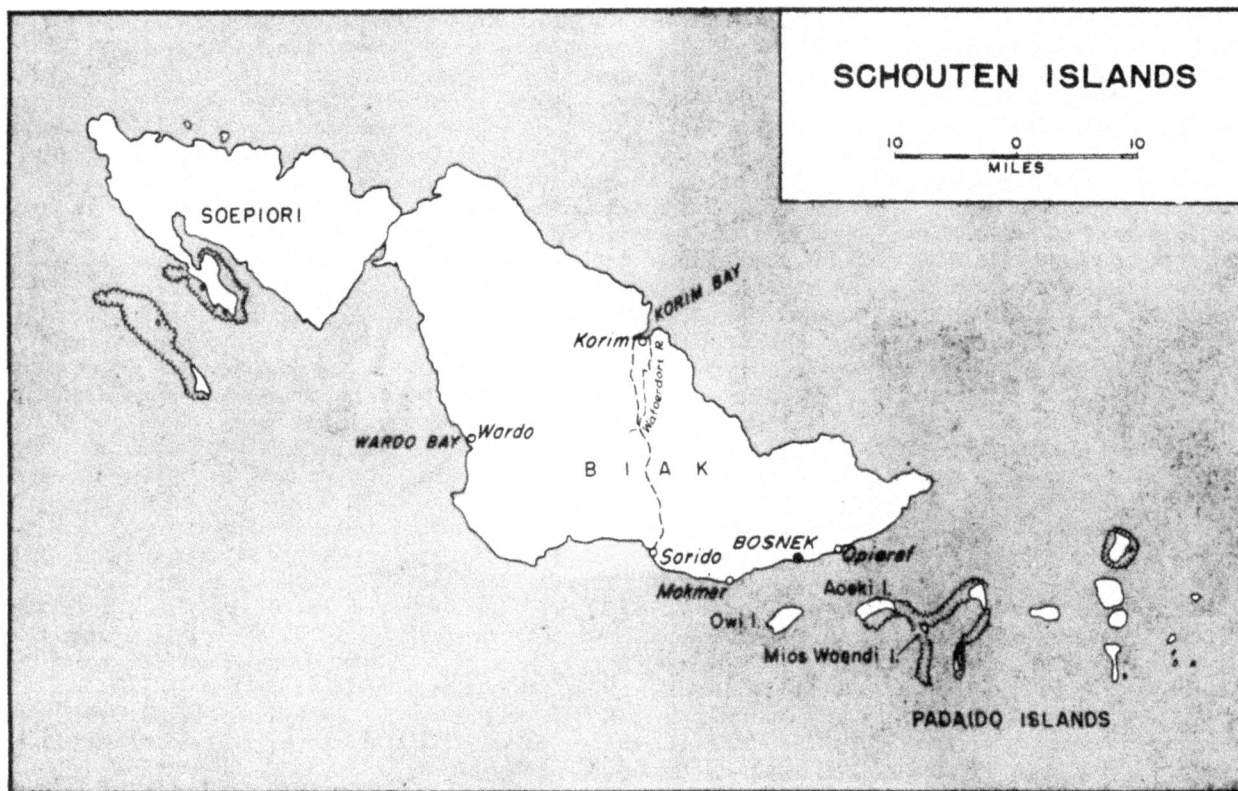

SCHOUTEN ISLANDS

10   0   10
MILES

mopped up the flatlands south of the bluffs with little opposition, but A Company, 1st Battalion, ran into trouble in an area between the two battalions' positions. Japanese trying to break out of the American trap attacked the company and forced it back to the battalion command post area.

The general northward advance since 23 June had been slow because of the terrain and also the necessity to coordinate movements with the front line of the 41st Division.

On the evening of 28 June, E and F Companies reached a new line of ridges and after a brief exchange of small-arms fire that left one rifleman wounded, the troops dug in for the night.

Second Battalion commander, Lieutenant Colonel James F. Pearsall, Jr., a Floridian who had graduated from West Point in 1937, ordered the two rifle companies to attack northeastward along the base of a cliff until E Company could seize the high ground.

The troops moved out at 0700 29 June and E Company came under heavy fire almost immediately. The F Company commander, Lieutenant Paul Austin of Fort Worth, TX, noticed a small rise to his front and ordered Lieutenant Alex Kramich to take it with his platoon. The GIs quickly eliminated the two machine guns on the hill. Next the company, two platoons abreast, moved up the side of a ridge to its left. At the crest, the Americans looked down on Japanese in bivouac. Every F Company weapon present opened up in a ferocious 30-second fusillade, wiping out the enemy force.

The company was ordered off the ridge to allow for an all-night artillery barrage, but before all the men had left the heights, Lieuten-ant Kramich sent a squad to reconnoiter the left flank. Enemy soldiers rose up out of spider holes and shot down the entire squad from close range.

Lieutenant Austin received that bad news when he joined Kramich and eight of his riflemen half-way up the side of the ridge at dusk. The platoon leader was certain seven of his men were dead along the ridge, which made withdrawal by the 10 men the only logical decision. But Austin hesitated. As he has written, he was overtaken by "a warm feeling, spreading over my entire being, accompanied by a sense of calmness and assurance." The company commander had to be sure a wounded man was not lying out in the bushes. He crawled toward the site of the ambush alone, first coming to a dead GI.

Lieutenant Austin crawled farther in the same direction and found another soldier lying on his back. To the officer's astonishment, the man blinked. It was Pfc Victor Reinick, who had been shot in the right thigh and could not move. With Japanese positions only 20 to 30 yards away, rescue was going to be difficult. But with Reinick helping as much as he could, Austin managed to pull the wounded man through the grass to safety without drawing enemy fire. Reinick was evacuated with the other Biak casualties and Austin did not see him until many years after the war.

It was then that Reinick described the ambush to his former company commander, who in turn has quoted the account: "It happened so fast, we didn't have a chance," Reinick recalled. "Sergeant (Duglo) Kinski fell, one of the medics was killed, and five others." Two bullets tore into Reinick's thigh, but while on the ground he was able to fire several bursts from his automatic rifle at the nearby enemy, allowing two or three fellow GIs to pull back.

When all was quiet, Reinick went on, Japanese soldiers looted and bayoneted the bodies, but before they could get to him, a mortar barrage drove them back.

The wounded soldier knew he would die if the Japanese came back, so he cried out to God in his mind: "Oh, God, send someone to save me." He recalled the moment. "There I was, 27 years old and never had said a prayer before in my life."

When Paul Austin and Victor Reinick were able to compare their individual accounts of the incident, both were amazed, Austin has written. "Vic has thanked me several times for saving his life. I sincerely hope he is also thanking the other party involved and our guardian angels," the former F Company commander said.

Task force headquarters soon learned the 34th Infantry would not be on the scene long. It was to be pulled out for another operation. Doe gave the regiment two more days to complete its mopping up before the troops would assemble on the beaches south of Borokoe Drome for sea transport.

On that date, 30 June, the most important phases of the Biak campaign were complete, with the major objectives in hand, though the operation continued until 20 August. The 34th Regiment left Biak on 15 July and returned to New Guinea.

Army battle casualties were counted at 435 killed and 2,360 wounded. Specific figures are not available for the 34th Infantry. One listing put the 41st Division's losses at 325 dead

20

and 1,700 wounded, from which it could be surmised that the 34th Regiment, as the other major combat unit present during most of the fighting, had suffered about 100 dead and 300 wounded. Perhaps typical of jungle warfare, non-combat casualties, which included illness, exceeded the battle numbers. On Biak, these were put at more than 7,000, though most recovered.

Diller, the heavy weapons GI who had helped with the nuns at Hollandia, described his introduction to the stark realities of war as he moved forward as part of a relief column on Biak: "I quickly came to realize that the enemy was shooting to kill. I saw men in bloody bandages ... . Others were carried on stretchers by four men struggling through ankle-deep, muddy terrain. As we got closer to the sound of gunfire, I noticed two covered bodies with the GI boots sticking out from under a poncho."

The operation for which the 34th Infantry had received an alert was on the nearby island of Noemfoor, but the regiment did not go in. The next action would be in the Philippines.

LEYTE

Landing and Consolidation

Liberation of the Philippine Islands, which the United States lost to the Japanese in the spring of 1942 after the heroic stands at Bataan and Corregidor, was a prime American military objective in the Pacific war and virtually an obsession with the Southwest Pacific Theater commander, General Douglas MacArthur.

Any military outfit selected to play a leading part in such a campaign knew then or later it was at center stage of the biggest show around. Though troops of the 24th Infantry Division at the time may not have appreciated fully the significance of the moment, except to themselves personally of course, history puts their deeds in the larger perpective.

The fall of 1944 found the 24th Division

garrisoned at Hollandia, Dutch New Guinea, scene of the successful campaign the division had fought the previous spring.

High-level planners had determined that the entrance in the return to the Philippines would be through Leyte, which is part of the Visayan group in the central part of the island nation. The advantages were several: Invading forces could approach Leyte from the east through a wide and open gulf; the island was close enough to Luzon to be tactically desirable, and was thought to provide enough level ground to establish air bases. The air distance from the Leyte capital of Tacloban northwest to Manila was just 295 miles.

Optimistic reports about the number of Japanese defenders on the island led military planners to move the schedule ahead by two months. Initially, the Leyte invasion was slated for 20 December; now it would be 20 October, with the later date reserved for Luzon. MacArthur and ranking members of his staff knew the estimates of the enemy strength on the island were grossly understated, but were confident the stepped-up timetable was workable.

A week before A-Day, the huge armada that had assembled at Hollandia put to sea, bound for what the men called the Far Shore, Leyte, 1,300 miles to the northwest. Aboard the transports were troops of the 24th Infantry Division, commanded by Major General Frederick A. Irving, and the 1st Cavalry Division, actually a square infantry division consisting of two brigades. Together, the divisions formed the X Corps that would go ashore in the northern sector of the invasion beaches.

Charles E. Blunt, Assistant Squad Leader C Company 19th Infantry, remembers listening to Tokyo Rose during the voyage. She said she knew the "20,000 Devils from Hell," as she called the 24th Division, were on the move but their troops would be waiting for them.

The conquest of the northern section of Leyte would develop in three phases. After infantrymen secured the beachhead and the series of hills behind the beach, they would drive

northwest across the Northern Leyte Valley to Carigara Bay on the north shore, and then southward on the east side of a mountain range through the Ormoc Valley to the bay of that name. On the way, such names as Palo, Hill 522, the Mainit River, Breakneck Ridge and Kilay Ridge would become almost as familiar to men of the Taro Leaf division as some of the places back home.

The landing was scheduled for 1000. Hours before, reveille sounded aboard the transports, and troops dressed quietly by the red lights in the deep compartments where they were quartered. Some checked weapons, some lay on their bunks and smoked; there was not much talking.

The conventional pre-invasion naval and air bombardment raised the decibels to high level, churned the earth and sand ashore and knocked out some of the defenses. But not all of them. With the 19th singing the Aussie song, "I've got sixpence, jolly, jolly sixpence," the infantrymen boarded the landing craft for the 5,000-yard trip across the glassy smooth gulf toward Red Beach, the 24th Division's objective.

The two X Corps divisions would land abreast, the 1st Cavalry Division on the right and the 24th on the left, as would the 19th and 34th Regiments, the latter on the right. The 21st Infantry had a separate mission to land 30 minutes before the principal H-Hour on the islands of Dinagat and Panaon and secure the strait that separates Leyte from Panaon Island to the south.

The corps' landing beaches, Red and White, were each 2,000 yards long, with a 1,500-yard interval between them. The main first-day objective for the two 24th Division regiments was to seize the town of Palo, southwest of the landing site, and then push northwest abreast toward the interior. More specifically, the 19th Infantry was directed to take the most prominent topographical feature in the area, Hill 522 just north of Palo, and then the town itself, and the 34th was to be available to help in that battle. The planned push northwestward was aimed at occupying Highway 1 between Palo and Tanauan.

The landing beaches were narrow, but the sand was firm. Behind them lay marshes, coconut trees and jungle vegetation. Farther west were rice paddies and swamps and then a low range of hills before the island opened into the broad and fertile Leyte plain.

The Japanese had prepared the defenses elaborately. A stream had been converted into a tank trap for about 1,500 yards paralleling the beach. Pillboxes built from palm logs and connected by tunnels studded the island.

The two 24th Division regiments approached the beach by battalions in column. Troops made wet landings as boats crunched to a halt well short of dry sand. Typically, men started the walk ashore in hip-deep water.

The first five waves landed without significant opposition, but those behind them came under intense shore fire about 2,000 yards out and began taking many casualties. Four craft carrying the 1st Battalion, 19th Infantry, were sunk. The Company C commander, Captain Joseph C. McNeely, was killed; so were most members of an ammunition and pioneer squad.

Disgorging personnel and supplies on Leyte.

21

Two section leaders, a platoon leader and some of the headquarters personnel of the Cannon Company were lost to fire from the beach.

Captain McNeely and his runner were seated in the stern of the LCVP bearing C Company's 1st Platoon. Assistant Squad leader Blunt remembers a tremendous explosion at the front of the landing craft as an artillery shell shattered the ramp, spraying metal over the two squads in the craft. Water, pouring into the craft, mixed with the blood and looked like red wine. Blunt's squad leader, S/Sgt Gladys, lost an arm. The metal fragments killed Captain McNeely, and his runner lost an eye. Blunt noticed that another squad leader, Don Irwin, was bleeding badly around his face. He had evidently raised his head just prior to the explosion. He lost sight in both eyes.

The LCVP finally hit the beach, but the ramp was hanging down and of no use. Blunt and the remaining men in the squad jumped into six or seven feet of water. All came to the surface, waded in, and joined C Company for the attack on Hill 522.

Japanese batteries hit four LSTs, killing or wounding most of the division's headquarters personnel. Among those lost were Lieutenant Eugene Friedman, of the 13th Field Artillery Battalion, and Sergeant Theodartus, of the battalion's service battery. The Head-quarters Company commander and the division's quartermaster were among the wounded.

The 34th Infantry's assault companies, I and K, hit the beach on time, but about 300 yards north of their target area. Bunched together, they immediately came under intense rifle and machine-gun fire.

Paul J. Cain, platoon leader K Company 34th remembered 20 October as "a beautiful day, sun shining, and sea very calm." Navy rocket ships, gun boats, and other assault boats

Bombing Red Beach on Leyte before the landing. (Courtesy of Rudy Haukebo)

Members of Co. C, 34th Infantry after advancing to a bridge destroyed by the Japanese, sent a patrol across the Carigara River in native boats. Carigara, Leyte Island, P.I. 10-31-44. (Courtesy of Charles Card)

kept the enemy pinned down until about three minutes after the landing. Then "the Japs got out of their holes and opened fire from pillboxes, trenches, and a few who climbed trees. We were now about 30 yards in and within 15 yards of where the Japs were dug in."

A sniper peeled the bark off a tree next to Cain's head. He rolled over to his left just as Lieutenant Howell Barrow, I Company commander, came to the same spot looking for his company. Cain pointed to I Company's location to the right but to be careful as a sniper was zeroed in on this spot. Howell apparently did not hear him. As he stood up, the sniper shot him in the head. Riflemen Trank and James Sullivan both spotted the sniper and made short work of him.

As Cain's platoon moved along a Japanese trench, Captain Francis D. Wai, the assistant regimental S-2, joined the platoon. A lone Japanese sitting in the trench with water up to his waist fired one round, killing Captain Wai. Scout Chann on the other side of the trench quickly dispatched the Jap with a burst from his tommy gun.

Both I and K Companies, pinned down and out of position, presented a fat target for enemy artillery. When the regimental commander, Colonel Aubrey Newman, a burley red-haired South Carolinian who graduated from the U.S. Military Academy in 1925, arrived in the fifth wave, he promptly began leading by personal example.

Standing up in the face of the withering enemy fire, Newman hollered, "Get the hell off the beach. Get up and get moving. Follow me." The bellowed order had the desired effect. The men arose and followed their colonel through the Japanese beach fortifications. Company I advanced with little difficulty, but Company K ran into stiff opposition from a system of five pillboxes about 75 yards from the beach. The company knocked out the fortifications with grenades and small-caliber weapons. Leading the way was the company commander, Lieutenant Troy L. Stoneburner who demolished one pillbox himself. Lieutenant Stoneburner was later killed during the Leyte campaign.

Company L of the 3rd Battalion, which had been the reserve unit, was sent in to the left of Company K to fill the gap caused by the landing boats missing their assigned area.

The 34th Infantry's beach area was clear of the enemy shortly after noon. The next objective, about 150 yards to the west, was a line of trees that could be reached only through a waist-deep marsh. Behind a mortar barrage, the 3rd Battalion's three rifle companies advanced to the trees and beyond. The 2nd Battalion, which had landed behind the 3rd, passed through to occupy the beachhead objective, but the regiment pulled back to Highway 1 at Pawing in order to maintain contact with the units on either side.

Sometime after the initial waves, General MacArthur waded ashore in the 34th Infantry's sector, a scene recorded by newsreels for posterity and seen by millions of Americans of that and succeeding generations. However, his "I have returned" proclamation no doubt caused more than one 24th Division man to consider

the fact that the general was not alone on the beach.

The 19th Regiment's first waves also came in too far north, nearly on top of the 34th's positions. Most of the initial resistance was on the left where the lead battalion, the 3rd, encountered intense mortar and automatic weapons fire. Company I knocked out pillboxes and 75-mm guns. One soldier who distinguished himself was Pfc. Frank B. Robinson, who dropped three grenades down the port of one pillbox and pulled its machine gun barrel out of line; crawled to another and threw lighted paper inside so that a flamethrower that had failed to ignite was able to fire through the flames; then drew fire from a third fortification so that tanks could spot its location. He later was awarded the Distinguished Service Cross.

Company K did not come ashore until the sixth wave and encountered fierce opposition. One platoon was out of contact with the rest of the company until the following day and suffered heavy losses.

Because the landings were off target by as much as 800 yards, pre-determined assembly areas could not be used immediately and as a consequence most of the fighting was carried out independently by platoons and squads. By mid-afternoon, the 3rd Battalion, 19th Regiment, had established a beachhead.

The 1st Battalion, 19th Infantry, landed next and also missed the planned beach to the north. The troops adjusted with a leftward oblique maneuver to reach their assigned area, but the resistance was savage. Heavy fire quickly pinned down both B and C companies, leading the battalion commander, Lieutenant Colonel Frederick Zierath, to order both companies to disengage and reposition themselves. Colonel Zierath, from Wisconsin, was a 1933 graduate of the Military Academy at West Point. The B Company executive officer, Lieutenant Robert W. Buck, and several enlisted men were killed in the initial encounter. D Company also took early casualties. Sergeant Beslisle of Headquarters Company was killed as well.

The invasion was not many minutes old when Lieutenant Art Stimson, of Houston, TX, a member of the division commander's staff, planted the Lone Star state's flag on the beach, declaring the return to the Philippines official.

The 2nd Battalion, 19th Infantry, came ashore at noon and established a defensive line around the beachhead. Company G moved out in the direction of Palo and ran into stiff resistance from a cluster of pillboxes. The company in short order suffered 15 casualties, including Lieutenant Frank Bird, Jr.,who was seriously wounded. By the end of the day, the battalion had dug in along Highway 1, ready to strike toward its objective, Palo, the following morning.

The 1st Battalion, 19th, in the meantime, was preparing to assault Hill 522, its first day's target, at mid-afternoon. That the unit did not delay turned out to be one of the most fortunate strokes in the entire Leyte campaign.

Hill 522, just north of Palo along the banks of the river by the same name, commanded the entire beachhead. Americans knew it to be heavily fortified with an elaborate network of

deep trenches, pillboxes, tunnels, caves and coconut log platforms, with a concrete covered command post at the summit. Forced Filipino labor had developed the defensive works over the preceding weeks.

For all the importance the Japanese placed on that feature, they made a serious miscalculation. Under the naval, air and field artillery bombardment, most of the defenders abandoned the hill temporarily, expecting to return to their positions after the landing.

Three companies of the 1st Battalion, 19th Regiment, moved toward the hill in column at 1430, but Company A in the lead came under fire that pinned it down. Zierath took the rest of the battalion around the right flank and attacked the hill from the northeast, Company C on the right and Company B on the left.

The steep hill was a tough climb, made all the harder by the weariness of the troops who had been in combat all day. Private Clarence Schumacher of Chicago, in a contemporary account in the Chicago Tribune, related that the men "had to come up its face virtually on our hands and knees."

The ascent was not entirely unopposed, despite the departure of the main body of defenders. B Company reached the first crest at dusk and came under heavy fire from two pillboxes. Schumacher, in describing that action, reported his unit had seven casualties, one dead.

At about the same time, scouts of C Company reached the highest point on the hill, looked over and saw two platoons of Japanese coming up the other side. They shouted for the rest of the company to hurry and the GIs narrowly beat their enemy to the top. Consequently, it was the Americans who had the advantage of the high ground in the fierce firefight that followed.

The C Company commander, Lieutenant Dallas Dick, who had taken over when Captain McNeely was killed on the way into the beach, had more than his share of close calls even for an invasion. On the beach, a bullet hit his helmet, ricocheted and tore his shirt. Then on the crest of Hill 522, the officer was wounded in the leg, a shell went through the morning report he carried, and finally, a round knocked the carbine from his hand. Nevertheless, Dick remained in charge of his company until he was evacuated 48 hours later.

The hilltop battle left about 50 Japanese dead. Through the night, they made infiltration attempts and mounted one banzai charge against C Company, which the Taro Leafers beat back.

Schumacher, in the Tribune article, had this comment: "We stole this hill, and it's mighty lucky we did. If we hadn't slipped through the Japs on the beach that first day and climbed up one side of this hill before the Japs climbed up the other, we undoubtedly would still be fighting for it."

The division commander, General Irving, put it this way: "If Hill 522 had not been occupied when it was, we might have suffered a thousand casualties in the assault."

So the private and the general agreed on the importance of a tactical result.

The 1st Battalion losses in taking Hill 522

were 14 killed and 95 wounded. Among the latter, 30 were treated and returned to their units.

By the end of A Day, the 24th Division held a beachhead averaging a mile deep, was positioned across Highway 1, and its men were atop Hill 522 overlooking the town of Palo. Contact was being maintained with the 1st Cavalry Division on the right.

Associated Press correspondent Fred Hampton, who came ashore with the 19th Regiment, the "Rock of Chickamauga," described the experience graphically.

"MacArthur threw overpowering American forces ashore on Leyte today, but from where I hit the beach with a regimental commander (Lieutenant Colonel George H. Chapman, Jr., of Wyoming, who graduated from West Point in 1933) it was a grim and bitter business.

"We raced the last 500 yards to the beach in landing boats in a rain of shell fragments and machine gun bursts, and when after eternal minutes, we hit sand, we had to plow through waist-deep water and geysers thrown up by very near misses.

"Twenty feet from us a crouching soldier groaned and rolled over with a bullet through his chest. A medical corpsman, running toward a group of wounded in a palm grove, pitched forward on his face ...."

"Until midafternoon, ships unloaded doggedly under enemy fire while assault troops inched toward the Palo road about a mile inland ... . At long last, the struggling soldiers got some of our artillery ashore and began answering the Japanese, but at nightfall the beachhead was still pocked with snipers."

That was the first day. The second day was not 90 minutes old when a truly extraordinary action occurred on the 34th Infantry's outer perimeter along Highway 1. It was the occasion when Private Harold Moon became an honored name in the history of the Taro Leaf division.

Moon, of Albuquerque, NM, was part of G Company, 2nd Battalion. He was occupying one of the two forward three-man positions that first night when the Japanese attacked along the highway in battalion strength about 0130.

Within half an hour, the enemy had advanced to within a few yards of the defenses, and the crossfire of mortar and machine-gun fire killed or wounded five GIs in the two foxholes, all except Moon.

Now alone at his position, Moon, armed with a Thompson submachine gun, returned fire and yelled insults at the enemy and exhortation to the rest of the platoon. After 40 minutes of fighting, he was hit in the leg but that did not stop him. About 0300, the H Company heavy machine gun section to his right was knocked out, making him more vulnerable to the approaching Japanese. An enemy officer began tossing grenades at Moon from across the road, and the soldier fought back. The duel ended about an hour later when Moon shot the officer through the head.

But the battle was not over. Japanese fanned out and surrounded the 2nd platoon, which was beginning to run short of ammunition. When an enemy machine gun advanced to within 20 yards of his position, Moon stood

Landing on Leyte Island. (Courtesy of Rudy Haukebo)

to determine its exact location and directed friendly fire until the gun was destroyed.

Japanese, by now concentrating much of their efforts on this lone soldier, charged with bayonets fixed, but Moon fought them off, killing 18 and driving the remainder back.

Platoon Sergeant John Ferguson of Utica, KY, himself a casualty, called to ask if Moon was still there, but the private, spotting another Japanese machine gun, was silent. He raised up and let fly a grenade at the precise moment the machine gun cut him down. Moon, who had fought from his position for about four hours, died in the foxhole with the two buddies who had been killed in the initial attack. Later in the day, when G Company passed through the scene of the fighting, the men counted 200 dead Japanese within 100 yards of Moon's foxhole. Moon later was honored posthumously with the nation's highest decoration, the Medal of Honor.

The remnants of the 2nd Platoon, still in a precarious position, fought their way out in a desperation move led by Staff Sergeant Verdun Myers. He ordered the men who could still stand to fix bayonets, get up and charge. This they did, hollering and shouting and driving straight through the enemy lines to reach the inside of their own perimeter.

The Japanese continued the contact, however. They hit Company L on the 3rd Battalion's left; the company, supported by mortar fire, counterattacked. Efforts by the GIs to flank the enemy position failed, so Company L made a frontal attack that broke the Japanese drive.

By this time, daylight had come to the battlefield of swamp and jungle. Second Battalion Commander Lieutenant Colonel James Pearsall ordered mortar and artillery fire thrown against the Japanese positions and requested air strikes as well. The Japanese in turn shelled the American troops. Battery A of the 63rd Field Artillery Battalion poured 150 rounds into the enemy lines.

Artillery fire and carrier air strikes drove the Japanese back into the rice paddies, and the 2nd Battalion was able to mop up along the road. The Japanese lost 600 men in the early morning encounter. Company G, 34th Infantry, Captain Ben H. Wahle, Jr., commanding, which took the hardest blows, had 14 men killed and 12 wounded. The H Company machine gun section attached to Company G had three killed and a gunner wounded.

The battalion's next job was to take a mass of hills west of Pawing, an assignment given to E and F companies. The troops jumped off at 1400. E Company secured the northern knoll in 25 minutes without opposition, but F Company ran into trouble from the steep slopes, high grass and about 200 enemy troops.

The Japanese hit the 1st and 2nd squads of the 1st Platoon with rifle and machine gun fire just as the first troops were nearing the top of the southern knoll. From their higher ground, the enemy also rolled grenades down on the Americans, while others worked their way round the reverse slope and attacked the 2nd Platoon with grenades as well.

The two 1st Platoon squads were forced to pull back and the 2nd Platoon was unable to move forward, so the F Company commander, Captain Paul Austin, of Fort Worth, TX, ordered the troops to disengage for reorganization. His company by then had suffered 14 casualties.

Mortar fire was called in, but Austin decided to delay further ground attacks on the heights until the next day. With the 63rd Field Artillery Battalion marking the target, Navy planes pounded the ridge until the Japanese ability to resist was broken. The company, with regimental commander "Red" Newman along, occupied the hill the afternoon of 22 October without suffering another casualty, thus securing the Pawing area.

To the south, the 19th Infantry's next major objective was the town of Palo, but first there was some unfinished business on Hill

522. Both companies, B and C, attacked down the far slope of the ridge and effectively ended enemy resistance. About 50 Japanese were killed in this brisk firefight.

Supplies did not reach the top, nor were the wounded evacuated, until late that day. The next few days were spent sealing off the tunnels and taking care of Japanese stragglers who periodically popped out of the holes.

Three battalions, 2nd and 3rd of the 19th Infantry and the 1st of the 34th Infantry, participated in the drive on Palo and its outskirts on 21-22 October. The 3rd Battalion of the 19th Regiment jumped off at 1400 along the beach road after naval gunfire and a mortar attack hit enemy positions, but the GIs encountered stiff resistance that kept the lead company, I, plus elements of the anti-tank company, pinned down for the night. The 34th Regiment's 1st Battalion, which had been in division reserve, moved up on the left flank to join the fray.

The job of taking Palo went to the 2nd Battalion, 19th Infantry, which moved out the morning of 21 October. Near the junction of the beach road and Highway 1, mortar fire hit the advancing troops, killing the battalion sergeant major and another man and wounding two others. The troops also encountered a Japanese force of about 35, probably some of the enemy who had tangled with the 2nd Battalion of the 34th Infantry in the pre-dawn battle the same morning. Machine-gun fire scattered them, and an artillery barrage added its weight.

The troops moving toward Palo on the south side of Highway 1 came under artillery fire that killed one American and wounded one. That caused the column to quicken the pace into the town, which it reached at 1500 without further casualties.

The Filipinos joyously greeted the Americans as the liberators they were, but soon, the battalion commander, Lieutenant Colonel Robert S. Spragins, had to break up the reunion by asking the civilians to go into a church while the GIs finished securing the town.

Troops spread out in three directions, but only those who probed to the west, Company F, ran into opposition. Japanese were still well entrenched on that side of town. The resulting fight was so fierce and the prospect of Japanese infiltration of American lines so great that Spragins ordered the company to pull back into a perimeter around the town square for the night.

The howitzers of the 13th Field Artillery Battalion pounded the roads leading into Palo from the west late that night, hitting a house filled with ammunition to set off a fire that burned for three hours.

The Japanese launched a counterattack about 0300 toward the middle of town, which the outposts drove back. The enemy then hit the American left, at the point where companies F and G, 19th Regiment, joined, and a savage infantry firefight ensued. The battalion's 81-mm mortars fired all its ammunition. F Company's Captain Velt C. Jones called fire from B Battery of the 13th Field Artillery Battalion to within 100 yards of his lines; the 63rd Field Artillery Battalion joined as well. The barrages contributed greatly to breaking up the attack, as the 19th Regiment's commander, Colonel Chapman, recognized: "Defense of Palo was aided immeasurably by the performance of the 13th Field Artillery which laid down protective fire. It never fired a short round."

The "Chicks" defending Palo drove back Japanese attackers in all positions. The night's fighting was expensive for the 2nd Battalion, which lost 16 killed and 44 wounded in the three and one half hours of savage infantry combat in which the enemy directed withering machine gun, rifle and mortar fire into the American lines. Among the wounded was the battalion commander, Spragins, who was hit in the forehead by a mortar fragment.

The enemy losses were put at 91.

The 19th Infantry headquarters of Colonel Chapman, was able to move into Palo by early afternoon, at which time the 3rd Battalion relieved the 2nd in the town.

The latter immediately launched an attack on Hill B west of Palo, one of the two rises that guarded the approach on either side of Highway 2. The other one, on the north, was designated Hill C. Hard fighting would be required on and for the two hills before the Red Beach area could be called secure and the second phase of the Leyte campaign, the drive inland, could begin.

But even before that, the Americans still found trouble in Palo. On the night of 23 October, a Japanese raiding party, using Filipino workers as a front, got past outposts southwest of the town and managed to capture two machine guns and a 37-mm weapon. Armed with mines, grenades, rifles and even sabers, they created havoc in the interior, throwing explosives into houses, slashing tires, and pouring gasoline on vehicles and setting them afire. Enemy troops even broke into an evacuation hospital and killed some of the wounded.

Later, after the Japanese set up their guns on the bridge leading into Palo, Americans on the other side swept the span with heavy fire, taking a fearful toll on the raiders. Sixty dead were counted, but the American losses were

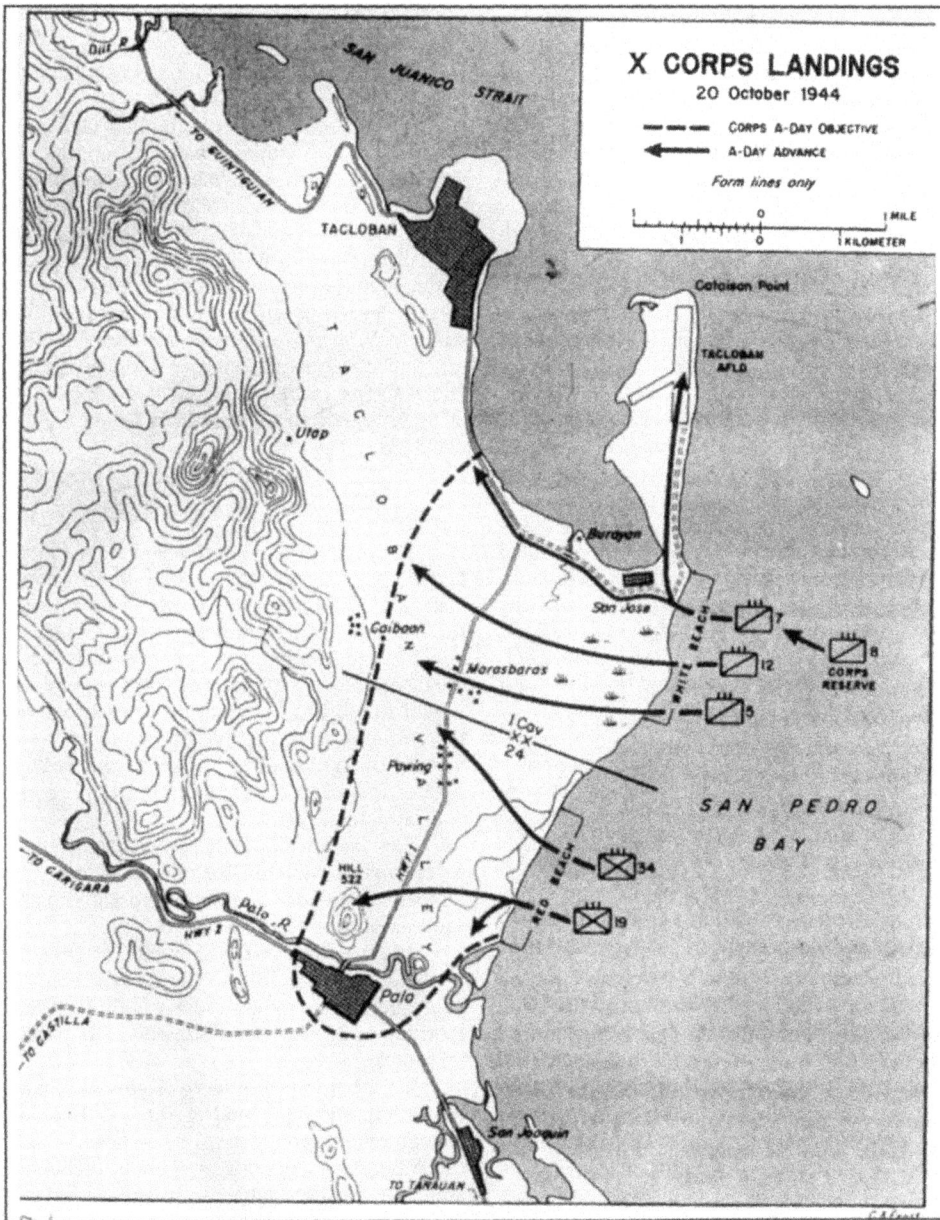

X CORPS LANDINGS
20 October 1944

CORPS A-DAY OBJECTIVE
A-DAY ADVANCE

Form lines only

Leyte

substantial also, 14 killed and 20 wounded. Nine of the 12 men guarding the bridge, six on either side, were casualties. Heroism was conspicuous. At one point, the regimental commander and Pfc. Sharpe, both covered by Pfc. Swarter, ran across the bridge. Private Malzahn, of the Signal Corps., remained at his post in the municipal building for two hours despite the constant zing of bullets hitting nearby. During that period, he received eight requests for artillery fire support. During the frantic encounter, quartermasters and engineers became infantrymen.

The 3rd Battalion's Company K, meanwhile, had moved out along Highway 1 to the south hoping to make contact with elements of the XXIV Corps. The company entered the town of San Joaquin on the morning of 24 October and secured it late that afternoon. Engineers went to work on a damaged bridge so armor could use it. The next day, the company pushed farther south and by mid-afternoon made contact with a unit of the 96th Division, the first between elements of the X and XXIV corps.

The rest of the 3rd Battalion, 19th Infantry, encountered little opposition in establishing a perimeter at Castilla, 8,000 yards southwest of Palo.

It was at this point that the X Corps commander, Major General Franklin Sibert, redeployed some of his force. He and the other ranking officers had anticipated heavier fighting in the 1st Cavalry Division's sector than in the 24th Division's. That was one reason for the order diverting the 21st Regiment on A Day to perform a separate mission. But it turned out that the 24th Division encountered the stiffer post-invasion resistance. Consequently, Sibert, before the fight for Hills B, C and other high ground west of the beachhead, transferred some 1st Cavalry Division units to the south to bolster the 24th Division's sector.

The initial assault toward Hill C came on the morning of 23 October at the hands of the 1st Battalion, 34th Infantry, and the 1st Platoon of the 603rd Tank Company, after an air strike battered the target area. In front of Hill C, in line east to west, were ridges known at Hill Nan and Hill Mike, which in their turn would have to taken first.

Company B, climbing Hill Nan, was near the crest when a machine gun opened up from 200 yards away. The Japanese on the reverse slope, employing a favorite tactic, hurled grenades down on the advancing American troops. The battle raged through the afternoon, with the company reaching the top only to be driven back. Similarly, the GIs repulsed Japanese counterattacks, but the machine gun continued its chatter.

Late in the day came the order to disengage so that artillery could go to work on the enemy positions. But the Japanese, apparently sensing an opportunity, counterattacked again, threatening the entire company. That is when two heroic soldiers took a hand and saved the withdrawal. Second Lieutenant Clarence Weigel and Staff Sergeant Hunt grabbed a bag of grenades and raced to the crest of the hill. There, exposed to murderous fire, they threw grenades down on the advancing Japanese as fast as they could pull the pins and succeeded in stalling the attack enough to allow the disengagement with few additional casualties.

Bombardment from 24th Division artillery pieces and 4.2-inch mortars throughout the night was so effective that the 1st Battalion occupied Hill Nan the next day without opposition. The 3rd Battalion, passing through the 1st, secured Hill Mike with equal ease.

The jumpoff for Hill C by the 3rd Battalion, 34th Infantry, came on the morning of 25 October when I and K companies moved out abreast and started the steep climb. K Company encountered no opposition in reaching its crest, but when I Company neared the top, the Japanese engaged in their standard reverse-slope defense with rifle fire and grenades, inflicting so many casualties on the company that a platoon from K Company was called upon to help. The battle continued throughout the day until at 1700, I Company reached and secured the top of the hill.

Meanwhile, Colonel James Pearsall ordered E Company of the 2nd Battalion to seize a small hill southeast of Hill C. The troops made their way up in single file through Cogon grass. The Japanese surprised the company by not waiting until the attackers neared the crest as they usually did. They opened fire while the riflemen were well below the top, pinning the Americans down. The 2nd Battalion countered with artillery and mortar fire for two hours, after which Company E took the hill with little trouble. The 34th Infantry thus held the high ground north of Highway 2.

The capture of Hill B on the south side of Highway 2, the job given to 2nd Battalion, 19th Infantry, required the best part of four days to complete. After its relief at Palo by the 3rd Battalion on 22 October, the 2nd under Colonel Spragins took a small ridge east of Hill B and then moved toward the main objective as the 13th Field Artillery Battalion and naval aircraft pasted the suspected enemy positions.

Company E in the lead ran into trouble as it reached the base of the hill. Well-concealed Japanese among the trees and on steep banks overlooking the road ambushed the passing Americans, precipitating a furious firefight. About 100 Japanese were killed before Company E pulled back to the ridge to the east for the night.

The 13th Field Artillery's howitzers pounded the hill again, and after machine-gun fire stalled a patrol, mortars neutralized the opposition and the battalion reached a lower crest of Hill B by mid-afternoon. During the day's fighting, the Battalion S-2, Lieutenant Joseph H. Maloy, was killed, and the same bullet went through the arm of Spragins, his second wound of the campaign.

The next morning, the battalion attacked the well-defended slopes rising above them, but in the face of stiff opposition, Spragins moved his troops around to the right until they took position overlooking a narrow asphalt road.

Companies G and E , 19th Infantry, moved out abreast on the morning of 25 October, first down the hill to the road and then up. When they reached the top, the Japanese met them with heavy fire. With the support of the 11th and 52nd Field Artillery battalions, the two companies fought a pitched battle with the entrenched enemy in what to that point was the bitterest combat the 2nd Battalion had experienced in the Leyte campaign.

E Company was pushed back, but Company G clung tenuously to the ridge. The latter company's 2nd Lieutenant Malcolm J. Watkins was killed and 2nd Lieutenant James B. Connell was wounded.

The day was nearly spent, but the battalion commander was not content to stop until his forces held the crest of Hill B securely in force. Spragins ordered the rest of the battalion to join Company G, which he sent out to a far ridge on the west. It was dark when, against the advice of one of his subordinates, the colonel instructed the battalion to move out. Maps were poor and the troops got lost, but about midnight they found themselves at the top of the hill in the midst of prepared - and unoccupied - Japanese positions. As on Hill 522, the enemy had left, this time for villages nearby to spend the night. Again, it cost them dearly. When daylight came, the 2nd Battalion could look down on Highway 2 from the secure crest of Hill B.

The 1st Battalion, having been relieved from Hill 522 previously, took and occupied Hill 85 to the south.

It was 25 October, and the first phase of X Corps' Leyte campaign was now complete, the result of six days of exhausting soldiering and often hard fighting. Much of the men's time was spent climbing steep inclines, or digging in on them, slogging through chin-deep swamps or thick jungle vegetation. The 24th Division's losses were 145 killed, 41 missing and 452 wounded. The beachhead was secure, the northern flank anchored, contact established with XXIV Corps on the south, and the high ground at the entrance to the Northern Leyte Valley occupied.

NORTHERN VALLEY

The main mission of the next stage of the Leyte operation was to capture the town of Carigara and secure the north shore on the bay of the same name. From the original beachhead, the direction generally was west northwest, and the 19th and 34th regiments would move out by separate routes toward the common intermediate objective of Jaro, a town on the southern edge of the valley where the Japanese were thought to have concentrated their forces.

The 1st Cavalry Brigade was reassigned to relieve the 24th Division of responsibility at its rear so the latter could proceed with its assault across the Northern Leyte Valley.

The 19th and 34th regiments, after seizing their respective hills the day before, did not pause before launching their drive inland the morning of 26 October along generally parallel routes.

On the north, following Highway 2, was the 34th Infantry. Its 2nd Battalion, in the lead, encountered small clusters of Japanese, whom the Americans disposed of without difficulty along the way. The Japanese had destroyed the bridges across some of the streams, so the 3rd Engineer Battalion built temporary spans in two

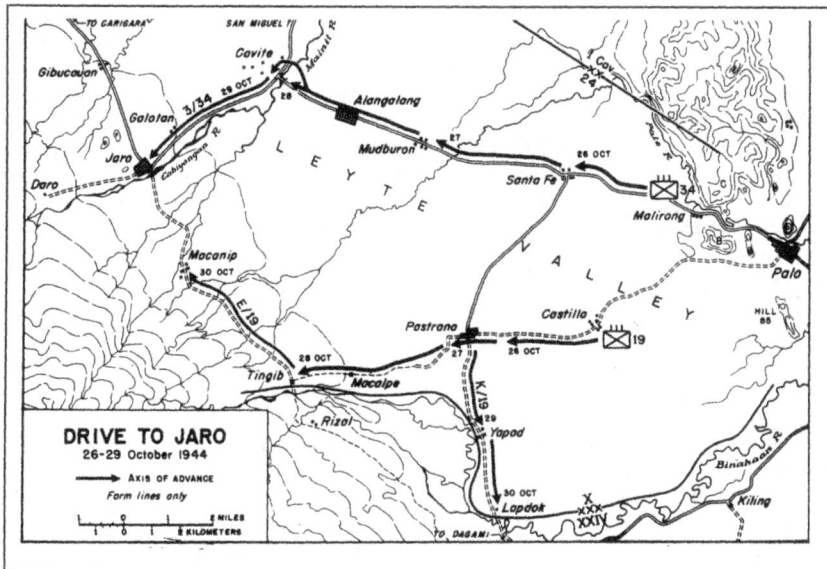

DRIVE TO JARO
26-29 October 1944

→ AXIS OF ADVANCE

Form lines only

cases and placed a Bailey bridge across the third.

The regiment's first significant action of the westward march occurred on 28 October when the 1st Battalion under Lieutenant Colonel Thomas E. Clifford, Jr., which had passed through the 2nd Battalion the previous day, reached the Mainit River bridge. That stream was just east of the town of Cavite, which was northeast of Jaro.

Company C made contact with Japanese on either side, suffering five casualties before pulling back. Companies A and B moved up on the left side of the road, and the 2nd Battalion took positions ready to join the attack as well.

But first, three batteries of the 63rd Field Artillery bombarded both sides of the river. The order of attack called for the 1st Battalion on the left to secure the eastern, or near, bank and five tanks to follow the assault companies. Regimental commander Newman ordered the 2nd Battalion on the right to cross the river at a ford about 500 yards downstream to the north, eliminate the enemy on the far side and then make contact with the Japanese at the bridge.

Enemy fire promptly pinned down the 1st Battalion at the water's edge, but Companies E and F managed to ford the stream in knee-deep water during a heavy downpour, climb the 20-foot bank through thick underbrush and organize the lightning drive toward the bridge.

Captain Paul Austin, F Company commander, described the fixed-bayonet dash that overwhelmed the Japanese force and secured the vital bridgehead on the west side of the Mainit River.

Austin positioned two platoons on either side of the road paralleling the river. On the right, the platoon leader was Sergeant Roy Floyd, of Eubank, KY, whom Austin described as a "soft-spoken, steely-eyed fighter with a natural-born gift for leading men into battle." Lieutenant Jack Calhoun's platoon took up position between the road and the river.

Austin ordered 60-mm mortars to lay down 50 rounds into the woods immediately beyond the open field directly in front of his force and directed a light machine gun section to fire into a line of trees on the right.

"I looked to my right at Floyd's platoon. He stood a few feet in front of his line of riflemen. I saw sun glistening on their bayonets affixed to the rifles. Floyd had come to fight.

"I looked to the left - 30 more bayonets. I said to each platoon, 'Don't stop until you get the bridge,'" the company commander related. He realized that 60 men had spontaneously made the same decision about fixing bayonets.

The running charge down the gravel road toward the bridge began, with Austin in the lead. The first sign of resistance came from an enemy mortar about 15 yards ahead, firing toward the 1st Battalion position at the bridge.

Sergeant Ernest Reckman, Valley Spring, N.Y., rushed to the mortar trench, tossed a grenade and eliminated the target.

"No one else broke stride," Austin recalled. "There was another puff of smoke much closer. I had a foot race with Reckman. It was a draw. The two (Japanese) in the trench were kneeling, heads bowed, awaiting death. It came quickly."

Reckman and another man then took out a third mortar.

Floyd and his 30 men halted at the edge of a deep draw and fired downward in a deafening volley that eliminated the enemy soldiers crouched below.

Meanwhile, the platoon on the left was firing into the trees on the river bank as the shouting riflemen continued their dash forward.

An enemy mortar shell exploded 10 yards in front of Austin, causing him to spin around to avoid the gravel and shrapnel and momentarily stride in the wrong direction. "I heard a voice to my right say, 'Uh, captain, uh, we're going this way.' I glanced at the man and saw a sly grin on his face. I could not restrain at smile at him when I saw the humor on his face.

"What a hell of a guy. In the middle of a bayonet charge, he was good-naturedly gigging his company commander for running in the wrong direction."

The bridge came into view from 200 yards away and the soldiers quickened their pace. The 60-mm mortar barrage churned the earth in the most likely enemy positions near the bridge.

Two of Floyd's men were killed about this time. Homer McClure, Chattanooga, TN, dueled a Japanese machine gun, but armed with only his M-1 rifle, which he fired furiously, he was overmatched and fell dead.

Clinton Short, Parkersburg, WVA, also died in the throes of aggressive combat. First he bayoneted a Japanese who had thrown a grenade at him and with his helmet knocked off from an enemy bullet, Short charged onto the next position. He was killed near the bridge.

By the time F Company reached the Mainit River span, the riflemen's ammunition was nearly exhausted. The dash had cost three F Company men killed and 11 wounded. Forty-two Japanese were killed defending the bridge.

Austin decided to set up his command post at the nearer of two poles at the bridge abutment and ordered Floyd to establish a position across the Jaro Road.

When the reserve platoon came forward, F Company established a semi-circle perimeter defense around the bridgehead. The weapons platoon set up mortars and machine guns to cover both roads approaching the bridge.

It appeared to Austin that the Japanese had prepared the bridge for demolition with the large pile of ammunition that they left on the bridge, which would have annihilated his command. However, he learned later that the three Japanese at the end of the detonation wire in a grove of trees were dead, two apparently killed by Floyd's men and the third a suicide. "Sergeant Floyd had not stopped until he had taken the bridge," Austin said.

Whether or not Colonel Pearsall knew the bridge was safe, he nevertheless walked across toward Austin, picking his way between the ammunition boxes. "I see you have captured the bridge, Paul. I will go back across and tell Colonel Newman," the battalion commander said.

Reflecting on the action, Austin credited Colonel Newman's accurate estimate of the best place to ford the river, just 50 yards beyond the Japanese left flank. "Second, the bayonet, when affixed to a rifle, adds another dimension to an assault of this nature. It calls for quickness. It calls for extra alertness and stamina. In bayonet training, yelling aloud is part of the learning process. F Company yelled and shouted during the attack partly to answer my shouts and partly because of the bayonets on their rifles," the captain remarked. Finally, he mentioned the revenge factor, in this case the unspoken remembrance of comrades recently killed on Hill 331, Joe Bartnichak, Louis Farmer, Ralph Dyer and others.

The next morning, the captors of the Mainit River bridge had the satisfaction of seeing jeeps, foot soldiers, trucks and tanks cross to continue the assault toward Jaro and up the Leyte Valley without the delay a blown bridge would have forced.

The 34th Regiment's 3rd Battalion, moving up behind, was in contact with the 19th Infantry to the south.

APPROACH TO CARIGARA

Responsibility for the southern prong of the 24th Division's drive west through the northern Leyte Valley was assigned to the 19th

Infantry, which on 26 October started from the advance perimeter it had established at Castilla, southwest of Palo.

The first objective was the town of Pastrana, about three miles away. The 3rd Battalion under the command of Lieutenant Colonel Elmer Howard, was the lead unit, and its I Company was at the point. The company, moving over a trail too narrow for vehicles, ran into heavy resistance at the edge of Pastrana about 1600.

A second thrust was undertaken by I and K companies abreast, but it too was halted by heavy fire from an unusual fortification, a star-shaped structure with a tin roof and sides banked with earth. on which grass grew. It was flanked by pillboxes and backed by a trench system. The fortification resembled native shacks clustered together, and was so odd in appearance that it aroused suspicion and eliminated the surprise element.

A third infantry attack by the two companies produced no headway and caused so many casualties that the battalion pulled back for the night.

It fell to the artillerymen and mortar crews to win this particular encounter, though employment of the big guns was hampered by the soft ground. Involved in the bombardment of the Japanese defenses through the night were Battery C, 11th Field Artillery Battalion, Battery A of the 14th Field Artillery Battalion, and the 13th Field Artillery Battalion. The three artillery units assumed the duty in tandem until daylight when the 4.2-inch and 81 millimeter mortars took over.

The night-long shelling flattened the defenses and enabled ground troops to enter and pass the town with minimum difficulty. Company K moved around Pastrana and set up a roadblock southwest of town to cut off any retreat, and the 1st Battalion moved in to help in mopping up stragglers.

The enemy still had a bite. A mortar round dropped into an aid station in Pastrana, killing three men from M Company; Captain James B. Jones, the 3rd Battalion S-3, was shot in the leg by a sniper. One of the more unusual spectacles anyone would see was an American bulldozer rumbling into town at its best speed with two GIs aboard. The other soldiers tried to wave it off because the vehicle was drawing Japanese fire from all sides, but the bulldozer made straight for the battalion headquarters, where, answering an emergency call, it dropped off blood plasma. The two men, Technician Fifth Grade Herritz, of Service Company, and Private Landrum, of Company B, 3rd Engineer Battalion, turned the dozer around, caved in the sides of a Japanese bunker that had been firing at them and left town as fast as they arrived.

With Pastrana secured, units of the 19th Infantry, protecting the 24th Division's southern flank, sent patrols out toward the south, southwest and west. The 1st Battalion set up a roadblock near Macalpe, west of Pastrana, and the 2nd Battalion pushed beyond to Tingib. Meanwhile, 3rd Battalion companies, having had their first hot meal of the operation, moved south to Ypad and then Lopdok, at the southern edge of the X Corps sector, to block any Japanese thrust from that direction.

The 19th regiment's units encountered the

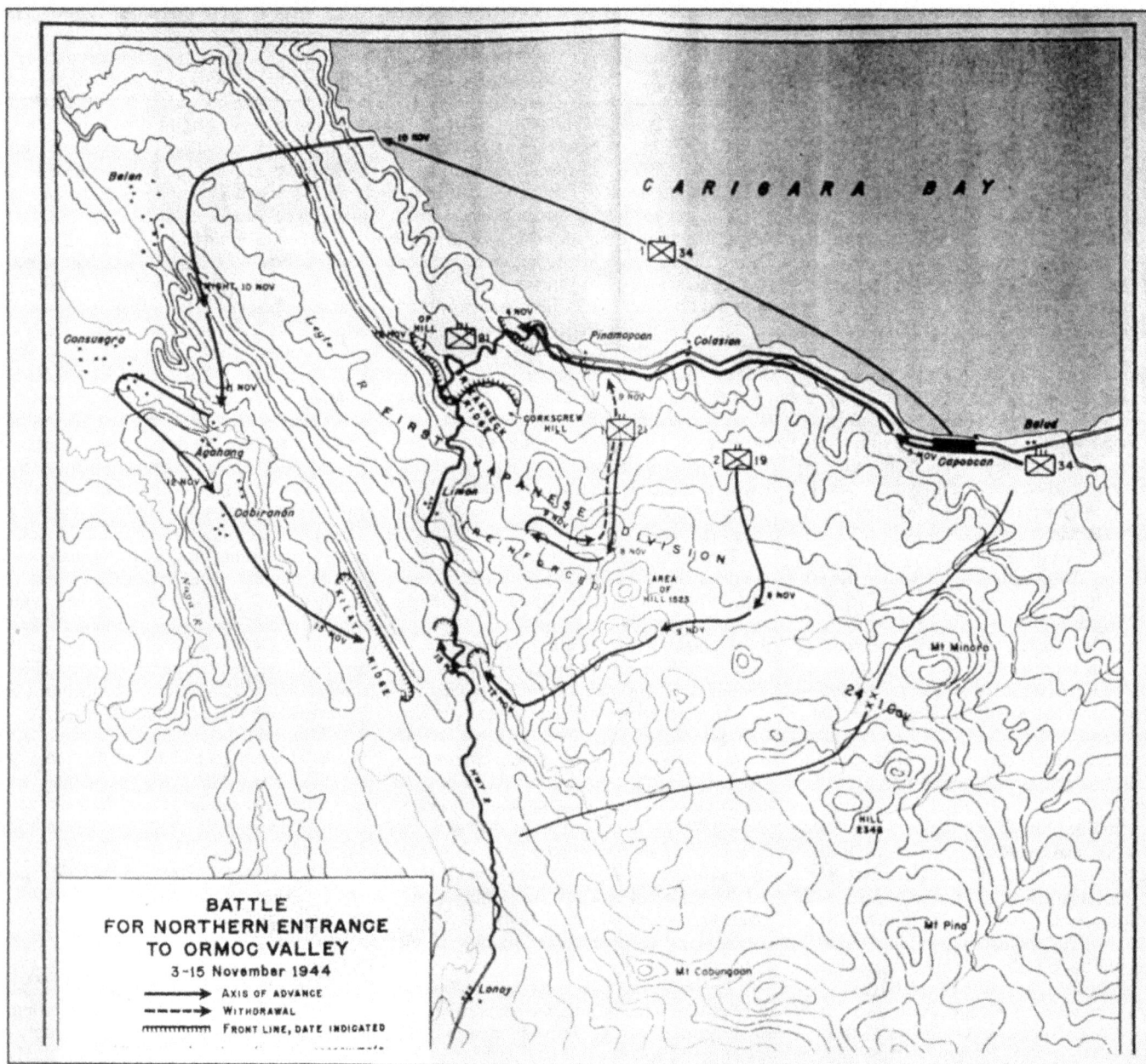

BATTLE FOR NORTHERN ENTRANCE TO ORMOC VALLEY
3-15 November 1944

→ AXIS OF ADVANCE
---→ WITHDRAWAL
⊞⊞⊞⊞ FRONT LINE, DATE INDICATED

enemy in strength of varying degrees. One of the sharpest clashes came when Company C of the 1st Battalion engaged about 100 Japanese at Rizal, southwest of Macalpe. Lieutenant William C. Naegele ordered a withdrawal so artillery could be registered on the enemy positions. The shell fire eliminated most of the Japanese force.

Ahead at the forward perimeter at Tingib, a Japanese horse convoy carrying 75 mm ammunition blundered into the American lines, one enemy soldier actually asking a GI manning an outpost a question. Second Battalion machine-guns and 37-mm canister fire left ammunition scattered and the road littered with dead Japanese and horses.

The 3rd Battalion's I Company threw back two small probes from the south, and by 30 October, leading elements of the 19th Infantry had progressed as far as Macanip on the road to Jaro from the southeast.

The evening before, the 34th Infantry's 3rd Battalion under Lieutenant Colonel Edward Postlethwait, a Missourian who had graduated from the Military Academy in 1937, had occupied Jaro without difficulty, but only after some hard fighting enroute.

The morning of 29 October, Postlethwait's battalion started down the road from Cavite southwest toward Jaro. L Company on the point ran into trouble just outside the village of Galotan, where the Japanese were fighting from under the town's shacks. Artillery fire was not effective in reducing the force, so two platoons attacked from either flank. Rooting the Japanese from their defensive positions was slow, bloody work, and the company suffered several casualties, including Lieutenant John B. Clark, who was wounded.

A GI force that had been sent wide to the right came under heavy fire from a wooded knoll. Artillery and mortar barrages drove the enemy back into position to menace the 3rd Battalion column that was moving forward.. Fortunately, however, the anti-tank platoon, which had been displaced forward, repelled the threat. The battalion entered Jaro at 1700, and on 31 October, 1st Battalion of the 19th Regiment closed on the town as well.

Carigara and the north coast, the division's objective in this phase of the Leyte campaign, was 10 miles northwest of Jaro, and the 34th Infantry commander, Colonel Aubrey Newman, put his men on the road the next morning.

At 0800, Company L of the 3rd Battalion jumped off. Dragon Blue did not have long to wait to meet resistance. Just outside Jaro, the column came under machine-gun fire from shacks lining the road. Tanks came up and took the enemy positions under fire and then withdrew.

Newman ordered the infantrymen forward slowly so that the Japanese could be located for effective artillery use. Lieutenant Lewis F. Stearns placed one squad of his platoon on each side of the road and he himself walked down the middle behind one tank and ahead of another. Once again, Japanese fire pinned the troops down, and once again, as at the beachhead, Newman provided personal leadership.

Lieutenant Stearns described the scene: "About that time, the colonel came up again and asked, 'What's the holdup here?' I told him he had better get down in the ditch, but he replied, 'I'll get the men going okay.'"

"The colonel started to walk forward and I called to the men, 'Let's go. The colonel is here.' They got up and started to move forward. Just as the colonel started to step off the bank, the Japanese opened fire with artillery and mortars. A shell landed right on top of the man next to the colonel, blowing him to pieces. I saw the colonel grasp his stomach and fall to the ground."

Stearns called for McPhail, the medic, who came up and started to dress the serious stomach wound while Giacomazzo, Colonel Newman's orderly, went back to get a Jeep.

"Colonel Newman was in complete command of his faculties," Stearns related. "he asked if we could remain in position and drop mortar fire on the enemy. I told him men were being killed every minute and we would have to do something and do it fast. The colonel thought for a minute. You could see he was in pain, but wanted to make a decision that would clear up the situation."

He decided to call for artillery fire, so Stearns sent a runner with that order and then disregarded Newman's request to be left where he was. "I told him we could not leave him there. We put him on a poncho and dragged him back to safety."

Lieutenant Colonel Chester Dahlen, the regiment's executive officer, took command and, after the withdrawal under cover of a second platoon, he ordered the attack to resume.

During the disengagement there occurred one of those oddities of war. A Japanese 37-millimeter shell went down the barrel of a 75 millimeter gun on a tank. Fortunately, the tank gunner had just opened the breach, which allowed the projectile to pass through and bury itself in a radio. Three men were wounded, but had a shell been in the tube, the entire crew would have been killed.

The artillery barrage ordered by Colonel Newman was lifted at 1230 and the 3rd Battalion moved out again, K Company on the left side of the road and I Company on the right.

But before the companies had gone far, Japanese poured artillery, mortar, rifle and machine gun fire into the columns. L Company tried to flank the enemy force on the left, but met stiff opposition from high ground commanding the road. The heavy fire drove back the L Company men, who were in open ground below the ridge. The rest of the battalion also had to withdraw through the 2nd Battalion positions. A day's fighting had not advanced the regiment beyond the outskirts of Jaro.

The 155-mm and 105-mm howitzers of the 11th, 52nd and 63rd Field Artillery battalions laid harassing and interdiction fire along the Jaro-Carigara road throughout the night, and the next morning, 31 October, the infantry attack resumed.

The plan of action called for the 3rd Battalion to lead the way, the 2nd Battalion to pass through and the 1st Battalion, which was the last unit to arrive from the Mainit River bridge,

to follow. The 19th Infantry, whose 1st Battalion was positioned at Jaro, was to continue to protect the 34th Regiment's rear.

Both the 2nd and 3rd Battalions engaged in fierce fighting early in the day. The 3rd Battalion's objective was to clear the hills west of the highway from which the Japanese had managed to create such havoc the previous day.

Thus Company L approached one ridge from the rear while Company I advanced astride the road. When the latter reached a stream, the troops came under heavy fire, then moved to the reverse slope of Company L's hill. When the I Company troops reached the top, they discovered a second hill farther west. A heavy machine gun raked the Japanese positions on the second hill. As I Company attacked, the reserve company, K, occupied the first hill and drove the enemy into L Company's position. The fighting was so intense that some of the Americans were pushed across the road for a time, but after three hours the troublesome high ground was cleared of Japanese.

The 2nd Battalion, meanwhile, had moved toward Tunga, the approximate halfway point between Jaro and Carigara. E Company, on the point, ran into resistance at the Ginagan River, which halted the advance until first tanks and then artillery brought their fire to bear on the enemy positions.

When E Company's mortar section and an anti-tank crew were pinned down and seeking to withdraw, Private First Class Laule, a Jeep driver, took charge of providing cover. Firing the .50-caliber machine gun mounted on the Jeep, he shouted for the other troops to pull back. As the last man reached safety, a shell hit the vehicle and killed Laule.

The 2nd Battalion continued its advance with Company G in the lead on the road and Company E on the left flank. At the Yapan River, the Japanese opened fire on Company G and American tanks moved up to help, whereupon the enemy concentrated its fire on the armored vehicles.

Company E also came under fire from a pillbox on a rise. A 105-mm self-propelled howitzer provided effective supporting fire. When that weapon's ammunition was exhausted, a second howitzer moved up, but it was quickly disabled by an enemy artillery shell.

Company E was given the unenviable task of protecting the damaged self-propelled howitzer against Japanese who had set up machine guns from which they could enfilade the position. It was a tough night for the company, but Easy held on. When a tank attempted to tow the howitzer, two of the three men handling the rope were killed. Then it was discovered that the gun couldn't be moved so the tank put a round through it to render the piece completely useless. Company E withdrew through Company F. Meanwhile, the battered Japanese force, many of them reinforcements who had come up the Ormoc road a week before, slipped away in the dark.

The day's fighting had cost the regiment 108 casualties, 42 of them in Company E alone.

The next morning, 1 November, under the plan sent down from General Irving the previous night, the 34th Infantry continued its push toward Carigara while the 19th Infantry protected the rear and flank against any Japanese attempt at reinforcement.

Companies A and B of the 1st Battalion, 34th Regiment, made a wide sweep to the right, or east, toward the town of Tuba, and met no resistance. The 2nd Battalion proceeded straight down the highway to Tunga, finding on the way much equipment the Japanese had abandoned in their hurried flight.

The two battalions converged at Tunga, rested, and moved forward again. By the end of the day, the point battalion, the 1st, was nearly to Sagkanan, the last town short of Carigara, and the rear unit, the 3rd Battalion, was in Tunga.

Elements of two American divisions, approaching from different directions, were at the threshold of the objective. The 1st Cavalry Division was coming down from the north and the 34th Infantry was poised to enter Carigara from the southeast.

The Americans were expecting a major fight. They had reason to believe 2,000 to 3,000 Japanese troops were in the town and they knew the enemy was capable of receiving reinforcements from Ormoc, which was not in the direction of the flank protection offered by the 19th Regiment. Furthermore, indications were strong that the Japanese had been busy building defenses in the town.

Accordingly, orders were issued for a saturation artillery bombardment in front of the American positions on the morning of 2 November before the infantry moved into the city. All available artillery units, except for one light battalion of the 24th Division, would be employed in the barrage.

The advance elements of the two divisions started their movements as planned. When they reached Carigara, they found that the Japanese had abandoned the town to take up strong defensive positions in the mountains southwest of Carigara.

In line, the 1st, 2nd and 3rd Battalions of the 34th Infantry made their way down the highway toward Carigara. Company G reconnoitered the left flank in case envelopment was necessary.

An hour later, the 1st Battalion halted at a bridge at the outskirts, waited for 90 minutes for elements of the 1st Cavalry Division to appear, and when they didn't show, sent patrols into Carigara. All was quiet, of course, but the 1st Battalion's crossing of a 180-foot bridge, which had been burned, was precarious. The battalion skirted the town on the west and moved up the coast as far as Balud before running into the only enemy fire the regiment encountered that day.

The 2nd Battalion, meanwhile, set up a perimeter at the Carigara River, and the 3rd Battalion dug in behind the 2nd Battalion. The 34th Regimental headquarters were established in the town.

The drive across the Northern Leyte Valley from the beachhead to Carigara Bay had been difficult and bloody. The Japanese had made careful selection of strong points from which to delay the American advance. But delay was all the enemy could do. When the enemy forced firefights, the American tactic of halting, withdrawing and allowing mortars, artillery and armor to go to work before the infantry proceeded, proved decisive in every case. So did the derring-do of small units, as at the Mainit River.

The Associated Press' Fred Hampton, in a dispatch dated 2 November, described the end of the 24th Division's valley operation as follows:

"The battle for the Leyte Valley, which started amid an artillery, mortar and machine gun barrage on Palo Beach 12 days ago, ended today when this embattled division raced down the last three miles of trans-valley highway and occupied this key city... .

"The irresistible advance split the Japanese forces in two, and rolled the remainder of the valley defenders into the mountains to the south. Scarcely a shot was fired as we occupied the town, which had been the goal of this hard-fighting division for almost two weeks of hot, dirty, sweaty and bloody battling along the network of village roads.

"General Kenneth Cramer (assistant division commander) said after we entered the town, 'We must have broken their backs in the Jaro fight. It was a bloody go, and I thank God we didn't have to fight like that all the way.'"

Hampton wrote further that the "'Victory Division'…bore the brunt of this battle for Leyte and fought with great courage and tactical brilliance... .I walked over many a blood smear on the road into Carigara today, red evidence of evacuations of Japanese dead and wounded.

"It is not a pretty picture, this backwash of war, but it is, to some extent, revenge for Bataan and Pearl Harbor." Had the wire service reporter been able to see into the future several months, he would have known that the 24th Division would exact even more direct revenge in the liberation of the Philippines.

The 24th Division apparently received its sobriquet, the "Victory" Division, from the Vs formed by two fingers lifted by cheering Filipinos shouting, "Vic-to-ree, Vic-to-ree."

Losses by the division's two regiments involved in the valley crossing (the 21st Infantry was still occupying its A-Day objective in the Panaon Strait area) were 210 killed, 859 wounded and six missing. But the Japanese were hurt far worse, with an estimated 2,970 killed.

To complete the liberation of Leyte, the U.S. Army would drive southward along Highway 2, which twisted through the plains and mountains from the northern Carigara Bay coast to the port of Ormoc, 25 miles away on Ormoc Bay.

The strategy was to push the remaining Japanese forces westward into the mountains where they could offer effective resistance no longer. The American forces were not fighting a static garrison, however. The Japanese could and did send reinforcements to Leyte that enabled them to put up a stubborn defense for weeks on end. In that respect, the American commanders feared the Ormoc corridor would become another Guadalcanal, where the Japanese were able to put ground troops onto the island in an almost continuous stream.

Again, it was the 24th Infantry Division that was chosen to spearhead the thrust southward through the Ormoc Valley. The 1st Cavalry Division, the northern component of X Corps, occupied Carigara, which freed the 34th Infantry to push westward along the coastal road to Pinamopoan, the point at which Highway 2 turns due south.

The regiment moved out early on 3 November by battalion in column, the 1st Battalion in the lead. The troops secured the first town, Capoocan, 10 minutes after entering and were on the coastal road again within a half hour.

Company B, on the point, had advanced about 1,000 yards when it ran into an entrenched force of about 100 Japanese on the bank of a stream. Mortar shells were dropped into the enemy position, but the company was forced to withdraw so that the guns of the 63rd Artillery Battalion could go to work.

Meanwhile, Colonel Clifford, 1st Battalion commander, directed a B Company platoon under Lieutenant Clarence Wiegel south to a ridge that paralleled the road. When Japanese were discovered on the reverse slope, A Company was dispatched as reinforcements. Guides led that company over the wrong trails and it

Mass on Leyte. (Photo Courtesy of J.H. Miller)

ran head-on into a well-hidden and entrenched enemy. The Americans made a frontal assault, but were taken under fire after passing the hidden positions. The company's losses were 11 killed and 13 wounded.

Colonel Clifford ordered C Company to join the fight with a left flanking movement to the next ridge. The two companies then launched an attack westward against the enemy across the stream.

When the leader of the advance squad of Company A was killed, Sergeant Charles E. Mower, of Chippewa Falls, Wisconsin, took command and started to lead his men across the stream. Hit by rifle fire at mid-current, Mower was seriously wounded but nevertheless found himself in an ideal vantage point to observe the movements of the enemy on the opposite side. Mower, half submerged, remained in his exposed position and maneuvered his men by voice commands and hand signals against the enemy. Two Japanese machine gun emplacements were destroyed and many soldiers killed as a result of Mower's directions. Finally, the Japanese became aware of what the wounded man in the water was doing and concentrated their fire on him. Mower was awarded the Medal of Honor, posthumously.

Company A withdrew, and after the artillery battalion turned its firepower on the troublesome ridge to the south, Company B attacked. Company C continued its flanking movement around to the south and eliminated the resistance in that area. The battle had lasted the better part of the day.

The initial resistance that morning led General Irving to order an amphibious maneuver across a stretch of Carigara Bay to a point beyond Pinamopoan, behind enemy lines. The mission, which the regimental commander, Colonel Chester Dahlen, assigned his rear battalion, the 3rd, was to determine the strength of the opposition facing the 1st Battalion in its westward march.

The initial plans were to send 17 LVTs (Landing Vehicle, Tracked, an amphibious landing vessel) loaded with troops, but when the 827th Amphibious Tractor Battalion arrived, it had only seven vehicles. That cut the force to Company K, plus a heavy weapons section, a medical detachment and forward observers from the 11th and 63rd artillery battalions.

The little fleet left Capoocan at 1430, navigating by the artillery fire that was falling on the target area, and reached its objective an hour-and-a-quarter later.

The landing was made with the support of .50-caliber machine gun fire from the LVTs. Once ashore, K Company moved inland by platoons in line and under fire from about 150 Japanese riflemen. One platoon took a small hill in the center of the front, from which a heavy machine gun provided effective fire. Two enemy artillery pieces, registered on the American troops, were taken out by mortars.

As the day ebbed, the volume of enemy fire increased and Japanese reinforcements were observed from the air on their way to the beachhead from two directions. When the battalion commander, Colonel Postlethwait, and the company commander, Lieutenant

Stoneburner, could not find a suitable place to dig in for the night, it appeared the amphibious force was in trouble.

The 11th Field Artillery observer called fire from his battalion that fell so close that shell fragments dropped on the K Company troops. The 63rd Field Artillery Battalion joined the bombardment of enemy positions.

Ten LVTs, the original fleet plus three more vehicles carrying two platoons of I Company as reinforcements, were sent to the beachhead, but the situation did not lend itself to a pitched battle there. Ammunition was running low, darkness was approaching and a satisfactory position could not be found. So with the I Company platoons providing cover on either flank, the landing troops withdrew. One Japanese counterattack was thrown back in the process.

When the LVTs had moved out to sea far enough, the 63rd Field Artillery directed its fire to the beach. The estimate of enemy killed in the encounter was 100, while the Americans lost one killed and four wounded.

Throughout the night, the 11th and 63rd Field Artillery battalions plastered the enemy positions in front of the 1st Battalion and dropped interdiction fire along the coastal highway. When the battalion probed forward the following morning, no Japanese were encountered. The enemy had left in the darkness, abandoning much of their equipment, including heavy weapons, ammunition dumps and documents.

The 1st Battalion moved west as far as Colasian, and the 2nd and 3rd battalions passed through. The 2nd Battalion set up a defense at Pinanopoan and the 3rd passed through and advanced about 1,700 yards beyond that town to a point just short of a mass of hills that would become known as Breakneck Ridge.

At this stage, troop movement paused while Sixth Army Commander General Walter Krueger considered the next deployment in light of the enemy's demonstrated ability to reinforce its army on Leyte via Ormoc Bay.

The general was worried about the possibility of a sea-borne assault against the American rear at Carigara Bay if all the United States forces concentrated on the drive south. The United States Navy didn't believe a Japanese amphibious landing likely, but Krueger decided not to risk it. His orders were to establish a defense against an assault from the bay before the American divisions embarked on the last leg of their campaign, the thrust through the Ormoc Valley to the bay to the south.

As a consequence, General Irving spread his four artillery battalions, which had been at Carigara, westward near the coast. The 13th and 52nd battalions moved to Colasian point on 4 November and the 11th and 63rd battalions took up positions on either side of Capoocan.

A battalion of 155-mm howitzers was emplaced about three miles southwest of Jaro where they would be within range of Ormoc 14 miles away to the southwest.

The 1st Battalion of the 19th Infantry was assigned to protect that heavy artillery unit. Another battalion of the regiment moved to the area of Pinamopoan, and the remainder of the

"Chicks" took station in the mountains around Jaro and Daro to protect the 226th Field Artillery Battalion and to guard the passes leading back into the Leyte Valley.

On 5 November, the 21st Regiment rejoined the rest of the division. X Corps Commander Sibert had made the decision several days before to bring the Gimlets from Panaon Island where they had landed on A-Day to secure the strait on the southeastern tip of Leyte. The regiment had encountered little resistance there and a battalion from another division took over the occupation.

The 1st and 3rd battalions of the 21st Infantry were transported by sea to Tanauan and then by trucks to Tunga, midway between Carigara and Jaro, where the troops bivouacked on 2 November.

Now the two battalions moved up to relieve the battered and weary 34th Regiment in front of Breakneck Ridge. The 34th Infantry had been in combat for 17 consecutive days since hitting Red Beach on 20 Oct. First to enter the key town of Jaro, the regiment was from that point the spearhead of the attack that secured the coast of Carigara Bay and positioned X Corps for the last phase of the Leyte campaign.

Now the 34th would pull back to occupy the coastal area at Capoocan, but first there remained some unfinished front-line business for a small force from the regiment, along with some field artillery observers.

On 5 November, the day the 21st Infantry relieved the 34th, Major Lemuel K. Blacker took a party of forward observers from the 52nd Field Artillery Battalion, accompanied by a patrol from the 34th Infantry, to a knoll on Breakneck Ridge known as OP Hill. From there the party directed fire on the area.

When Japanese of platoon strength attacked, the Americans found refuge in an abandoned pillbox, and Lieutenant Colonel Frederick R. Weber, the 21st Regiment's commander, sent two companies from the 3rd Battalion, K on the right side of Highway 2 and I on the left, to rescue the observer party. K Company overcame opposition, secured the northern slopes of the hill, and accomplished the rescue mission. I Company, after a stiff fight, captured high ground known as Corkscrew Hill.

In order to hold their positions, both companies needed more ammunition, but supply trucks were stopped by enemy riflemen who shot out the tires, forcing the vehicles to withdraw.

That meant the ammunition and other supplies had to be hand-carried to the troops, who were so far out in front of the rest of the regiment that the quantity reaching them was quite thin. For the Gimlets, engaged in their first major action on Leyte, the experience must have reminded them of Hollandia the previous spring. As the point regiment in that attack, the 21st Infantry men were at the far end of a precarious human supply line that was barely adequate to sustain them in combat.

Filipinos helped carry supplies to the front line troops and assisted in other ways. They carried litters to evacuate casualties, served as guides, and volunteered for work details to free up American soldiers for combat. Some, like

15-year-old Adriano Villamor, served as cannoneers in the 11th F.A. Battalion. Villamor later became a lawyer, a judge, and mayor of Jaro.

Throughout the remainder of 5 November and the following morning, the Japanese kept the pressure on K and I companies. Three enemy night attacks were thrown back, and after daylight, mortar and artillery fire became so heavy that the American troops withdrew and rejoined the rest of the 3rd Battalion at Colasian.

The 1st Battalion, 21st Infantry, took up the fight that day, but failed to secure positions on the northern approaches to Breakneck Ridge. And that night, on the eve of the concentrated 21st Infantry assault on the ridge, it was the Japanese who launched an aggressive move against the 2nd Battalion, which occupied a center position astride Highway 2. The two-hour attack, supported by mortar fire and grenades, did not succeed in breaking the American perimeter.

BREAKNECK RIDGE

Breakneck Ridge, an irregularly shaped complex of hills, knolls and rocky ravines situated a little more than a mile south of Carigara Bay, represented the first natural barrier for entry into the Ormoc Valley from the north. Highway 2, single width and unpaved, twisted and wound its way over and through the hills making up the ridge system for a distance of about four miles.The Japanese had built formidable defenses on the high ground, including their characteristic trench networks as well as spider holes, many on reverse slopes invulnerable to direct fire.

Even the natural features conspired to make Breakneck Ridge easier to defend than attack. The hills were densely overgrown with shoulder-high Cogon grass, sharp and impenetrable, which the Japanese cut short in places for fire lanes. The deep hollows were heavily forested, and the persistent rainfall rendered the steep slopes treacherous most of the time.

As 6 November came to a close, the Japanese held the northern slopes of the system of ridges and the approaches to them. The main U.S. attack was scheduled for the following morning.

Opposing the Americans was the First Imperial Division, a fresh, veteran unit that had served for several years in Manchuria. The 21st Regiment did not know it at the time, but the GIs probably were outnumbered three to one.

With the 3rd Battalion, 19th Infantry, attached to the 21st Regiment, four battalions were deployed for the 7 November assault. The 2nd Battalion, 19th Infantry, would join the fight forthwith as well.

The attack was by columns of battalions, with the 2nd Battalion, 21st, in the van. The first objective was a branch ridge 400 yards to that unit's front.

E Company on the right reached the ridge against only light opposition, but G Company, east of the highway, ran into trouble from about 200 Japanese entrenched on the forward slope. Self-propelled guns came up, but they were unable to reduce the enemy strongpoint. Two

tanks also lent their fire, but an enemy soldier disabled one by planting a magnetic mine against the side. The other vehicle then withdrew.

At this point, with the attack momentarily stalled, the 21st Regiment underwent reorganization. Colonel William Verbeck, who had been X Corps G-2, took over as regimental commander from Lieutenant Colonel Weber, who became the executive officer. That freed Lieutenant Colonel Seymour Madison, the previous executive officer, to assume command of the 2nd Battalion, while Major Lamar Little shifted from the 2nd Battalion to the 1st as commanding officer. Weber, incidentally, remained in his new post for the remainder of the campaign and earned praise from Verbeck as an excellent and loyal executive officer.

Colonel Verbeck, a decorated and wounded veteran of fighting in Alaska, was an imposing figure physically and in other respects. He stood 6 feet 5 inches, spoke fluent Japanese and was conversant in Tagalog, the national language of the Philippines.

Captain Malcolm D. Aitken, S-3 for the regiment's 3rd Battalion, recalled his first impression. "The 3rd Battalion had been driven off the high ground to the south the previous day, after having been virtually surrounded. We were dragging our tails, frankly, and I probably showed it."

After an initial exchange, the new regimental commander commented: "Captain, I know what you all went through yesterday and I'm proud of the 3rd Battalion. Now what do you say we walk back down the road so I can meet the rest of your great group."

Later, Aitken told the battalion commander, Lieutenant Colonel Eric Ramee, he thought he was bringing in the grand prize. "I decided that this was a man I could follow to hell, if necessary. And as it turned out I did, several times."

One of Verbeck's first moves was to order L Company to make a flanking maneuver to the east to try to seize the high ground that had been denied Company G from the front. But the enemy forced L Company to pull back. F Company also had withdrawn from earlier positions because of a misunderstanding in orders, and now the two companies made contact.

Thus the 21st Regiment's night perimeters after the first day of the attack were at the edge of Breakneck Ridge. In their first three days of Leyte combat, 5-7 November, the Gimlets engaged in sharp and costly fighting, losing 40 killed, three missing and 117 wounded.

Meanwhile, on 7 November, the 2nd Battalion, 19th Infantry, after having made a hurried trip from Jaro to the coast, was ordered to seize Hill 1525 on the far southeastern end of the ridge mass. Because the outfit's kitchens were still at Jaro, the troops moved out with only two-thirds of a ration per man.

The mission, assigned to the Chicks' Company G, went awry when guides led the troops far to the east of the intended destination.

Colonel Verbeck that night ordered an artillery barrage against the positions in front of the 2nd Battalion of his regiment and then

renewed the attack the following morning. He directed the 1st Battalion to take Hill 1525 and make contact with the 2nd Battalion, 19th Infantry, from which point the American troops could flank the enemy from the south.

In the midst of these plans for offensive action, violent tropical weather pounded the battlefield. A typhoon moved in from the west on the morning of 8 November. It was vividly described by a 24th Division soldier, Jan Valtin, in his book, *Children of Yesterday*:

"From the angry immensity of the heavens, floods raced in almost horizontal sheets. Palms bent low under the storm, their fronds flattened like streamers of wet silk. Trees crashed to the earth ...the howling of the wind was like a thousand-fold plaint of the unburied dead. The trickle of supplies was at a standstill. On Carigara Bay the obscured headlands moaned under the onslaught of the ...seas ... Massed artillery barrages sounded dim and hollow in the tempest. Trails were obliterated by the rain. The sky was black."

When the typhoon struck, Johnny Rodriguez of C Company 21st and a buddy, Wilson Cannon, were caught in the open with no time to dig in. Cannon was very cold and his teeth were chattering. Rodriguez sat down and wrapped his arms around Cannon to keep him warm during the night. Their helmets were the only protection from the deluge.

The 3rd Battalion was in a perimeter in a coconut grove near the beach at Pinamopoan when the typhoon struck. It was into that situation that a lieutenant colonel from Sixth Army headquarters paid a visit, giving Captain Aitken a chance to make his case for supply relief on behalf of the regiment.

The line companies had been in combat for five days without hot food, and the forward units were down to about one unit of fire. Also, no replacements were in sight for the regiment, which had suffered about 10 percent casualties.

Pleas for resupply went unheeded. That night, as typhoon winds continued to blow and torrential rains fell, a large coconut tree fell directly on the hole where the Sixth Army visitor and two lieutenants were sheltered under a poncho. The officers were not injured by the tree, but they were trapped for a time in the water-filled hole and nearly drowned. It took the efforts of several soldiers to free the men.

Despite the storm, the 24th Division battalions launched the day's scheduled attack. It was harder going for the 21st Infantry. The 2nd Battalion routed Japanese from their spider holes and caves with flame-throwers and doggedly ground out an advance. Company E moved forward until it reached the site of a bridge the Japanese had blown and there came under mortar, rifle and automatic weapons fire from the flanks.

That, in fact, was the pattern of much of the day's fighting, as the enemy infiltrated in small groups and took the 2nd Battalion under fire from concealed positions on their flanks and rear.

Nevertheless, Company F fought its way to its objective, the southeastern crest of Breakneck Ridge, and when night came the company was still in contact with a hostile force.

GIs, marching to battle, strive to be optimistic, showing true grit.

The enemy strength in front of the 21st Infantry enjoyed excellent defensive positions. As one example, Japanese soldiers occupied the steep sides of a gulch at the destroyed bridge where E Company was stalled.

The 1st Battalion moved out the same morning, 8 November toward Hill 1525, an uncertain undertaking considering the poor quality of the available maps. But by late afternoon, the unit reported digging in under automatic weapons fire at the southern base of the hill.

The 2nd Battalion, 19th Infantry, meanwhile, was attempting to reach the same objective. G Company drove a Japanese force off a bridge where the advance had been held up the day before. By the time the remainder of the battalion had caught up, the enemy had abandoned much of his equipment, including a field order left on the body of an officer.

Lieutenant Colonel Robert Spragins, battalion commander, determined his unit was still east of Hill 1525, so he ordered Company E to occupy a ridge 1,000 yards to the west to provide an observation post into the Ormoc Valley.

While the two forces were locked in battle on Breakneck Ridge itself, the positions to the north behind the main front were not quiet either. On the night of 7 November, a suicide squad of about 25 Japanese, some of whom could speak English, attacked the perimeter of the 19th Infantry's 3rd Battalion at Pinamopoan. Fifteen of the enemy were killed, including one who had strapped a land mine to his stomach. A bullet detonated the explosive.

Nor had the 34th Infantry been idle since the 21st Regiment had relieved the regiment in its forward position. The 1st and 3rd battalions and elements of the 19th Regiment probed the mountainous region on patrols out of the coastal towns of Capoocan and Colasion Point. The 34th Infantry's 2nd Battalion patrolled the Sinayawan-Mount Badian area in response to reports of heightened enemy activity. (Detailed accounts of 34th Regiment's actions during the battle of Breakneck Ridge will appear in a subsequent chapter.)

Foul weather spawned by the typhoon continued to drench the battlefield the night of 8 November and into the following morning as the 21st Regiment troops, weary, muddy, and soaked after four days of hard combat, prepared to jump off again.

Two battalions abreast, the 2nd, less Company F, on the west side of the highway and the 3rd on the east, moved forward against the heights of Breakneck Ridge. Heavy American artillery barrages had preceded the infantrymen and now as the attack progressed, howitzers and mortars continued to rain fire down on targets in front of the advance. Rifle companies, using grenades and flame-throwers, reduced the resistance before them.

By the end of the day's intense fighting, both battalions had improved their positions. It took less than two hours for Company I to reach the crest of an intermediate ridge that ran southward toward the middle of the main ridge line. A short time later, Company L passed through the Company I position to attack the center of Breakneck Ridge, and after several hours of hard fighting against strong opposition, managed to seize the top of the hill in its sector.

On the right of the American lines, E Company, which had held a perimeter at the gulch site of the blown bridge for two days, moved away from that position and swung farther west to occupy high ground at the rear of the Japanese overlooking the bridge location. G Company maneuvered even farther to the right to attack OP Hill, one of the first-day objectives. Forward observers continued to direct artillery fire against targets of opportunity.

Both E and G companies west of the highway reached their objectives as well, but the latter, in the face of blistering enemy fire, was forced to retire about 300 yards north on the eastern slopes of a ridge and reorganize. G Company then threw back an evening counterattack. Each of the rifle companies, having dug into night-time perimeters, received reinforcement from a platoon of heavy machine guns.

Action to the southeast in the vicinity of Hill 1525 remained confused and difficult on 9 November. The 1st Battalion, 21st Infantry, had orders to leave one company, A as it turned out, on the western slope of the hill and move west-northwest to cut the Ormoc Road near Limon so as to block the escape route of the Japanese from Breakneck Ridge.

Heavy enemy fire from the front and both flanks stalled the battalion temporarily but did not prevent the unit from nearing Limon. However, back on the hill, A Company found itself beleaguered by a superior enemy force and was barely hanging onto its position. As a consequence, orders came for the rest of the battalion to abandon the Ormoc Road mission and fall back to the hill in relief of A Company. Upon the arrival of these troops, enemy pressure continued, forcing the battalion to retire another 3,500 yards to Pinamopoan, where the unit established a beach perimeter.

The two battalions in the vicinity of Hill 1525, the 1st of the 21st and the 2nd of the 19th, still had not made contact with each other; nor would they that day.

The latter battalion, still probing westward in search of the hill, moved out in that direction the morning of 9 November to join Company E, which had preceded the main body the previous afternoon.

When Colonel Spragins learned of A Company's troubles about noon that day, he ordered F Company forward in a forced march to pick up E Company with the intention of having both join the battle.

Slippery trails and felled trees, no doubt from the typhoon, hampered the march, and the column did not reach the last ridge until late in the afternoon. The 2nd Battalion troops could see Carigara Bay and the Ormoc Valley, but they heard no sound of firing that would tell them a battle was being fought; nor did their patrols turn up any sign of friend or foe.

The battalion thought it was on the western slope of Hill 1525, but by this time, it became evident that the hill wasn't what the maps had shown it to be. Instead of a single hill, it was a long ridge with many knobs and knolls.

Spragins was told the hill had been lost that day and it was his battalion's assignment to retake it, in a night attack if possible. However, the location of the hill proper was still unknown and the resumption of fighting would have to wait until daylight.

The same day, 9 November, the Japanese succeeded in reinforcing Leyte through Ormoc, though U.S. air attacks succeeded in disrupting the operation. The infusion of fresh enemy troops was part of the offensive plan outlined in the captured document mentioned above. That alerted the Sixth Army commander, General Krueger, to the need to resume the drive south in earnest and to protect the mountain passes into the Northern Leyte Valley, which the Japanese hoped to recapture.

The coordinated drive over and through Breakneck Ridge to Limon and Ormoc Bay was set for the morning of 10 November, and as before, it was the 24th Division that drew the spearhead assignment.

General Irving ordered the 21st Infantry to attack the center, while a battalion from each of the other regiments established strong flanking positions on either side. The 2nd Battalion, 19th Infantry, its frustrating odyssey in search of Hill 1525 over, was assigned to set up a roadblock on Highway 2 about a mile south of Limon. The 1st Battalion, 34th Regiment, was to sweep far to the right and occupy Kilay Ridge.

"Success of the Leyte campaign depends upon quickly and completely destroying hostile forces on our front," General Irving told his troops before they jumped off that sodden morning after rain had saturated the front throughout the night. Also falling on the Japanese positions were artillery shells from a 10-minute barrage.

The Gimlets' 1st Battalion, having reorganized after its foray on Hill 1525, moved out from its beach position and passed through the ridge perimeters that the 2nd and 3rd battalions had established the previous day.

Company A, the lead unit, passed through the E Company position. Company G captured OP (Observation Post) Hill, and Company I occupied the site of the demolished bridge. Company L seized the elevation in its own area.

The attack seemed to be going well, but an attempt by the 1st Battalion to take a ridge 200 yards to its front, an assault Colonel Verbeck had ordered, was unsuccessful and the troops had to fall back to previous positions.

Japanese on the reverse slopes of OP Hill also resisted the 2nd Battalion's efforts to move down the ridge toward them. To make matters worse, enemy soldiers after dark managed to cut the telephone lines from 21st Regiment headquarters to its battalions.

Howitzers poured white phosphorus shells and other ordnance on the enemy during the night. Company C of the 85th Chemical Battalion added 4.2-inch mortar rounds. Captain Aitken, for one, was effusive in his praise of that unit, and indeed all support elements. "Their awesome accuracy and the devastating effect of their HE (high explosive) and WP (white phosphorous) fire saved countless American lives, and we worshipped them." Others he mentioned were the engineers, artillerymen, the armored force, forward observers, liaison men, intelligence personnel, and the 7th Portable Surgical Hospital, about which the S-3 said, "Coolness under fire seemed to be their watchword, and their unfailing professionalism doubtless permitted some of us to return to our families in more or less whole condition ..."

On 11 November, the 1st and 2nd Battalions abreast launched a renewed attack. Fire from Japanese in strong positions east of Corkscrew Ridge kept the 2nd Battalion immobilized, and the 1st Battalion, after penetrating to a point 300 yards south of the main ridge, also encountered stiff opposition.

Armor from the 44th Tank Battalion came up and took out about 25 enemy positions, but one tank was lost when it went over the edge of a road.

A remarkable feat of bridge building made the tank operation possible. It was the work of the 1st Platoon, A Company, 3rd Engineer Battalion. The company commander, Captain James Latane, measured the gap to be spanned and had timbers cut to the precise size. The pieces were trucked forward to the site and quickly assembled. It was virtually a pre-fab

ricated bridge, which the engineers put together under fire.

The regimental commander, Colonel Verbeck, personally led the tank column to the top of the ridge, despite the fact the targets were several hundred yards forward of his command post and he had only the regiment's Intelligence and Reconnaissance Platoon for cover. The fire the tanks delivered against the entrenched Japanese positions on the reverse slopes and in the wooded ravines was considered to be the key action in the regiment's breakthrough. The A Company tank commander, Captain Julian Van Winkle, arrived at the forward regimental command post holding his lower abdomen with two gunshot wounds. The company commander had refused to leave the scene of action until the mission was complete and then he walked back under his own power.

By day's end, the 1st Battalion held its objective, a ridge 300 yards southwest of OP Hill. On 12 November, the 3rd Battalion, with armored support, passed over the crest of Breakneck Ridge before noon, and the 1st Battalion enveloped the Japanese left flank.

"The enemy response to the successful advance of the 21st was violent and non-stop," Aitken recalled. "Artillery and mortar rounds as well as heavy machine gun fire fell in all advance positions." In the ensuing days, all three battalions engaged in fighting against company-size units, with bayonets often used by both sides.

The Japanese hold on Breakneck Ridge was starting to give way.

In fighting on 13 November, the 1st and 2nd battalions made significant advances. By the following day, the 21st Regiment had broken the major resistance and occupied all of Breakneck Ridge proper. Japanese forces remained on some secondary heights, however, and were continuing to put up a fight.

The 1st Battalion, the unit farthest forward, attacked south toward Limon in companies abreast on 14 November. Company A was astride the highway; Company B was on the west and Company C on the east. The battalion encountered stiff resistance but ended the day within 1,200 yards of Limon.

That night, the 2nd Battalion beat off three determined Japanese counterattacks, and the following day, all three battalions encircled and reduced enemy strongpoints.

A casualty late in the battle was I Company commander Lieutenant Dale E. Johnson of Manhattan, KS, who was crouching in a forward observation post when he was killed by a sniper. He and Aitken had been friends since Schofield Barracks days. Long weeks in combat had numbed men to news of losses. "But this time I broke down as I watched them load his body in the back of a 2 1/2 ton truck, with many others," Aitken recalled.

After 12 continuous days of grinding combat, the 21st Infantry was relieved on 16 November by the 32nd Division's 128th Regiment. The 21st troops walked back to Carigara and the following day moved by truck to the area of Jaro.

The battle of Breakneck Ridge had been a bloody one for the 21st Infantry, which suffered 630 casualties, killed, missing and wounded. The Gimlets killed 1,779 Japanese.

On 18 November, the 11th F.A. Battalion was in position near Colasian in direct support of the 24th Division's continued attack on Breakneck Ridge and the approaches to the Ormoc Valley. At about 1100, Japanese artillery fire began falling on battalion headquarters, seriously wounding in the shoulder John Berry, the battalion Operations Sergeant.

In short order, a tremendous artillery barrage turned the entire headquarters area into a terrifying scene of chaos and destruction. Colonel Hodges, the battalion commander, could hear the cries of the wounded above the shouts of men and the din of artillery bursts. In the second gun section of B Battery, bright flames from exploding shells igniting powder charges shot high in the air. The sharp cracks of small arms ammunition sounded like a string of firecrackers.

Some of the men of B Battery and Battalion Headquarters ran to a small stream bed for cover; others dove into their foxholes. With the shelling and noise intensifying, Colonel Hodges made his way to B Battery, directly in front of the fire direction center, to determine the damage. There he saw an incredible, unforgettable sight: Staff Sergeant Howard W. Wagner, blood streaming down his face, driving his bulldozer through the artillery barrage. On his own initiative, realizing the extreme danger facing B Battery, he was moving dirt to extinguish the burning powder and cover the exploding .30 caliber ammunition. These shells could have hit highly sensitive fuses stored nearby, setting off a chain reaction and possibly causing the entire ammunition pits to explode.

Sergeant Wagner's open, exposed position astride the bulldozer made him especially vulnerable to shell fragments. With total disregard for his own safety, Wagner drove the bulldozer back and forth with extraordinary courage and skill until the fires threatening the powder charges and small arms ammunition were extinguished.

The sergeant dismounted from the bulldozer near the second and third gun sections to discuss the situation with the B Battery commander, Captain James Will, and the executive officer, Lieutenant Will Chilcote. Suddenly several shells landed a few yards away. A shell fragment tore a large gash in Sergeant Wagner's leg, giving him his second wound of the day. A short time later, while being moved to a jeep for transportation to a medical unit, a large shell fragment caused a very serious wound in his side, necessitating evacuation to the 1st Field Hospital. After his return to the United States, Sargeant Wagner required long and extensive medical treatment and rehabilitation.

Staff Sergeant Wagner was one of eight men of the 11th Field Artillery Battalion to earn the Silver Star during World War II.

FLANK BATTLES

The success of the Breakneck Ridge battle before and after the relief of the 21st Infantry owed much to the heroic action of units of the 24th Division's other two regiments over the course of several days in three major locations.

24th beach landing on Leyte.

Assault landing on Leyte.

These were the 1st Battalion, 34th Infantry, which occupied the high ground west of the ridge; the 2nd Battalion, 19th Infantry, whose roadblock to the south held off repeated Japanese reinforcement efforts; and elements of the 2nd Battalion, 34th, which took up a position along a Japanese infiltration route.

The 2nd Battalion, 19th Infantry, started moving west on 10 November toward the Ormoc Highway south of Limon to establish the roadblock as ordered. The mission was to drive a wedge between the Japanese troops still in front of American units engaged on Breakneck Ridge and any enemy force coming up from the south.

Lieutenant Colonel Robert Spragins, battalion commander, did not want his troops to exhaust themselves fighting their way through to the objective. The men already were on short rations and had been in continuous combat since A Day, 20 October. So he chose a circuitous route hoping to avoid contact. Any Japanese the unit encountered, he hoped to kill so that the larger elements could not be warned of the 2nd Battalion's approach.

The tactic was mostly successful for the first two days, though the trek over difficult terrain in a constant rain was arduous. On 12 November, with the Ormoc Road just 1,500 yards away, the lead company, G, came under fire. The company was able to advance to the road, but heavy resistance continued from high ground west of the highway.

The selected location for the roadblock spread over elevations on either side of a saddle in the highway about 2,000 yards south of Limon. But the battalion still had to take this objective, and the supply situation was becoming desperate. The troops had to resort to raiding the packs of dead Japanese for rice and finding edible vegetation. An air drop missed the mark, and led to clashes between American and Japanese soldiers, all of whom were seeking the same prize of edibles.

According to H Company machine gunner Frank Fantino of Torrington, CT, the men were reduced to eating the pulp of the sago palm tree. A Filipino guide with the battalion showed them how to cut it to get the inside pulp. It had no taste but at least put something in

their stomachs. Rations did come down one day. "Big deal!" By the time the squad leaders divided the rations, each man received just one spoonful of a mixture of cereal, corn, meat, and raisins.

Spragins' major push to seize the desired terrain astride the Ormoc Road started on the morning of 15 November when Companies E and G and a platoon from F Company jumped off for the hill south of the saddle. Fantino was too weak to lift the gun tripod by himself and had to get two buddies to set the tripod on his shoulders. The rest of the battalion remained behind with the executive officer, Major Charles Isackson.

G Company crossed the road without drawing fire, but once the troops started moving up the hill, fire from well-fortified positions pinned down two platoons. Spragins redeployed E Company to the northern slope, which it took with little difficulty, thus establishing what would become the west perimeter.

When Isackson's detachment formed the east perimeter, the roadblock was in place, but the attack that put the battalion in position had cost a number of casualties. Attempts were made immediately to establish contact with the 1st Battalion, 34th Infantry, on Kilay Ridge 700 yards to the west, as a route for evacuating casualties, but the enemy was too strong between the two positions and the idea had to be abandoned.

The 2nd Battalion's roadblock paid off quickly. Late on the night of 15 November, a Japanese truck convoy came up from the south. American machine gun fire set four of the vehicles on fire and created havoc among the enemy troops.

Three hours later, an enemy infantry column also tried and failed to penetrate the American blockade, suffering heavy losses from the machine guns. After daylight, an artillery duel rocked the perimeter. It was the first of five days of grim defensive combat. The battalion was constantly besieged by an enemy of superior numbers while enduring the privations of hunger, thirst and the harsh elements. The Rock of Chickamauga was proving once again to be worthy of the name.

Pfc Fantino will never forget the guard-

ian angel who took care of him during this time. With his machine gun dug in on the side of a hill overlooking the road, one of three Japanese spotted him and threw a grenade that landed at his feet. It settled in the mud before exploding. Fantino was covered with mud but no fragments.

A weapons carrier, firing its machine gun, tried to run the road block gauntlet. Fantino crouched low in his foxhole with just his hands protruding above his head firing his machine gun at the weapons carrier. After three bursts, he poked his head up and saw his tracers hitting the carrier. The Japanese machine gunner was not in sight. Despite absorbing more bullets and nearly rolling over a bank, the carrier moved out of range.

Later a Japanese tank came into view. Its first round hit just below Fantino's machine gun, lifting the gun about a foot, but not exploding. The second round was long, landing between his gun and the foxhole above him, but also not exploding. The third round, which would have split the bracket, did not come.

Many wounded were forced to lie for days in muddy foxholes, receiving only the most rudimentary medical care, but it was the best that medics could offer. The west perimeter particularly suffered in that regard. The battalion surgeon, Captain Edward Croxdale, was on the east side and three times attempted to cross with patrols to the west only to find the resistance too great.

The morale of the wounded and able alike remained high, however. Typical was the casualty who after receiving no treatment for days concluded he would recover without it. "Captain, if they don't get me out of here pretty soon, I'll be well and won't have a chance to see those white sheets and pretty nurses," the soldier told an officer.

A relief column, elements of the 3rd Battalion, 34th Infantry, arrived 19 November The party consisted of I and K companies, troops from M Company, an anti-tank platoon, an ammunition and pioneer section, artillery, medical and radio detachments. Also on hand was the Cannon Company of the 19th Regiment. The relief troops brought food and started making plans to carry out the wounded on litters fabricated from small trees and parachute fabric.

Orders came for the battalion to withdraw on 20 November, but Japanese attacks through the first half of the day stalled the effort. The enemy launched banzai charges against both perimeters at dawn. The GIs repulsed them, but the west perimeter absorbed a renewed assault. Finally, a platoon of G Company, 19th, threw back the last attack, killing 70 of the enemy.

The withdrawal over the next three days was an epic event in itself. Before starting the withdrawal, each man was fortified with 10 "D" rations (chocolate bars). Facing the chest-deep, swift-running Leyte River, the Battalion used two parallel ropes fashioned from vines to maintain footing during the crossing. It was Spragins himself who led a group of men across to secure the first line on the far bank. The battalion accomplished the maneuver without losing a man, a pack or a weapon.

The carrying party of the 3rd Battalion, 34th Infantry, which was ahead of the 2nd Battalion, 19th, on the trail, engaged in a brisk firefight on 21 November, and fell back to a point where it joined the 19th Regiment men.

With the two battalions now together, the tortuous trek continued under the rear-guard protection of K Company, 34th Infantry, and elements of the "Chicks."

It was hard going. Litters had to be passed hand to hand in the rugged terrain. It took four hours for the procession to pass one particularly steep point where a long human chain had to handle the litters. Bearers, quickly fatigued, required frequent relief. The roadblock defenders and the carrying party combined accounted for 26 litter cases and 40 walking wounded. There would be more casualties before the destination was reached.

On 23 November, the last full day on the trail, the column came under enemy fire from knee mortars and other weaponry, resulting in the loss of two dead and three wounded. The fatalities were a blinded casualty and the soldier who was leading him.

The column reached Pinamopoan on 24 November, Thanksgiving Day, and enjoyed their first hot meal in two weeks. Company F aid man, Richard C. Watson of Daleville, IN, started the 23-day combat ordeal at 170 lbs. and came out at 98 lbs.

The roadblock operation had cost the 2nd Battalion 31 dead, all of whom were given religious burials, plus two missing. In addition to the 55 wounded who were successfully evacuated, 241 men were hospitalized for skin disorders, foot ulcers, battle fatigue and exhaustion.

The 2nd Battalion, 19th Infantry, received a Presidential Unit Citation for its feat of arms. The citation stated in part: "For five days, surrounded, attacked repeatedly, unable to evacuate its wounded, and with ever increasing attrition from hunger and exposure, the battalion held. It broke up four enemy truck columns, dispersed three strong foot columns, neutralized four field pieces, and artillery observers directed devastating fire on numerous concentrations [of the enemy]."

The battalion was also known as the "Lost Battalion." Back on the beach in a hospital, a sergeant from Division Headquarters asked Pfc

An M-7 supports 24th Infantry Division soldiers advancing on Leyte Island.

Frank Fantino if the men had expected to come out of their roadblock position alive. Fantino answered, "Of course; we all did." The sergeant replied, "Division Headquarters didn't. They were writing you guys off the books. They called you the 'Lost battalion.'"

During and after the 2nd Battalion's action on the Ormoc Road, the 1st Battalion, 34th Infantry, was engaged in desperate defense of a height known as Kilay Ridge to the west. The terrain feature dominated the road, whose occupation by American troops was necessary to protect the flank of the main force driving south from Breakneck Ridge toward Limon and to prevent Japanese reinforcement of the front from that direction.

On 10 November, Lieutenant Colonel Thomas (Jock) Clifford, battalion commander, was ordered to prepare for rapid movement. His unit, down to 565 men after 21 days of continuous combat, boarded 18 LVTs for the seven-mile trip across Carigara Bay from Capoocan to the disembarkation point.

Once having landed, the battalion moved quickly inland without opposition, arriving at Kilay Ridge at the rear of the enemy lines on 13 November. To that point, supply was the unit's most serious problem. The departure had been so abrupt that accompanying rations were inadequate and resupply efforts along the way were only partly successful. Except for the help of Filipino guerrillas, the situation would have been worse.

The Americans found well-prepared fortifications atop Kilay Ridge, but no Japanese to man them. It was obvious from the honeycomb of trenches and gun emplacements that the enemy expected to occupy the ridge later.

Clifford ordered his troops to establish their own defensive positions for maximum tactical advantage. The ridge, running northwest to southeast, was about 900 feet high, its crest broken by a series of knolls. To the east were other high points that partly obstructed the view of Highway 2. Included were hills designated Ridges Numbers 2 and 3, which also would have to be held by the battalion.

As mentioned above, the effort made for

contact between the 1st Battalion, 34th, on Kilay Ridge and the 2nd Battalion, 19th, on the Ormoc Road, never achieved more than tenuous success because of the strength of the Japanese positions between them.

The first significant action occurred on 15 November when an A Company patrol clashed with about 50 Japanese on Ridge Number 2, which was about 600 yards east of the battalion's main positions.

The intensity of combat stepped up markedly on 17 November. A platoon of Company B on Ridge Number 2 and elements of first Company D and then Company B on Ridge Number 3, about 600 yards to the south, tangled in an increasingly fierce encounter with about 200 Japanese.

As that fight raged, Clifford went to the scene. While he was there B Company suffered six casualties, one of whom could not walk out because of a thigh wound. The battalion commander himself carried the man on his back for a mile over a difficult trail to the command post. Clifford was awarded the Distinguished Service Cross for this action.

Company B by the end of the day was cut off from the rest of the battalion. This was the first of several times during the Kilay Ridge fight that a unit would be isolated from the main force.

But Clifford was not willing to give up what his troops painfully had gained. He sent a carrying party to resupply the besieged company and then Company C to relieve it. The latter company did so on 18 November, but under heavy rifle fire, and the firefight continued.

Meanwhile, Company B, in a new position on the south flank of Kilay Ridge, was the target of an attack that threatened to surround it again. Artillery fire was directed on enemy positions, but Company B was running low on ammunition. After going forward to inspect the situation, Clifford ordered the company to pull back. For the same reason, the colonel also ordered the withdrawal of Company C from Ridge Number 2 to Kilay Ridge. On the morning of 20 November, the Japanese attacked in force, but the Company C positions had been vacated a half hour before.

By this time, conditions for the battalion were starting to deteriorate. Not only was ammunition becoming critically low, but rations were inadequate, the men were never dry, the constant rain kept the ridges muddy and slick, ranks were being depleted by sickness as well as battle casualties, sleep was fitful and sporadic at best and enemy fire persistent.

At the north end of the ridge, the concern was keeping the supply line to the town of Consuegra open in the face of reports that strong Japanese columns were converging on the ridge from two directions.

The enemy launched a fierce attack with fixed bayonets against the perimeter at midafternoon on 22 November, nearly surrounding Companies A and B. The fight lasted into the darkness, and Clifford ordered Company B to break out through Company A.

That night, General Gill, commander of the 32nd Infantry Division, to which the battalion was temporarily attached, ordered Clifford to hold the ridge at all costs. Two days later, after relative quiet had returned to the front, Gill sent the following message to the battalion commander: "You and your men are doing a superb job. Hang on and keep killing the Japs…" They would do both, hang on, and kill more enemy, a total of about 900 before the battle was over.

The fight reheated on 25 November with another heavy perimeter attack against Company A. The regimental commander, Colonel Dahlen, told Clifford that his battalion was "in a tight spot," because the 32nd Division could give him no immediate help.

Clifford knew that his small and dwindling force was surrounded on at least three sides and an enemy attack could come from about any direction. The crucial supply line to the north was still open, but for how long, the battalion commander couldn't know.

At 1930 on 28 November, the Japanese launched their main attack in the attempt to drive the Americans off Kilay Ridge. Enemy mortar and heavy machine-gun fire was directed against outposts; GI mortar crews responded with a barrage of their own. Company C on the south came under ferocious assault. The charging Japanese reached Company C lines with bayonets fixed and combat became hand to hand. The forward platoon pulled back to the rest of the company, which was separated from the rest of the battalion.

The fight continued through the night and by morning, Company C was still cut off. A reinforced platoon from Company B broke through to Company C, but the ammunition shortage was acute. A party carrying ammunition to the beleaguered company was pinned down by Japanese blocking the trail.

The supply line from Consuegra was still open, however, and a party entered the perimeter carrying, among other things, Thanksgiving rations – five days late.

Clifford asked for reinforcements, and got them. Late in the afternoon, 2nd Battalion of the 128th Infantry arrived on the ridge. On 1 December, both battalions took up the task of driving the Japanese off the ridge and putting

down resistance, but even with the fresh troops, hard fighting continued.

On 2 December, commanders halted the ordered withdrawal of Clifford's battalion when a company of the 128th Regiment encountered stiff opposition in attempting to reclaim a hill. However, on 4 December, the 1st Battalion, 34th Infantry, started coming off the ridge in earnest and over the next two days the Red Dragons made their way back to Pinamopoan.

The battle of Kilay Ridge had cost the battalion 26 dead, two missing and 101 wounded. Sickness also took its toll to the point that the battalion's effective strength dropped to less than 400.

The 24th Division report on the Leyte campaign stated: "Colonel Clifford finally had to order the battalion surgeon to evacuate only the worst cases. The remainder fought with what strength they had left, and often on sheer nerve alone."

The 2 December order for Clifford to withdraw his battalion, issued by General Gill, included this message: "You and your men have not been forgotten. You are the talk of the island, and perhaps the United States. Army beat Notre Dame, 59-0, the worst defeat on record." The latter must have pleased Clifford, who had been an All-American football player at West Point.

The 1st Battalion, 34th Infantry, received a Presidential Unit Citation for its defense of Kilay Ridge. The citation stated in part: "Ten major and 17 minor engagements took place during the next 14 days as the Japanese made desperate attempts to retake Kilay Ridge…Elements of the battalion were cut off four different times but fought their way out and regained contact with our own troops. Three times the battalion gave ground, but by prompt counterattacks regained the lost positions … .

"The bold and determined action of the [battalion] in maintaining for 25 days the hazardous position behind enemy lines, then courageously participating in the attack, so harassed the enemy that he was unable to withstand our main attack southward through Limon."

The main drive down the Ormoc corridor and the two main blocking operations on the highway south of Limon and Kilay ridge occupied the 21st Infantry and one battalion each of the 19th and 34th regiments for various periods in November and December 1944, but other elements of the 24th Division were busy also, often in contact with the enemy.

Most of their work either was in protecting the flanks along the path of the southward thrust or guarding the supply lines behind that offensive. Japanese penetration of the defensive perimeter in the beach area would have had serious consequences for the entire operation.

The 1st Battalion, 19th Infantry was attached to the 1st Cavalry Division while shielding corps artillery shelling Ormoc and patrolling trails to lake Davao. In carrying out the latter mission, Company A reinforced spent nine extremely hard days contending with the steep terrain and foul weather typical of the environment. The troops tried three times to

cross mountain passes and engaged in sharp fights each time. The entire unit nearly drowned in a flash flood that cascaded down a gorge. Battle casualties were light, but when the company was relieved - by an entire regiment, incidentally - attrition from sickness and exposure had reduced its effective strength from 191 to 120.

The 24th Cavalry Reconnaissance Troop carried out a deep probe in enemy territory when the force penetrated nearly to Delores where as many as 600 to 800 Japanese could be observed.

The 3rd Battalion of the 19th Regiment, besides defending the beach area, helped with the hand-supply train for the 1st Battalion, 34th, on Kilay Ridge. Both the 1st and 3rd Battalions, 19th Infantry were assigned on 19 November to the Sixth Army as part of the Western Visayan Task Force.

With the 1st Battalion, 34th Infantry, engaged and the 3rd Battalion committed either to holding Hill 1525 or evacuating the 19th Infantry wounded from the Ormoc roadblock, it fell to the 2nd Battalion, 34th, to stretch itself thinly along the beach perimeter to secure the American supply line and prevent Japanese infiltration.

From 8 November to the end of the Breakneck Ridge battle, all three rifle companies of the 2nd Battalion plus the heavy weapons company exchanged fire with the enemy, inflicting and taking casualties.

At one point, Japanese broke through the line near Colasian and set up a roadblock. Native supply carriers fled, and the Cannon Company was pressed into service to replace them, further reducing its strength. Colonel Dahlen converted the anti-tank company into a temporary rifle company and put those troops plus cooks and clerks into the line.

The hastily organized unit attacked, and over the next two days forced the Japanese from their positions while occupying three hills.

The saga of Company G in maintaining a ridge-top blocking position over more than three weeks played a key role in the success of the operation on Breakneck Ridge.

The company under command of Captain Ben Wahle headed south out of Capoocan early on 8 November toward a position about five miles south. The mission was to occupy a point on the major Japanese infiltration route up the Ormoc corridor. Dense jungle and poor maps made the going tough, but the unit found high ground on the trail near the village of Sinawayan where Wahle decided to set up his defensive perimeter.

G Company's strength at the time was 87 men; in addition, a heavy machine gun section from H Company had been attached. F Company also accompanied the column, but the next day, the battalion commander, Colonel Pearsall, recalled those troops to Capoocan.

After a few days of comparative quiet, the Japanese attacked a patrol and then followed the Americans back to the perimeter. Eric Diller, a member of H Company, described the encounter. Pfc. Angelo Montaglione, the patrol scout, ran back to friendly lines. "Where are they," Diller asked. "Right behind us," the scout answered. Diller then noticed the blood on Montaglione's fatigues. The soldier had been hit three times in the thigh, causing life-threatening wounds considering the terrain and the isolation of the unit. But the soldier survived that action, and the war.

When the attack against the perimeter came, the Americans answered with machine gun fire and grenades, several thrown by Diller. "Our section leader, Sergeant Carey, moved 10 feet in front of our position and squatted down when an enemy grenade exploded." Diller recalled. "I raised my head and asked him if he was OK. He nodded and almost simultaneously an enemy bullet pierced his head, killing him instantly."

Diller credited a G Company BAR man, Pfc. Leo Gomolchak, with a major role in driving off the attack. "He calmly stood behind a huge tree ... and blasted away, a real unsung hero." After the fight, 42 Japanese bodies were found.

The attacks, which in the beginning came from the south, gradually moved around the perimeter until Captain Wahle was convinced his company was surrounded. He alerted his platoon sergeants to the possibility of a fixed-bayonet breakout in case the position was overrun.

Supplies also began to grow short, making a diet of coconuts and rain water necessary. The stench of decaying bodies fouled the air.

Pfc John J. Breeden of Gordonsville, VA, relieved the tension and improved morale with an impromptu mail call. He slipped down the trail through the Japanese lines, picked up G Company's mail at 34th regimental headquarters, and made it back to the company undetected by the Japs.

On 20 November, G Company fought its biggest battle on the hilltop, an all-night affair against a company-size force that hit the perimeter on the south and west sides. Wahle recalled that bodies were stacked so high they blocked the fire lanes. Seventy-one enemy dead were counted at daylight.

"I can't praise my men enough for their willingness to stand and fight it out with a very determined enemy. Never once did I hear anyone mention giving up. This is the true test of combat seasoned soldiers," Wahle wrote years later.

Finally, late in November, Colonel Pearsall ordered F Company under Captain Paul Austin and the anti-tank company to relieve G Company, but finding the outpost was not easy. When the relief troop was about a mile away, Austin asked for gunshots from G Company so he could determine the bearing.

The three companies stayed on the hill for three more days. On 2 December orders came from battalion headquarters to return to Capoocan.

Captain Wahle counted 37 Japanese attacks against this force for which he estimated the enemy paid with more than 200 killed.

WINDING UP LEYTE

After the 21st Regiment was relieved on Breakneck Ridge, it took over the defense of the artillery units firing on Ormoc and in addition patrolled the area. On 8 December, the unit moved to the Capoocan-Carigara area for pa-

trol duty until first the 3rd Battalion and then the 1st and 2nd Battalions were placed under Sixth Army control for the next operation, Mindoro.

The last action on Leyte involving the 24th Division was conducted by the 34th Regiment and the 24th Cavalry Reconnaissance Troop on the Leyte Peninsula on the far northwest corner of the island. The 1st Battalion had no sooner arrived at the beach after its epic struggle on Kilay Ridge than the regiment was alerted on 7 December to move against an estimated 2,000 Japanese who had landed at San Isidro on the west coast of Leyte after an American air attack had wrecked their convoy offshore.

Colonel William Jenna, regimental commander who had been on sick leave in the United States, returned to his post on 23 December in time to lead the final mop-up of organized Japanese resistance on the peninsula.

The 1st Battalion 34th under Colonel Clifford was ordered to proceed overland from the east toward San Isidro while Companies F and G of the 2nd Battalion 34th conducted amphibious operations from LVTs and LCMs as they moved down the coast. When Company G reached San Isidro Bay, it encountered machine gun fire and abandoned a frontal attack. A site farther south was selected for landing, which was accomplished with difficulty when the craft became mired in mud.

The first major contact came on 10 December when a 17-man patrol from Company C came under attack by more than 100 Japanese in a fixed-bayonet banzai charge. The combat was hand-to-hand, during which a platoon leader, 1st Lieutenant Oakley Storey, killed a Japanese with the enemy officer's own saber.

Later that night, repeated attacks by Company F against strong Japanese reverse-slope positions led to equally savage fighting during which the company lost six killed and 10 wounded. But 73 enemy died.

The 34th Regiment's drive to clear the peninsula of Japanese was relatively quiet until 22 December when an enemy force was routed from the town of Tuktuk after it was caught between one platoon each from Companies A and C and a mortar squad that moved up the Nipa River.

The 24th Cavalry Reconnaissance Troop, moving down the west coast from the far corner, attacked an enemy concentration, but found itself threatened from the flank and nearly trapped against the sea. Platoon leader, 1st Lieutenant Charles Dyer, was killed in the action and the patrol escaped only by commandeering a sailing boat after dark and putting out into the bay. An American PT boat rescued the soldiers.

Finally, on 28 December, the coordinated attack of the 1st and 2nd Battalions against light resistance succeeded in the capture of San Isidro, the last major objective on the Leyte peninsula.

On 5 January 1945, the 34th Infantry was relieved by elements of the 77th Division. The regiment had engaged in 78 consecutive days of combat, a record for the Southwest Pacific Theater.

The 24th Infantry Division lost 558 men killed, and 1,784 wounded, a total of 2,342, during the Leyte operation but also left behind at least 7,252 – and probably more – dead Japanese.

It was on Leyte that the 24th Division earned the accolade, "Victory Division." Consider these facts: (1) The liberation of the Philippines was, short of forcing the surrender of Japan itself, the major American objective of

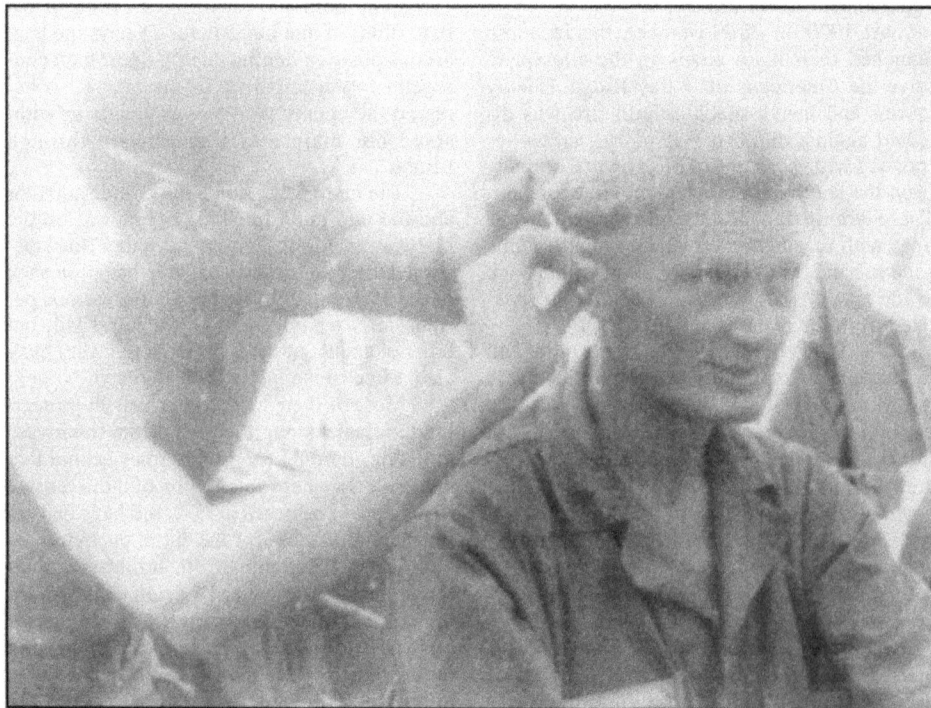

Leyte: Barber - Sgt. James Mims, customer - Lt. Zenon Rybel. Photo Interpretation Team. Even in combat, whenever circumstances permit, soldiers maintain pride in appearance. (Courtesy of J.H. Miller)

Maj Gen Roscoe B. Woodruff, Commander of the 24th Division, November 1944 - August 1945.

the Pacific war; (2) the capture of Leyte was the key to that liberation; (3) the 24th Infantry Division, fighting from 20 October to 5 January, from Red Beach on the east coast to San Isidro on the west, was, more than any other single unit, instrumental in seizing the island. Victory Division fits.

The senior Japanese commanders recognized the strategic importance of the Leyte campaign in more sweeping terms. Vice Admiral Kondo wrote the following: "Once Leyte falls into the hands of the enemy, he will be able to build up a base for the intensive bombardment of ... and for the recapture of the Philippines. Moreover, it will mean the severing of all sea communications between Japan and the south. Therefore the battle for Leyte is a battle for Japan and the decisive battle for GEA (Greater East Asia), a battle which Japan must win."

The Japanese admiral was prophetic. His opinion was reinforced in even more specific terms after the war by General Yamashita at his war crimes trial in Manila. The 24th Division commander at the time, Major General James A. Lester, was a member of the trial tribunal. As related by Ken Ross at the 24th Division's 1996 reunion in Minneapolis, General Lester had quoted Yamashita to this effect: "Japan lost the pacific war in the battle for Leyte during the Philippines campaign. Leyte was lost at the battle of Breakneck Ridge, and the battle for Breakneck Ridge was lost to your Colonel Verbeck (commanding officer of the 21st Infantry)."

The 24th Infantry Division started the crucial campaign with Major General Frederick Irving in command and ended it under the command of Major General Roscoe Woodruff, who took over on 18 November.

General Irving's son, Colonel Frederick F. Irving USA (Ret), gives these reasons for his father's relief:

"The 24th Division under General Irving had borne the brunt of the fighting on Leyte since its landing on October 20. Despite having only two regiments from October 20 until November 5 (the 21st Infantry had been detached to secure the strait separating Leyte from Pinaoan Island to the south), the division secured its initial objectives and fought its way some 35 miles across the northern Leyte Valley to capture Carigara, the entrance to the Ormoc Valley.

"Heavy rains had impeded progress and now intensified. The 24th was chosen to lead the attack south to capture Ormoc. However, the road from Carigara to Pinamopoan, over which all supplies had to pass, had dissolved in a sea of mud. General Irving warned that it would not support a major offensive until repaired, but was ordered by higher headquarters to proceed. The division pushed on, but progress was slowed by the mud and heavy enemy resistance. General MacArthur's headquarters was anxious to secure Leyte and move on to Mindoro. Sixth Army headquarters felt the pressure and decided they should relieve General Irving despite his warning.

"The officers and men of the 24th Division felt that General Irving had been made a scapegoat for the mistakes of higher headquarters. This was substantiated by the fact that the 32nd Division, which relieved the 24th south of Pinamopoan, drove less than eight miles down the Ormoc Valley by December 21st, five weeks later, even though supported by elements of the 1st Cavalry and 24th Divisions. This in spite of the fact that the 7th and the 77th Divisions had landed south of Ormoc on December 7th and November 28th and diverted a substantial portion of the Japanese defenders.

"These facts, in retrospect, show how unjustified the decision was to relieve General Irving. He later commanded the 38th Division in fighting on Luzon and went on to a distinguished career, retiring as Superintendent of the United States Military Academy at West Point."

LUZON, MINDORO AND THE WESTERN VISAYAN ISLANDS

The next major step in the Philippine campaign was the recapture of the principal island of Luzon, but a preliminary objective was Mindoro where military planners wanted to establish air bases for the support of the main effort.

Mindoro, the third largest island in the group, is directly south of Luzon. An inhospitable place of pestilential weather and forbidding terrain, it was sparsely populated. Japanese defenders numbered about 1,000.

The invasion of Mindoro was scheduled to precede that of Luzon by 15 days to give the infantry time to seize the airfield site on the southwest corner of the island and the engineers time to do their work.

After a 10-day delay, the Mindoro operation was set for 15 December. The assault troops at the principal landing site on the southwest coast were the 19th Regimental Combat Team, operating independently of the 24th Division at this point, and the 503rd Parachute

Infantry. They were part of the Western Visayan Task Force under the command of Brigadier General William C. Dunckel.

The 3rd Battalion, 21st Regiment, also was to go in on the northeastern side of the island from which point the troops could feint movement against Luzon just across a strait to the north. The Western Visayan Task Force put to sea from the eastern shore of Leyte on 12 December, and Army personnel suffered their first casualties long before they reached their destination.

On 13 December, the dreaded kamikazes, then a new weapon in the Japanese arsenal, dropped out of the sky upon the convoy transiting the Mindanao Sea and crashed into the cruiser *Nashville*. General Dunckel was wounded and his chief of staff was killed.

Later, on 21 December, the ship carrying the 3rd Battalion, 21st Infantry, toward Mindoro also was hit by a suicide plane. Six infantrymen were killed and 32 were wounded.

The invasion itself was less eventful except for an ongoing air-sea battle off the landing beaches as the Japanese continued their kamikaze tactics. The 19th Regimental Combat Team and 503rd Parachute Infantry landed abreast with little opposition and by late afternoon had secured a beachhead seven miles deep. Ineffective resistance in the far southeast part of the landing zone near Caminawit Point led to five enemy killed, two wounded and one captured.

The first day's progress put the infantry past the San Jose airstrip, a prewar emergency landing field, but engineers, who already were on the job that first day, chose another site for the airfield about three miles south.

The second day of the operation also went off smoothly. In fact, the Western Visayan Task Force suffered no ground casualties on 15-16 December. On 17 December, the town of San Jose itself was occupied. The invasion force consolidated positions, strengthened beach positions and started patrol action to the north and east.

John I. Lowgren of Torrance, CA, remembers that "Mindoro was a vacation for K Company 19th...got restful sleep for a change." Little or no opposition during the landing; patrols found negligible resistance inland. C Company's Sergeant Charles E. Blunt of Brisbane, CA, and his rifle squad with attached machine gun squad, had the luxury of sleeping in tents after first bunkering the machine gun with sand bags and barbed wire and digging individual foxholes.

Engineers completed the first airfield on Mindoro on 20 December, and had the second ready for limited use on the 23rd. The aircraft based on the island helped counter the Japanese air attacks against the airfields and the troops on the ground. The severest threat to the American presence on Mindoro was from the skies and sea, and made the airport construction performed by the engineers all the more heroic.

The GIs of the 19th Infantry found the dogfights overhead fascinating but sometimes destructive. Sergeant Blunt remembers one intrepid kamikaze pilot diving his Zero into a ship apparently loaded with gasoline and bombs an-

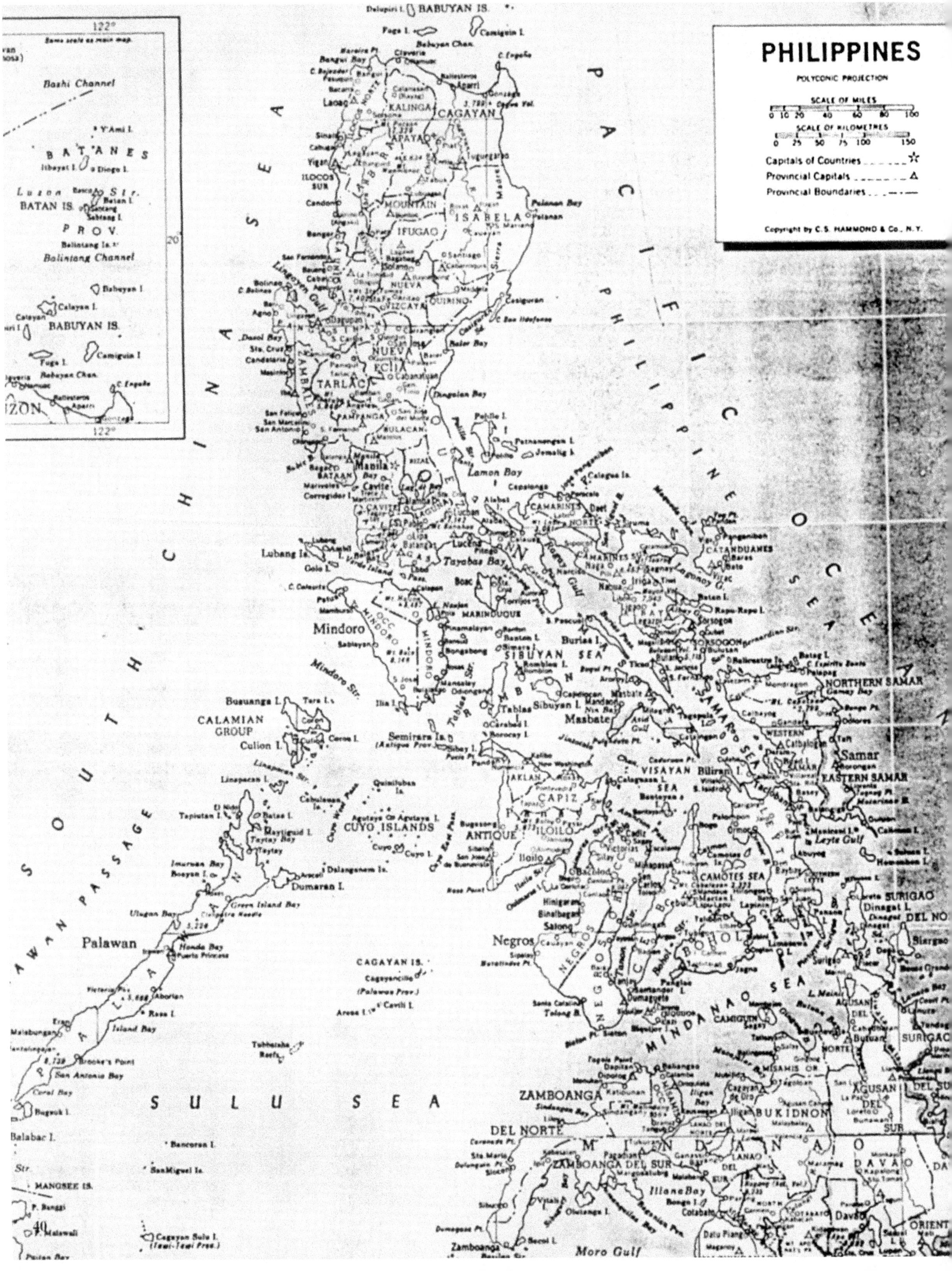

PHILIPPINES

POLYCONIC PROJECTION

SCALE OF MILES

0 10 20 40 60 80 100

SCALE OF KILOMETRES

0 25 50 75 100 150

Capitals of Countries .... ☆
Provincial Capitals .... △
Provincial Boundaries .... —·—·—

Copyright by C.S. HAMMOND & Co., N.Y.

BABUYAN IS.

BATANES

BATAN IS. PROV.

Bashi Channel

Bolintang Channel

BABUYAN IS.

Luzon

ILOCOS SUR

KALINGA

CAGAYAN

APAYAO

MOUNTAIN

ISABELA

IFUGAO

QUIRINO

NUEVA VIZCAYA

Laoag

Vigan

San Fernando

NUEVA ECIJA

TARLAC

PAMPANGA

BULACAN

BATAAN

RIZAL

Manila ☆

Manila Bay

Corregidor I.

CAVITE

LAGUNA

BATANGAS

QUEZON

Lamon Bay

Tayabas Bay

CAMARINES NORTE

CAMARINES SUR

CATANDUANES

ALBAY

SORSOGON

Mindoro

OCC. MINDORO

OR. MINDORO

MARINDUQUE

ROMBLON

MASBATE

SIBUYAN SEA

NORTHERN SAMAR

WESTERN SAMAR

EASTERN SAMAR

Samar

CALAMIAN GROUP

Culion I.

CUYO ISLANDS

ANTIQUE

CAPIZ

AKLAN

ILOILO

Iloilo

CEBU

Negros

NEGROS OCC.

NEGROS OR.

BOHOL

LEYTE

SOUTHERN LEYTE

Leyte Gulf

SURIGAO DEL NORTE

SURIGAO DEL SUR

Palawan

Puerto Princesa

CAGAYAN IS.
(Palawan Prov.)

Cuyo

Dumaran I.

Brooke's Point

Balabac I.

MANGSEE IS.

Tubbataha Reefs

SULU SEA

ZAMBOANGA DEL NORTE

ZAMBOANGA DEL SUR

Zamboanga

LANAO

BUKIDNON

MISAMIS OR.

MISAMIS OCC.

AGUSAN DEL NORTE

AGUSAN DEL SUR

CAMIGUIN

MINDANAO

MINDANAO SEA

COTABATO

DAVAO

Davao

Moro Gulf

Illana Bay

SOUTH CHINA SEA

PACIFIC OCEAN

PHILIPPINE SEA

PALAWAN PASSAGE

CAMOTES SEA

VISAYAN SEA

SAMAR SEA

BOHOL SEA

40

chored in Mangarin Bay. The resulting implosion as the ship went down created a twenty-foot wall of water which washed away and destroyed the machine gun bunker and barbed wire. The two squads had time to race away from the beach amid falling pieces of metal.

An enemy surface fleet moved close ashore on 26 December and undertook a thunderous bombardment of American positions. While friendly casualties were not great, naval shelling has been described as an especially unnerving combat experience for ground troops, even those who are veterans of land-based attacks.

The Japanese were persistent in their aerial campaign against the Mindoro invaders and the offshore shipping on which the Army units depended for supply. From 15-29 December, the enemy flew 334 sorties against the San Jose area. That is a daily average of 20 planes making three attacks each.

Starting on 19 December, the 19th Regimental Combat Team and 503rd Parachute Infantry spread out along the southern, western and northwestern shores to track down Japanese stragglers and to secure areas against the possibility of enemy reinforcements. The troops set up sites for radar stations and provided protection for them.

The 3rd Battalion, 21st, which had come through repeated air attacks while at sea, landed on 24 December. Colonel William J. Verbeck brought the rest of his 21st Regiment ashore on 30 December and deployed his troops in a defensive perimeter adjacent to the Bugsanga River, which flowed past San Jose in a southwesterly direction.

The regiment was given the task of clearing out the northeast corner of Mindoro as a diversion, as noted above, and also to liberate more Filipino civilians. About 135 Japanese were killed and 300 others driven into the interior high country by the Gimlets and guerrillas, at a cost of one dead and seven wounded in the 21st Regiment.

Early in January 1945, the 21st Infantry was in operation along the west coast of the island. Lieutenant Colonel Eric P. Ramee's 3rd Battalion cleared out enemy strongholds in Bongabong sand Pinamalayan. The 2nd Battalion advanced through the mountains to Gusay in mid-January against scattered opposition. Headquarters personnel moving with the 2nd Battalion, having been told by Filipino civilians of a Japanese patrol approaching the perimeter, ambushed the enemy soldiers. In a brief but sharp firefight, all the Japanese were killed, except one man who escaped.

Colonel Verbeck described the action in verse, one stanza of which follows: "An old man and his daughter, led the Jappies to the slaughter;

And they wandered into camp without a qualm;

So entirely unsuspecting, in a close group all collecting;

And our men were hiding, waiting cool and calm."

As the 21st Regiment drove toward Calapan, the largest town on Mindoro's northeast coast, the 3rd Battalion joined the force. The Gimlets, after meeting stiff resistance along the last eight kilometers, entered the town on 24 January.

During the Mindoro operation, K Company, 21st, under the command of Captain Milton E. Wilson, was diverted to the island of Marinduque about 30 miles off Mindoro's north coast. The reported enemy strength there was about 100 men in two garrisons. Shortly after the company landed on 5 January, the troops encountered stiff resistance at Boac and put out the call for bazookas, explosives and medical supplies. These were delivered by Navy PT boat. Company K secured the island during the week ending 11 January.

For the entire Mindoro operation, which essentially was concluded by the end of the month, ground forces of the Western Visayan Task Force suffered 16 killed, 71 wounded and

four missing in direct contact with the enemy, plus other losses from Japanese air attacks.

The capture of Mindoro was significant for several reasons. The primary purpose was to provide a base for air support for the main effort on Luzon, but the island also became a major staging area for other land operations in the Philippines as well as a base from which to secure the water passages through the Central Visayas. Moreover, by taking the northeast corner of Mindoro, the Allies ensured that the Japanese would not be able to reinforce Luzon from the south. The Japanese might also shift troops from the Lingayen Gulf area to southern Luzon to repel a possible amphibious operation from northern Mindoro.

The Japanese were still active on Mindoro in March 1945. They erected an observation post with a huge telescope on the side of 8,491' Mount Halcon, the third highest mountain in the Philippines. From this perch, they could observe and report on allied shipping in the Verde Island Passage separating Luzon and Mindoro. During a week-long mopping-up operation in Northern Mindoro, the 2nd Battalion 34th Infantry found several pockets of Japanese. G Company destroyed the OP and captured the telescope, but lost one man killed and seven wounded. Among the wounded were Jack Calhoun, the company commander, who returned to the company for the Mindanao campaign, and veteran fighter Verdun Myers, Harold Moon's Platoon Sergeant on Leyte, who took three machine gun bullets in his left elbow.

The southern Luzon campaign, the responsibility of the Eighth Army and more particularly the 11th Airborne Division, kicked off on 31 January 1945 with an invasion at Nasugbu Bay on the island's west coast about 45 miles southwest of Manila. Attached to the airborne division were two battalions of the 19th Infantry and the Cannon Company of the 21st Regiment. Cannon Company so distinguished itself in the drive from Nasugbu to the capital city that it was presented a Presidential Unit Citation.

The next mission for the 21st and 19th Regiments was to secure small islands on the western approaches to the Visayan Passages to ensure those waterways were firmly under allied control.

A reinforced company of the 19th Infantry's 1st Battalion landed on Verde Island in the strait between Luzon and Mindoro on 23 February. After three days of fighting, during which the American troops killed 20 Japanese and captured three 75-mm guns, the company returned to Mindoro. However, the guerrilla garrison left behind was not strong enough to cope with the continued resistance, so men from both 24th Division regiments returned 1 March to crush the remaining opposition. Six Americans were wounded. Japanese losses were about 80 killed.

The Lubang Islands, which guarded the western entrance to the Verde Island passage, lay about 55 miles west. After a small reconnaissance force landed on the main island of Lubang on 27 February, the reinforced 1st Battalion, 21st Infantry, came ashore unopposed the next day and chased the Japanese garrison

Troops relax, taking break from "daily grind" in Philippines. (Courtesy of J.H. Miller)

into the interior. The defenders' ranks were swollen by the presence of troops who had fled from southern Luzon under the assault of the independent 158th Infantry.

A contemporary news account of the initial landing on Lubang by the rubber-raft force of 14 men appeared in the hometown paper of Pfc. Charles W. Feeback, Jr., of Carlisle, KY. The story described a sharp 15-minute fight during which the small American force virtually wiped out a Japanese garrison in the town of Lubang. Feeback's Bronze Star citation states, "Operating under cover of darkness they established themselves so as to destroy the garrison of twice their number ... and then proceeded to Port Tillic." There, according to the citation, the troops made contact with naval forces by native canoe and provided information that caused an air strike to be called off, thereby saving the civilian population from destruction.

As a footnote to this action, reports 30 years later told of two Japanese on Lubang who were harassing fishermen. One soon was killed by gunfire and the other, a Japanese army straggler from World War II, surrendered and was returned to Japan. In the 1945 news account, there was mention of two Japanese who escaped when the American advance force eliminated the garrison at Lubang town. Feeback, then a Phoenix, AZ, businessman, surmised that the Japanese soldier who returned to Japan was one of the two enemy soldiers who had fled his group's attack in 1945.

On 9 March, Company E, 19th Infantry, relieved the 1st Battalion and spent the rest of the month clearing the island before turning mop-up operations over to the local guerrillas. About 230 Japanese were killed before Lubang was secured. American losses were 10 killed and 20 wounded. No Japanese were found on any of the other islands in the group.

Next, the 19th Regiment turned its attention to two islands in the Sibuyan Sea east of Mindoro, Simara and Romblon, which are about 25 miles apart.

The plan was for reinforced companies of the 1st Battalion to land simultaneously on each of the islands on the night of 11-12 March. The expected surprise, it was hoped, would offset the disadvantages of darkness, heavy seas and rain squalls.

The rubber-raft landing on Romblon by C Company 19th went off well, but poor visibility and mixed signals from guerrillas ashore forced troops to delay the invasion of Simara until dawn.

The fighting on both islands was difficult and costly. The company assigned to Simara took 10 days to clear the island of the stubborn enemy, killing 120 but losing 10 dead and 20 wounded of its own. That company, leaving the rest of the job to the Filipinos, moved over to Romblon to help conclude that operation.

After the landing, the C Company riflemen engaged in house-to-house fighting and drove the Japanese out of the town of Romblon and into the hills. An American patrol, maintaining contact with the enemy, was cut off and pinned down by the Japanese, who held the high ground.

A relief patrol poured enough fire into Japanese positions to allow the first unit to escape with their casualties, but the Chicks remained at a disadvantage to the Japanese holding the crest of the hill.

Mortarmen laid down a barrage and drove the enemy off the top, enabling C Company to charge up the height. Lieutenant William C. Naegele leading the unit received orders by radio to pursue the enemy.

With no heavy weapons support available, Lt. Naegele moved his platoon into position to resist an expected Japanese attack. He placed Sergeant Charles E. Blunt's first squad on the right, a machine gun squad with Roy Welch gunner in the center, and the second squad on the left. Despite laying down a base of fire, the platoon came under heavy fire from Japanese snipers and a machine gun as a Japanese officer waved his Samurai sword to signal a banzai charge.

With several men already killed and wounded, the first platoon started moving back toward the beach. Sergeant Blunt, although wounded in the lower leg by a grenade, led his squad down a steep ravine to avoid the Japanese attack. Sitting down facing four directions, the squad waited while Japanese soldiers beat the brush with machetes looking for them. When darkness came, Blunt led his squad to the beach. Blunt and one of his squad members, Pfc Gene Welsh, who was also wounded, recovered together in a makeshift hospital and later in a field hospital on Mindoro.

The 19th Infantry troops put down the island's last resistance on 3 April with a loss of 15 killed and 35 wounded. About 140 Japanese were killed.

ZIG ZAG PASS

Meanwhile, the 24th Division's 34th Regiment was busily engaged in the main event, the hard fighting on the principal island of Luzon. After the 34th Infantry's 78-day ordeal of combat on Leyte, the outfit needed substantial replacements for the new operation, which 43 officers and 796 enlisted men fresh to the theater provided. The 34th RCT (regimental combat team) and the 38th Infantry Division comprised the XI Corps, whose assignment was the invasion of the western Luzon coast in the San Antonio area of Zambales Province. The 24th Division's 11th F.A. Battalion of 155mm howitzers served with the 38th Division Artillery during the operation.

The landing site was about 20 miles northwest of Subic Bay, which was also near the location of the San Marcelino air base. Both Subic Bay and San Marcelino were military targets of significance.

Besides seizure of those installations, another objective of the assault was to close off Bataan Peninsula to any Japanese withdrawal from the north, similar to the maneuver of the Americans and Filipinos in 1942 when the Japanese invaded Luzon. Then, the Allies were able to fight a long delaying action on Bataan, and the U.S. Army was not interested in allowing a repeat performance in reverse.

Invasion day was 29 January. The four regiments of XI Corps, with the 34th on the right, went in abreast. Rather than enemy fire, the first waves were greeted by cheering Filipinos. In fact, no opposition from the completely surprised Japanese was encountered the first day. The only Army casualty was a 38th Division man who was gored by an angry carabao.

The 34th RCT's objective was Subic Bay and the town of Olongapo on the harbor's north shore. As the American troops would discover, about 50 well-positioned Japanese defended Olongapo. They held advantageous high ground and well constructed fortifications. A bridge near the approach to the town had been rigged with explosives as well, but would do the defenders no good.

Leading the American attack was the 24th Reconnaissance Troop, followed closely by the 3rd Battalion under the command of Lieutenant Colonel Edward M. Postlethwait, who had led the unit throughout the Leyte fighting.

The reconnaissance troop dashed along Route 7 and reached the north shore of the bay by dark. The next day that force, led by Lieutenant Richard V. Collopy, exchanged fire with the entrenched enemy as the American troops tried to round a hairpin turn short of the objective.

A rifle unit, I Company, commanded by Lieutenant Paul J. Cain, came up to try to dislodge the Japanese. Cain sent a platoon onto a ridge to protect the company's left flank and another to occupy a cemetery on high ground. Lieutenant Kenneth Yeomans' 2nd Platoon was assigned to knock out a pillbox straight ahead. One of his squads was pinned down, however, and the battalion commander called for heavier firepower. A 75-mm self-propelled mount of the regimental Cannon Company blasted the enemy machine-gun positions and succeeded in silencing the opposition at that point.

Meantime, a sergeant in Lieutenant Lewis Richtiger's 1st Platoon put on a demonstration of superb marksmanship by picking off in succession three Japanese soldiers trying to blow the bridge into Olongapo 300 to 350 yards away.

Another example of GI competence occurred after the enemy blew a hole in the approach road, creating a tank trap. Men of Company C of the 3rd Engineer Battalion used steel mats to effect a quick repair and the attack forces were soon rolling over the bridge.

The Japanese withdrew late in the afternoon, ending the action. American losses were three killed and one wounded from I Company plus an artillery observer and a member of Cannon Company who were wounded.

On the third day ashore, 31 January, a patrol from L Company, 3rd Battalion, 34th Infantry, crossed the line separating the Zambales and Bataan provinces, thus claiming the proud distinction of being the first American liberators to return to that storied and tragic peninsula.

The next phase of the battle was to drive eastward along Route 7 through Zig Zag Pass to seal the base of Bataan. Selected as the spearhead was the 152nd Regiment of the 38th Division, which passed through the 34th Infantry northeast of Olongapo on 31 January to begin the advance to Dinalupihan that the corps commander, Major General Charles P. Hall, expected to end the Zig Zag phase of the operation no later than 5 February.

Thus began what would become known as the Battle of Zig Zag Pass. The Japanese had prepared their defenses better than the American Army commanders anticipated. The pass, which begins about three miles northeast of Olongapo, was a notably rugged and densely jungled piece of real estate through which Route 7 contorted itself for about three additional miles. The foliage was so dense that the highway could be impossible to see from as close as five yards off to the side. The Japanese had established a series of mutually supporting strong points over a length of about 2,000 yards running along a northwest-southeast axis on either side of Route 7 at the pass. A similarly well constructed second line lay about 900 yards to the east. The strongpoints consisted of foxholes dug atop knolls and knobs and connected by trenches or tunnels running along the ridges. Pillboxes built from logs and covered with dirt were strategically located. All the positions were well-camouflaged in the thick foliage. The troop concentration numbered no fewer than 2,100 well-supplied enemy. They were armed with heavy machine guns, mortars and artillery. The Japanese field pieces were well-scattered for defensive purposes but for the same reason they were less able to deliver concentrated fire.

A company-size Japanese outpost about midway between Olongapo and Zig Zag Pass offered resistance to Company A 34th on 31 January, but the 152nd Infantry overcame and bypassed that force the next day. The regiment pushed on to begin the climb into the teeth of the enemy defenses. By the second day, 1 February, the 152nd Regiment began to be heavily engaged as American troops on the left encountered the strong points of the Japanese right.

Over that day and the next, the 152nd Infantry found itself in a bitter struggle against the entrenched enemy in an area where Route 7 forms a huge horseshoe curve open on the north end. Because of the confusion of battle, difficult terrain and poor maps, it was never quite clear, even to the commanders in the field or the rear, where the various American units were located. At times it was thought the leading elements were nearly across the horseshoe, at others it appeared they had not yet reached the first, or western, leg.

Company C, 34th Infantry, attacking along Highway 7 Zig Zag Pass, 3 February 1945. (U.S. Army Photo, courtesy of Charles W. Card)

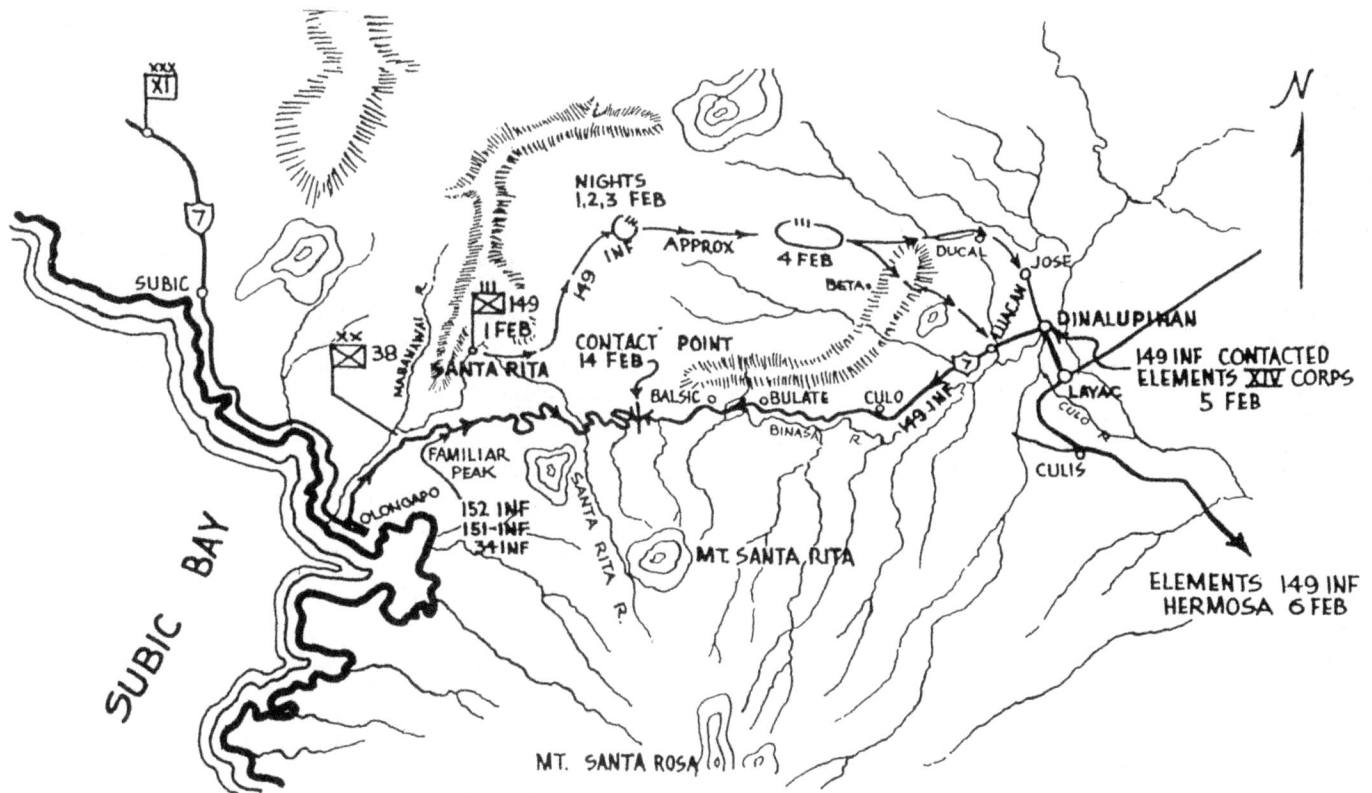

OLONGAPO – DINALUPIHAN
ZIG-ZAG PASS   SCALE 1:180,000 APPROX

Zig Zag Pass

Regardless, the opening stage of the Battle of Zig Zag Pass brought the 152nd Regiment to grief, cost its commander his job and ultimately had the same effect for the 38th Division commander as well. General Hall arrived at the front on 2 February and concluded the unit's performance was less than satisfactory. As a consequence, he ordered the 34th Infantry at Olongapo to move up and pass through the 152nd to take the point of the attack. The latter regiment would follow behind to clean up any pockets of resistance the Dragons bypassed.

General Hall's impatience was based in part on his mistaken belief that the infantrymen were opposed only by relatively small outposts manned by second-string troops instead of a sizable, well-equipped, combat-seasoned force that had given itself every defensive advantage.

The 34th Infantry went into Zig Zag Pass on the morning of 3 February in line of battalions in order of their numbers.

The 1st Battalion, 34th Infantry, came under mortar and artillery fire as the troops moved through the 152nd Infantry's position. The battalion commander, Lieutenant Colonel Charles Oglesby, sent Companies A and C to follow the horseshoe path of Route 7. Within that giant loop in the road were many smaller ones so that at most points, the visibility for the advancing men was quite short, no farther than the next bend. The troops were moving up the east leg when they encountered a "tank trap" camouflaged as a tree felled across the road and engaged a small enemy force in a brief firefight.

Oglesby also ordered Company B to attack eastward across the open end of the horseshoe, a maneuver that brought sharp enemy retaliation against all three rifle companies.

With the two regiments still in the process of relief and withdrawal within a tight area along the twisting road, Japanese were able to pour fire down on the entire force. With remarkable accuracy, the barrage of 90-mm mortar shells and 105 mm artillery fell on the American positions. When the GIs noticed that the Japanese did not require bracketing fire to register on the target, they knew they were fighting first-rate combat troops.

The barrage reached the rear battalion, the 3rd, killing one man and wounding five. The dead soldier was one of the replacements who had come ashore 29 January and had been in the Philippines only about two weeks.

As the day wore on, Oglesby concluded it would be folly for his force to turn the far corner of the horseshoe before a strong pocket of resistance could be eliminated on a key height that dominated the terrain east of the highway.

Accordingly, he ordered Lieutenant Oakley Storey's Company C to leave the road and move northeast. Contact led to a fierce firefight, which was followed throughout the rest of the afternoon by enemy rifle and machine gun fire from the ridge.

Unable to make significant headway despite artillery and heavy weapons support, the latter from Company D, Storey withdrew and dug in for the night.

Meanwhile, the battalion commander had sent A Company, led by Lieutenant Gilbert Heaberlin, southeast off the road toward a hill called Familiar Peak in an attempt to outflank

the enemy left and relieve pressure on both Companies B and C, which, it was now clear, were up against a solid wall of resistance.

The heavy jungle and poor maps made orientation by the company guesswork at best. Further, the Japanese saw a ripe target of opportunity in the isolated American unit and would mount three fanatical banzai attacks against the company during the evening and night.

Heaberlin's troops had dug in on a knoll about halfway between the horseshoe and Familiar Peak. A seven-man patrol led by Sergeant Garrett probed into the jungle and became lost in the dim dusk light. When an enemy patrol opened fire, Garrett threw a couple of phosphorus grenades hoping his company would see the smoke and reveal its position to the patrol. It worked out that way, and the patrol scurried back to the perimeter unharmed.

The Japanese launched their first attack before Company A was completely dug in. As a replacement soldier, Bill McKenna, recalled, "My hole was only about three inches deep and I literally crawled inside my helmet."

The first attack was repulsed, giving McKenna and his foxhole partner Tony Ratto time to prepare better for the next one. The screaming Japanese again rushed the men of Company A, who this time fixed bayonets and pulled their grenades. McKenna, Ratto and the others poured M-1 fire into the figures coming out of gloom to drive the enemy back once again.

The third attack was weaker. Afterwards, friendly artillery fire closed off the American positions to the Japanese.

To the northwest, Company B, which had encountered stiff opposition from a ridge line, was forced to slide back to the southeast, repeating the experience of a battalion of the 152nd Infantry. The unit dug in for the night a short distance east of the northwest corner of the horseshoe.

First Battalion casualties for the day were 13 men killed and 26 wounded. Company A's figures of two dead and four wounded covered the entire three days the unit was encircled southeast of the road. Company A's relatively few losses, indeed its very survival, was a tribute to the 63rd F.A. Bn. that continued to drop rounds within 25 yards of the company's position. The artillerymen's accurate fire kept the enemy at bay from the trapped unit, and no round fell short.

The line at the end of the day extended diagonally from Company B's position near the northwest corner of the horseshoe 400 yards southeast past the eastern leg of Route 7 to Company C's position.

The official U.S. Army history of the Luzon campaign, *Triumph in the Philippines*, carried this passage appraising the first day's action by the 34th Infantry: "If one thing was obvious by dusk on 3 February, it was that the 34th Infantry had employed insufficient strength for the task at hand – it had committed only one battalion to do a job that three battalions of the 152nd had been unable to do."

The regimental commander, Colonel William Jenna, undertook to rectify that situation the following day by assigning all three battalions to the battle. The 1st Battalion was directed to attack the Japanese on the dominating high ground east of the horseshoe from which the enemy had employed such effective resistance the day be-

fore. The 2nd Battalion would work north of Route 7 and try to flank the Japanese right and clear them from the northeastern corner of the horseshoe. The 3rd Battalion, essentially in reserve, would follow the 2nd as it advanced.

The 34th Infantry, after initial success on 4 February ran up against continued stubborn resistance as the day wore on. Japanese forces, using mortars and artillery effectively, refused to be dislodged from their defensive positions in the pass.

The 1st Battalion lost ground and by the end of the day had to dig in farther south on the eastern leg of the horseshoe than it had the night before. The 2nd Battalion's Company E enjoyed some success in reducing enemy strongholds along the road, but late in the afternoon F and G companies had to fall back to Route 7. Because the 2nd Battalion had not made a net gain forward, the 3rd Battalion remained in reserve and did not join the action.

The hard day had cost the regiment two high-ranking casualties. Both the executive officer and the 1st Battalion commander were wounded and knocked out of action.

The first occurred when Lieutenant Colonel Chester Dahlen, the regimental executive, came forward to Company E's position. That company, led by Captain "Tuffy" Pullen, was the leading element in the 2nd Battalion's attack and had reached the curve out of the horseshoe where the road forms a figure two.

The company was meeting fierce resistance from machine guns and mortars and the immediate terrain made artillery support dangerous for the friendly troops.

While Dahlen, 2nd Battalion commander Major Harry Snavely and the artillery forward observer were standing beside the road considering the artillery adjustment problem, an incoming round burst low over the three. Only Dahlen was hit. A fragment put a large wound in his buttock.

But the colonel, who had served as regimental commander on Leyte after Red Newman was wounded, now determined that the division's artillery was firing at too low an angle. While waiting for medical treatment, Dahlen ordered the forward observer to have the 63rd Field Artillery Battalion adjust to high-angle fire.

Japanese riflemen took advantage of the lull in the artillery support, shooting the two medics carrying Dahlen and cutting the wire to the rear.

Two wiremen, Sergeant Hanford Rants and Pfc. John Six, exhibited great heroism in restoring communications. When they started back to find and splice the break, they discovered a Japanese soldier had about 10 yards of the road covered.

The two GIs raced through the rifle fire, repaired the break, and returned under the sights of the same rifleman. But the pair hadn't seen a second break in the wire and had to repeat the feat, making another run for it with bullets zinging around them both ways.

Colonel Oglesby was far forward with Company B about mid-day when a hand grenade came virtually out of nowhere. The explosion caused multiple wounds in his face, chest and arm. The 3rd Battalion executive officer, Major Carl O. "Speedy" Mann, took over the 1st Battalion.

Another key casualty on 4 February was Captain Rucker Innes, G Company commander, who was wounded in a thunderous mortar barrage toward the end of the day.

Earlier, Snavely had sent first Company F and then both Companies F and G on flanking missions from the northeast corner of the horseshoe in an effort to position them to attack from the rear the Japanese force holding up Company E. F Company's point platoon, climbing a narrow jungle trail, was near the crest of the key Japanese defensive terrain in the area when it came under withering fire from about 100 Japanese riflemen. A second attempt to reach the top from a different angle had the same result.

Snavely ordered the two companies to withdraw and dig in on the first good defensive ground. That process had hardly started when the mortar attack exploded with devastating force among the troops. Casualties were one dead and 24 wounded in Company G, Innes among them. Company F experienced 11 killed, 51 wounded and one missing. Lieutenant Jack L. Calhoun, executive officer, took over Company G.

The number of sudden casualties put heavy demand on the medical personnel and the two Portable Surgical Hospitals to the rear near Olongapo. Ambulances were on the road between the front and the hospitals throughout the night.

The 152nd Infantry once again was heavily engaged in the Zig Zag that day as well, but its 1st Battalion in attempting a wide sweep against the Japanese right north of Route 7 was driven back by a thundering artillery and mortar barrage. The ridge north of the horseshoe remained in enemy hands despite four major American attacks.

The 34th Infantry's first two days of combat in Zig Zag Pass were costly. The regiment lost 41 men killed, 131 wounded and six missing, while making no substantial gains beyond the positions of 2 February except for extending the front somewhat to the north and pushing a short distance past the eastern arm of the horseshoe.

It was at this point that General Hall conceded the fact that the forces under his charge were up against a main line of resistance, not mere outposts. The XI Corps commander also decided the next phase of the fight would go better under unified command, so at 2200 4 February he attached the 34th Infantry to the 38th Division led by Major General Henry Jones. Previously in the Luzon operation, the 34th RCT had operated directly under corps control.

The plan called for the 34th Infantry to clear the horseshoe area and continue driving east south of Route 7, while two battalions of the 152nd attempted to flank the Japanese north of the highway. The other battalion of the 152nd was south of the 34th Infantry, a split that troubled regimental commander Jenna sorely, but he could not persuade General Jones to change it.

One weakness in the plan recognized by Jones, and Jenna, too, as it turned out, was the limitations on artillery support. The division commander would rather have spent a day or two softening the Japanese stronghold with a concentrated barrage, but the speed that Corps Commander Hall was insisting upon did not allow for such a delay.

As happened the day before, the initial attack on 5 February went well. The 2nd Battalion, 34th Infantry, which had been under mortar fire during the night, attempted to outflank a Japanese strong point near the northeast corner of the horseshoe. The movement put the unit north of Route 7, which interfered with plans for artillery support of the 152nd Infantry, but the advance nevertheless was progressing.

The day was one of fearsome battering by Japanese mortars and artillery. The commanders of both B and C Companies, Lieutenant Thomas Rhem and Lieutenant Oakley Storey (for the second day in a row), respectively, were wounded. But the most telling hit was on the 2nd Battalion command post where four high-explosive rounds fell, blowing away equipment and papers and killing three and wounding four 2nd Battalion enlisted staff.

Front-line troops on 5 February felt they were operating at a serious disadvantage because of a peculiar restriction General Jones had placed on division artillery. Essentially, except for fire east of the Santa Rita River, call missions would have to be processed through channels with a loss of precious time.

Jenna sent the following message to General Jones: "I am convinced that the entire Japanese position opposing XI Corps cannot be cracked unless there is a withdrawal to a point where entire Corps artillery and all available air work it over with every possible means for at least 48 hours. My 1st and 2nd battalions have suffered terrific casualties and it is becoming questionable how long they can hold up under this pounding … ."

It was apparent the colonel and the general agreed on the need for sustained artillery bombardment of the Zig Zag defenses, but the division commander had his boss to contend with and did not reply to Jenna's message.

The regimental commander thus decided on his own to pull his 1st Battalion, which was continuing to take casualties from artillery fire, back west of the horseshoe. The 3rd Battalion had moved forward and was crossing the open end of the horseshoe and provided the cover for the withdrawal of the other two battalions. The 1st Battalion and the forward elements of the 3rd came under fire during the process, which was completed by late afternoon. The entire 34th Infantry was by then west of the horseshoe bend in Route 7.

The battering the regiment had endured over the previous three days caused General Hall to order its relief by the 38th Division's 151st Infantry. After coming ashore on 29 January the 34th Regiment suffered 325 casualties and 25 psychoneurosis cases, practically all in the Zig Zag Pass combat of 3-5 February, including a large number of key personnel. The total was 40 percent of the casualties the entire regiment had suffered in 78 days on Leyte. Even among the non-casualties many men were not considered combat effective at the moment, which demanded that the regiment be pulled out of the line.

Zig Zag Pass had been an exceptionally tough fight in every respect. The 2nd Battalion surgeon, "Doc" Cameron, observed, "The Zig Zag is the only time I ever saw an American soldier break down emotionally. These dazed kids were coming in crying and when I asked them what unit they were in they didn't know."

The next day, General Henry Jones was relieved of his command of the 38th Division. He felt he had reason to believe that the 34th Regiment had been manipulated by General Hall to justify his dismissal. As Jones interpreted events, when the corps commander ordered the 34th Infantry, then operating under corps control, to replace the 152nd Regiment as the spearhead at Zig Zag, success would have been a reflection on the effectiveness of the 38th Division. When the 34th Infantry could not penetrate the stiff defenses, as Jones saw it, the regiment was placed under his command so he could be blamed.

Regardless, subsequent events vindicated both the 34th and 152nd regiments. It took the entire 38th Division, including the 149th Regiment pushing from the east, another 10 days of hard fighting to vanquish the Japanese entrenched among the jungled ridges of Zig Zag Pass. Moreover, by then substantial aerial and artillery bombardment was available to support the infantry effort.

The 34th Infantry did not have much in the way of territorial gains to show for its three-day ordeal in the pass, but there can be no question that the troops discovered and defeated several Japanese strongpoints that the 38th Division men did not have to contend with.

General Hall, in an optimistic mood at the end of the day, 5 February, offered a brief compliment in his report to 6th Army Commander General Krueger. "The 34th RCT has done a good job since being here. I am taking it out of the line and substituting for it 151st Infantry."

Perhaps his comment was related to his stated opinion that the defenses American troops encountered in Zig Zag Pass were the strongest he had ever seen.

The 34th Infantry's departure from Zig Zag Pass did not end the 24th Division's role in the battle. Colonel Joseph H. Hodges' 11th F.A. Battalion remained until the battle ended ten days later. The 11th had replaced the 38th Division's 150th Battalion of 155mm howitzers, which were enroute from Oro Bay, New Guinea, when the Zambales Operation began. The heavy 155s were considerably more effective in destroying Japanese log and dirt bunkers than the 105s.

The 11th Field supported many attacks by the 38th Division's 149th, 151st, and 152nd Regiments. Utilizing a "rolling barrage" that sometimes fell as close as 100 yards in front, one battalion of the 152nd Infantry on 9 February fought its way successfully 600 yards across a rough, jungle-covered valley. Colonel Hodges said this was the only time the 11th F.A. Battalion fired a rolling barrage in its five Pacific campaigns.

Observation was so limited in Zig Zag Pass that the artillery observation planes were used round-the-clock to direct artillery fire. Colonel Hodges, a veteran of all the 24th Division campaigns, said Zig Zag Pass was the only time he had seen observation planes sent up at night to adjust artillery fire.

The light planes usually flew low and were vulnerable to Japanese rifle and machine gun fire. One 38th Division plane, flying along the front lines, had already been destroyed by a 155mm "Long Tom" rifle round fired from deep in the rear. On 8 February, one of the 11th F.A. pilots, 1st Lieutenant Hollister G. DeMotts, was shot down while adjusting fire for the 38th Division's 138th F.A. Battalion. 1st Lieutenant Willis L. Chilcote, commanding C Battery 11th Field sent a patrol, which found the downed plane and recovered DeMott's body. Chilcote deduced from the evidence that DeMotts was hit in the air, managed to land the plane without extensive damage, but died from enemy rifle fire while on the ground.

CORREGIDOR

The name that in the spring of 1942 was known the world over as the symbol of desperate American military resistance to overwhelming Japanese force became a battleground once again nearly three years later, with different results.

Corregidor, an island three and one half miles long and a mile and a half across at its widest point, guards the entrance to Manila Bay. Stretching across an east-west line, the island lies a short distance off the southern tip of the Bataan Peninsula. It is tadpole-shaped, with the large head pointing toward the South China Sea and the slender tail into the bay.

Topographically, the features include the sandy, wooded tail on the eastern end rising gradually to Malinta Hill at about the mid-point, a 350-foot height extensively undermined with tunnels. To the west, the terrain dips to a 500-foot wide waist called Bottomside with beaches on either side. From there, the ground rises to a higher level called Middleside and thence even higher to Topside on the far western end.

Though Corregidor in February 1945 did not represent a major piece in Japanese defensive plans, the American forces knew it had to be taken to eliminate a constant source of potential harassment. Also impossible to overlook was the emotional aspect of the operation. Because the island was the last bastion before allied surrender of the Philippines in 1942, its recapture would be a special event.

The enemy garrison consisted of about 5,000 men, mostly naval troops, which was far in excess of the U.S. intelligence estimate of about 850

The job of taking Corregidor fell to the reinforced 3rd Battalion of the 34th Infantry, commanded by Lieutenant Colonel Edward Postlethwait, and the 503rd Parachute RCT. Attached to the battalion for the operation was A Company of the 34th's 1st Battalion. Together the units formed the Rock Force under the command of Colonel George M. Jones, the 503rd regimental commander.

The invasion, a joint airborne-amphibious operation, was set for 16 February. The 503rd RCT was to be flown from Mindoro and dropped on Topside, while the 34th Regiment men would go ashore on the south beaches of Bottomside two hours after the initial parachute landing.

Though the paratroopers, by their sheer numbers if nothing else, would represent the main body of attackers, the amphibious phase was crucial. The seaborne assault was necessary to open up supply and evacuation routes to and from Topside, and also to avoid the necessity of the 503rd RCT having to take Malinta Hill in an attack across the low, open ground of Bottomside. The amphibious troops' mission was to seize Malinta Hill immediately and thereby cut the Japanese forces on the island in two.

Extensive air and naval bombardment preceded the landing, and on the morning of 16 February, cruisers and destroyers moved close ashore and let fly salvoes that churned the sands of Bottomside.

The 3rd Battalion, which had arrived at Mariveles Harbor at the south end of Bataan the previous day with the 151st RCT, loaded onto 25 LCMs manned by the 592nd Engineer Boat and Shore Regiment for the two-hour trip around the west end of the island to the south beaches. The invasion shore was designated Black Beach, a 200-yard strip of sand. The first troopers of the 503rd had started descending on Topside two hours before.

The amphibious invasion started at 1028, two minutes ahead of schedule. The initial waves, men of K and L companies, encountered little opposition, and quickly rushed forward to begin the assault on Malinta Hill. But as the Japanese recovered from the stunning bombardment, they took the invaders under machine-gun fire from two locations, Ramsay Ravine at the left rear and the bluffs at San Jose Point at the southwest corner of Malinta Hill. Enemy gunfire hit some of the boats carrying M Company before they reached shore. I Company hit the beach and raced across the narrow neck to the north shore.

Thirty minutes after the first infantrymen landed, K and L companies were atop Malinta Hill without losing a man. So surprised was the K Company commander, Captain Frank Centanni, that he looked around and exclaimed, "I'll be damned." I Company was not so lucky. Three minutes after hitting the beach, Lieutenant Phil Nast, the weapons platoon leader, was filled by a mortar fragment in his chest two inches from his heart. Overall, casualties during the first half hour were two dead and six wounded. But the fighting would soon get much worse, and two days later, Captain Centanni himself would be among the dead from a Japanese bullet.

The 3rd Battalion also learned the beach was heavily mined when the unit's vehicles crunched ashore. One after the other, a medium tank, an M-7 self-propelled mount of the regiment's Cannon Company, and a 37mm anti-tank gun detonated mines and were destroyed. One account had the battalion losing one half of its vehicles to mines and anti-tank fire from the caves in the cliffs within the first half hour.

The troops of K and L Companies, after their hands-and-feet scramble up steep Malinta Hill, could look back at the increasing violence on the beach. Jan Valtin, a member of K Company and author of the post-war book, *Children of Yesterday*, described the scene: "Right and left the hillsides spewed fire. Fifties tore through the landing craft and thirties hammered the plates and the ramps. Mines popped. Pieces of jeeps and tanks and tank destroyers were flying in the sunshine. But a tank and a self-propelled gun crawled up the beach and plugged away at the pillboxes."

Valtin remembered the big blue flies that swarmed in huge clouds on Corregidor, increasing the misery of infantry combat. Bill McKenna, a member of A Company, remarked on the flies also, as well as the odor from rotting corpses that hung in the air on the island. "The ugly flies swarmed everywhere. They clung to fatigues and exposed skin ... The smell on Corregidor pervaded everything. It was said that men on ships anchored offshore in Manila Bay would get sick from the smell from a distance of two miles away," McKenna wrote. Ten days after the invasion, a C-47 sprayed the island to solve the fly problem, but the stench remained.

The parachute drop had been as successful as the amphibious landing that first morning. The Japanese, already off-balance by the pre-assault bombardment, evidently were surprised by the airborne attack. By nightfall on 16 February, the forward elements of the 3rd Battalion, 34th Infantry were within 250 yards of the 503rd RCT positions at the head of Ramsay Ravine. With about 2,000 paratroopers on the ground, commanders decided to cancel the scheduled drop for the next day.

At 1000 17 February, less than 24 hours after the seaborne-airborne invasion had begun, the two commanders, Lieutenant Colonel Postlethwait of the 3rd Battalion and Colonel George Jones of the 503rd RCT met at what had been San Jose. It was like Stanley meeting Livingston, according to the After Action Report. The immediate concern was securing the

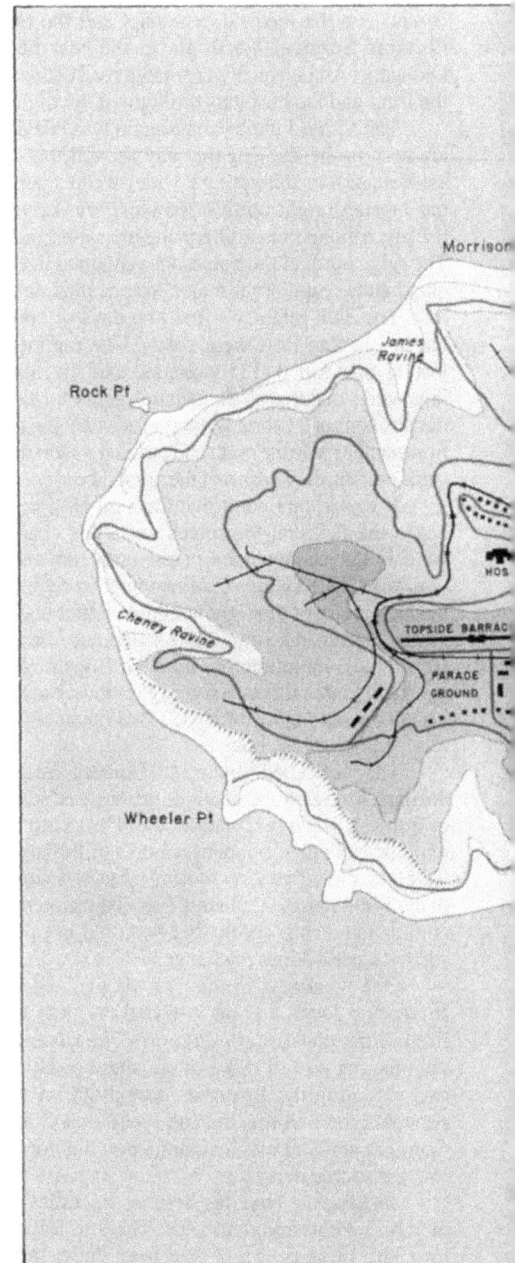

Morrison

James Ravine

Rock Pt

Cheney Ravine

TOPSIDE BARRAC

HOS

PARADE GROUND

Wheeler Pt

evacuation route for the substantial number of casualties among paratroopers, to which the 3rd Battalion set about doing.

The larger battle plan called for the 34th Infantry troops to finish securing Malinta Hill and then contain the remaining enemy troops in the island's tail to the east while the 503rd RCT reduced the opposition on Middleside and Topside. When those tasks were completed, the American force would then overrun the enemy east of Malinta Hill.

The terrain of Corregidor dictated a generally uncoordinated series of small-unit mop-up operations. Though the 3rd Battalion 34th soldiers had reached the top of Malinta Hill the first day, the fighting on that height was by no means over.

The two companies that had taken the hill were under no illusions about what was beneath them as they occupied that high ground. Malinta Hill was honeycombed with tunnels in which were stored vast supplies of incendiary material besides the Japanese soldiers. The hill could erupt in volcanic violence at any moment.

K Company held the north end of the hill, L Company the southern hump. The companies' task was to keep the Japanese confined in the tunnels and deny them freedom of movement on the island. To that end, three men were assigned to block an east-west road and remained at their post for eight consecutive days, 16-23 February. They fought off repeated fanatical attacks from Japanese who were wielding rifles, bayonets, pistols and grenades. Twenty-three enemy died in the attempt. Valtin wrote: "Each of these three men lost 20 pounds in a week. You should know their names. They might mean little to you but they mean a lot to us." He identified them as Sergeant Lewis Vershun, Private Emil Ehrenbold, and Private Roland Paeth.

On the first night, a series of brisk Japanese counterattacks against the Dragon Blue infantrymen holding the north slope of Malinta Hill cost the Americans 10 battle deaths.

Firing erupted in the K Company sector shortly before midnight. In the darkness, the chatter of automatic weapons, the burst of mortar shells and the shouting of men created a chaotic situation. Adding to the confusion was the fact that phone wires were cut and communications were disrupted.

Heavy fighting continued throughout the night for K Company, and casualties were substantial.

I Company under Lieutenant Paul Cain, which had crossed Bottomside after landing and took up positions at North Dock, passed the first night with only an infiltration attempt to contend with. The next day, the company took up the job of clearing the area.

The procedure included tossing grenades into bomb craters, where enemy usually were hiding, and then assaulting the positions. This method accounted for about 40 Japanese killed. The company employed a flamethrower against a large camouflaged cave where the Japanese had secreted a big gun.

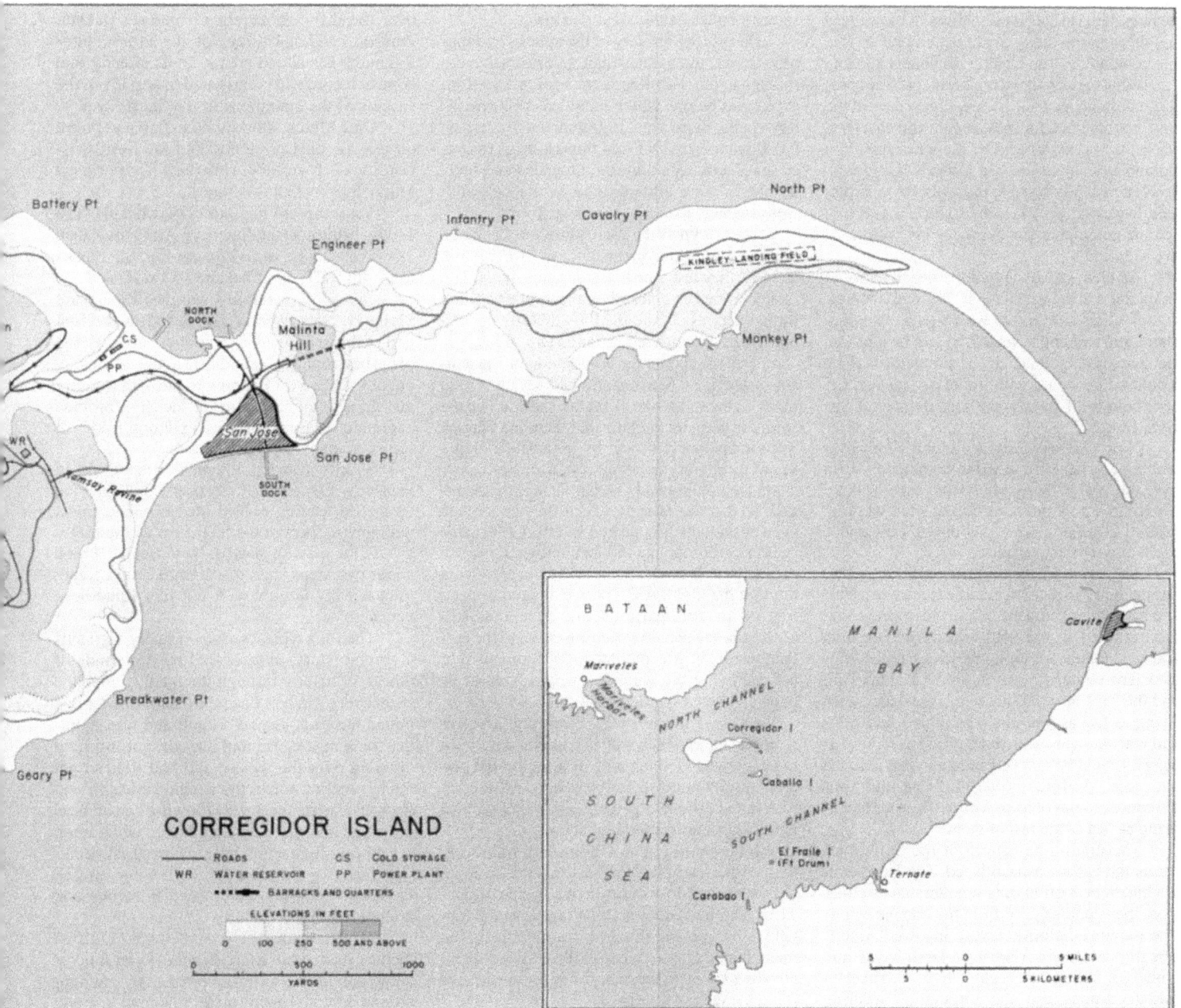

CORREGIDOR ISLAND

About mid-afternoon on 17 February, I Company relieved the battered K Company, and A Company took over North Dock from Lieutenant Cain's company.

I Company had to turn back enemy forces trying to chase the Americans off Malinta Hill. One tactic employed by Cain's men was to roll grenades onto the attackers. Sergeant Persinini described the technique: "You pull the pin, let the lever fly off and gently lay it over the side of the hill into the lap of the upclimbing (Japanese), then watch him go back down the hill and take a couple of climbers with him."

A humorous story is associated with I Company's assault on Corregidor. While the company was still fighting in Zig Zag Pass, two men in the weapons platoon complained that the third man in their hole, a new replacement, was not carrying a weapon and woke them up to fire at noises he heard when he was on watch at night.

When the platoon leader, Philip H. Nast, confronted the replacement, the man replied, "I am a conscientious objector." "How in hell did you get here in a rifle outfit?" Nast demanded to know. "I didn't want to hide behind my religion," the man said. He had gone all through basic training, through the replacement depot, and up to a line company before making his beliefs known.

What to do with the replacement? The company commander, Paul J. Cain, suggested that the man become Nast's messenger, and that was where he was assigned. But the messenger in a platoon is also the platoon leader's bodyguard. So Nast instantly became probably the only platoon leader in the US Army to have a non-rifle bearing conscientious objector as his bodyguard in combat.

As their LCVP neared the beach at South Dock on 16 February Nast, with his "bodyguard" at his side armed with a pack, two canteens, and two empty hands, had an inspiration. He quickly explained to his protector that he would be occupied with important matters the next couple of days and "why don't you just GET LOST?"

Nast was severely wounded soon after landing and never returned to I Company. "But over the years," he wrote, "from time to time, my mind wandered back to the man who assaulted Corregidor armed with two canteens, a pack, and two empty hands."

The mystery was finally solved 53 years later during the 1998 reunion in Little Rock when Nast and his former company commander were reminiscing about the war. Cain remembered the man and specifically the night after Nast was evacuated. The company was on top of Malinta Hill, and the Japs hit hard that night. Grenades were flying as fast as pins could be pulled, and rifles and machine guns were being fired as rapidly as triggers could be snapped and new clips jammed into place. "And there on the line," Cain said, "was the conscientious objecor with a rifle in his hands, firing as fast as the rest of them."

The night-time pattern of the Corregidor campaign had been established. The 3rd Battalion had to beat off nightly counterattacks either from the island's tail or from the tunnels below. The daytime fighting mostly involved American troops clearing Japanese from caves and tunnels or failing that, sealing them up. The 34th Infantry troops also concentrated on securing the roads to Middleside as supply and evacuation routes for the 503rd RCT.

I Company's Vic Backer described the enemy's last attempt to retake Malinta Hill, on the night of 20 February. "The First Platoon, led by Sergeant S. Schorr, stood the brunt of the attack all night long and held the (Japanese) at bay," Backer recalled. Before dawn, the platoon was starting to run short of ammunition, but Backer credited a soldier named Sam Snyder with averting disaster. "Quickly grasping the situation, he jumped out of his foxhole and creeping and crawling under fire, rounded up and distributed all available ammunition to the beleaguered men." By dawn, Backer wrote, many dead enemy lay only a few feet from the I Company position.

I Company had to clean out the North Dock area a second time before the campaign ended, and it was there that Sergeant Owen Williams gave his life but saved his squad. When the group ran into a grenade ambush, Williams immediately sounded a warning, which allowed the rest of the squad to take cover. But the sergeant's shout gave away his position and a sniper's bullet fatally wounded him.

Despite the ferocity of the attacks by Japanese troops, the greatest danger of massive casualties to the 34th Regiment's force was from explosives below, which included 35,000 artillery shells, more than 10,000 powder charges, 2,000 pounds of TNT and thousands of rounds of small arms ammunition, grenades and mortar shells. Also underground in the labyrinth were as many as 2,500 Japanese troops.

The GIs knew the enemy might set a charge off at any time, and on the night of 21 February, at 2130, they did. The blast was enormous. The tunnel entrances belched fire, debris was flung far in every direction, the hills literally opened up. Rocks were hurled as far as two miles.

That afternoon, the 3rd Platoon of Lieutenant Heaberlin's A Company had set up a road block on the south side of Malinta Hill. When the Japanese blew up the hill, six GIs in the platoon were immediately buried by a landslide, and a squad of infantrymen was stranded. Secondary detonations continued to alter the face of the terrain, so that the road on which the platoon had been positioned disappeared and the hill became a sheer cliff dropping 150 feet to the sea.

Efforts to rescue the detachment continued through the night. A PT boat managed to get a line up to the men, and one rifleman, Bill McKenna succeeded in getting down to the surface where he was picked up by a rubber raft, but retrieving the wounded would have to be done another way after daylight.

At mid-morning 22 February, a squad member, Joe Froelich who had mountain-climbing experience led the way in bringing the platoon survivors down to the beach. All but six men in the 3rd Platoon were killed or wounded in the blast and subsequent action.

If the explosion on Malinta Hill was costly to the Americans, it was disastrous for the Japanese who had lost control of the detonation. Their goal had been to allow troops in the tunnels to escape and mount a counterattack, but many Japanese were killed in the blast and about 50 others trying to break out of the west entrance fell to American gunfire.

Two nights later, more underground explosions rocked Malinta Hill, but they were mostly suicidal on the part of the Japanese.

On 24 February, the American forces launched the final assault on the tail of Corregidor, and by the end of the second day, organized resistance ended. Tragically, however, the Japanese were capable of a final act of death and destruction. At 1100 on 26 February, the underground Japanese arsenal at Monkey Point blew up with tremendous force, killing at least 200 Japanese and 50 Americans.

The 3rd Battalion, 34th Infantry, was not on hand for that final pyrotechnic display. The unit had been relieved the day before by the 151st Infantry of the 38th Division to go to Mindoro where the 24th Division was staging for the Mindanao operation. For the battalion, so recently engaged in the bitter fighting at Zig Zag Pass, its gallant action on Corregidor resulted in the award of the Presidential Unit Citation.

Sixth Army commander, Lieutenant General Walter Krueger, wrote the following on 10 March as the 34th Regiment left his command: "Fighting with skill, courage and great gallantry over the difficult terrain of historic Bataan, Zambales and on Corregidor, the 34th Infantry Regiment has added greatly to its already fine combat record and contributed materially to the success of the operations of the Sixth Army."

On 2 March, the American flag was raised once again on Corregidor, and the fortress island was formally returned to General MacArthur by Colonel Jones.

Its recapture had not come cheaply. The 11-day battle cost the American Army more than 1,000 casualties, including for the 3rd Battalion, 34th RCT, 38 killed and 153 wounded.

One of the wounded was 2nd Lieutenant Philip H. Nast, who is mentioned in the first part of this section on Corregidor. Nast was one of the new replacement officers assigned directly out of OCS at Fort Benning to the 34th Infantry just prior to embarkation for the Zig Zag Pass operation on Luzon. He was platoon leader of the I Company weapons platoon.

Shortly after landing on Corregidor on 16 February, Lieutenant Cain sent Nast's platoon up a road leading to Topside to make contact with the troopers of the 503rd Parachute Infantry. As the platoon started, Nast recalls "I took about two steps, saw black smoke, and something hit my left chest. It felt like I had been punched."

Then as a typical serious casualty, Nast tells a graphic story, experienced by thousands of others, of his trip through the medical pipeline to recovery. "When I came to, Sam Snyder had pulled me back behind a knoll and was shouting for a medic. He had already put my field dressing over the wound and had tried to get me to swallow one of the wound tablets (if you want an experience, try swallowing one of these pills, big enough to choke a horse, while lying flat on your back with a hole in your chest, drinking water from a canteen). Sam came up wth the school solution; he crushed the tablet and poured it into the wound.

"I was loaded onto a stretcher, and two medics carried me to the beach. If you think it takes guts to be an infantryman, try running around a "hot" beach (under machine gun and small arms fire) standing up carrying a stretcher. If I could have gotten off and walked, I would have. I tip my Combat Infantryman's Badge to all medics who served in the field in comabt.

"When I got to the aid station on the beach, a Medical Captain looked at my chest and told me that I had a sucking wound. Fortunately that meant nothing to me. As I lay there I remember the sun was terribly hot and bothered my uncovered chest and eyes. As I was being given plasma, the Doc told the man who was holding the bottle to stand in such a way that his body cast a shadow on my face. I don't know who had more guts—the doctor for telling the medic to stand that way on a "hot" beach or the medic who carried out his order.

"I came to again to find that I was once more on a stretcher. I was placed on the deck of an assault boat as more wounded were loaded on board. The boat was almost full when I heard explosions close to us. One of the medics shouted to the coxswain that the Japs were trying to hit us with mortar fire and that he should get us out of there.

"The next thing I remember was lying on the top deck of an LST. A doctor was moving from man to man. He would check the wound and then say something to other men who were with him. He examined me, said something, and moved on as two men picked up my stretcher and carried me to the tank deck (I later learned that the doctor was conducting triage, the sorting of and allocation of treatment to patients according to a system of priorities designed to maximize the number of survivors).

"I floated in and out of consciousness for an unknown period of time. When awake I noticed a great amount of activity at the far end of the hold. A medic approached and said I was about to be moved. I asked if I could have a shot before being moved. I had not had a great deal of pain. My main discomfort came from difficulty in breathing because my left lung had collapsed. Whatever the shot was they gave me was great. I just didn't give a damn. The doctor could have told me they were going to cut off my head and sew it back on and I would have told him to go ahead.

"They moved us to the top deck, and I saw heaven. A big white ship loaded with beautiful women, all looking down at us. I was transferred to that white cloud half expecting to be issued GI wings and a harp. Not so. The ship was for real. It was the hospital ship "Hope," and the beautiful women were Army nurses who were on the way to Lingayen Gulf to join a hospital there. It turned out that many of the nurses had sailed from San Francisco on the "General Howze" that had carried so many of the recent replacements in the 34th to Hollandia where the nurses disembarked while we traveled on to join the 24th Division on Leyte. A number of the nurses came to visit me and to inquire about many of the other men.

"I was carried below to a soft bunk with clean sheets. Soon a big, and I do mean big, and very pretty Navy nurse came to my bunk, took one look, and disappeared. She soon returned with a basin of hot water and a cloth and proceeded to give me a bath. How she knew that I had not had a bath in over a month I'll never know. The bath was followed by a bowl of straw-berries and cream. It may not have been real cream, but after a diet of C and K rations, it sure tasted like cream.

"Some of the other patients were not as fortunate as I. Across the aisle from me was a man whose whole body appeared to be covered with gauze. I was told he was Navy and had suffered severe burns.

"A day or so later, I was taken by a corps-man to X-ray. The medics wanted to know where the shell fragment had lodged. Unfortunately, because the left chest cavity was filled with fluid, the X-ray revealed nothing. Sooooo- a doctor soon appeared at my side with a slender piece of metal and said he would probe and try to determine the direction the fragment had taken. He then proceeded to insert that metal object into the hole in my chest. I felt no pain, but there is something very unpleasant about watching a piece of metal disappear for a number of inches into your body.

"My stay on the Hope (about a week or so because we first went to Lingayen to drop off the nurses) was not at all unpleasant. I had to sleep sitting up to relieve the pressure on my heart, but it sure beat sleeping where the rest of my outfit was. I was on a soft diet, baby food mounds of yellow (carrots) and greens (peas), pureed stuff, not too tasty, but D bars weren't so hot either.

"My only unpleasant experience on the Hope was when a nurse told me that the ship was unarmed, but she felt that was alright because it was brightly lit, so the Japs would know it was a hospital ship and would not bomb it. I didn't bother to tell her that combat medics removed the Red Crosses from their helmets because they made such good targets. Otherwise, the trip was a pleasant cruise. The trouble started when we arrived in Hollandia.

"After a number of days following assignment to the 54th General Hospital, a medical Lieutenant Colonel said they would have to aspirate me because of the fluid in my lung. The next day an orderly brought a tray covered with a towel to my bedside. I wish the tray had stayed covered, because when the doctor removed the towel, I saw the biggest hypodermic needle ever invented by man. The doctor was a kind and feeling man. He asked if I would prefer to have him stick that bayonet in the front of my chest or in the rear. I elected to have him approach me from the rear. It was not too bad for me because I didn't have to watch, but the rest of the guys in the ward did. They soon learned to read a book or hobble off to the head when they saw my tray coming.

"The first aspiration was done four times. The doctor kept asking me how I was doing and I kept saying, 'Fine, doc; keep going.' Shortly after he finished, I began to have trouble breathing and was spitting up a white foam. A nurse saw this, picked up my hand, saw that the nails were turning blue, and raced off. She returned with a few other people and an oxygen tank and mask. And then all was right with the world! My heart had been pumping against the fluid, and when too much was taken off at once, the heart began to beat so fast that the blood could not pick up sufficient oxygen.

"After four or five weeks at the 54th, and a visit by my battalion commander, Colonel Postlethwait, I was transferred to a general hospital in New York state. I returned to limited duty in September 1945."

MINDANAO

The main objective in the reconquest of the Philippines was the occupation of the principal island of Luzon, which General Douglas MacArthur initially planned to complete before moving forces into the southern islands.

However, events dictated a change in the timetable. Unspeakable atrocities committed by Japanese naval personnel in January and February against the civilian population caused the high command to step up the schedule and free the populated areas of the nation with all possible speed. That meant use of troops already in the area, as opposed to waiting for the armies fighting on Luzon to finish that operation.

MacArthur entrusted the liberation of the southern islands to the Eighth Army, commanded by Lieutenant General Robert Eichelberger. By the second week of April 1945, only the section of Mindanao east of the Zamboanga Peninsula remained in enemy hands.

The task of securing that territory fell to the 24th and 31st Infantry Divisions, comprising X Corps under the command of Maj. Gen. Franklin C. Sibert, a Kentuckian who had graduated from West Point in 1912. Sibert was a seasoned Pacific warrior who had commanded the 6th Infantry Division in the advance west from Hollandia on the northern coast of New Guinea and X Corps throughout the Leyte campaign.

Mindanao is the principal island in the southern Philippines and the second largest in the archipelago. While it did not hold the strategic importance of Leyte or Luzon, Mindanao nevertheless was defended by about 43,000 Japanese troops, ensuring a hard and prolonged

Members of the 1st Bn, 34th Regimental Combat Team, 24th Division, march on to Digos, Mindanao, P.I., on the next to the last day of the march, 26 April 1945.

fight. Its recapture was essential to the conclusion of the Pacific war.

The main objective of the attacking forces was Davao, a port on the eastern side of the island and location of the largest enemy concentration. The invasion, however, would be on the opposite side of eastern Mindanao at lightly defended Illana Bay, about 100 miles northwest of Davao.

The 24th Division, after participating in action on Luzon and several smaller islands, was encamped on the southwestern corner of Mindoro, one of the islands elements of the division had helped capture. Plans called for the division to embark on LSTs (Landing Ship, Tank), the workhorses of the Pacific invasion forces, from San Jose on about 10 April.

First came the intricate job of loading under the direction of an officer who assigned space aboard the ship for vehicles and units according to a schedule devised to prevent beach crowding. The loading officer was equipped with drawings of the ship's deck and tiny scale drawings of the vehicles that could be cut out and fitted into the diagrammed spaces of the vessel.

A snag developed in the loading for the 2nd Battalion, 34th Infantry, when a large number of 55-gallon oil drums was added to the cargo without warning. These had to be loaded first, a process that took longer than expected. The drums also occupied space previously assigned to other units. The battalion exec, Major Tommy Cathcart, took a personal hand by stripping to the waist and helping in the sweaty task of loading the drums. Some units took longer than anticipated; some had more or fewer vehicles than promised. Somehow, some way everything scheduled to be loaded was tucked aboard.

The loading officer was never happier than when the bulldozer operator, always the last man to board and the first to leave the ship, removed the sand accumulated at the ramp and just squeezed the 'dozer in as the ramp slowly ascended.

The initial plans called for the Mindanao landings at Malabang by the 24th Division, commanded by Major General Roscoe B. Woodruff. A class of 1915 graduate of West Point, Woodruff had commanded the division on Leyte under General Sibert in the X Corps. Assistant division commander was Brigadier General Kenneth F. Cramer, and the division artillery commander was Brigadier General Hugh Cort.

Two days before the invasion date, 17 April, developments dictated a change. Filipino guerrillas had succeeded in taking Malabang, and Marine Corps aircraft already were operating from the airstrip nearby, thereby making action by the Taro Leafers against those objectives unnecessary.

Under the new plan, the 24th Division would put only a battalion ashore at Malabang, while the remainder would land down the Illana Bay coast at Parang in Polloc Harbor. Two branches of the Mindanao River empty into the bay in that area, and the Americans needed to secure the mouths, which was another reason for selection of the invasion site.

The 31st Division was scheduled to follow the 24th Division ashore on 22 April. Generally, the 24th Division was to proceed eastward by river and highway to Davao while the 31st, upon reaching a main north-south artery about midway across that section of the island, would drive to the island's northern coast.

The major Japanese units in eastern Mindanao were the 100th Division, commanded by Lieutenant General Jiro Harada; the 30th Division, under Lieutenant General Gyosaku Morozumi; and the 32nd Naval Special Base Force headed by Rear Admiral Naoji Doi. The 100th Division and the naval troops held the southeastern third of eastern Mindanao, including Davao; the 30th Division defended the rest. Nearly impenetrable mountains separated the two bodies of Japanese troops.

The operation started as scheduled on the morning of 17 April 1945. First ashore were troops of the 533rd Engineer Boat and Shore Regiment, 3rd Engineer Special Brigade, on Ibus Island off Malabang. Company K, 3rd Battalion, 21st Infantry, landed without opposition on Bongo Island outside Polloc Harbor. The rest of the battalion went ashore at Malabang to the welcome of the guerrillas.

The main body of the 24th Division landed by regiments at Parang. In the van was the 19th Infantry, followed by the remainder of the 21st. The 24th Reconnaissance Troop reconnoitered the shores of Polloc Harbor and rode LVTs into the northern arm of the Mindanao River.

Among the first ashore was an oversized squad led by Private First Class Frank Fantino, a veteran of previous combat who would rapidly earn his non-com stripes during the campaign then starting. Fantino was a member of H Company, 19th Infantry. His superiors had handed him his first leadership assignment, to land and move inland a short distance and find a good location to set up a heavy machine gun.

The amphibious craft took the squad of 14 to the water's edge. "It couldn't go any farther because the terrain rose steep and had too much jungle," Fantino has written in his account of his experiences. "We rushed out without any opposition and moved inland until we reached the top of a hill about a quarter mile inland. We located a good spot for our gun with a good field of fire, deployed the men to protect the gun, and waited for (Japanese) or orders, whichever came first."

Opposition being light to non-existent in the early going, orders came first.

Jan Valtin, a 24th Division soldier who wrote a history of the Taro Leaf in the Pacific, *Children of Yesterday*, recorded that the first division casualty on Mindanao was 21st Regiment commander, Colonel William J. Verbeck, who was washing his face in front of his command post when a sniper's bullet grazed his back. It was his fourth wound of the war.

About the same time, General Woodruff stepped into a spider hole and cracked some ribs.

Valtin credits two GIs, Sergeant Robert McKenzie of Syracuse, N.Y., and Sergeant Paul Salas of Richmond, CA, with killing the first two enemy soldiers in the battle for eastern Mindanao. The pair were probing through a coastal swamp when they came upon the Japanese.

On the first afternoon, the 19th Regiment secured the entire Parang area. By the end of the day, the landing force had seized 35 miles of coastline and assault companies had penetrated five miles inland while fording three rivers.

Even though early resistance was negligible, the natural features made the going difficult. The withdrawing Japanese had burned the 240-foot bridge over the Ambal River, forcing combat engineers to undertake immediate bridge-building operations. Crocodiles infested the waterways, and at times infantrymen waded in water shoulder deep.

The commanders had expected the inva-

Pfc. Bob Bauer of Dubuque, IA, and Pfc. Joseph Condo of Columbus, OH. 34th Infantry Mortarmen, put captured Jap bicycle to good use. Digos, Mindanao, 26 April 1945. (Courtesy of Charles W. Card)

sion troops to spend three or four days establishing a firm beachhead. When that goal was accomplished before the end of the first day, they did not hesitate to launch the drive inland immediately.

The first objective was Fort Pikit, 35 miles away, at the junction of Route 1 and the Mindanao River. The plan was for the 19th Infantry to travel by highway and the 21st Infantry aboard LCMs upstream.

The move eastward started on 18 April, the day after the invasion. The river convoy made 20 miles by dark. Naval and engineer gunboats lent their support the next day, 19 April, and the group reached Paiduk-Pulangi, nine miles short of Fort Pikit, by nightfall.

In his book, Valtin described the Navy crewmen, in the unaccustomed role of jungle fighting, raking the shores with machine gun fire as they guided their vessels up the river. At one point, the sailors fired at movement ahead only to find it was an Army barge coming their way. "The Army-Navy duel ended when the ships met head-on in the bend in the river," the author wrote.

Meanwhile, the 19th Regiment, moving over a poor road, did not match the pace of the water-borne troops. The road was so overgrown with cogon grass that frequently it was no more than a tunnel through the vegetation.

Besides the handicap of the narrow trail, men of the 19th Infantry were harassed by Japanese troops and slowed by the heat and the necessity of hand-carrying supplies.

One skirmish by 19th Regiment troops on 19 April resulted in 18 enemy dead. The same day, 21st Infantry men encountered 80 Japanese near Lomopog.

General Woodruff, fearing the 21st Regiment was getting too far ahead, ordered the unit to draw back downstream for 10 miles. Crews of five engineer LCMs remained forward to hold Paidu-Pulangi for the night and the next day.

The 3rd Battalion 34th Infantry, under Lieutenant Colonel George (Bugeye) Willetts, came forward by river and overland, reaching Fort Pikit on 21 April, finding the five boat crews already there. Two days later, the 19th Regiment also reached Fort Pikit.

By the end of the day 22 April, 3rd Battalion 34th, against only light resistance, had pushed on to reach the key road junction at Kabacan, nine miles northeast of Fort Pikit. At Kabacan, the island's two main highways joined. They were Route 1 and what was commonly called the Sayre Highway. First Battalion, commanded by Major Carl O. (Speedy) Mann, was on the march close behind the 3rd from Pikit, and the 2nd Battalion was enroute by LCM up the Mindanao River.

Major Harry L. Snavely's men of the 2nd Battalion had finally received their marching orders at dusk after remaining behind two days to unload the LSTs. They marched in darkness in regular company formation with full pack several miles to the river to board the LCMs. Then came a restful time of boating up the river. General Eichelberger wrote in Our Jungle Road to Tokyo: "There hadn't been a military adventure quite like this since federal gunboats operated on the lower Mississippi during the Civil War." Without sleep for 48 hours, the 2nd Battalion bedded down near Fort Pikit on 22 April.

The 24th Division since landing less than a week before had made a lightning thrust into the middle of eastern Mindanao, arriving considerably earlier than X Corps expected. That fact was of major strategic importance. Because main Japanese forces on the island had become hopelessly split before they could react to the Americans, the eventual outcome of the eastern Mindanao campaign was effectively decided in the first few days.

Corps Commander Sibert now could execute his two-pronged plan, sending the 31st Division, then unloading, up the Sayre Highway and the 24th Division the remaining 50 miles southeast to Davao Gulf.

The division's next objective was Digos, a town near Davao Gulf about 20 miles southwest of Davao. From there, the troops would drive on Davao and seek to destroy the Japanese 100th Division.

Once again, the 24th Division troops knew speed was to their advantage. The faster Digos could be reached, the less time the enemy would have to set up defenses along Route 1.

The Digos region was amply defended by the Japanese, whose combat force there included about 3,350 men, but they had anticipated a seaborne assault, not one from overland. It was not until 22 April, five days after the fact, that General Harada, the 100th Division commander even knew of an American landing. Even then, he still thought the operation at Parang was a feint and awaited what he thought would be the main assault from Davao Gulf, with his weaponry pointed in that direction.

The 24th Reconnaissance Troop moved out from Kabacan on the morning of 24 April followed by the 34th Regiment. The 1st Battalion led the advance. The 2nd Battalion passed through the 3rd and marched to Kidapawan, 20 miles beyond Kabacan.

The next day, the 2nd Battalion shuttled by truck another 20 miles to Dalapuay and took over the lead on 26 April.

With G Company in the van, the enemy pinned the battalion down with intense fire from small arms, automatic weapons and anti-aircraft guns situated in three pillboxes at the Digos crossroads. The "pow-pow" of these guns, sounding like canister as the rounds cut through the trees, dropping leaves on the troops huddled below, added a new dimension to the fighting. H Company opened up with its 81 mm mortars, but had to move its guns to the side when a round dropped short among friendly troops.

Throughout the day of 27 April, all three of the 2nd Battalion's rifle companies in their turn pounded the Digos defenses. After the initial thrust, G Company withdrew while division cannoneers fired an artillery barrage and then renewed the attack, suffering five casualties. After further artillery support and an air assault on the enemy position, E Company took up the fight but without taking the position. Finally F Company attacked, but had to disengage. During the night, with the 2nd Battalion dug in at the front of the Japanese stronghold, the enemy evacuated the position, leaving 25 dead.

Effective resistance at Digos had ended and Davao lay only 20 miles up the coastal road. General Eichelberger was elated. In Our Jungle Road to Tokyo, he wrote of the Taro Leafers' swift thrust across eastern Mindanao: "Only 10 days after the original landing, the 24th Division had fought its way 110 miles across Mindanao to the Gulf of Davao. Not three or four months - as General MacArthur had predicted - but 10 days. It was a remarkable achievement, truly one for the history books. It was the longest sustained land advance of Americans in the Pacific."

The drive was all the more impressive for the conditions men of the 24th Division encountered on the way. The Japanese had blown about 100 bridges across the jungle streams that flowed across the island terrain, forcing the combat engineers into almost constant bridge-building activity. Through jungles and over

Mindanao River. (Courtesy of Charles W. Card)

mountains, the infantrymen force-marched their way while coping with ambushes, land mines, crocodiles and the uncertain temperament of native tribes.

An encounter with one islander, however, gave a 19th Regiment officer an interesting surprise. As related by Valtin in *Children of Yesterday*, Lieutenant Robert Drennan of Rock Hill, S.C., was leading his platoon when a Moro waved a paper in front of his face. "You from 19th Infantry?" the native inquired.

"How did you know?" Drennan replied. The officer then read the paper. It was a discharge certificate from the 19th Regiment issued in Hawaii in 1924 to Private Maximo Cabayan.

Cabayan told the lieutenant, "I weesh to serve my old outfit." And so he did, as a scout and interpreter.

The experience of a battalion of the 19th Infantry, also described in Valtin's book, illustrates the natural perils of crossing the island. On a rainy night with the river raging below

them, 900 men under the command of Lieutenant Colonel Joy K. Vallery of Lincoln, Neb., crossed a foot bridge that had been devised by the engineers. For the first 50 feet, the men had a hand-hold; for the last 50 feet, they had to walk on the log with nothing to hold to while crocodiles filled the river below. The only loss in the maneuver was a single steel helmet.

The drive to the gulf had completely disrupted Japanese plans. General Harada had designed his defenses to repel an American invasion in Davao Gulf. His main armament was pointed toward the beaches and ill-suited to resist an overland attack on his right flank. The Davao area was particularly valuable because of six airdromes, which the Japanese had used to stage their westward advance to the Dutch East Indies early in 1942.

General Woodruff described the Japanese defenses in his After Action Report: "Along the shore of the gulf affording the best landing area, the Japanese had constructed underwater obstacles of palm logs and barbed wire concealed

at high tide when amphibious landings are made. Assault boats, hitting the obstacles 50 to 75 yards from shore, would have floundered and become easy targets for Japanese gunners. Back of the beach Japanese concrete bunkers with interlocking bands of crossfire raked the beach. Next came a tank ditch covered by another row of bunkers. Then a third row of bunkers built of palm logs and then a line of ingeniously constructed individual defenses and supporting pillboxes. Everything was superbly camouflaged."

With Digos in hand, General Woodruff hestitated not a second. While the 34th Regiment held the crossroads, he immediately dispatched the 19th Infantry northward to capture Davao and one battalion of the 21st to Mintal, an important road junction about four miles northwest of the gulf and eight miles west of Davao. Unknown to the Americans at the time, Mintal was located on what turned out to be the first Japanese main line of resistance.

While the 2nd Battalion 34th secured Digos, the regiment's 1st Battalion commander took advantage of the distraction of the enemy and, fording the Digos River, moved around the north flank of the Japanese at the crossroads and east onto the road to Davao. The battalion seized the high, forbidding cliffs in the vicinity of Tagabuli Bay overlooking the road. This move, effectively preventing the Japanese from occupying this strong defensive terrain, was a factor in the 19th Infantry's swift move to Davao. General Woodruff later determined that five Japanese battalions in the area could have been diverted to the natural defensive position and seriously changed the course of the campaign.

The 19th Infantry advanced northward 20 miles from Digos along the coastal road on the western side of Davao Gulf and occupied Davao City 3 May. For some inexplicable reason (perhaps another example of the inability of the Japanese to change plans and adjust to changing conditions), the enemy did not contest the passage of the 19th Infantry across his entire front. General Woodruff was astonished, but delighted.

During the drive northward, the 11th F.A. Battalion established its gun positions on 1 May inside abandoned Japanese bunkers at Matina Airdrome on the outskirts of Davao. The enemy had used the bunkers with their earthen six-foot-thick sides to protect its planes. Colonel Hodges, the battalion commander, had placed his headquarters and fire direction center in one of the bunkers.

Japanese manning five-inch naval guns on a hillside 500 yards away had watched the battalion dig in. One gun zeroed in on the battalion headquarters bunker. After one long round followed by a short, the next round plowed into the bunker and showered dirt and shell fragments on the CP and first aid tents. Colonel Hodges expected the gun to "fire for effect" but that was the only round.

The 11th's guns were not in position to return fire, but a nearby battery of 105s quickly silenced the naval guns. Japanese energy in digging the thick revetments had saved the battalion from harm.

The 19th Infantry's crossing of the broad

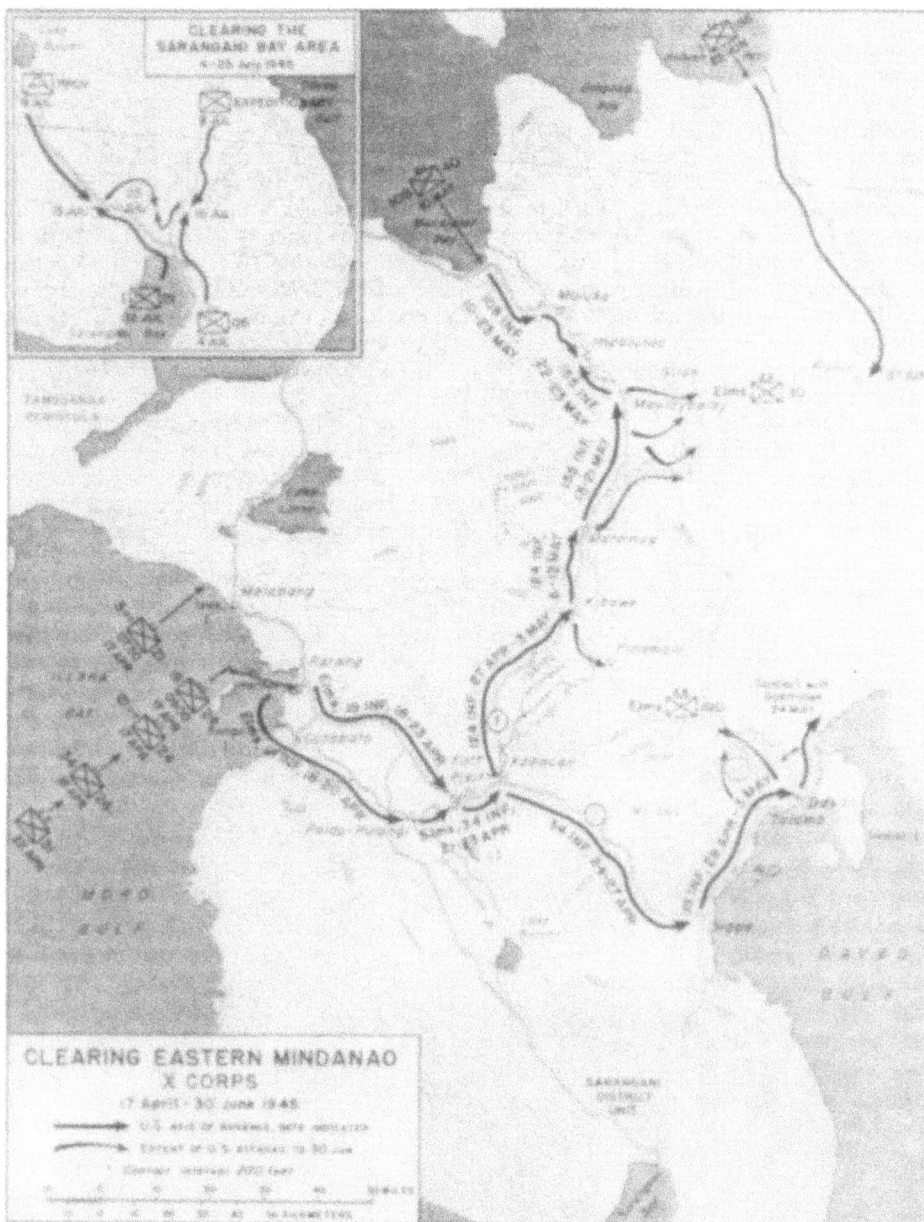

Clearing Eastern Mindanao.

Davao River and entry into Davao were made easier by the deceptive tactic of the regimental commander, Colonel Thomas (Jock) Clifford. He ordered an artillery barrage at the most logical crossing site, and the Japanese answered. Then, having convinced the enemy that would be the crossing point, Clifford sent his men across several miles upstream. They were in Davao before the Japanese had a chance to recover.

One hero of this exploit was Sergeant Alfred A. Sousa of Honolulu, a combat engineer. At the selected crossing point was an old bridge with a 40-foot gap blown out in the middle. Both ends were mined. According to an account in *Children of Yesterday*, Sousa swam to the far end, disarmed the mines, swam back and then directed the construction of a makeshift bridge of ladders, tree trunks, timbers and ropes.

Leading the infantry across was a rifle platoon commanded by Lieutenant Clifton Ferguson of Indianapolis. Also in the first contingent into Davao were Clifford and Assistant Division Commander Cramer.

At the gates of Davao, enemy artillery was said to outnumber the division's pieces by three to one. One artillery officer, Lieutenant Colonel Harold E. Liebe of Tacoma, WA, gave his account of the fight at Davao where, he said, infantry at a bridgehead were taking heavy casualties from Japanese naval artillery. "My men decided to do something about it. They manhandled a 105 mm howitzer across the river and up a hill on nothing but their muscles and guts. From then on it was a point-blank duel. It was firing by bore-sighting, that is you look down the barrel of your howitzer until it is on target. After an hour of dueling, we knocked out the competition." (*Children of Yesterday* - Valtin.)

The capture of Davao positioned the 24th Division for the main effort of the Mindanao campaign, the defeat of the Japanese 100th Division, which had withdrawn to strong defensive positions in the rising terrain two to four miles inland from Davao Gulf and paralleling the northeast coast. The enemy line extended from Catigan in the south, a point 13 miles southwest of Davao, to about 12 miles north of that city where the line could be anchored in the hills.

The Davao River, running south-southeast into the gulf, split the Japanese front. On the right, or west of the river, were five infantry battalions; on the north were four battalions and some air force service troops. The center in the Mintal area was where the Japanese were the strongest. Defensive positions were established in depth along Route 1-D, which ran inland from the coast.

Since the Japanese posture was strictly defensive, the Americans of the 24th Infantry Division had no choice but to eliminate the enemy garrison by offensive warfare.

Triumph in the Philippines, the official U.S. Army history of the campaign, included this observation: "From the theater point of view, the 24th's future operations would be mopping up, although tactically speaking the division was about to enter upon a frontal attack as rough as any the U.S. Army had engaged in the Philippines."

Sirawan, Mindanao July 1945. Platoon is 3rd G Company 34th, Platoon Sergeant Whitaker. In forefront Platoon Leader Mann. (Courtesy of David Mann)

General Eichelberger put the "mopping up" concept in its proper perspective.: "If there is another war, I recommend that the military, and the correspondents, and everyone else concerned drop the phrase 'mopping up' from their vocabularies. It is not a good enough phrase to die for."

Author Jan Valtin , observing that the battle for eastern Mindanao for the Americans was one to re-establish "face" in a final way. He wrote: "The dogfaces who fought and won this 'battle of prestige' fought it without enthusiasm but with a sullen and melancholy hatred."

A recurring theme sounded by the Mindanao warriors was the comparison to other Philippine fighting. General Cramer, as quoted in *Children of Yesterday*, made this observation about Davao: "It looked like a cinch. But after a few minutes it was worse than anything Leyte ever had. Artillery seemed to be firing at us from point-blank range and mortar shells were falling all around. Guesses are never good enough. You never know really what's going to happen, until you go in there to get shot at. That's the only reliable source of information."

Other men called the fighting on Mindanao "as bad as Breakneck Ridge, and bigger." The difference in strategic importance between Leyte and Mindanao was obvious, but for sheer savagery of action and tenacity of the enemy, the southern island campaign was regarded by the fighting men as every bit as tough and perhaps more so.

In those early days of May, some manpower adjustments were in order. Generals Sibert and Eichelberger recognized that the extended supply lines for both divisions on the ground required more troops if the impending offensive actions were to be successful. So the 162nd Regimental Combat Team of the 41st Division, then at Zamboanga, was brought over to protect the line from Illana Bay to Kabacan. That movement also allowed Sibert to release the 21st Infantry from Corps reserve to participate in the main assault against the 100th Division.

The Mindanao campaign now unfolded into four distinct phases. First, the 24th Division had to locate the enemy, pinpoint his defenses, and determine his capabilities, all by patrolling and probing. This period also was one of consolidating and stockpiling supplies at Davao and Talomo, making the airfields operational and bringing up reinforcements to guard the line of communications.

After their initial inertia, the Japanese put up a stout resistance along their first defensive line. Piercing this line constituted phase two.

Behind the first line of defense, the Japanese had constructed a second. Anchored at Wangan on the west, the line ran through Ula east to Mandog on the Davao River. The third phase, cracking this line, proved to be tougher, at least for the 34th Infantry in the center, than destroying the first.

The fourth phase was the pursuit of the enemy beyond Calinan into the rough, jungled mountains where the Japanese hid until the war ended.

The arena for the rest of the campaign was a gradually rising plain formed by the principal natural features, the Davao and Talomo rivers. The division's axis of attack was northwestward along Route 1-D, a hard-surfaced road that started at Talomo on the gulf and wound between the two rivers through Mintal and Tugbok to Calinan. Always on the attackers' left was Mount Apo, at 9,369 feet the highest peak in the Philippines.

Much of the fighting would be done in an environment that could only be described as forbidding. The area west of the Davao River and north toward Calinan was the location of overgrown and neglected hemp plantations. The plants, resembling banana trees, grew to a height of about 20 feet. Originally set about 10 feet apart, the hemp, or abaca plants, were heavy with shoots, about a foot in diameter and only about a foot apart at the time of the battle. The men who had to fight among the hemp plants found visibility virtually zero and the temperatures almost unbearable because the canopy held the already oppressive heat close to the ground.

Captain Malcolm D. Aitken, S-3 and later executive officer of the 1st Battalion, 21st Infantry, described the defenses the Japanese had developed in the area in their long anticipation of the American attack. "Caves, tunnels, interlocking trenches serving strategically placed pillboxes, all overgrown with jungle vegetation, or dug in hundreds of impenetrable abaca groves .... Spider holes and well-camouflaged strongpoints abounded in these groves."

Sergeant Fred Livingston, of Boyce, TX, learned about the subterranean installations of the enemy in an explosive way when he led a detail to blow up a Japanese cave just below the crest of a ridge facing the Talomo River. Under covering fire from his men, Livingston threw a dynamite charge into the mouth and then dived down the hill to escape the effects of the anticipated blast. There was one explosion, then two and then three. As Valtin described the scene, "The hill bubbled, flames shot from other concealed tunnels. The whole hillside disintegrated. The men were stunned and deafened by the blasts, which continued to come in split-second intervals. Concussions slammed them into the ground, lifted them into the air, and slammed them down again. Smoke and dust covered the summit. Rocks, sprays of earth, smashed corpses and fragments of broken trees rained down on the hillside." What the Americans had thought to be a single cave was a labyrinth of tunnels filled with ammunition and fuel.

The environment contributed to the nature of the warfare the American GIs found themselves in. The battle for Mindanao was marked by countless encounters at extremely close range between small units, sometimes two or three men. Ambushes, booby traps, mines and rigged bombs were common. Often it would be daylight before a GI discovered the dead enemy at his feet, or in his foxhole, whom he killed during the night's darkness.

Close-quarter action often had bizarre results. Sergeant William Braswell, of Jacksonville, FL, on one occasion tried to retrieve an enemy grenade that had lodged between the shoulder blades of a fellow GI. Just as he reached for it, however, the grenade exploded, killing the other man and blowing off Braswell's own hand at the wrist.

The 21st Infantry jumped off against the formidable center of the Japanese line on 30 April for seven weeks of hard and continuous combat that provided little relief for the infantrymen. The initial objectives were Libby Airdrome, two miles off the coast northwest of Talomo, and Mintal. The airdrome was in front of the enemy positions, but the defensive line was on high ground overlooking the field.

The 1st Battalion, 21st, commanded by

Major Nicholas E. Sloan, bypassed the airdrome to the west and drove directly on Mintal, arriving there on 3 May. The rest of the regiment took Libby Airdrome on 5 May, but could advance no farther up Route 1-D. That put the battalion at Mintal in peril for a time of being surrounded and possibly annihilated.

During a sudden firefight in the push to Mintal, Johnny Rodriguez of C Company recalled an odd experience with Ramon Tapia, a recent replacement. After diving into the nearest foxhole, Rodriguez noticed that Tapia kept his head down. He told the new man to keep his head up, that he couldn't see a thing with his head down, that they were too far back to get hit. "Oh yeah," Tapia said, "What about this bullet?" A bullet had just lodged in the log in back of them.

Next, the 34th Infantry tried to bypass the enemy's Route 1-D positions by driving north on the east bank of the Talomo River. Then on 8 May, 1st Battalion of the 21st Infantry also crossed to the east side of the river near Mintal, but enemy artillery, mortar and machine-gun fire drove that unit back to the western bank two days later.

Two battalions of the 21st started moving north along the east bank of the Talomo River

Members of Co. A, 34th Infantry Regiment, 24th Victory Division, move up along the Digos road, Mindanao, P.I. (Courtesy of Charles W. Card)

toward Mintal on 12 May and over the next three days managed to reduce Japanese positions and clear Route 1-D all the way to Mintal, a feat that established a good supply route and secured the division's left rear.

The Gimlets were under frequent attack as they approached Mintal, and the enemy action intensified after the GIs entered the town. The 1st Battalion officer Aitken described one attack and the heroism of the battalion surgeon, Captain J. W. Cathcart.

"One night before we took Mintal, we were hit with two grenade and machine gun assaults, one early and one after midnight. In the latter ... Cathcart crawled across the perimeter to minister to a critically wounded soldier who had been shot or bayoneted in the throat. This was an incredibly brave act in light of the seldom-broken rule prohibiting any movement in the perimeter at night ... .

"Without any skilled help, and with only a flashlight under a poncho, this intrepid medical officer was able to insert a makeshift tube in the soldier's windpipe and to restore his breathing," Aitken recalled.

Captain Cathcart later was killed in action. (The medical officer is not to be confused with Major Thomas Cathcart, 2nd Battalion executive officer in the 34th Infantry) Captain Cathcart had been wounded while treating casualties from a 1st Battalion patrol, and as he was being carried from the field, the doctor and the litter bearers all were cut down by machine-gun fire.

Another heroic battalion surgeon, Captain Stanley Luria, treated 262 casualties in one five-day, five-night stretch. The doctor worked in his tent under artillery and mortar fire, and sometimes in foxholes using his flashlight to see and his poncho for cover. Remarkably, none of the 262 men died.

Medical personnel routinely risked their lives in various ways. Captain Paul E. Byrd, a medical officer from West Fargo, ND, was roused at 3 a.m. to deliver plasma to the front. Five men in a Jeep roared down a dark road, going around blown bridge sites, for 10 miles to get their precious cargo where it was needed. On the way back, the party was ambushed and four of the five were wounded. As the driver backed down the road, the men who were able jumped out and did battle until American infantrymen arrived to rout the enemy.

At the Mintal perimeter another attack during heavy rain reached such intensity that a call was made for supporting fire from the 52nd Field Artillery Battalion.

The position at the main point of attack was manned by the Headquarters Company of the 1st Battalion, 21st, and a .50 caliber machine gun operated by Lieutenant Arominski of the Pioneer Platoon.

"I began to listen for the .50 caliber machine gun, and when it finally did open up, my feelings were mixed," Aitken recalls. "On the one hand I was confident that nothing could stand up to those deep-throated bursts, but on the other hand, I knew that 'Ski' wouldn't fire unless and until he had something to shoot at, so that meant that we were in danger of being overrun.

"Ski's gun seemed to turn the force of the attack aside, and when the artillery shells started to fall, there was only sporadic firing by the enemy."

During the battle for Mintal, another 21st Regiment soldier, Pfc. James H. Diamond of Company D, distinguished himself conspicuously over the period of a week, 8-14 May. Armed with a submachine gun, Diamond charged and killed a Japanese soldier who was about to throw a grenade at his section. Then, while firing on the enemy, the soldier also directed artillery and heavy machine-gun fire on enemy pillboxes that were pinning down two American machine-gun sections, thus enabling them to set up and bring their weapons to bear on the Japanese. Later, Diamond volunteered to help evacuate soldiers under heavy fire from a bridgehead. On 14 May, the soldier was leading another patrol to bring out wounded, and as he secured an abandoned machine gun, Diamond was fatally wounded. The fire he drew allowed the rest of the patrol to reach safety. For his heroism, Pfc. Diamond, of New Orleans, LA, was awarded the Medal of Honor.

Four officers of 1st Battalion, 21st Infantry, took on the role of litterbearers for a wounded GI during the fight for Mintal when their bridge game was interrupted by enemy fire. The officers, like the other fighting men on the island, had to seize their brief pleasures where they could find them. For Sloan, Aitken, Captain Ed Farmer, the battalion S-3, Captain Jim Doyle, the battalion adjutant, and Captain Warren McNamara, Company D commander, that meant bridge.

The battalion had just pulled back into Mintal in mid-May. The reserve company, Company D and the Headquarters Company established a rough perimeter, and a column of battalion vehicles pulled off on the other side of the road. So the officers determined they had time to get in some bridge.

However, machine gun fire opened up on the opposite side, and one man was hit. The others, pinned down, were unable to help, but the four-man hole where the officers had been playing cards was in such a line that they could approach the wounded man without serious exposure. The four officers determined to crawl to the casualty, but as soon as they moved, the machine gun fired again. However, it soon was clear that the gunner could depress his weapon only so far, so the officers flattened out and crept across the road to the wounded man, dragged him onto the litter and pulled him to cover behind the truck. With no sign of a medic, each of the four officers grabbed a corner of the litter and made a run for it back across the road and on to the battalion aid station.

With that, the foursome resumed their bridge game.

Another incident in the 21st Regiment's westward drive was revealing of Colonel Verbeck's qualities. Three officers were lying prone while conferring because of heavy frontal fire that had stalled the unit's progress toward the town of Bayabas. They heard a voice behind them, "Break out the canteen cups." It was the regimental commander, in a time and place he wasn't expected. He held two canteens, one filled with 190-proof GI alcohol and the other Coca Cola. After the colonel poured everyone a drink, he inquired of the situation. He then recommended pulling back to the perimeter and hitting the strongpoint the next day.

Early the next day, Colonel Verbeck himself led a contingent of Filipino troops in bypassing the strongpoint and entering Bayabas.

While the 24th Division's other two regiments were fighting their way up Route 1-D, the 19th Infantry was operating in the Davao area. Starting on 10 May, some elements reduced Japanese strongpoints in the hills north of the city, while others moved onto the high ground west of the Davao River. One battalion cleared Samal Island in the gulf where Japanese artillery had been firing on American troops in the city.

On 15 May, the 34th Infantry took over the area south of Davao from the 19th Regiment.

The plan for the next phase of the Mindanao offensive called for the 21st on the left and elements of the 34th on the right to attack north abreast on either side of the Talomo River against the Japanese center, while the 19th Regiment prepared to strike north and northeast from Davao to clear the coastline and link up with a guerrilla unit, the 107th Division.

Inasmuch as the Americans thus far had ignored the enemy flanks, the Japanese reorganized their defenses and concentrated on the middle.

The 100th Division commander pulled two battalions from the flanks to reinforce the center and shifted the bulk of his army west of the Davao River, leaving Admiral Doi with his naval force east of the river.

The entire 24th Division renewed its attack on 17 May. The 19th Infantry moved northward and a week later made contact with the guerrilla unit. With Route 1 north of Davao now secure, the Chicks were in a position to turn westward toward the left flank of the Japanese line.

The 21st Infantry, on the division left, advanced along two parallel tracks, one on Route 1-D and the other by a minor road east of the Talomo River. The regiment's left took three days to reach Tugbok on Route 1-D one mile northwest of Mintal. Resistance, stiff on that side, was even tougher on the right where Japanese poured artillery, mortar, machine gun, rocket and rifle fire into the Gimlets.

Crossing the Talomo River was a challenge for the 1st Battalion, 21st. The commander, Major Nick Sloan, and his exec, Captain Aitken, conducted a reconnaissance upstream to find an alternative location to the bridge site that Japanese artillery had destroyed. On the way, a grenade tossed out of a spider hole wounded Aitken in the shoulder but he continued on.

The 3rd Battalion engineers repaired the foot bridge and the battalion crossed in two hours under artillery fire, aided by answering fire from the 52nd Field Artillery Battalion and 4.2-inch mortars.

It was not until 27 May, 10 days after the 21st Infantry launched the attack that elements on the right drew even with the remainder of the regiment by seizing a junction about a mile east of Tugbok. The 21st Regiment held that

Medical technicians of the 1st Bn., 19th Regimental Combat Team, 24th Division, are on the march from Parang, Mindanao, P.I., to Ft. Pikit. In the left column, the fourth soldier from the front is Pfc. Edward Bettencourt of 1st Bn Medical Aid station. The Filipino directly behind him is Jeremias Bejarin, one of several natives who assisted the soldiers in carrying supplies. (Courtesy of Charles W. Card)

and G companies joined the two platoons on the hill and extended the perimeter. As the companies dug in, snipers were active. They shot one G Company man outside the perimeter. A Hawaiian sergeant, Thomas Martin, never hesitating, bounded to him and dragged him back inside the perimeter. Another sniper shot an F Company man.

Soon after dark, the Japanese unleashed murderous fire using knee mortars, 20 mm anti-aircraft guns, machine guns, rifles and rockets. Miraculously, there were no casualties. American mortars and artillery finally silenced the enemy at about 2200, but the rocky ground made sleep impossible for the rest of the night.

Each GI regardless of rank knew that the first move in the morning would be to clear the area in the abaca from whence came the previous night's firing. Third platoon G Company drew this job. With no heavy weapons preparation and no supporting fire, the platoon moved in a line across an open field into the grove. No firing greeted them; the Japanese had fled.

The 21st and 34th regiments, despite what might seem to have been modest territorial gains northwest along Route 1-D and the Talomo River, had accomplished a major feat toward defeating the Japanese on Mindanao.

By reaching Tugbok, the 24th Division had cracked the strong center of the enemy lines, and when General Woodruff realized that, he immediately made plans for the next phase.

The Japanese commander also took steps to prolong the defensive battle he was fighting by falling back to a second line approximately three and one half miles north of Mintal. The new line, centered on the town of Ula, was anchored on the right at Wangan, about four miles west, and on the left at the Davao River. East of that stream, the last defensive position was at the town of Mandog.

The new round of combat would begin with the Japanese significantly weakened. The 21st Infantry had decimated one independent battalion. Five other enemy battalions, four regular and one provisional, were at about half strength as the result of the fighting through 28 May.

The 24th Division plan called for a continued drive north-northwest along a broad front, again with the 21st Infantry west of Route 1-D and the 34th along that road and a secondary road one mile to the east.

On 28 May, the 3rd Battalion 34th Infantry made contact with the 21st Infantry at the road junction one mile east of Tugbok. From the junction, a secondary, unnamed dirt road ran north about six miles to an east-west road that led to Calinan, the last large settlement on Route 1-D before the road became a dirt trail into the mountains. The 34th Infantry now had two avenues of attack, the dirt road and Route 1-D.

Since the main road would require rebuilding of about 12 bridges, General Woodruff decided to use the secondary road as the main route for supply and line of attack.

The terrain was quite different from the hilly country the 34th had just left. The new area was a flat plateau with occasional rises, crossed by streams, with some forests. The 3rd

---

ground for two more days before being relieved by the 34th Infantry.

On 14 May, Colonel William Jenna, 34th Infantry commander, returned to the United States and the executive officer, Lieutenant Colonel Chester A. Dahlen took over. A native of Minnesota and West Point graduate in 1933, Colonel Dahlen had commanded the 3rd Battalion 21st Infantry at Hollandia. As regimental exec, he replaced Colonel Aubrey Newman (division chief of staff during the Mindanao operation) after the latter was seriously wounded on Leyte. Dahlen too was wounded at Zig Zag Pass on Luzon. He eventually rose to corps command and retired as a major general. Succeeding Dahlen as regimental exec was Lieutenant Colonel James F. Pearsall.

To almost the end of May, the 34th Infantry had three battalion-size, separate offenses under way between the Talomo and Davao Rivers. The 1st Battalion attacked the enemy's line in the Matina area, and the 3rd Battalion attacked north, east of the Talomo River in conjunction with the 21st Infantry. The dirtiest job the regiment faced was clearing the coastal hills between the two rivers. The Japanese were constantly launching harassing attacks from this area on the Route 1-D supply line from Talomo to Mintal.

The bulk of this nasty job fell to the 2nd Battalion. The enemy had established its initial main line of defense from west of Mintal east along the coastal hills to the Davao River and beyond. As events were to show, capturing these hills was the key to breaking the enemy's line. Japanese occupying the heights had made supplying the 21st Infantry's forward battalion extremely hazardous by their harassing forays against supply columns. The key

terrain feature, Hill 550, was assigned to 2nd Battalion, 34th.

On 15 May, F Company 34th relieved the 2nd Battalion 19th, which had held the southern reaches of the hill mass since early in the month. The enemy gradually increased pressure on F Company so that by 18 May the rest of the battalion moved to the Hill 550 area.

The 34th regimental S-2, Captain Lloyd F. Van Dusen, accurately appraised the situation: "Indications are that the enemy's main line of defense has been located on high ground to the front. A determined defense from well-prepared positions may be expected on this ground." One action is indicative of the fighting in the area.

G Company moved by truck on the morning of 19 May and debarked in the rear of F Company. The area was dominated by an oval-shaped hill with forests 100 to 200 yards away to the west and south, and abaca the same distance to the north. An F Company platoon, commanded by Lieutenant Delmont E. MacAnallen, of Akron, OH, had taken the hill, but needed reinforcement to repel an expected Japanese attack. Captain Rucker Innes, G Company commander, fully recovered from his wound in Zig Zag Pass, sent one platoon commanded by Lieutenant David Mann, of Norfolk VA, dashing up the hill during a lull in the fighting. Each man had to run a gauntlet of rifle fire through an open space to reach the top. The two platoons, one from each company, formed a perimeter around the top of the hill and awaited an attack that never came. Incidentally, the two platoon leaders, McAnallen and Mann, had attended Officers Candidate School together.

Late in the afternoon, the remainder of F

Battalion would move northwest on Route 1-D, the 2nd Battalion on the dirt road and the 1st Battalion farther east.

The 19th Regiment's mission now was to clear the Japanese left east of the Davao River. That attack started on 29 May from the coast north of Davao. Two days later the Chicks were near the main line of defense, which they overran in the ensuing days. By 7 June the troops were near Mandog. Air and artillery support helped the attackers overwhelm the Japanese, whose last major defenses on the east side of the river were in a state of collapse. It took the 19th Regiment another nine days to mop up the last of the organized resistance in and around Mandog before General Woodruff pulled the regiment out and allowed guerrillas to take over. What was left of the Japanese defenders in that area faded into the hills to the north and avoided any further serious fighting.

During the 19th Infantry's advance, H Company's Frank Fantino, who had come ashore as a private first class and would leave as a staff sergeant, demonstrated how the seasoned non-coms helped the newly minted junior officers who continued to arrive in the battle zone.

"We moved in single file along a mountain jungle trail and came to a meadow and crossed it," he wrote years later. "Just on the other side of the meadow we came to a Japanese-dug trench ... ."

The trench was unoccupied, so Fantino and a second lieutenant who had not been in combat before continued on into the jungle where they came under machine gun fire.

"The lieutenant and I dove behind a very small mound and tried to see where the gun position was located but we couldn't see farther than 50 feet into the jungle," Fantino recalled. The officer turned to Fantino and suggested, "Maybe we should get the machine gun up here and put down covering fire for the riflemen in front us."

"I said, 'Lieutenant, those GIs are gone by now and we're alone out here, and I don't think you'll be able to get a gun crew together. You remember that trench we passed a little while ago? If you want me, I'll be in that trench,' " Fantino recalls replying.

The H Company sergeant dashed back to the trench during a lull and found three men from a rifle company there also. The trench was under heavy enemy fire, but soon the second lieutenant joined them. All five men in turn evacuated the trench hot spot and reached a jungle position safely. In the meantime, the enemy had withdrawn.

On 30 May, 2nd Battalion 34th launched its attack on Ula in the center of the Japanese second line, the key to General Harada's defense. All companies moved by truck to an assembly area in preparation for the attack north and west to seize Ula and a bridge over the Talomo River 1,500 yards west of Ula. The objectives lay 2,000 yards ahead through extremely dense abaca growth. The only routes of advance were along narrow straight paths, which furnished admirable lanes for Japanese machine gun fire. The battalion jumped off at 1015 in column of companies, sequence E, G and F.

Following an artillery and 81 mm mortar barrage, Company E advanced along a path 200 yards east of the secondary road. At 1050 enemy machine guns, rifles and mortars from well-camouflaged positions bordering the road halted the company in its tracks. Employing mortar and rifle support fire, the company advanced 1,500 yards to secure a vital trail junction. Company G followed, deploying on both sides of the trail into the dense abaca to mop up and clear out the continuous series of spider holes and entrenchments. Company G passed through Company E and moved to the west of the unnamed road where the GIs came under intense machine gun fire. The two rifle companies consolidated their positions and dug in for the night.

At one point during a firefight with Japanese 100 yards distant in abaca, a platoon of G Company advanced along a ditch, using the dirt from the trenching as cover. Suddenly a BAR man, Leo Gomolchak, screamed, "Oh, my head," and slumped into the ditch behind the bank. Blood was evident when he removed his helmet. But then, flashing his trademark grin, he held his helmet aloft and pointed to two neat holes through his steel helmet and liner with only a graze on his neck. Gomolchak would take home the ultimate war souvenir and a Purple Heart too! The company commander, Jack Calhoun, radioed the platoon to withdraw. In one of the incongruities of war, hardly an hour after its harrowing firefight, the platoon was eating a delicious hot dinner topped by a dessert of blueberry cobbler.

During the night the Japanese inflicted several casualties in the G Company perimeter with mortars. Two enemy soldiers carrying dynamite were blown up trying to infiltrate the perimeter. Company F renewed the attack at

Above photos: A patrol of the Antitank Company, 34th Infantry, 24th Division, moves out to rescue some Filipinos near Digos, Mindanao, P.I., led by some of the Filipinos who managed to escape on the possibility that the patrol might be intentionally led into an ambush. (Courtesy of Charles W. Card)

0915 on 31 May and by 1225 had pushed to within 300 yards of Ula before machine gun fire stopped the riflemen. Company G on the left side of the road and F Company on the right finally seized the crossroads town of Ula at 1600. Major Jack Matthews, the regimental S-3, sent a platoon north on the road to draw fire. Fortunately, the enemy machine gunner missed the entire platoon not more than 200 yards to his front. Major Matthews assumed command of the 1st Battalion on 10 June, and was succeeded in the S-3 slot by Captain George H. Ellis.

The 34th Infantry resumed the attack with battalions abreast, the 3rd on the left, the 2nd in the center and the 1st on the right. The attack became a daily routine of following a road or trail to the next crossroads. The enemy would defend one crossroads, then withdraw and defend the next.

G Company, now reduced to two platoons of 20 men each, followed the secondary road for the next 10 days. With the platoons rotating in taking the lead, the company would attack northward each day. If stopped before reaching the next crossroads, the company would dig in for the night and resume the attack the next day.

On 3 June Lieutenant Colonel Lester L. Wheeler assumed command of the 34th Infantry when Colonel Dahlen rotated home. Colonel Wheeler was a 1935 graduate of West Point and had been Division G-2 on Leyte. He came to the 34th from the 19th Infantry where as a battalion commander he had recently directed an unheard-of dawn attack on a key Japanese stronghold after an overnight march. Colonel Wheeler would retire as a brigadier general.

On 4 June, after a sharp fight ended with G Company capturing a crossroads, E Company passed through and seized another. Always near the front, Major Snavely and four others were wounded by an artillery round. Supported by two soldiers, Snavely limped back down the road. Major Cathcart, the exec, assumed command of the 2nd Battalion.

On 9 June, the 34th Regiment was approaching the end of the enemy's defensive belt north of Ula. Tanks were the normal complement when troops advanced along the road. The tankers would not move unless surrounded by infantry, so fearful they were of Japanese placing box mines in the treads or hitting the tank with a Molotov cocktail or a rifle grenade.

The normal procedure was for the tank to fire a round with his 75mm gun down each side of the road to stun any enemy lurking in spider holes. The infantry then would clear each side of Japanese for about 50 yards. Then the tank would move forward and the process would be repeated.

First Battalion 34th veered east toward the Davao River in an attempt to cut off enemy units, but by the time the troops reached the river bank on 9 June most of the retreating Japanese had escaped.

The maneuver by the 1st Battalion brought the 34th Infantry units close to the 19th Regiment forces then in the process of capturing Mandog the same day. Thus the entire 100th Division's second line of defense east of Ula

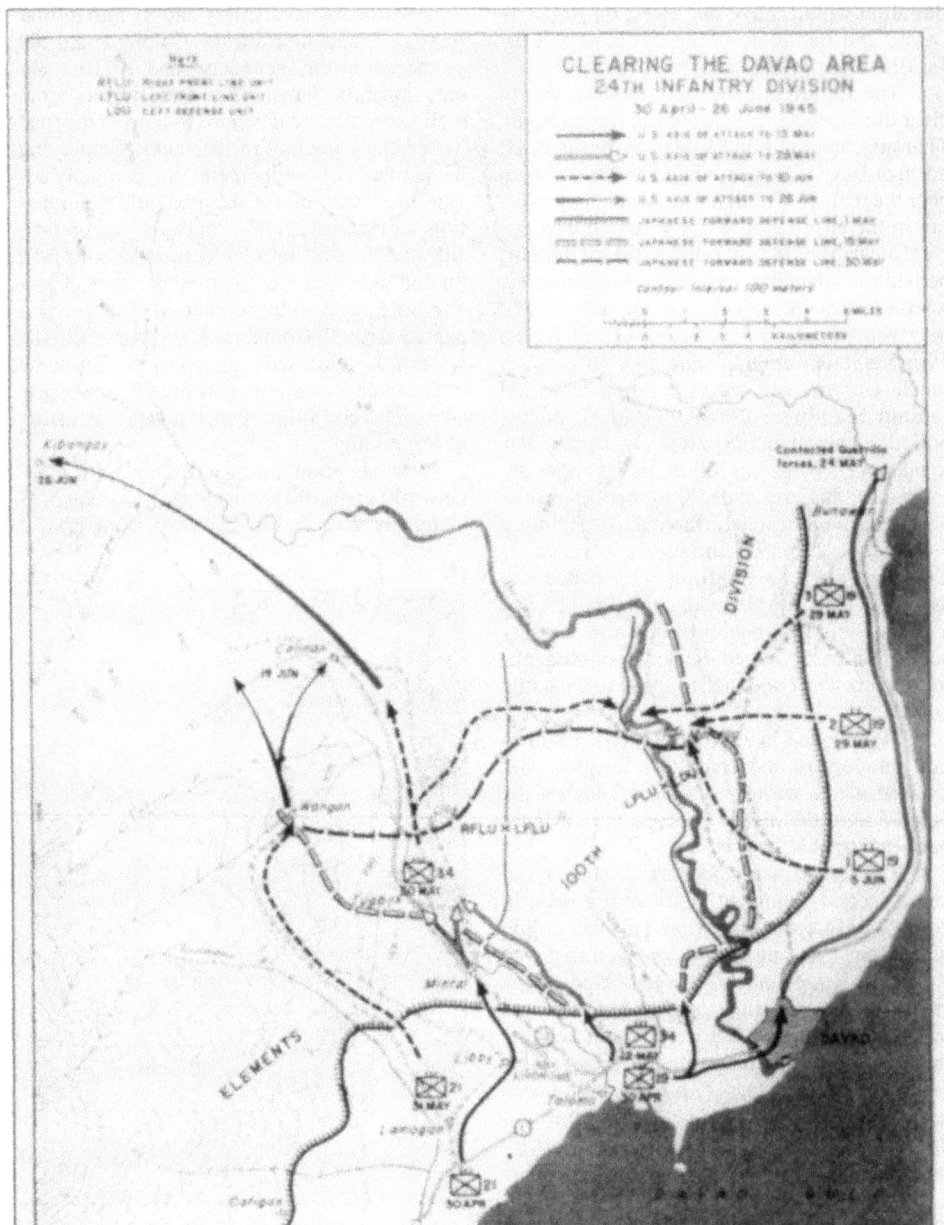

Mindanao

had fallen apart under the relentless American pressure.

To the west, also on 9 June, the Japanese center was collapsing under the assault of the remainder of the 34th Regiment and the attached 3rd Battalion, 163rd Infantry. Those troops had pushed three miles beyond Ula and were encountering little organized resistance.

The 21st Regiment's attack on the left of the U.S. line progressed at about the same pace. The troops pushed their way up the secondary roads west of Route 1-D until they reached Wangan, anchoring the Japanese right, on 9 June. The following day, enemy troops in that sector were in general retreat.

The 24th Infantry Division from Wangan on the west to Mandog east of the Davao River, a distance of 10 miles, had by the end of the day on 10 June completely overtaken the second line of defense and defeated the Japanese 100th Division. The enemy now was preparing to withdraw into the mountains to the west, necessitating pursuit and mop-up by American units.

The Mindanao campaign to this point had cost the 24th Division 350 killed and 1,615 wounded. Japanese 100th Division losses were estimated at 4,500 killed. The U.S. Army cemetery on the island was the site of frequent burial ceremonies. One scene, described by author Valtin, was that of the division chaplain, Major Paul J. Slavik, of St. Paul's Church in New York City, standing in the ever-expanding cemetery under artillery fire passing overhead and pronouncing religious rites over the open graves of the recently fallen.

On 10 June, the 21st Infantry and three battalions of the 41st Infantry Division attacked toward Calinan.

The presence of the 162nd and 163rd regiments of the 41st Division enabled the 34th to be relieved on 13 June. All battalions of the regiment had been in almost daily contact with the enemy for five weeks. The men boarded trucks at Ula for a three-day rest at Daliao on the gulf.

Although a beaten force, the 100th Division retreated in an orderly fashion and was still capable of occasional savage outbursts.

On 15 June, the 34th Infantry began the relief of the 21st Infantry, another regiment that needed a respite from continuous combat.

As with most units in extended combat, the fighting had taken a heavy toll on the 21st Regiment's company commanders. By mid-June, three had been killed and most of the others wounded. One of those was the Company M commander, Captain William M. Langford, who died in a suicide grenade attack on 15 June, the day before he was scheduled to rotate stateside.

B Company commander, Captain Theodore Crouch, who typically was far forward in any action, was another who lost his life. In early June with the 1st Battalion moving north from Monterey, one of B Company's outposts outside the perimeter where the battalion had dug in for the night was overrun.

"Ted and I had been in the CP with two of the other company commanders when we heard automatic weapons fire coming from the B Company sector," Captain Aitken recalled. "Ted immediately gathered up his helmet and carbine and took off running toward the sound of gunfire. Several of us urged him to send a patrol out to take care of the problem, but Ted ignored us."

While Captain Crouch and others were trying to help wounded B Company men, he was mortally wounded. Aitken recommended Captain Crouch for the Medal of Honor for that and other actions, and it was approved through all command levels in the Southwest Pacific, but the War Department changed the decoration to the Distinguished Service Cross, which was awarded posthumously after the war.

Other 1st Battalion casualties included the C Company commander, Captain John A.

Childs, whose wounds forced his evacuation to the United States; and A Company commander, Captain Robert "Ace" Malone, who also was wounded and knocked out of action. Succeeding him was the battalion S-2, Captain Philip S. Irons III, who at 23 was one of the youngest men of his rank in the regiment. Irons had earned the Silver Star and the Bronze Star in the Leyte and Lubang actions.

The 3rd Battalion, 21st, also suffered a severe loss on 25 May when its commander, Major Tom Suber, later lieutenant colonel, fell seriously wounded by machine gun fire just after the battalion had taken its objective east of Tugbok. Suber was evacuated to the United States and survived his wounds.

In a special commendation to the 21st Infantry dated 20 June, provided by Francis E. Haugh and Wilber Vander Vorst, Colonel Verbeck reviewed the 21st's performance. The regiment had counted 2133 enemy dead and captured 14 prisoners, which was 42 percent of the 5149 dead reported by the 24th Division.

The 24th Division was now entering the fourth phase of its campaign in eastern Mindanao - pursuing the enemy into a remote mountain sanctuary.

The 19th Infantry took Mandog on 15 June, crossed the Davao River and began operating close to Route 1-D in the ever-narrowing front. The division front had contracted from 20 miles in length in early May to about four miles at Calinan between the Davao and Talomo rivers. The 34th Infantry was generally astride Route 1-D, the 162nd Infantry was on the left pushing westward.

The Japanese were expected to conduct a vigorous defense of Mount Monoy, which dominated Route 1-D west of Calinan. However, E Company 34th sent a platoon to the top

unopposed. The enemy had not taken advantage of this natural defensive position, thereby allowing the 1st and 2nd battalions of the 34th Regiment to attack with a secure right flank.

The annual summer rains finally arrived about 20 June, making the last two weeks of the campaign anything but pleasant. GIs slipped and slid climbing the mountain trails, carrying all their equipment with them. Foxholes filled with water at night. K rations were the only food that could be transported forward under these conditions.

On 24 June, A Company 34th and some elements of the 19th Infantry that had taken up a position with the company endured one of the bitterest experiences that can come to fighting men in war, death among their number from friendly fire. At a bridge over the Tamogan River, American planes dropped about 12 bombs on A Company and strafed its position, killing five men and wounding 20. The men on the ground finally were able to place recognition panels.

That same day, the 24th Division suffered another huge loss when Colonel Thomas (Jock) Clifford, commander of the 19th Regiment, was killed in a mortar attack at Tamogan. According to historical accounts, the first shell wounded Clifford and a second round landing on the same spot killed the colonel and wounded the man who had gone to his aid.

Company H machine gunner, Alvin F. Buchholz of Grand Junction, CO, was assigned to a detail to guard those removing Colonel Clifford's body. He remembered seeing Clifford's jeep damaged by the mortar shell that killed him. Colonel Clifford had been driving to the front when he was hit in what appeared to be a previous enemy bivouac. Japanese bodies and equipment were strewn over the area.

Colonel Clifford, winner of the Distinguished Service Cross for his heroism on Leyte, was one of the 24th Division's premier fighting men. He arrived in the Southwest Pacific with the Taro Leaf division early in 1944 and at one time or another served in all three infantry regiments.

Before the division sailed for the Southwest Pacific, then-Major Clifford commanded the 1st Battalion, 21st, a unit known popularly as "Clifford's Rangers."

Colonel Clifford, still commanding that battalion, led the vanguard unit inland on New Guinea to the key objective, the Hollandia Airdrome.

He was commander of the 1st Battalion, 34th Infantry, that fought so magnificently on Kilay Ridge in protecting the flank for the main attack on Breakneck Ridge on Leyte in November 1944.

Assuming command of the 19th Regiment upon Colonel Clifford's death was Lieutenant Colonel Walter S. Wickbolt. In the 21st Regiment, the commanding officer, Colonel Verbeck, was elevated to division chief of staff. One of the division's most decorated soldiers, he earned during his tour the Silver Star with Oak Leaf Cluster, the Bronze Star with two Oak Leaf Clusters, and the Purple Heart with three Oak Leaf Clusters. Verbeck subsequently achieved the rank of major general.

The division's farthest point of penetra-

Lt. Gen. Robert L. Eichelberger, CG, 8th Army, recrosses partially wrecked bridge across the Davao River, on his way back from the front lines at Davao City, Mindanao.

tion up the Kibawe-Talomo trail was achieved by troops of the 3rd Battalion 34th Infantry on 26 June when they reached the mountain barrio of Kibangay two miles beyond the Tamogan River.

At this point, the Japanese were able to halt their head-long retreat and reorganize their defenses. The enemy held their posiitons until the middle of July and then, with supplies running short, the Japanese took for the mountains to survive as best they could.

Late that month, the 24th Division troops were relieved by guerrillas of the 107th Division.

With the battle winding down, Japanese civilians on the island started to surrender. The largest group of these, 71, was captured by G Company 34th on 27 June when they emerged from a school building led by an English-speaking man carrying a white flag.

Coincidentally, the Mindanao campaign ended on the Fourth of July for the 2nd Battalion 34th. In one glorious display of fireworks, the men fired most of the heavier ammunition. The next day they started slogging back down the trail, with loads lighter and spirits bolstered by the thoughts of no more fighting on Mindanao.

General Eichelberger had declared the eastern Mindanao campaign to be concluded on 30 June but some American troops continued to fight in the mountains through most of July. Additionally, another operation, clearing Sarangani Bay on the south end of eastern Mindanao, also took place that month.

Ironically, General MacArthur, when he was contemplating his return to the Philippines, initially planned to begin the liberation with a two-division invasion at Sarangani Bay. Now that was to be the location for the last attack originated against Japanese troops in the Philippines campaign. The operation was under the command of Brigadier General Kenneth Cramer, assistant 24th Division commander.

About 2,000 Japanese were defending the area when the assault opened 4 July with the landing from PT boats by the 24th ReconnaissanceTroop of the 24th Division on the southwest coast of the bay. Several other units participated, including the 1st Battalion 21st, which landed on 12 July on the northwest shore. The next day, that battalion made contact with a provisional infantry battalion from Fort Pikit about 60 miles beyond the bay's northwest corner. The various units converged on the main body of Japanese hiding in the hills and valleys of the area and brought organized resistance to a halt on 25 July. Mop-up and pursuit operations continued until 11 August, four days before V-J Day, when most of the participating units returned to Davao. Securing the Sarangani Bay areas had cost the combined American-Filipino units 13 killed and 13 wounded, against 450 Japanese dead. For the entire Mindanao campaign through 30 June, total Japanese killed was put at 10,540, of which the 24th Division accounted for 6,585. Filipino-American units killed another 2,325 by the end of the war.

The 24th Division, which had been totally engaged on Mindanao throughout the battle, lost 540 killed and 1,885 wounded, a total of 2,425, compared with 544 killed, 1,784 wounded and 14 missing, a total of 2,342, on Leyte.

Men of the 24th Division continued to take casualties right up to the end and even after the hostilities supposedly were over. Valtin in *Children of Yesterday*, reported skirmishes after 15 August, including the loss of two 21st Regiment men who were killed after the ceasefire while watching a movie.

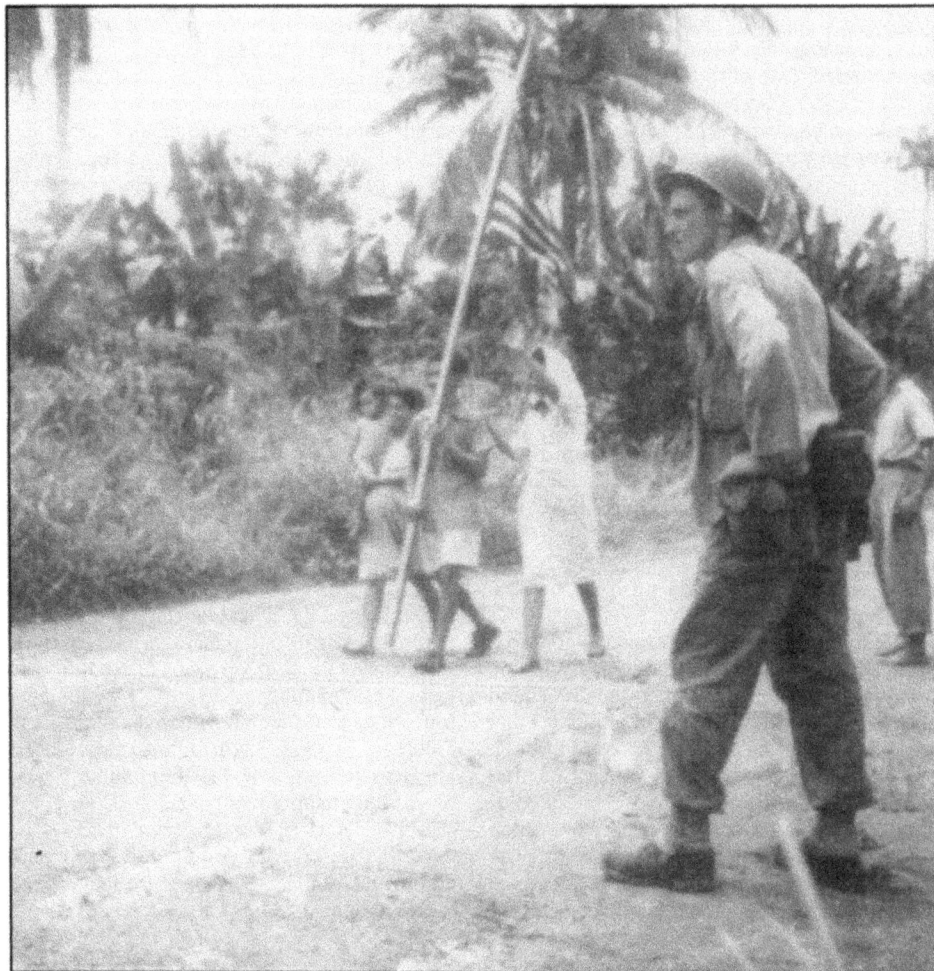

One of a group of Filipinos carries the American flag as the Filipinos happily greet the newly arrived 24th Division troops, Davao, Mindanao, P.I. May, 1945. (Courtesy of Charles W. Card)

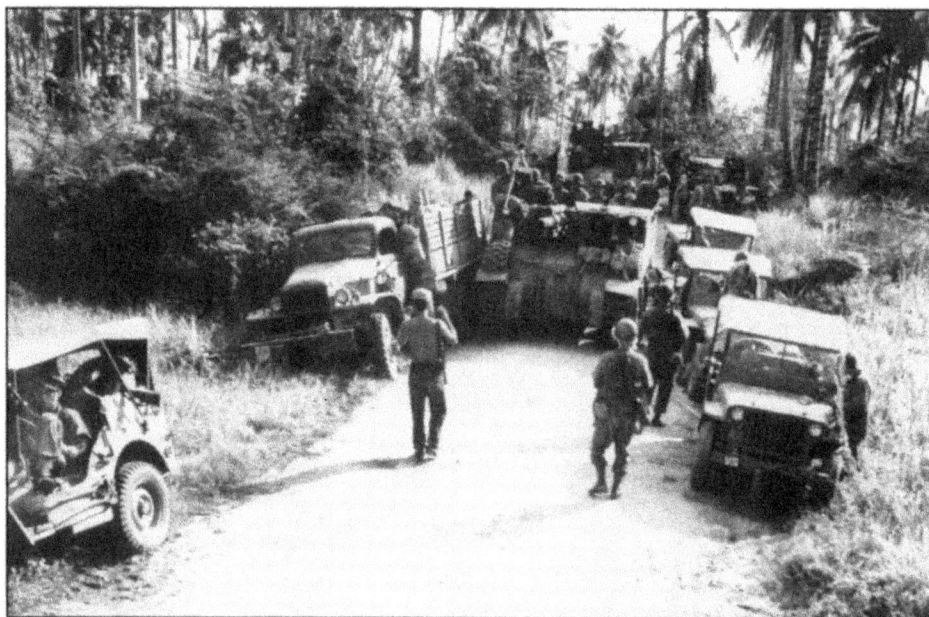

Smaller vehicles move to the side of a narrow road to permit a tank to pass as the 24th Divsion prepares to cross a bridge into Davao, Mindanao. (Courtesy of Charles W. Card)

One of the late deaths was that of Colonel Frank McGee, commanding officer of two guerrilla divisions, first the 106th and then the 107th. He was attached to the 24th Division as officer in charge of guerrilla units in the division's sector.

He had been discharged from the U.S. Army for disability after World War I and was living on Mindanao when World War II broke out. Colonel McGee volunteered for active service again and did not surrender in 1942. After surviving nearly four years of war in the Philippines, he was killed by a Japanese sniper on 7 August.

Finally, it was finished. The campaign to recapture eastern Mindanao was over. The liberation of the Philippine Islands was accomplished. World War II, as of 15 August 1945 was a total and unqualified victory.

For the men who came ashore at Illana Bay 17 April, Mindanao had been a long, dirty, steaming grind of deadly combat against an enemy that possibly was all the more dangerous because his mission was defense. Unlike typical island campaigns, the Japanese on Mindanao did not allow themselves to be virtually annihilated. Of the total military and civilian Japanese in eastern Mindanao as of 17 April, estimated at 55,350, more than 34,000 survived and turned themselves in.

The campaign officially was listed as having lasted 75 days, but many of the 24th Division men were engaged in combat operations for 100 days or more. For the soldiers who arrived off New Guinea for the Hollandia invasion on 22 April 1944, and then fought their way through to the end, it was a long stretch of combat indeed, some 15 months with little respite.

Casualty figures were not exact for all operations; therefore the total cannot be precise either. But from what is known, the 24th Infantry Division lost approximately 1,400 killed and missing and 4,900 wounded in action at Hollandia, Biak, Leyte, Mindoro, the Western Visayas, Luzon and Mindanao.

At the end of that last campaign, the combat warriors were being replaced by the occupation troops, those freshly arrived from the United States who were too late to take an active part in the fighting.

Jan Valtin, in *Children of Yesterday*, described what the new men saw as they disembarked: "They stared at the burned houses, the decapitated palms, the wrecks of trucks and airplanes littering the roadsides, the listless and emaciated natives, and they leaned forward to decipher the signs at junctions along their dusty course."

For the men who had helped liberate the island, indeed the Southwest Pacific, from the grip of the aggressor and survived, leaving this place was a welcome relief. For them it was time to go home.

Men of the 24th Division crouch at the side of one of the streets leading into Davao, as firing and shell fragments fall about them. (Courtesy of Charles W. Card)

OCCUPATION OF JAPAN
1945-1950

The post-World War II occupation assignment of the 24th Infantry Division pre-ordained its fateful role as the first combat unit into Korea after the outbreak of hostilities on the peninsula on 25 June 1950. For the second time, the division's motto, "First to Fight," would be confirmed in fact and in deed..

After V-J Day in August 1945, the 24th Division, then on Mindanao in the southern Philippines, prepared rapidly for occupation duty in Japan. The men received issues of heavier clothing for the coming fall and winter in the colder climate to the north, and they underwent training in language, customs and the way of life of the land of the defeated enemy. The transition from war to peace was no minor adjustment.

During the last two weeks of August, American troops encountered and sometimes killed isolated Japanese on Mindanao, but gradually the wartime footing began to loosen.

An after-action report of the 34th Regiment carried entries that typified the garrison routine during the early part of September. The regimental perimeter was relieved and the trenches filled in. Inspections, training and retreat were daily events. Recreation included volleyball, softball and basketball. Movies were shown three times a week and the Red Cross supplied Coca Cola each day. The censorship of mail ended.

The men kept fit with five-mile marches, and took training tests during the first half of October. Finally, they dismantled the recreation halls and other buildings, stacked the lumber neatly and thoroughly policed the area.

The division, under the command of Major General James A. Lester, embarked on 15 October, bound for Shikoku, the smallest of the four main Japanese islands. The 19th and 34th regiments encamped on that island, and division headquarters was set up in the Matsuyama City Library. The 21st Infantry billeted at Okayama on the southeast coast of Honshu, the largest Japanese island.

The landing plan resembled a wartime operation. The 34th Infantry, for instance, went ashore in columns of battalions as determined with precision beforehand. As the plan stated: "The first landing battalion will secure the initial beachhead, the second landing battalion will advance along and secure the main highway, and the third landing battalion will pass through the other two battalions and secure a military objective in the Castle Hill area, Matsuyama. "

This occurred on 22 October. Four days later the regiment completed the unloading and settled in a garrison previously occupied by Japanese troops. Off-post passes were issued as of 26 October.

The 24th Division landed on Shikoku six weeks after the signing of the peace treaty. By this time, Japanese actions on Honshu had shown that the military and the general populace would cooperate with the Americans. However, nobody could be sure, especially in the first days of the occupation of Shikoku, one of the four main islands.

Therefore, as described by Charles R. Lewin, who served on the division G-2 staff as Division Historian and Public Relations Officer from February until September, 1946, the division's strategy to combat overt, hostile activity was based on two considerations: (1) preparation for mob violence, and (2) preventive measures to preclude adverse activities by the Japanese.

The division's being combat ready during the landing and for several days afterward discouraged any mob violence that might have been in the offing. In addition, the occupation troops received training in how best to control mobs.

The division used constant surveillance as a preventive measure to discover any seditious activities by the Japanese. Several officers highly proficient in the Japanese language reviewed carefully all Japanese newspapers and other publications distributed in the 24th's sphere of control. In addition, line companies dispatched patrols into the hinterland to observe and report suspicious activities. American Nisei (second generation Japanese) soldiers checked Japanese school textbooks for adverse content.

Probably the best preventive measure was to make sure American soldiers did not antagonize the Japanese such as desecrating their shrines, being rude and abusive to Japanese citizens, going into shops and taking goods without paying for them, and consorting with Japanese women in public.

Any of these actions could easily create animosity among the Japanese. The most volatile of these potential problems was the US troops' desire for companionship with Japanese females. Co-mingling confined to out-of-the-way places would be less offensive to the Japanese people than open displays of affection.

American commanders swiftly and decisively solved this problem at the outset of the occupation. If a member of the American forces were caught kissing, embracing, or fondling a Japanese female in public, he faced appropriate disciplinary action by the Provost Marshal. Some GI's were indiscreet and punished; but the practice of co-mingling was never rampant and there was no indication that the Japanese committed any acts of violence based upon public consorting by the American forces.

The early job of occupation was far from a routine mission. Duty was multi-faceted, with its moments of tedium as well as enjoyment. Listed below are some examples of various activities engaged in by the 24th Divisioin personnel:

- Demilitarizing the wartime power;
- Destroying Japanese caches of weapons and ammunition. Each man was allowed to send home a Samurai sword, Japanese rifle, and bayonet boxed up by Japanese workmen;
- Ferreting out secret societies;
- Training in military maneuvers, including plenty of target practice;
- Establishing functioning civil government;
- Working with Japanese authorities to improve public sanitary conditions, especially the discouraging of certain excretory customs of the Japanese;

Troops display trophy of war.

Typical view a GI got when he rode on a Japanese train in Kyushu, providing GIs glimpses of the "everyday" Japanese. (Courtesy of Dr. Charles R. Lewin)

- Cooperating with Japanese officials to control sexually transmitted diseases;
- Banning GI truck drivers from pulling up behind a Japanese trolley car and then pushing it down the street. All the while the irate conductor shouts misunderstood invectives.
- Urgently training U.S. soldiers to drive their military vehicles "on the wrong side of the street." The British left an odd legacy as to which was the "right side of the road."
- Abolishing swimming in creeks, and also in reservoirs that the Japanese had constructed to hold water to fight the fires caused by the bombs dropped by Americans planes. This taboo against swimming was necessary because the GIs were becoming seriously ill with schistosomiasis, a horrible affliction caused by

a blood fluke lurking in the contaminated waters.

Meanwhile, the division emphasized education and recruitment, the latter to refill the depleted ranks caused by redeployment.

The work on Shikoku was completed in mid-February 1946. Then the division headquarters shifted to Honshu for a short time before the entire division took up occupancy on the Japanese island of Kyushu. Division headquarters on this southernmost island was established at Kokura in the northwest corner where it would remain for the balance of the occupation period.

The 19th Infantry set up first at Ota and then at Beppu on the east coast of the island. The 21st was assigned to Camp Wood at

24th Military Police Platoon 1946 Kokura, Japan. (Courtesy of Russell Arnold)

Members of the 19th Infantry Bn Medics. Beppu, Japan. (Courtesy of K.E. Kunkel)

Headquarters Battery, 13th F.A., 24th Division at Camp Haugen, Japan. July 1952. (Courtesy of George Lyon)

"H" Company, 19th Infantry Regiment at Camp Haugen, Japan. 1952. (Courtesy of Joseph O'Connell)

"A" Battery, 13th F.A. Bn., 24th Divsion at Camp Haugen, Japan. April 1952. (Courtesy of John Dennis)

Officers of the 13th F.A. Artillery Bn at Camp Hakata, Kyushu, Japan 1947. (Courtesy of J.M. Williamson)

I and E section Division Headquarters, 24th Infantry Division, Kokura, Japan, July 1947. Front L-R: Dykes, unknown, St. Peter and unknown. Back L-R: Schrumpf, unknown, unknown, Mahoney and Raines. (Courtesy of L.V. Schrumpf)

Gen Woodruff with Japanese Officer. (Courtesy of J.H. Miller)

Jap Planes-Shikoku, Japan.

24th Infantry Divsion at Camp Younghans, Japan. May/June 1953. (Courtesy of Carl Groth)

Kumamoto, and the 34th Regiment encamped just outside the port city of Sasebo, location of a former Japanese naval base that would become a major American naval installation during the Korean War. The 34th Infantry's Japanese home was Camp Mower, named for Sergeant Charles Mower, a "Dragon" who had been awarded the Medal of Honor posthumously for heroism in the Philippines during World War II.

By 1950, soldiering in Japan had settled down into pleasant garrison duty with relatively comfortable living, Japanese girlfriends and other amenities. The Americans and their erstwhile enemies developed a cordial relationship.

Through natural attrition, transfers and rotation, the number of combat veterans in the division diminished to about 15 percent of the personnel in the five years after World War II. The remainder were post-war enlistees or draftees, mostly young men in their late teens who had come into the Army in the late 1940s for what seemingly was to be a peacetime hitch.

KOREA

THE BEGINNING 1950-1954

When the North Koreans crossed the 38th Parallel in force on 25 June 1950 to launch the three-year conflict, the 24th Division was at about two-thirds strength. The three infantry regiments had just two battalions each and the artillery battalions only two batteries each. The other division components, such as the engineers and the tank company, were proportionately under-strength. Instead of the authorized personnel of 18,804 officers and men, the 24th Infantry Division counted only 12,500 at the outbreak of war, a number that was hastily supplemented from other units to bring the total strength to 15,965 before the division departed for the war zone.

Equipment also was found wanting. The division's armor authorization called for 142

tanks. It had 20, and those were the light M-24s. The available 2.36-inch bazookas were too small to be effective against the big Russian-made tanks. The artillery batteries were short of anti-tank rounds, and no anti-tank mines were immediately available for the coming combat. Some of the ammunition was too old for maximum effectiveness. Even the C-rations had been on hand too long.

The division commander since the previous October, succeeding Albert C. Smith, was Major General William F. Dean, a 50-year-old ROTC officer from the University of California at Berkeley, who had led the 44th Infantry Division in Europe during World War II. As commander of the 7th Infantry Division during the occupation period, Dean had also served as military governor of Korea. Personally and as part of the 24th Division's history, Dean would write a dramatic chapter in the weeks and years ahead.

A quick look at the map of the region would have told anyone what war in Korea would mean to the 24th Infantry Division. Kokura was directly across the Korea Strait from Pusan, the southeasternmost city in Korea. No American troops were closer to the action and none could get there faster.

But the division's first mission associated with the Korean War involved no troop movement or fighting. By pre-arrangement in case of any emergency in Korea, the 24th was to receive, assist and dispatch evacuees from the country.

The first contingent of American women and children sailed from Inchon on a Norwegian freighter, which docked at Kokura on June 28. Men of the 24th Infantry Division worked around the clock helping the dependents, who arrived with few personal belongings, to receive the care and attention they needed and start their trip to other points in Japan.

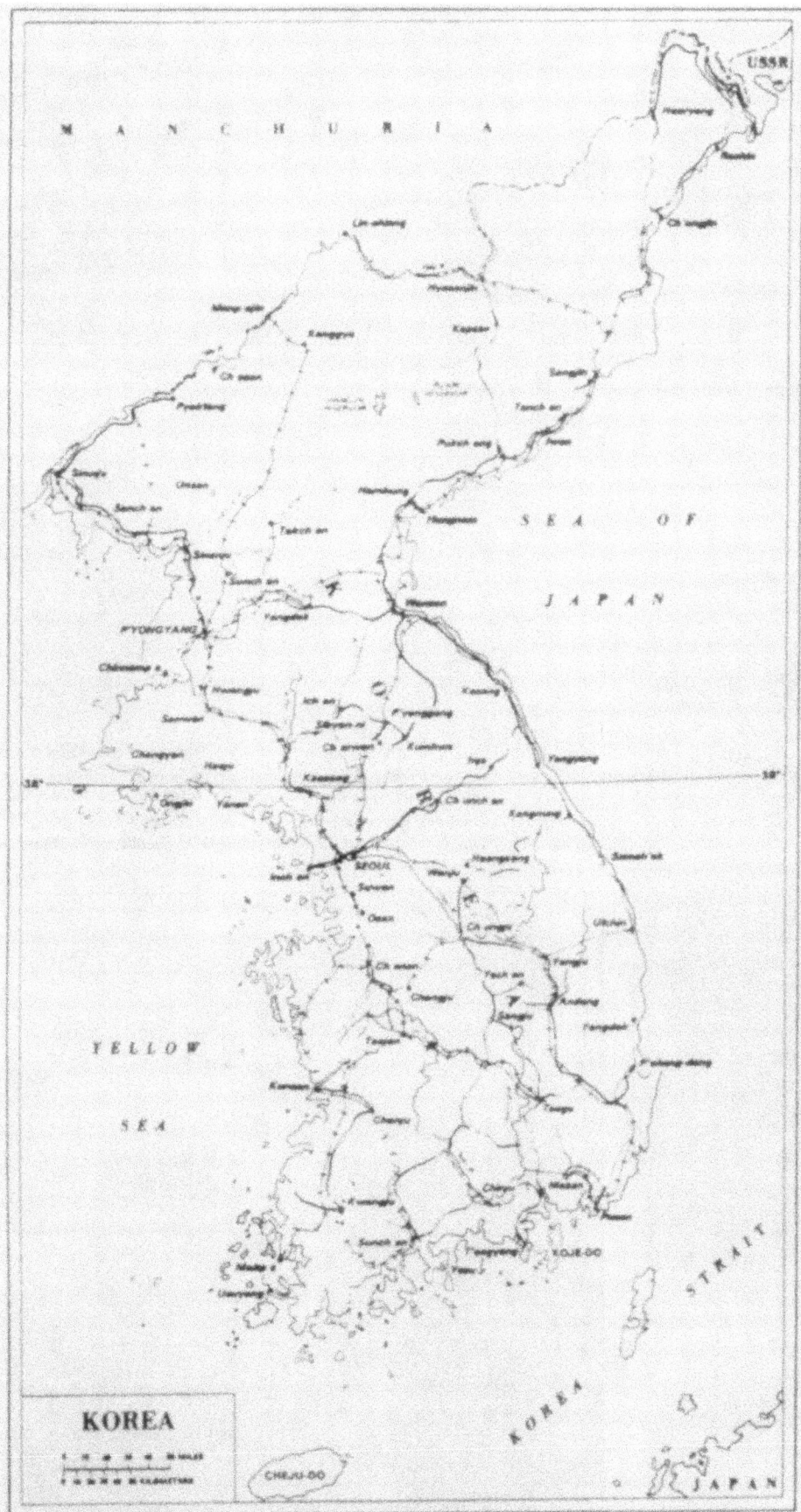

Truce Tent and Fighting Front, U.S. Army in the Korean War. Office of the Chief of Military History, U.S. Army, Washington, D.C., 1966. (Courtesy of Walter G. Hermes)

In the confusion caused by the North Korean Army's swiftness in overrunning South Korean territory in the first hours of the invasion, the American military contingent in the country evacuated also. In fact, flights carrying members of the Korean Military Advisory Group reached Japan even before the ship carrying the civilians sailed into Kokura.

Dean got his orders on 30 June: Take his division to Korea and also assume overall command of the land expeditionary force. His job was to be a two-hatter for the few days it would take for American authorities to realize the war would require the entire Eighth Army, and then some.

The task of pulling the division together and moving it across the straits to the mainland of Korea presented a formidable logistical problem for the commanding general. The 24th's elements were scattered throughout southern Japan. Two of the regiments, the 21st and 34st, were at home in the Kyushu camps, Kumamoto and Sasebo, respectively, but the 19th Infantry, ordinarily billeted at Beppu, was on amphibious maneuvers on 30 June near Yokohama.

On that day, the division's tank company, reconnaissance company and some of the engineers were at Yamaguchi on Honshu, the artillery battalions were based near Fukuoka and the signal company, quartermaster and ordnance units and the rest of the engineers were at headquarters at Kokura.

Dean got the main body of his division moving from various Japanese ports by sea toward Pusan as rapidly as he could. It is fair to say that in American military history, no outfit was thrust from peacetime duty to full-blown ground combat so abruptly as was the 24th Infantry Division in those first days of July 1950. Before or since, there never has been anything to compare with the situation the division faced at that time.

Before any ground troops disembarked from ships onto Korean soil, General Dean and the vanguard of 24th Division fighting men would have already arrived there after having made the trip by air.

For the general, just getting to the war was an adventure of its own. He was forced to take three stabs at it during the first two days of July. The first time, the C-54 transport carrying him, his staff and his Jeep could not land on the dirt strip outside of Pusan because it had been chewed up by the heavy planes that took the first troops into the country. A smaller craft was able to get down on the second trip, but then the pilot couldn't find Taejon, the actual destination, in the dark, so the party returned to Japan once again. The third trip was plagued by fog, but on Dean's instructions, the pilot flew out over the Yellow Sea off the west coast and followed the Kum River to Taejon, the headquarters of the hastily assembled military expeditionary force. Taejon, due south of Seoul, was about midway down the peninsula from the 38th Parallel close to the western side. That city, which Dean knew from his days as military governor, would play a pivotal role in his life.

"Moving Up," 1st Bn 19th Infantry Korea. (Courtesy of James F. Hill)

The obiquitous jeep plays key role in Korea.

Korea, TK-35, 34th Tank Co., 90mm. (Courtesy of D. Baillie)

Looking out to Kumsong Valley from MLR just before the drive for Kumsong. Co M 19th Infantry Regiment 24th Infantry Division 75MM Recoiless Rifle Platoon. (Courtesy of Joseph S. Barto)

Taken in the mess hall of "B" Battery 13th Field Artillery Battalion, Camp Hakata, Japan, just a few months before the war in Korea. (Courtesy of Ellsworth "Dutch" Nelsen)

At right: Located in Beppu, Kyushu, Butsudan, one of the largest idols in Japan, was one of the cultural sights GIs could visit before and after Korean Campaign. (Courtesy of Dr. Charles R. Lewin)

TASK FORCE SMITH

The urgencies of the military situation in South Korea a week after 135,000 North Korean troops poured across the border were such that the high command did not believe it advisable to wait for sea transportation to put the first GIs on Korean soil. An airlift was required.

The decision came on 30 June, the day General Dean received the order to take his 24th Infantry Division to Korea. A smaller advance unit, a token force in actuality, would have to leave immediately.

Dean reportedly became the object of criticism by military strategists for committing his forces piecemeal, and he himself was none too pleased about having to do so, but evidently believed he had little choice. If it had to be done, he wrote, the ideal officer had been selected to command the advance unit, Lieutenant Colonel Charles B. (Brad) Smith, commander of the 1st Battalion, 21st Infantry. Smith, 34, of Lambertsville, N.J., was a West Pointer, Class of '39, who had fought in the Pacific during World War II.

Task Force Smith, as the unit was called, was destined to fight the first land battle by Americans in the Korean war and thus became part of the lore of that conflict.

Smith was informed of his assignment by the 21st Infantry commander, Colonel Richard W. Stephens, just hours before departure, at the regimental heaquarters at Camp Wood in Kumamoto. "The lid has blown off - get on your clothes and report to the CP," Stephens ordered.

The assembled task force consisted of the battalion's B and C companies, reinforced with riflemen from the 3rd Battalion, plus half of the 1st Battalion's Headquarters Company, one half of a communications platoon , two 75-mm recoilless rifles, two 4.2 inch mortars, six 2.36-inch bazooka teams, and a weapons platoon for each company consisting of a .50 caliber machine gun, two .30 caliber machine guns and two 60-mm mortars. In addition, a detachment of the division's 52nd Field Artillery Battalion, consisting of five 105-mm howitzers, joined the force after it landed in Korea. Initially, plans called for four each of the recoilless rifles and 4.2-inch mortars, but transportation problems caused by bad weather and poor runways forced a reduction to half the number of those heavy weapons that could be taken.

Task Force Smith reached the front with 540 men, 406 in the two rifle companies and 134 artillerymen. Only one-third of the officers and fewer than one half of the non-coms had combat experience, and most of the enlisted men were younger than 21. Riflemen carried 120 rounds of .30 caliber ammunition each and two days of rations.

Smith recalled his orders from General Dean as follows: "When you get to Pusan, head for Taejon. We want to stop the North Koreans as far from Pusan as we can. Block the main road as far north as possible." Already in Taejon was Brigadier General John Church, chief of the General Headquarters Advance Command. Army headquarters in Japan had sent him and his staff to Korea to provide the initial liaison and coordination for the military effort. He would have further orders for Smith.

The task force's trip by truck from Camp Wood to Itazuke Air Base took five hours in the torrential monsoon that had hit the area. At 0300 1 July, the 24th Division soldiers boarded C-54s for the short flight across the Korea Straits to the dirt strip outside Pusan where they landed. Troops were greeted there and in other towns later by cheering civilians and flag-waving children. They were made to feel like liberators.

First came a 12-hour train ride to Taejon where Church assigned the task force to take up blocking positions in two locations, one company each at Pyongtaek, which was on the main road south out of Seoul, and at Ansong several miles to the east.

From Pusan, the soldiers of Task Force Smith had followed the historic Korean invasion path. It pointed northwestward through Taegu and Taejon and then northward toward the capital. Over many centuries through countless wars, other soldiers and armies had traveled the same route. Now, however, it was the mechanized North Korean Army driving in the opposite direction, brushing aside everything that stood in its way.

General Church told Smith that one objective of his force was to stiffen the spine of the South Korean Army whose performance in the first days after their country was invaded was hardly inspiring. As the general put it, "We have a little action up here. All we need is some men up there who won't run when they see tanks. We're going to move you up to support the ROKs (Republic of Korea troops)." There was considerable understatement in the general's words. There would be more than a little action, the mission would involve more than standing firm against tanks, though the men of Task Force Smith certainly would do

Korean Memorial at Osan, Korea, Memory of 24th Infantry Div., 21st Inf. Regt. 1st Bn. Korea "Task Force Smith" 1st American G.I. killed on this hill from "B" Co. 1st Battalion, 21st Inf. Reg. He was Kenneth Shadrick from West Virginia.

that, and there would be no ROKs around to support when the unit reached the fighting front.

The position selected for Task Force Smith would have been hard to improve from a defensive standpoint. At Pyongtaek, an arm of the Yellow Sea reached nearly to the town, while Ansong was bounded on its east side by a high ridge line. Thus natural barriers protected the flanks on both sides of a relatively narrow pass. Even with those advantages, Task Force Smith was too small for the job expected of the unit, and everyone knew it.

To say the GIs were ill-prepared for what was about to happen would be no exaggeration. Many assumed they had gone to Korea on a short-term mission. Their meager ammunition and rations allotment tended to confirm that fact. So it appeared to be something of a lark, an adventure, a break from soft garrison duty for an interlude of real soldiering before returning to the barracks life of Japan, where confidently, many had left their money, clothing and other personal effects.

Coupled with typical Yank cockiness was a serious underestimation of the enemy, whom the men of the task force assumed to be a peasant army that would be awed by the first look at an American uniform and readily subdued. No matter how small their numbers in the field at the moment, they were still part of the United States Army, victors in Europe and the Pacific in the greatest of all wars.

Colonel Smith did not keep his troops long at Pyongtaek and Ansong. Consistent with Gen. Dean's orders to engage the enemy as far to the north as possible, Smith reconnoitered beyond Osan and selected a position between that town and Suwon, which is 20 miles due south of Seoul. There he would be able to keep his little force together, not divided as at Pyongtaek and Ansong.

By the time Task Force Smith reached its new position, the force had been in Korea four days, moving ever northward by train and truck. The rain had been nearly constant and for early July, the temperature was unseasonably cold. Mosquitoes infested the land like a biblical plague, and the GIs' noses told them all they cared to know about rice paddies and the human excrement that fertilized them. Some of the soldiers already were sick from contaminated local water. South Korea, to put it mildly, was significantly lacking in charm. More than that, the young soldiers, some of whom had taken their first airplane ride on the trip from Itazuke to Pusan, had received a preliminary look at the ugliness of war on their way up to the front. They had seen an ammunition train blow up and they had witnessed a South Korean Army officer force one of his men to kneel and then shoot him in the back of the neck for crimes not explained to the Americans.

The native army showed further signs of the same lack of enthusiasm General Church had suggested. When the South Korean truck drivers who were supposed to take the unit north beyond Osan discovered the direction of travel, they invited themselves out and the Americans had to take the wheel themselves. Then Smith was surprised and dismayed to find no South Koreans on the three hills he had selected for his troops. His little force was all alone in the strange and menacing land.

In the wet and chill darkness early on 5 July, 406 riflemen alighted from the trucks and began to climb the scrubby, rocky hills that commanded the main road between Suwon and Osan on either side to find the places where they would dig in and wait. The ground was stubborn and the ponchos most men were wearing against the continuing downpour made the job even more awkward. Foxholes completed, many of the troops found time for a couple of hours' sleep before daylight exposed the flaws in their positions to the practiced eye of the battalion executive officer, Major Floyd "Mother" Martin.

Martin earned his nickname because he was diligent in looking after his men. He was an old-timer with 24 years of service behind him. Martin started with the New York National Guard in 1926, was called to active duty in 1940 and spent World War II in Alaska. Now the officer was about to lead men who were not even born when he put on his first khakis in combat more terrible than any of them could possibly imagine.

Down below on the road, communications men were laying telephone wires back to the artillery units. The men earlier had unloaded and stacked the ammunition, but for some reason they hadn't carried it up the slopes to the hillside troop emplacements.

The line Smith established covered about a mile overall, athwart the main road and bending back southward along the railroad tracks east of the road. The 4.2-inch mortars were sited about 400 yards to the rear on the reverse slope.

Four of the artillery battery's 105s were in place about 2,000 yards behind the infantry and the one howitzer supplied with six HEAT (High Explosive Anti-Tank) projectiles was in position in a bend of the road about halfway between. Incidentally, the six shells capable of penetrating tank armor represented exactly one-third of such ammunition that was on hand in Japan at the time of the deployment. That fact is indicative of the United States' deplorable condition of readiness to fight a major land war in the Far East in 1950. If another is needed, consider that the only bazooka ammunition available was 2.36 inch, which the Army found in 1945 to be ineffective against tank armor. None of the heavier 3.5-inch rockets were available in the Asian theater at that time.

Soon the men of Task Force Smith would pay dearly for their superiors' lack of preparedness for a sudden outbreak of hostilities that called for American participation.

It was a few minutes past 0700 when movement on the road to the north gave the first indication that tanks were coming. Smith, standing in the steady downpour and scanning the distance through binoculars, saw them. So did a 21st Infantry radio operator who reported to the command post, "I guess this is it. I see tanks coming." In a scene described in Max Hastings' book, *The Korean War*, Sergeant Loren Chambers of B Company, holder of five Purple Hearts from World War II and about to win his sixth this day, spotted the column of green-painted tanks clanking down the road from Suwon and identified them accurately to his platoon leader as T-34s. That heavy Russian-built tank was considered by some military men as the best armor used in World War II. At the outset of the Korean War it was clearly superior to the light armor the 24th Division was bringing to the conflict.

It took an hour or more for the lead enemy tanks to close the range sufficiently, which gave the American troops along the ridge line ample time to watch, exchange excited observations and anticipate what the rest of the day would be like. The platoon leaders walked back and forth in front of the foxholes offering counsel and admonition.

Finally, when the head of the North Korean column was about a mile from the front line, a company commander, Captain Richard Dashner, called for artillery support. The howitzers barked their first rounds at 0816 hours. At 700 yards, the 75-mm recoilless rifles added their fire against the tanks and when the enemy armor drew abreast the bazooka teams went to work. The shooting war had started. Baker and Charlie companies, 1st Battalion, 21st Infantry, and the 52nd Field Artillery Battalion were facing an armed enemy. The United States Army was back in action, and once again, the 24th Infantry Division was First to Fight.

As the opening shots were fired, it was late afternoon of the Fourth of July back home in the United States. A people who were generally oblivious to the lethal fireworks on three remote hills in a country few had heard of two weeks before were waiting for darkness to fall so their own benign fireworks displays could begin in celebration of the holiday. It was rather ironic.

The American Army gunners and bazooka crews taking aim on the North Korean tanks coming down the road into their midst were hitting the mark, but with little effect. The standard artillery shells did not penetrate the armor, nor did the recoilless rifles or the 2.36-inch rockets.

The tank column kept moving, turning their 85-mm guns and machine guns on the infantry occupying the high ground that overlooked the road through a saddle in the terrain.

The ineffectiveness of the small bazookas did not diminish the valor of the effort being made by the soldiers carrying the weapons. One was Lieutenant Ollie Connors, of Tupelo, MS, who took the hand-held weapon and went after the North Korean tanks with a fury, firing 22 rockets in all at close range and succeeding at least in knocking the tracks off one tank. It was only the shouted warning, "Behind you, lieutenant," from a soldier nearby that allowed Connors to wheel and see a tank's threatening cannon in time to avoid the fire and get off a round of his own.

The task force's artillery commander, Lieutenant Colonel William Perry, with Sergeant Edwin Eversole, led five other bazooka teams, but as in most anti-tank experiences of the day, the rockets did no damage to the enemy's armor.

The inexperience of the soldiers showed in one instance. Lieutenant Philip Day, a B Company platoon leader, helped a recoilless rifle team position the awkward weapon to fire on the tanks. However, it was sited on a forward slope and the backblast from the first round slammed the rifle into the hillside, forcing the team to strip and clean it before resuming fire. The crew succeeded, but a short time later, an 85-mm shell knocked the weapon out of action. The force of the explosion sent blood gushing from Day's ears.

The one weapon to which the enemy tanks were not invulnerable was the 105-mm howitzer closest to the line with its six armor-piercing projectiles. These shells were used up quickly but not before rounds found their targets and disabled two lead tanks. Then occurred a singular event that nearly all chroniclers of the engagement recorded, but unfortunately the account remains incomplete in one important detail. Three North Korean tankers bailed out of their crippled and burning vehicle. Two came out with their hands held high as in surrender, but the third emerged firing his burp gun in the direction of the American lines. Return fire cut down the enemy soldier, but a GI, an assistant machine gunner, also fell dead, by all accounts the first of more than 36,000 American servicemen who would be killed in action in the war. No one knows his name, and that is regrettable.

The column contained 33 tanks in all. Most passed through on the way to Osan, firing on the Task Force Smith positions as they went by but not stopping to engage the Americans otherwise. And there was nothing the GIs could do to stop them. The tanks inflicted about 20 casualties, dead and wounded, on the 24th Division unit. One of the wounded was Colonel Perry, who was hit in the leg by small-arms fire, but refused to leave the field. The only American howitzer put out of business was the forward gun, which was hit by a single 85-mm shell from the third tank through. Contrary to fact, Smith assumed his artillery battery had been severely damaged and had taken serious casualties.

The commander's lack of information was due to the communications woes that plagued the operation almost from the start. Telephone lines between the forward positions and the artillery, somewhat suspect as to condition in the first place, were chewed up by the tank traffic. Rifle and machine gun fire that continued to rake the road throughout the battle prevented communications men from replacing them. The wetness caused the radios to function poorly and finally give out altogether. So by 1100, about 45 minutes after the last of the tanks had passed, not only was there no contact between infantry and artillery within the unit, there was no way for Task Force Smith to communicate with headquarters at Taejon or the Army forces immediately to the rear at Pyongtaek and Ansong.

The encounter between the North Korean tanks and the American blocking force was over at about 1015. Smith's task force, with its limited anti-tank firepower, managed to stop four tanks and inflict minor damage on three others, which were able to keep moving.

The second phase of the battle of Osan opened about 1100 when an enemy convoy of infantry-laden trucks covered by three tanks at the head of the column moved down the road toward the American lines. The tankers who had passed through earlier evidently did not warn the foot soldiers behind them of the Americans' presence, an oversight that would give the GIs an initial but short-lived advantage in the coming exchange.

The North Korean force in a column six miles long consisted of two regiments, about 4,000 to 5,000 men in all, of that army's 4th Division. When the communist force was about 1,000 yards away, mortar, machine-gun and rifle fire erupted from the American lines. The immediate result was chaos in the North Korean convoy. Trucks caught fire and exploded. Infantrymen abandoned their vehicles and took refuge in ditches or scattered in confusion and disarray. The enemy troops had not expected this. Task Force Smith's mission was to block and delay the enemy advance, and the halted column testified to at least momentary success.

The North Koreans quickly reorganized and mounted a frontal attack with about 1,000 men against B Company on the east side of the road, which the GIs succeeded in fighting off. Task Force Smith found itself outnumbered at least eight to one. Those would be long odds if the defenders were in the Alamo. But in the field with no way to protect the flanks, the odds were impossible.

As the Americans held off the enemy at their front, the North Koreans used their enormous numerical advantage to spread out and begin an envelopment maneuver. If the battle were to proceed toward its inevitable conclusion, the little American force would be surrounded and annihilated or captured.

At this stage, Colonel Smith was facing limited and unpleasant choices. With no chance of reinforcement or air support (heavy skies and rain kept the aircraft away) staying put would mean loss of the unit. If he counterattacked, he would be forfeiting the good defensive positions the high ground afforded, and if he fell back down the Osan road he would chance another encounter with the tanks that had passed through earlier. Smith could be certain of one thing: Enemy armor was between his task force and the nearest American troops.

North Koreans flanking Americans on the west gained higher ground, causing Smith to tighten his line by withdrawing C Company from that side of the road and placing the entire force in a circular perimeter on the east side. Soon, however, enemy troops were firing down on the GIs from elevated positions east of the railroad tracks. North Korean mortar fire intensified and American casualties mounted. Wounded men lay in rows below the front-line position as medics did their best to provide relief.

The plight of the small force, and its frustration, was illustrated in a telephone dialogue between Sergeant Loren Chambers and another GI, as described in John Toland's book, *In Mortal Combat*:

Chambers called for 60-mm mortars.
"Won't reach that far."
"How about some 81s?"
"We don't have any."
"Hell ... throw in some 4.2s."
"We're out of that too."
"How about the artillery?"
"No communications."
"How about the Air Force?"

"We don't know where they are."
"Then damn it, call the Navy."
"They can't reach this far."
Finally the exasperated first sergeant exclaimed, "Send me a camera. I want to take a picture of this." Chambers was wounded by a mortar fragment a few minutes later.

By about 1430, the already difficult situation had become untenable. The force was nearly surrounded, except for a narrow corridor on the left, and ammunition was running low. There was nothing to do but to withdraw, a dangerous and difficult maneuver in daylight when it means disengaging from contact with an attacking enemy force.

Smith came to the decision reluctantly, believing at the time he would always regret giving the order.

It was during the retreat that Task Force Smith suffered its worst casualties and the breakdown of order and discipline. Up to that point, the casualties numbered 30 to 40, including those who had been hit by fire from the tanks earlier in the day.

Only the able and the walking wounded would withdraw. The unit would have to leave its dead and seriously wounded behind, a bitter experience for all concerned. Among the unnamed heroes of the day were a medic and two senior non-coms who refused to leave, choosing instead to remain behind with the wounded. Their fate was not recorded, which unfortunately precluded their receiving the recognition they deserved.

Toland wrote of six wounded men lying on the ground as a lieutenant passed. "What is going to happen to us, lieutenant?" one cried out. The officer gave him a hand grenade with the words, "That's the best I can do for you."

C Company under Captain Richard Dashner was first to move down the slippery, muddy hill toward the rice paddies to the east. Retreat along the road, still being raked by fire, was out of the question.

The withdrawing GIs were under heavy mortar fire from well-chosen positions, including as the process wore on from those the American infantrymen had just left. Every account of this action tells of the panic and chaos. Task Force Smith had ceased to be an organized unit as men made a headlong rush for survival. When soldiers on the hill saw others leaving, the fear of being left behind became overwhelming.

Lieutenant Day, late of the recoilless rifle experience, recalled the disorder. "It was every man for himself," he was quoted in Max Hastings, *The Korean War*. "Guys fell around me. Mortar rounds hit here and there. One of my young guys got it in the middle... . There wasn't much I could do but pat him on the head and say, "Hang in there."

Day told of another man who was hit in the throat but survived by holding the wound together with his hands for the rest of the day.

As the soldiers tried to run through the rain-soaked bogs and flooded paddies, they jettisoned equipment, helmets, anything that would slow them down. That included combat boots, which became too much to pull from the sucking mud.

The confusion and loss of unit cohesion

was not confined to the rank and file. Command order and communications collapsed also. For instance, a platoon of Company B led by Lieutenant Carl Bernard, who had been a Marine enlisted man during World War II, did not get the word that the task force was pulling out. He discovered that dismaying fact only when he noticed a slackening of fire from nearby American positions and sent a runner to check. When the man returned, he exclaimed, "They're all gone."

So Bernard, who had been wounded in the face and hands by a grenade, organized his own retreat. He split his platoon plus some walking wounded he gathered on the way into two groups. Without a compass, the officer used the map of Korea he found in an abandoned schoolhouse as a navigational tool. He reached American lines five days later.

Other clumps of men from Task Force Smith straggled back along various paths toward the friendly forces of their own army. Captain Dashner managed to reach Taejon in two days with more than half of his Company C. Floyd Martin and his team at the battalion command post tried to burn papers, but they were wet and had to be buried instead. The troops walked south along the railroad tracks until they came upon the trucks of American gunners and boarded the vehicles.

Meanwhile, Colonel Smith, lacking radio or telephone communication with the howitzer battery, went personally to tell the artillerymen that the infantry was leaving. It was then that he discovered the field pieces basically undamaged and communications men still trying to string cable to the forward positions. But of course it was too late for that.

The gun crews disabled their pieces by removing the sights and breech blocks. They and the two lieutenant colonels, Smith and Perry, loaded onto trucks and headed south. The artillery's rolling fleet had been barely damaged, but the infantry's truck park had been demolished by enemy fire.

Smith soon discovered where the enemy tanks had gone. At Osan, the Americans found North Korean tanks crews casually resting and smoking. The soldiers of both armies stared wide-eyed at each other as the trucks rolled past, but oddly, no one made a hostile move. The Americans made an abrupt turn east on a dirt road along the north edge of Osan and kept going.

Along the way, the trucks picked up about 100 infantrymen emerging from the rice paddies in the flight from the battlefield that lay to the northwest.

The column reached Ansong that night. General Dean, meanwhile, was in Pyongtaek fearing the worst about Task Force Smith. When four drenched survivors stumbled into headquarters with tales of terror from the front, it was easy to believe that the unit had been virtually wiped out. However, Perry, arriving from Ansong, hobbled in on his wounded leg with a more realistic assessment of the situation.

Over the next several days, as stragglers continued to show up at various places along friendly lines, the count revealed 184 Americans killed, wounded or missing out of an origi-

nal force of 540. By unit, casualties included five officers and 148 enlisted men in the two 21st Infantry companies and five officers and 26 men in the 52nd Field Artillery Battalion. Twenty-eight of the artillery losses were among the forward observers and volunteer weapons crews.

The overall casualty rate, 35 percent, was enormous for a one-day battle, but was less than Dean had come to expect and at least was short of annihilation.

Some of the individual heroism was conspicuous enough to be recognized. Lieutenant Connors, the fighting bazookaman who made North Korean tankers know he was there, won the Silver Star. So did a couple of private first class machine gunners. Vern Mulligan of C Company killed six North Koreans in a firefight at close range, and Florentin Gonzalez volunteered to remain with his gun to cover his platoon's withdrawal and was still at his post when the position was overrun.

The unit's two senior officers, Colonel Smith and Colonel Perry, were awarded the Distinguished Service Cross for their part in the action. Smith, incidentally, remained in Korea until late in the year and eventually retired from the Army as a brigadier general.

Back on the battlefield, meanwhile, a scene was unfolding that would have sickened and infuriated the surviving GIs had they witnessed it. It would have given them a better idea of the kind of people they were fighting. It was described in Toland's book, *In Mortal Combat*.

The North Koreans occupying the field coldly shot any wounded Americans who seemed defiant, sparing only those who begged for mercy. Later the dead from Task Force Smith lay scattered about, many with their mouths open. A North Korean thought it amusing to throw a handful of dirt into each gaping mouth with the words, "The Americans are still hungry even though they're dead. Here, have some earth to eat." For some reason, the South Korean villagers thought it was funny also.

The battle of Osan, the first land engagement for American troops in Korea and the first encounter between Americans and Communists in the post-World War II era, must be considered a defeat on the simple basis of the final outcome.

And while there might be some who would dwell on the disorderly retreat in full flight off the ridge, that fact is secondary to a far more important one. For several hours an American Army unit, previously untested in combat and hopelessly outnumbered and outgunned, stood and fought bravely without hope of relief or reinforcement and without much prospect even of survival.

The contemporary news accounts were remarkably accurate, all things considered. The Associated Press dispatch in 5 July editions in newspapers back home, led this way: "U.S. troops outnumbered 8-1 held off the best Communist division and 40 tanks for six hours in the first engagement of the war."

That sentence is a concise summation. Task Force Smith put in a long day on 5 July 1950, and wrote a proud chapter in the 24th Infantry Division's history.

TO TAEJON

When troops of Task Force Smith fell back to friendly lines, they mingled with the 1st and 3rd Battalions of the 34th Infantry, which had taken up positions at Pyongtaek and Ansong, respectively. Those points on the map, it will be recalled, were earlier identified as having excellent defensive qualities because of the estuary of the Yellow Sea on the left and a high ridge line on the right. So when Task Force Smith, which earlier had been ordered to set up a blocking force at the two locations, moved north of Osan, General Dean quickly assigned the newly arrived 34th Infantry to the Pyongtaek-Ansong line.

This was an improvement in numbers, of course, since the blocking units now were battalion size, not company. But the force still had no tanks or artillery and little in the way of anti-tank weaponry to counter the big Russian-made T-34s now bullying their way down the invasion route at the head of large infantry units.

After the initial airlift of Task Force Smith, the remainder of the 24th Division began making its way by sea at the best speed manageable from Japan to Korea, landing at Pusan in stages. The 34th Regiment was first to arrive and was in position on 5 July, the day of the battle north of Osan fought by the half battalion of the 21st Infantry led by Colonel Charles B. Smith.

While that fight raged toward an uncertain conclusion, insofar as the division or 34th Regiment could know, the force at Pyongtaek had its first encounter with the enemy and took its first casualty. Brigadier General George Barth, acting division artillery officer on loan, had ordered bazooka teams forward based on reports of tanks in the area. After the GIs spread out along a ridge line, an enemy T-34 was spotted about 1,500 yards to the left. Also about that time a North Korean ammunition convoy heading for Task Force Smith appeared, but fortunately was halted by Lieutenant Charlie Payne and his men.

The GI bazookamen moved to within about 500 yards of the big enemy tank and fired the first round. It appeared to have scored, but as other soldiers learned before and after, the light weapon then available had little effect on the heavy armor. North Koreans piled out of the tank and machine gun fire erupted from that direction. A young GI fell in the bean field in which the bazooka team was taking cover. His name was Shadrick, dead at 19 from a gunshot in the chest. The team fired all its ammunition, futilely, and then withdrew carrying Shadrick, the first combat death suffered by the 34th Regiment in Korea.

Subscribers to the New York Herald-Tribune would read correspondent Margaret Higgins' account: from the scene: "The medics brought the dead soldier's body in here, tenderly lifting him from the Jeep. The lifeless form was shrouded in a blanket which kept the pelting rain off the blond young face. As medics brought the body in, one private said bitterly, 'What a place to die.'" Earlier, in Toland's book, Higgins was quoted as saying Shadrick seemed to have a surprised look on his face when he was brought in.

Maj Gen William F. Dean, Commander 24th Division, June 49 - July 50.

Twenty-four hours after Task Force Smith's men peered northward through the chill dawn rain to see a juggernaut approaching, the Dragons of the 34th Infantry had approximately the same experience the morning of 6 July.

The stories told by the 21st Regiment men retreating from Osan did not inspire confidence in the soldiers of the 34th. Neither did the long columns of pathetic civilian refugees or what the American Army perceived to be a lackluster effort by the South Korean Army. However, subsequent reports indicated that some ROK units actually did a creditable job fighting during those early days. It was just hard for the GIs to see that sometimes.

Dean, in his book, *General Dean's Story*, recounted the chaos and suspicion that reigned among the senior South Korean officers at the outset of the conflict. The ROK chief of staff's job changed hands three times in short order, but one, the American general remembered, had the idea of letting enemy tanks pass through and building traps behind them. In the absence of a better anti-tank tactic, Dean thought it might have worked.

Even before the fate of Task Force Smith became known, Dean sensed trouble based on the reports of enemy tanks south of Osan, undoubtedly those that had drawn first blood early the morning of 5 July. One of them, of course, had skirmished with the bazooka patrol that day.

The first heavy encounter involving the 34th Infantry Regiment occurred the next day when North Korean armor and infantry crossed the shallow river north of Pyongtaek with little difficulty, despite the Americans having blown the only bridge.

The 1st Battalion put up some resistance, but soon fell back to a point below Chonan, the next city to the south. At Ansong to the east, the 3rd Battalion reportedly withdrew without being attacked.

When Dean discovered that the 34th Infantry had abandoned those solid defensive po-

sitions so quickly, he was upset, to put it mildly. The peninsula bulges to the west below Pyongtaek, meaning the left flank of the regiment now was exposed and would remain so.

By the time the commanding general reached the scene, the entire 34th Infantry was south of Chonan, to his great distress. In his book, Dean took personal responsibility for any mixup in communications, but nevertheless he replaced the regimental commander and gave the job to Colonel Robert Martin, whom Dean knew from the war in Europe. Martin was doing staff duty in Tokyo and Dean asked for him by name to take the field combat assignment.

Dean's initial orders to the 34th Infantry the evening of 6 July were to dig in and hold in place, but he soon directed the regiment back to Chonan to make its stand. Charley J. Cole of K Company remembers making it back to Chonan walking and running in 10 hours. The company commander, Captain Earl N. Hill, shuttled 15-20 men at a time in his jeep and trailer. According to Cole, "Some guys were walking barefooted because they had so many blisters on their feet."

K Company dug in near the train depot in Chonan in a drenching rain. Cole ate his first meal in two days: soggy bread and mashed potatoes in a canteen cup! He was surprised to find the battalion's duffel bags stored in the train depot. Several men stacked the duffel bags six feet high and four feet thick and made a barricade.

On 8 July, enemy tanks and infantry entered the city and began pounding the beleaguered defenders. When the North Koreans struck at about 0510, Cole and a buddy used this barricade to repel the first elements. Martin, cut off from his headquarters, took a bazooka and with Sergeant Jerry Christenson, rushed into the street. The bazooka and an 85-mm cannon from a North Korean tank fired at each other simultaneously. Martin was cut in half by the enemy shell, but the sergeant survived. The colonel, whose regimental command lasted just 48 hours, had succeeded in that short time in instilling the unit with his own fighting spirit. He was awarded the Distinguished Service Cross.

But Chonan was a lost cause. The 1st and 3rd battalions of the 34th Infantry were taking a fearful battering in the city, and after the death of the commanding officer, resistance disintegrated and troops began pulling back toward the south once more.

Charley Cole felt that he may have captured the division's first prisoner. He came across a knocked-out North Korean tank, which had run up a telephone pole at a 30-degree angle. After capturing one of the tankers nearby, Cole marched him south by prodding him occasionally—not always softly—with his bayonet.

On heights overlooking the town from the south were Dean and Eighth Army commander General Walton Walker, who that day had given the 24th Division commander the good news that the entire Eighth Army, meaning three other infantry occupation divisions from Japan, was joining the war.

Dean had ordered the light tanks attached to the 19th Regiment forward to help support

the evacuation of Chonan. When the first platoon came over the hill, Walker asked its commander, a young lieutenant, what his intentions were. "I'm going to slug it out," said the officer, who to Dean had the look of a man who did not expect to survive the experience. Walker had other ideas and he calmly gave the lieutenant what in Dean's mind was "as fine a lecture on tank tactics as you could hear in any military classroom."(Walker had been XX Corps commander in General Patton's Third Army in Europe during World War II.)

Walker had advice for Dean also, in part on how to deal with the fact that his regiments had only two battalions each. This deficiency was more than a shortage of manpower, though it was certainly that too. Army combat doctrine is based on the triangular organization, which meant two units could be committed and a third held in reserve. Dean and his regimental commanders did not have that luxury and would have to try to work around it.

The division's immediate concern was finding the next line of defense in light of the enemy breakthrough at Chonan. South of that city, the road splits, one leg branching southeast toward the cities of Chonui and Chochiwon, the other running due south toward Kungju. Both roads eventually reach the all-important Kum River, occasioning this Dean order: "Hold Kum River line at all costs. Maximum - repeat maximum - delay will be effected." The fate of the key city of Taejon, then the provisional capital, south of the Kum depended on how well that order was carried out.

Dean gave the exhausted, decimated 34th Infantry the easier assignment on the road running due south. The general put the newly arrived and fresh 21st Infantry under Colonel Richard W. Stephens, nicknamed "Big Six," to defend the main road heading eventually toward Taegu and Pusan. The 19th Regiment also was in the country, holding a reserve position on 8 July, meaning that one week after the fateful order in Japan, the entire 24th Infantry Division now was deployed in Korea, though it remained understrength and inadequately equipped.

President Truman already had offered his unfortunate description of the war as a "police action," a fact not lost on some of the infantrymen doing the fighting. During the battle of Chonan, one sardonic GI, spying an unfamiliar brigadier general on the street, cracked, "Hey, the commissioner is here to hand out our police badges."

Colonel Stephens, a South Dakotan who graduated from the Military Academy in 1924, offered a less witty but more direct commentary on President Truman's choice of words when, as quoted by Army historian Roy Appleman, he said, "The men and officers had no interest in a fight which was not even dignified by being called a war." Stephens would retire a Major General.

The bewildered troops and their equally perplexed commanders, viewing the chaos of the countryside and the political and military instability of the native ally, could not at this stage hope to defeat the well-armed, well-organized enemy then enjoying massive superiority in men and equipment. The Army's mis-

71

sion was to hold and delay as much as possible until reinforcements arrived and a counteroffensive could be organized. On this day, the 24th Division, already shocked and beaten back by a brutal and motivated enemy, surely felt lonely, isolated and desperate.

As expected, the North Korean 4th Division attacked down the road toward the 21st Infantry's positions at Chonui and hit the regiment hard. However, Stephens' Gimlets, at the moment even more understrength than usual because Task Force Smith's half battalion was not yet on the scene, fought back gallantly and in a furious counterattack succeeded in regaining some lost ground. To date, it was the most enouraging infantry action of the war. It was then that the American GIs discovered the first atrocities of the conflict, the bodies of six of their fellow soldiers with their hands tied behind their backs with barbwire and bullets in their heads. The North Koreans did not always take prisoners, and as that fact became more widely known among the American GIs, it heightened their willingness to fight. There was no percentage in surrendering.

The 21st Infantry punished the crack 4th North Korean division so severely that the enemy's 3rd Division was called in to relieve it. The fight raged for four days, as the American regiment, now including the soldiers who had survived the fight at Osan on 5 July, gave ground grudgingly in falling back to Chochiwon, and finally to the Kum River on 12 July. Dean was effusive in his praise of the performance of Stephens and his men for maximizing the delay and making the enemy pay a high price for its progress. At one point, the regimental commander was well in front of his own lines and cut off from his command post, but managed to find his way back.

The gallant battle at Chochiwon cost the 21st Regiment dearly. The unit was down to 1,100 men, fewer than half the number that came over from Japan, so Dean moved the fresh but green 19th Regiment, the storied "Rock of Chickamauga," up to a strategic point on the Kum River to relieve the 21st. As the two regiments passed each other, the condition of the 21st Infantry did not encourage the 2,276 troops of the 19th Regiment, under the command of Colonel Guy Meloy, Jr., who had not led troops in battle before. Meloy was a 1927 Military Academy graduate from Maryland, who would retire as a full general.

Dean assigned the "Chicks" to the location where the Seoul-Pusan highway crosses the Kum River at Taepyong-ni, about 20 miles northwest of Taejon, which he reasoned was the most likely point of the North Koreans' next main effort.

At this stage, the American Army had been fighting in Korea for a week, and two of the 24th Division's three regiments had been severely mauled. The 21st Infantry, which had suffered 1,433 casualties to that point, took up positions east of Taejon and south of the South Korean sector to serve as a reserve unit in case the North Koreans broke through there.

The next phase of the desperate fight for South Korea, the battle of the Kum River, was about to begin.

The North Korean 4th Division, after its

5th RCT tank assigned to the 24th Division was painted with tiger stripes on the front and gun barrel to represent 1950 - Korea's year of the Tiger. (Courtesy of Richard Clayton)

painful encounter with the 21st Infantry, turned its attention to the 34th Regiment holding the left flank at Kongju., about eight miles downstream from the 19th Infantry's position. On the right flank to the east was a ROK outfit.

The 34th Infantry was under the command of its former executive officer, Colonel Robert "Pappy" Wadlington, 49, who had taken over when Martin was killed. The regiment fought first on the north side of the Kum River, but later was forced to withdraw to the opposite bank to establish its defense.

North Koreans launched their attack against the 34th Infantry Dragons on the morning of 14 July. Two companies of the 3rd Battalion, I and L, held the forward positions with the 1st Battalion in reserve. About three miles to the rear was the 63rd Field Artillery. No fire was forthcoming from that source because the artillerymen were depending upon direction from the air, and Communist Yak aircraft had driven the American planes away. With mortar and armor support, North Korean infantrymen began crossing on barges about two miles downstream from the L Company position on the left. When mortar and machine-gun support of the company did not materialize, the lieutenant in command decided to withdraw without making contact with the enemy and was relieved of command as soon as he arrived at battalion headquarters.

The Kum River was at its low summer level, nearly dry in some places, and presented little trouble for either infantry or the T-34 tanks in making the crossing.

The loss of the regiment's left flank allowed the North Korean troops, to pour through the gap in strength and bypass I Company without the necessity of a frontal assault. Other enemy troops infiltrated and overran the artillery batteries with the loss of ten 105-mm howitzers, ammunition and about 70 vehicles.

At the height of the battle, Eighth Army commander Walton Walker took to the air to see what was happening to the 34th Regiment. As the 4th North Korean division crossed in

ever increasing numbers in multiple locations, many of them wading, tanks on the far side poured their 85-mm cannon fire into the American defenders on the south bank. Artillery shells also fell among the GIs of the 34th Infantry. The river was "running red," according to one observer.

Toward the end of that bad day, Wadlington ordered the 1st Battalion to counterattack in an effort to reclaim lost ground, including the 63rd Field Artillery position, but the effort was to no avail. So Wadlington's regiment pulled back to the town of Nonsan, southwest of Taejon.

As is nearly always the case, the loss of an engagement did not negate the personal heroism of many of the men. In this desperate fight on the Kum River, there were no rear-echelon troops. No matter what the normal duties of the soldiers might have been, they fought as infantrymen.

From the air, Walker could see the obvious. The forced withdrawal of the 34th Infantry made the position of the 19th Regiment to its right virtually untenable. Faced with defending 30 miles of front along the Kum River, the untested regiment was stretched tightly and its left flank was wide open. Already, tanks and self-propelled guns were firing on the American infantrymen.

To protect the flank as much as possible, the 19th Regiment's commander, Meloy, ordered a company of the 2nd Battalion, two light M-24 tanks and two .50 calibre machine guns to guard against attack from that direction. The unit, under the command of Lieutenant Colonel Thomas McGrail, represented two-thirds of the force Meloy had hoped to keep in reserve while the 1st Battalion held the forward positions.

The diversion of his reserve force would, to Meloy's mind, result in dire consequences for many of the men in his regiment.

Initial encounters between the Chicks and the North Koreans were sporadic and, from the American standpoint, successful, even reassuring. Infantry probes near a blown bridge over the Kum and some shelling was about all the action the line experienced until about 0300 on 16 July.

Then a flare dropped from a North Korean airplane signalled a full-scale tank and artillery barrage, followed by an infantry crossing in a gap between C and E companies. Commanding C Company was Lieutenant Henry McGill, who was assured by his 1st Platoon leader, Lieutenant Thomas Mahler that "We're doing fine" about 30 seconds before Mahler was dead from a burp-gun bullet through the head.

The savage fight raged for about three hours before North Koreans of the 3rd Division overran C Company and flooded through the breach in huge numbers. The entire 19th regiment was in danger of being cut off from the rear.

Meloy tried to organize a counterattack using cooks, bakers, drivers, mechanics, clerks and other auxiliary-type personnel, but the effort fell short. He himself was seriously wounded while trying to mount a second assault and later was evacuated on a tank. Meloy turned the 19th Infantry over to the 1st Battalion commander, Lieutenant Colonel Otho T. Winstead, who was killed later in the day.

Meloy ordered a withdrawal of the regiment toward Taejon, but enemy troops were at the Chicks' rear in strength and set up an extensive roadblock. Some vehicles, including the tank carrying Meloy and the international journalist, Margaret Higgins, managed to evade the roadblock, but about 500 men remained trapped.

Meloy was convinced that had he been able to keep his 2nd Battalion intact and in reserve, he either could have prevented the North Koreans from setting up the road block or he could have driven them off.

A relief force of light tanks and anti-aircraft guns came up from the south in the attempt to open the road, but enemy fire inflicted heavy casualties on the Americans and turned the tanks back.

Surgical Technician Rodolph Mullins, assigned to the 1st Battalion 19th Infantry, remembered that the battalion was "bottled up" all that day of 16 July. The fighting was so intense that the artillery with the battalion was firing direct fire. Several artillerymen were among the 60-70 casualties "stacked up" at the battalion aid station.

The only way out for the trapped infantrymen was to climb the steep slopes on either side of the road, which, considering the number of wounded who had to be carried, required almost superhuman effort. Major Fentsimacher, the battalion S-2, gave the order to withdraw. All vehicles and equipment that could not be carried were destroyed by bayonetting the tires and exploding thermite grenades on the engine blocks. One group of about 100 made it to the top of the slope, but it was obvious that with the North Koreans in close pursuit, the 30 wounded on litters could be taken no farther.

Herman G. Felhoelter, a Roman Catholic chaplain from Louisville, KY, volunteered to remain behind with the wounded men while the others continued to make their escape.

From the next hill, a sergeant turned and saw through his binoculars the horrifying sight of a massacre. The North Koreans had caught up with the Americans. They slaughtered the helpless men while the chaplain prayed over them and then they murdered him as well. Father Felhoelter was awarded the Distinguished Service Cross.

As one of those who escaped, T/5 Mullins had a harrowing experience on the march that unusually dark night. During a rest stop, M/Sergeant Raymond Stafford from New Mexico asked Mullins to go back down the trail to make sure there were no stragglers. After going several hundred yards, Mullins started back. Suddenly, he bumped into someone.

"I was scared to death," Mullins recalls. "I didn't know what to do." The two stood on the trail for what seemed an eternity, each with a gun in the other's ribs. Mullins reasoned that if he said anything in English he would be shot if the other was a North Korean. If he tried to say something in Korean and the other was a GI, he would be shot. Finally both slowly withdrew, and Mullins found his way back to his comrades. He never knew whether his adversary was a GI or a Korean.

At the request of GRS (Graves Registration Service) Mullins went back to the area in September to identify battle sites. He found several bodies, still on litters, of men who had been massacred with Chaplain Felhoelter.

Before the battle of the Kum River erupted in the 19th Regiment's sector, Dean had moved the battered 21st Regiment up to a reserve position behind the 34th. The division commander's hope was to coordinate the withdrawal of the two regiments in the line, but now with the 19th Infantry fighting for its very survival, the entire defensive structure was shattered.

The Chicks who managed to elude the North Korean trap withdrew all the way back to Yongdong, the rear division headquarters 30 miles southeast of Taejon, to reorganize. Some elements of the 2nd Battalion remained to participate in the next major battle - for Taejon.

Both General Dean and General Walker, Eighth Army commander, knew Taejon could not be held long. It was a matter of one day, two at the most. The real defense of the peninsula would have to take place farther to the southeast, in what would forever be known as the Pusan Perimeter. But that would come later.

The job of defending Taejon fell mainly to the 34th Infantry, plus the 2nd Battalion soldiers of the 19th Regiment, who most recently had been bloodied in the attempt to break up the roadblock south of the Kum. The divison had only two battalions of artillery with which to counter the attack soon to come.

Dean made the unconventional choice to remain in Taejon rather than at division headquarters in Yongdong, because, as he later explained, he wanted to be where the immediate decisions had to be rendered. Either way, he later reflected, it probably would not have made much difference in the outcome of the battle.

American troops were deployed thinly north and west of the city. Walker flew over the area and was encouraged to see that the units of the 24th Division were positioned defensively as well as they could be, which gave him hope Taejon could be held until 20 July, his goal.

For the beleaguered Taro Leafers, who in two weeks of bitter fighting against overwhelming odds had stood alone, American help was arriving. The sister division, the 25th, was already in Korea, but was occupied to the east bolstering the efforts of the ROK troops. The 1st Cavalry Divison, despite the name, another infantry outfit, was just then landing at an east coast port and would be in the line south of Taejon in a couple of days.

On the evening of 19 July, 1st Battalion, 34th Infantry, held the forwardmost position on a ridge along the main highway northwest of Taejon near the airport. Behind that unit the 3rd Battalion also occupied high ground about a half mile outside the city. Elements of the 2nd Battalion, 19th Regiment, were situated to the northeast.

The North Korean 3rd and 4th Divisions had hit the American defenses throughout the day on 19 July, but not in great strength. However, in the darkness, imaginations sometimes worked overtime. Lieutenant Robert Herbert, a platoon leader in G Company of the 19th Infantry, twice that night was dispatched with his unit to check out rumors that E Company had been wiped out. When he arrived, he found everything under control.

About midnight, the enemy launched the main assault against Taejon. What happened between then and late in the afternoon could be variously described as chaotic, confused, desperate, and infernal.

Colonel Red Ayres, commander of the 1st Battalion, 34th Infantry, already had heard the rumble of tanks from his command post. Then, just before midnight, he learned enemy forces had been seen on a road south of town, suggesting, accurately as it turned out, that the North Koreans were moving around to the rear of the American positions. About three hours later, Ayres discovered the North Koreans had penetrated his line on the main road. The enemy 4th Division was taking out the battalion's right flank, and within an hour, small arms fire began hitting the CP itself. It was time to evacuate.

Communications ranged from minimal to abysmal, mostly due to malfunctioning equipment but also human misunderstanding. Shortcomings in the flow of reliable information accounted for many of the problems of that day, including the fact Dean and Lieutenant Colonel Wadlington, the 34th Infantry's exec, at one point labored under the assurance at the regimental command post that the western defenses were still intact when in fact they were nonexistent. Lack of reliable radio contact also allowed the North Koreans to move around to the south of the city and block escape exits without the knowledge of many of the troops and their officers.

That maneuver, incidentally, was available to the communist army because the Yanks did not have sufficient numerical strength to protect their flanks. The North Koreans also were able to occupy a key road out of the city because the division reconnaissance company, originally assigned to that area, was released to the control of the regiment, which sent it north.

The new 34th Infantry commander was Colonel Charles Beauchamp, who had been borrowed from the 7th Division to replace the late Robert Martin. Beauchamp was a West Pointer, Class of 1930, from Michigan. After 15 days of combat by the regiment, he was the fourth officer to lead it.

Throughout most of the battle of Taejon, Beauchamp was away from the command post, suffering from communications troubles and misapprehensions of his own. One series of the colonel's experiences may illustrate how it was going for American troops that day. When Beauchamp heard tanks had been seen east of the city, he assumed they belonged to the 21st Regiment. Learning the truth, he organized a defense at a pass and tried to hail an infantry company passing through for help, but the company commander misunderstood the order and continued on. So Beauchamp hurried to the 21st Regiment's headquarters only to find that the regiment had been given no part in the defense of Taejon. Nevertheless, the colonel latched onto some tanks as well as the company that had passed earlier and returned to the scene of action. But by that time, the enemy had destroyed the defensive force left behind and now stopped the U.S. armor with anti-tank mines. Added to those woes, the infantrymen were running out of ammunition.

By afternoon, North Korean tanks and a large number of infantry were in the blazing city; many roads leading out of Taejon were blocked or were under enemy fire. The best outcome any GI could imagine was to escape that holocaust.

The fighting was desperate, and often heroic. A collection of KPs, clerks and messengers mounted a counterattack at the edge of the city. Headquarters personnel led by the regimental operations officer, Major S.C. McDaniel, went forward to keep snipers pinned down in order to allow an artillery unit to withdraw with its weapons intact. The artillerymen had considered pulling the breech blocks and abandoning the weapons. McDaniel, incidentally, was another officer from the 7th Division. He replaced Major John Dunn, who had been wounded and captured at Chonan. McDaniel also was captured the day of the Taejon battle, but did not emerge from prison camp. Because his efforts on behalf of fellow prisoners were so effective, many believe his captors murdered him.

The gallantry of Sergeant George Libby, of the 3rd Engineers - the famed "Pacific Engineers" - was particularly conspicuous. Libby, fighting as an infantryman as were his fellow engineers, twice crossed an open road under heavy fire to retrieve wounded men. He was firing his carbine at enemy infantrymen when he noticed an artillery tractor in the road. He put a wounded man aboard, and then stationed himself so as to shield the driver from North Korean small-arms fire. He was hit several times, but the tractor managed to move beyond enemy range. Libby, who died of his wounds, was awarded the Medal of Honor.

The division's transportation officer, Captain Raymond Hatfield, tried desperately to get his supply train out of Taejon to Yongdong, and stubbornly refused to leave the rail yard until the move was accomplished. He paid with his life. When American troops retook Taejon weeks later, they found Hatfield's body. After the war, Dean recommended him for the Silver Star.

Lieutenant Herbert, of G Company, 19th Infantry, who had spent much of the night on wild goose chases, finally set up a defensive road block west of the city and remained there long after most other units had begun pulling out. During the flight from Taejon later that day, it was Herbert's refusal to stop to rest — after a lieutenant colonel had called for a break - that saved him and about 60 other men. Based on what Herbert could see from the next ridge, it appeared the superior officer and his contingent were killed or captured by the pursuing North Koreans.

Dean's tank-hunting foray through the streets of Taejon has been widely discussed over the years. Whether it was foolish derring-do or inspirational heroism, the episode is much a part of the Dean lore, and no history of the battle of Taejon can overlook it.

The commanding general had awakened early on the morning of 20 July at the 34th Regiment command post to the sound of firing and the odor of cordite, which told him that the enemy was at the gates of the city, or inside it, and therefore help would not arrive from the other Army divisions in time to hold Taejon. Confirmation of that fact came from his aide, Lieutenant Arthur Clarke, who reported that North Korean troops and tanks had been seen in the city. The regimental command had no contact with two battalions, the 2nd from the 19th and 1st from the 34th and did not know where the flanks were.

Dean's first anti-tank expedition failed. The bazooka rounds fired by a nervous enlisted man missed. Then came the famous incident of the general firing at enemy armor with his side arm. He later tended to debunk the significance of that action. "I wasn't silly enough to think I could do anything with a pistol. It was plain rage and frustration," he wrote in his book, *General Dean's Story*. But because some of the survivors of Taejon later reported that they had last seen the division's commanding general banging away at North Korean tanks with his .45, that is the image that stuck.

When he set out in search of tanks that morning, Dean concluded there was no more general officer's work to be done at the moment. In fact, he wrote that most of his deci-

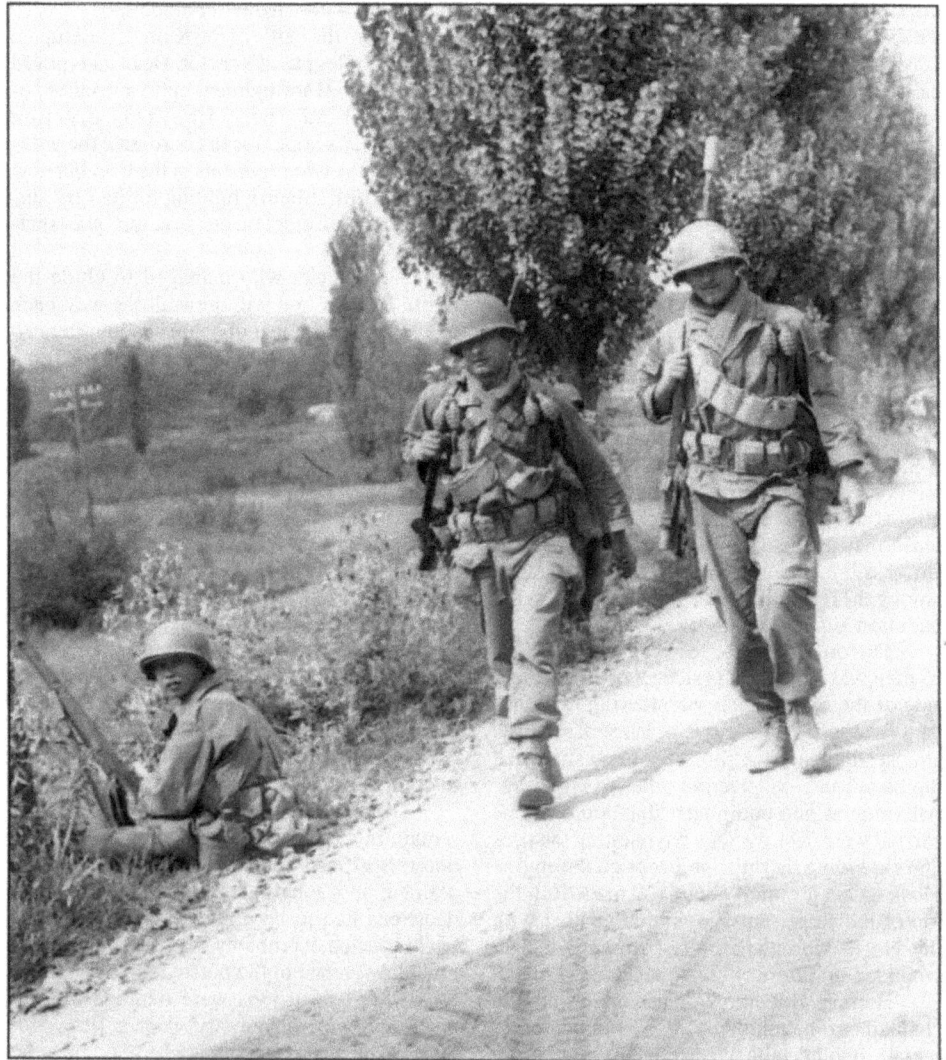

Richard Mercy (left) and Robert Mercy (right) advancing toward Taejon. Sept. 1950.

sions that day could have been made by any competent sergeant.

The criticism directed at Dean from some fellow officers derided his decision to take to the streets to fight like an ordinary foot soldier instead of taking care of his larger responsibilities.

But Dean, having obtained the newly arrived 3.5-inch bazooka rockets, did succeed in destroying an M-34 tank, and more than that, destroyed the myth of the big tank's invincibility. The 3.5-inch ammunition, better configured to penetrate tank armor, was first used in Korea at Taejon. So perhaps there was a larger purpose to Dean's infantry-soldier activities. Besides that, the situation in the city was so desperate, with 24th Division men falling back uncertainly and straggling through the streets, the inspirational value of the general fighting alongside should not be discounted.

With North Koreans closing in on three sides, Beauchamp and Dean decided by midafternoon that Taejon would have to be abandoned. By late afternoon convoys were forming to move out toward the southeast.

It was late afternoon when the order sounded to evacuate the town. Because of smoke, fire, resistance, lack of communications, the scarcity of open exit routes and general pandemonium, it was a scene of chaos. General Dean's last radio message as division commander was, "Enemy roadblock eastern exit of Taejon. Send armor immediately."

The first convoy was ambushed. The Dean party followed at high speed under sniper fire, dodging burning vehicles by such close margins the men could feel the heat. Buildings also were on fire, and on one street that the jeeps and trucks traveled, American infantrymen were engaged in a furious firefight along the side.

The Jeep carrying Wadlington got lost and ended up on a dead-end street near a school. He and the others, under heavy fire, had to abandon their vehicle and escape on foot. The same fate at the same dead-end befell another column of vehicles a short time later.

In the smoke, noise, and gunfire, it was hard for drivers to stay together and remain on the right road. Dean's party missed the turn onto the road to Pusan, but had to continue on hoping to find an alternative route. The second Jeep and L Company followed the lead Jeep on its erroneous path.

But taking the right road was no bargain either. The original head of the column, which did not miss the turn, later came under heavy mortar fire. The lead half-track was hit and set afire, the second also was destroyed, and machine-gun fire raked the column. When GIs scrambled to the side of the road for cover, North Korean troops rose from a rice paddy firing burp guns.

The Dean column picked up walking wounded and casuals as it went. When the group later ran into a North Korean roadblock it had to abandon its vehicles. The men, 17 Americans and one South Korean, remained pinned down by the side of a road by rifle and machine-gun fire but managed to crawl away only after dark. Dean made the observation that Clarke, an air officer by training, was in this circumstance functioning admirably as an infantry officer.

The battle of Taejon was over. The 24th Infantry Division had lost 922 men killed and 228 wounded. The majority of those killed were first listed as missing, suggesting whole units had been overrun and annihilated. Those Taro Leafers who escaped the burning city would fight another day, and soon.

The remnants of the 24th Division reeled back to the south, southeast and southwest from Taejon. Lieutenant Clarke made it to Taegu and reported the circumstances of General Dean's disappearance down a mountainside. The commanding general had gone for water in the darkness and become permanently separated from the column. (See appendix for more complete description of Dean's experience.)

With Dean now missing in action, Walker gave the job of 24th Division commander to Major General John Church, who, it is recalled, had been sent with a small advance party to Taejon from headquarters in Tokyo at the outset of the war, preceding even Dean and his staff.

With total personnel losses now put at about one-third and with even the inadequate equipment with which the division had entered hostilities depleted further, the battered and exhausted 24th was placed in Eighth Army reserve behind the 1st Cavalry Division.

The respite was to be short-lived. Walker learned that the North Korean 6th Division, essentially fresh, had driven south along the west coast from the Yellow Sea estuary below Pyongtaek. Dean's fear that loss of that position opened the west side of the peninsula to the enemy was proving to be prophetic.

The enemy 6th Division moved to the southwest corner of Korea and then swung east along the south end, taking dead aim on Pusan. The enemy drive to flank the American forces on their left included a second prong farther north by the battle-tested 4th Division, which on 24 July stood at Kochang.

The 24th Division would have to go back into action before it had enough time to recover from the delaying action its regiments had been fighting since 5 July far to the north at Osan.

"I'm sorry to have to do this, but the whole left flank is open and reports indicate the Koreans are moving in," Walker told Church. General Douglas MacArthur, the overall United Nations commander, detected a serious mistake by the North Korean 6th Division. It dawdled on its trip south and then east toward Pusan by rolling up the South Korean ports instead of pointing the spear straight at the main objective.

The 34th Regiment was sent to oppose the North Korean 4th Division at Kochang. The communists attacked the weary GIs almost immediately and forced them to begin a withdrawal that would not stop until the regiment was behind the Naktong River.

To the south facing the oncoming 6th Division was the 19th Regiment, for which no river defense was available to the rear. The Naktong turns abruptly east toward Pusan north of the area the Chicks were assigned to defend.

Reinforcements were moving into the 19th Infantry's sector. Two battalions of the 29th Infantry (independent regiment) arrived in Korea from Okinawa and were sent directly to the front without benefit of additional training or without even having time to prepare their weapons adequately. Included in the contingent were 400 troops fresh from the United States. The battalions, under the command of Lieutenant Colonel Harold Mott were attached to the 19th Infantry. They were the first ground troops to arrive in Korea from anywhere other than Japan.

Mott ordered his 3rd Battalion to occupy Hadong, an important crossroads town 35 miles southwest of Chinju, the location of 19th Infantry headquarters near the southern tip of the peninsula.

After spending their first night in combat sloshing through rice paddies, and hoofing over ridges, the 700 men reached their objective, the Hadong Pass on 26 July. But an ambush by North Koreans from high ground soon overwhelmed K and L companies, and Mott and his entire staff were hit in the early moments. The reserve force, I Company, came up in an effort to relieve the besieged troops and it too found itself trapped in the same rice paddy under murderous small-arms and mortar fire from above.

Some of the Americans fought their way out of the ambush, but they left 300 to 400 dead behind. The 3rd Battalion, which had expected to oppose 500 enemy, found themselves outnumbered many times over in the Hadong Pass battle. It was a bitter, bewildering introduction to combat for raw troops who had arrived in Korea only the day before.

The stunned survivors of the Hadong massacre fell back toward the next town to the east, Chinju. Reinforcements for the battered 19th and 29th regiments hurried to the front. They were fresh from the United States, and most had never been in combat before. Many bewildered young men died west of Chinju that night, 30 July, hardly knowing where they were in that strange land, what outfit they belonged to, who their officers were, and without even having their names entered on the company rolls. That was one of the more pathetic aspects of those desperate, early days of the Korean war.

Chinju was lost by the following day, and now it was Masan the GIs had to defend or else the enemy would have a clear route to Pusan itself.

PUSAN PERIMETER

With reinforcement by the 27th Regiment of the 25th Division, the American infantry held Masan. The Chicks occupied the northernmost road encircling the hills west of the town and the 27th positioned itself on the south. The enemy made its attack in the latter direction and failed to crack the 27th Infantry's lines.

Thus the stage was set for the six weeks of savage combat that would forever be known as the battle of the Pusan Perimeter. Eighth Army Commanding General Walton Walker determined that the retreat would have to come to a halt if the country was to be saved. Finally at the southeast corner of the peninsula he had a defensible line and there his army would make its stand.

To emphasize his point, Walker on 29 July made his famous "stand or die" declaration to his staff at the 25th Division headquarters. His statement in part: "A retreat to Pusan would be one of the greatest butcheries in history. We must fight until the end... If some of us must die, we will die fighting together. Any man who gives ground may be personally responsible for the death of thousands of his comrades... I want everybody to understand that we are going to hold this line. We are going to win."

This was more than the military equivalent of a half-time pep talk. Walker meant what he said, because essentially he was right. Loss of the perimeter area, with the network of rail lines and roads inside the line, would make a counteroffensive nearly impossible and in effect drive the American forces out of Korea.

His fight-to-the-death edict, however, produced sardonic reaction from some of the 24th Division men. Sergeant C.W. Menninger, 3rd Battalion, 34th Infantry, remembered an older non-com rolling his eyes and commenting, "Fight to the death? What does he think we've (been) doing for a month?" (*From The Korean War, an Oral History, Pusan to Chosin*, by Donald Knox)

As July turned to August, the monsoons changed to uncharacteristic drought in South Korea, and the heat was almost unbearable, worse than anything most of the men had ever experienced. Temperatures reached 120 degrees at times and soldiers who made the mistake of drinking water from rice paddies, which were fertilized with human excrement, suffered terribly from bloody dysentery.

Casualties from heat exhaustion at times exceeded battle losses, which was understandable. Men were lugging heavy equipment over mountainous terrain and many were not in shape for such rigors. The first combat soldiers to enter the Korean conflict were not fresh out of boot camp and advance infantry training, but came directly from the relatively sedentary life of occupation garrison duty.

The Pusan Perimeter was roughly shaped as a rectangle 50 miles wide and 100 miles long, anchored on the east by the Sea of Japan and on the south by the Korea Strait, which meant that for the first time, there would be no opportunity for the North Koreans to flank the American and ROK lines.

Along the north side of the perimeter, the ROK sector, was a mountain barrier. The western defensive line formed along the Naktong River, which snaked from north to south before turning east toward Pusan. That stream, shallow enough during August 1950 to be forded in many places, ranged from a quarter mile to a half mile wide. The second largest river in Korea, it flowed through a narrow valley between high ground on either side, the elevations greater on the west bank. Just inside the northwest corner of the perimeter was the key city of Taegu, then the provisional capital and Eighth Army headquarters.

Walker deployed three divisions along the 100-mile western front, the 1st Cavalry Division on the north, the 25th Division on the south, below the confluence of the Naktong and Nam rivers, and the 24th Division in the middle covering a front of 34 miles.

The division, down to 9,882 men at the start of the perimeter campaign, was considered by that time to be at only 40 percent combat strength based on manpower and equipment, and might have been even lower if fatigue and morale were taken into account.

One soldier's description of his unit's arrival behind the perimeter line gives some idea. Pfc. Leonard Korgie, L Company, 34th Infantry, which had fallen back from Kochang, said, "When we drove into the Pusan Perimeter you never in your life saw a more beat-up bunch of soldiers. God, we were tired. We had had no rest or letup anywhere on the road. ...The heat was atrocious.

"Inside the perimeter, the company stopped by an apple orchard and dropped in place. No one unhooked his gear. I collapsed with head resting inside my helmet. I don't remember moving until the next day.

"The guys were very quiet. They realized what they'd been through and much more was coming. Many faces that I'd known were missing. I thought of the days to come." (*The Korean War*, Knox)

The 24th Division survivors may not have realized it at the time, maybe no one did, but the tide of the war already had turned in favor of the American forces, mainly because of the sacrifices of the "First to Fight" division.

True, the enemy onslaught had rolled back the men of the Taro Leaf all the way from Osan starting on 5 July, but in the cold calculations of war, their blood and the ground they gave had bought the necessary time. As Harry J. Middleton wrote in *The Compact History of the Korean War*, the "hard investment the Eighth Army had made was beginning to pay off."

Reinforcements now in the country raised allied manpower numbers beyond those of the invaders, and more men and hardware were arriving all the time at the teeming port of Pusan, now to be protected at all costs.

One of the new arrivals early in August was 2nd Lieutenant Harry Maihafer, of Syracuse NY, one of many members of the West Point Class of 1949 who would be filling platoon leader slots and other combat roles in Korea. Now a retired colonel living in Nashville TN, Maihafer is author of *From the Hudson to the Yalu*, which chronicles the Korean War experience of his West Point class. (Of 574 graduates that year, 248 went to Korea. Twenty-six died there. Among the infantry officers, the mortality rate was much higher, one in five. Of 90 '49'ers assigned to infantry divisions, 17 were killed in action or died of wounds, and one died in a prisoner-of-war camp. The 24th Infantry Division had 21 members of the Class of 1949, of whom five were killed in action, one was captured, and one died a natural death.)

Maihafer, an armor officer, initially was assigned to the 24th Infantry Division's 78th Tank Battalion. Upon disembarking at Pusan, he and others traveled by train to the town of Miryang, camp-site of the division's replacement company, and then by truck forward to Yongsan.

The young lieutenant came under fire for the first time his first morning in Yongsan, which, as he wrote in *From the Hudson to the Yalu*, came as something of a shock "because this had never happened before ...." It was what combat soldiers call "seeing the elephant."

The shelling caused several casualties among American personnel, including a young corporal who on the truck ride had regaled Maihafer with war stories. Now he had a piece of shrapnel in the leg, which gave the newly arrived 2nd lieutenant a look at the fear and shock that can overtake a wounded man.

The 78th Tank Battalion had been shattered in previous combat and for the moment, the outfit was not going to be rebuilt. Thus the tank officer Maihafer would become an infantry officer instead. He was assigned to the 21st Regiment where he would serve until, as a captain several months later, he would become aide to the 24th Division commanding general.

On the first of August, this remained the crucial question: Could the Americans and South Koreans hold the perimeter against the only tactic left to the North Koreans, frontal assault?

The line was thin. Some companies stretched across 4,000 yards of frontage. The 24th Division was exhausted, and some elements of the others, American and South Korean, were of questionable fighting ability.

Walker's tactic, which he employed masterfully, was to plug his best units, his "fire brigade," into the line when and where they were needed the most. The outcome often was precariously in doubt, but the defense held.

The first major test came in the 24th Division sector in the battle of the Naktong Bulge, an area so-called because of the way the river sweeps to the west opposite the town of Yongsan.

The unit farthest forward at the bulge was the 3rd Battalion, 34th Infantry, under the command of Lieutenant Colonel Gines Perez, newly arrived from the United States. He deployed his three rifle companies, I, L and K, from north to south in that order, with gaps of two to three miles between each, which the troops tried to compensate for with trip wires, flares and booby traps. Illustrating the sparseness of the defensive line best was the fact the battalion's sector of 15,000 yards was 50 percent longer than infantry doctrine at the time envisioned a full-strength division holding.

North of the 34th Infantry's sector was the 21st Regiment, while the 19th Infantry, just arrived from its action in the Masan area, was in a reserve position.

Starting on the night of 5 August, the entire North Korean 4th Division poured through the thin defenses and established a bridgehead east of the Naktong. This created a dangerous salient and threatened the town of Yongsan itself.

The North Koreans, pushing equipment on rafts, waded across initially but reinforcements later made use of underwater bridges built with sandbags and rocks so that troops could walk to the opposite bank.

The first night of the battle, initial contact was made by a patrol from L Company, which the company commander, Captain Douglas Syverson, sent across the river as a listening post. With Pfc. Korgie were Corporal Ed Metowski, Frank Pollock, Eugene Singleton and Alvin Ginn, among others.

Noises to the front led the men to open fire, which brought enemy soldiers down on them from all sides. Korgie ran for his life to reach his platoon command post. From there, he and another soldier emptied their M-1s at about 15 North Koreans coming up the hill toward them. Korgie took to running parallel to a group of enemy troops, who evidently thought he was one of them, until, by dint of luck and extraordinary effort, Korgie eluded the North Koreans and ended the harrowing experience.

The main enemy thrust, which penetrated the gap between I and L companies, bypassed the 3rd Battalion forward hilltop positions and drove southeast through a draw toward the 4.2 mortar emplacements, which they overran, and onto the battalion command post.

A second crossing was attempted farther north in the 21st Regiment sector, but the enemy, after encountering a mine field and taken under artillery fire, was routed by the Gimlets' machine gunners and fled west in disarray.

Perez and headquarters personnel, alerted to the approach of the North Koreans, made it back three miles to the 1st Battalion command post of Lieutenant Colonel Harold Ayres to give him the news.

At 0520, the regimental commander, Colonel Charles Beauchamp, informed General Church of the breakthrough: "Enemy are across river in force in center of my sector. It's pretty dark and situation is obscure. I am committing my reserve at daylight to clear up the situation."

B Battery of the 13th Field Artillery Battalion lay in the path of the advancing enemy and at 0830 began to take small arms fire. The artillerymen withdrew with one howitzer and several vehicles, but had to abandon four field pieces and nine vehicles. Casualties in the encounter were two killed, six wounded and six missing.

Colonel Ayers sent C Company forward by truck and ordered A, B and the weapons companies to follow on foot under the leadership of the battalion executive officer.

Ayers himself moved out ahead of his troops to the area of the abandoned 3rd Battalion command post and came under fire from the high ground there. When C Company, under the command of Captain Clyde Akridge, arrived, the colonel ordered an attack on the hill. Akridge was wounded three times in the early going and had to be evacuated. That put Lieutenant Charles Payne in command of the company and the fight continued.

American mortarmen poured fire on the hill, which the enemy held in strength, but the mortar sergeant, standing to direct fire, was killed immediately. Other weapons personnel were hit as well. Ayers, who was nearby, made a dash across rice paddies to reach the positions of A and B companies. Two of his staff were hit on the way.

The enemy force on the hill was too strong for C company to dislodge, and the number of dead and wounded mounted. Payne and a platoon leader, Lieutenant McDonald Martin, who was wounded, made it to a nearby grist mill. Some members of the company were already there and other survivors of the savage fighting on the hill joined them. For the next several hours a desperate battle raged.

Heroism was conspicuous among the American troops. For instance, Robert Witzig, who had fired the last of the 60-mm mortar ammunition, helped drag wounded to a nearby culvert. Later in the grist mill, he volunteered to go for help. An explosion knocked him unconscious and put three wounds in his back. As he came to, he killed a North Korean with his .45-caliber pistol as the enemy soldier was reaching for a grenade. After Corporals John Nearwood and Harold Tucker dragged Witzig back to the mill, the wounded GI manned a Browning Automatic Rifle and continued fighting. Nearwood volunteered to seek help and was quickly killed.

"Hour after hour we held the North Koreans off. At first we let them get within eight or 10 feet of the mill. Then we'd fire a volley and the enemy would fall back," Payne said. (*The Korean War*, Knox)

The North Koreans took many casualties with each rush at the grist mill, but so did the Americans. The GIs stacked their own dead for protection against the onslaught.

Payne described another incident: "There was a young soldier who held his dying buddy in his arms. He wouldn't or couldn't put him down, just kept adding bandages to his wounds. I told him we needed his rifle, his buddy was dead, and he had to get into the fight."

Company A, 34th, under Captain A.F. Alfonso reached the grist mill, but unfortunately, a tank accompanying the force, thinking the building was held by the enemy, put a round through it and mortally wounded three C Company men.

Payne himself was knocked unconscious by the blast and GIs loaded him onto a truck with the dead. The vehicle came under fire and rammed into a ditch, which revived the lieutenant. Bleeding from the mouth and nose and nicked by many fragments, he was able to crawl away and then walk to safety. Payne was one of about 35 C Company survivors.

Company A drove on west to the river where it joined part of L Company still holding its position.

B Company meanwhile was engaged on a height called Cloverleaf Hill. That hill combined with Obang-ni Ridge formed a backbone about midway between the Naktong and Yongsan. The road to the town wound through a pass between the ridges, Cloverleaf on the north and Obang-ni a little lower, on the south.

Closer to the river, I Company and other elements withdrew toward the 21st Regiment's zone, but the regimental executive officer, Colonel Wadlington, arrived to lead them back toward their former position. The 24th Reconnaissance Company and I Company attacked North Koreans occupying a hill in that area, but were driven back with substantial casualties.

The 24th Division commander, General Church, alarmed at the number of North Koreans east of the Naktong, committed the 19th Infantry to the battle. The regiment, attacking on the northern flank of the 34th Infantry, trapped about 300 enemy troops about a mile from the river and killed most of them.

The first day of the battle had been a hard one with heavy American losses, but the 24th Division had counterattacked effectively and still held important ground.

Throughout the night, division artillery, consisting of 17 105-mm howitzers and 12 155-mm pieces, interdicted the crossing sites.

Nevertheless, the North Koreans continued to pour reinforcements across the river into the bulge at several crossing points. As happened before, enemy troops trying to cross in the 21st Infantry zone were driven back.

Attempts by the 19th Infantry and B Company of the 34th at counterattacking on 7 August met little success. The weariness of the troops, plus the scorching heat and shortage of rations, all contributed to lack of progress. At day's end, the North Koreans occupied the heights, Cloverleaf and Obang-ni ridges, overlooking the pass on either side.

A fresh regiment, the 9th Infantry of the 2nd Division under the command of Colonel John Hill, entered the fray the following day to reinforce the 24th Division.

The new troops took over the main effort against Cloverleaf and Obang-ni, relieving B Company of the 34th Infantry on the former. Near the river, the enemy occupied a hill overlooking A Company's position and was attempting to move more forces across the Naktong on 8 August when an A Company .50-caliber machine gun dispersed the North Koreans.

Later in the day, the North Koreans registered mortar and artillery fire on A Company's hilltop position and then stopped, leading Captain Alfonso to believe, accurately as it turned out, that the enemy planned a coordinated attack that night. So he received permission to withdraw his company and the remaining members of L company. The troops managed to reach 1st Battalion lines by daylight 9 August but not without taking some casualties along the way, notably by a platoon that stayed too close to the road.

Farther south near the river, K Company, 34th, came under attack by enemy troops who overran a forward observation post. The company, as ordered, held, and the reorganized L Company deployed behind its right flank.

While the 9th Infantry continued to fight at the strategic pass, the 2nd Battalion, 19th Regiment, succeeded in taking several hills north of Cloverleaf, including Ohan Hill. However, by 10 August the battalion was down to about 100 effective soldiers in its rifle companies.

General Church placed all troops in the bulge under the command of the 9th Infantry's Colonel Hill and ordered a coordinated attack for 11 August. The plan called for the 9th and 19th Regiments to drive southwest through the bulge, the 34th Infantry to protect the southern flank, and the 1st Battalion, 21st Infantry, to move to the southern part of Obang-ni Ridge.

The plan basically fell apart when the North Koreans themselves launched an attack that collided head-on with the American effort. The major part of the 4th North Korean Division was across the river and for the first time, enemy armor and heavy weapons were within the bulge.

The enemy stalemated the 9th and 19th regiments that day and drove the 21st Infantry from its assembly area before it could begin the ordered maneuver.

Moreover, North Koreans threatened the town of Yongsan itself as they penetrated deeper into the salient. The North Koreans wiped out a squad from K Company, 34th Infantry, and seized the bridge it was guarding over the Naktong. General Walker ordered a battalion of the 27th Infantry, 25th Division, into that area.

The North Koreans set up a roadblock east of Yongsan, which caused Hill to shift troops from Cloverleaf to that area. Additionally, a hastily assembled force from eight different units, clerks, cooks, reconnaissance troops, and military police, found itself pressed into front line duty to block further penetration by the North Koreans east of Yongsan. In charge of this outfit of about 135 men was Captain George B. Hafeman, commander of the 24th Division Headquarters Company. These troops manned passes at Singong-ni and Wonjon and throughout the day, 12 August, fought off North Korean attackers. But they held. On three occasions, armored vehicles delivered food, water and ammunition to the troops at Wonjon.

The effort at the two passes plus that at four other outposts manned by engineers succeeded in relieving the pressure on Yongsan. Early on the morning of 14 August, 3rd Battalion, 34th Infantry, learned of Colonel Hill's order for L and K Companies to withdraw from their isolated hilltop positions on the Naktong and move behind the 1st Battalion as regimental reserve. The two gallant companies had held their lonely positions for eight consecutive days after the first enemy attack bypassed them on 5 August.

Hill resumed his offensive on the rainy morning of 14 August against the enemy holding Cloverleaf and Obong-ni. In the three days since the earlier effort came to naught, neither side had made headway. The 13th Field Artillery Battalion, commanded by Lieutenant Colonel Charles W. Stratton, pounded the ridges with a 10-minute barrage and the infantry, elements of the 9th RCT and all three regiments of the 24th Division, jumped off.

The fighting was savage up and down the line and casualties were heavy. That night, North Koreans virtually surrounded the 1st Battalion, 21st Infantry, south of Obong-ni at the far end of the battle line. Colonel Brad Smith's battalion fought its way out of the encirclement and held its new position with the help of a counterattack by the 3rd Battalion, 34th Infantry, which included K and L companies, the two units that had just come down from their river positions.

First Battalion, 34th Infantry, whose three rifle companies were down to less combined strength than that of one company, nevertheless was fighting fiercely on Obong-ni Ridge. The first day of the attack, B Company nearly reached the crest before being thrown back. On the morning of 15 August, A Company's 2nd Platoon, led by Sergeant 1st Class Roy Collins, crossed a shallow saddle to attack enemy troops on the reverse slope of a knoll. The two forces exchanged grenades and rifle fire from as close

General Matthew Ridgway, Commander-in-Chief, United Nations Command, April 11, 1951. (U.S. Army Photo)

as 10 paces. A North Korean soldier trying to surrender could think of nothing else to do than to tackle Collins around the waist, according to the account of this battle by Roy Appleman in *South to the Naktong, North to the Yalu.*

Less than an hour after the platoon launched its attack with 35 men, 25 had been killed or wounded. One of the casualties was Pfc. Edward O. Cleaborn who stayed behind after the last 10 withdrew in order to get in one last shot. He was killed in the attempt. Three more of the nine wounded men the survivors carried out died before they reached the aid station.

Despite the bravery and determination of the troops, Task Force Hill could not dislodge the North Koreans. The colonel was using all the forces at his command and there were no reserves to bring up.

General Walker, who did not share General Church's accurate estimate that the Americans were fighting the entire North Korean 4th Division, decided he would have to put more troops into the field. Testily he told the 24th

Division commander, "I am going to give you the Marine brigade. I want this situation cleaned up, and quick."

It took two days of fighting, 17-18 August, to accomplish the objective of driving the North Koreans from the bulge. The line of battle had the Marine brigade, essentially the 5th Marines plus artillery, attacking Obong-ni Ridge and the 9th Infantry in front of Cloverleaf. On the flanks were the 24th Division units. First Battalion, 21st Infantry, was on the left, and on the extreme right, ready to retake Ohang Hill, was the 19th Infantry. The 24th Regiment, 25th Division, was just to the right of the 9th.

The Marines, whose regimental commander persuaded General Church, against the latter's better judgment, not to order a coordinated attack against both main ridges, discovered they could not take Obong-ni while its right was exposed. So late in the afternoon of 17 August, after 24th Division artillery raked the ridge lines with air-burst projectiles, Marines and Army attacked in concert and succeeded.

Fighting was heavy on the right as well. Troops of the 19th and 34th regiments had been in contact with the enemy in previous days. Elements of both had narrowly averted being surrounded. One officer, Captain Barszcz, commanding officer of G Company, 34th Infantry, particularly distinguished himself in the action.

Now the 24th Division troops drove southwest from the northern part of the bulge and captured high ground near the Naktong River. On the morning of 19 August, Marines and 34th Infantry troops linked up at the Naktong. The routed enemy fled across the river in disorder, the 4th Division utterly defeated by the 24th Infantry Division and attached units.

Army casualties in the battle of the Naktong Bulge were 71 killed, 286 wounded, and 563 missing. Most of the missing were later listed as dead.

The 2nd Division relieved the 24th Infantry Division along the Naktong, and then, after six weeks of non-stop infantry combat of the most desperate nature, the Taro Leaf division underwent reorganization.

On 25 August, the division strength was 10,600 and needed about 8,000 replacements plus major resupply of arms, equipment and vehicles to bring it up to wartime strength.

General Walker ordered the battered 34th Regiment and 63rd Field Artillery Battalion reduced to the status of paper units. Of the approximately 2,000 men who entered Korea with the 34th Regiment on 3 July, only 184 remained in late August, making the unit's casualty rate more than 85 percent. These included 98 killed, 569 wounded, 773 missing and 274 non-battle injuries. The huge number of missing men testifies to the kind of combat the regiment engaged in, suggesting that the North Koreans had overrun and cut off units, leaving many troops unaccounted for.

Remaining troops and equipment in the deactivated units were transferred to other 24th Division outfits. Men of the 1st Battalion, 34th Infantry, joined the 19th Infantry's new 3rd Battalion, and the 3rd Battalion of the 34th, was absorbed into the new 2nd Battalion, 21st Regiment. Personnel and hardware of the 63rd FA Battalion were distributed among the new C batteries of the 11th, 13th, and 52nd Artillery battalions.

To replace the paper units, General Walker transferred three units to the 24th Division. They were the 5th Regimental Combat Team, (which had come into the country earlier and was in the line near Masan,) as its third infantry regiment, the 6th Medium Tank Battalion and the 555th Field Artillery Battalion, the "Triple Nickel," which also had engaged in heavy fighting on the south end of the perimeter.

The 19th Regiment and the 11th FA Battalion took on the status of reserve units attached to the 2nd Division, the 21st Infantry went into Eighth Army reserve, and the rest of the division assembled about 12 miles southeast of Taegu.

Two of the 24th Division's new units, the 5th RCT and the 555th FA Battalion, shared the Taro Leafers' Pineapple Army lineage from Hawaii. Additionally, the infantry regiment and the artillerymen enjoyed a close bond with each other.

The 5th RCT included many men of Hawaiian descent and also some veterans of the famed 442nd Regimental Combat Team and the 100th Battalion Combat Team, highly decorated Nisei units from World War II.

The 5th RCT was commanded by Colonel Godwin L. Ordway, West Point Class of 1925 from Maryland, and the Triple Nickel was under the command of Lieutenant Colonel John H. Daly, a Texan who graduated from the Military Academy in 1936. The two units arrived in Korea together on 31 July and the next day were in the vicinity of Masan attached to the 25th Division.

Eighth Army had hurried the newly arrived troops to the southern anchor of the forming perimeter defense where enemy troops driving toward Masan were applying the greatest pressure.

A few days later, Task Force Kean under the 25th Division commander came into existence to launch an attack westward along the Masan-Chinju corridor.

This combined Army-Marine unit included the 5th RCT and the 555th FA Battalion. During the week of 7-14 August, the American force engaged in bitter fighting in the hills and passes west of Masan after the offensive collided head-on with one launched at the same time by the North Koreans.

The 5th RCT's 1st Battalion commander, Lieutenant Colonel John P. Jones, suffered serious wounds early in the fighting, and temporary command of the infantry battalion passed to the artillery officer, Colonel Daly, who had been wounded himself.

Later, the battalion command went to

Outpost Spring 1951, (L to R) Sgt. Tom Kilfoyle, Sgt. Dan Garcia, Cpl Charles B. Fender.

Lieutenant Colonel T.B. Roelofs. His C Company particularly absorbed horrendous punishment. At one point, only 23 survivors from an original company force of 180 could be found.

The regiment's 2nd Battalion, commanded by Lieutenant Colonel John Throckmorton, found itself beyond a pass and well forward of the rest of the outfit, the result of division orders to hold the main body in place.

During a battle in the pass that came to be known as Bloody Gulch, enemy troops virtually surrounded the 555th FA Battalion and decimated the unit. First, North Korean armor pounded the artillery positions and then the infantry closed in. Three of the 555th's 105-mm howitzers continued firing for several hours before the North Korean troops overran the battalion.

The battle on 12 August cost the Triple Nickel all eight of its 105-mm howitzers in two batteries. The battalion's casualties were estimated at 75 to 100 killed and 80 wounded On the day after the fighting, only 20 percent of the unit were present for duty. Five weeks later, troops of the 25th Division found 55 bodies of 555th artillerymen in a house at Taejong-ni.

So the new units did not arrive in the northern sector of the defensive perimeter later in the month as combat virgins. One of the 5th RCT men had distinguished himself in battle conspicuously while the regiment was still at the south end of the front lines. Company C held a position near Sobuk San Mountain late the night of 25 August when about 100 North Koreans tried to break through the perimeter. Master Sergeant Melvin O. Handrich, of Manawa, WI, went forward under fire to direct mortar and artillery fire. The following morning, he did the same when another group of North Koreans attacked. During the close-quarter engagement, Sergeant Handrich rallied elements of his company to continue the fight. Despite serious wounds, the soldier refused evacuation and continued to direct his company's fire from a forward position. Finally, the enemy overran his position and mortally wounded the sergeant. Near his body lay more than 70 dead North Korean soldiers. Sergeant Handrich's country awarded him the Medal of Honor.

By the time the 5th RCT was assigned to the 24th Division, the 2nd Battalion's Colonel Throckmorton had replaced Colonel Ordway as regimental commander.

It was not long before elements of the 24th Division were back in the front lines fulfilling Walker's "fire brigade" role, the desperation tactic that kept the buckling Pusan Perimeter from giving way entirely.

For the month of August, total 24th Division casualties were 1,941, the most of any of the Eighth Army's four divisions in the field. As the month waned, there was trouble everywhere, from the ROK positions in the east, to the mountains north of Taegu, to the Naktong bulge area, to the southern flank held by the 25th Division.

First General Walker ordered the 21st Infantry into position north of Taegu, but before the regiment could reach its destination, the general directed Colonel Richard Stephens to turn the Gimlets around and rush to Kyongju

in the far eastern sector. There the front held by the ROK divisions was on the verge of collapse under the onslaught of North Koreans who threatened to sever the Taegu-Pohang-dong link.

The 21st Regiment was to be part of a new ROK-American task force formed under the command of Major General John B. Coulter to avert disaster at the eastern anchor of the line.

The regiment first took up position north of the town of Angang-ni, near the point of enemy penetration. But ROK losses overnight prevented the American attack, and then the emphasis shifted to Pohang-dong on the coast where the North Koreans had driven to a point southwest of the town.

B Company, 21st Infantry, supported by tanks, counterattacked successfully in that zone on 28 August, advancing a mile and a half from the southern edge of Pohang-dong. The next day, the action was repeated, and troops of the 21st Infantry took over a 1,000-yard sector northwest of the coastal town.

Despite aerial and naval support and hard fighting by American and ROK troops, the lines continued to sag and some South Korean units were near collapse.

ROK forces lost a key height, Hill 99, and K Company, 21st Infantry, got the assignment to retake it on 2 September. But resistance by the deeply entrenched enemy was too great. Hurling grenades down onto the American GIs

Start of attack on Oct 14, 1951. (Courtesy of H.W. Rhoades)

"I" Co 21st Christmas 1950. Front Row L to R: Pfc. Gilbertson; Lt. Lynch, CO; Lt. Maihafer, Plt. Ldr. Standing in Doorway: is Pfc Gary Watercamp. and to his immediate right is Keith Hagan (Courtesy of Keith Hagen)

climbing toward the crest, the North Koreans inflicted heavy casualties. By mid-afternoon, K Company could account for no more than 35 men. Two tanks of the 6th Tank Battalion also were lost in the attack. One hit a land mine and the other threw a track.

Coulter withdrew the 21st Infantry from Pohang-dong and positioned the regiment near Kyongju to the southwest. The newly formed 2nd Battalion under the command of Lieutenant Colonel Gines Perez, formerly of the deactivated 34th Infantry, took up a horseshoe-shaped defensive position on the east side of Angang-ni, while the rest of the regiment deployed north of Kyongju.

On the night of 3 September, the ROK front in the Angang-ni area disintegrated. Enemy troops entered the town and the fighting was so confused and the forces so intermingled that 2nd Battalion forces had to hold their fire for fear of hitting friendly troops. "We couldn't tell friend from foe," Perez said.

The next day proved to be one of extraordinary action by the 2nd Battalion, particularly G Company. As day broke on 4 September, the company found itself alone and nearly surrounded. The ROK troops were gone. So the company withdrew eastward to the bridge over the Hyonsan-gang River.

The remainder of the battalion, on orders form Colonel Stephens, pulled back to join the rest of the regiment north of Kyongju. That movement required Perez' men to fight their way through an enemy roadblock east of the river. When they discovered G Company missing, Stephens ordered the battalion to return. That meant the troops had to shoot their way back to the bridge, pick up G Company and then fight through the enemy positions once again – the third time that day – before reaching the regimental position. Tanks led the column, firing straight down the road and into the hills on either side. Three Patton tanks were lost on the way when enemy fire knocked the tracks off.

The same day, General Walker, alarmed at the North Korean gains in the eastern section of the perimeter, ordered the remainder of the 24th Division to Kyongju. Only the day before, the division had received orders to leave its reserve position near Taegu and go back to the Naktong bulge area to relieve the Marines. The troops bivouacked for the night in a typhoon-spawned downpour. The new order came before the Taro Leafers could move into position at the bulge.

The assistant division commander, Brigadier General Garrison Davidson, arrived at Kyongju on 4 September, and the 19th Regiment and other 24th Division troops traveled through the day over muddy roads to reach the town before midnight. By 0700 6 September, the division was in place. Davidson was a 1927 West Point graduate from New York.

Coulter had sent the 21st Infantry into a huge gap between two ROK divisions northwest of Kyongju earlier and now ordered the regiment to attack in that direction.

On 6 September, 24th Division Commander Church took over the task force from General Coulter, who went back to Taegu. One of General Church's first decisions was to recall the 21st Infantry from its mountain attack and redeploy the regiment near Kyongju. Then he moved his command post four miles south into open country.

Early on the morning of 8 September, a North Korean platoon-sized patrol had sliced in behind the 3rd Battalion of the 21st Infantry, trying to get at a supporting tank unit. They were driven off, but on their way north, they blundered into a position held by I Company of the 21st. A sharp fight ensued, but the enemy was driven off by a counterattack led by Lieutenant Tom Hardaway, West Point Class of 1949. The enemy suffered severe casualties, many as a result of grenades hurled by young Hardaway, who was killed during the action and was awarded a posthumous Silver Star.

A week-long battle between ROK troops and North Koreans opened up in the hills bordering the valley between Kyongju and Angang-ni. The 3rd Battalion, 19th Infantry, joined the fighting early on 9 September.

North Korean forces drove K Company from Hill 300, about midway between the two towns, and then held on against counterattacks. The 13th Field Artillery Battalion lent fire support to a ROK regiment which held Hill 285 farther north. Heavy downpours soaked the battlefield during these engagements while an overcast sky prevented air support.

A ROK regiment captured Hill 300 on 11 September, and the Chicks' 3rd Battalion re-

8th Army Reserve area 3rd Platoon, M Company, 19th Infantry, Chunchon, Korea. September 1951. (Courtesy of Joseph S. Barto)

Cleaning mess gear, M Company, 19th Infantry, 75 MM Recoiless Rifle Platoon. September 1951, Chunchon. (Courtesy of Joseph S. Barto)

Chunchon, Korea Sept 1951. Co M 19th Infantry 24th Infantry Division. Just before church services. George Cochran (L), One-Eyed Rielly (R).

Third Platoon B Company 19th Infantry, Korea, July 1951.

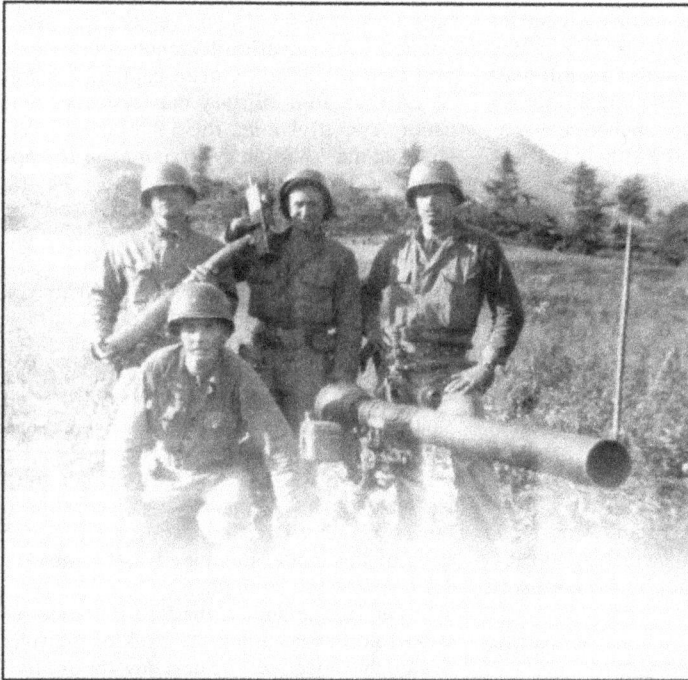

"M" Company, 19th Infantry Regiment, 24th Infantry Division 75mm Recoiless Rifle Platoon. Chunchon, Korea. Sept. 1951. Back row L to R: Joseph Barto, Medlock, and Joe Mangrum. Front row L to R: George Cochran. (Courtesy of Joseph Barto)

"M" Company, 19th Infantry Regiment, 24th Infantry Division 75mm Recoiless Rifle Platoon MLR. Kumsong, Korea. Oct. 1951. Joseph Barto (standing), Reilly (left) and Gilisspe (right). (Courtesy of Joseph Barto)

Some of the 5th RCT crossing the Han River in 1951. (Courtesy of Richard Clayton)

Ed Jackson taken just before he was captured. (Courtesy of Ed Jackson)

"I" Co 21st. April 1951. (L to R) Cpl. Robert Abher 57 gunner; Sgt. Keith Hagen, radio; Capt. Ruff Lynch wounded on this hill around April 25, 1951: Lt. Harris. (Courtesy of Keith Hagen)

Sept. 1951, Korea. I and R Section, Hq. Co. 3rd Bn., 19th Inf. Regiment. Front row L to R: Gene Voglesong, Bob Beam, and Richard Woodland. Middle: Oscar Welton. Back row L to R: John Herter, Bud Botomiller, Leo Piccinin, Bill Newby, Joe Goss, and Delmar Johnson. (Courtesy of Richard Woodland)

lieved the South Koreans. The enemy body count was 257, plus much abandoned equipment and weapons. The fighting for the hill cost the American battalion 37 killed, including eight lieutenants.

A large force of North Koreans also threatened Yonil Airfield from the southwest. The field, near the coast south of Pohang-dong, was not being used except for emergency landing and refueling, but the Air Force was still evacuating bombs, fuel and equipment.

Church assigned the assistant division commander, General Davidson, to form a task force and go to the assistance of the ROK units defending the air strip. The force comprised the 19th Infantry, less the 3rd Battalion, the 13th FA Battalion, Battery C of the 15th FA Battalion, the 3rd Battalion of the 9th Infantry, the 3rd Engineer Combat Battalion, the 9th Infantry Regimental Tank Company and other assorted units.

The task force spent 10 September making the circuitous trip to its destination and the following day launched the attack. The 1st Battalion, 19th Regiment, took the first hill mass without opposition, but the 2nd Battalion, passing through, encountered entrenched enemy on the next hill to the west and was held in check for the rest of the day.

On 12 September, after Australian planes dropped napalm, the 2nd Battalion resumed the attack and took the height, Hill 482, about noon, thus ending the enemy threat to Yonil Airfield.

The perimeter battle in the east at last was coming under control. The ROK forces took over the sector and on 15 Sept. the 24th Division moved to Kyongsan, southeast of Taegu, to regroup.

BREAKOUT

In mid-September, the Eighth Army stood poised to break out of the perimeter and in effect retrace the 24th Division's path northwest back toward Seoul. The movement was made possible by the invasion at Inchon, a west-coast port near the South Korean capital. General MacArthur, in a military masterstroke, sent ashore two divisions, the 1st Marine Division and the 7th Infantry Division, on 15 September. The landing succeeded in relieving enemy pressure at Pusan and allowed the American-ROK troops to fight their way out of the pocket.

The 5th Regimental Combat Team played a key role toward that end with the capture of the town of Waegwan on the east bank of the Naktong northwest of Taegu in a five-day battle, 16-20 September. In the process, the unit shattered the North Korean 3rd Division and the enemy flank in that sector.

The 5th RCT, the 24th Division's third regiment that had been temporarily attached to the 1st Cavalry Division during the first two days of the battle, numbered 2,455 men, or 1,194 below full strength.

On 16 September, the 2nd Battalion attacked northward along the bank of the river toward the objective. The next day, the 3rd Battalion joined the battle and the 1st Battalion deployed for action as well. The terrain feature of greatest tactical importance in the area was Hill 238 southeast of Waegwan, against which the 5th RCT launched a full regimental attack on 19 September. The first day, the regiment gained much of the height and the battle continued the next morning against the well-bunkered enemy. The 3rd Battalion took control of the hill, with heavy losses to the defenders while the 1st and 2nd Battalions pushed westward toward Waegwan, which leading elements entered by mid-afternoon.

By this time, the NK 3rd Division had begun a panicked retreat across the river north of the town, abandoning many of its weapons to the advancing American troops.

The same day, 20 September, the 5th RCT under command of Colonel John Throckmorton captured its final objectives east of the Naktong, including Hill 303 by the 2nd Battalion north of the town. The regiment's losses on the last day of the battle were 18 killed, 111 wounded and three missing. By the end of the day, the 1st and 2nd battalions were west of the river.

The 5th RCT's clearing of the strategic ground opened up a crossing for the 21st and 19th regiments west of Taegu, scheduled for 18 September. That was the day the 5th RCT and the 6th Tank Battalion returned to 24th Division control.

The 21st Infantry's maneuver hit a snag when the unit discovered that the I Corps engineers had not bridged the Kumho River, a tributary of the Naktong the troops would have to cross first.

The 3rd Engineer Battalion thus had to reinforce an underwater bridge previously used by the 5th RCT and also to fashion makeshift ferries to float the vehicles to the opposite bank. The engineers engaged in constant sandbagging to keep the bridge usable, resulting in a traffic backup of five miles east of the Kumho.

General Church now realized his evening crossing of the Naktong could not be accomplished, so his revised goal became to clear the river before daylight of 19 September. Other-

June 1951 C Company 19th Regt. 24th Division. Michael A. Antosh with a captured chrome plated 1927 Thompson sub-machine-gun.

wise, the enemy might catch the troops in a vulnerable position.

It was 0530 when the first wave of boats entered the Naktong from the east bank with 1st Battalion, 21st Infantry, troops. They landed in a firestorm of enemy machine guns slashing into both flanks. Artillery and mortar shells fell on both banks, some from Hill 174, the height that dominated the west bank near the landing site.

Seventeen-year-old BAR-man William E. Anderson of Wilderville, OR, remembered that C Company spent the night before in an orchard under tank or anti-tank fire, waiting for the plywood boats that didn't arrive until after daylight. The men carried the boats about 1/4 mile across a sandy beach before pushing off for the far shore. There were no casualties in Anderson's boat, but boats in the next wave were hit hard with machine gun bullets, mortars, and small arms fire. Many died crossing the sandy beach trying to reach the river.

Anderson's squad leader, Sergeant Robert Niarhos, directed his squad toward a machine gun firing from a low hill to the left front. He probably thought he had lost another new man when he saw Anderson fall headfirst in a smelly rice paddy. But Anderson rose and continued on.

After capturing the hill, the squad started moving over the top. ROK (Republic of Korea) soldier Song Chang-Bum, who was attached to the company as a rifleman, stepped in front of Anderson and took a bullet into his shoulder. Anderson tried to find him during a visit in 1996 to express his gratitude, but Mr. Song had died six months previously.

When C Company ran out of ammunition later in the day, Interpreter-Rifleman Lee Sang Yun volunteered to replenish the supply. He went back to the river and rowed across the river still under fire alone in the engineer's boat. He collected machine gun ammunition and rowed back across. Mr. Lee was a civilian who never served in the ROK Army. Anderson found him after 46 years by placing an ad with photograph in a Seoul newspaper, and the two renewed a close wartime relationship.

The 1st Battalion, continuing to cross under fire, suffered 120 casualties, but once on the west bank, the troops reorganized and captured Hill 174.

The 3rd Battalion made the trip across the river that afternoon. The 2nd Battalion followed during the night and the next morning. Once on the far bank, the Gimlets pushed northward to or beyond Waegwan.

The crossing site for the 19th Infantry and the 24th Reconnaissance Company was two miles south. The 2nd Battalion made the trip on the afternoon and evening of 19 September under fire, suffering 50 casualties even before leaving the east bank. Resistance lightened on the west side, however.

The reconnaissance company crossed that night and then passed through to the west. By 20 September the regiment had completed the crossing and was holding high ground on the far side.

Getting the two infantry regiments across the Naktong had been a hazardous operation for the 3rd Engineer Battalion, which lost 10 men killed and 37 wounded. The attached Koreans also suffered losses.

By 20 September, all three infantry regiments of the 24th Division were firmly implanted on the west bank of the Naktong, and over the next two days, the division's artillery, armor, transport and service units would make the crossing over hastily built bridging. Corporal Joseph J. Drozd, Company B 21st Infantry, remembers riding the fourth of five Company A, 6th Battalion tanks as combat patrols began probing to the north.

Roy Appleman, in *South to the Naktong, North to the Yalu*, wrote of the action that with the exception of delays in bridging the Kumho, the 24th Division's five-day operation "left little to be desired." The division on 22 September was positioned on the west bank of the river ready to follow through on its progress.

From that appraisal, it seems clear that the rigors of seven weeks of bitter ground combat had hardened the erstwhile garrison troops into an outfit ready to take the fight to the enemy. The route would be up the main Taegu-Kumchon-Taejon-Seoul Highway. Before the push began, Colonel Richard Stephens, the regimental commander, stood on a truck and delivered a pep talk to the troops, which was recorded in Harry Maihafer's book, *From the Hudson to the Yalu*:

"We're breaking out of the Naktong Perimeter, and the 21st is going to spearhead it. I want you to be aggressive, bold, and to move fast. If anyone delays you, move around them. We have the numbers now to overflow 'em, so don't worry about leaving any enemy bypassed; there'll be lots of people behind you to mop up."

Stephen's talk had its effect. Pfc. Leonard Korgie told of a patrol moving toward Waegwan led by Lieutenant Williamson, former first sergeant of L Company, 34th Regiment, who had won a battlefield commission. "Lieutenant Williamson decided to march down

Korea - August, 1951 - Michael A. Antosh, C Company, 19th Regt., 24th Inf. Division with captured Russian PP SH - 44 Submachine gun.

85

the hill. Down we went – yelling, swearing, firing like hell. Some North Koreans jumped from their holes and immediately went down; others raised their hands in surrender, but stupidly held onto potato-masher grenades. We didn't hesitate – tore their heads off." (*An Oral History*, Knox)

The Americans were on a roll after the perimeter breakout, but along the way were grim reminders of the earlier retreat. The 21st Infantry's Korgie again: "One day we passed the hill I'd been chased off of in July when the North Koreans had us on the run. Graves Registration teams were bringing the bodies down…There were a lot more of them than I realized."

Sergeant Dews, E Company, 21st Regiment, had his own impression of the drive: "The wary and cautious 24th Division went more slowly than the recently arrived units. It had sold this real estate with the lives of its own brave men and did not intend to let the enemy get behind it again."

The first major objective west of the Naktong was the city of Kumchon. As the 24th Division launched that thrust, the 1st Battalion, 19th Infantry, captured the town of Songju. On 21 September, General Church started the attack along the main highway, his regiments in echelon with the 21st Infantry in the lead.

In front of Kumchon, the enemy fought a stubborn rear-guard action that found opposing tanks slugging it out with each other. D Company, 6th Medium Tank Battalion, lost four Patton M46 tanks. Later, when the battle had been fully joined, action cost the battalion six more tanks. The 5th RCT passed through the 21st Regiment to take the lead in the infantry fighting for Hill 140, which cost the 5th Regiment about 100 casualties. Meanwhile, the 19th Infantry had to fight off bypassed enemy forces along the road back toward Waegwan.

After the battle, the 24th Division advanced with little trouble for another three days before the troops ran into another pocket of resistance 10 miles east of Taejon. The North Koreans had hoped the bulk of its force could escape via this route. The 1st Battalion, 19th Infantry, now on the division point, attacked the force holding the heights at the town of Okchon.

On 27 September, the 24th Division approached Taejon, the scene of the fierce battle on 20-21 July when the outnumbered and outgunned Taro Leafers were driven from the provisional capital. One tank gunner may have expressed the sentiment of the division with this little tune: "The last time I saw Taejon, it was not bright or gay; today I'm going to Taejon and blow the place away."

Scouts of the 2nd Battalion, 19th Infantry, and engineers of C Company, 3rd Engineer Battalion, reached the edge of the city late in the afternoon and an hour later, the 19th Regiment secured Taejon. It was fitting that these units were the first into Taejon, because the Chicks and the engineers had been among the last to leave the burning city in July.

Many enemy tanks were destroyed in the fighting, and this time, it was the North Koreans who were being taken prisoner. Troops of the 24th Division captured enemy equipment and even liberated four U.S. howitzers that had been lost the first time through.

The recapture of Taejon also revealed the enormity of North Korean atrocities, the mass execution of civilians and American GIs. Miraculously, two U.S. soldiers, presumably 24th Division men, had survived the massacre by feigning death. The dirt covering them was shallow enough that they could get air.

On 29 September, General Church moved his command post to Taejon, from where he could direct the division mission of protecting the lines of communication back to the Naktong River. The 24th Division stretched for about 100 miles, from the Kum River held by the 19th Infantry back to the Waegwan bridges, covered by the 24th Reconnaissance Company. The 5th RCT was in the Kumchon area while the 21st Infantry was situated between Taejon and Yongdong.

CROSSING THE PARALLEL

The next phase of the Korean War came early in October when the Eighth Army gathered to launch a major offensive across the 38th Parallel into North Korea on the west side of the peninsula. The spearhead was to be the 1st Cavalry Division, with the 24th Division and a South Korean unit protecting the flanks.

Significant action occurred between 9-14 October in the Kumchon area north of Kaesong, the town captured by the North Korean invaders the first day of the war in June.

West of Kaesong was the town of Paekchon where advancing 1st Cavalry Division troops bypassed North Korean units.

The enemy troops, though clearly on the run, proved they could still be dangerous.

On 13 October, a company-size enemy force ambushed a battery of the 77th Field Artillery of the 1st Cavalry Division. A soldier bearing the news of the ambush managed to run back to Paekchon where the command post of the 21st Infantry's 3rd Battalion was located.

The battalion commander, Lieutenant Colonel John McConnell, dispatched I Company, led by Captain Floyd Gibson, to relieve the beleaguered unit. Company I, in a picture-book use of fire and maneuver, which might have won praise from the Fort Benning Infantry School, employed mortar and small-arms fire to disperse the enemy, rescued the artillerymen and captured 36 North Koreans in the process.

Two days later, in an effort to speed the advance toward the North Korean capital of Pyongyang, I Corps ordered the 24th Division to attack on the corps' left toward the town of Sariwon and then proceed northward to the capital.

The 21st Regiment moved out to the west toward Haeju against significant resistance. The tank-infantry force reached Haeju on 17 October and secured the town after defeating a force of about 300 North Koreans.

C Company's William Anderson remembers the day the company halted its advance in a broad valley to observe an aerial dogfight. A NK Mig was machine-gunning a P-51. There were several passes, but the P-51 could not maintain the pace. The Mig made a really wide turn and came in behind the P-51. The latter started a long dive towards mountains across the valley and appeared to be diving straight into a mountain. At the last second, he pulled up sharply, but the Mig on his tail bored right into the mountain, producing a huge fireball.

Farther east, the 19th Infantry was trailing the 5th Cavalry in approaching Sariwon, and with a British brigade also on the road, a traffic jam delayed the whole process.

The Corps commander, General Frank Milburn, created even more tension by establishing competition between the two divisions, the 24th and the 1st Cavalry. Whichever reached Sariwon first would win the privilege of leading the corps attack into Pyongyang. The Taro Leafers were at a disadvantage due to a more circuitous route over bad roads.

The British 27th Brigade actually reached

A scene of devastation after artillery bombardment. Just below the 38th Parallel. (Courtesy of Glenn White)

the town first. Along the way, one officer driving southward toward the edge of Sariwon was amazed to see two columns of Koreans coming toward him. Actually, they were North Koreans being forced northward by the 19th Infantry toward a city they thought their countrymen still occupied. The U.N. forces thought the Orientals were South Koreans coming up with the 24th Division, and the enemy soldiers thought the white Britishers were Russians. It was very confusing.

Since 1st Cavalry Division soldiers had been with the British unit, the American division won the honor of leading the way into Pyongyang starting the next day. But the 24th Division entered the capital as well.

The Eighth Army continued to roll rapidly west and north, the 24th Division on the left near the Yellow Sea coast. Leading the drive was the Australian brigade, which encountered heavy resistance at the town of Chongju toward the end of October.

His troops exhausted, the Australian commander asked for relief by the 24th Division, and General Church immediately ordered the 21st Regiment to pass through and lead the surge.

On the evening of 30 October, the 2nd Battalion under the command of Lieutenant Colonel Gines Perez moved out. Not long after midnight near the village of Kwaksan, the column ran into a North Korean ambush of armor and infantry. With Perez and regimental commander Stephens directing the action from their radio Jeeps, the battle raged under the moonlight. Enemy shells failed to penetrate American armor, but the same could not be said on the other side. It was a far different story than in the beginning, when North Korean tanks were impervious to the bazookas in the field at the time and the light U.S. armor was hard-pressed to compete.

By daylight, the North Koreans withdrew, leaving 50 dead, five disabled tanks and other heavy weapons. Colonel Perez was awarded the Distinguished Service Cross for this and other action.

Resistance lightened after that engagement, permitting the Gimlets to advance with impressive speed, though troops were periodically slowed, sometimes having to reduce bypassed enemy pockets. Sergeant Warren Avery, G Company of the 21st Infantry, recalls a fierce fight at an abandoned gold mine the North Koreans were using as a stronghold.

"Around dusk they hit us ... I dueled all night with a North Korean. He shot green tracers at me; I shot red tracers at him. ... About 2 in the morning I finally hit him. The sluiceways caught fire and the North Koreans were silhouetted in front of the flames. It became a shooting gallery," Avery said. (*An Oral History* - Knox.)

By noon, 1 November, the 1st Battalion was at the outskirts of Chonggo-dong, 18 miles from the Yalu River and the border with Manchuria.

That afternoon, seven North Korean tanks and 500 infantrymen attacked the 1st Battalion. Taking the fight to the enemy was Company A of the 6th Medium Tank Battalion, commanded by Captain Jack G. Moss, which met the enemy head-on in a brief but fierce tank battle that destroyed the North Korean armored force against only slight damage to two American tanks. The attacking infantry force retreated after suffering about 100 casualties.

While the 21st Infantry drove northwest along the coast, the 19th Regiment to its right advanced due north from Chongju to Kusong. The division's third regiment, the 5th RCT, following a British brigade, was farther to the right still.

The 5th RCT had been the first 24th Division unit to cross the Chongchon River and by 28 October was in full march toward the town of Taechon. Short of that objective, the regiment engaged and destroyed a North Korean mechanized force and captured 89 troops, including two Chinese who turned out to be stragglers and not part of the organized enemy unit.

Between Taechon and Kusong, Colonel Throckmorton's 5th RCT encountered a large enemy concentration of 5,000 to 6,000 men supported by tanks and other heavy weaponry. In hard fighting, the regiment managed to drive through the enemy, capture Kusong on 31 October and continue the attack the next day to secure a key road junction north of the town. The enemy lost 300 to 400 troops in the engagement plus many vehicles and weapons.

To this point, it appeared U.N. forces on the spearhead of the drive toward the Yalu River were able to dispatch in relatively short order whatever North Korean units were opposing them.

By midday on 1 November, leading elements of the 5th RCT were 10 miles north of Kusong, while on the same day, as stated above, the 21st Infantry to the west had just defeated the enemy in a tank battle at Chonggo-dong. Then everything changed, including the lives of the soldiers in the field, the direction of the Korean War and indeed, history itself.

Airplanes flying over the front dropped messages to both regiments calling a halt to their advance and, at least in the case of the 21st Infantry, ordering consolidation of positions and preparations for defense in depth.

For a force that was winning every encounter decisively, the order was "like a bolt out of the blue," as some in the 1st Battalion, 21st Infantry, put it.

That battalion, commanded by Lieutenant Colonel Charles B. Smith, was the leading element of the regiment, and thus won the distinction of the deepest Eighth Army penetration toward the Manchurian border in the Korean War. The battalion also fought the northernmost Eighth Army action of the war at Chonggo-dong that day. What a strange coincidence that the battle would involve Colonel Smith's troops, some of whom had been with him as part of Task Force Smith at Osan on 5 July when they were the first American ground unit to engage the North Koreans.

A C Company 21st patrol actually penetrated to the Yalu River. William Anderson, promoted to be a BAR-man corporal, has a vivid recollection of urinating in the Yalu.

As the troops and their commanders would soon learn, it was the full-scale commitment of Chinese combat troops to the Korean War that so radically altered their mission.

Actually, the U.N. ground forces had two new enemies: the Chinese and cold weather. In North Korea, winter comes early. By 1 November the sting already was being felt. As it developed, the American Army and Marine Corps were ill-clothed for combat over the frozen and snow-covered landscape that lay ahead. And as fate would have it, the winter of 1950-51 was uncommonly severe in Korea and elsewhere.

As a portent of things to come, Pfc. Robert Harper, Headquarters Company, 3rd Battalion, 19th Infantry, related that as early as 28-29 October, enemy radio traffic carried voices that sounded like Chinese. A company-strength patrol went forward to investigate, and Harper was part of a wire team assigned to lay lines back to headquarters. "It was Halloween and colder than a witch. No one had been issued winter gear yet. .... We waited and we froze. It was very dark," Harper said. The patrol returned to report a large enemy force in front of the American positions. "We went up faster than we'd gone down and entered our lines about daylight. It had been a long, cold night. But it hadn't been as long, nor as cold, as the nights to come." (*An Oral History* - Knox.)

The entry of the Chinese into the war meant that U.N. forces would have to fight an army of almost unlimited manpower in the enemy's own part of the world. The human waves that fell upon the Americans and others from this point on were the result. Though the Chinese suffered grievous personnel losses, the mass attacks still came.

The first orders called for an I Corps withdrawal south of the Chongchon River, but Eighth Army Commanding General Walton Walker wanted to maintain a bridgehead north of the river to hedge against the prospect of resuming the offensive. Drawing the bridgehead assignment were the 27th British Brigade on the left and the 19th Regiment on the right in the area of Anju.

The units were in place on 3 November, and the following day an enemy force crossed the Kuryong River, a Chongchon tributary flowing from the north, and managed to get to the rear of the 1st Battalion, 19th Infantry. They captured the battalion radio, but the Chicks, after destroying equipment, were able to withdraw to the east to friendly positions with little loss.

The regiment's 3rd Battalion tried to drive through and link up with the 1st Battalion. However the enemy forces between them were too strong, so division commander Church ordered the 21st Regiment to recross the Chongchon to the north side and help clear the enemy from the 19th Infantry's sector. He also assigned his assistant division commander, Brigadier General Garrison Davidson, to take command of all 24th Division troops north of the river and coordinate those bridgehead operations.

The 2nd and 3rd battalions, 21st Infantry, launched an attack on the morning of 5 November, after the enemy had made a further penetration during the night, and restored the 19th Regiment's positions. The 3rd Engineer Combat Battalion once more fought as infantrymen in protecting the Chongchon bridges at Anju.

Desperate action erupted on the night of 5-6 November on the extreme left flank of the 19th Regiment's position where the 2nd Battalion held an isolated height, Hill 123. A five-mile gap in the lines existed from that point to the British positions farther west.

Communist troops, following telephone lines, came up from the rear and surprised E and G companies, killing many men as they lay in their sleeping bags, and overrunning the battalion positions. The other two battalions of the regiment, with artillery support from the south side of the river, drove back enemy attacks that night in hard fighting.

Several E Company men gave their lives in heroic action during the battle for Hill 123. Corporal Mitchell Red Cloud gave the first alarm to his company of the approach of the Chinese when a group charged him from about 100 feet away. He leveled his BAR at the oncoming troops, and after he was wounded, Red Cloud regained his feet, wrapped one arm around a tree and continued firing his automatic weapon at point blank range until he was killed. Many Chinese dead were found in front of his body.

Pfc. Joseph W. Balboni, also a BAR man, stood his ground against a charge of Chinese troops from about 75 feet, firing his weapon until he too was mortally wounded. Seventeen dead enemy soldiers were counted in front of his position.

Red Cloud earned the Medal of Honor for his gallantry and Balboni the Distinguished Service Cross. In the same action, Lieutenant Leslie Kirkpatrick, West Point '49, was killed when he left his foxhole to go to the aid of a wounded comrade.

At the same time bloody engagements were taking place at the bridgehead, the 5th RCT in position to the east was locked in bitter combat with Chinese troops south of the river.

The regiment took its place on 3 November at the town of Kunu-ri behind the Republic of Korea II Corps, whose troops held a key elevation, Hill 622, three miles northeast.

A heavy Chinese attack on the hill the next day broke the ROK lines, and troops began pouring back through the 5th RCT position. Captain Hubert H. Ellis, C Company commander, halted the retreat and forced the ROK soldiers to regroup and counterattack. The effort was a success in that after the hill changed hands several times during the day, by nightfall the South Koreans held the most important ridge.

The momentum of the Chinese drive carried to the 5th RCT lines where heavy fighting ensued, often at close quarters. At one point, the regiment had to withdraw about 1,000 yards, but by the end of the day Colonel Throckmorton's troops had driven the division-size enemy force back, thus saving the position at Kunu-ri and protecting the right flank of the Eighth Army.

One of the heroes of the day was Lieutenant Morgan B. Hansel of C Company, who charged Chinese machine gun positions alone. His action saved his platoon as a fighting unit, but he lost his life. Lieutenant Hansel was awarded the Distinguished Service Cross.

The battles on either side of the Chongchon River ending 6 November also marked the end of the first phase of the Chinese intervention. The enemy force withdrew northward after heavy losses from engaging U.N. troops, and by 7 November, the 24th Division units were able to achieve their limited objectives with little resistance.

Despite the presence of Chinese in force, General MacArthur ordered a general offensive by the Eighth Army along a 75-mile front for 24 November, the day after Thanksgiving, from the Chongchon River line.

But Eighth Army Commander Walton Walker, in an extraordinary move, visited the 24th Division command post on the eve of the attack to instruct General Church in effect to withdraw at the first sign of Chinese troops. The 21st Infantry was to lead the attack, and the word to Colonel Richard Stephens was that "if he smells Chinese chow, pull back immediately." (*In Mortal Combat*, John Toland.)

At dusk the next day, a massive Chinese counteroffensive began. The equivalent of nine U.S. divisions swarmed across the front and fell upon the Eighth Army, and the rapid fallback to the south began.

One of General Walker's legacies was the salvation of the Eighth Army, one result of his prescience about the coming of Chinese hordes.

3rd Platoon, Company "C", 6th Tank Bn., 24th Inf. Div., Korea, 1951. (Courtesy of David E. Teich)

1st Lt. David E. Teich and Sgt. Bailey of 3rd Platoon, Company "C", 6th Tank Bn., 24th Inf. Div., Korea, 1951. (Courtesy of David E. Teich)

"Pass-in-Review," 11th F.A. Battalion, Korea, 1953. (Courtesy of Neil Estes)

The rapidity of the Army's withdrawal and the effectiveness of its rear-guard combat was mistaken by some in the press for a panicked retreat.

On 23 December, the Eighth Army having established a defensive line behind the Imjin River below the 38th Parallel, General Walker decided to take a Jeep trip to the front and while there, present his son, Lieutenant Sam Walker, with his second Silver Star. The younger officer was a company commander in the 19th Infantry. On the way, the Jeep collided with a ROK vehicle on an icy road, and the general was killed instantly.

By this time, the shivering troops in battered infantry units were cruelly aware that the "home by Christmas" hope so prevalent in the previous weeks had been only so much wishful thinking.

Morale was precarious by this time, which General Matthew Ridgway the new Eighth Army Commander recognized as he described the men's unresponsiveness and lack of alertness. Lieutenant Maihafer, a platoon leader in I Company, 21st Infantry, who had returned to his unit after suffering a leg wound in September, told of the reluctance of the GIs to come down off the snow-covered hills even for the special Christmas Day dinner the cooks had prepared. They would rather eat C rations at the top of the ridge than expend the effort to come down for a good meal. Maihafer took the unusual step of ordering his men off the hills, for which some expressed later appreciation.

The C Company 21st plan for feeding Christmas dinner called the relief of men on line in shifts. The Chinese brought an abrupt halt to this plan by shelling the company kitchen before all the men had a chance to eat.

The Chinese delivered their next blow on New Year's Eve against the I and IX Corps. The 24th Division was positioned in the center of the Eighth Army line with the 1st Cavalry Division, the ROK 6th Division and the British 27th Brigade.

Along a 44-mile front, the Chinese waves surged forward through the white landscape to the eerie accompaniment of bugles and screams. After holding out several hours, the ROK 6th Division gave way, allowing the Chinese to stream through a breach between two 24th Division regiments.

The U.N. forces fell back to a bridgehead in front of Seoul, and then on 3 January 1951, General Ridgway, ordered another "retrograde movement" across the Han River out of the capital toward Suwon.

By mid-January, the tide turned again, slowly, as Ridgway ordered a limited counter-offensive and allied forces made small gains against often stiff resistance.

During the month, a new commanding general took charge of the 24th Division. Replacing General John Church, who had led the Taro Leafers for six months in triumph and hard times from the perimeter almost to the Yalu River, was Brigadier General Blackshear M. Bryan, a Louisianan who graduated from the Military Academy in 1922. He received his second star a few days after taking command of the division.

As the division joined in the grinding push northward, the 5th RCT was in action near Subuk. 2nd Lieutenant Carl H. Dodd, of Kenvir, KY, led his E Company platoon in an attack on Hill 256. Intense fire initially stalled the assault, but Dodd reorganized his men and then single-handedly destroyed a machine-gun position. His inspired platoon then fixed bayonets and overcame the enemy positions. Dodd again reorganized his small force and led it onto the hill proper, throwing grenades and firing his rifle. With his last hand grenade, the young officer destroyed an enemy mortar and killed its crew. Later, after rearming himself, Dodd led a final bayonet charge to eliminate the last positions. For his heroism, Dodd earned the Medal of Honor.

(Dodd died on 13 October 1996 in his native Kentucky at the age of 71. On that occasion, his former company commander, retired Colonel Bill Conger of Birmingham AL, made this comment, "He was one of the rare infantry soldiers that is able to take command in the firefight and understand what's going on. Dodd was all fired up when I last saw him on that hill. It takes a man of unusual ability to live in a combat environment and have the presence of mind to do what he did…." Conger had been wounded just before Lieutenant Dodd's heroic action.)

Two subsequent allied pushes, Operation Killer from 27 February to 7 March, and Operation Ripper, 7 March-4 April drove the Chinese back across the Han River and then to the 38th Parallel. The capital city of Seoul once again was in friendly hands, this time for keeps.

On the first day of Operation Ripper, 7 March, Company I, 19th Infantry, was in battle near Yonggong-ni. Sergeant 1st Class Nelson V. Brittin, of Audubon, NJ, volunteered to lead his squad up the hill his unit was trying to take. In the initial attack, Brittin hurled grenades at enemy positions and shot Chinese soldiers as they fled. He himself was wounded by a grenade but refused treatment and continued the attack. After his squad had moved about 100 yards up the hill, the unit encountered more heavy opposition, and once again, the sergeant charged a concealed machine gun and silenced it before enemy fire mortally wounded him. Brittin had killed 20 enemy soldiers and knocked out four enemy weapons. For his gallantry, Brittin earned the Medal of Honor.

The U.N. advance now was peninsula-wide and deliberate, but Ridgway had no complaints. He wanted mutual protection of the flanks the broad progress afforded.

After General Douglas MacArthur was relieved in April, General Matthew Ridgway became U.N. commander and General James Van Fleet took over the Eighth Army. By a convergence of circumstances, that historic change in command was accomplished at the 5th RCT command post and in the near proximity of the 24th Division commanding general, Blackshear Bryan, and other division personnel.

Harry Maihafer, then aide to General Bryan, was on hand and related the events in his book, *From the Hudson to the Yalu*. Secretary of the Army Frank Pace was on a tour of the front on 12 April 1951 when he and his entourage stopped at General Bryan's division headquarters. The party proceeded to the regimental command post. While at the 5th Infantry headquarters, an urgent message arrived from the Eighth Army chief of staff for Secretary Pace.

He listened to it twice, and then took General Ridgway outside, despite a hailstorm. "General Ridgway, it's my duty to advise you that you are now the supreme commander of the Pacific. General MacArthur is relieved."

Maihafer and the others did not know exactly what was up, but they could tell it was important.

By mid-April, allied forces were beyond the 38th Parallel again. What followed over the next several days was the largest single battle of the Korean War.

The goal of the Eighth Army was to seize the "Iron Triangle," an area in the form of a triangle with Chorwon and Kumhwa at its base and Pyonggang (not to be confused with Pyongyang, the North Korean capital) at its apex. The Iron Triangle was coveted by both sides because of its key road junctions.

On the right of the I Corps sector, the 24th Infantry Division had continued in the attack, with armored patrols from the 6th Medium Tank Battalion striking northward toward Kumhwa while the 19th and 5th Regiments relieved the 21st Regiment on line. The 21st then moved to reserve positions along line "Kansas," an Eighth Army designation for a stretch of defensive terrain above the 38th parallel.

On 22 April, a prisoner revealed that the Chinese would attack at dark. In a massive attack, the CCF (Chinese Communist Forces) launched its long-expected Fifth Phase offensive, hurling 350,000 men toward the U.N. lines to start the largest single battle of the Korean War.

Dug in with the 24th Division was the 8th Ranger Company, Captain Herbert commanding. In March 1951, a Ranger company had been assigned to each of the six divisions in Korea. Colonel Robert W. Black (USA ret), then a platoon leader in the Ranger company, has given a good account of the 24th Division's reaction to this Chinese offensive in his book, *Rangers in Korea.*

The Chinese attack hit the 24th Division at a center ridge occupied by the 2nd Battalions of the 5th RCT and the 19th Infantry, "then flowed like water along the 24th Division line. The whole front was a roaring crescendo of fire." At 0250 hours on 23 April, the 6th ROK Division, on the 24th Division's right, crumbled under the onslaught. The ROK's pell-mell retreat caused a huge chasm that threatened to shatter 8th Army's lines.

The 5th and 19th regiments began pulling back under a curtain of American artillery fire. On that day division artillery fired 15,712 rounds, its greatest single-day total of the three-year conflict. The Chinese dead piled up, but live Chinese kept coming.

At 0855 hours the 24th Division was ordered to withdraw to line "Kansas" and defend. General Bryan placed the 19th Infantry on the left, the 21st Infantry on the right, with the 5th RCT in reserve. I Corps informed the division that the nearest friendly troops on the division's right were approximately 13,000 meters to the rear. General Bryan sent the 8th Rangers into this void to find out what was on his right flank.

At 2000 hours 23 April, 87 enlisted men and three officers of the 8th Ranger Company passed through the 2nd Battalion 21st Infantry and began the long, arduous climb to the high ground on the right flank of the 24th Division. The route of march would take them over steep, difficult Hills 628, 1010, and 1168. Lieutenant Black remembered that "the men carried heavy burdens for such a climb. Combat packs included two days' rations and mountain sleeping bags. Each rifleman had four bandoliers of ammunition with 48 rounds per bandolier. Each Browning Automatic Rifleman carried his twenty-pound weapon and twelve magazines with twenty rounds per magazine."

By 0600, 24 April, the Rangers had occupied Hill 628 after dispersing a Chinese patrol with artillery fire. After breakfast the Rangers began the four-hour ascent of even steeper Hill 1010. From this critical terrain feature, the Rangers could see ridgelines that had offered natural avenues of approach to the 6th ROK Division area and southwest to the right flank terrain occupied by the 21st Infantry. They could see large numbers of Chinese passing to the east in the U-shaped gap between the 24th Division and the 1st Marine Division, the next stable unit to the east. As Eighth Army moved reinforcements to shore up the sides of the bulge created by the disintegration of the 6th ROK Division, the 8th Rangers watched from their perch on Hill 1010 the movement of elements of four Chinese Field Armies pouring south through this huge hole in the lines.

Chinese pressure began to threaten the 24th Division. At 0807 hours 24 April, the 19th Infantry reported its position untenable. A battalion of the 5th RCT was sent to assist. To give further protection to the right, the 3rd Battalion of the 5th was moved to the right rear (south) of the 21st Infantry to block the Chinese penetration into the Division rear. This position was approximately 4000 meters to the rear (south) and 2000 meters west of the Ranger position on Hill 1010.

Enemy patrols began to probe the Ranger position at dusk, hitting several squads atop Hill 1010. At midnight Captain Herbert dispatched several reconnaissance patrols which passed Chinese patrols as commanders on both sides sought to determine relative strengths on opposing hills. A Ranger patrol went back down the slope and found Hill 628 now occupied by the enemy. But carrying parties from the 2nd

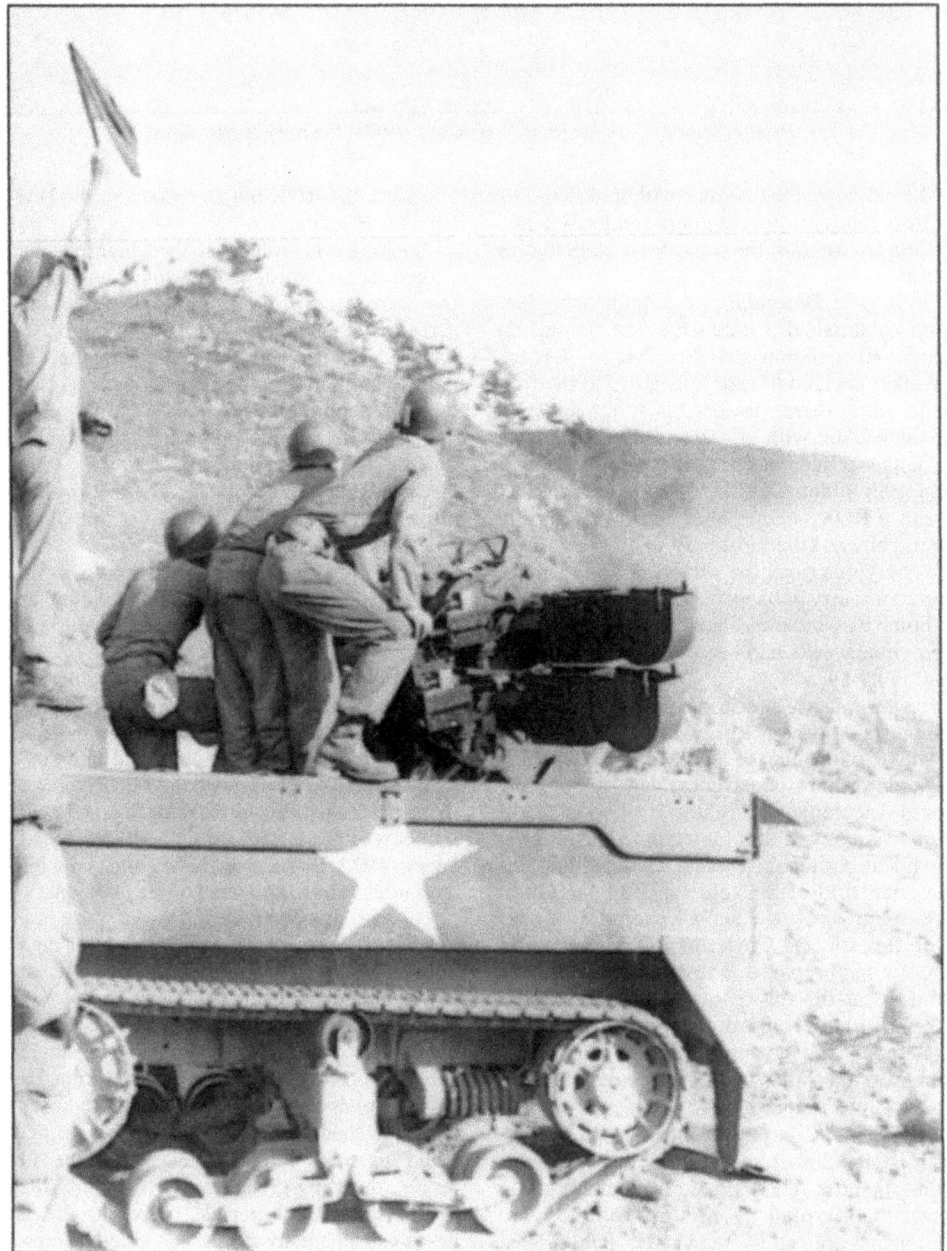

While the 26th AAA AW Bn(SP) was located near Masan, South Korea, in Sept. 1953, "B" Battery conducted M-16 service practice at a firing range near Pusan. The only indentifiable person in this photo by the vertical white stripe on the rear of his helmet is 1st Lt. Roy H. Wells, "B" Battery Executive Officer. (Courtesy of Roy Wells)

In Sept. 1953 the 26th AAA AW Bn(SP) was located near Masan, South Korea. "B" Battery had just been released from attached status with the 1st Bn., 19th Inf. Regt., 24th Inf. Div. and returned to the control of the 26th. This is 1st Lt. Ellis I. McKinnon shown in the motor pool. (Courtesy of Roy Wells)

Battalion 21st Infantry slipped through with food, ammunition, and water for the Rangers.

With such wide gaps between units, the situation was ideal for Chinese infiltration. At 0245 on 25 April, the 24th Division switchboard came under fire as well as the division airfield. Chinese fired on the 5th RCT rear command post at 0330.

Just prior to dawn twelve to fifteen ROK soldiers, who had become separated from their unit and bypassed by the CCF, joined the Rangers. When they were brought inside the perimeter, they gasped repeatedly in stumbling English, "Many, many Chinese!" The Chinese had reached their high-water mark. Eighth Army ordered its forces to withdraw to Line "Delta" below the 38th parallel.

At 0500 forward elements of the 24th Division started the daylight withdrawal. The Ranger company was detached from the 21st Infantry and attached to the 3rd Battalion 5th Infantry. The Rangers started retracing their steps off Hill 1010 toward Hill 628. The company could never establish radio contact with the 5th RCT. All messages had to be relayed through 2nd Battalion 21st Infantry.

When the column was halfway between Hill 1010 and Hill 628, a message from 2nd Battalion 21st Infantry warned them to avoid Hill 628 because a friendly patrol had met heavy resistance there. A short time later a message from Division G-3, relayed by the 21st Infantry S-3, instructed Captain Herbert to continue south along the ridge across Hill 628 to prevent the 3rd Battalion 5th RCT from being cut off by the enemy.

The enemy had indeed occupied Hill 628 and was prepared to contest every foot of the Rangers' path across the hill. The Rangers were soon engaged in a crisp firefight on a narrow ridge with steep sides that prevented the traditional base of fire and maneuver. A misstep, and a man would tumble down the ridge. An

enemy force coming from Hill 1168 rained their firepower on the rear of the company. At 0821 25 April, the 2nd Battalion 21st Infantry reported to Regiment, "Ranger Co completely surrounded, still in radio contact with them." The Rangers, at a greater range into enemy territory than the other division units, were engaging forces that threatened the north flank of the 3rd Battalion 5th RCT and east flank of the withdrawing 21st Infantry.

All morning the Rangers attempted to contact the 5th RCT to which they were now attached - but in vain. At 0830 Company L 5th RCT, 2500 meters south of the Ranger position, moved north to assist the Rangers. However, Company L came under intense small arms fire and withdrew at 1008 hours. Back on the ridgeline the Rangers were using their heavy firepower to grind their way forward but at a price of mounting casualties. Captain Herbert was hit hard in the neck and shoulder. The executive officer, Lieutenant Giacherine at the rear of the company, took over. Through radio contact with the 2nd Battalion 21st Infantry, the 52nd Field Artillery laid a curtain of fire around the Rangers.

At 1005 with the rest of the 21st clear, the 2nd Battalion 21st Infantry began its withdrawal. Two platoons of Company C 6th Medium Tank Battalion were in the valley, forward of the 21st's position, covering the move by fire. By 1026 the 2nd Battalion reported that all its troops were on the road. Still engaged heavily with the enemy, the Rangers could see the tanks on the valley floor. At great risk to themselves, radio operator E.C. Rivera and Nick Tisak climbed to the top of Hill 628 under small arms fire and finally made radio contact with the tanks, the Rangers' only hope for survival.

Giacherine had already picked out a route off the ridge, even though it meant going deeper into enemy territory. He requested a linkup with

the tanks at a point 3000 meters northeast of the Ranger position. At 1105 hours 21st Infantry reported, "3rd Platoon C Company 6th Tanks remaining to assist Ranger elements that will be down in about one hour."

Under Lieutenant Giacherine's direction, the Rangers began a fighting withdrawal from Hill 628. A six-man force under Master Sergeant Ellis served as point; the wounded went next followed by the rear guard. Few men could be spared to help the wounded; many men walked off the ridge holding their entrails to prevent their spilling from gaping abdominal wounds. Captain Herbert's neck wounds could not easily be bandaged; he came down with his fingers jammed into the bullet holes to stanch the bleeding. For some, the withdrawal was a race down the slopes, firing into enemy foxholes on each side.

The Chinese pursued the Rangers closely and nearly overwhelmed the rear guard. Only napalm from a Navy F4U Corsair and accurate artillery fire directed by an observation plane saved the Rangers from destruction.

The Rangers and the four tanks of Lieutenant David Teich's 3rd Platoon C Company 6th Tank Battalion arrived at the prearranged rendezvous point within fifteen minutes of each other. The wounded were placed on the tanks, then the other Rangers and ROK soldiers climbed on board. The S-3 journal of the 6th Tank Battalion shows the following message from C Company at 1200 hours: "3rd Platoon on his way back, 107 men with him, 25 WIA."

According to Robert Black in *Rangers in Korea*, General Bryan summed up the action by "congratulating the 8th Rangers, telling Lieutenant Giacherine that the Rangers had revealed to him that the entire right flank had been exposed, and the Ranger action had prevented the 21st Infantry Regiment, if not the entire division, from being cut off."

The courage of Lieutenant David Teich and the men of his 3rd Platoon of C Company 6th Tank Battalion deserves special recognition. Unescorted by infantry, the crews of four tanks remained some 3500 meters in advance of friendly forces to aid the Rangers. They did this with the full knowledge that friendly forces had withdrawn and enemy troops were occupying the vacated positions.

The 21st and 19th regiments were able to withdraw in good order, but the Chinese managed to get behind the 5th RCT and maul the unit severely. The regiment suffered 800 casualties in that one night. Seven Patton tanks also were lost.

Also taking a beating in the same engagement was the 555th Field Artillery Battalion. The Triple Nickel had been decimated at the Pusan Perimeter in August and now it happened again. The unit had to abandon 13 105-mm howitzers and 60 vehicles. John Toland's book, *In Mortal Combat*, included this passage: "The next morning Corporal Don Hansen (a Marine) ... was scanning the road below his ridge with glasses. He could see hundreds of bodies, smashed trucks, tanks, ambulances, and guns. On both sides of the road, tents were torn down and there were more bodies than he could count. It was total devastation, a gruesome scene. He didn't know he was viewing the remnants of a regiment of the ROK 6th Division and the 555 Artillery Battalion, the Triple Nickels."

That same day, 26 April, Company C, 21st Infantry, was locked in battle with enemy forces near the town of Mugok. Sergeant 1st Class Ray E. Duke of Tennessee led a patrol to Hill 503 to rescue several soldiers who were pinned down by enemy fire. The patrol regained the position, but Duke was wounded by mortar fragments. When the platoon withdrew, Duke learned some of the wounded had been left, so he reorganized his force to retrieve them. "We'll never make it, Sarge, there's too many of them out there," one GI protested. "We ain't leaving our men out there," the sergeant retorted.

The platoon launched a furious charge using bayonets and rifle butts to smash through the Communist lines. After the wounded were recovered, Duke rallied the men for a second charge. Duke, wounded for the third time in an enemy counterattack, refused to withdraw with his platoon.

His troops last saw him leaning against a boulder still firing into the enemy closing in on his position. The Chinese captured Sergeant Duke, who died in a POW camp 11 November 1951. His country honored the Gimlet hero with the Medal of Honor.

When the fury of their assault had spent itself, the battered Chinese units pulled back, leaving the front relatively quiet for the next three weeks.

However, on 16 May, the enemy launched its second spring offensive, and once again the 24th Division, with the others, engaged in hard fighting. The 5th RCT, in a forward position at the outset of the attack, absorbed the initial blow and slowed the enemy surge. That regiment then withdrew through the 19th Infantry, which for the next three days hurled back Chinese trying to dislodge the Chicks from "Barbed Wire Hill."

The 24th Division surprised the Chinese by counterattacking. Allowing the enemy no time to rest, recoup or reorganize, the Taro Leafers drove forward and utterly defeated the force opposing them. The division captured 3,955 prisoners over a six-day period.

It was during the same period that swarms of Chinese troops attacked the 21st Regiment command post, igniting a pitched battle with medics, cooks, clerks, administrative noncoms, and security personnel. The large groups of enemy soldiers in friendly rear areas were the battered remnants of the Chinese 180th Division attempting to escape the encirclement of American forces.

The battle of 27 May, as described in the 24th Division newspaper Taro News, dated 30 May 1951, began when enemy soldiers attacked the medical unit at the 21st Infantry CP. The medical personnel inflicted substantial casualties on the attackers but soon were overwhelmed by vastly superior numbers and other headquarters soldiers joined the fray.

Other headquarters soldiers joined the fray, which was fought with bayonets, rifle butts and hand-to-hand and raged throughout most of the morning. The headquarters personnel held their ground until the 2nd Battalion, 5th RCT, arrived to smash the enemy from the rear and flanks and put down the last resistance. When the fighting ended, the 21st Regiment's CP area was littered with Chinese dead.

The 5th Regiment's 2nd Battalion had spent the previous night engaged with an enemy company until moving to the aid of the headquarters. The American troops then continued aggressive patrols throughout the remainder of the day, netting about 1,200 prisoners.

June brought another offensive as allied troops kept pressure on the Chinese and North Koreans. C Company 21st Infantry, commanded by Captain Ernie Denham, launched an attack on a forbidding height called Granite Mountain, the top of which could be reached only by a narrow ridge. That restricted the assault to one platoon at a time. The 1st Platoon and then the 2nd were driven back with heavy losses by ferocious small arms fire, mortars and grenades.

Finally Denham led the 3rd Platoon up the ridge. The GIs were greeted by a firestorm as the Chinese held nothing back. A 120-mm mortar exploded near the company commander, mangling one of his legs and severing the other. As the American platoon fell back, the Chinese counterattacked, and Denham feared he would be left to be captured.

However, an unlikely force of Korean irregulars led by a C Company sergeant, Henry Cecil, repulsed the enemy and carried Captain Denham back to the base of the hill. A Navy doctor who was on detached service with the Army, and with whom Denham had had a casual drink weeks before, took a second look at the gravely wounded officer, whom he had first considered a hopeless case, and initiated treatment.

Cecil's background, described by Harry Maihafer in From the Hudson to the Yalu, was unusual. During the Depression year of 1933, he was among prisoners released from the Army stockade at Fort Leavenworth with the understanding they leave the continental United States. He went to Hawaii, enlisted in that territory's National Guard, fought in the Pacific in World War II, and after the war was assigned to the 24th Division. He and another soldier recruited and trained a force of about 100 Koreans into an irregular force in the weapons platoon. It was that contingent that rushed the hill and rescued Captain Denham.

By summer, the Korean conflict entered a new phase in which it became more a war of attrition from strong defensive positions, reminiscent of World War I, than the war of movement of the first year.

The 19th Regiment, however, launched a maneuver on 4 July - one year less one day after the first 24th Division action in Korea - that took the Chicks behind Chinese lines where they punished the enemy in four days of fighting.

Four weeks later, a 19th Infantry soldier, Sergeant 1st Class Stanley Adams, of Olathe, KS, distinguished himself in battle. His A Company platoon was about 200 yards forward of the company position when about 250 enemy soldiers attacked early on 2 August. Adams led 13 other soldiers in a bayonet charge against the advancing enemy. A leg wound failed to stop him. Four times the concussion from grenades knocked Adams down and still he continued until his force made physical contact with the enemy. Using his bayonet and rifle butt, Adams overcame one Chinese after the other. When the enemy withdrew, they left behind more than 50 of their dead. Sergeant Adams earned the Medal of Honor.

That month, the 24th Division went into Eighth Army reserve and returned to the front in October with orders to seize strong defensive positions in the heights above Kumsong in preparation of winter operations. The division secured its objective within three weeks.

It was in that area on 15 November that Pfc. Mack Jordan of Collins, MS, gave his life in heroic action that earned him the Medal of Honor. Jordan, of Company K, 21st Infantry, was a squad leader in the 3rd platoon engaged in a night attack against a key position. Jordan first crawled forward and took out a machine-gun position with grenades. He then charged enemy soldiers, killing some and forcing others to retreat. Explosives severed both of his legs, but Jordan still fought on long enough to keep the enemy at bay while the rest of his platoon regained the position and continued the battle.

A change of division command in December brought Major General Henry I. Hodes to succeed General Bryan. General Hodes, from Washington, D.C., was a West Pointer, class of 1920.

Finally, after 18 months of combat up and down the war-ravaged peninsula, the 24th Infantry Division, except for the 5th RCT, came off the line for the last time in mid-January 1952. Taking the division's place in the bunkers near Kumsong was the 40th Infantry Division.

It was back to Japan for the Taro Leafers with all the comforts of civilization, but absent the old pre-Korea garrison duty complacency. This time, training for combat readiness reached a high level of intensity, from amphibious operations to ski training.

Division command changes came more rapidly now. In February, Major General George W. Smythe relieved General Hodes, and in November 1952, Major General Charles L. Dasher, Jr., took over.

General Dasher led his troops back to Korea in mid-July 1953, but the armistice halted the fighting on 27 July before the bulk of the 24th Division engaged the enemy again. However, the two units whose early losses were so great that it was necessary to reduce them to paper status were heard from once again. The 63rd Field Artillery Battalion delivered fire against the enemy in the I Corps sector for the last nine days of the war. And the 34th Infantry once again was a line regiment At the end, the regiment held a blocking position behind the 2nd Division's 23rd Regiment, which absorbed heavy blows in the last Chinese mass attacks.

The cease-fire brought a new mission for the men who wore the Taro Leaf - prisoner repatriation. The Army assigned the 19th Infantry to Cheju-do, where the allies held anti-communist Chinese POWs, and the 21st Infantry to Koje-do, the camp for the hard-core doctrinaire communists. Both islands were off the southern coast of the country. The 34th Regiment went to Pusan where it organized Task Force Olson to escort freed prisoners to Inchon, from whence they would sail to Taiwan.

The overall operation, dubbed "Big Switch," was fraught with potential trouble, but it went off smoothly under the direction of the 24th Division men.

The division took up semi-permanent encampments in South Korea and continued training. In October, the division got another commanding officer, Major General Carter B. Magruder.

The 34th Infantry effected another prisoner transfer in January 1954, again without incident.

On March 1, the 24th Division relieved the 45th Division, a National Guard outfit slated for return to the United States. The new commanding general was Major General Paul D. Harkins, who had commanded the departing 45th Division. He succeeded Brigadier General Carl I. Hutton, former 24th Divison artillery commander, who had taken over from General Magruder in January.

The Korean War had cost the "First to Fight" 24th Infantry Division 3,735 killed and 7,395 wounded seriously enough to require hospitalization. The division's performance also earned this accolade from General Matthew Ridgway: "With unexcelled fighting spirit and efficiency the men of the division have con-sistently displayed the greatest gallantry and devotion to duty. Their record is a proud one of great combat achievement, of unswerving loyalty and sacrifice."

But even General Ridgway at that early date may not have realized how much the brave men of the 24th Infantry Division had accomplished. To look at South Korea in 1996, a thriving, increasingly democratic, largely Christian nation, a dependable ally and vibrant economic power and trading partner demands a playback to 1950 when that nation literally was saved because one U.S. Army division, undermanned, underequipped, underprepared, nevertheless threw itself into the breach. That is quite a legacy for any military unit.

LATER YEARS
1954-1996

The deactivation of the 24th Infantry Division after the Korean War, the first of two periods of dormancy for the Taro Leaf, lasted until 1 July 1958 when the division was reactivated in Germany.

The outfit that had spent its entire previous existence in the Pacific now found itself in a different geographic setting and a new situation. Instead of engaging in the hot wars of the islands and the east Asian mainland, the men of the 24th Division took on the role of cold warriors in the tense atmosphere of postwar Europe.

The 24th Division relieved the 11th Airborne Division, also a veteran of the Philippine campaign of World War II, at Augsburg and Munich, but the troops barely had their barracks bags unpacked before they were off on a mission that could have turned hostile quite easily.

The 24th Division, two weeks after activation, was urgently dispatched to Lebanon where communists were threatening the established government. The Taro Leafers remained in the volatile Middle East for two months, contributing to the maintenance of the region's stability (admittedly a relative term) before returning to Germany.

Two years later, in July 1960, 24th Division was put on alert for possible movement to the Belgian Congo in central Africa, then in the throes of the revolution that would end colonial rule and create the new nation of Zaire. Orders to the Congo never came, but in that situation the face of the new role to be played by the U.S. Army began to come into focus. Units could expect to be deployed any time from any point to any of the many potential trouble spots of the world.

And in Germany, the focal point of the American-Soviet, East-West confrontation, there was trouble enough, or at least the chance for it. This may have been peacetime technically, but Army duty in Germany during the 1960s was not of the traditional garrison variety. Exercises were rigorous and the state of readiness remained high.

The East German Communists erected the infamous Berlin Wall in August 1961 to prevent refugees from fleeing to freedom in the west. The structure succeeded in that purpose

Camp area near North Korea. (Courtesy of James Bell)

Home of "C" Company, 21st Gimlets, 24th Infantry Division. 1956. (Courtesy of James Bell)

93

to a high degree, but it also came to symbolize the Cold War and starkly emphasize the differences between the two systems.

The wall also increased the volatility of the Berlin flash point. Three months after its erection, the 1st Battalion, 19th Infantry, arrived in Berlin to bolster the allied forces there. Other 24th Division units followed.

For a time, a genuine crisis situation persisted as American and Soviet tanks faced each other at Checkpoint Charlie. Reserves were called up by the U.S. military and no one was quite sure whether war would break out once more.

"A lot of soldiers were scared while in Berlin because of what just a small incident might have started," Lawrence A. Babits, a member of the 1st Battalion, 21st Infantry, during that period recalled. He now is a faculty member at Armstrong State College in Savannah, GA, not far from Fort Stewart, home of his old division.

But thanks to the peacekeeping efforts and deterrent strength of the 24th Division and other NATO units, war did not break out in the 1960s and history later would record the end of the Berlin Wall and the demise of European communism. The soldiers of the World War II and Korean Victory Division had their part in another triumph, the battle that didn't have to be fought.

The division's European deployment, during which it was paired with the 10th Panzer-Grenadier Division, lasted for 10 years.

Starting in September 1968 and over the following 12 months, the 24th Infantry Division moved to its new home, Fort Riley, KS, the first time the unit had been stationed in the United States. There the division was deactivated for the second time, on 15 April 1970. Most of the troops and equipment were absorbed into the 1st Infantry Division, then just back from Vietnam.

The 24th Division's hiatus was not permanent, however. Its third incarnation had its origin at Fort Stewart on 21 October 1974, when the 1st Brigade was formed as the nucleus of the soon-to-be reactivated division. That event occurred at the post on 21 September 1975.

Lieutenant General Donald E. Rosenblum, USA (ret.) writes of the reactivation:

"I arrived at Fort Stewart on 12 January 1975 as the junior Brigadier General in the US Army. In addition to the post personnel there were about 300 enlisted and officers who were wearing the 24th patch. They were in the process of provisionally organizing. I appointed myself as the CG of the 1st Brigade (Separate), 24th Infantry Division. We were to consist of 3 Infantry battalions (2nd of the 19th, 2nd of the 21st and 2nd of the 34th), one Artillery battalion (1st of the 35th), a Support battalion which would be the forerunner of the DISCOM, an Engineer Company, a cavalry troop, and a Headquarters & Headquarters Company. From that initial formation the Division would come. We were later told that the 48th Infantry Brigade of the Georgia National Guard would be our "Roundout 3rd Brigade," which meant that we would have two Regular Army Brigades along with our Division Artillery to support the

Infantry as well as a DISCOM, Cavalry Squadron, Engineer Battalion, Aviation Battalion, and separate companies. The National Guard's Brigade's supporting units would be integrated.

"We immediately decided that the 24th would be a Disciplined, Trained, Physically Fit Organization. Everyone was indoctrinated with that, and all newly arrived personnel were briefed on the great history of our 24th. We instituted the greeting of "Victory"—"First to Fight" when salutes were exchanged as well as painting the V on the camouflage cover of the helmets. Since we had no barracks, I signed a lease with the Adjutant General of Georgia and we leased a goodly portion of the National Guard area at Fort Stewart. The barracks were 40-man, open bay, cinder block buildings without heat or air conditioning. Latrines and showers were next to the barracks so the troops had to go outside to use the facilities. In spite of the spartan living conditions, the 24th had the best reenlistment rate in all of Forces Command for 2 years.

"On 22 September 1975 we were formally activated as a Division. The Secretary of the Army, Martin R. Hoffman, passed me the Division Colors and we were officially the 24th Infantry Division. Our training was tough and realistic, and we continued to hammer at the theme of Disciplined, Trained, Physically Fit soldiers and units. Our first test came after we were less than one year old. We participated in a joint readiness exercise against the 82nd Airborne Division at Eglin Air Force Base. Our 2nd Brigade had 13 people so they exercised on maps. There was little doubt in the entire Army's mind after that exercise that the 24th Infantry Division was in fact a top-notch organization. From sergeants to generals who observed the operation there was disbelief how professional our soldiers, non commissioned officers, and officers were. We were professionals.

"In August of 1976 we hosted the annual convention of the 24th Infantry Division Association. Each member had a young soldier from his old outfit as an escort. Our soldiers were visibly impressed with the Association members. The highlight of the weekend was a Division Review. We invited the Association members to come forward and "take" the review. As the colors of the various units passed in review and dipped, it was quite emotional to see the response of the Association members. The soldiers of the 24th will never forget the Association and its members.

"We who were in the leadership positions realized that if we did things right that Fort Stewart/Hunter AAF would be a place where soldiers and their families would want to be stationed with the 24th. Somehow I still believe that we did things properly and got the 24th Division off on the right foot. In addition we fostered a great relationship between the Division and the Association."

The 2nd Brigade was provisionally organized in 1976, shortly before the division participated in the Joint Readiness Exercise, Brave Shield IV, in October in the Florida panhandle.

With the formal activation of the 2nd Brigade on 14 June 1977 and the inclusion of the round-out unit, the 48th Infantry Brigade of the

Georgia Army National Guard, the division was at full strength.

The 24th Infantry Division took on the designation of Mechanized on 30 September 1979, which meant the addition of armored personnel carriers, tanks and more support personnel.

A year later, the division became part of the Rapid Deployment Force, and its personnel were trained accordingly by rotation at the National Training Center at Fort Irwin, CA. The unit would have to be ready to respond quickly to a variety of contingency missions as the need arose.

DESERT STORM

Eleven years passed before that need arrived in a major way. On 2 August 1990, tanks and men of the Iraqi army crossed the border into Kuwait in a massive invasion that set the world on edge. Saddam Hussein's aggressors not only wholly occupied their immediate neighbor to the south, they also threatened Saudi Arabia and indeed the stability of the entire strategic region.

Under the leadership of the United States, an allied coalition began to come together and deployment of military forces began.

One of the first to move was the 24th Infantry Division (Mechanized) out of Fort Stewart under the command of Major General Barry R. McCaffrey. Starting on 7 August, just five days after the invasion, 26,000 troops of the 24th Division made the long cross-ocean transit to the Middle East as part of Operation Desert Shield.

For the next six months, the 24th Division and other coalition military units prepared themselves in the Arabian desert for the day they once again would engage an enemy in a shooting war.

The air offensive started on 17 January 1991, and it was devastating in its effectiveness over the following five weeks. But just as had been true in war historically, it takes ground troops to occupy territory and drive the enemy from it. Modern technology had not changed that reality.

Across the frontier to contest the American and coalition forces was the vaunted Republican Guard, supposedly the elite unit of what commentators repeatedly reminded everyone was the world's fourth largest army. Land mines planted thick and wide were said to pose a dire threat to any men and machines that dared to venture forward.

For three weeks before the ground war began, the 24th Division engaged in cross-border forays for reconnaissance, to set electronic devices and identify crossing points, among other missions. The division suffered its first combat deaths in the ground war during this period.

The coalition's ground forces jumped off for the attack into Iraq early on the morning of 24 February. Desert Shield had become Desert Storm.

What happened next amazed the world. The power, efficiency, technical dominance and superb preparation of the American military machine revealed itself on the sands of that ancient land.

General McCaffrey issued this statement

2-7 TAC in Iraq. 1991 Front row L to R: Pfc Debolt, Sgt Mau, and Pfc Barton. Standing L to R: Cpt Caruso, Csm Moore, Ltc Ware, Maj Stenson, and Ssg Campbell. (Courtesy of Kim Stenson)

to his troops before the invasion: "Soldiers of the Victory Division ... we now begin a great battle to destroy an aggressor army and free two million Kuwaiti people ... . By force of arms, we will make the Iraqi war machine surrender the country they hold prisoner ... .

"There will be no turning back when we attack into battle ... .We have the weapons and the military training equal to the task. We pray that our courage and our skill will bring this war to a speedy close ... . We shall do our duty."

The 24th Division launched its attack at 1500 the first day, 11 hours after the initial jump-off and 15 hours ahead of its own schedule, which the high command had moved up.

In a lightning thrust, the mechanized infantry of the 24th Divison rolled 370 kilometers through and around the enemy army. It was said the division went farther and faster than any mechanized force in military history.

During the 100 hours of ground combat, the 24th Infantry Division (Mechanized) fought battles at Talill and Jalibah air bases and the Basrah Plain, and after the official cease-fire at the Rumayah Oil Field. The Taro Leafers succeeded in severing the line of communication between the field and the enemy capital of Baghdad and destroyed the 26th Commando Brigade, the 47th and 49th Infantry Divisions, and four Republican Guard divisions. Troops of the 24th Divison captured more than 5,000 enemy soldiers and disarmed many more.

The initial assault across the frontier was by three brigades abreast: the 197th under Colonel Ted Reid on the left, the 1st commanded by Colonel John LeMoyne in the center and the 2nd led by Colonel Paul Kern on the right.

The units reported no early resistance, but a howling sandstorm through the afternoon and night kept visibility at near zero. All three brigades reached intermediate objectives in their drive toward the Euphrates River Valley during 25 February, destroying enemy equipment and capturing Iraqi troops.

A fierce battle erupted on the night of 26 February involving two battalions of the 7th Infantry, part of the 1st Brigade. Hundreds of flaming targets were visible in the desert as the 2nd Battalion of Lieutenant Colonel Chuck Ware and the 3rd Battalion of Lieutenant Colonel Dave Jensen slugged it out with the 26th Iraqi Commando Brigade. Hundreds of rounds of mortar and artillery rounds fell in the 1st Brigade positions, but fortunately they were largely ineffective.

The 4th Battalion, 64th Armor, under Lieutenant Colonel John Craddock, came upon a large ammunition storage site north of Highway 8, and despite multiple anti-tank rocket hits that damaged his tank, the battalion continued the attack. Craddock was awarded the Silver Star for the action.

According to Major Kim Stenson, S-3 of the 2nd Battalion, 7th Infantry, the 1st Brigade's objective for the day was Highway 8, the main line of communications between Kuwait and Baghdad, and therefore the main line of retreat for Iraqi forces fleeing Kuwait.

Assisting the 1st Brigade's drive with accurate fire were artillery units, the 1st Battalion of the 41st Field Artillery under the command of Lieutenant Colonel John Floris, and the 212th FA Brigade, which fought a heavy gun duel with Iraqi artillery battalions and destroyed four of them.

Weather continued to present a problem. On the second day of the attack, heavy rains slowed down the 197th Brigade and some units became bogged down in mud on the afternoon of 26 February.

Only a few hours later, sandstorms again plagued the fighting men. With visibility reduced by the blowing sand, a platoon from the 1st Battalion 18th Infantry suddenly found itself surrounded by a superior enemy force. Against heavy fire and overwhelming numerical odds, the platoon leader, Lieutenant Larry Aikman, Jr., led his men in successfully fight-

ing their way out of the encirclement and rejoining the battalion. Aikman was able to provide valuable information about Iraqi positions and strength. For his bravery and leadership under fire, Aikman was decorated with the Silver Star.

Troops of the 24th Division continued to overwhelm pockets of the enemy on their swift push toward the airfields. When scouts of the 2nd Battalion, 18th Infantry, discovered about 300 infantrymen and their vehicles, fire was called from the 4th Battalion, 41st Field Artillery under the command of Lieutenant Colonel Bill Engel. The result was 49 Iraqis killed, rolling stock destroyed and the surrender of the rest of the dispirited force.

The 2nd Brigade opened the main attack on Jalibah Air Base on the morning of 27 February after the 1st Brigade had conducted a fixing attack along the approach, and artillery units pounded targets in a tremendous barrage. The assault was a coordinated artillery, armored and infantry onslaught. Tanks of 1st Battalion, 64th Armor and 3rd Battalion 69th Armor under the respective commands of Lieutenant Colonels Randy Gordon and Terry Stanger engaged the enemy southwest of Jalibah, allowing the 3rd Battalion, 15th Infantry of Lieutenant Colonel Ray Barrett, to clear the airfield by 1000.

The attack netted 2,000 enemy soldiers, 80 anti-aircraft guns and an entire tank battalion. The American troops blew up the airfield's fuel and ammunition supplies and destroyed 20 Iraqi aircraft.

General McCaffrey flew into the captured base to congratulate personally the 2nd Brigade commander, Colonel Paul Kern, whose unit now was being recognized as the star of the campaign.

Talill Air Base was the objective of the 197th Brigade holding down the division's west flank. Early in the afternoon of 27 February, 2nd Battalion, 69th Armor, initiated a raid to suppress enemy fire, and then, after air and artillery support, the armored unit penetrated the main entrance to the field despite a 20-foot berm guarding the base. Exchanges were brief but sharp before the brigade secured the field.

The Victory Division's next major objective was Basrah to the east, and no time was lost launching the attack. At 1300 27 February, only three hours after the seizure of Jalibah, the 1st and 2nd brigades and the attached 3rd Armored Cavalry Regiment commanded by Colonel Doug Starr were on the move abreast, from left to right in the order named. The main line of attack was in the 1st Brigade zone.

The force encountered heavy but largely ineffective artillery fire. Within hours, the opposing Iraqi army was utterly defeated. The Americans seized 1,300 bunkers of artillery, 500 one thousand pound bombs and other munitions. Thousands of terrified and bewildered Iraqis surrendered and then were beneficiaries of the remarkable compassion shown them by soldiers of the 24th Division.

About 0330 28 February, just an hour and a half before the division planned to continue the attack, the command post was notified that a cease-fire had been called for 0800. The division suspended further combat operations immediately in order to avoid unnecessary American casualties.

Despite the official truce, coalition troops, including those of the 24th Division, continued to take sporadic mortar and artillery fire the remainder of 28 February and throughout 1 March. Many skirmishes were reported.

Early on the morning of 2 March heavy movement of vehicles east of the division's farthest penetration indicated that remnants of the defeated Iraqi army were attempting to escape through the 24th Division's sector and onto the north. Major Stenson, the 2/7 S-3 remembers excellent visibility of the Iraqi column 2500 meters distant, several kilometers long, bumper to bumper. As a result, 1st Brigade commander Colonel LeMoyne requested an air cavalry troop and within 10 minutes the unit was on station.

The 1st Brigade moved forward with two infantry battalions abreast. The 2nd Battalion, 7th Infantry under Lieutenant Colonel Chuck Ware on the right came under fire from anti-tank weapons, but did not return it inasmuch as the enemy soldiers surrendered immediately.

However, when battalion scouts rounding up prisoners were fired on again, Lieutenant Colonel Ware received permission to return fire.

The American force effectively boxed the Iraqis in by use of the air cavalry troop to the north and fire ordered by General McCaffrey on the south. Lieutenant Colonel Tom Stewart, commander of the 1st Battalion, 24th Aviation, sent an Apache company on the attack. The pilots fired 107 Hellfire missiles, of which 102 scored direct hits.

Next, Colonel LeMoyne committed Lieutenant Colonel Craddock's 4th Battalion, 64th Armor to the battle. The tanks attacked from south to north along the entire length of the enemy columns.

By afternoon, the Battle of Rumayah Oil Field was over. It may have been one of the most one-sided in American Army history. The 1st Brigade and its attached units destroyed 187 armored vehicles, 34 artillery pieces, 400 trucks and other vehicles, nine rocket-launcher systems and seven missile systems. In addition thousands of Iraqi soldiers fled back into the Basrah pocket, and hundreds more were captured. Some trudged northward on foot.

The Victory Division's losses were one soldier wounded, an M-1 tank destroyed when an enemy tank next to it exploded, and one Bradley damaged.

Total combat casualties for the 24th Division during the 100-hour ground war were eight killed and 36 wounded.

General McCaffrey appraised the campaign this way: "I should underline that the valor, energy and training of the American soldiers won this great victory that freed Kuwait."

After the fighting, the 24th Division soldiers quickly shifted to humanitarian pursuits, building camps for the thousands of refugees and providing them with food and medical care.

Fittingly, given the spearhead role played by the Taro Leafers, President George Bush announced that the 24th Infantry Division (Mechanized) would be the first unit home.

On 6 March the first contingent left the Persian Gulf; two days later the division was relieved west of Basrah by the 1st Cavalry Division, which had a long history of fighting alongside the 24th Division. The two divisions went in abreast at Leyte in 1944 and together helped hold the Pusan Perimeter in 1950.

The Victory Division returned home to Fort Stewart where General McCaffrey, reflecting on the recent action, commented in a speech: "They attempted to run an operation against us, and they couldn't."

In some ways he spoke of a far different Army than the ones that had gone before. The division General McCaffrey led was high-tech and mechanized, its destructive power almost beyond comprehension.

But the modern 24th Division had one thing in common with its forebears: Whether the principal weapon is an M-1 rifle or a computer operated missile system, the indispensable component of any combat infantry division is the fighting man who must defeat the enemy on the ground where he finds them.

Generations of American soldiers wearing the Taro Leaf patch have demonstrated that fact repeatedly with honor and courage.

Lieutenant General Joseph DeFrancisco writes as follows of the final deactivation of the 24th Division:

"I took command of the Division on 15 June 1994. By that time, my predecessor, MG, later LTG Paul E. "Gene" Blackwell, had firmly reinstituted policies and procedures necessary to refocus the Division after returning from its brilliant performance in Desert Shield/Desert Storm. Our finely tuned deployment readiness posture and tough, realistic battle-focused training paid great dividends in the following months.

"During the 1994-1996 time frame, National Command Authorities called on the 24th numerous times in emergency situations. Large elements of the Division deployed to Cuba and Surinam for refugee operations, to central Georgia for flood relief support, and to Haiti, Kuwait and Saudi Arabia in response to threats to international security. The largest deployment was to Kuwait and Saudi Arabia in October 1994. Operation Vigilant Warrior included the movement of the Division CP and one brigade to Kuwait while a second brigade deployed to Saudi Arabia, all in response to threatening moves by the armed forces of Iraq.

"Training deployments included three iterations of Intrinsic Action in Kuwait, Operation Iron Falcon in the United Arab Emirates, Operation Bright Star in Egypt, three rotations to the National Training Center at Fort Polk, Louisiana, and seven rotations to the National Training Center at Fort Irwin, California. Throughout, the Division, its troops and junior leaders excelled in all facets of soldierly performance.

"The Iron Fist of XVIII Airborne Corps, as we were known, remained the Army's most modernized heavy division throughout this period. We fielded numerous major systems and pieces of advanced equipment including the Paladin 155mm self-propelled howitzer and the newest heavy equipment transport system.

"Due to a Department of the Army decision, the Division officially reflagged to the 3rd Infantry Division on 15 February 1996. On 25 April that year, we held a reflagging ceremony at Fort Stewart and, with all due respect and solemnity, cased the colors of the Victory Division. It is the fervent hope of many that those proud colors will someday fly again."

APPENDIX

GENERAL DEAN'S ODYSSEY

The conventional combat role of Major General William F. Dean as commander of the 24th Infantry Division lasted only three weeks. Yet that officer without question is one of the most notable figures ever to wear the Taro Leaf patch.

Battle at Rumalyah oil fields in Iraq. Persian Gulf War. 1991. (Courtesy of Kim Stenson)

MG William F. Dean, USA-Ret., May 21, 1981.

As recorded in a previous chapter, it was Dean who led the vanguard of American combat troops into Korea at the outset of war in 1950. A prisoner of war for three years, Dean, acclaimed the "hero of Taejon," survived to wear his nation's highest military decoration, the Medal of Honor.

Not long after his release from North Korean captivity in 1953, Dean described the experience in an autobiography, *General Dean's Story*, written with the assistance of William L. Worden. It is from that book that this chapter is drawn. All the factual presentations herein are attributed to that book, though some inferences, interpretations and commentary along the way are this author's own.

The history of the 24th Infantry Division and Dean's personal experience took separate directions from the moment around midnight of 20-21 July 1950, when the general took a headlong plunge down a mountainside and became forever separated from the small column of American soldiers trying to reach allied lines somewhere south of the city of Taejon, which had just fallen to the North Koreans.

The tumble down the steep slope knocked Dean unconscious and injured his shoulder. He had stepped out of the line because he thought he heard the trickling of water and wanted to find it. Before that happened, the general was helping carry a badly wounded man, which caused him and the others to fall behind the main body of the group, 17 Americans and one South Korean.

The casualties had consumed all the available water, and Dean considered the need for resupply rather urgent. His aide, Lieutenant Arthur Clarke, who was leading the column, at one point vetoed the general's water expedition as being likely to bring the North Koreans down upon them again. Later, Clarke, realizing the commanding general was missing, ordered a halt for the remainder of the night and the following day while waiting in vain for Dean's return.

Clarke succeeded in leading the column to rejoin American forces two days later. Dean spent his three years of captivity in the sad belief that Clarke probably had been killed, but as it happened, the young officer survived the war and now lives in Ft. Collins, CO. Dean held the same belief about another of his aides, Captain David Bissett, who had been constantly agitating for a line command. Dean assumed that after his own capture, Bissett would succeed in becoming a company commander, but higher authorities recognized the officer's organizational talents and he was diverted back to staff work. Bissett too managed to prove his former boss wrong and live through the war.

Thus began Dean's solitary odyssey through the rugged and confusing terrain of south central Korea armed only with Clarke's .45. Dean had lost his own side arm sometime during the withdrawal action, and the younger officer, having been wounded in the shoulder, relinquished his own as being useless to him.

This was not completely foreign territory to Dean. Two years before, the officer had served an occupation tour in South Korea as military governor. But on this trek, he had no compass and had to rely on his instincts and general knowledge of terrain to keep him moving in the right direction.

Inasmuch as Dean could not know how far the American and Republic of Korea troops had been pushed toward the southeast corner of the country, he was unable to pinpoint his destination. But the objective always was the same: Get back to his division, wherever it was, resume command and rejoin the fight.

Early in that particular ordeal, Dean determined one thing: He would avoid being taken prisoner at all costs. His main concern was the propaganda value the communists would be able to realize from the capture of a general officer.

Laboriously, and not always in a straight line, Dean made his way in the direction toward friendly lines, the enemy having passed through. That left the general behind their lines on the north. The injured shoulder from the fall down the hill made the going painful. And food was a constant problem.

Early in the trip, Dean came upon an American lieutenant, Stanley Tabor from the 19th Infantry, who also was trying to find his way back to his own lines. This party of two stayed together two or three days, but one night as they attempted to elude hostile riflemen while crossing a rice paddy, Tabor disappeared. The general thought the lieutenant was behind him, but when he looked back, Tabor was gone. With the possible exception of the brief glimpse at what Dean thought were American POWs marching in the snow near the Yalu River late that fall, Tabor's was the last American face the commander of the 24th Division would see for more than three years.

Dean had a special appreciation for Tabor, who had insisted on staying with the injured general even though as a younger man and unhurt he would have had a better chance of making it back alone, as Dean suggested. Dean learned later that Tabor too was captured, but did not survive to see freedom again.

Overall, Dean spent 35 days on the trail

trying to reach his division. Toward the end, he assumed his destination had to be Pusan, the port city on the extreme southeastern corner of the peninsula, beyond the city of Taegu. The general had discerned the military situation correctly in that regard, but never came within 120 miles of Pusan at any point.

Throughout the ordeal, Dean had little to eat and suffered much digestive distress of both extremes. Dysentery would plague him greatly during the early weeks of his captivity.

Experience taught Dean to move at night and hide during the day, and to give the villages a wide berth. However, on occasion, his audacity in the opposite direction paid off. He once walked straight through the middle of a town without being bothered. He also was successful at times in enlisting the help of South Korean civilians, who brought him food, primarily rice for which Dean developed a taste.

Once, the general was sheltered and fed by a farm family far up in the mountains for several days, but the Koreans became alarmed for their safety and considered it prudent to send the American officer on his way.

There were innumerable close calls and near misses. Once Dean was surrounded by a makeshift local militia in brush and weeds and somehow managed to slip through the cordon and escape.

The end of his flight finally came on 25 August near the city of Chinan, when Koreans who had seemed helpful and in whom Dean placed his trust turned him in. The general was armed with his .45 throughout the ordeal and was determined, if the occasion arose, to choose suicide over capture.

He never had that chance. When the time came, Dean was overpowered in a surprise attack by a large gang of men and had no opportunity for successful resistance or to take his own life. Thus it was some satisfaction to the soldier that though he was captured, he never surrendered.

During the winding, meandering foot trip toward the south, Dean never came close to reaching the lines of his division, but he did approach to within earshot of artillery fire, which gave him encouragement that the retreat may not have been as far as he earlier believed.

After his capture, Dean was taken to the police station in Chinan, due west of Taegu and directly south of Taejon. He spent the first night in a cage, literally, but shortly later began the trip northward by truck. One stop was in the familiar city of Taejon, where he had the strange experience of seeing his old Jeep. Eventually, Dean and his guards reached the North Korean capital of Pyongyang and then to the town of Sunan a short distance farther north.

During the early months of Dean's captivity, he was moved frequently, usually by truck and most often to houses, though he spent some time in public buildings. Though the general repeatedly asked to be sent to a prisoner-of-war camp, that plea was never granted. Later, when he learned what the American prisoners in those camps endured, he concluded that he was fortunate not to have been there. Nevertheless, Dean's firm belief was that as the senior American POW, his place was with the men of lesser rank where he at least could

97

exercise such moral authority as was possible to help ensure humane treatment of the other Americans, hundreds of whom no doubt were members of his 24th Division.

Dean was listed initially as missing in action and many assumed he was dead. His helmet liner with the two stars was found at Taejon, giving credence to that conclusion. However, in January 1951, his POW status was revealed.

Life in the various Korean houses was decidedly unpleasant for the captive during the first year and a half. The dwellings were poorly heated, if at all; sleeping conditions were exceptionally crowded. The typical room was eight-feet square and might have to accommodate as many as seven people, Dean and his guards. The houses were devoid of furniture. Except for what seemed to be arbitrary rules that made life even more uncomfortable than it had to be, Dean did not encounter sadism or much gratuitous cruelty. As an example of the strange rules, he was not allowed to lie or stand during the day. Sitting was the only permissible position. And the Koreans were reluctant to let their two-star captive exercise in the early going, mainly out of their insistence that he not be seen. Yet, in most ways he lived as the Koreans did and ate what they ate, which primarily was rice, various soups and some meat - pork and chicken mainly.

In the fall of 1950 during the big allied push northward, Dean was moved all the way to the Yalu River, and beyond into Manchuria briefly, obviously to prevent his liberation by American forces.

On the Korean side, Dean was billeted in the city of Manpo, and it was there, in a driving snow and sleet storm, that Dean caught a glimpse of a group of men he took to be other American prisoners of war. They were plodding wearily, their heads bent against the brutal weather.

The Koreans kept the stay in Manchuria as short as possible before they hustled their high-ranking prisoner back across the bridge. They clearly were anxious about the possibility of his being seen by the Chinese. Later, Dean was told that he was the only allied POW under the control of the North Koreans; the others were all held by the Chinese, though in due time the Chinese became aware of his presence.

As the war's fortunes shifted again, it was considered safe to bring Dean south to the Pyongyang area again. He was settled in a house in January 1951 and there began his worst year. Food was at its poorest, living conditions were uncomfortable, restrictions were at their highest and oddly enough, the captors seemed to have lost their interest in their prisoner.

Overall, it must be said that the North Korean treatment of Dean was comparatively decent, all things considered. He was not physically abused in any overt way, though the threat of torture early in the three-year ordeal resulted in the only case of personal animosity felt by Dean toward any of his captors, insofar as the book revealed.

During that stage, Dean was being kept under intense questioning, at times for many continuous hours. The Communists were after vital military and political information, such as the defense plans for Japan. Some were known by Dean and some were not, but either way, he was going to tell his captors nothing that would be any help to them. They also were eager for Dean to sign something, virtually any piece of paper the interrogator could take back to his superiors. One pressing issue was American air raids, some of which came close to the locations where Dean was being held. The North Koreans considered the air raids atrocities and wanted Dean's signature on documents so stating. He did agree to write a letter to American authorities, which the Reds no doubt considered a concession but which was intended by Dean to convey the message to his country's military that the bombing raids were not as effective as they should be. The language contained veiled suggestions that might have led the astute reader to understand how to improve the air war.

It was during the height of North Korean questioning that a Colonel Kim lost his patience and began talking of torture. He mentioned such unspeakable horrors as forcing water under pressure through the mouth or rectum, driving shoots under the fingernails and setting them afire (the thought of that one made Dean wince), and an electric shock treatment.

At this point, Dean, still in bad physical conditions from his ordeal before capture, more or less assumed he would not survive captivity, but he did not intend to go out quietly. More than that, he feared that in his weakened state, torture might cause him to say more than he should. So drastic action was called for.

Dean noticed that a guard had the habit of propping an automatic weapon in a corner of the room next to the one in which he was being held.

Dean's plan, if he could catch all the guards either asleep or paying no attention, was to crawl the few yards to the gun and fire a burst in order to draw Kim into the open. The next rounds would be for the North Korean colonel, and the last one would be for himself.

Dean was certain he could operate the weapon, a submachine gun with a drum magazine, without difficulty. Before his capture, he and his aide, Lieutenant Clarke, had familiarized themselves with one like it in Taejon.

Sure enough that morning, the guard dozed and Dean reached the gun. But it jammed, and the noise of the American trying to get the weapon to fire awoke the soldier. In an instant, North Koreans were all over the general, but they did not use more force than was necessary to subdue him. The incident brought a North Korean general into the picture and when Dean told him of Kim's torture threats, that was the the last of the contact between the colonel and the prisoner. It was obvious that the North Koreans had no interest in losing their two-star prisoner to suicide or in any other manner. Other indications of the same thing were the number of times Dean was able to bluff his captors through tough talk. The North Koreans usually would give in rather than retaliate. As for Colonel Kim, Dean made more than one mention of the hope he someday would meet his tormentor again under different circumstances.

No other North Korean earned the general's wrath. Though he liked some guards more than others, Dean noted the kindness and consideration of many. One man walked for miles through snow and bitter cold to deliver a letter he thought Dean would want to see. The captive knew most or all of the men by name, and one in particular, an enlisted man named De Soon Yur, Dean developed a genuine and lasting fondness for. "It is possible for men to be enemies and friends at the same time, and we were," the general wrote.

Though Dean was given propaganda material to read and was shown movies glorifying communism, his book does not reveal intense efforts at brainwashing on the part of his captors. Late in his captivity, the North Koreans made one serious effort to lure the American to their side, suggesting in a casual way that he was in the wrong army and offering him a corps command. Dean's answer was too unequivocal for them to pursue the matter any further. Earlier, an officer persuaded Dean to agree to go to China with him. Dean regretted his affirmative answer almost immediately and was quite relieved when the trip was turned down by higher authority.

The long-awaited truce on 27 July 1953 meant repatriation would not be far behind. It happened the first week in September. As General Dean rode in a Jeep from Kaesong to Panmunjon on that day, he noticed a column of trucks stopped alongside the road. They were full of American soldiers who also were on the way back to freedom. Some of them recognized the general as he passed and shouted greetings. "Those wonderful Yankee voices," as Dean called them, were the first of their kind he had heard in more than three years.

When the Jeep reached the head of the line, the vehicles proceeded to the exchange point where an American Army colonel welcomed home the commanding general of the 24th Infantry Division.

Dean did not consider himself a hero, and the reader of his biography is forced to believe the man was not engaging in false humility.

Fortunately, his country did not agree with the general's self-appraisal.

BELATED RECOGNITION

It took more than 40 years for one 24th Division soldier's heroism to be recognized by his country. Wayne "Johnnie" Johnson, of Phoenix, AZ, was an 18-year-old private first class in the 21st Infantry when he was captured by the North Koreans in July 1950 near Chochiwon. He had been at the front six days.

Through more than three years of captivity in North Korea, Pfc. Johnson secretly recorded the deaths of hundreds of his fellow prisoners, listing name, rank, hometown, unit and date. About 100 of those deaths occurred during a nine-day "death march" along the Yalu River in November 1950.

Even though record-keeping of any kind was against the rules of the North Korean captors, Johnson defiantly maintained his list. "I just felt like someone would want to know when these people died," he said.

Many of the names were those of his fellow 24th Division soldiers. The Associated Press cited two as examples: Pfc. William Griffith, Pittsburgh, PA, 1 November 1950, a member of the 34th Regiment; and Private Leonard Provost, Santa Clara, NY, 2 February 1951, who was in Johnson's regiment, the 21st.

Once a guard found his list , which the prisoner had hidden in the mud wall of his prison shack. Johnson was beaten severely and warned against further attempts to record the information. But he had kept a second copy and continued to maintain the list.

Finally as repatriation neared in August 1953, Johnson secreted the paper in a toothpaste tube and was able to smuggle it out. He told debriefers of the list but it was treated with little interest at that time. However, in 1996, a researcher came across the information, and Johnson at last received the recognition he deserved. Because of the chronicle the soldier kept at great risk to himself, the fate of hundreds of Americans, who otherwise would still be listed as missing and unaccounted for, has become known to the military and most important, their families.

For his courage and determination, Wayne Johnson, in August 1996 was awarded the Silver Star.

MEDAL OF HONOR

Twelve soldiers of the 24th Infantry Division between 1944 and 1951 so distinguished themselves with sacrificial and intrepid acts on the battlefield that the United States honored them with the highest combat decoration this country can bestow, the Medal of Honor.

The battle for Leyte in World War II was the occasion for two of those, the battle for Mindanao one, and the war in Korea the other nine. Eight of the 12 men were killed in the action for which they earned the medal and one more did not survive his resulting enemy captivity.

Medal of Honor awardees, their units, the dates and locations of the pertinent action are listed in order as follows:

Private HAROLD H. MOON, JR., Albuquerque, NM, Company G, 34th Infantry, 21 October 1944, near Pawing, Leyte;

Sergeant CHARLES E. MOWER, Chippewa Falls, WI, Company A, 34th Infantry, 3 November 1944, near Capoocan, Leyte;

Pfc. JAMES H. DIAMOND, New Orleans, LA, Company D, 21st Infantry, 8-14 May 1945, Mintal, Mindanao;

Major General WILLIAM F. DEAN, Berkeley, CA, commanding general of the 24th Infantry Division, 20-21 July 1950, Taejon, Korea;

Sergeant GEORGE D. LIBBY, Casco, ME, Company C, 3rd Engineer Battalion, 20 July 1950, Taejon, Korea;

Master Sergeant MELVIN O. HANDRICH, Manawa, WI, Company C, 5th Regimental Combat Team, 25-26 August 1950, near Sobuk San Mountain, Korea;

Corporal MITCHELL RED CLOUD, JR., Friendship, WI, Company E, 19th Infantry, 5 November 1950, near Chonghyon, Korea;

1st Lieutenant CARL H. DODD, Kenvir, KY, Company E, 5th Regimental Combat Team, 30-31 January, 1951, near Subuk, Korea;

Sergeant 1st Class NELSON BRITTIN, Audubon, NJ, Company I, 19th Infantry, 7 March 1951, near Yonggong-ni, Korea;

Sergeant 1st Class RAY E. DUKE, Whitwell, TN, Company C, 21st Infantry, 26 April 1951, near Mugok, Korea;

Sergeant 1st Class STANLEY T. ADAMS, Olathe, KA, Company A, 19th Infantry, 2 August 1951, near Sesim-ni, Korea;

Pfc. MACK A. JORDAN, Collins, MS., Company K, 21st Infantry, 15 November 1951, near Kumsong, Korea.

Only General Dean, Lieutenant Dodd and Sergeant Adams lived to receive the Medal of Honor personally. Sergeant Duke survived the immediate combat but died in a North Korean POW camp on 11 November 1951. The others were killed in action and received their decorations posthumously, as did Sergeant Duke.

Following are passages from each man's Medal of Honor citation:

Private HAROLD H. MOON, JR.: "He fought with conspicuous gallantry and intrepidity when powerful Japanese counterblows were being struck in a desperate effort to annihilate a newly won beachhead.

"In a forward position, armed with a submachine gun, he met the brunt of a strong, well-supported night attack which quickly enveloped his platoon's flanks. Many men in nearby positions were killed or injured. Private Moon was wounded as his foxhole became the immediate object of a concentration of mortar and machine gun fire. Nevertheless, he maintained his stand, poured deadly fire into the enemy, daringly exposed himself to hostile fire time after time to exhort and inspire what American troops were left in the immediate area.

"A Japanese officer, covered by machine gun fire and hidden by an embankment, attempted to knock out his position with grenades, but Private Moon, after protracted and skillful maneuvering, killed him.

"When the enemy advanced a light machine gun to within 20 yards of the shattered perimeter and fired with telling effects on the remnants of the platoon, he stood up to locate the gun and remained exposed while calling back range corrections to friendly mortars, which knocked out the weapon.

"A little later he killed two Japanese as they charged an aid man. By dawn, his position, the focal point of the attack for more than four hours, was virtually surrounded. In a fanatical effort to reduce it and kill its defender, an entire platoon charged with fixed bayonets. Firing from a sitting position, Private Moon calmly emptied his magazine into the advancing horde, killing 18 and repulsing the attack.

"In a final display of bravery, he stood up to throw a grenade at a machine gun, which had opened fire on the right flank. He was hit and instantly killed, falling in the position from which he had not been driven by the fiercest enemy action.

"Nearly 200 dead Japanese were found within 100 yards of his foxhole. The continued tenacity, combat sagacity and magnificent heroism with which Private Moon fought on against overwhelming odds contributed in a large measure to breaking up a powerful enemy threat and did much to ensure our initial successes during a most important operation."

Sergeant CHARLES E. MOWER: "He was an assistant squad leader in an attack against strongly defended enemy positions on both sides of a stream running through a wooded gulch. As the squad advanced through concentrated fire, the leader was killed and Sergeant Mower assumed command.

"In order to bring direct fire upon the enemy, he had started to lead his men across the stream, which by this time was churned by machine gun and rifle fire. But he was severely wounded before reaching the opposite bank. After signaling his unit to halt, he realized his own exposed position was the most advantageous point from which to direct the attack, and stood fast.

"Half submerged, gravely wounded but refusing to seek shelter or accept aid of any kind, he continued to shout and signal to his

MG Blackshear M. Bryan, CG, 24 Division and M/Sgt Stanley Adams, Medal of Honor Recipient-1951. (Courtesy of H.J. Maihafer)

squad as he directed it in the destruction of two enemy machine guns and numerous riflemen.

"Discovering that the intrepid man in the stream was largely responsible for the successful action being taken against them, the remaining Japanese concentrated the full force of their firepower upon him, and he was killed while still urging his men on.

"Sergeant Mower's gallant initiative and heroic determination aided materially in the successful completion of his squad's mission. His magnificent leadership was an inspiration to those with whom he served."

Pfc. JAMES H. DIAMOND: "When a Japanese sniper rose from his foxhole to throw a grenade into their midst, this valiant soldier charged and killed the enemy with a burst from his submachine gun. Then, by delivering sustained fire from his personal arm and simultaneously directing the fire of 105-mm and .50 caliber weapons upon the enemy pillboxes... he enabled (the American crews) to put their guns into action.

"When two infantry companies established a bridgehead, he voluntarily assisted in evacuating the wounded under heavy fire, and then, securing an abandoned vehicle, transported casualties to the rear through mortar and artillery fire so intense as to render the vehicle inoperable, despite the fact he was suffering from a painful wound.

"The following day he again volunteered, this time for the hazardous job of repairing a bridge under heavy enemy fire. On 14 May 1945 when leading a patrol to evacuate casualties from his battalion, which was cut off, he ran through a virtual hail of Japanese fire to secure an abandoned machine gun. Though mortally wounded, he reached the gun. He succeeded in drawing sufficient fire upon himself so that the remaining members of the patrol could reach safety. Pfc. Diamond's indomitable spirit, constant disregard of danger, and eagerness to assist his comrades will ever remain a symbol of selflessness and heroic sacrifice to those for whom he gave his life."

Major General WILLIAM F. DEAN: "In command of a unit suddenly relieved from occupation duties in Japan and as yet untried in combat, faced with a ruthless and determined enemy, highly trained and overwhelmingly superior in numbers, he felt it his duty to take action which to a man of his military experience and knowledge was clearly apt to result in his death.

"He personally and alone attacked an enemy tank while armed only with a hand grenade. He also directed the fire of his tanks from an exposed position with neither cover nor concealment while under observed artillery and small-arms fire.

"When the town of Taejon was finally overrun, he refused to ensure his own safety by leaving with the leading elements, but remained behind, organizing his retreating forces, directing stragglers, and was last seen assisting the wounded to a place of safety.

"These actions indicated that Major General Dean felt it necessary to sustain the courage and resolution of his troops by examples of excessive gallantry committed always at the threatened portions of his front lines.

"The magnificent response of his unit to this willing and cheerful sacrifice, made with the full knowledge of its certain cost, is history. The success of this phase of the campaign is in large measure due to Major General Dean's heroic leadership, courageous and loyal devotion to his men, and his complete disregard for personal safety."

Sergeant GEORGE D. LIBBY: "While breaking through an enemy encirclement, the vehicle in which he was riding approached an enemy roadblock and encountered devastating fire, which disabled the truck, killing or wounding all the passengers except Sergeant Libby.

"Taking cover in a ditch, Sergeant Libby engaged the enemy and despite the heavy fire crossed the road twice to administer aid to his wounded comrades. He then hailed a passing M-5 artillery tractor and helped the wounded aboard. The enemy directed intense small-arms fire at the driver, and Sergeant Libby, realizing that no one else could operate the vehicle, placed himself between the driver and the enemy, thereby shielding him while he returned the fire.

"During this action, he received several wounds in the arms and body. Continuing through the town, the tractor made frequent stops and Sergeant Libby helped more wounded aboard.

"Refusing first aid, he continued to shield the driver and return the fire of the enemy when another roadblock was encountered. Sergeant Libby received additional wounds, but held his position until he lost conciousness. Sergeant Libby's sustained, heroic actions enabled his comrades to reach friendly lines."

Master Sergeant MELVIN O. HANDRICH: "His company was engaged in repulsing an estimated 150 enemy who were threatening to overrun its position. Near midnight on 25 August, a hostile group over 100 strong attempted to infiltrate the company perimeter. Sergeant Handrich, despite the heavy enemy fire, voluntarily left the comparative safety of the defensive area and moved to a forward position where he could direct mortar and artillery fire upon the advancing enemy.

"He remained at this post for eight hours directing fire against the enemy who often approached to within 50 feet of his position.

"Again, on the morning of 26 August, another strong hostile force made an attempt to overrun the company's position. With complete disregard for his safety, Sergeant Handrich rose to his feet and from this exposed position fired his rifle and directed mortar and artillery fire on the attackers.

"At the peak of this action he observed elements of his company preparing to withdraw. He perilously made his way across fire-swept terrain to the defense area where, by example and forceful leadership, he reorganized the men to continue the fight.

"During the action, Sergeant Handrich was severely wounded. Refusing to take cover or be evacuated, he returned to his forward position and continued to direct the company's fire. Later, a determined enemy attack overran Sergeant Handrich's position and he was mortally wounded. When the position was retaken,

over 70 enemy dead were counted in the area he had so intrepidly defended."

Corporal MITCHELL RED CLOUD, JR.: "From his position on the point of a ridge immediately in front of the company command post, he was the first to detect the approach of the Chinese Communist forces and give the alarm as the enemy charged from a brush-covered area less than 100 feet from him. Springing up, he delivered devastating point-blank automatic rifle fire into the advancing enemy. His accurate and intense fire checked this assault and gained time for the company to consolidate its defense.

"With utter fearlessness, he maintained his firing position until severely wounded by enemy fire. Refusing assistance, he pulled himself to his feet and wrapping his arm around a tree continued his deadly fire again, until he was fatally wounded.

"This heroic act stopped the enemy from overrunning his company's position and gained time for the reorganization and evacuation of the wounded."

1st Lieutenant CARL H. DODD: "Dodd, given the responsibility of spearheading an attack to capture Hill 256, a key terrain feature defended by a well-armed, crafty foe who had withstood several previous assaults, led his platoon forward over hazardous terrain under hostile small-arms, mortar and artillery fire from well-camouflaged enemy emplacements, which reached such intensity that his men faltered.

"With utter disregard for his safety, Lieutenant Dodd moved among his men, reorganized and encouraged them, and then singlehandedly charged the first hostile machine gun nest, killing or wounding all its occupants.

"Inspired by his incredible courage, his platoon responded magnificently and, fixing bayonets and throwing grenades, closed on the enemy and wiped out every hostile position as it moved relentlessly onward to its initial objective.

"Securing the first series of enemy positions, Dodd again reorganized his platoon and led them across a narrow ridge and onto Hill 256. Firing his rifle and throwing grenades, he advanced at the head of his platoon despite the intense concentrated hostile fire which was brought to bear on their narrow avenue of approach.

"When his platoon was still 200 yards from the objective, he moved ahead and with his last grenade destroyed an enemy mortar, killing the crew.

"Darkness then halted the advance, but at daybreak, Dodd, again boldly advancing ahead of his unit, led the platoon through a dense fog against the remaining hostile position. With bayonet and grenades he continued to set pace without regard for the danger to his life, until he and his troops had eliminated the last of the defenders and had secured the final objective. Lieutenant Dodd's superb leadership and extraordinary heroism inspired his men to overcome this strong enemy defense ... ."

Sergeant 1st Class NELSON V. BRITTIN: "Volunteering to lead his squad up a hill, with meager cover against murderous fire from the enemy, he ordered his squad to give him support and, in the face of withering fire and bursting shells, he tossed a grenade at the nearest enemy position. On returning to his squad, he was knocked down and wounded by an enemy grenade. Refusing medical attention, he replenished his supply of grenades and returned, hurling grenades into hostile positions and shooting the enemy as they fled. When his weapon jammed, he leaped without hesitation into a foxhole and killed the occupants with his bayonet and the butt of his rifle. He continued to wipe out foxholes and, noting that his squad had been pinned down, he rushed to the rear of a machine gun position, threw a grenade into the nest, and ran around to its front where he killed all three occupants with his rifle.

"Less than 100 yards up the hill, his squad again came under vicious fire from another camouflaged, sandbagged machine gun nest well-flanked by supporting riflemen. Sergeant Brittin again charged this new position in an aggressive endeavor to silence this remaining obstacle and ran directly into a burst of automatic fire, which killed him instantly.

"In his sustained and driving action, he had killed 20 enemy soldiers and destroyed four automatic weapons. The conspicuous courage, consummate valor and noble self-sacrifice displayed by Sergeant Brittin enabled his inspired company to attain its objective ... ."

Sergeant 1st Class RAY E. DUKE: "Upon learning that several of his men were isolated and heavily engaged in an area yielded by his platoon when ordered to withdraw, he led a small force in a daring assault which recovered the position and the beleaguered men.

"Another enemy attack in strength resulted in numerous casualties but Sergeant Duke, although wounded by mortar fragments, calmly moved along his platoon line to coordinate fields of fire and to urge his men to hold firm in the bitter encounter.

"Wounded a second time, he received first aid and returned to his position. When the enemy again attacked after dawn, despite his wounds, Sergeant Duke repeatedly braved withering fire to ensure maximum defense of each position. Threatened with annihilation and with mounting casualties, the platoon was again ordered to withdraw when Sergeant Duke was wounded a third time in both legs and was unable to walk. Realizing that he was impeding the progress of two comrades who were carrying him from the hill, he urged them to leave him and seek safety. He was last seen pouring devastating fire into the ranks of the onrushing assailants."

Master Sergeant STANLEY T. ADAMS: "At approximately 0100, Sergeant Adams' platoon, holding an outpost some 200 yards ahead of his company, came under a determined attack by an estimated 250 enemy troops. Intense small-arms, machine gun and mortar fire from three sides pressed the platoon back against the main line of resistance.

"Observing approximately 150 hostile troops silhouetted against the skyline advancing against his platoon, Sergeant Adams leaped to his feet, urged his men to fix bayonets and he, with 13 members of his platoon, charged this hostile force with indomitable courage. Within 50 yards of the enemy, Sergeant Adams was knocked to the ground when pierced in the leg by an enemy bullet. He jumped to his feet and ignoring his wound continued on to close with the enemy when he was knocked down four times from the concussion of grenades which had bounced off his body.

"Shouting orders, he charged the enemy positions and engaged them in hand-to-hand combat where man after man fell before his terrific onslaught with bayonet and rifle butt.

"After nearly an hour of vicious action, Sergeant Adams and his comrades routed the fanatical foe, killing over 50 and forcing the remainder to withdraw.

"Upon receiving orders that his battalion was moving back, he provided cover fire while his men withdrew. Sergeant Adams' superb leadership, incredible courage and consummate devotion to duty so inspired his comrades that the enemy attack was completely thwarted, saving his battalion from possible disaster."

Pfc. MACK A. JORDAN: "As a squad leader of the third platoon, he was participating in a night attack on key terrain against a fanatical hostile force when the advance was halted by intense small-arms and automatic-weapons fire and a vicious barrage of hand grenades.

"Upon orders for the platoon to withdraw and reorganize, Pfc. Jordan voluntarily remained behind to provide covering fire. Crawling toward an enemy machine gun emplacement, he threw three grenades and neutralized the gun. He then rushed the position, delivering a devastating hail of fire, killing several of the enemy and forcing the remainder to fall back to new positions.

"He courageously attempted to move foward to silence another machine gun, but before he could leave his position, the ruthless foe hurled explosives down the hill and in the ensuing blast both legs were severed. Despite mortal wounds, he continued to deliver deadly fire and held off the assailants until the platoon returned."

24TH INFANTRY DIVISION

"The Victory Division"

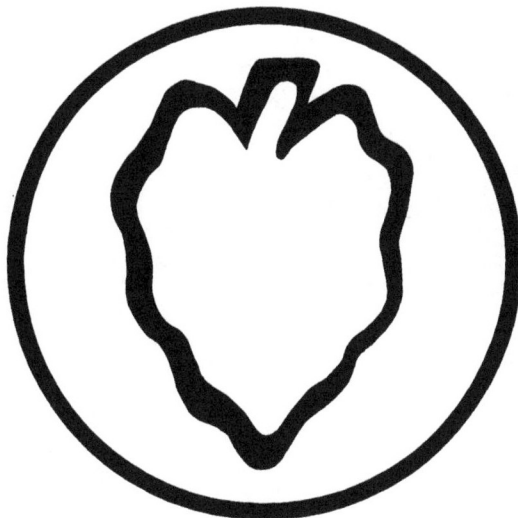

First to Fight
"Jungle, Snow, and Sand"

24TH INFANTRY DIVISION
SPECIAL STORIES

So, You Want to be Airborne!

by Malcolm D. Aitken

After elements of the 24th Division had completed their mop-up of positions on the island of Mindoro, we entered into still another training cycle, and life became boring again. During this period, I spent many a night in poker games, quite often with officers of the 503rd Parachute Infantry RCT, bivouacked nearby. During the day, I watched the 503rd troops going through their endless practice jumps and at night I listened to my poker playing buddies, many of whom were going through the same jumps during the day, recounting their exciting stories of previous airborne assaults at night.

Before long, the boredom and the exposure to the airborne mystique got to me, so I approached one of my poker-playing friends to see how I could go about transferring to the 503rd. I was told that the Airborne RCT was short of officers, and that the CO, Col. Jones, was anxiously awaiting additional company grade officer replacements before their next mission, which wasn't too far distant.

An appointment was arranged for me with Col. Jones, and I went through the Battalion Commander and Regimental Commander of the 21st to request permission to seek a transfer to the 503rd. To my surprise, I received quick approval but, unexpectedly, Col. Verbeck, the Regimental CO, directed me to also obtain the approval of the Division Commander.

Now I had more than a speaking acquaintance with Maj. Gen. Roscoe B. Woodruff, the Division Commander, as we had met on the volleyball court on numerous occasions when our Regimental Officers team had taken on the Division Headquarters team. I felt reasonably confident that he would remember me from those occasions, rubber-stamp the request - no problem. When I reported to the General, I stood at attention after explaining my presence, but received neither recognition nor permission to stand at ease.

General Woodruff whirled around in his chair, grabbed the EE-8 phone crank and gave it a twist, and asked the operator to connect him with the CO of the 503rd. When Col. Jones came on the line, the conversation went like this: "Jones, this is Woodruff. I understand that you've been soliciting one of my officers for transfer to your regiment." Brief silence. "Well, then hear this. If you want someone to test your parachutes, I'll send you over some sacks of sand, but until then you will discontinue your officer recruiting in this Division; is that clear?" I presume it was clear to Col. Jones, because the general then rang off, turned to me and asked: "Any questions?" I had none," so he dismissed me. Within two weeks, the 503rd had jumped on Corregidor, suffering many casualties, and we were on board ship headed for Mindanao.

Commentary:
24th Division's Occupation of Japan, 1947-1949

by J.M. Williamson

At the end of World War II the 24th Infantry Division/Artillery relocated to Fukuoka, Kyushu, Japan at Camp Hakata, a former Japanese naval base. The artillery units were engaged in a number of missions not normally performed by tactical units. These included those installation functions normally performed by Post, Camp and Station units.

I, Joseph M. Williamson, then a lieutenant colonel, commanded the 13th Field Artillery Battalion during the period January 1947 to July 1949. My duties, in addition to normal tactical unit command duties, included that of Provost Court Officer for the adjudication of alleged violations of the occupation rules by the Japanese in the Fukuoka area. I had an office, court room and small civilian staff located in the city of Fukuoka. I would usually hold court once a week. I also coordinated with Japanese authorities in matters pertaining to support from the U.S. military. I have a photo showing me conferring with the governor of Fukuoka Prefecture during "Operation Earthquake," a disaster relief plan. Since there was no military police unit assigned to the area, my battalion was given the mission of providing this service. One of my batteries was stationed in the city of Fukuoka with personnel on a rotating basis. Another duty not included in the normal artillery mission was to plan for the defense of the Army Air Corps Itazuke Air Field. Other officers from my unit were detailed to other functions not related to artillery. One served as a military government official in the Fukuoka area; another served as the Post Exchange Officer; another as Provost Marshal in Fukuoka.

One outstanding event was the 13th Field Artillery Battalion being selected as the unit to be reviewed by Lt. Gen. Robert Eichelberger, Commanding General Eighth Army on 5 March 1947. His reviewing party included Maj. Gen. Roscoe Woodruff the I Corps Commander; Eighth Army Chief of Staff, Maj. Gen. Clovis Byers; and Maj. Gen. James Lester, Commanding General, 24th Infantry Division. An interesting side-lite of this inspection was that the World War II combat boots with their rough finish were not really intended to be shined. So the Army did not provide a product for this purpose. I directed that axle grease used for vehicles be rubbed on them. It was better than nothing.

In 1947 and 1948 my unit did normal garrison duties and conducted unit training which included field firing of weapons. Maneuvers were conducted with the 19th Infantry Regiment under tactical conditions. These were conducted in the Kurume, Hijudai and Saitogaki areas.

An interesting arrangement during the occupation at this time was the attachment of Japanese labor units to units. The one attached to my battalion performed various duties under the control of a "labor boss," an English speaking Japanese national. I had two English speaking Japanese girls doing clerical duties in my headquarters. The battalion "adopted" a Japanese orphan as its mascot. A uniform was fitted to him. He was a great morale booster.

The battalion often had to improvise to get the job done. The axle grease I mentioned for shining boots is an example. Another example included cutting up the standard issue long planked dining tables with benches and building tables and chairs for seating four individuals.

Although I was reminded that I could be court-martialed for the destruction of government property, it was not long before the other units had done the same thing. I could mention others but one innovation did not turn out as expected and now over 50 years later can be considered as humorous. I asked the culprit to relate the episode to me. A copy of the letter I received is enclosed. The Art referred to in the letter is the former battery commander of Mr. Rhodes, Arthur Travis, then a captain.

By the time that I was reassigned to the United States in July 1949, the division artillery was reduced to a skeleton command. Troop strength was greatly reduced and most of the vehicles had been placed in limited storage.

Ole Glory with Mt. Fuji in the background of Camp McNair, Japan. July 1952. (Courtesy of John Dennis)

GOING SOLO

by Marion Thacker

On 9 August 1950 my best buddy, Bobby E. Lawson, was substituting for our driver who was so tired that he was getting dangerous for us to let drive. We knew about the dangers of going through the pass toward Tugbok but we did it to kick off a counter attack that eventually fizzled and died. But Lawson, being new to the trade, didn't know how far he should back over the pass, as no one had told him, before we opened up and sent everyone on the opposite hill scurrying for cover. The North Koreans had zeroed in on the pass with one of their anti-tank weapons that was just a little bit larger than our own 50 caliber bullets. It was a very long rifle with a very high muzzle velocity and was pulled around on two wheels. Lawson backed into the pass and slowed down and they opened up with their anti-tank rifle. Unfortunately the shell hit Lawson in the back of the neck, proceeded to cut the steering wheel in two, bending the two jagged ends into the dash and proceeded on through the dash to hit the left front tire. We sent Lawson back for medical help but, to no one's surprise, he died soon after reaching the hospital. We bent out the steering wheel as best we could and took the M-16 halftrack back to Yongsan, where the 26th AAA had its Command Post (CP), to try to get repairs. We pretty much ruined the tire getting it there but I guess it was already in bad shape.

On 10 August 1950, we were settling in to await the tire from Japan. Grant Agne, who I know today, came into the CP wearing only his pants. He reported that several of them who were on outpost or infantry duty at Agok were going back along this road and decided to take a bath in a nearby pond or stream. All of them were captured except Grant and Norman McLeod, a medic that just recently died. I believe that he died last year or the year before. McLeod had run with Grant and took a bullet and was grievously wounded. Grant had tried to hide him and came on in. By the time we got out there he had moved himself. We quickly made up a volunteer crew and took a tire from a truck and put it on the left front of the halftrack Even though it was much too small the lugs all fit the wheel. As I recall, this all volunteer crew consisted of lst Lt. Daniel Boone of Kentucky as commander; Albert Lewchuck from New Jersey as driver; an Indian or Oriental kid who I didn't know was the gunner. He told me that he was a replacement. But, there were several Indians in the outfit that I didn't know as they pretty well kept to themselves; Kenneth Lewis from Pennsylavania as cannonier and myself from Kentucky aa cannonier. Our intent was to find the medic and rescue as many of the guys as we could.

The upshot or end result was that we never found the medic, and ran through a road block about 3/4 miles long. Boone was wounded. I thought that Lewis was wounded too. The guy I didn't know, who was our gunner, was killed. I know this for a fact for I tried to take him out of the turret so that I could use the quad-fifties, and I eventually got burned real bad. Thank goodness Lewchuck was unharmed. I think that

if he had been, we would all have been captured had we wrecked and more than one of us would have been dead. We were going as fast as the halftrack would go, about 44 mph in a vehicle which could usually do 48 mph.

The crux of the story is, I was the only one shooting at the North Koreans. My job became very clear to me then, I couldn't let the Koreans onto the road and possibly get us stopped. I had to do all in my power to prevent Al Lewchuck from being hit. As the North Koreans seemed to be poor shots, even with a machine gun, and were stupid enough to concentrate on the only guy shooting at them, I just kept shooting. About then a bullet hit me and my glasses, leaving a bleeding gash through my left eyebrow. I took a little more shrapnel in the face then heard a bullet hit something just over me; then I felt the coolness of gasoline pouring over me. I had no idea where the gasoline was coming from and gave it very little thought.

As I couldn't see very well, I decided to just shoot at the horizon as I could distinguish the sky and the earth. I hoped that this would keep them off the road. Pretty soon I felt a difference in temperature for I had broken into a sheet of flames. I suspect that a tracer bullet had ignited the gasoline. I didn't know what had been hit or where the gasoline was coming from. I never thought about it much, as I couldn't stay there. I yelled at Al as I was bailing out of the halftrack, "I'm burning," and hit the ground rolling, but I guess that my clothing was pretty well consumed by the time that I quit rolling. Someone was tugging on my clothing and I thought, "Oh no, the dirty SOBs are going to torture me." I opened one eye a crack to see if I could see an advantage of any kind and to my amazement saw Al Lewchuck bending over me. He was pulling the still smoldering clothes off my body as best he could. I then opened both eyes and saw that little puffs of dust, dirt, or sand were jumping up around us. I don't know what I said to him but he grabbed my good arm and stood me up and said, "Come on Diggah (they called me Digger for a long time) Lets get atta heah." I tried to run back to the halftrack but was pretty slow; this was the last time that I

was on my feet for eight or nine months, but I eventually got there, but I don't remember ever getting on it. I remember that I was happy to see that the halftrack was out of the line of fire. Al is dead now, but I saw him before he died. It broke my heart to see him suffering from the cancer that he had. I had just recently realized that Al had come from a place of safety into an unsafe place to get me. I tried to get Al a Silver Star Post for this deed but the Army wanted me to pay for it, investigation and all. Without knowing what this could eventually cost me, I couldn't see myself signing a blank check for them. I finally sent it to a congressman from New Jersey and never heard any more about it. You've heard of black holes but I don't think this one was black.

I recall waking up on a stretcher in Agok. Agok was a small village near where my comrades were doing outpost duty. I could hear much gunfire and begged the medic for a gun with which to defend myself. He steadfastly refused thinking, I suppose, that I wanted to kill myself, but the thought had never entered my mind. I passed out again and woke up again the next day, 11 August 1950. As we were leaving the place we were meeting a convoy of trucks which someone said belonged to the Wolfhounds of the 25th Division.

With my limited vision I could see that the trucks were coming pretty close to the guy's feet that was laying across the hood. I yelled, "Watch that man's feet." Just then the truck we were meeting lurched in the muddy road and did indeed hit them. Someone raised from the cab over which I was placed on a stretcher and told me, "Don't worry, he really didn't feel anything as he was already dead." I don't remember any more about that trip.

The next time that I awakened a little was when they were loading me on a helicopter. I was an unhappy person, for the rotor in my face was about to drive me nuts. A medic tried to fix it for me. He told me that I was lucky that I was getting out of that hell-hole and going back where I could get all the cold beer that I wanted whenever I wanted it. I tried to hit him and then passed out again.

24th Motor Patrol Company. Korea. (Courtesy of Charles Lacroix)

I briefly awakened on a deck of some sort with many men on stretchers. A non-com was walking among the stretchers with several bottles saying Bourbon, Scotch, Gin, and something else but I had quit listening and said Scotch He pulled a glass out of his pocket and poured from one of the bottles. I tried to reach for it and discovered that I had bandages all over me, but my face. He held the glass to my lips and I'm sure that I drank the whole thing. That was about the best drink of Scotch that I can ever remember having. But, I passed out that time too, for I don't even remember my body or head hitting the stretcher.

The next thing that I remember is a bit weird. I was in charge of a group of people in a cave in which water was rising but I could see the glow around the bend ahead. I must have been the only person who could see it for I had to keep driving the people to keep the water from inundating them. This was a recurring dream but it all finally came into focus for me. Black curtains were drawn up tightly about my bed. The glow was from a ceiling light which was just out of sight behind the curtain, and water was coursing through my bandages making me feel cool. I yelled and a nurse who had been sitting outside the curtain stuck her head inside and asked, "Did you make a noise?" I thought that woman had the biggest eyes that I had ever seen. I said, "I guess I did and I'm so hungry I could eat a horse." She said, with her big eyes shining, "Just a minute," and disappeared. I soon discovered that I could have given her much more than a minute for I had them to spare over the next year. Soon there were four men bending over me. One said, "I'm your doctor. You are in the Tokyo Hospital and I understand that you are hungry." I said, "I sure am," and he said, "What would you like." I said, "I would like the biggest steak that you can find." He said, "It will be up shortly." Pretty soon I got a little cup of steak broth which was good even if it fell far short of my expectations.

I stayed awake this time and pretty soon the pain started. I don't remember much of anything else for several months except once a General Collins came through. Someone whispered that he was the Chief of Staff. He was looking for someone that he could give a medal to so that he could get his picture taken. They brought him in to my bed and told him aside, "This man is in about as bad a shape as they get." I wish they had told me instead of him but back then I was pretty courteous. Back then I could still hear pretty good. But, the Purple Heart doesn't have my name on it. To this day I haven't gotten the set of orders for the Purple Heart that he awarded me that day nor have I gotten a copy of the picture.

Sometime in 1951 I was getting about well enough to get out of the service. I retired 31 October 1951, so they brought me a paper to sign. It had the wrong serial number on it so I pointed this out to them and felt that it would be changed as they wrote it boldly with a pencil in the block. I now have a copy of that paper but there is no change on page two. it never occurred to me then that all of my medical records were under this erroneous serial number. So if there is someone out there who has serial number RA 13 373 209 please contact me. This number is from West Virginia, Virginia, Washington DC, Maryland, or Pennsylvania. My real number is RA 15 378 209 and is a Kentucky number. The 15 was issued in Kentucky, Ohio, parts of West Virginia, Indiana and parts of Illinois.

None of the volunteer crew of which this is written ever got an award of any kind for their efforts. This is one reason that I'm pretty sure that Boone was wounded, for he is now deceased. He was a good officer. He and Grimes and Blalock were all good officers. I don't know what to say about Harrison and Garvey for I never saw either of them in the field after we went to Korea.

As I was in a Navy hospital I saw a lot of Marines. Forgive me if I see them all with their chests covered with Bronze and Silver Stars. I guess that I grew a bit skeptical when I'd see many medals on a chest, for in the Army they were scarce as hen's teeth among enlisted men. My feeling was that the senior officers got DSCs. The junior officers got Silver and Bronze Stars. Enlisted men got zilch, and it didn't even have a ribbon on it. I have great hopes that this all changed sometime after I was gone, for all that I saw from the Korean War later on were Marines.

CHAPLAIN O'GARA

by Donald E. Montgomery

On a cold Korean night in the early 1950s, I was driving our 19th Infantry Regiment Chaplain, Reverend Donald B. O'Gara, to an urgent meeting at 24th "Victory" Division Headquarters. Recently I'd been promoted out of a rifle company to regimental headquarters, so I naturally took great pride in my newly assigned jeep. I kept it in tip-top shape and developed a reputation for quick, reliable trips. At this particular time, we were practically flying along the dark, unpaved, Main Supply Route (MSR), churning up huge, billowing clouds of dust behind us.

Out of the alert corner of my right eye, which was scanning the dark roadside for hidden dangers, I also noticed the kindly Reverend's lips moving rapidly as if in earnest, silent prayer. It was common knowledge enemy Chinese and North Korean Communist infiltrators were lurking about, so I assumed our Chaplain was praying because he was frightened. Seeking to calm him down and bolster his spirits, I ventured some words of comfort.

"Don't worry, sir, I've got my forty-five right here at my side!" I emphasized this assurance with a sweeping right-arm gesture, loudly slapping the big pistol holster fastened to my cartridge belt.

Instantly the good Reverend snapped out of his prayerful reveries and said, "It's not the enemy I'm worried about, it's your driving!"

I was so surprised by his quick, witty reply, I almost drove off the road.

What a bright, spirited, kindly person was Chaplain O'Gara! It was said of him he was much too old to be a chaplain in Korea in 1952-54, but, as the story was told, he begged his bishop in his native San Francisco to let him go, and the bishop let him have his way. Believe me, the troops in the 19th were mighty glad Chaplain O'Gara got to serve them.

In spite of many adverse situations, Chaplain O'Gara cheerfully persisted and lightened the burdens of us all. He never complained about the tough conditions. Instead, he brought comfort, sympathy, and good humor to many a sad and frightened soldier far from home.

Many are the stories told about Chaplain O'Gara. For example, I'm thinking about the time the Red Cross told a soldier his mother died, but it was really the mother of another soldier in the 19th who had the same name. Both soldiers knew each other through frequent mail mix-ups and other confusions, but this was the worst mix-up of all, since the news reached the wrong boy. A few days later, Chaplain O'Gara got the tough job of correcting the error.

On another occasion, early one evening, Chaplain O'Gara was called to L Company of the 19th to give last rights to a soldier who choked to death on a chicken bone. I didn't witness the tragic affair, since I only drove the Chaplain over there and waited for him in my jeep. Later, on the way back, however, the Chaplain told me about it, and that the unfortunate soldier had a wife and two small children back home. Combat deaths were rare in Korea at that time after the truce was signed, but other kinds of deaths unfortunately occurred, and Chaplain O'Gara usually had to deal with them.

There were other memorable incidents I can recall involving Chaplain O'Gara's sojourn with the 19th. Of those, one particularly unusual one stands out. It happened the day before the good chaplain rotated back to the USA.

Several of us were standing on a hillside in the middle of the afternoon, shaking hands with Chaplain O'Gara and bidding him good-bye. While we were there, a few other well-wishers and farewellers arrived, creating a small circle of troops around the chaplain. Then the regimental supply sergeant showed up. When it was the sergeant's turn to say something, the rest of us waited while he stepped forward and, choked with emotion at the thought of Chaplain O'Gara's leaving, suddenly handed the good reverend a shiny .45 caliber pistol.

Chaplain O'Gara hesitated a moment while the rest of us froze in disbelief. Sensing everyone's hesitation, the supply sergeant cheerfully said, "It's OK, Reverend, the serial number is listed as missing in combat!"

We lower ranking onlookers began biting our lips and tongues to avoid open laughter at so bizarre a presentation. Chaplain O'Gara, however, without batting an eye or flinching or smirking, kindly thanked the sergeant for his generous gift and sentiment. Then he carefully handed the pistol back, declining the gift with the excuse he might get into trouble with the MPs (Military Police) if they caught him smuggling such a weapon out of Korea. The good reverend never suggested the pistol was an inappropriate gift for a chaplain, nor did he ridicule the sergeant in any way or hurt his feelings.

Not much more than a year before Chaplain O'Gara's death on 11 March 1984, I

USO girls in Kyushu, Japan. (Courtesy of Francis Haugh)

found him in a Los Gatos, California Jesuit retirement home. My wife and I visited him with our unusually large family of four boys and four girls. It was our one big family vacation of a lifetime before our older children began leaving the roost, and it was a chance for some snow-bound Minnesotans to spend Christmas in California visiting Disneyland and other well known places. I also wanted my do-it-yourself army to meet an unusual chaplain and former acquaintance.

Chaplain O'Gara was now living in a beautiful setting overlooking the San Francisco Bay Area from a southwestern perspective. He looked the same as I remembered him, and looked so much his lively, spirited self, I had no idea he'd been ill with leukemia and other problems leading to his passing a year later.

Graciously the good chaplain took my large family on a tour of the place, showing us splendid views of the bay area and pointing out several tourist attractions, including an enormous dirigible hangar in the distance at Moffit Field in Sunnyvale, where the Goodyear Blimp sometimes parks.

Chaplain O'Gara seemed his old self from Korean War days, even commenting to my wife about my talkative tendencies, if not my driving. My wife, of course, much to my annoyance, kept agreeing with him and he loved it. When my family of 10 climbed into our rented passenger van to depart, he helped my wife into the right front passenger seat on the opposite side of the van from where I was standing. Eyes twinkling, he said to her in a hushed tone deliberately loud enough for me to hear, "Now you know what it was like for me in Korea."

God bless Chaplain O'Gara! He was the only one in the 19th who could put me down like that and get away with it. He knew it, too, and relished throwing me his playful barbs. Hey! I admit I tend to be a bit puffed up now and then and am no humble soul like he was. I know my shortfalls, too, and it's a certainty I'm no saint. It's also a certainty I'm privileged to have known and served Chaplain O'Gara. Who could forget him?

A NEW YEAR'S EVE PARTY IN KOREA

by Donald B. Perrin

I was the medic assigned to A Company, 1st Battalion, 19th Regiment, 24th Infantry Division. C Company was out in front of our positions about one mile while we were set up on the right-hand side of the road. Company B was on the left-hand side. On a small hill on our right flank was the ROK outfit. To their right was the 25th Division. On a ridge off a high range around noon on 31 December 1950, the Chinese began sending us mail and it continued on into the night. When dark fell, Company C fell out and in behind us, as the Chinese troops were closing in on their positions. Unknowing to us, during the night the ROK outfit said they were confused and withdrew without telling anyone. We were shelled all night long. The bugles were blowing like crazy. At first light I looked out of my foxhole and as far as you could see were Chinese troops coming at us. Just then we realized that the Chinese had surrounded us during the night through the gap the ROK had abandoned. They also had the high ground and were firing down on us. The decision was made for us to cross over the road to B Company, as the ridge was a little higher. We fought our way with C Company across and along the road. We suffered tremendous losses. When we got across the road, we were caught in a crossfire between B Company and the Chinese. I called it the killing field because that's what it was. I was patching up the wounded as best as I could. I saw a guy in front of me take one in the head and saw it come out the back. I was helping the wounded through the field and passed him up, knowing he was dead. Just then he called to me and said, "Doc, where are you going?" I couldn't believe it! I stopped and patched him up as good as possible and had him hang on to my carbine for me to lead him out, as there was blood all over his face,

Just at that time Bazellies' ammo bearer got hit and he was screaming for me to help him,

but he was dead as soon as he was hit. Bazellie was furious. He opened up a new box of ammo and threw it in his machine gun. He looked at me and said, "Give my regards to Broadway, Doc." We were really getting clobbered, bodies were everywhere. Bazellie rose up with his machine gun in his hand and, going full blast, charged the Chinese position. It seemed as though the enemy was so startled that they let up on the fire in the ravine. Soon enough Bazellie's gun was answered and we knew the result. It gave us a chance to get a few more men out of the crossfire. I don't think any of us would have made it if it had not been for Bazellie. I was helping the last man through the pass into B Company when a Chinese ran right over my head and pointed his weapon straight at me. I rose up and he just stood there with his gun pointed at me. Just at that time someone shot him. I couldn't believe he didn't pull the trigger. As we all joined up with B Company we were being shelled with 120 mortars. I made two more trips back into the field trying to bring someone out alive but to no avail. Our wounded were getting wounded again and I noticed the Chinese had cleared a draw that I could get some of the walking wounded out, I hoped. We had three medics on the hill and the area was so small. I went to the CO and told him I would try to get as many walking wounded out as I could. He said it would be a miracle if I could do that. J.B. Hunt, the first sergeant, must have thought I was nuts the way he looked at me.

I got 18 men together that I thought could make it, including the man with the head wound. As I got them all ready to move out, I looked back at the command post and Sgt. Hunt was just staring at me. I often wondered what he was thinking but he never said a word. We moved down the ravine. When I got to the bottom I went out on the iced-over rice patty and came under fire. I tried to crawl on the ice but I couldn't, as I had an overcoat on. I took off my aid bag and laid it on the hump of a hill until I could get my overcoat off. When I put my aid bag back on, the firing stopped. I moved the men out onto the next ridge where our other troops were supposed to be. We were traveling on the backside of the ridge when I came under fire again. I got all the men down. I looked around and saw a Chinese waving a flag at me off to my left. He motioned me to come on down, so I did. He informed me that it was not the Chinese that were firing at us but one of our own. He said if I surrendered my weapon to him we would be granted safe passage through the Chinese lines. They wanted the United States to know they were going to honor the Geneva Convention Agreement. The North Koreans did not honor the Agreement and that is why medics had to carry guns and not wear any markings of any kind on us. The Chinese who stopped us spoke better English than I did. He told me he was a graduate of Berkley University in California. I went up over the hill and called out to one of our Officers. He said he would go with us. The Chinese said no way he could go with us. I finally got him to agree to let us pass. The Chinese told me to stay on the top of the ridge. Our lines were about eight miles ahead. The temperature was around 0 degrees during the day. It really helped out with the wounds that were bleeding. That's the only way these guys got out alive. Late that night I got our guys into ambulances. I was exhausted after two days on the move but the C.O. of the C.O. whose lines we came through asked me to fill in as they were expecting the Chinese to hit them that night and their medic had been killed. I restocked my aid bag off the ambulance and fell in with the 25th Infantry Division. The Chinese didn't attack that night. I guess they were worn out also from the two days of fighting. I fell asleep that night and my feet froze for the second time. The next day I had to be evacuated back to my own outfit or what was left of it. It was one hell of a New Year's Party. The slues were lit up all night with shells and flares. Years later I wrote to Sergeant Hunt to ask him what he was thinking. He said it was so hectic that day he didn't remember much of anything. I still have the nightmares they said would go away and I am still suffering with my feet and back which is another story.

Thank you for letting me bend your ear. I had 13 months under fire from July 1950 through September 1951. I have seen a lot of guys get Congressional Medals of Honor but none who deserved one more than Bezellie. He, like thousands of other guys, only received a Purple Heart but deserved it more than most who received medals.

"I" Company, 21st, 24th. Standing is Walter Kamp. Seated are Griewahn, Warrener, Morgan, Hagen, Honeycult, Maihaifer, Lynch and Gibertson. (Courtesy of Keith Hagen)

PACKED LIKE SARDINES

by Alan J. Shields

After 13 months of basic training and Louisiana maneuvers to prepare me for combat, my war began at Camp Stoneman, north of San Francisco. At Stoneman we were again punctured, reamed and generally mistreated. In addition to lectures on the dangers which faced us when we encountered the Japanese we were also informed about the dangers of the tropics, Malaria, Dengue, Elephantitus, and Jungle Rot. And last, but not least, primitive native populations (some that still practiced cannibalism). We also were told that we should make possible arrangements for loved ones with written wills and set up beneficiaries for our GI insurance prior to embarkation. The last week in April 1944, we were loaded on trucks at Camp Stoneman and taken to the Fort Mason Pier just south of Fisherman's Wharf. Here we were loaded on a dull battleship gray, refitted passenger liner.

The sky was clear as we passed Alcatraz and headed into the setting sun. I stood on the fantail and stared at the Golden Gate Bridge until it was swallowed up by the sea. I'm sure I was not alone wondering if I would ever pass this way again, or would this be a one-way trip

They had stripped the four passenger decks of all cabins and replaced them with five tiers of bunks. They packed 5,000 of us on that ship. Conditions aboard could not have been much worse on the old slave ships. The heat as we neared the equator was intolerable. The heads overflowed most of the time and more than a few guys were seasick. It could be really nasty if someone in a bunk above you was sick.

Having spent a year and a half in the Maritime service I found the congestion aboard difficult to accept. On a merchant vessel this size there would be no more than a crew of 35 or 40. They took away all of our weapons and ammunition prior to our boarding, which probably saved few lives. We had two meals a day. Beginning at six bells (seven AM) we lined up with our mess kits and wormed our way up and down companion ways until we arrived at the galley where we were given beans and soft boiled (often raw) eggs, a slice of toast and some swill that was not even close to being coffee. Then you entered the dining hall where tables were bolted to the deck, no chairs, where you stood until you finished your so called breakfast. Upon finishing your meal you immediately got in another line which would eventually take up back up to the deck where two GI cans full of hot water (one soapy) were available to wash and rinse 5,000 mess-kits. After an hour or two on deck it was time to get back in line for the second meal. As we neared the Equator the heat below decks became unbearable. However, there wasn't sufficient room for 5,000 on deck. More than a few fights resulted from someone stepping on someone. Since we traveled without lights stepping on another body was a real possibility. Having spent some time in the Maritime service I knew a few places which afforded a little bit of privacy. Shortly after dark each night I would slip into one of the lifeboats for a rather peaceful night's sleep. I also figured that if we were torpedoed I wouldn't have to worry about getting a seat in a life boat.

With 5,000 GIs aboard, plus crew, even well-working heads would not be sufficient. Two urinal troughs were set up on the fantail. I wouldn't say they were foul smelling, but one had no difficulty finding them in the dark. Because of possible Japanese submarines we had to zig-zag all the way to New Guinea. The only highlight of the trip was the initiation of the members of the ship's crew who had never been across the Equator before, and we were all given a certificate stating that we crossed the International dateline.

We arrived at Oro Bay the first week in June 1944. The Replacement Depot was a huge tent city on the edge of a dense jungle. I was told that it was usually a week before we would be sent north to various units. I couldn't believe the beauty of New Guinea. The clear blue water, the white sandy beaches and palm trees. How could there be a nasty war somewhere near here.

Limbo - could best describe life at the depot. We were housed eight to a tent and slept on uncomfortable Army cots. Never in my life, before or since, have I felt as helpless, or maybe insignificant would be a better term, as I did at the replacement depot. I had absolutely no control over my life, present or future, and it was doubtful that I ever would again. I was at the bottom of the food chain. I swore then and there that if I were able to survive, I would go back to school and complete my education.

The second morning at the depot a young lieutenant rousted out a bunch of us for a detail to spray some of the surrounding jungle to help limit the number of malaria-carrying mosquitoes. We had only gone about 50 feet into the jungle when I saw a snake that was about 20 feet long and as big around as my thigh hanging from a tree. I screamed and the lieutenant drew his 45 and fired, again, again and again. I don't think he even hit the tree. The snake showed up the next morning curled up on the floor of one of the tents, where it was sleeping off a meal of a pet wild pig one of the guys had caught. I was very pleased that that one experience with a python was my one and only encounter with a snake the whole time I was overseas.

My first encounter with death and the casual way it was often treated occurred about the third day at the Depot. A captain stuck his head in our tent and asked six of us to grab our rifles and fall out for a firing squad. Some nut had fallen out of a palm tree and broken his neck, but he was to be given a burial with full military honors. We were to fire three rounds in the air over his grave. The cemetery overlooked the bay and was about five miles up a very steep mountain road. We played poker in the back of an ambulance, got out and fired three rounds, got back in the ambulance and continued our game. I never even knew the name of the guy. I was going to help bury a number of nameless people in the next 14 months. All who died were given, as was this no name guy, a decent burial if possible, and parents were told that their son died in the defense of his country. You don't write parents and tell them that their stupid son fell out of a palm tree.

The next leg of our journey was a two-day trip up the coast of New Guinea to Lae aboard a battered old tramp steamer. It was a real pleasant experience for me as I established a friendship with some of the black gang who were fellow members of the National Maritime Union. We swapped stories about fun in Baltimore, Brooklyn, Boston, and the scenic North Atlantic. They invited me to have some good fresh food and a few cold beers. It was going to be a long time before I would have any more good food and cold, warm, or even hot beer.

The Replacement Depot at Lae was a boardwalk city built up over some really deep, sloppy, mud. I neglected to say earlier that we arrived in New Guinea in the winter. Winter this close to the Equator means rainy season, jungle, mud, malaria, jungle rot, dense rain forests and lots of creepy crawlers. After two days of filling out additional forms and getting more probes and shots we were loaded up again on LCIs (Landing Craft Infantry) and shipped up the Coast to Hollandia in Dutch New Guinea. This was the Staging Area for the 24th Infantry Division. The Division, in its first combat action of the war, had taken Hollandia and the Japanese airbase two weeks prior to my arrival.

I arrived along with a bunch of other replacements at Hollandia. At 24th Division Headquarters I was told that I should report to E Company, 21st Infantry Regiment about a mile up a rather primitive road, actually two deep tire tracks. Upon arrival at E Company Headquarters I was sent first to the supply tent where I was issued an M-1 rifle, a bayonet, a bandoleer of ammunition and two hand grenades, then told to follow a muddy trail about 100 yards to a bunch of tents and ask for a Sgt. Arona. It was then that I finally arrived at my destination - lst Squad, First Platoon, E Company, 21st Infantry Regiment, 24th Division. Sgt. Arona looked at my size and stated that he thought I would make a good first scout (to replace the scout I was to later find out they lost in the invasion of Hollandia) and he sent me back to the supply tent to turn in my rifle and draw a Thompson submachine gun and a number of clips. For the next seven months, until being hospitalized for three months with malaria and jungle rot, I led my squad, often my platoon, and occasionally my company, into whatever action we were assigned, the most devastating being Breakneck Ridge in Leyte.

A Night the Lights Went Out

by James W. Mims

After the 24th Division was relieved on Leyte, the Division CP pulled back and reoccupied a site we had previously used. It was in a palm grove on the west side of the road, and north of Jaro. The 38th Division CP was located a couple of miles south of us.

One night about 8:30 the lights were all on, and many were enjoying a movie set up on the steep bank of a small creek inside our perimeter. The action had moved on over Ormoc way, and we were enjoying the peace and quiet, as was the 38th CP.

All at once, BAM! BAM! BAM! BAM! BAM! Five explosions blasted out!

All lights were quickly doused, people ran into palm trees and each other, fell over chairs and tent ropes, hit each other in the head with flashlights, and caused all manner of injuries in a mad dash to find shelter. One of my lieutenants, Zenon Rybel, dived under our truck, forgetting that we had partially dug it in, and suffered a substantial cut on his scalp. The medics had to shave his head around the place to sew it up, making him look like a tonsured priest, so we called him "Father Rybel" to his further discomfort! (He declined to put in for a Purple Heart!)

We later learned that the same panic hit the 38th CP, and the following morning both they and we had quite a lineup at sick call with fellows seeking appropriate repairs!

But we never found out what happened. The blasts were right between our two CPs, fortunately, and could have been mortars, artillery, or bombs, although we heard no planes. Just one of life's little mysteries!

No Atheists in Foxholes

by William T. Llewellyn

During World War II occurred one of the most significant events of my life. I was 19 years old at the time, and our Infantry Regiment had just recaptured the town of Olongapo and the Subic Bay Naval Base in the Bataan Corridor north and east of Manila on the island of Luzon in the Philippine Islands. Three miles from Olongapo a narrow road called Highway 7 wound upwards through dense jungle and twisted back and forth through rugged terrain. This stretch of twisting road was known as Zig Zag Pass, and the ensuing battle of Zig Zag Pass changed my life. The jungle was so thick that there was no visibility five yards from the road, and yet the Japanese could observe every movement coming up the road from observation posts high in the hills ahead and were dug in with well camouflaged positions connected by tunnels. From the moment our Battalion entered the Zig Zag, it came under intense heavy mortar and artillery fire that seldom let up for the three days that we were there. We advanced 200 yards up the road, fell back 100 yards, advanced 150 yards, fell back 200 yards, each time digging new holes or falling back into old positions. At one of these positions I shared a hole with an 18-year-old replacement who had joined us after the Leyte campaign and was in his first battle. We could hear the thump as the Japanese dropped their mortar shells in the tubes and the interlude of several seconds while the shells were in the air, and then the explosion in the trees around us and the whine of shrapnel as they would land. Many combat veterans have experienced the same agonizing fear and know

Just me and my foxhole. (Courtesy of J.B.Frank)

this feeling. The suspense while not knowing whether you live or die while the shells are in the air can be unbearable, and the replacement was sobbing next to me in the hole, and I suddenly started saying the Lord's Prayer over and over, which I had done many times before. I didn't know what else to do, but here was something I could relate to because of my background. I grew up in the LaGrange Congregational Church but never believed I would ever need the Lord at such an early age. The praying I did calmed and strengthened me, and I put my arm around the sobbing soldier and tried to comfort him. I would like to think I helped him but believe I did. I found out later he had never been to church. He had not become acquainted with the Lord as I had in Sunday School, and he had nothing to grasp onto. He didn't know how to pray, yet I had felt God's presence as soon as I started praying.

Our battalion was relieved on Zig Zag Pass after three days and suffered 50% casualties, including 90% of the officers and non-commissioned officers of Battalion Headquarters Company. During that war I found that people with a strong faith in God were the strongest people in difficult situations. I have called on the Lord many times since. He has never let me down, and he didn't in Zig Zag Pass, the most intense three days I will ever experience, where I put Him to the ultimate test.

LEYTE LANDING

by George P. Losio

My remembrances of the Leyte landing 20 October 1944 as a private with the 19th Infantry Provisional Battalion, 24th Division: It was early on the morning of the 20th. I had been sick with dysentery from tainted bully beef on the way to the invasion and felt weak and out of sorts. We had just received bandoleers of ammo and were getting ready to go down the Jacob's Ladder when I noticed that the wrong ammo had been issued. I immediately reported this and was given the assignment of opening up boxes of Ml ammo which was the proper issue. In the process of opening up these ammo boxes with my bayonet, the only tool I had at the time, I severely cut my hand. Now I was feeling weak from dysentery and had a gash. I did not seek medical attention as there were all kinds of things happening. We finally went down the Jacob's Ladder and boarded LCVP 7/9 for the landings. I was aboard USS *Fuller*. We then circled the mother ship and then proceeded to the beach under the roar of rocket-firing LSTs and battleships. We were under heavy shore battery fire and before reaching the beach received a jolt and started sinking. We were rescued by another Fuller craft LCVP 7/18 and after much difficulty because of a ramp that would not go down went over sides with bullets whizzing all about. On landing we loaded our Mls and prepared for battle. I did, however, manage to let the Ml bolt slam up against my thumb. I can still feel the throbbing. We were landed in the wrong spot and for the balance of the day were on our own. Japanese squads were visible running across, not too many yards away.

Well I will stop here but give you some personal information. Pvt. George P. Losio, citizen soldier, Company A, 1st Platoon, 2nd Squad.

SOMEWHERE AROUND THE 38TH PARALLEL

by George E. Lyon

This was a time of change for the outfit. There were so many men with excessive combat time being rotated back to the States that it was kind of hard to remember all of their names. Now, a large majority of the men were being supplied by either Reserve or National Guard. This fact alone should have been a good indicator to the strain being placed upon America's military might.

Our battalion commander was Major Leon Kosmacki. His staff of officers included, to name a few, Capt. James Graham, battalion communications; Captain Voss, fire direction control; Capt. Kenneth P. Jones, Lt. Chausee, Lt. Lawrence Tassie, Lt. Cardona, forward observer and pilot of one of the L-19 planes.

Headquarters Battery officers were: Capt. Norman A. Robinson, CO; Lt. David Spencer, communications officer; Lt. Nolan, motor officer; Lt. Carew was a battery officer, but I don't recall in what capacity. This was by no means, the full compliment of our officers, only the ones that I can remember.

At full strength, Headquarters Battery of the 13th Field Artillery Battalion numbered around 149 men. They permitted me to have two clerks, at my request, to maintain the huge volumes of paperwork and assist in setting up and tearing down of our command post.

Two clerks, Cpl. Glass and Pvt. Nelson, got me away from the administrative duties and allowed me to concentrate on what I considered important things, like security and the overall functioning of the men of the Battery.

At this late date I know it would be impossible to name all the men; however, I can still remember a few: Mike Nacarotta, David Butler, Milton Lindberg, Asa Page, Daly, Kern, Rebeinspies, Ernest Lynch, Albert Cardona, Jack Talmadge, Folse, Higgins, Vrobel, Smith, Fincher, Zwicky, Stookey, Synadinos, Kirkpatrick, Dean, Ellis, DeSantis, Robert Sullivan, Pierce, Harvey, Canepa, O'Keefe. The only other name I can pull up is First Sergeant Curtis of A Battery.

Weapons of the 13th Field Artillery were 105 mm Howitzers. A short barrel weapon designed to fire at high angles of elevation, which made them very efficient in the hills of Korea. Their short effective range also necessitated their being in close proximity to the front lines and this could be hazardous to a fellow's health. For the close in type fighting of the Korean war, I would say the 105 Howitzers and mortars were the weapons most used - other than personal weapons of the soldiers.

Taking the post of first sergeant put me in the position to inherit a house boy, a young Korean lad about 20 years of age. He carried the nickname of George, but his real name was Kim Yong Guk. Smart as a whip too. He had a very good understanding of the English language and could even write it a little. George did my laundry, the cleaning up around the command post and assisted the two clerks in tearing down and setting up camp whenever we had to move.

The only creature comfort I had was an old homemade bunk, also inherited from the previous first sergeant. It was wider than the run of the mill Army cots. With two clerks and a house boy, made it easier to move from place to place.

I suppose I had been there maybe a week when the division made a big push and we had to move up. I got my first taste of the Gypsy type migration. The need to move and re-establish new gun positions and fire direction control didn't allow time to fool around with folding and precise packing. Vehicles were assigned to each section and if they couldn't get all their accumulated gear on it, the excess remained behind.

What really amazed me was the efficiency with which these men piled everything on their vehicles. Tied it all down and with stuff hanging over the sides, flapping in the breeze, moved with the most unmilitary procedure from one

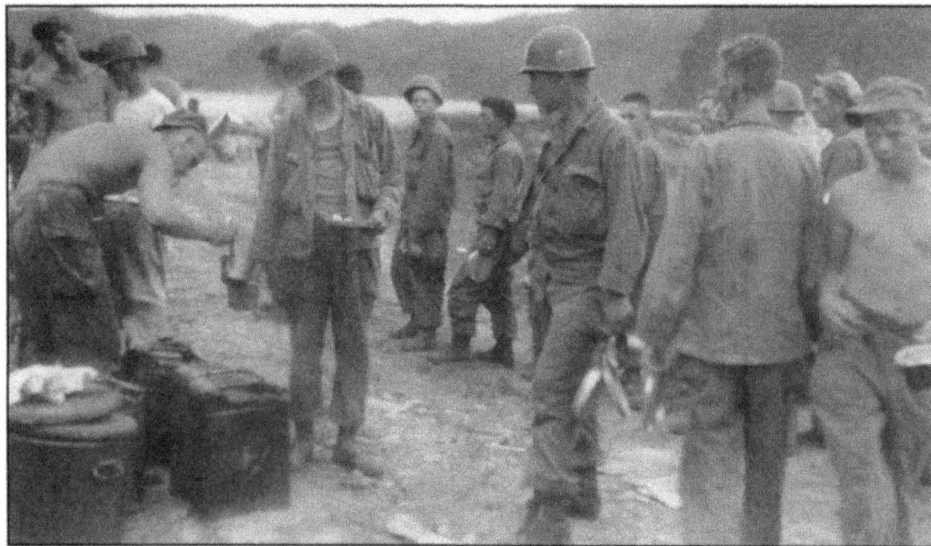

Hungry and tired soldiers enjoy mess, "But it ain't like Mom's home cookin."

place to another to become again in short order a fully functional combat unit.

It looked very undignified for the type military I was accustomed to, but it worked and I sure wasn't going to change that. Our communications section, or wire section as they were called, were always last to move out as they policed up all the communications wire, then laid it in the new position. Without question, these men worked harder than any of the others and the work was more dangerous too.

Headquarters Battery was not a firing battery as the other four batteries were. We were more of a support for the others, maintaining the communications for the battalion, maintaining the fire direction control, forward observers and battalion headquarters.

This first move put us in a bad position, but it couldn't be avoided. Our outfit squeezed into a small valley between two pretty high hills and a couple of well placed mortars could have played havoc with us. Everyone sensed that we were vulnerable and the tensions began to mount; rumors of infiltrators didn't help matters much either.

Security established with machine gun outposts and guards scheduled, we settled in for the night. Fire direction control being a 24-hour operation, the officer of the day, sergeant and corporal of the guard were stationed there.

Sometime in the wee hours of the morning, I woke from a deep and troubled sleep to hear the sound of heavy breathing at the entrance to my tent. Pulling the 45 caliber automatic from its holster hanging on my bunk, I was just before putting a round in the chamber when the guard spoke and identified himself.

I don't know how it happened, but I had failed to schedule a relief for him. As the guard's post was right outside my tent, I tossed him a blanket and told him to bed down right there. I imposed a penalty on myself and stood watch on the machine gun outpost for the rest of the night.

Somewhere Captain Robinson came up with an old World War II Quonset Hut which we erected for a recreation hall. We were honored with one USO Show featuring an Evelyn Page before we had to advance again and leave the hut for some other lucky outfit.

Peace negotiators at Panmunjom started back to work after a 64-day delay caused by North Korean disagreement. Our side wanted to have a buffer zone about two and one half miles wide between us and the Red Army as a cease fire zone.

I could only wonder why someone didn't try to dispel the nasty rumors that the only reason we were in this God forsaken place was to protect the vested interest of the three major oil companies of the United States. I don't know that any of that was fact, but there were rumors.

I kept telling myself that I was here because my country was in jeopardy and they needed me. However, I found it odd that the country we were supposedly trying to save would bill the United States for 160 million dollars for damages created by and against them by the North Koreans. Not only that, but the United States paid the bill.

It sure does make a fellow curious, doesn't it? It almost gives you a feeling that for the United States to prosper they have to have a war of some type going on. How different things would be if all nations were required to have the same size budget for peace as they did for defense.

Well, it won't serve any useful purpose to dwell on the likes of that way of thinking, so we best get on with the business at hand. By the latter part of October 1951, we were in the position that we would remain in for the balance of our tour in Korea.

During all of our moving around, this was the only camp site that I personally selected. Given grid coordinates of an approximate area, I was to take a platoon of men, select a camp site to accommodate our Battery and clear the area of all mines.

Some six or eight miles from our present location and in the area of Kumsong, we found what appeared to be the perfect site. From the main road, this area lay across a small shallow stream of swift flowing water. Consisting of two fairly large rice paddies, it was bordered on two sides by hills. I figure this was the north end of the Kumhwa Valley, because behind us it was clear for what looked like 20 miles.

The North Koreans must have retreated too fast to mine this area, for we found nothing. We started probing, but got braver as we went along and finally one guy said he would take the truck and drive over the entire area, and did, before I could stop him.

I reckon I made the right choice because when I brought the captain to look at the site and explained the reason for selecting it, he said, "We'll move in the morning."

In my mind I had the camp laid out already, so it was just a matter of telling each section where they would set up. The move and set-up worked out so smoothly, I received compliments from the battalion commander.

Having been without proper bathing facilities for so long, the next thing we did after putting in the latrine was build a shower. The stream close by supplied the water and scrounging a little pipe put us in business. It was fancy enough for front line bathing and appreciated by all, including visitors from other units.

Sharing the facilities paid off in the nature of a heater for the water supplied by neighboring outfit. So now we were going first class. The heater was probably one of the best things we had going for us right then, as the weather was turning cold.

Moving on into November, the camp began to take on the appearances of a permanent type installation. Sandbagged sidewalls for the tents and a real sure enough guard post at the entrance to our area, manned 24 hours a day. My two clerks, and George the house boy, secured a truck load of empty ammo boxes from the firing Batteries and proceeded to build us a real orderly room.

One day, the captain stopped me during one of my rounds of the camp site. I usually did this a couple of times a day to see if we could improve on our conditions any. We talked for awhile about things in general when out of the clear blue sky, he said, "Sarg, how would you like a promotion to Lieutenant?" I didn't answer right off, just stood there, contemplating the answer I would give. I knew of the need for officers as forward observers and I knew also the dangers involved in that capacity, as we had already lost several.

"The major wanted me to ask if you would accept a commission as a second lieutenant," he said.

"Look, captain, I appreciate the consideration and all and I'm not trying to be smart, but I doubt there's anyone here that can run fast enough to pin a set of bars on my shoulders," I told him.

I had spoken the magic words. He laughed, put his arm around my shoulder and said, "Atta boy, Sarg, I like you just the way you are." I have no idea what he told the major but I'm sure he never used the same terms as I had.

I have no explanation as to the camaraderie that developed between myself and the captain. It just did. Ever so often in a fellow's lifetime he will run across people like this. They share a small corner of your life that's not available to everyone. Maybe it was the charisma of two individuals thrown together by extenuating circumstances, or the knowledge that you have someone you can trust and depend on if put to the test.

Clearly, both sides in this so called police action were getting a belly full of killing each other off because things seemed to be winding down a bit now. Probes and skirmishes were getting to be farther apart. The firing batteries of all front line artillery were being limited to the number of rounds of ammo that they could fire each day.

At one time, the forward observer would call for fire on anything that moved. Now they were having to locate concentrations of troops and even then they had to be strategical. The forward observer kept a record of coordinates fired, and as troops re-occupied a position, could readily call fire in on them. Operating both from the ground and air, the observer was a most valuable man.

A Mire Situation

by George F. Lance

While stationed up north with the 21st Regiment, our company area was located on what had at one time been a rice paddy. The area had been leveled out along an adjoining small mountain area that contained various ammunition bunkers. The main road going past the company area was dirt, as was everything else in sight. With the exception of the mess hall, the orderly room and one or two truck repair bays, the only other covered structures were squad tents. Each tent had a wooden floor, two pot belly stoves and two small light bulbs overhead. The only electric power was each evening from dusk to about 9:00 p.m., when a small engine generator was operated. This generator was located within the company area at a central location to all the facilities.

Service Company seemed like a stop-off point for many new officers coming into the Regiment. They would be there from a week or two up to a month or two. Most came and went and we often were unaware there had been a change. However, one new commander arrived and promptly was annoyed by the loud sound of the electrical generator operating each evening. He ordered the truck service personnel to move it to a location back near the mountain, where it would not be so evident. They carried out their new orders by picking the small generator up on the hook end of a large truck-mounted hydraulic wrecker and driving around the mess hall to gain access to the space that ran across the foot of the mountain range. That is where all the fun began.

As luck would have it, we had been in the Korean "Monsoon" rainy season for at least a couple of weeks. It had rained and rained and rained. The dirt grounds and road had deep gullies washed out everywhere. When the wrecker drove up around the mess hall it was leaving deep scars in the mud in what was normally a decent walking area. When it rounded a left turn and got around the small covering where we all washed our mess trays, the right side of the wrecker sank straight down so that the bed of the wrecker was flush with the ground. There was no way it could get itself out of the mire. Of course the generator, which probably didn't weigh more than 750 pounds, was still on the hook and of no use to the whole company for a number of days. Retrieval of the wrecker and other items proved to be quite a challenge.

The following day Tank Company sent a tank retriever over to assist. Of course he had to come in the same way around the mess hall, so the scars from the wrecker's tires were now increased in size at least five-fold. The retriever set up some distance away and tried to winch the wrecker out of the mire. It didn't work. The retriever tried a new position and ended up stuck itself. Tank Company then sent a second retriever, who got the first one out and then together they tackled the wrecker. They finally succeeded, but you can imagine how the entire company area looked by now. They had deep tracks cut in the earth all around the mess hall and other facilities. About this time there was a let-up in the rain, so the engineers were out on the main roads trying to repair the wash-out damage. It so happened that a large bulldozer was working on the road near our area, and the company commander persuaded the operator to come in and level out the damage his idea had caused. The operator agreed but it was not too long until he too was stuck in the mire. This time a detail of "volunteers" were recruited to go and it was not too long until he too was stuck in the mire. This time a detail of "volunteers" were recruited to go and carry long telephone like poles in and place them under the tracks of the dozer so that it could get traction to back out of its predicament. Eventually he got the area reasonably level and our daily routine returned to normal. The Company Commander who started the ruckus was reassigned and we never heard anymore about him.

DEAR JOHN

by George F. Lance

The eight-week Leadership School, under the command of the 3rd Battalion, had three individual classes underway at any given time.

Each class was housed in a two-story barracks building. A fourth barracks was used to house all the personnel that had been culled from the classes, while they awaited new orders to move on to another assignment. This group of drop-outs were utilized within the battalion to pull various details from KP to cutting grass.

Among this group was one individual who was constantly in trouble - I'll call him "John." He had failed the course somewhere along the line and ended up in barracks #4. Each day he was given a detail to carry out. I recall coming back to our company area in a marching formation, four abreast. As we marched up the company street, there was John using a water hose to water the grass around the front of the barracks buildings. Of course he turned the hose on the men as they marched past - which was funny and yet sad that he did not have better control of himself.

Another day, John was appointed to an ammo detail on one of the firing ranges. He came back to the company area with a handful of firecrackers that simulated machine gun fire. Later in the evening he waited for GIs to be sitting on commodes in the latrine and then he'd light them up and throw them inside. Needless to say it was a dangerous game.

Still later, John dropped an M-8 grenade in an empty commode in barracks #4. The resultant explosion destroyed all the porcelain bowl and base that rests on the floor. The only thing remaining was the heavy white porcelain ring around the top where the seat normally rests - which was still fastened to the inlet water pipe coming out of the wall. That was the last straw and the company commander filed papers for a court-martial. In the weeks that followed, it was discovered that John's true age was only 16, so they dropped all charges and dismissed him from further service within a couple of days.

TAKING OUT THE TRASH

by George F. Lance

I shipped overseas late in the month of October. We were placed on a Liberty ship, which was not very large or stable in a rough ocean. The first day I was on guard duty on the triangular shaped "forecastle" of the ship - the most forward part just ahead of the bridge where the anchor winches and other like machinery are kept. This was an off-limits area for the troops. I had the watch from 4:00 p.m. to midnight. We put out from Seattle at dusk and the water was rough well before we got near the ocean. Since I was topside and out in the open air, my biggest concern was hanging on while the ship dipped and soared in the rough water. However, it was not long before the other GIs below started to come up for air - and told me stories of how bad conditions were below.

At midnight I was relieved and went below to get warm and some sleep. The sickness was all around from the moment I stepped into the ladder well, and no one had exaggerated the true conditions. Guys were laying everywhere and it was not a pretty scene - nor did it help my sense of smell or the urge to upchuck myself. I made it to my bunk, which was about six decks down. My bunk was on the main aisle about four bunks back of the forward latrine which was located in the bow of the ship. The latrine was also triangular shaped and was directly below the forecastle area I had been guarding. I had the second bunk from the bottom. The rack was four bunks high, with one guy below me and two above. It so happened that our bunks were in line with one of the "hold" access areas of the ship. In other words, we were along the left or port side of the ship and there was an identical set of bunks on the right or starboard side. Between us in the center of the ship, left to right, was a large open area with a floor made up of heavy steel planks that could be removed to allow access to the decks below. This steel flooring was recessed about two inches below the regular deck level where we walked and our bunks were positioned.

The open area was about 20' x 20' in size, and on the front and rear ends we had placed everyone's bags one side of the ship to the other. A lot of guys would gather on top of these bags to pass the time talking, sleeping or whatever, as it gave them more space than in the cramped quarters of their bunk. Within this aisle area was a large galvanized type trash can. It was contained within the recessed area of the removable floor by the 2" lip. The trash can was intended for trash of any kind. However, it had been used frequently by guys that were making a dash to the latrine because of sea sickness but felt they couldn't make it in time. As a result, the paper trash and other garbage was mixed with this very undesirable bodily refuse.

I managed to get to my bunk without losing my own dinner and fell off to sleep. I did not do too bad through the remainder of the night and early morning. However, I recall becoming conscious to the drone of the ship and propeller shaft, and the fact that the ship was bobbing terribly in the water. I was also aware that the propeller was lifting out of the water on a forward tilt since I could hear the shaft and screw speed up momentarily, then come back under load as the stern settled back in the water and pressure was reapplied to the drive line components. We were also bobbing left to right, first one front corner and then the other. I was also conscious of a sliding noise and a bang, followed by a similar noise and then another bang. I finally opened my eyes and took a look around. The cause of the noise was the trash can sliding back and forth across the open area, stopping at the lip of the deck floor on either side in rhythm with the rocking of the ship. There were numerous GIs on the duffel bags and I swear a number of them had bets going as to which poor guy was going to "get it" when the ship dipped far enough to tip over the can. Although I was aware, I was too lazy to move and do anything about it. After what seemed like an eternity, sure enough the ship took a big dip and the can came toward us swiftly. It dumped its smelly contents across the walking aisle next to our bunks, and a fair amount of the trash spilled out over the guy who was asleep in the bunk under me. At that point I jumped out and assisted him and we were good friends the rest of the trip. Neither one of us could eat anything but crackers for the first two weeks. Although it was not funny

Early morning attack 14 October 1951 by "E" Company 21st Inf. (Courtesy of H.W. Rhoades)

at the time, it now seems funny to recall after so many years of living on the solid land.

BEHIND CLOSED DOORS

by George F. Lance

A warrant officer was in charge of the Personnel Section, which was housed in a metal Quonset hut about 20' wide and 80' long, with a wooden floor and wooden bulkheads at each end. The front had a single wooden door leading to the dirt road out front. The building was located on a hill about a mile from Regimental Headquarters. We were taken to the job each morning in a 6 x 6 and brought back at noon for lunch. The same routine was followed again in the afternoon. Each clerk within the section was responsible for all the personnel records for two rifle companies within the 21st Regiment.

One day a low ranking officer that was newly arrived from the States made his appearance. He was directed to the clerk in charge of the rifle company to which he had been assigned. I do not recall what it was the officer wanted, but vividly recall his storming out of the office in a wild rage after not obtaining what he desired. His feet stumped on the wooden deck with each step and he slammed the door so that it shook the building. We could hear his jeep start up and drive away.

Unknown to the young officer was the fact that the regimental commander happened to be at the rear of the building talking with the warrant officer in charge. After witnessing the poor display by the younger officer, the CO waited for a short time and then called the headquarters building. He asked for the young officer that had just stormed out. After identifying himself, he asked the lieutenant to return to Personnel and "close the front door properly." We all waited with anticipation for the inevitable. Sure enough, a short time later we heard the approach of the jeep, which stopped out front. A moment later the front door gently opened part way, then was reclosed very

quietly. We heard the jeep turn around and the sound fade in the distance.

LOST IN A JUNGLE

by Jack Jorgensen

I arrived at the replacement depot at Buna in August 1944. One of the other arrivals had a brother who was killed earlier in New Guinea and was buried at the cemetery there. He had promised his family that he would visit the cemetery if he happened to be in New Guinea. By chance, that is where he was shipped. He asked for someone to go with him, but since it was off-limits no one volunteered. I did not know the man, but felt sorry for him and agreed to go with him, and then another, whom neither of us knew, also agreed to go. We started walking to where we heard the cemetery was and caught a ride with one of the guys working at the cemetery. He got us in and we looked at the thousands of crosses, but as the day wore on, it was getting toward 1:00 or 2:00 in the afternoon, we decided to return to camp and maybe look some other time. We were afraid to go out the main gate because it was off limits and we thought we would be in trouble, so we decided to walk into the jungle and circle around to the road again. We started off and could find no side trail, and finally we just took off on what looked like a jungle trail. We got hopelessly turned around and it was getting toward dusk. We came across a native village, but they would not speak to us or do anything to indicate they understood us. We were getting very thirsty as we had no water, and also scared because we had no guns. We thought we were heading to the ocean and followed the trail until we did come to the ocean. It was pretty dark by then but we could see a little. We followed the ocean until we came to a river entering into the ocean. We tried to wade across the river, but it was too deep. We finally waded and swam and made it to the other bank when we heard a shout and a half dozen soldiers coming toward

us. Luckily they were an Australian unit and when they found out who we were and where we were from, they had a jeep haul us back to our camp. It was close to midnight when we arrived. We went directly to our tents, and none of the officers ever found out we were gone.

OUR FIRST ENGAGEMENT

by C.W. Johnson

The long, slow and tortuous train ride from Pusan northward had given us too much time to dwell on our situation. The "Police Action" was about to begin. Our imaginations were in high gear. We passed a train filled with wounded South Korean soldiers. The bloody bandages only made the butterflies in our stomachs flap their wings that much harder.

It didn't help our nerves one bit when suddenly the lights went out all over the train. We had reached an area near the front where hostilities could break out at any time. The blackout was a safety measure to avoid us from being seen. The locomotive snaked on through the dark Korean countryside for several more miles. As quietly as a train could be, we heard the steam hissing from its engine. The clickety-clack of the wheels were muted by our pounding hearts.

The first battalion of the 34th Infantry Regiment was left there in the middle of nowhere in the darkness. Company A, followed by B, C and D, struggling under the weight of our gear, began the search for a place to dig in. After a long trek through several rice paddies, our site was chosen. In the pre-dawn hours we began to prepare our position. We could see the flash of artillery in the distance. The war was getting closer. From our hill, we saw a bridge in the road to the north. Our mortars zeroed in on the bridge. We waited. It rained during the night and the heat and humidity were terrible. I was standing in water over my ankles. That day and all through the night, we waited.

The morning brought with it the thickest fog I've ever seen. We could see barely a hundred yards. It was six hundred yards to the bridge. We could hear noises from beyond the bridge. The sound of engines and clanking metal could only mean one thing. Tanks! Time was standing still. Finally, the sun began to burn away the fog, slowly at first. Our visibility increased bit by bit until the bridge came into view. A murky shadow appeared in the roadway and later became the first of 13 tanks that I counted before the column disappeared around a curve.

I had brought a camera with me, for no good reason except that it cost plenty and I didn't want to lose it. I began scanning with the viewfinder. Across the horizon, perhaps a mile away, was the whole North Korean army! Panning closer, the lead tank was approaching the bridge! I saw its turret swing in my direction just as our mortars opened fire. The first couple missed and in that moment I saw a ring of smoke from the gun still pointed at me. I clicked the shutter and closed the camera. An instant later the shell landed several yards up the hill behind me. For us, the war had begun! In the

113

ensuing hours we would be scattered, overwhelmed by their sheer numbers. We managed to destroy a couple tanks but lost 19 men and a good officer in the effort. The order to withdraw never reached them at their outpost.

As green as I was at that time, I knew enough to stay close to our veterans. Most of us were in shock and needed to be pointed in the right direction. It would take the rest of the day to regroup; however, in the days and weeks to follow we did our best to slow the advance of North Korea. The war lasted over three years and cost us over 50,000 casualties. Was it worth it? It began and ended at or near the 38th Parallel. No territory changed hands! I didn't even save the picture I had taken on day one. In my panic to leave my foxhole that day, all I could think of was my rifle and ammo. I did make a grab for my camera on my departure but succeeded only in picking up a pair of field glasses. We traveled light after that and even the field glasses were discarded later. Somewhere on a hill in Korea, if it hasn't been discovered, lies my camera with a picture of the first shot fired at us in the Forgotten War.

"C" Company, 19th Infantry, 24th Division. L to R: Sgt Charles E. Blunt, S/Sgt Jugewieski, and Sgt Donald Erwin enjoy a comparatively substantial meal, for a change.

MEMORIES OF THE 19TH INFANTRY IN KOREA, 1950

by Ret. Major Robert G. Fox

In January 1950, I was initially assigned to the 24th Infantry Division, Kokura, Japan. Later, I was detached to the 19th Infantry Regiment as the CMP detachment CO/PM.

My first encounter prior to 25 June 1950 was with missionaries, medical personnel and their families. My MP detachment was assigned the responsibility for the safety and security of the personnel and their property (what there was of it) as they were housed within the 19th Regiment Camp Chickamauga.

The 19th Regiment was alerted prior to June 25 (Captain Greathouse/Greenhouse became the camp commander and PM left behind due to age). He, along with a few of my MPs, support troops, civilians, Japanese help and security guards, assumed the responsibility for the operation of the camp and the evacuees from Korea.

The 19th Regiment moved immediately to the 24th Division Headquarters, Kokura, for personnel build up, supplies, weapons and ammunition. These items were totally inadequate in quantity and quality. Medical supplies were nonexistent as our medical supplies through the years had a way of ending up within the black market operations.

Our equipment and supplies were loaded on 6 by 6 trucks, jeeps and trailers, then we moved out to the Port of Sasebo. The first major set back was the lack of sea transportation. None available, no LST, nothing; no Navy, no Army TC. We ended up with the beat-up, rusted, old Japanese tramp steamers/cargo ships. Another problem was loading. The port facilities did not have the heavy-lifting capability to pick up loaded vehicles. All vehicles had to be downloaded, then uploaded aboard ship in order to make available every

inch of space, which was very limited on the tramp steamers/cargo ships belonging to the Japanese. Slow boat to Korea.

Arrived at Pusan, and what a mess. The Koreans refused to off load the Japanese ships. No love loss between them. Red influence, union strike, whatever the reason, I do not really know. The American troops, plus the Japanese crews, ended up loading the ships. I can remember spending two miserable exhausted nights trying to sleep on a pile of rice sacks that were crawling with lice and other bugs looking for a free lunch.

After completing the download, officers were assembled. Colonel Meloy, Regiment CO, presented the battle plans and issued map overlays. After briefing the staff and BN COs, Colonel Meloy said, "Fox, I want you to take your six tanks and 24 MPs to Taegu. You are my advanced element. Set up regiment headquarters when you get there. The rest of the 19th will follow up behind you." He said this with a slight grin on his face. All the other officers broke up laughing for we had no tanks and none since we arrived in Japan. The only armored vehicles were in Toyko with the First Cavalry - Pride and Joy of Doug Out Dug - General MacArthur, Emperor of Japan. This remark broke up a great deal of tension one has prior to confronting the unknown.

I departed from Taegu at 0500 with six jeeps and 24 MPs poorly equipped and no training for combat. Our small arms consisted of a 45 caliber automatic per troop, one 30 caliber carbine per jeep, and a basic load of ammunition and rations for one day. We had no medical supplies. We had communications, as I had the same vehicles used for MP duty in Beppu. I believe this is the real reason we were selected as the advance element. Additionally, I was old Infantry/Airborne from WWII and the 5250 Tech Int from the Philippines to Tokyo with MI, G-2, GHQ and the occupation forces until 1946.

Prior to the move out in the morning, I spent most of the night bargaining for a 30 caliber machine gun, rifles, and ammunition. It cost me two cases of cigarettes and one case of beer that we had confiscated from the Koreans, who had stolen it from us. I never smoked - it was the beer that killed me to give up as water was not fit to drink and is what ended my stay in Korea and resulted in the trip to Osaka General Hospital. I could only secure one 30 caliber machine gun and two cans of ammunition, 250 rounds per can. The M-1 rifles were hard to come by. They were worth their weight in gold. No luck. I went back to the compound for a few winks of rest.

With a 30 caliber machine gun mounted on my jeep, we left the compound in Pusan at 0500 and headed for Taegu. It was very hot and humid. There was no wind. We were traveling over dusty, winding roads and across rice paddies when we were caught in the middle of one field by three fighters. My provost sergeant was the first to spot three small specks in the sky. If we saw them, we knew they could not miss us in the open and so vulnerable. Since the mountains would force them to make a fighter pass across the road bed with the sun to their back, I ordered the men to hit dirt on the right bank.

The fighter peeled off in perfect formation for the attack. Upon closer observation, it appeared as though the fighters were P-51 Mustangs, WWII vintage. They made the attack without firing a round and continued on what I assume was a recon mission. Fighters once committed to the attack find it difficult to back off and not fire a burst or two, or were they like us - short on ammunition or none at all? That was the only eventful part of the trip. I might add the fact that we did not fire a round could be a factor.

When I arrived on Taegu, I secured the university (its building and grounds) as the 19th

Regiment CP. I secured the town civic center building as my headquarters and CP. First thing we all did after securing the area was to clean up. The well out back was a God send.

The first casualty I encountered was not from enemy fire. One of our own 19th troop leaned out too far while passing through a narrow tunnel. He was dragged the entire length along side and bottom - one could not recognize him as a human being. It was alleged that he was pushed out, as he was regarded as one of the 19th no good SOBs. This was never proven nor was there time to investigate it before contact was made with the enemy.

My mind is a complete blank from this time on and has no recall. I remember waking up in a field ambulance with eight other troops, stacked four high each side, mass of sweat, shaking all over, and begging for water. A medical officer (a lieutenant whose name I cannot remember but who saved my life) came over to me and said, "Hi pal, I am getting you out of this stinking mess. It is a hell hole. I am sending you home to Japan by air evacuation."

The 19th Infantry Regiment and the 24th Infantry Division were totally under strength and lacked adequate equipment, material, rations, supplies, and ammunition to wage war. We were taken out of a soft, cat-like occupation life in the beautiful hot spring center of Beppu, Japan located on the ocean with the mountains in the background. We were caught with our pants down - off to war (police action) for which we were not prepared.

Other than the OPS officers, BN COs and staff, most of the company grade officers were West Point, with no YMI or combat experience. Of the 83 officers with the 19th, I am told that only eight survived the Korean War. I know I ended up in the Osaka General Hospital. It was there that I saw Colonel Meloy, who had been hit in the leg, a clean hole through his heel while diving head first into a foxhole. The OPS officer was there also. I have to give him credit. He was determined to get out of the hospital and back into combat. That was where the promotions were, if you lived. My mission ended with the Korean War. I was transferred to the Air Force and sent stateside for R/R, additional training, and assignment Security Y-80 WAFB Germany.

REMINISCENCES
OF WORLD WAR II

by Gilbert Hilkemeyer

Amid all the muck and the blood and the killing and confusion of battle a certain grim humor develops among the troops. It is absolutely essential if you wish to keep your sanity. After many years most of it does not seem funny at all; none of it produced leg slapping guffaws. But it provided a therapeutic relief. A non-participant would not see anything funny at all.

"King" Company landed on Red Beach in Leyte with a full complement of five officers. Two days later I was the only officer remaining. We had had one platoon leader killed and the company commander and the weapons platoon had been wounded on the landing craft coming in. Another platoon leader was wounded on the second day with a flesh wound through the buttocks; four holes. He was able to walk out. The situation prompted one GI to say "You're the only officer left, how come you haven't been hit?" My only comment could be "A telephone pole makes a poor target for a nearsighted Japanese" (I was six feet two and weighed somewhat under 170 pounds.)

We arrived in the village of Pastrana late in the afternoon. Another unit was pinned down ahead of us facing a star shaped fort. The order came down. "Dig in" and dig in we did. It was growing dusk but we were concerned about exposing ourselves too much so the digging in the hard soil was difficult. We crawled into our holes for the night while the shelling of the fort continued.

At dawn some wit in the company asked, "Why is your hole so long, so narrow and so shallow?" Our position there was of not much value, so we pulled back and moved to the left of the fort to set up a road block at the edge of town on the road from Dagami where the following night we had some heavy action with an unsuspecting Japanese patrol that did not know we were there. The next day the shelling continued. My curiosity got the better of me and I went to a place where I could watch the mortar shells hitting the fort. A little quarter inch sliver of hot metal hit just below my left eyebrow. It was almost spent because it barely broke the skin and hung there until I pulled it out. Not much humor there. Later our kitchen caught up with us, the first time since our landing. You might know what our meal would be. It was Spam with reconstituted potatoes (the cubed kind), green beans and reconstituted lemon drink made with heavily halizoned water. My utensils were a cut off section of banana stalk for a plate, my mess spoon, combat knife and canteen cup. I think the cooks were somewhat amused about how our eating habits had changed.

Soon we moved to a perimeter in the vicinity of Carigara. We dug in on a slight slope in a driving rain that was a part of the monsoon that had hit. In the morning I complained to the sergeant, whose hole was just uphill from mine, that the water he was bailing out of his hole was running into mine. His answer was, "Half the time I was using my helmet for a bed pan." I believe that he was suffering the same from the man uphill from him.

There came a day of sunshine and since we were in theoretical reserve we were tapped for a carrying party to supply Col. Jock Clifford's lst Battalion of the 34th Regiment on Kilay Ridge. Half the men carried a case of ammo or rations. The other half carried the extra packs, and each man carried his own weapon. Early in the morning we met a guide who was to take us around the right side of Breakneck Ridge. We were well on our way when we heard a zipping noise coming through the kunai grass. Then a voice from below, "Get off that hill, we're attacking it this morning." We sustained several wounded, none very serious. It was not determined whether the firing was friendly or enemy. We sent the wounded back, reorganized and went on our way, delivering our load at Consuegra. We stayed the night and returned.

On the way back we crossed a bare domed hill where our artillery had caught a large number on the enemy in the open with a "time on target" barrage. There were so many bodies that we could not walk straight across. I was eating my last rare caramel cube out of my last "k" ration. Later I mentioned to a friend that every time I ate a caramel cube the scene came back quite vividly. He said, "It's a sign that you're losing it." Many years later, it is still quite vivid. Later in the day as we came down the lower portion of Breakneck Ridge we met three glum looking correspondents. We told them, "You want to see a war, go up around the corner." I don't think they did. The fighting there was over, but the bodies, both enemy and friendly, had not been moved and there was an overwhelming odor. We finished our mission without further incident.

By the time we made the landing at Parang in Mindanao, I had been assigned company commander of Cannon Company. It seemed my lot that my assignments usually came just prior to embarking for a new beachhead, never giving me time to get acquainted with the men. We landed as a unit, but there was a very brief time that we could function that way. The Japanese had burned or blown up every bridge on the road to Davao. So immediately our mounts were left behind with their platoon leaders and I started walking with regimental forward. This amounted to the colonel and a handful of people. We walked most of the way to Davao. It was quite some time before my jeep caught up. The mounts arrived just in time for the assault on the city of Davao. The engineers had a really difficult time rebuilding or bypassing all the bridges. One day during our walking we were far from anywhere. Our canteens were empty and we were thirsty. We came to a small pool of water along the road. A spirited debate developed as to whether it was a small spring or just gathered rain water. The consensus was that it was a spring and we cleaned it out to make it flow. It was just a puddle. We ended up drinking muddy halizoned water. This is something they didn't teach at the Infantry School.

As we reached the Davao River, Sergeant Sousa of the engineers was repairing the bridge, and the division commander and some Filipino dignitaries were ferried across along with flag waving and speeches. About that time, a Japanese machine gun opened up. Even generals and dignitaries hit the mud when machine guns opened up. Someone silenced the gun and the ceremonies proceeded.

As soon as the Infantry had cleared out Davao and moved up the coast, the city was placed off limits for our personnel. Rear area was already anticipating the end of combat. I received a communication from division that one of my sergeants had been caught there by the MPs and to reply by endorsement thereon what I had done about it. I called him in and we discussed it. My answer was that I had reprimanded him. My reprimand to him was for being dumb enough to get caught.

The war was over but Japanese did not recognize it. We pursued them into the hills. The First Battalion came upon a cache of goods that had been moved from a store in Davao. Soon everyone, including the major in command, was dressed in colorful shirts and other gear, having put aside their cruddy uniforms. About that time a division inspection team arrived. That ended that. The team was dressed in clean, pressed fatigues having had access to laundry service. They did have the good grace not to discipline the major.

We moved to the beach in preparation for the invasion of Japan. Winter uniforms were being issued. Mine required extensive alteration; all available seamstresses were pressed into service so that all personnel would be decently dressed.

We moved into pyramidal tents complete with cots and floors. While I relaxed on my cot during noon break in just my shorts some men commented that I reminded them of the pictures coming from Europe of the death camps. I was under 135 pounds. We played volley ball on the beach but had to delay in the middle of our game for a short time while the engineers removed a buried anti-tank bomb that was located where the server stood.

Every effort was made by command to bring back peace time discipline. A firing range was set up; one of my men was cited for displaying his unloaded weapon in a dangerous manner. Division and regiment kept levying work details throughout the day. It kept the company commander busy keeping a scorecard because someone from division would come out and count the men that were out for training.

Though a number of us had enough points for return to the States, we moved with the division to Japan. While waiting to report to the replacement depot, Special Services broke out a *set* of horseshoes for relaxing. A Japanese civilian was carefully watching the shoes as they were tossed from peg to peg. A friend next to me expressed his opinion, "Pretty soon they will be teaching us how to play horseshoes."

SKOSHEE

by Norm Dixon

We were getting ready for the big October push and the last thing I needed was a monkey, but I bought one from a guy who brought it back from Japan On R&R. It's name was Skoshee and he was very cute. Skoshee hung on to my lower leg and rode nearly everywhere I went and everyone thought he was very cute. But cute began to run a little thin when he got loose from me while lined up outside for breakfast and jumped right into the vat of egg batter and began to eat. I got out of that one without being lynched.

Another time when I returned to my pup tent I found Skoshee playing with the five hand grenades that I had left hidden there. Needless to say I was sweating on that one too, the pup tents were set up quite close to one another. The final straw was when Skoshee crawled into my sleeping bag one cold October night and defecated while I was in it. What a mess! I could never get the smell out no matter how many times I scrubbed it.

We were about to jump off on the assault near Kumhwa and Kumsong and I couldn't imagine what I would do with a monkey during the action. Besides, by this time Skoshee was no longer cute. I hated him! Finally at the last minute a tanker was taken in by this little demon and since he was being rotated back to the States I agreed to sell Skoshee for what I paid for him plus a ride in his Sherman tank.

MY FIRST THREE WEEKS IN US ARMY SERVICE

by Dick Fisher

There are many experiences I could submit, but the one I choose to submit is one that a great many members of the 24th Division experienced. I have never seen it recorded any where, however.

I received my draft notice about the middle of September 1942. After my physical examination, I was ordered to report for transportation to Indiantown Gap Reception Center. We were told not to bring any valuables (watches, cameras, etc.) because as soon as our basic training was complete, we would be given a "Delay En route" to our duty station, so that we might go home and recover "Our Valuables."

When we arrived at the Center, we got the usual treatment (uniforms, physical exams, intelligence and aptitude tests), the seemingly daily short-arm inspections.

On the third day, a sergeant came around and called off a lot of names, of which mine was one. He told us to pack everything into our barracks bag except our toilet articles, canteen cup and our knife, fork and spoon. We would be moving out.

When we got to the train, it was a train of day coaches and it was headed west. The Know-It-Alls (recruits who had been at the center for two weeks or more) told us we wouldn't be going very far. If you were going very far they told you to take your mess kit too. I remembered them that evening as I ate my dinner from a paper plate.

We sat up all night on the day coach. The next morning we were in Chicago and transferred to a train of sleeper cars. The route from Chicago was weird. We traveled south through the Midwest to El Paso, TX, then west along the Mexican border to Los Angeles, CA, then north to Pittsburg, CA. The train stopped there at 2:00 in the morning. Our car was greeted by a medical officer, who informed us that we were (1) at Camp Stoneman (2) that Camp Stoneman was a Port of Embarkation, and (3) that we would be sent overseas within two weeks. We had been in the Army eight days. He then took us to barracks where we were able to take a shower and clean up after our five day trip across the country.

One week later we were taken to one of the San Francisco docks and loaded onto the USS *President Johnson*. That night we sailed out of the harbor. I remember looking up as we went under the Golden Gate Bridge, where we could see a guard waving good-bye.

The next morning a convoy formed bound for we knew not where. The *President Johnson* had probably been a freighter, but the Army had turned it into a hell-hole. The enlisted men's accommodations were no different from so many other ships, but the *President Johnson* was not equipped to handle that many humans who required toilet facilities. To solve the problem, a shack had been set up on deck. There was a metal trough on one side to serve as a urinal, and on the other side was a "six-holer." Sea water was pumped through each trough to flush it out. When the sea got a little rough, well you can probably imagine the mess.

The most memorable event occurred after three days at sea. At about 2-3:00 a.m. (I am not sure exactly because as I already noted, I will be picking up my valuables on my "Delay En route" after I have completed basic training, so I didn't have a watch) an alarm sounded on our ship. Seven shorts and one long. We had been informed that meant Prepare To Abandon Ship. At this point we had been in the Army 15 days.

Most of us were asleep at the time. The alarm woke us in a hurry, and we got up on deck as quickly as possible. Leaving the ship in a lifeboat was a frightening prospect because the seas were fairly rough and the weather as cold. Plus the fact that none of us had ever been to sea before.

After waiting for about 45 minutes, with no explanation, the All Clear sounded and we went back to our cots. I'm not sure many of us slept. If we did, we probably dreamed about that "Delay En route."

The next day, the reason given for the Abandon Ship alarm was that one of the ships in the convoy "zigged" when it should have "zagged" in the convoy route. My experiences with the "Delay En route" have made me wonder about the Official Version of anything connected to the Army.

Two days later we arrived at Honolulu. We were transported to Schofield Barracks where we were placed in the capable hands of a cadre from the 34th Infantry Regiment. After basic, I was assigned to the 34th. .

I finally got that "Delay En route" on 13 November 1945. My discharge says that I served two years, 11 months, 20 days overseas and 26 days continental service.

As I said at the beginning of this story, it is not unique in the 24th Division or in many of the Hawaiian units, because the men in that group and an earlier group from the Mid-west were used for replacements in all of them. However, I have never seen it recorded anywhere.

A LETTER TO MY WIFE

by Bob Moncur

July 28, 1951

Today we finally came back to our rear area for a couple of days, but only after each company had a crack at taking that hill and failing. Now they say that we are going to go back and take a hill that we had before and pulled off of. That should give you an idea of how much sense there was to our latest operations. We just take a hill, pull back after taking it, and then go back a week later and have to fight for the same hill. I pray every night that they do something about this cease-fire before these people go completely crazy and have us all either dead or in the hospital. We took our crack at Razor-back Hill on the second day with our platoon and the third in the attack, and the second platoon in reserve. We were to go up one finger to a saddle and the third was to go to our right up to one of the peaks and give us any help they could. As it turned out, we were the only platoon engaging the enemy and the third was in no position to help us at all. We moved out with our bedrolls because if we took the hill we were supposed to hold it that night, and then pull back the next day. My squad was third in the approach and we were just about up to the top when the lead squad got hit. They were firing back and forth when I decided to take a look at the situation for the machine gun. I took off my bedroll because it is practically impossible to move with a blanket swinging on your back. The chinks were just throwing hand grenades then, but as I got up there we started to draw automatic weapons fire from both flanks and the front. We were in no position to do anything without support so we were ordered to pull back, but there were two wounded men that we had to get out. Most of the men pulled back to the protected slope but there were still a few of us there and we had to get the last wounded man out. We got the wounded man out of the ditch and down below and then there was just a BAR man and I left to cover the withdrawal. There were bedrolls laying all over the hill and empty BAR clips (which are almost impossible to replace) so I started heaving rolls back down to the men and stuffed my shirt with empty clips. By this time the BAR was out of ammo so the gunner had his carbine and I had mine, so we just kept firing and clearing the hill of equipment. By some trick of fate we both ran out of ammo at the same time so we both had to reload our clips right there. The man who started taking the wounded man out had to leave him, so on the way back I tried to drag him down, but he was

too heavy, so I called Kirk (the BAR man) to give me a hand. The Chinks were heaving grenades all over the place and the wounded man had died already, but we still tried to get him out. Just as Kirk got over to me a Chink grenade landed right in between us, so I just yelled, "grenade," and we both took off to the side of the hill - and it went off without touching either of us. By this time the Chinks had moved back down and were throwing out a lot of fire and lots of grenades so we had to leave. If the man was still alive we never would have left him but there was nothing we could do for him. After we all got down, Kirk told me that if I hadn't gone up there and called him he probably would still be up there. The platoon sergeant said that he was going to put a few other fellows and me in for a decoration, but all I wanted was to get out of there like I was and to see my buddies get out. When we got back today the platoon sergeant told me that he is going to have to find a new squad leader for my squad because I won't be here too long. I sure hope it means what I think it does and if so I just have to sweat out a couple of more operations and then our prayers will be answered.

PRESS RELEASE

by Charlie Card,
taken from the Memphis Commercial Appeal

With the 24th infantry Division in the Philippines the platoon of Lt. Thomas C. Rhem out-banzaied the Japanese in one action in the Philippines.

One company of this crack "Victory" Division was cut off and Lt. Rhem received orders to break through to it. His platoon was already only a skeleton force from more than a month of steady fighting.

There was only one way to accomplish the mission, and that was by cool daring.

Lt. Rhem radioed the isolated company

to stay down, then he lined up his men, fixed bayonets, and gave each one three grenades. They pulled the pins and let go their grenades in quick volleys, then charged the Nips with rebel yells.

Straight through the Japanese lines they tore. So terrified were some of the enemy that they were caught praying. The skeleton platoon killed 25, captured five light machine guns, and not a man was even wounded.

THE WAR'S CHRISTMAS PAUSE

by Nicholas Marasco

The 34th Infantry Regiment spent four Christmases overseas during WWII. The first, shortly after the Pearl Harbor bombing, was noted by our being thrust into a war with loaded weapons, blackout, half rations, extensive guard duty, etc.

The second Christmas, also on Oahu, Hawaii, was a little better with food and late packages from home. The third in Australia provided excellent food and timely Christmas packages from home.

On 24 December 1944, Company L of the 34th Infantry was moved by landing craft to the Calubian Peninsula of Leyte Island of the Philippines.

In the barrio of Calubian at the foot of the mountains, was a bombed out church where our Catholic chaplain said a mass. The next day, Christmas 1944, Captain Stearns demanded and received of Colonel Postlethwait, our portable kitchen and our Christmas mail and packages brought up to us. He said, "My men are going to have their Christmas." We had fruit cakes, candy, cookies and canned goods in our packages from home. Since we were moving out that night with no way to carry all those goodies into combat, we gave most of it to the Filipinos who had not had anything like it under the Japanese, especially the children. They milled around us and squealed with delight at every cookie, candy bar or stick of gum given to them.

Pete Millard had just returned from furlough and brought me four cans of my favorite hometown Genesee beer from USA. Dibbler, Schuler, Millard and myself went into the Barrio on the beach to cool our beer in the ocean. There we chatted with and took pictures of the children, women and guerrillas who flocked around us.

It was the best Christmas in years for the Filipinos and also for us because we were able to do something for those children. Their joy and laugher made our Christmas very real. Like a miracle, Captain Stearn's demand that his men have their Christmas was to include the entire barrio, men, women and children.

Our mission was to cross the Calubian Peninsula under the cover of darkness so that we could overlook from the mountain top, the ocean on the other side. There was to be an invasion by our troops there and were to cut off any Japanese attempting to escape into the mountains.

As darkness came, the third platoon started

21st Infantry on parade at Kyushu, Japan. 1946. (Couretsy of Francis Haugh)

up the mountain to 10 miles behind the Japanese lines with a guerrilla guide, and maybe light from the "Star of Bethlehem," to guide us.

At daylight, we arrived overlooking the ocean on the other side of the peninsula and dug in our positions and the war went on.

MY TIME IN KOREA

by Richard S. Clayton

When I landed in Korea, my assignment was to Company G, 3rd Platoon, 3rd Squadron, 5th RCT which was attached to the 24th Division. I was one of the first replacements for Company G. Although with the 5th RCT, I spent an entire year serving with the 24th Division.

To look at me as a young soldier in my uniform, the patches I wore did not tell of all my assignments. Missing was the 5th RCT patch that was not authorized until 1952. In its place on my right shoulder was the 24th Division patch which I proudly wore throughout my military career. Incidentally, the 5th RCT patch was finally sewn on my uniform 10 years ago.

One of my most vivid memories is that of the winter of 1950 in Korea. Living in Pennsylvania, I am no stranger to harsh winter weather, but the memory of that one remains. The temperatures were -30 to -40 degrees below and it made me think what it must have been like at Valley Forge all those years ago. Nothing since has come close in comparison.

Like any soldier put in that situation, Korea was not a conflict nor a police action for those of us that experienced it, it was war.

Our motto for the 5th RCT was, "I'll try sir," and to this day we still live by that.

WE HAVE NOT FORGOTTEN

by Tony Alvarez

Only a medic knows you can't be there 10 months and not daily risk it all. Close calls caring for wounded while under fire, you can't escape all the agony you share with your infantrymen, the hardships, fatigue, losing your buddies, some of whom died in your arms. I am not, was not, ashamed to admit I cried then and I still do. Some events are preserved; the memories are still here and its like the very first moment. At first I couldn't talk about it. I felt guilty; yes, I felt guilty that some of my buddies didn't make it, or that they lost limbs. I was scared for I administered first aid and they didn't make it, or lost limbs. Just did what I could with what I had. I've always had fears and dreams of trying again, of those scenes of meeting my buddies hurting, without limbs, and I would blame myself and think, why? How? How did I make it and they didn't. I was afraid to meet someone I attended; were they all right? All there? Did I do enough? Once I met two who remembered me giving them first aid. My memory went blank on names and faces but I did remember the places, the action, but then there were so many I was afraid of whatever hurt they went through.

It's been a long 54 years since I last saw you. To be sure, the last time we had a good reason to enjoy an ice cold beer or any drink, we were at Schofield Barracks doing our best to spend our company funds before we left for Korea. The password for that night was "Poffinoarger."

With Capt. Chas. B. Gault OIC of entertainment, we had a great party in the old hospital hall and the hula show in the company game room that was our last company get-together. We left on three different ships: the *General Mann, Brewster* and *Gaffey*. So I never saw some of my buddies again. As you know some didn't make it, medics went fast. I did see some Stateside. They did receive the Bronze Star and Purple Heart and they thought all the original 5th RCT Combat Medics had one or the other, or both. Well I didn't. Someone forgot I was there for at least 10 months and had many, many close ones while caring for the wounded. I was hit three times by shrapnel sliver splinters. One time I went to 5th RCT aid station to have shrapnel removed. Sgt. Bill Wood did remember me. My blank head didn't want to admit it, but we talked about the same places, actions. He would start and I would finish his conversation. We remembered old buddies, even their nicknames. Seems as if we met before. I'm sure you remember those days. I remember I was so fatigued, I didn't care if I got mine just so it was fast. I didn't want to know and hurt like my buddies. Ten months is a long time; it didn't take me long the way things went to know we were forgotten. When is enough enough? Over there it never seemed to end. Anytime there is too long; in no time at all you're not sure of anything. You just follow those infantrymen, you learn fast. You don't forget those who didn't make it. The front soldiers sure don't forget what their buddies went through and it makes them go on and on. There's no stop for them. It gives you the will to go on to follow them. You want to be there if need be. You pray that somehow the need will soon pass, then end. We don't care we are here forgotten, for we did not then and now. We have not forgotten.

MY BAPTISM OF FIRE

by Joseph J. Drozd

Several days after the outbreak of hostilities in Korea, 15 June 1950, a large group of NCOs and enlisted men were transferred from the 35th Infantry and 27th Infantry Regiments of the 25th Infantry Division to the 24th Infantry Division via rail from Kyo to Sasebo and by Japanese ferry boat to Pusan, South Korea. We camped in the Pusan Stadium overnight; the next morning the men were assigned to the 1st Battalion. My friends and I were assigned to Company B, 21st Infantry. It was nearly noon when the troops boarded a train and headed north. At certain railroad stations the train stopped briefly while Korean women came to the rail cars and offered some green tea to drink. At the last stop, south of Chonan, we disembarked and formed into a column of twos and marched from the train station while a Korean two or three piece band played *God Bless America*. Our group marched up the dirt road and set up defense positions on a hill; I could hear South Korean Army Cavalry withdrawing all night long. The next day we marched north to another large hill and by early afternoon had dug in our defensive perimeter. During the afternoon we had noticed a couple of farmer's down in the valley, strolling in their field of crops, looking up at our positions. We fired a shot their way and they ran off. Later on, we heard they were North Korean Army soldiers dressed in civilian clothes reconnoitering our defense perimeter. This was a favorite tactic of theirs during the early days of the war.

Elements of Task Force Smith had withdrawn to regroup; we were ready to face the enemy. The next day, 6 or 7 July, around mid-morning a fog rolled up the hill and dissipated

North Korean exchange at Yong Dung-po during 1953. (Courtesy of William Healy)

and then the North Korean Army attacked the hill. Commie machine gun fire raked the hill, along with artillery and T-34 tank fire.

A squadron of P-51 Mustang fighters (5th Air Force) arrived and promptly began strafing the enemy troops, empty shell casings (50 caliber) falling on us. Cpl. John L. Garland and I were in our foxhole and every time I popped my head up for a quick look, machine gun bullets ripped the soil about two feet above our foxhole. Amid the shelling I could hear a guy from Alabama in the next foxhole shouting, "Lordy Lord," so great was his fear.

I think Lt. Col. Smith was with us and as we were about to be surrounded the order came down the line, "Every man for himself." I swiftly sprang out of our foxhole, with Cpl. Garland right behind me, and ran around the side of the mountain, a section which was recently plowed, with machine gun bullets ripping at our heels. I noticed a 1st lieutenant running behind us and he went down. I hesitated for second, thinking he was hit, but he yelled, "Keep going," I only tripped." We finally ran out of the gunner range. Other men had run around to the other side of the hill and down onto the dirt road. We joined a group of NCOs at the base of the nearby hill where Sgt. Brown grinned and said, "Joe, this sure isn't like maneuvers on Mt. Fuji, is it?" I grinned back and said, "It sure as hell isn't!" This was in reference to the 35th Infantry Regiment, 25th Infantry Division's advanced infantry maneuvers on Mt. Fujiyama near Tokyo just three months ago.

This group was hiking along the trail and came to a fork in the trail. I decided to take the left fork with the thought in mind that a small group had a better chance of making it back to our lines. Cpl. John L. Garland of Erwin, TN; Cpl. Ralph E. Harless, Huntington, WV; and Cpl. Roy C. Miller, Des Moines, IA came with me. As I was the senior NCO, I was the leader of our group. The other men continued on the

main trail. Along the path we passed a Korean farmer, his wife, one child and a cow who were in hiding. I nodded "Hello" and kept on going.

Soon we heard burp gun fire from the ridge over to our right. (An experienced combat infantryman can distinguish between US Army and North Korean army machine gun or burp gun fire, that is, a burp gun has a faster rate of fire and a higher pitch.) We kept moving and were fired upon by Commie guerrillas, we circled the area and picked up the trail again. An American soldier came walking down the mountain towards us, clad only in fatigues, bare feet, no cap, no equipment or rifle. He was a young blonde haired fella; I asked what outfit are you from? He answered "Company C." I told him to come with us, he adamantly refused and went his own way. Our canteens were empty, we're very thirsty and we see a Korean farmer near a field. We approached him, asking for water. I motioned towards the rice paddy water. I immediately became suspicious of the man and told my men not to drink this water. About 200 feet away was a large natural pit with a farm house on it. I ordered my men to stay at the top rim and cover me while I went down to check the well. As soon as I got near the well, three Koreans barged out of the farm house. They were mean looking and of military age. My sixth sense told me to get out of there fast. We moved out quickly. I told my buddys I felt these were the men, Commie guerrillas, that fired at us earlier.

As we circled through the mountains, I climbed to the top of one for a look around and I could see the 52nd Field Artillery Battery withdrawing down the dirt road, and the Air Force pounding the Communists. We hastened our pace and marched down the mountain trail and on to a dirt road (it was late afternoon). As we rounded a corner into a small village, we saw a column of two 2-1/2 ton trucks and several jeeps waiting for stragglers. Here was Margaret "Maggy" Higgins, female war correspondent in fatigues, standing near the trucks with an Army officer. I placed my men wherever there was room in the jeeps; there being no more empty space, I sat on the right front end of a jeep hood.

Maggy Higgins took a photograph of us, titled "GI Jeep Column," which was published in *Time Magazine*, 24 July 1950. We had just made it; five minutes later the column drove a few miles to a village, re-grouped in a schoolhouse, had chow and went to Massachusetts. Here I met Sgt. Bennett who related to me that their group was ambushed by Commie guerrillas. He, being the last man in line on the trail, dove into the bushes and escaped, the rest were killed. This was the burp gun firing we had heard back in the mountains. Sgt. Brown and Sgt. Owens were in that group. It was sad for me to hear of this for I personally knew these two men. The US Army lost some very good NCOs that day.

The next morning we marched up the dirt road and onto a hill and set up a defensive perimeter, awaiting the next Commie attack. After this second battle the group united with their respective units. Company B's commanding officer was Capt. John "Jack" J. Doody, a fine officer and leader.

My group of men jokingly referred to ourselves as the 21st Infantry Regimental Mountain Goats because of the frequent climbing of hills, day and night, both fighting and shifting positions. The Korean War was very hard on the infantrymen, physically and mentally.

THE NAKTONG RIVER CROSSING AND HILL 1157

by Joseph J. Drozd

My unit was trucked to a staging area near an orchard adjacent to the Naktong River around 2:00 a.m. on 15 September 1950. All three battalions of the 21st Infantry made the crossing. We were to have air and artillery support. Men spread out in the orchard to await the crack of dawn; jump off time. The engineer unit had an assault boat with an engineer for each squad of infantrymen.

As we began to move out, our forward observer from the 52nd Field Artillery and his driver were killed by a direct mortar hit on their jeep. We picked up our assault boat and engineer at the edge of the orchard and started carrying it towards the water. The sandy section of the dry riverbed was tough walking in with machine gun bullets whizzing by and mortar rounds exploding nearby. After carrying the boat for about 50 feet, I noticed a boat at the water's edge just sitting there, no one near it. I yelled to my squad leader, Sgt. Gilbert, "Let's drop this boat and board that empty one." This we did, and ran amid machine gun bullets to the river edge. Two ROK soldiers were in our squad; they were up front, I was in the rear of the boat with Sgt. Gilbert and the engineer. We paddled out into the river and saw several boats floating downstream with dead Americans lying in them. Suddenly, machine gun and mortar fire hit very close to us, the ROKs dropped their paddles in the boat and crouched down. I immediately moved forward, moved the ROK soldier aside, took his paddle and started to call cadence, so we all can paddle in unison. Sgt. Gilbert took over calling cadence.

The boat slowly started to move across the portion of the Naktong with the swift current. Machine gun fire raked the water about 10 feet to our left front and mortar rounds exploded in the water to our right front, splashing water on the men. This is when I started to pray intensely to God for protection. It seemed like forever, but we finally got to the enemy side of the Naktong River. The river bank was about three feet high with about two feet of land to stand on. The boat hit the shore, with men jumping onto the small shoreline. Our BAR man, Pfc. Raymond Wirth of Buffalo, NY, jumped into the water at the rear of the boat, thinking it was shallow. He got a shock; the water was still way over his head. Two men quickly grabbed his wrists and pulled him up onto the boat; he would have surely drowned. His BAR got clogged up with water and silt and the engineer had a brand new BAR. I ordered him to exchange his with our BAR man, seeing

Marilyn Monroe, one of the favorite "Pin Ups" for GIs, on tour to build troop morale. (Courtesy of Neil Estes)

that he was to go back across the river and we needed a good working BAR.

The men spread out along the river edge, machine gun fire and mortar rounds raking the water behind us. I judged the angle of fire coming from the mountain and we fired a fusillade in that direction. In a few minutes a 1st lieutenant came over and asked if we were Company C, and we said, "No, we're Company B, 1st Platoon." He ordered us to attack the mountain. We moved out through a cornfield, bullets whizzing through the cornstalks and up the hill. We came across a young North Korean soldier, looked about 16-years-old, who was hit in the stomach and lying in a gully. By his glassy eyes, I could see he was dying. A few moments later, one of our platoon leaders, a 2nd lieutenant, came by saying, "I got me a gook." He had killed the wounded and dying boy.

Our squad advanced up the hill and came across a Russian-built automatic weapon with a bipod, similar to our own BAR, with blood all over the buttstock. I think this was the result of the rifle fire I had directed on the hill from the river edge. We continued to advance up the hill, all this time without artillery or air support. About three-fourth's of the way up the hill, I looked back and could see the combat engineers building a pontoon bridge across the Naktong; they also took a direct hit from enemy mortar fire. Looking beyond the river I could see the elements of the battalions marching forward in a column of twos with Patton tanks. I saw a mortar round hit directly on the infantry/tank column, men hit the dirt, the column moved forward, several men lay there, dead or wounded. Finally a flight of Navy Corsairs flew over us and the enemy mortar fire ceased. When the flight flew away, the enemy mortar fire started up again.

When we reached the top of the hill, a North Korean sniper fired at me; the bullet hit the dirt about five feet to my right and waist high. Thank God for his poor eyesight. The squad took cover immediately. A sniper had been in hiding somewhere behind us. The strange thing is, he didn't fire at us again.

The combat engineers got the pontoon bridge built, the tanks came across with the infantry. The enemy mortar crew must have retreated, for the firing stopped. This squad and one officer was assigned to go on a combat patrol riding five tanks from Company A, 6th Tank Battalion. I rode on the 4th Tank in the column. We headed north along the mountain road, came to a bad section of road; four tanks made it and the edge of the road collapsed sending dirt and rocks cascading down the mountainside. The fifth tank had to turn back. The mission of this patrol was to link up and make contact with elements of the US Army's 2nd Infantry Division. This was done late in the afternoon of 15 September 1950. In this combat episode, our squad didn't lose one man.

In the meantime, we by-passed some 5,000 North Korean troops sitting along the mountain tops. These troops later surrendered. The 21st Infantry Regiment, the "Gimlets," continued northward. This was the end of my experience of Naktong River Crossing and Hill 1157.

My home away from home. (Courtesy of Ed Jackson)

STILL OF THE NIGHT

by Edward V. Jackson

In mid to late 1961 the Berlin Wall Crisis was in progress. The 24th was all over Germany, including Berlin. We had units from Ft. Stewart, GA and Ft. McClellan, AL brought over and attached to the 24th in Augsburg. The 21st Infantry, from late summer through winter, 1961-1962, participated in Summer Shield, Autumn Shield, under 7th Army, 7th Corps control. During these maneuvers, I drove HQ 11 for the HQ&HQ Co. CO.

During one of these operations we went far north, I believe near Bremen. During the FTX we were opposed by some Special Forces. Their mission was to infiltrate and capture 21st Infantry BG commanding officer.

Our position was in a forest with a plowed field between us and the enemy. We were supposedly in a rear area. At about 2:00 a.m. I was on guard duty to the rear perimeter on a wooden point that stuck slightly into the plowed field. I had excellent cover and view to my left, right and forward. I was very isolated as we had few guards and no officer or NCO checking on us. It was a moonlit night and we were under black-out. It was dead silent. The stillness was broken by machine gunfire far down my left flank, then silence.

Very soon I observed three people crawling towards me at about 75 yards across the plowed field. As they approached I slowly stood completely concealed behind a large tree. The edge of the field was 10 feet away and in the darkness I was invisible. When the three characters got about 20 feet away, still crawling, I had already decided there'd be no, "Halt who goes there?" If this were actual combat I would not make a decision that would cost my life or allow my HQ be attacked.

I emptied my M1 at the three before they had the chance to split up or even get up. (It was blanks however.) There was no return fire from the other side of the field.

Not knowing they were dead they rushed me, overpowered me and dragged me across the field. My shouts for help went unanswered and I was captured by the Special Forces.

I hope they learned a lesson that they used if they ever saw actual combat. Drivers were required to carry the division code book, even on guard, which I felt was ridiculous. So I suggested my captors search me. The 24th Division also learned a lesson.

During exercise "Spearpoint" we joined the 1st British Corps and Canadians again far to the north in tank country. I believe near the gap. At this time and until I left Germany in March 1962, I drove the 21st Infantry Battle Group Command Truck, the M114 war room APC. It was no coincidence that things were heating up in Berlin and along the Iron Curtain. Troops from the 21st that were on ships going home had their ships turned around to bring them back to Germany. Countless units were attached to or took the place of 24th Division units all over Germany, including Berlin. Heroes all.

The beginning of the end of the Iron Curtain, the Berlin Wall, the Communist Eastern Block armies, the Soviet Block. The Berlin Wall Crisis was almost the third world war. Because of the presence of battlefield atomic weapons it would have been a massacre and carnage of unbelievable proportions. They would have lost, most of us would have been left in fields of white crosses. The troops from Italy, France, Spain, England, Norway, etc. would have finished it up. We'd have occupied Russia and that would have been a disaster.

Some shots were fired, people suffered and died; it was scary. But we "Cold War" vets of all Allied nations "won our war." Thank you, President Reagan and President Gorbachev.

Korea will still have to be dealt with. The 50th anniversary of that one won't be a celebration. I was there 1 January 1960 through 28 March 1962 and am proud of it and my comrades in arms. We'd have given them a taste of "The Victory Division."

24TH DIVISION INFANTRY COMBAT COMMANDERS

World War II (1941 - 1945)

24th Division
Major General Frederick A. Irving
Major General Roscoe B. Woodruff - 18 November 1944
Major General James A. Lester - August 1945

Assistant Division Commander
Brigadier General Kenneth F. Cramer - Leyte through Sarangani Bay

19th Regiment
Lt. Colonel George H. Chapman, Jr. - Hollandia, Leyte
Colonel Thomas E. Clifford, Jr. - Mindanao (KIA 24 June 1945)
Lieutenant Colonel Walter S. Wickbolt -24 June 1945

1st Battalion
Lieutenant Colonel Frederick R. Zierath

2nd Battalion
Lieutenant Colonel Robert S. Spragins
Lieutenant Colonel Joy K. Vallery - Mindanao

3rd Battalion
Lieutenant Colonel Elmer Howard
Lieutenant Colonel Lester L. Wheeler - Mindanao to 3 June 1945

21st Regiment
Colonel Charles B. Lyman - Hollandia
Lt. Colonel Frederick R. Weber - Leyte
Colonel William J. Verbeck - Leyte, Visayas, Mindanao

1st Battalion
Lt. Colonel Thomas E. Clifford, Jr. - Hollandia
Major Lamar Little - Leyte
Major Nicholas E. Sloan - Mindanao

2nd Battalion
Lieutenant Colonel Seymour Madison - Leyte

3rd Battalion
Lieutenant Colonel Chester A. Dahlen - Hollandia
Lieutenant Colonel Eric P. Ramee - Leyte, Mindoro
Major Thomas Suber - Mindanao (WIA 25 May 1945)

34th Regiment
Colonel William W. Jenna - Hollandia, Biak, Leyte, Luzon, Mindanao
Colonel Aubrey S. Newman - Leyte (WIA 1 November 1944)
Lieutenant Colonel Chester A. Dahlen - Leyte 1 November 1944, Mindanao 14 May 1945
Lieutenant Colonel Lester L. Wheeler - Mindanao 3 June 1945

1st Battalion
Lieutenant Colonel Thomas E. Clifford, Jr. - Leyte
Lieutenant Colonel Charles E. Oglesby - Luzon (WIA 4 February 1945)
Major Carl O. Mann - Luzon 4 February 1945, Mindanao
Major Jack Matthews - Mindanao 10 June 1945

2nd Battalion
Lieutenant Colonel James F. Pearsall, Jr. - Hollandia, Biak, Leyte
Major Harry L. Snavely - Luzon, Mindanao (WIA 4 June 1945)
Major Thomas Cathcart - 4 June 1945

3rd Battalion
Lt. Colonel Edward M. Postlethwait - Hollandia through Corregidor
Lieutenant Colonel George Willetts - Mindanao

Korea (June, 1950 - July, 1951)

24th Division
Major General William F. Dean
Major General John H. Church - July 1950
Major General Blackshear M. Bryan - January 1951
Major General Chares L. Dasher, Jr. - November 1952

Task Force Smith
Lieutenant Colonel Charles B. Smith

19th Regiment
Colonel Guy S. Meloy, Jr. - (WIA 16 July 1950)
Colonel Ned D. Moore

1st Battalion
Lieutenant Colonel Otho T. Winstead - (KIA 16 July 1950)
Lieutenant Colonel Robert L. Rhea

2nd Battalion
Lieutenant Colonel Thomas M. McGrail

3rd Battalion
Not activated until 31 August 1950
Lieutenant Colonel Harold B. Ayers

21st Regiment
Colonel Richard W. Stephens

1st Battalion
Lieutenant Colonel Charles B. Smith

2nd Battalion
Lieutenant Colonel Gines Perez - 25 August 1950

3rd Battalion
Lieutenant Colonel Carl C. Jensen - (KIA 12 July 1950)
Lieutenant Colonel John A. McConnell

34th Regiment
(Deactivated 31 August 1950)
Colonel Robert R. Martin - (KIA 8 July 1950)
Lieutenant Colonel Robert L. Wadlington - 8 July 1950
Colonel Charles E. Beauchamp

1st Battalion
Lieutenant Colonel Harold B. Ayres

2nd Battalion
(Not activated)

3rd Battalion
Lieutenant Colonel Gines Perez - to 25 August 1950

5th RCT
Colonel Godwin L. Ordway - 25 August 1950
Colonel John L. Throckmorton - 15 August 1950

1st Battalion
Lieutenant Colonel John P. Jones - (WIA 11 August 1950)
Lieutenant Colonel T. B. Roelofs

2nd Battalion
Colonel John L. Throckmorton - to 15 August 1950

3rd Battalion
Lieutenant Colonel Gines Perez

24TH INFANTRY DIVISION VETERANS' BIOGRAPHIES
SUBMITTED BY MEMBERS OF THE ASSOCIATION

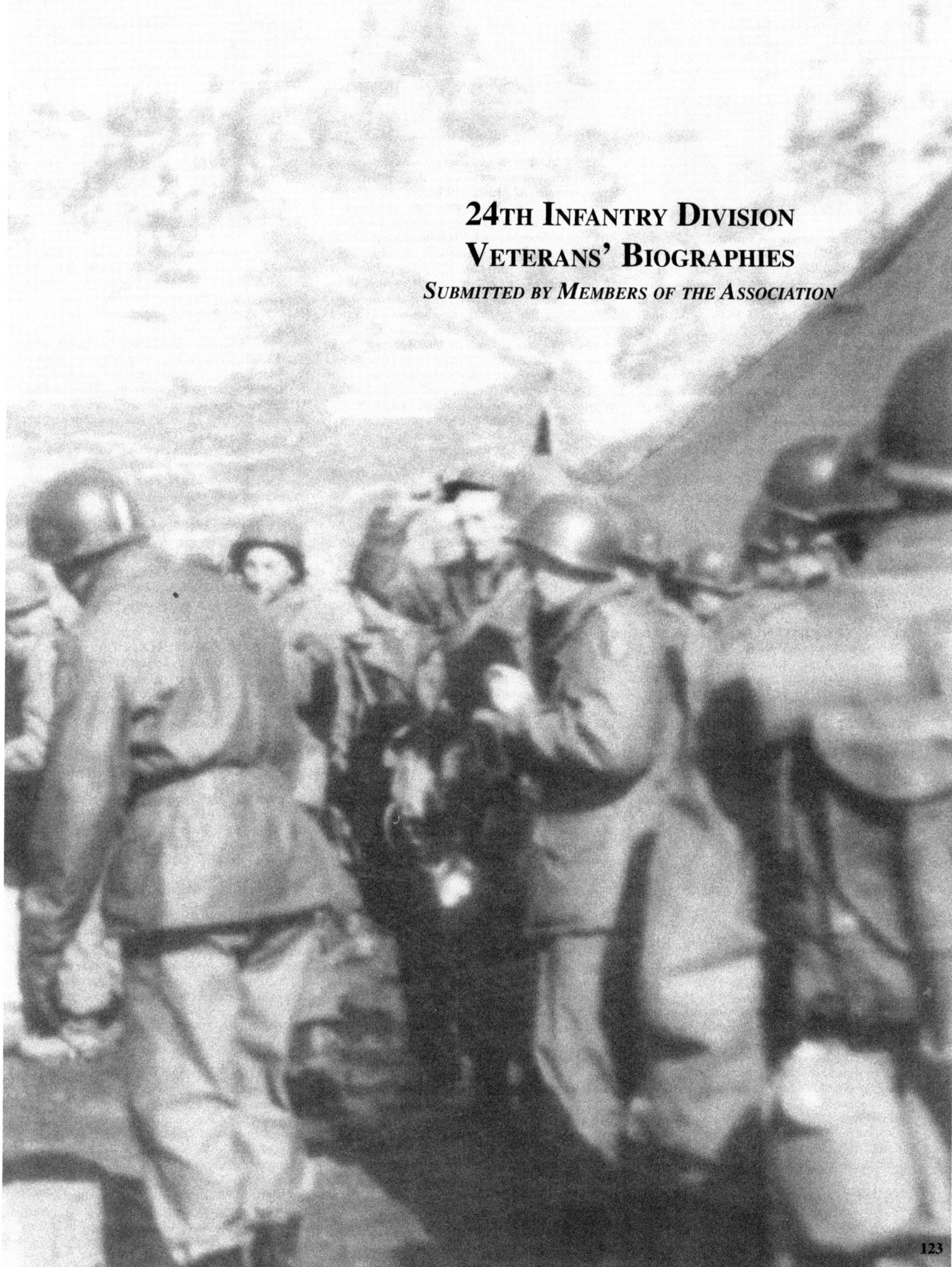

JOE E. ABERNATHY JR., born Feb. 17, 1929 in Gaylesville, AL. He graduated from Gaylesville High School and was drafted into the Army Dec. 5, 1950, taking his basic training at Camp Chaffee, AR.

From Seattle he was sent to Camp Drake, Japan and on May 5, 1951 to Pusan, Korea. He was assigned to the 24th Div., 19th Regt., Co. K, 3rd Bn. He attained the rank of master sergeant and 4th platoon sergeant.

The division was sent to Camp Haugen, Japan in February 1952, rotated home by way of Camp Stoneman, CA to Camp Chaffee, AR and processed for 30 day leave.

Returned to Camp Chaffee, sent to Ft. Ord, CA then to Camp Roberts, CA for remaining six months where he was a platoon sergeant for new trainees. Released from active duty in September 1952 and stayed in the inactive reserve for five years.

Married Martha Stewart and they live in Carrollton, GA. They have one daughter, Anita, who is married to Jerry Haynes and has two children, Matt and Katie. Joe was a banker for many years and retired Dec. 31, 1993 as vice president, West Georgia National Bank, Carrollton, GA.

WILFORD R. ACKER joined the service on Nov. 15, 1944, and served with Co. A, 21st Regt. He served in the Pacific, Philippines, Leyte, Mindanao and the Occupation of Japan. He was discharged on Nov. 15, 1946, with the rank of technical sergeant.

DALE S. ACKERMAN joined the service on March 8, 1940, and served with HQ Co., 21st Inf. Regt. He participated at Pearl Harbor and in New Guinea. He was discharged with the rank of staff sergeant. Dates served: 1940-45.

MALCOLM D. AITKEN, born April 3, 1919 in Philadelphia, PA. He was called to active duty as a 2nd lieutenant, Infantry, Nov. 1, 1941 and assigned to the Army Counterintelligence Office in Honolulu, HI.

Transferred to 21st Inf. Regt. in April 1943 at Schofield Barracks and assigned to Co. K. He accompanied the 24th Inf. Div. through Australia, Goodenough Island, Hollandia, Panaon, Leyte, Mindoro, Mindanao and Sarangani Bay. His last assignment as WWII ended was as battalion executive officer, lst Bn., 21st. Following the end of WWII he accompanied the division to Japan and participated in the occupation.

Aitken separated from the service in May 1947. Among his decorations are the Bronze Star w/OLC, Purple Heart and the Combat Infantry Badge.

He received his BA degree in police administration and MS in administration of criminal justice from San Jose State University, CA. He is married and has four daughters, one son and seven grandchildren.

BENEDICT J. ALES, born Dec. 22, 1928. He enlisted in the Army Jan. 18, 1948 and was assigned to M Co., 34th Inf., 24 Inf. Div. in Japan and Korea.

Memorable Experience: The men were ordered by Maj. Rosen to counterattack a village which was heavily wooded and infested with heavily camouflaged North Koreans. The enemy opened up fire and guys were being hit and dirt kicking up all over. Then Cpl. Ales took his water-cooled .30 cal. machine gun crew to an exposed open rice paddy and started working over the trees and enemy started dropping as he yelled "Water-Cool's gonna get you gooks." He silenced them and Maj. Rosen had them withdraw being they were outnumbered. But the North Koreans were knocked off balance and caused a lot of confusion. Cpl. Ales never received any recognition for his daring, brave action. The situation was so chaotic the next few weeks, nobody had time to write him up for the award.

He was discharged Jan. 23, 1952. Awards include the Combat Infantry Badge and Purple Heart w/cluster.

Ales and wife, Grace, have four children: Pat, Tina, Joe and Benita, and six grandchildren: Ben, Pat, Kate, Steve, Sara and Grace. He is retired.

ANTHONY ALICKNOVIC joined the service in June 1941, and served with the Co. E, 34th Regt., 24th Div. He participated in the South Pacific, Hawaii, Australia and San Francisco. He was discharged with the rank of staff sergeant. Dates served: June 1941 to April 1946.

GEORGE WELDON ALLARD, born Aug. 12, 1922, Wichita Falls, TX. He enlisted in the Army in October 1942; assigned to 1st Bn. HQ 21st Reg. 24th Div. in Hawaii, November 1942 with duty in communications as a radio operator.

Memorable Experience: he was on first wave at Hollandia and they managed to work their way toward airfield. I don't recall how far, but they had air support. A note was dropped from the air and he gave it to Col. Jack Clifford who read it, then folded and handed it back to Allard who has kept it all these years.

The note dated April 23, 1944 read "We have been bombing and strafing a grove loaded with motor vehicles. Position about one-mile west of Hollandia Air Field. Believe we have also located barracks in that area which we'll give a good working over. We think you are doing a grand job. Good Luck.

Air Coordinator
Pilot, Lt. Cmdr. W.I. Martin
Flt. Surgeon Ridley
Radioman Williams
Torpedo Squadron 10
USS *Enterprise*
SSgt. Allard was discharged in November 1945. He received all the usual unit award plus the Purple Heart.

He has been a musician most of his life and worked in some great bands. He was also a funeral director and is now retired. Married Mary Ann and has two daughters, Lydia De'Ann and Tammy De'Renda and one grandchild, Brooke Ashley Bazor.

BENJAMIN R. ALLEN joined the service in April 1945 and served with HQ and HQ Co., 1st Bn., 19th Inf. Regt. Participated in the UN Offensive, Oct. 12, 1950, to Nov. 2, 1950; CCF Intervention, Nov. 3, 1950, to Jan. 24, 1951; UN Counter Offensive, Jan. 25, 1951, to April 21, 1951; CCF Spring Offensive, April 22, 1951, to July 8, 1951; and the Summer Offensive, July 31, 1951, to Sept. 9, 1951. He was discharged with the rank of staff sergeant. Dates served: September 1950 to October 1951.

ROBERT L. ALLEN, born May 7, 1932. He en-

listed in the service Nov. 30, 1951 and served in the Artillery. Assignments include basic training at Camp Polk, LA; survey scout with 37th Inf. Div.; FECOM assignment with C/63rd FABN/24th Inf. Div.; 4th FABN, 212th Bde. and 214th FA Bde.

Discharged in September 1953 as an E-5 and retired in July 1985 as colonel 0-6. His awards include the Meritorious Service Medal, Good Conduct Medal, Army Achievement Medal, Reserve Achievement, United Nations, Korean, National Defense and NG 20 year.

Accomplishments: OHNG direct commission, completed artillery branch and assoc. advance course at Ft. Sill; completed Command and General Staff College via USAR and Ft. Leavenworth, KS; commander, B/136 FABN and worked with regulars 1977-84.

Civilian activity as senior manufacturing engineer with GM as tool and die maker, tool and die designer, prod. supervisor, general supervisor, tool and die maintenance; he retired from GM after 36-1/2 years and from the USA with 33-1/2 years. Robert and his wife, Barbara, have two children, Alesia and Charles.

ROBERT W. ALLEN joined the service on Sept. 4, 1944, and served with Co. I, 21st Regt. He participated in the ETO, Rhineland and Central Europe. Dates served: July 19, 1952 to Feb. 2, 1954. He was discharged with the rank of sergeant first class. His awards include the Korean Service Medal and Bronze Service Star.

WILLIAM GARRISON ALLEN joined the service on June 27, 1941, and served with the Service Co., 34th Inf. Regt. He participated in the Pacific Theater; Hollandia, New Guinea; Leyte; Southern Philippines, where he was wounded in action; Oahu, Thailand; Australia; Good Enough Island; Biak; Mindanao; and Shikoku.

He was awarded the Purple Heart and Bronze Star w/Arrowhead for opposed landing in Leyte, Oct. 20, 1944; OLC added Sept. 14, 1945. Commanded the 3rd Bn., 34th Inf. Regt. from July 24, 1945, to Oct. 26, 1945. The battalion went into Japan as part of the Army of Occupation in October 1945. Maj. Allen received the Bronze Star Medal (2nd OLC) for ground combat on or about June 11, 1944, by executive order. Dates served: June 7, 1941, to April 7, 1946.

He joined the USAR and was recalled during the Korean War, serving from June 21, 1951, to Nov. 20, 1952. He was discharged with the rank of major.

MAURICE K. ALLGEIER JR. joined the service on Dec. 20, 1965, and served with the HHC Co., 1st and 19th Regt. He was stationed at Reese Kaserne, Augsburg, Germany. He joined the USAR and was promoted to sergeant major. Dates served: May 1, 1966, to Dec. 1, 1967. He is still in the active guard Reserve at Camp Pike, AR.

GUSTAVO ANTHONY ALVAREZ, born in San Diego, CA and enlisted in the Army in January 1949. Attended Medical Field Service School, Brooke Army Medical Center, Ft. Sam Houston, TX; assigned to Medical Co., 5th RCT, Schofield Barracks, HI, 1949-50; Korea, 1950-51, 5th RCT, 24th Div., combat medic.

Returned to the ZI in June 1951 and assigned Medical Section, 6004 ASU, Ft. MacArthur, CA; TDY Norton AFB, San Bernardino, CA in connection with Army display medical aid station exhibit. Returned to Ft. MacArthur for the sad duty of participating in burial service with full military honors for their fallen comrades.

Discharged in June 1952 and served with the National Guard as staff sergeant E-6, Co. B, 40th Maint. Bn. during Vietnam, 1963-66.

Married Nancy Garibay and they have three sons: Henry, Rick and Michael; daughter, Priscilla; grandsons: Tim, Henry Jr., Steven, Chris and Michael Jr.; granddaughters, Alysia and Eleanna. Employed three years as clerk, US Civil Service (Navy) and retired after 31 years with the postal service.

FISHER AMES joined the service in August 1943, and served with H&H Co., 19th Regt. He participated in New Guinea, Leyte, Mindeoraand Mindanao. He was discharged with the rank of T5. Dates served: April 1944 to July 1945.

DONALD A. ANDERSON joined the service on Jan. 16, 1946, and served with the 13th FA, B and C Batteries, 24th Inf. Div. Participated in the Central Cabaret "Beer Hall", Fukuoka Kyusha and as a battery clerk at a MP compound in Fukuoka. He was discharged on Nov. 12, 1948, with the rank of T4.

HORACE ANDERSON, born March 14, 1931. He enlisted in the Army on Dec. 7, 1947 and took basic training at Fort Jackson, SC. Went to Korea in June 1948, 7th Inf. Div. and left June 1949; Hawaii, 5th RCT, July 1949; Korea, July 1950. Rotated in April 1951 to Fort Benning, GA.

He was wounded at Naktong and again on Hill 256. Anderson was discharged Dec. 8, 1951 as sergeant first class. His awards include the Combat Infantry Badge, Silver Star, Bronze Medal w/V, UN Service Ribbon, Vietnam Campaign Ribbon, Purple Heart w/cluster, Korean Occupation Ribbon and Korean Service Ribbon.

Memorable experiences include receiving his master license in US Merchant Marines; serving with a great bunch of men in the 5th RCT, US Infantry and his four years in the Army. He retired from the Merchant Marines June 1, 1997 as master of steam and motor vessels and also as first class pilot in all waters of the Great Lakes.

His wife Ernestine passed away in 1990. He has two married daughters, Deborah Coleman and Robin Sanchez, and six grandchildren: Larry, Andrew, Aaron, Anthony, Jennifer and Julia.

MARSHALL H. ANDERSON, joined the service on Feb. 7, 1947 and served with HQ Btry., 13th FABN, Aug. 4, 1950 to Aug. 20, 1950 as a corporal; served with C Btry., 13th FA Aug. 21, 1950 to Oct. 4, 1951, as a sergeant; and with HQ Btry., 24th Div. September 1956 to May 1957, as an artillery sergeant.

Participated in the Korean War Aug. 4, 1950 to Oct. 4, 1951. Anderson retired Jan. 1, 1968 with the rank of first sergeant. Awards include the Bronze Star Medal and Korean Service Medal w/6 Bronze Service Stars.

WILLIAM E. ANDERSON, born Dec. 17, 1932. He enlisted in the Army Infantry March 25, 1950 and took his basic training at Fort Riley, KS. After a brief furlough he was shipped to Korea in August 1950.

Assigned as automatic rifleman, 1st Squad, 2nd Plt., Co. C, 21st Inf. Regt. 24th Inf. Div. from August 1950 to December 1951. Discharged April 26, 1953, Fort Ord, CA with the rank of temporary corporal, Replacement Depot.

Awards include the Bronze Star, Purple Heart, Good Conduct Medal, Distinguished Unit Citation, Korean Service Medal w/Silver and Bronze Service Stars, National Defense Service Medal, UN Service Medal, Combat Infantry Badge, ROK Unit Citation, Korean War Service Medal and Korean Peace Medal.

Spent three years in US Army Reserve and six years in US Coast Guard Reserve. He retired as a police officer, city of San Jose, CA, then spent 20 years in banking and worked his way up to vice president in asset control.

He received several commendations in law enforcement. One that especially stands out was going into the flooded and freezing waters of Guadalupe Creek in an effort to rescue a young boy who had fallen into the creek.

He married Connie Irene Crowell-Johnson June 6, 1952 in San Jose CA. Children are Danille Jo Johnson, Michelle Ruth Johnson and Rebecca Ann Anderson; eight grandchildren and five great-grandchildren. (Kari, Laura, Steve, David, Duane, John, Jamie and Katie.) He is retired and nursing many old injuries in the rural area of Wilderville, OR.

LEWIS R. AHNERT joined the service on Jan. 19, 1943, and entered active duty on June 7, 1943. He served with B Btry., 13th Field Regt. He participated in New Guinea and the liberation of the Southern Philippines. Dates served: June 7, 1943, to Dec. 20, 1945. He was discharged with the rank of T5. Awards include the Asiatic-Pacific Theater Ribbon, Philippine Ribbon w/2 Bronze Stars, Good Conduct Medal and WWII Victory Medal.

MICHAEL A. ANTOSH joined the service in July 1950 as a light weapons infantryman, and served in Co. C, 19th Regt. He participated in Korea, many battles and many wounds. He was discharged with the rank of sergeant. Dates served: April 1951 to March 1952.

RUSSELL ARNOLD joined the service on Feb. 8, 1945, and served with the 24th MP Plt. He participated in the Philippines from September 1945 until Japan in July 1947. He was discharged with the rank of staff sergeant.

CHARLES ASHLEY, born Oct. 13, 1918. He enlisted in the Army June 10, 1943 and assigned to 21st Regt. as a machine gunner and later as field radio and wireman in the South Pacific.

Memorable experience was on Mindanao when the Japanese had blown out a bridge and their ammo was on the other side. They made a make-shift foot bridge and six of them crossed to get the ammo under heavy sniper and artillery fire. Two men were killed and two refused to go back again, so Charles and Cpl. Whitsler were left to do it alone. Their outfit took a great loss but if they hadn't got the ammo it would have been the end of all of them.

He was discharged Nov. 10, 1945. Awards include the Bronze Star, Philippine Liberation Medal, Asiatic Campaign Medal, Good Conduct and WWII Victory Medal. He was told he earned the Silver Star and possibly Medal of Honor, but never got them.

Worked as construction worker (equipment operator) and is now retired and enjoys golf in summer and billards in winter; also writing poetry and oil painting.

He married Anne Ashley and has two children, Geraldine and Dennis; and four grandchildren: Cindy, Mike, Pat and Jenny.

FRANK A. ATHANASON, born Aug. 1, 1926, Augusta, GA. In 1945 he took infantry basic training at Camp Blanding, FL then went to Artillery Officer Candidate School at Fort Sill, OK, graduating as second lieutenant Dec. 7, 1945. He is listed in the Hall of Fame at Fort Sill.

From 1945-50 he served in various troop assignments in Germany and the US. During this period he was commissioned in the Regular Army; 1950-51, he served a 14 month tour in Korea with the 555 FABN which was part of the 5th RCT attached to the 24th Inf. Div. He was wounded April 21, 1951.

Returning from Korea, he served on ROTC duty at the Univ. of Washington and with the 3rd Armd. Div. in Germany until 1959 when he attended the Command and General Staff College at Fort Leavenworth, KS. In 1960 he was assigned to the Pentagon in the Office of the Chief of Research and Development.

Following a tour in Vietnam, he commanded artillery battalions in the 11th Air Assault and the 5th Mech. Div. Also served as G-4 5th Mech. Div. before going to the Army War College in Carlisle, PA. Upon completion of the Army War College, he served in the office of Secretary of Defense as division artillery commander, 3rd Inf. Div. a second tour in Vietnam; chief army section, JUSMAGG and as the NATO liaison officer in Greece.

Athanason retired in April 1978 after 32 years of active service. His decorations include the Silver Star, Bronze Star, Purple Heart, Air Medal and Legion of Merit. He joined MOPH in April 1979.

He has a BS in political science from the Univ. of Washington and an MA in Middle East history from LaVern University.

C.H. ATKINSON JR. (BRONKO) joined the service on Sept. 13, 1941, and served with the 24th Div., MP Co. until 1943; then HQ Btry., 63rd FA. He participated at Pearl Harbor, Hollandia and the Philippines. He was discharged with the rank of private first class. He was awarded the American Defense Medal w/star, Philippine Liberation Medal w/2 stars and Asiatic-Pacific Medal w/3 stars. Dates served: 1941-45.

JOHN F. AUNGST was inducted into the service on Sept. 17, 1942, attended basic training at Ft. McClellan, AL and Camp Butner, NC. He was shipped overseas to Oahu, HI on March 5, 1943. Joined Co. C, 19th Inf. Regt., 24th Div. on March 10, 1943. He then went to Australia Aug. 8, 1943, then to Good Enough Island Jan. 1, 1944.

Shipped out to Hollandia, New Guinea April 1, 1944, for their first campaign and saw the first combat. He shipped out of there in October 1944 and landed on Leyte, Philippine Island Oct. 20, 1944, with the first wave in the Philippines. Spent 40 days in combat on Leyte and shipped out with task force to Mindoro to set up security for engineers to build airstrips for planes to refuel to hit Luzon. He then went to Luzon for one month and back to Mindoro for another month, to Romblon for two months and back to Mindanao. He then went to Mindoro and was in combat there until the war was over. He spent 33 months overseas.

He was discharged with the rank of technical sergeant.

PAUL AUSTIN, Major, joined TXNG, 144th Regt., 36th Div. in Fort Worth, TX, June 1937. Called to active duty with the division in November 1940, commissioned 2nd lieutenant Class #39 at Infantry School, Fort Benning, GA, July 1942, and became I&R platoon leader 34th Inf. on Oahu in October 1942.

Participated in Hollandia Operation as F Co. Executive and on Biak as F Co. Commander and commanded throughout Leyte Campaign. In mid-December 1944 he became S-3 2nd Bn. Closed out his service in Pacific Theater as 2nd Bn. XO in ZigZag Pass. Discharged as major in October 1945.

VAUGHAN P. AUSTIN JR. was inducted into the service in January 1949 and served with the 11th FA BN, HQ Btry. He participated at Korea. He was discharged in December 1951 with the rank of private first class. He was awarded three Battle Stars.

LOUIS AVANZINO joined the service on Nov. 13, 1944, and served with Cannon Co., 21st Regt. He participated in the Southern Philippine liberation. He was discharged with the rank of sergeant. Dates served: May 6, 1945, to November 1946.

WARREN G. AVERY joined the service on June 18, 1949, and served with G Co., 21st Regt. He participated during the Korean War, 1950-51. He was discharged with the rank of sergeant first class. Dates served: September 1950 to November 1951.

DAVID L. AYERS, born March 18, 1932. He enlisted in the US Army March 28, 1949 and took his basic training at Fort Ord, CA. He was assigned to 11th FA, B Btry., October 1949 as #1 man on #2 gun and went to Korea and fired the first shot from the 11th FABN in 1950.

Pfc. Ayers was discharged June 20, 1950. He was wounded twice but never awarded any medals, not even the Purple Heart.

He worked odd jobs until 1955 when he went to work for the railroad as a switchman and retired 27 later in 1981 as a conductor. He is now enjoying hunting, fishing, traveling and going to 24th Division reunions.

Married Barbara in February 1954 and they have two children, Gerald and Denise; and one grandchild, Alyssa Lee Ann Spargo. They spend winters in their motor home in southern Arizona and summers in Colorado.

RAYMOND D. BACH joined the service on Sept. 1, 1943, and served with the Cannon Co., 21st Inf. Regt. He was released on Feb. 15, 1946, with the rank of corporal.

Recalled on Sept. 1, 1950, and participated in the Korean War April 19, 1952.

ROBERT H. BACON enlisted in the Regular Army and was sworn in on July 9, 1940, at Philadel-

phia, PA. He served with Co. I, 19th Inf. Regt. He was an eye witness to the Battle of Pearl Harbor; member of the first task force to Canton Island; fought Japanese jungles of New Guinea; jungles of Moratai, Halmaherah and Luzon; and participated at Finschaaffen, Sarmi and Hollandia. He was discharged with the rank of staff sergeant. He is a life member of the 24th Div. and Pearl Harbor Associations. Dates served: July 9, 1940, to July 22, 1945.

PAUL E. BADER, born May 25, 1925. He enlisted in the Army July 13, 1943 followed by 17 weeks basic training at Camp Fannin, TX. Joined the 24th Div. Feb. 4, 1944 and was assigned to Co. G, 34th Regt.

He participated in the following campaigns: Hollandia, Biak, Leyte, Luzon, Mindanao and was wounded on Bataan at Zig Zag Pass.

T5 Bader was discharged Jan. 5, 1946. Decorations include the Victory Medal, Asiatic-Pacific Theater Ribbon w/3 Bronze Battle Stars, Philippine Liberation Ribbon w/2 Bronze Battle Stars, Good Conduct Medal, Purple Heart Medal, GO 19 9 Gen. Hosp. 45, Bronze Star Medal GO 26 24 Inf. Div. 45, Combat Infantry Badge.

Memorable experiences include combat in Leyte Campaign, Red Beach; the road block at Pawing; Mainit River Bridge; Battle for Jaro; 20 days on the ridge line at Sinawayan; Battle of Zig Zag Pass, Luzon.

He attended Michigan State University and received BS and MA degrees; returned to MSU and completed 60 hrs. of course work toward PhD. Served as a high school teacher and counselor, took a position as the associate director of admissions at MSU and worked 12 more years as a school administrator at the K-12 level, then took a civil service position with the state of Michigan for 11 years. He retired from the state of Michigan Civil Service in 1984 and taught at Lansing Community College five years after retirement.

Married E. Laurencine Jan. 18, 1947 and they have two adopted children, John E. Bader and Jodie Marie Mataya, and three grandchildren: Robert E. Hughes, attending Arizona University; David Mataya, 16; and Alicia Mataya 12 yrs. Bader has been retired since 1984 and enjoys reading, gardening, fishing and playing with his computer.

DAVID BAILLIE joined the service in July 1950 and attended basic training at Ft. Benning, GA, 30th Inf. Regt., 3rd Inf. Div.; and Infantry School instructor. He served with 24th Inf. Div., 34th Regt., 1950-51; 1st Cav. Recon, 1952-53; and 34th Tk. Co., 24th Inf. Div., 1957-58; and 1st Cav., 9th Regt.., B Tp., 1958-59. He participated in three tours of Korea, 1950-51, 1952-53 and 1957-58.

Spent three winters in Korea and several more summers and Japan too. Served approximately six years in the National Guard, until discharged with the rank of E-7. Dates served: 1950-62.

WILLIAM W. (BILL) BAIR, born May 20, 1927, Williamsport, PA. He entered military service July 20, 1945 and took his basic infantry training at Camp Fannin, TX. Assigned to Fort Benning, GA and was honorably discharged Dec. 16, 1945 with the rank of tech 5.

Bair was recalled to military service Feb. 18, 1953 as second lieutenant. He attended Associate Infantry Company Class 24 at Fort Benning, GA and was assigned to 8th Inf. Div. at Fort Jackson, SC. He joined

G-21 of 24th Inf. Div. at Chuchon, Korea, then assigned to Korean Military Advisory Group. He was honorably discharged Feb. 4, 1955 with rank of first lieutenant.

His medals include American Theater, Victory Medal, National Defense Service, Korean Service, UN Service and the Commendation Ribbon w/Metal Pendant.

Graduated from Penn State in 1952 with engineering degree. He married Shirley A. Peacock Jan. 26, 1952. They have three grown children and six grandchildren. He retired as senior engineer after 34 years with Bethlehem Steel. He is a member of the 24th Inf. Div. Assoc.

FREDERICK E. BAKER JR., born July 16, 1930 in Concord, NH. He enlisted in the National Guard July 9, 1948 and was discharged Sept. 1, 1949. He enlisted in the US Regular Army Sept. 2, 1949 with infantry basic training at Fort Dix, NJ.

Assigned to 9th Div., 60th Inf. Regt., 2nd Bn., US 4th Army, Fort Bliss, TX; 213th AW SP BN in 1950; 21st AW SP BN from Fort Bliss to Camp Zama, Japan, October 1950, US 8th Army; assigned to 52nd AW SP BN and attached to 24th Inf. Div. Dec. 13, 1950, Pusan Korea. He made staff sergeant in 1951 while in Korea. He had various ground support missions with the 24th Inf. Div.

His last days in Korea were on line at Kumhwa near Kumsong, Oct. 31, 1951.

Most honored military decoration is three Bronze Combat Service Stars. Returned Stateside Dec. 3, 1951 and was Discharged at Fort Devens, MA Jan. 4, 1954.

THOMAS W. BAKEWELL was inducted into the service on Sept. 2, 1941, and served with the 724th Ordnance Co. He participated in the Pacific, Hollandia, Leyte and Mindanao. He was discharged with the rank of 1st lieutenant. Dates served: April 1943 to September 1945.

JOSE A. BALTAZAR joined the service on Jan. 6, 1943, and served with Co. B, 3rd Eng. (C) Bn. He participated in Hollandia, Dutch New Guinea, Leyte, Mindoro, Mindanao, Philippine Islands and Asiatic-Pacific Theater. He was wounded in Leyte on Oct. 31, 1944. He was discharged with the rank of staff sergeant. Dates served: April 1943 to September 1945.

JOHN H. BARGER joined the service on Sept. 3, 1940, and served with HQ & HQ, 24th Div. Arty. He participated in Hollandia, Philippine Islands, Pacific, Pearl Harbor and Good Enough Island. He was discharged with the rank of staff sergeant. Dates served: Sept. 3, 1940, to June 24, 1945.

AARON D. BARNES joined the service in March 1943 and served with Co. G, 19th Inf. Regt. He participated in the Pacific Theater; Hollandia, April 1944; Leyte, October 1944; Mindoro, December 1944;

Luzon, January 1945; Mindanao, April 1945; and the Occupation of Japan. He was discharged with the rank of staff sergeant. Dates served: 1943-46.

CLAUDE E. BARRICK JR. joined the service in February 1952 and served with the Service Btry., 11th FA Regt. He participated in Japan and Korea. He was discharged with the rank of corporal. Dates served: 1952-54.

JOSEPH S. BARTO, born in June 1929, Lorain, OH. He was employed at Thew Shovel Co. in Lorain when drafted in January 1951 during the Korean War. After completing training at Fort Knox, KY, he shipped out from Fort Lawton, Seattle, WA, Pier 21 aboard the ship USS *Marine Lynx* bound for Yokohama, Japan.

Left Sasebo, Japan for Pusan, Korea assigned to Co. M, 19th Inf. Regt., 24th Inf. Div., 75 mm Recoilless Rifle Platoon. He attended 19th Inf. NCO School and became a gunner. His outfit was pulled from Reserve to assist 14th Inf. 25th Div. in Kumhwa Valley, Korea where he was wounded in September 1951. Returned to East Central Front to begin Operation NOMAD, the drive for Kumsong. He participated in CCF Spring Offensive, Summer and Fall Offensive and the second Korean winter during the Korean War.

The 24th Div. was replaced in Korea by 40th Div. He boarded the ship USS *Menefee* in Inchon Harbor bound for Yokohama, Japan in January 1952. He was on the 19th Inf. track team at Camp Haugen, base of the 19th Inf. Regt. on northern Honshu.

He rotated to the States aboard USNS *Anderson* for San Francisco, CA and Camp Stoneman. Boarded plane for Midway Airport Chicago, IL and was discharged from Fort Custer, MI in October 1952.

Decorations include the Combat Infantry Badge, Purple Heart, Korean Service w/3 Bronze Stars, UN Service (Korea), WWII Occupation (Japan), National Defense, Good Conduct, President of Korea (Rhee) Citation.

JACK P. BARTON SR. joined the 24th Div. on May 1, 1944, and served with Co. A, 21st Regt. He participated in too many theaters, campaigns and battles to mention. He was discharged with the rank of sergeant first class. Dates served: 1948-51.

ANTHONY R. BASILONE joined the service on May 14, 1941, and served with Co. L, 21st Regt. He participated in Pearl Harbor, Central Pacific, New Guinea and the Asiatic-Pacific Theater. He was discharged with the rank of corporal. Dates served: June 1941 to November 1945.

ERNEST BAYNE, born June 9, 1931. He enlisted in the Army in November 1948 and participated in the Occupation of Japan in 1949; went to Korea, 1950-51, as a wireman for 13th FA and FO many times, he kept all lines open for the artillery.

Memorable experience was as radioman up on a hill calling for a fire mission for his lieutenant.

Cpl. Bayne was discharged Aug. 8, 1952. Awards include the Bronze Star, Silver Star, Army of Occupation Medal (Japan) and Korean Service w/Silver Star.

He retired from Hertz Car Rental and now raises African gray parrots, Tiels and Budgies (all exotic birds).

Married Dorothy and they have five children: Dan, Steve, Terry, Tracy and Linda; and eight grandchildren.

RICHARD G. BEARD joined the service in August 1946 and served with Co. B, 6th Med. Tk. Bn. He was discharged with the rank of sergeant. His awards include the Good Conduct Medal, WWII Victory Medal, Army of Occupation Medal, National Defense Medal, Korean Service Medal w/6 Bronze Stars, UN Service Medal and the Republic of Korea Presidential Unit Citation Badge. Dates served: July 1950 to July 1953.

ED BECKER joined the service in September 1949 and served with Co. H, 21st Regt. He participated in the Pusan Perimeter break through to Yalu River back to the 38th. He was discharged with the rank of corporal. Dates served: August 1950 to November 1951.

GLENN EDWARD BEHRENDS, born June 1920 Monticello IA. As a youth he worked farms, helped start Agri-lime business (rock quarry). In the winter time worked as handyman and clerk for Gamble Store.

He married Jan. 1, 1942 and was drafted Feb. 4, 1942. His basic training was at Paine Field, WA then sent directly to Schoffield Barracks Radio School in Hawaii. After 15 months was sent to Australia and Camp Caves. Spent three months with Navy on Ferguson Island, rejoined 24th Div. Another detail with Navy, rejoined 24th at Hollandia, NG. Spent time on Islands of Pacific and on to Leyte, PI. Oct. 20, 1944.

The end of December 1944 rotated to States after three full years and was discharged July 14, 1945.

He spent 20 years as a farmer, seven years in lumber yard and was trucker for 13 yrs. He raised five children and slipped into retirement at 62 years of age. Glenn and his wife did some traveling with 5th wheel until 1990 when they sold RV and bought a new mobile home, putting it in a park in Monticello, IA.

CHARLES L. BELANGER joined the service in January 1949 and served with Co. A, 21st Regt. He participated in Korea, Pusan Perimeter, the break to the north to the Yalu River and the Chinese Counter Offensive. He was wounded on Jan. 3, 1951, north of Seoul. He was discharged with the rank of corporal. Dates served: 1950-51.

JAMES C. BELL, born Sept. 30, 1936. Enlisted July 20, 1955 in the Army. Basic training at Ft. Jackson, SC then went to Korea where he was assigned to Co. C, 21st Gimlets 24th Div. as an infantry man.

Other stations include 537th FA, Ft. Sill, OK; 0, Germany, 78th Ord. Co.; 1960-64, 58th Ord. Co., Ft. Campbell, KY; 1964-65, Korea and 501st Int. Unit. 1965-66, Ft. Campbell, KY, 2/11th Arty.; 1966-67, Vietnam, 2/13 Arty.

He was shot Aug. 18, 1967 and evacuated to Japan, then to Ft. Gordon, GA for physical therapy; 1968-70, Ft. Jackson, SC, training troops; 1970-74, C Trop, 1st Sqdn., 4th Cav., Germany; 1974-77, 16th Inf., 4th Bn., Ft. Jackson, SC, training troops.

Retired Oct. 1, 1997 as SFC. Awards include the

National Defense Service Medal, Vietnam Service Medal, RVN Campaign Medal, Purple Heart, Bronze Star Medal, Vietnam Cross of Gallantry w/Palm, Army Commendation Medal, w/OLC, Good Conduct Medal, 1st thru 7th Awards.

Memorable Experiences: touring Germany and other countries; being shot at by an old lady and kid; living in tents in Korea with no heat.

After military retirement he went into law enforcement with Jackson County Sheriff Dept. and served 16 years as a deputy, investigator and captain. Then went to Section AL where he served as chief of police until retirement in 1998.

Married Eva Jean Bell and has one child, Patricia Ann Gifford, and two grandchildren, Ashley Nicole Gifford and Lamonda Rose Gifford.

JOSEPH BELL, born Dec. 28, 1928 Peeksill, NY. Enlisted in the Army in September 1946. Basic training was at Fort Bragg, NC. Served 15 months in Beppu, Japan, 1947-1948 with HQ Co., 1st Bn., 19th Inf. Regt. in the Ammunition Pioneer Platoon. Discharged from the Army in March 1948 and recalled to active duty in December 1950. He was assigned to Post Signal Office at Camp Breckinridge, KY as an electronics technician.

Released from active army duty to reserve status in December 1951. He holds the Occupation Medal and WWII Victory Medal.

Married Irene D.H. Dittmer in March 1953 and has one child and two grandchildren. He retired in 1985 after 30 years as a Dept. of Defense (DOD) civilian employee with the US Army Electronics Research and Development Laboratories and the Satellite Communications Agency. Fort Monmouth, NJ as a communications specialist and is currently employed as a technical consultant with Systems Technologies Inc.

He has a certificate in electronics technology from Madison Institute and an AAS degree in electrical engineering technology from the New York Institute of Technology. As a DOD employee, he participated in the development and testing of electronic communications equipment including a satellite communications earth terminal designed to operate with the worlds first synchronous orbit communications satellite.

LAURENCE BENSON joined the service on Jan. 18, 1961, and served with Co. B, HHQ, 2nd Bn., 2nd Inf.; and 2nd Bn., 19th Inf. He was discharged with the rank of private first class. Dates served: June 1961 to January 1964.

LOUIS H. BERGIN joined the service in June 1939 and served with 2nd Bn., HQ Co., 21st Inf. Regt. He participated in the Pacific and Pearl Harbor. He retired on September 30, 1964, with the rank of CWO4. Dates served: 1939-44.

JOHN R. BERNING joined the service in October 1953 and served with HQ Btry., 11th FA. He was discharged with the rank of 1st lieutenant. Dates served: June 1954 to July 1955.

BARNEY B. BERTINUSON joined the service on Oct. 26, 1942, and served with Co. D, 24th Med. Bn. He participated in New Guinea, Southern Philippines, Mindanao, Leyte, Mindoro, and three weeks during the Occupation of Japan. He was discharged with the rank of sergeant. Dates served: Nov. 10, 1942, to Nov. 27, 1945.

CHARLES BEST, born Jan. 2, 1924 and enlisted June 13, 1944 in the Army. Stationed in the Philippines and Occupation of Japan.

He was discharged as T/5 May 15, 1946. Awards include the Combat Infantry Badge, Asiatic-Pacific Theater, Philippine Liberation Service, Victory Medal, Bronze Arrowhead Medal, Japanese Occupation Medal.

As a civilian he spent most of his time as a mechanic and garage operator. Claims to be retired but does security work for Board of Public Utilities in Kansas City.

He and wife Marie have no children.

ROBERT JACKSON BEVINS joined the US Army on May 9, 1951, and served in the 24th Inf. Div., 24th CIC Det. He participated in Japan and Korea. He was discharged on April 17, 1954, with the rank of sergeant. Awards include the Korean Service Medal w/Bronze Star, UN Service Medal, National Defense Service Medal, Good Conduct Medal and Commendation Medal. Dates served: January 1953 to April 1954.

CHARLES J. BIANCO, born Nov. 18, 1924 and enlisted Oct. 15, 1940 in the Army. He enlisted from Binghamton, NY at 15 years of age in the 27th Inf. Div. but transferred to the 24th Div. 34th Inf. Regt., H Co. (was anxious to get into combat).

Participated in invasions at Dutch New Guinea, Biak, Leyte, Luzon, Mindoro and Mindanao (where he received a severe head wound from a motor shell).

He was discharged May 3, 1946 as PFC. Awards include two Purple Hearts. Sixteen men in his section got the Bronze Star in Leyte and he was told Sgt. Goldstein was putting him in for a Silver Star for saving about 15 men from K Co. Sad to say (for his grandchildren's sake) he didn't get either one.

Memorable experiences include volunteering for patrols with lead scout on many occasions; helping three Philippine children who accidentally detonated a Japanese grenade; helping in the rescue of 100 missionaries in Hollandia; and knocking out two pill boxes in Mindanao.

He was a scoutmaster for 10 years, member of Scouts Order of Arrow, received Life Oak Award in Scouting and is very active in church and school activities with wife, Johanna, and their six children: Mark, Charlene, Michael, Lynne, Eric and Joseph; and 12 grandchildren: Melissa, Stephen, Christina, Daniel, Saerica, Meghan, Ashley, Charles, Jonathon, Frank, Victoria and Logan.

Retired and stays at home, his disability doesn't allow for many actives.

RICHARD C. BIGGS joined the service on Feb. 15, 1941, and served with Co. B, HQ 1st Bn., 3rd Bn., Regimental S-3 and executive, 19th Regt. He partici-

pated in Pearl Harbor, Tanahmerah Bay, Leyte and Mindoro. He was discharged with the rank of major. Dates served: June 1941 to March 1946.

JOSEPH G. BISHOP joined the service on Dec. 22, 1947, and served with Co. F, Service Co., 5th RCT Regt. He participated in Mason, Taggu, Pusan Defense Perimeter, July to September 1950; breakout, September 1950; Chinese Intervention and recapture of Seoul, November 1950 to June 1951. He was discharged with the rank of corporal. Dates served: 1949-51.

BERNIE EDWARD BJORKMAN joined the MNNG on Aug. 27, 1940, and was released from active duty on Nov. 15, 1941. He was recalled on Jan. 21, 1942, to Camp Chaffee, AR, and served with HQ Co., 1850th Service Unit before transferring to infantry. He then joined the 24th Inf. Div., Service Co., 19th Inf. Regt. He participated in New Guinea, Luzon, Southern Philippines, Leyte, Mindoro. He was discharged on Oct. 5, 1945, with the rank of master sergeant.

WILLIAM (BILL) H. BLAND, born July 30, 1933 enlisted Feb. 20, 1951 in the Army. Basic training was at Camp Cooke, CA then sent to South Camp, Fuji, Japan and Korea front lines for six months with 63rd FA Bn. Chief of Section B Battery.

He was discharged Dec. 23, 1953 as sergeant E-5. His awards include the Army Occupation Medal (Japan) US Service Medal, National Defense, Korean Service Medal and Good Conduct Medal.

After his discharge, he farmed four years, worked at Chevrolet Plant, K.C. Leeds, MO, 10 yrs., Donaldson Co. Inc. 29 yrs., UAW Local 710 (served as vice-president and president).

He married Denise Joy Bland and has three children: Russell, Randall and David; 10 grandchildren: Valerie, Melanie, Justin, Nathan, Eric, Alicia, Marcey, Tammy, Tamie, Tanya; and five great-grandchildren. He retired July 1, 1996 after 39 years with UAW Union.

LESLIE L. (DOC) BLOUIN, born Aug. 3, 1929 DeLamere, ND. Enlisted in the Army January 1949. Basic training was at Fort Riley, KS; Signal School, Ft. Monmouth, NJ; joined the 13th FABN 24th Inf. Div.

In June 1949 he was at Camp Hakata, Japan. He was deployed to Korea with the 13th FA as part of the 24th at the end of June 1950 and served 13 months returning to the States in July 1951 as an SFC, E6 with an assignment to Ft. Sill OK, Ft. Chaffee, AR and Ft. Sill.

Following a short assignment in Germany he had a 17 month break in service. He re-enlisted in November 1955 and joined the 24th in Korea with the 19th Inf. Regt. HQ on the DMZ. After 16 months he was assigned to 2nd Inf. Bde. at Ft. Devens, MA. In January 1959 he was sent to Germany to the 34th Signal where in March of 1962 he received an appointment as an electronic maintenance warrant officer.

In September 1962 he was assigned to the Signal Corps New Equipment Introductory Company at Ft. Monmouth; January 1965, 1st tour in Vietnam as advisor to The Vietnamese 7th Inf. Div. Signal CO at My Tho in the Delta; a tour in Germany to the 68th Signal Bn.; back to Vietnam as an advisor to the 2nd

Corps Logistical Command at Nha Trang; back to Germany for the terminal assignment where he retired July 31, 1971.

Following retirement he attended the University of Nebraska to complete his undergraduate degree then returned to his family in Germany, where he sold life insurance for two years. In 1974 he returned to the States to work for the Navy as a civilian in electronics spares and repair parts procurement where he retired after 22-1/2 years as a GS-13 giving him a total of 45 years government service.

He and his wife Doris have been married for 39 years and have one daughter, a son and five grandchildren. They enjoy all types of dancing, are fully retired and enjoying the opportunity to travel.

CHARLES E. BLUNT, born May 8, 1923 enlisted January 7, 1943 in Infantry. Basic training with 83rd Bn. at Camp Roberts, CA. He joined 19th Inf. Regt., 24th Inf. Div. in May 1943, Schofield Barracks, Honolulu HI; Brisbane, Australia; Rockhampton, Goodenough Island, Hollandia, New Guinea, Leyte, Philippines, Mindoro, Romblon, Mindanao.

He was discharged Dec. 12, 1945 as sergeant squad leader, Awards include the Purple Heart, OLC, Combat Infantry Badge, American Theater w/3 Bronze Stars, Good Conduct Medal, Asiatic-Pacific Theater, Ribbon, Philippine Liberation Ribbon, Freedom Medal and on May 25, 1999 (after 54 years) he received the Bronze Star Medal.

He was a shop foreman, general office equipment in San Francisco, CA; 1947-50 worked as tech for Wells Fargo Bank San Francisco. He joined the US Government at the Presidio of San Francisco as tech then promoted to inspector. He retired February 1980 and went into partnership in travel business then sold out and became sales manager of VISTA Travel in San Francisco, CA, 1984. He and wife escort cruise groups all over the world and so far have been on 44 cruises. He received the first sustained Superior Performance Award at the Presidio of San Francisco plus several other awards.

Married Helen Blunt and has a daughter, Barbara Eyler, from his first marriage; Richard Blunt, Christy Cambell, Robert Blunt; grandchildren are Tommy, Tim, Dawn, Mark, Matthew and Travis.

CLARE W. BOAK joined the service in April 1945 and served with HQ Co., 63rd FA. He participated in the South Pacific, Philippine Liberation, Occupation of Japan. He was a radar operator during the Vietnam War; then went to Alaska from 1950-53. He was discharged with the rank of sergeant. Dates served: 1945-53.

JOSEPH H. BOATWRIGHT joined the service on Jan. 9, 1942, and served with the Service Co., 34th Regt. He participated in every operation involving the 34th Regt. plus Corregidor. He was discharged with the rank of 1st lieutenant.

RICHARD N. BOHLS, born Nov. 27, 1931, Omaha, NE and enlisted January 1949 in the Army. Basic training was at Camp Chaffee, AR. Assigned to I Co., 21st Inf. Regt. August 1950; 1st Plt. 4th squad/asst. gunner 3.5 rocket launcher.

Early October 1950 1st Plt. came upon a North Korean equip depot with a number of new Russian vehicles that were disabled when abandoned. Richard recognized the missing parts and with the help of comrades rounded up enough parts to put three jeeps and two trucks in running order. Richard maintained these vehicles until April 1951.

He was then assigned to getting ammunition and rations to the troops of I Co. when on front line duty. In late summer 1951 he was given the duty of field first sergeant. When more training programs were set up the troops were moved to different areas for classes. This was one of the duties to get the troops there.

Discharged in June 1952 as SFC, E-6. Awards include the Combat Infantry Badge, Army Presidential Unit Citation, Korea Presidential Unit Citation, Korean Service Medal w/6 stars, UN Service Medal and Good Conduct Medal.

As a civilian he built several experimental aircrafts and received his private pilot license in September 1974.

Employed 30 years as electronic tech and R&D Development, 14 years with University of Texas at Arlington Civil Engineer School. He is now retired.

Married Mary Ann and has six children: Richard Jr., Glen A., Sheila, Shirley, Sylvia and Shawn; 13 grandchildren and one great-granddaughter.

SHUCKRY BOJRAB, born June 29, 1927 and enlisted September 1946 in the Army. Trained in Camp Polk, LA then sent to Japan, Camp Hakata, 13th FA as a light truck driver. He carried 155 Howitzer, cannoners and sergeant to practice. After serving with 24th he was discharged, but stayed with Navy Reserve for six years. Received Medal for Occupation of Japan.

At Camp Hakata, Japan he was a light truck driver and helped with first elections. He drove a captain and sergeant to different poles to check votes. The people were nice to us.

He belonged to the Masonic Lodge Shriners, VFW American Legion Post 42, TPA, Scottish Rite

Married Louise and had three children: Adam, April and Jodi; and seven grandchildren: Carly, Tye, Amara, Tim, Stacey, Trudi and Travis. He retired from Falstaff Brewery after 32 years and now helps his wife with crafts. He uses a scroll saw to cut out wood for her to paint.

EARSEL E. BONDS joined the service on March 15, 1948, and served with HQ & HQ Co., 1st Bn., 21st Regt. Participated in Korea from July 1, 1950, to May 15, 1951. He retired on March 15, 1968, with the rank of E-7.

GEORGE L. BOUCHAR, born Jan. 11, 1924 and enlisted Sept. 22, 1944 in the Infantry, Co. B, 34th Regt. Participated in combat at Davao, Mindanao and Philippine Islands as a rifleman. IRTC Ft. McClellan, AL.

He was wounded on a mountain top overlooking Davao Gulf May 7, 1945 and was brought down from the mountain top on a stretcher to field hospital, then evacuated by air to Leyte then back to the States.

He was discharged Aug. 24, 1946 as PFC. Awards include the Combat Infantry Badge and Purple Heart.

Worked in insurance field, real estate broker and retired from US Postal Service. Now enjoys family, golf, travel and bowling.

Married Lorraine and has six girls, one boy and 16 grandchildren.

R.S. (BUCK) BOWEN, born Sept. 27, 1915 and enlisted September 1943 in the Infantry. Stationed at Camp Roberts, CA; Camp Stoneman CA and was assigned to Co. G, 34th Regt., 24th Inf. Div.

He joined the company at Hollandia, went to Leyte, Luzon, Mindoro, Mindanao and Japan on occupation duty for about three months. He has several memories of different places and times, but the landing on Leyte wins the prize.

Discharged January 1946 at Ft. Chaffee, AR as T/5. Awards include the Combat Infantry Badge and Bronze Star.

After being home a few years and working in the Post Office he joined an Army Postal Unit of the ADG Dept. and served four years. He was discharged with the rank of tech sergeant.

Married Bula Ferle Bowen and has two children, Travis and Kelly. Worked for Purolator four years then US Postal Service, starting at level 3. He retired in 1974 as tour superintendent (level 18).

RAYMOND G. BOWERING joined the service on Sept. 11, 1946, and served with HQ Co., 2nd Bn., 19th Regt. He participated in the Occupation of Japan, Camp Chickamauga, and Beppu, Japan. He was discharged with the rank of sergeant. Dates served: 1946-47.

KEITH F. BOYD, born Feb. 7, 1924; enlisted September 1943 in the Army; and served in combat infantry mortar section in New Guinea and Philippines.

Attended many military schools: OCS; Military Management, March AFB; Arctic Survival, Ladd AFB, AK; Squadron Officers School, Irvine, CA; Ground Operations Officer, Irwin, CA; Pacific Region Staff College as a seminar advisor, McChord AFB, WA; Command and Staff College, Maxwell AFB, AL.

He was wounded at Luzon and at Mindanao. Discharged Oct. 10, 1945, Medical Percy Jones Hospital, Ft. Custer, MI. Awards include the Combat Infantry Badge, Bronze Star, Purple Heart w/OLC, Good Conduct Medal, Asiatic-Pacific, American Defense, Philippine Liberation, WWII Victory Medal, American and Philippine Presidential Citations.

He has Ph.D. in nutritional science, Life Science Institute, TX; DCH doctor of clinical hypnotherapy, Ervine, CA. He was Alaska territorial police officer, general building contractor for CAP Air Search and Rescue w/44 missions. He retired in 1980 as lieutenant colonel. Also, a civic leader, honorary mayor of the "high desert" (California) and a professional gaming investor (gambling).

In June 1945 he met President Truman at Hamilton Field, San Francisco, CA. In June 1977 he met and had a long chat with Prince Charles at Atlanta, GA.

He is divorced and has one daughter, Kathleen Wicker, and two grandchildren, James and John Wicker.

ROBERT F. BRABHAM joined the 24th Div. on June 7, 1942, in Hawaii. He served with the Div. HQ, AG Office. He participated in Southwest Pacific, New Guinea and the Philippines. He was discharged with the rank of sergeant. Dates served: 1942-45.

ALBERT H. BRADEN JR. joined the service on Aug. 15, 1941, and served with the 1st Bn., Med. Det. Co., 21st Regt; commanding officer, 24th Div., Med. Bn.,; and 24th Div., HQ. He participated in Hawaii, Australia, Good Enough Island, Hollandia, Dutch New Guinea, Leyte, Mindoro, Luzon and Mindanao. Returned to the states in October 1945. Received honorable discharge on Feb. 25, 1946, with the rank of major. Dates served: 1942-44.

CHARLES BRADLEY joined the service on June 9, 1944, and served with Co. A, 19th Regt. He participated in Leyte, Mindoro and Mindanao. He was wounded by Japanese mortar. He was discharged with the rank of corporal.

EDWIN G. BRANDAU was inducted into the service on Aug. 26, 1941, at Ft. Sheridan. He attended basic training at Camp Roberts, CA, with the 88th Machine Gun Bn., 24th Div. He served with Co. K, 34th Regt. Participated in three Asiatic-Pacific Theaters: Hollandia, Biak and Leyte. He was discharged with the rank of staff sergeant. Dates served: December 1941 to January 1945.

WILLIAM W. BRASWELL (WOODY) joined the service in November 1940 in Jacksonville, FL, and was assigned to the 31st Div. He served with Co. B, 19th Inf. Regt. He participated in the Pacific, Mindoro and Mindanao. He was discharged with the rank of technical sergeant. Dates served: November 1944 to May 26, 1945.

CHARLES E. BRAULT, born Sept. 8, 1928 in Linton, IN. He was drafted into the Army out of Muskegon, MI in October 1950 and sent to Camp Picket, VA for a couple of months of unit tank training. He never had even one day of basic infantry training.

In March 1951 he was sent to Korea where they took five days and nights training just running up and down the mountains. They said it was to shrink their stomachs in case they couldn't get food to us. It worked; that was the most meaningful training he had.

Sent to Love Co. Squad, 21st Regt. on the front line that had only five men. He had a choice of being the machine-gunner or the 1st scout. He didn't like the idea of carrying the machine gun up and down those hill, so took the 1st scout job. He spent nine months in combat as a rifleman (never fired a M-1 rifle until actual combat).

Left the front line around midnight, New Year's Eve 1951 as the 24th Div. went back to Japan. He was out on ambush patrol at the time and remembers it was at least 20° below zero.

He attained the rank of sergeant and was discharged in July 1952. Medals include the Korean Service Medal w/2 Bronze Stars, UN Service Medal and the Combat Infantry Badge (the most meaningful).

He was never recruited by any of the Veterans organizations until the 1990s when these ranks started to thin out, and he never heard of the 24th Inf. Div. Assoc. until 1995.

He retired from the Shaw Walker Office Furniture Co. and is enjoying his retirement.

THOMAS C. BREAZEALE joined the service on June 10, 1942, and served with Cannon Co., 19th Inf. Regt. He participated in Hawaii, Australia, Hollandia, Leyte, Mindoro and Mindanao. He was discharged with the rank of 1st lieutenant. Dates served: October 1942 to April 1946.

JOHN J. BREEDEN, born Dec. 3, 1923 and living in Washington, DC when he was drafted on Jan. 28, 1943. Sent to Gainsville, TX for basic training; to Alexandria, LA for jungle warfare training; Ft. Ord, CA then by SS *General Brooks* to SWPA.

Arrived in New Guinea in September 1944 as replacements for the 24th Div. Assigned to Co. G, 34th Inf.; trained for invasion of Leyte; received a head wound Oct. 21, 1944 and spent two days in a field hospital.

Memorable Experiences: They were running across a clearing taking a bridge when a machine gun opened up and some men were hit. Breeden got weak in the knees and went down. A GI stopped and got him by the arm and said come on I'll take you over. He looked up to see who this brave man was, but he had no face. It was just cloudy, smoky and it was a clear day. Later he asked the guys which one helped but "they were looking out for themselves" was all he ever got out of them. He believes it was his Guardian Angel. He was with Co. G the whole time and promoted from PFC to T5 to Buck Sergeant and later to staff sergeant as a squad leader. Also remember a time at Bataan when Co. G was going through a banana grove and the tank was knocked out. He jumped in a ditch for cover and landed in a nest of red ants. Wow! He came out of ditch fast.

Discharged Jan. 9, 1946. Awards include the Purple Heart and Combat Infantry Badge. He loves his country and would do it all again if he had to.

Married Eva and they have three children: John J. Jr., Carol Harris and Brenda Lopez; and four grandchildren: Christopher, Larry, Tara and Kimberly.

JAMES B. BROCK, born July 19, 1922, Conover, NC. He joined the Army Nov. 30, 1940 and was sent to Schofield Barracks, 1941-1943.

Left New Guinea for the States in December 1944 and was assigned to the Armored School at Fort Knox, KY until his discharge June 9, 1945, Fort Bragg NC.

Awards include the American Defense Medal w/ Bronze Service Star, Asiatic-Pacific Theater, Campaign Medal, w/2 Bronze Service Stars, Good Conduct Medal, Combat Infantry Medal and Pearl Harbor Medal.

He worked in the trucking industry, was a Trailways bus driver and heavy equip operator. James has been retired since 1985.

Married Hazel on Sept. 20, 1945 and they have two sons, David, Roswell GA and Michael, Savannah GA; five granddaughters: Kelly and Lindsey, Roswell, GA; Magan, Marley and Mickie, Savannah, GA.

JAMES F. BROGAN joined the service in August 1941 and served with HQ Co., 34th Regt. He participated in Southwest Pacific. He was discharged with the rank of staff sergeant. Dates served: 1941-44

EUGENE P. BRODERICK joined the service in February 1948 and served with Co. A, 21st Regt. He participated in Huachan Res., Kumwha, and Kunsung Valley. He was discharged with the rank of sergeant. Dates served: May 1951 to April 1952.

LUTHER V. BROOM joined the service on Sept. 1, 1943, and served with Co. D, 19th Regt. He joined the 24th Div. in Hollandia; participated in the invasion of Leyte and Mindoro; went to Luzon with the 3rd Bn.; was wounded taking airfield at Mallia; evacuated to a hospital; and rejoined his company on Mindoro. They then went to Mindanao on a 150 mile march across the island. He was wounded one-half mile north of Davao City on May 7, 1945. He stayed in the hospital until Feb. 23, 1946, and was discharged with the rank of private first class.

GERALD F. BROWN, born Oct. 21, 1932 and enlisted in the Infantry at age 17. Attended basic training school at Fort Riley, KS; joined Co. A, 34th Inf. Regt., 24th Div. in August 1950 in Korea. The unit became Co. I, 19th Inf. Regt. He was assigned to Fort Sill, OK in September 1951; assigned to 4th Inf. Div. in Germany, January 1953; Fort Carson, CO June 1956; ROTC University of Missouri, June 1957; 7th USA Aviation Group, Germany September 1959; Ft. Sill, OK June 1963; ROTC University of Kansas, December 1964; 2/17th Arty., Vietnam, May 1967; Ft. Sill, OK August 1968, duties as communications chief.

Brown retired July 1, 1970 as master sergeant. He received the Combat Infantry Badge, Bronze Star, Meritorious Service Medal, Army Commendation Medal, Purple Heart, Good Conduct Medal, National Defense Medal, Distinguished Unit Citation, Korean Service Medal, Vietnam Service Medal, Army Occupation Medal (Germany), RVN Medal w/Dev-60, UN Service Medal and Korean Unit Citation

He worked as an electronics specialist with Kansas Dept. of Transportation for 24 years.

Married Vinnice M. Board in March 1950 and had five children and 11 grandchildren. They both retired in February 1944 and are living in Hutchinson, KS.

MYRL BROWN joined the service on March 8, 1943, and served with Co. M, Machine Gun, 34th Inf. Regt. Participated in Buna, Leyte, Bataan,and Corregidor. He was wounded on Bataan on January 30 and Corregidor on Feb. 17, 1945. He was discharged on Dec. 12, 1945, with the rank of corporal.

JOHN H. BRUENING joined the service on May 19, 1941, and served with Co. B, 52nd FA Bn. He participated in Hawaii, New Guinea and the Philippines. He was discharged with the rank of private first class. Dates served: May 19, 1941, to Sept. 16, 1945.

ALVIN F. BUCHHOLZ, born Sept. 26, 1925 and was inducted Dec. 2, 1943 in the Army. He began basic training at Camp Roberts, CA, assigned to Co. A, 88th Inf. Tng. Bn. Participated in invasion of Leyte (Oct. 20, 1944), Mindoro, Mindanao and spent time on Luzon.

On July 20, 1944 he went to New Guinea Replacement Depot, at Hollandia. In October 1944 assigned to the 24th Div., Co. H, 19th Regt. Arrived back in the States Jan. 25, 1946 and was discharged Jan. 30, 1946 as staff sergeant.

Received the Asiatic-Pacific Service Medal, Philippines Liberation w/2 stars, WWII Victory Medal, Distinguished Unit Citation and Bronze Star.

He worked four years in a grain elevator company, five years deputy county assessor for Burlington County and 32 years with the state of Colorado. He retired in Grand Junction, CO.

He and his wife, Lorena, have four sons: Bradley, Doyle, Ronald and Gregory; one granddaughter, Marie. He enjoys restoring old farm tractors and playing golf.

HOWARD W. BUCKLES joined the service in May 1952 and served with the 11th FA, Service Btry. Regt. He participated in the Korean War. He was discharged with the rank of corporal. Dates served: February 1953 to April 1954.

EUGENE K. BUCKLEY, born June 25, 1932 and enlisted in the Army Sept. 9, 1949. Assigned to Co. H, 19th Inf., 24th Div., Unit 2 as ammo bearer.

He was discharged June 30, 1951 as private first class. His awards include the Purple Heart, Combat Infantry Badge, Army of Occupation with Japan Clasp, Korean Service Medal and UN Defensive Medal. He worked as a model maker for a Hyd. Mfg. Co.

Married Adeline and has six children: Joe, Mike, Alan, Brett, Janet and Jeannine; nine grandchildren and two great-grandchildren. He is now retired.

JOSEPH BUCKOVICH joined the service in 1943 and served with Co. G, 19th Inf. Regt. He participated in New Guinea and the Philippine Islands campaigns. He was discharged with the rank of technical sergeant. He received the Silver Star for the Mindanao campaign. Dates served: 1943-45.

EUGENE H. BUGNER joined the service on Jan. 19, 1951, and served with the HQ Co., 13th FA, 24th Div. He participated in Korea. He was discharged with the rank of corporal. Dates served: August 1951 to January 1953.

ERNEST R. BURLINGAME enlisted in the Army 1948 in Ohio. He was sent to Cleveland, Oh for a physical and then to Ft. Knox, KY where he joined the Third Armor Division, 1st Platoon, C Company. After basic he was sent to Seattle, WA where he sailed to Japan. he was later reassigned to the 1st Cavalry Divsion, H Troop at Camp King. Later he became a

Supply Sgt for D Company MP Compound and was sent to Camp Wood. This is when the Korean War broke out.

He remembers being on night watch and hearing a clanking sound and reporting it to his officer. He was told to go back on watch.Later when daylight broke he says all hell broke loose. He also remembers witnessing a sergeant being shot in the back of the head.

MATTHEW W. BUSEY joined the service in February 1943 and served with the 6th MTB. He participated in the EAME campaign, Korea and Vietnam. He was discharged with the rank of 1st lieutenant. Awards include the EAME Medal w/2 stars, Korean Service Medal w/5 stars, Arrowhead, Presidential Unit Citation, Vietnam Service Medal w/2 stars, Silver Star, Bronze Star, Purple Heart, Vietnamese Medal of Honor w/3 stars and the Vietnamese Cross of Gallantry. Dates served: 1948-51.

ALFRED I. BYRD joined the service on June 8, 1940, and served with Companies C and B, 11th FA. He participated in Pearl Harbor and the Asiatic-Pacific campaign. He was discharged with the rank of T-5. Dates served: June 8, 1940, to Dec. 5, 1944.

JOHN F. BYROM joined the service in July 1943 and served with Co. M, 3rd Bn. Staff, S-2, 21st Inf. Regt. He participated in the Pacific Theater, Philippines and Japan. He was discharged with the rank of 1st lieutenant. Dates served: August 1945 to August 1946.

PAUL J. CAIN, born April 5, 1915 in Ivesdale, Champaign County, IL. He was drafted in February 1940, did his basic training at Camp Croft, SC, transferred July 1942 to Officer Candidate School at Ft. Benning, GA and commissioned 2nd lieutenant, Infantry, October 1942.

Joined Co. K, 34th Inf. in Oahu, HI, April 1943; accompanied unit to Australia, Goodenough and participated in invasion of New Guinea at Hollandia and later in action on Biak. With 1st Plt., Co. K, 34th Inf. he was leader in assault wave landing on Leyte, P.I., Oct. 20, 1944.

Transferred to company commander Co. I, 34th Inf., November 1944; made beach landing at Zambales, Luzon, P.I. and attack on Kalakan Point, Olongapo on Subic Bay. Made February 16 assault landing bottomside Corrigidor, P.I.; Apr. 19, 1945 landed at Cotabato, Mindanao, P.I.; Aug. 14, 1944 war ended and he returned home to Illinois in November 1995.

Transferred to 85th Div. Reserves and retired as major S-3 in 1975. Decorations include the Combat Infantry Badge, Silver Star, Bronze Star w/2 clusters, Bronze Arrowhead and Unit Citation.

He is a life member, 24th Infantry Division Association, Reserve Officers Association, American Legion and Knights of Columbus.

Married Florence Wise Cain and has two children, Michael and Christie; and four grandchildren.

WILLIAM B. CALDWELL III joined the service in September 1949 and served with Co. C, 34th Regt.; A Co., 34th Regt.; HQ Co., 1st Bn.; HQ Co., 3rd Bn., 19th Regt.; Co. L, 19th Regt.; and HQ Co., 3rd Bn., 19th Regt., Korea. He participated in the Pusan Perimeter Defense; breakout, 1950; Yalu, 1950; and Defensive, 1951; and Counter Offensive, 1951. He was discharged with the rank of lieutenant general.

PAUL M. CAMPBELL, born Jan. 24, 1925 and enlisted Oct. 28, 1943 in the Army. Took his basic training at Camp Fannin, TX; went to Replacement Depot, New Guinea and joined the 24th Inf. Div. at Hollandia. He remained with the 24th until May 21, 1945 when he was wounded on Mindanao.

After being wounded he was flown to 126th General Hospital on Leyte, then to 1st Convalescent Hospital on Leyte where he remained until the first A bomb was dropped on Japan. Shortly after he was sent back to the States, hospitalized at Borden Gen. Hosp., Chickasha, OK until his discharge Jan. 29, 1946 as sergeant.

Decorations include Combat Infantryman Badge, Asiatic-Pacific Theater, Campaign Medal w/2 Bronze Stars, Good Conduct Medal, Purple Heart and Victory Ribbon

After being wounded May 21, 1945 was flown to 126th general hospital on Leyte, from there to 1st convalescent hospital on Leyte, remained until the first bomb was dropped on Japanese, shortly after was sent back to the states arriving Sept. 21, 1945, was hospitalized at Borden general hospital at Chickaska, OK until being discharged Jan. 29, 1946 at Ft Sam Houston, TX separation center.

Retired from Federal Civil Service in 1975 after 26 years of service at Tinker AFB, OKlahoma City, OK. He raises beef cattle in his retirement years.

Married Wanda Faye had four sons, one daughter, and 11 grandchildren.

WILLIAM G. CAMPBELL, born Feb. 3, 1917, San Antonio, TX. He joined the Army in April and took his basic training at Ft. Sill, OK. Sent to Ft. Ord, CA; Brisbane, Australia; joined 24th Div. at Rockhampton and assigned to survey section, HQ Btry., 52nd FA.

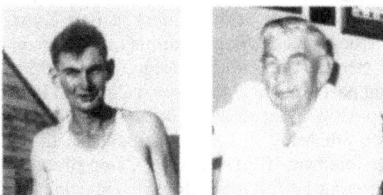

Made Hollandia landing, Red Beach landing, Leyte, Mindoro and Mindanao. After bomb was dropped went to Japan.

Discharged Dec. 7, 1945, at Ft. Bliss, TX. Awards include the four Bronze Stars, Asiatic-Pacific, Philippine Liberation, Combat Stars (5), Bronze Arrowheads (4) and Bronze Star.

Received BS degree, 1938 and taught adult school for veterans; pursued master's degree in education and spent 25 years as elementary school principal. He re-

tired in 1978 after 35 years as educator. Also raised cattle and had an orchard after retirement.

Memorable experiences include surviving the entire Leyte and Mindanao operations. Also, the close relations with others at the time has never been equaled in his 81 years.

He and his wife Patricia had one son William G. Jr., daughter Alyson Campbell McHatton, two grandchildren, Robert and Christi McHatton.

CHARLES CARD, born May 5, 1924, Mt. Vernon, OH and enlisted in May 1943 in the Army. Assignments as rifleman, BAR company messenger, Co. B, 34th Regt., 24th Inf. Div., Hollandia, New Guinea, Leyte, Mindanao, Philippines, Shikoku, Japan.

Discharged Jan. 6, 1946. Decorations include the Bronze Star Medal w/OLC for Leyte frontal attacks, Kilay Ridge Campaign, Presidential Unit Citation, CBI Badge and Philippine Liberation Medal.

Earned BSC degree from Ohio University in 1948. Was manufacturing manager with Dow Chemical Company and Dresser Industries in location in Ohio, Connecticut, Wisconsin, Chicago, Texas, covering plants throughout US, Canada, Mexico and Brazil. Retired from Dresser in 1989.

Married Martha and has two children, Bill and Sue; two grandchildren, Kristin and Julie; and one great-granddaughter, Halley.

Enjoys traveling, golfing, writing, teaching and placement consultant part- time.

DAVID "PAUL" CARPENTER joined the service in 1944 and served with Co. A, 21st Inf. Regt. He participated in the Mindanao campaign. He was discharged with the rank of 1st sergeant. Dates served: 1945 to November 1947.

EDSON A. CARPENTER joined the service on July 20, 1941, and served with Co. A, 767th Tk. Bn, 19th Regt.; and Co. I, 19th Regt. He participated at Pearl Harbor, Philippine Islands, New Guinea, Hollandia, Admiralty Islands and Leyte. He was discharged with the rank of staff sergeant. Dates served: 1941-45.

TOMAS CARRILLO joined the service on Dec. 17, 1947, and served with Co. E, 21st Regt. He participated in the UN Defensive, UN Offensive, CCF Intervention, first UN Counter Offensive and CCF Spring Offensive. He was discharged with the rank of 1st lieutenant. Dates served: 1950-51.

GEORGE H. CARTER, born April 23, 1926, Willow Springs, TX. He enlisted Aug. 14, 1944 at age 19. Assigned to 19th Inf., Co. B, 1st Bn. After the war was over he transferred to HQ Co., 1st Bn. 19th. Continental service was eight months and three days and foreign service was one year six months and 20 days.

Memorable experience was when platoon crossed Davao River on a plank, make-shift foot bridge and dug in that night in a cemetery. The Japanese fired over their heads all night.

Discharged Nov. 6, 1946 as PFC. Awards include the Asiatic-Pacific Campaign Ribbon w/Bronze Star, Good Conduct Medal, Purple Heart, Distinguished Unit Badge, Army Occupation Ribbon, Japan Victory Ribbon and three Overseas Badges.

A farmer at heart; after the service he stayed home for one year to recover from malaria and yellow jaundice. He then married his childhood sweetheart, Vera A. Blalock, and they had three children: Linda, Carole and George H. Jr. He retired from Shell Oil after 38 years, moved back home and built their home near Lake Livingston at Point Blank, TX.

JOSEPH K. CASKEY, born April 8, 1920. He enlisted in January 1941, serving with the Army 13th FABN as battery officer and battery commander. Discharged in February 1945 as captain.

Returned to college (Tulane University) and graduated from law school. Practiced law for five years; worked for an oil company, then started his own oil and gas business in 1970.

Married Sara and has three sons: Keith, John and Bill; and two grandsons, Simon and Theodore. He is retired but still involved in the oil and gas business in a small way.

ELVIN CHINIGO joined the service in August 1946 and served with the HQ Co., 1st Bn., 21st Regt. He participated in Korea, Task Force Smith, up to the Yalu and back. He was discharged with the rank of corporal. Dates served: 1948-51.

IRVING L. CHRISTENSEN was inducted into the service on Sept. 14, 1954, and served with the 724th Ordnance, Regt. Bn., Co. A. He participated in Korea; served as a welder; helped support the 34th Regt. and 62nd Artillery. He was discharged in July 1956 with the rank of corporal.

MORRIS L. CHURCHILL SR., born Sept. 17, 1931 in Philadelphia, PA. He enlisted Aug. 17, 1954 in the Army; attended QM Basic Officer Course as a 2nd lieutenant in 1954.

Overseas assignment was in Kobe, Japan as commander, Supply Center. Other assignments include: XO, 24th S&T Bn., Germany, 1965; supply officer, 45th Spt. Gp., Pleiku, Vietnam; commander, EES Depot, Germany, 1971-74..

Retired Aug. 31, 1974 as lieutenant colonel (Ret). Decorations include the Legion of Merit, Bronze Star Medal, Meritorious Service Medal w/OLC, Army Commendation Medal and numerous service medals.

Member of DAV, American Legion #114 and TROA. Belongs to senior golf and bowling leagues, and is deacon and treasurer of the Mt. Olive Baptist Church, Centreville, VA.

Graduated from USA Command and General Staff College, industrial college of the armed forces and obtained a master's degree in microbiology in 1970 while in service.

Married Mattie Toon and has three daughters and one son: Madelyn, Maurene, Maria and Morris Jr. He is a devoted church member and enjoys golf and bowling weekly.

WILLIAM E. CLARK, born Dec. 24, 1917 and enlisted in the Army in September 1942. He served in European Theater of Operations, Corps of Engineers

May 15, 1944 through Dec. 30, 1945; released ERC Jan. 6, 1946 with the rank of sergeant.

Decorations include the Good Conduct Medal, American Campaign Medal, EAME Service Medal, one Bronze Star and WWII Victory Medal.

He was recalled to active duty Oct. 30, 1950, arrived in Korea and assigned to 24th Inf. Div., 19th Regt., L Co., as squad leader 1st Squad, 3rd Plt.

Decorations include The Combat Infantryman Badge, Korean Service Medal, three Bronze Stars, American Defense Medal And UN Service Medal.

RICHARD S. CLAYTON, born April 4, 1933 and enlisted in the Army in 1950, age 17. He received his basic training at Fort Knox, KY and was assigned to Co. D, 33rd Med. Tank Bn. Embarked from Camp Stoneman, CA, landing in Korea in September 1950, then assigned to Co. C, 3rd Plt., 3rd Squad, 5th RCT, attached to the 24th Div. Later baptized, Nov. 8, 1950 by Chaplain Darrell F. Joacluin and witnessed by Thomas J. Utley.

Experienced some tough times in winter of 1950 and 1951. In May 1951 he was slightly wounded by shrapnel from a mine, returned Stateside and assigned to the US Army hospital at Camp Pickett, VA. After about a year he was re-assigned to Germany, serving with the 7th Chemical Depot Co., 7th Army.

Medals received include the Purple Heart, CIB, Good Conduct Medal, Army Occupation Medal, National Defense Service Medal, Korean Service w/4 BBS, UN Service Medal and Korean Presidential Citation. He was discharged in April 1954.

In 1956 he married Anna and has two daughters, Connie and Carol, and seven grandchildren. Retired from construction work, he now resides in Meadville, PA.

GRAY I. CLAWSON joined the service on June 10, 1946, and served with Btry. A, 63rd FA BN. He participated in Korea. He was discharged in July 1952 with the rank of 1st lieutenant. He joined the National Guard and USAR and was discharged on May 7, 1980.

LAFAYETTE A. COCHRAN joined the service on May 21, 1941, and served with the 24th QM Truck Co. He participated in Leyte, Hollandia, Mindoro, Pearl Harbor, New Guinea and many others. He was discharged with the rank of T-5.

THOMAS F. COCHRAN, born Dec. 13, 1931 and enlisted in the Army on April 13, 1948. His assignments include basic training at Fort Knox, KY; "B" Troop 8th Cav. Regt., Camp Omiya, Japan, rifleman; Service Co., 34th Inf. Regt., Sasebo, Japan, assistant post exchanger manager; I Co., 34th Inf. Regt., Camp Mower, Japan and Korea, sniper; Tokyo QM Depot, 8th Army and Japan Logistical Cmd., warehouse foreman; 101st Abn. Div., Camp Breckenridge, KY, testing NCOIC; SCARWAF, (Special Category Army With Air Force) engineers, France, Germany, England, truckmaster, operations sergeant and project NCO; transportation research and engineering command, Fort Eustis, VA, administrative supervisor and project coordinator; transportation supply depot activity, Ascom City (Bupyong), Korea, Sergeant Major-First Sergeant, Seattle Sub-Sector Command, Fort Lawton, WA, advisor to USAR; US Army Recruiting Cmd., Rock Island, IL, recruiter; Security Platoon, Honor Guard, 101st Abn. Div., Fort Campbell, KY, 1st sergeant; US Southern Cmd., Quarry Heights, Ca-

nal Zone, administrative assistant to the Secretary Joints Staff; 4th Admin. Co., 4th Inf. Div., Pleiku and An Khe, Vietnam, NCOIC Admin. Services Div., "B" Co., US Army Trng. Ctr., Ft. Campbell, KY, 1st sergeant, HQ Co., US Army Garrison, 1st sergeant.

He retired Oct. 31, 1971 as 1st sergeant. His awards include the CIB, Bronze Star w/3 OLCs, MSM, Meritorious Service Award w/3 OLCs (state of Tennessee), GCM w/3 Silver Loops, Army of Occupation Medal (Japan, Germany), NDSM, Korean Service Medal w/ star, Vietnam Service Medal, UN Service Medal, RVN Campaign Medal w/2 stars, Presidential Unit Citation, Valorous Unit Award, Meritorious Unit Commendation w/star, ROK Presidential Unit Citation, Vietnam PUC, RVN Gallantry Cross w/Palm, RVN Civil Actions Honor Medal.

In 1986, he received a direct commission as captain in the Tennessee Defense Force and went on to become a LTC and resigned in 1992 due to conflict with duties at Ft. Campbell, KY to return to the 101st Abn. Div. home from Desert Storm. Was the Ft. Campbell and FORSCOM nominee for the Secretary of Defense Equal Employment Opportunity Award for Excellence in 1978. Was civilian employee of the year at Ft. Campbell in 1995 in the administrative/ specialist category. Has been awarded more than 100 certificates of achievements, commendations for federal service and a Commendation and an Ambassador of Goodwill Award from governor's of Tennessee for his work with military organizations after retirement.

His most memorable experience was being the 51st president of the 24th IDA (1997-1998).

Married Jacqueline Louise (Devereaux) and has three children: Marviene Marie Farrington, Terence Vincent Scott Cochran and Gregory Alan Cochran. They have six grandchildren: Gary Dale and Kyle Jarrod Farrington; Scott Anderson, Elizabeth Ann, Thomas Chell and Alan James Cochran (deceased).

He is the Chief of the Logistics Support Branch, Readiness Business Center at Ft. Campbell, KY. He is also the executive secretary for the 3rd/34th and 2nd/ 21st Inf. Bn. Assoc. (units of the 24th Inf. Div.), the first to fight in Korea. In August 1998, he took on the task to provide information and assist the Korean Freedom League in erecting a monument in Chonan, Korea recognizing the 34th Inf. Regt. and all those members who perished there, killed in action or taken prisoner and never accounted for. That monument is to be completed for dedication on the 50th anniversary of the battle which was July 5-8, 1950.

EARL N. COLBEY joined the service on Feb. 28, 1948, and served with the Med. Co., 21st Regt. He participated in Task Force Smith and was a POW from July 6, 1950, to Aug. 23, 1953. He was discharged with the rank of corporal. Dates served: 1948-53.

CLARENCE A. (BUD) COLLETTE, born Nov. 25, 1929, Los Angeles, CA and drafted into the Army in January 1951. His basic training was at Ft. Ord, CA.

He served 11 months in Korea, 1951-52, with the 5th RCT, 24th Inf. Div.

He was wounded and taken to a MASH unit, then air evacuated to another field hospital for surgery. After two weeks there, he was taken by hospital train to Pusan, where he stayed for over a month in the Swedish Hospital.

With a wobbly knee he volunteered to go back to the infantry. His regiment was in a reserve position and he knew he would go home soon after he got back. He arrived back in California in May 1952, had his leave and was assigned to Camp Irwin, near Death Valley, CA. He was there from July to his discharge in October 1952. he served in the National Guard as the 1st sergeant of an infantry battalion headquarters company for three years.

Married Jean M. McDonald in January 1953. They have two grown children and two grandsons. He retired after 33 years with Pacific Telephone Company. Veterans organizations include MOPH, DAV and VFW. his most honored military decoration is the Combat Infantry Badge.

WILLIAM (BILL) COLLINS, born Nov. 3, 1926 and enlisted September 1946 in the Army. He was assigned Beppu, Japan, January 1947 to February 1948 with Occupation Forces. He served as motor sergeant 1st Bn., 19th Inf. Regt.

Discharged March 4, 1948 and is a lifetime member of VFW and member of American Legion. After 39 years he retired in 1984 from NJ Transit, then was in transportation consulting business, 1984-95.

Married Mary Robertson in June 1948 and has two children, Kathleen and Bill Jr. (deceased); and two grandchildren, Bill (17) and Chris (7). He is the owner of a small Marina in Sewaren, NJ.

ERNEST COMPTON joined the service on July 24, 1940, and served with Co. I, 34th Inf. Regt. He participated in the Southern Philippines and New Guinea. Discharged with the rank of sergeant. Awards include the Combat Infantryman Badge, Good Conduct Ribbon and the Asiatic-Pacific Theater Ribbon w/2 Bronze Stars. Dates served: July 24, 1940, to July 12, 1945.

WILLIAM A. CONGALTON JR. joined the service in July 1949 and served with Co. E, 19th Regt. He participated in Naktong River, Pusan Perimeter; battle at Sang-Pum-Ni. He was discharged with the rank of private first class. Awards include the Purple Heart, Silver Star and Combat Infantryman Badge. Dates served: 1949-52.

WILLIAM E. CONLEY joined the service on Aug. 23, 1946, and served with the 24th MP Co. He was discharged with the rank of private first class. Awards include the WWII Victory Medal and Army Occupation Medal (Japan). Dates served: Aug. 23, 1946, to Dec. 6, 1947.

JOHN J. CONLON joined the service on Nov. 12, 1934, and served with the Service Btry., 7th FA; K Co., 19th Inf.; Parachute School. He was discharged with the rank of 1st lieutenant. Awards include the American Defense, American Campaign, Asiatic-Pacific and WWII Victory Medals. Dates served: 1934-45.

RICHARD L. CONNOLLY joined the service on Feb. 15, 1943, and served with HQ Btry., 24th Div. Arty. Participated in Hollandia, New Guinea, Leyte, Mindoro and Mindanao, Philippine Islands. Discharged with the rank of corporal. Dates served: Oct. 6, 1944, to Dec. 26, 1945.

JOSEPH J. CONOYER joined the service on Oct. 24, 1942, and served with Co. C, 3rd Eng. He participated in the South Pacific, New Guinea and the Philippines. He was discharged with the rank of T/4. Dates served: October 1942 to November 1945.

DUANE L. CONWAY, born March 26, 1928 and drafted Oct. 23, 1950 in the Army. Basic training was at Camp Atterbury, IN; he was assigned to the 24th Div. in 1951 and attended their Signal School. Upon completion was assigned to HQ Co., 2nd Bn., 21st Regt.

Discharged July 22, 1952, and transferred to ERC for five years. He attained the rank of sergeant. Awards include the Combat Infantry Badge, UN Service Medal, Korean Presidential Unit Citation, Korean Service Medal w/2 Bronze Stars.

Used the GI Bill and graduated from Slippery Rock State College, Slipper Rock, PA, with a BS in social studies and geography. He taught at North Allegheny schools, Pennsylvania grades 7-12; got his master's in counseling and guidance from Westminister College, New Wilmington, PA and spent 20 years in guidance before retiring in 1986 from North Allegheny. Received counselor Emeritus in PSS, CA, CPA Assoc. of Secondary Schools and college admission counselors. Active in Ingomar Methodist Church Men's Prayer Group, treas. for 30 years of the Quiet Fund (helping needy in the area), past president of Slippery Rock Univ. Alumni Assoc. (received Past President Award in 1996), board member 12 years, member of the PA Korean War Veterans and was auctioneer at their 2nd reunion in 1998.

Married Dorothy Book, an elementary teacher, in 1956. No children. He is retired and keeps busy working in his garden and taking care of his lawn and traveling to Florida for the winters.

HAROLD L. COOLEY joined the service on Nov. 27, 1950, and served with Co. K, 19th Regt. He participated in three battles at Korea. He was discharged with the rank of sergeant first class. Dates served: May 1951 to February 1952.

JOSEPH PATRICK CORMIER, born June 30, 1930 and enlisted in the Army Dec. 30, 1949. Basic training was at Ft. Dix, NJ, assigned to Ft. Bragg, NC, transferred to HQ Co., 1st Bn., 21st Inf. Regt., 24th Div. at Kumotmota, Keyushu, Japan February 1950; airlifted to Korea July 3, 1950 Task Force Smith, July 5, 1950.

Discharged May 29, 1952 as corporal (T). Awards include the Combat Infantry Badge, Military Service Medal, Army Commendation Medal, Occupation Medal (Japan), Bronze Unit Emblem, Dist. Unit Emblem, three Bronze Service Stars to ROK PUC, CIB, Korean Service Medal, One Overseas Bar, UN Service Medal and Special Certificate of Valor, TFS. Owned and operated Plumbing and Heating Company, 1960-95, and is now retired.

Married Oct. 24, 1953 to Denata G. Cyr and has four children: Donna, Patricia, Michael and Laurie Ann.

LEONARD P. COSENTINI joined the service in October 1950 and was sent to Korea in December

1950. He served with Co. L, 19th Regt. He was wounded on April 12, 1951. Discharged in 1952 with the rank of sergeant. He was awarded a Battle Star.

EUGENE P. COYLE joined the service on Dec. 1, 1950, and served with the Med. Co., 19th Regt., 2nd Bn. He participated in Korea. Discharged with the rank of private first class. Awards include three Battle Stars and Combat Infantryman Badge. Dates served: July 8, 1951, to March 1952.

HERMAN V. CRITCHFIELD, it was in May 1950, that this 25-year-old corporal, US Army took a short discharge from an artillery battalion in Ft. Carson, CO and re-enlisted for the Far East Command. He reported to Bremerton, WA, boarded a ship for Japan and was assigned a pusher for the galley detail.

Was assigned to the 24th Inf. Div., and arrived in Kyushu July 1, 1950; went by ferry to Pusan, Korea. His first day in combat he was assigned as chief of section for the forward howitzer. When they left the forward position all his personal belongings were left in the truck at that position. He had just purchased a new "Ike jacket" before he shipped out of California. The jacket cost him $17 and he will always remember the loss.

He has reminisced this day many times with others who were there at the same time and yes, asked the question "How the hell did we get out of there alive?"

PAUL A. CSISZAR, born Jan. 5, 1933 in Kalamazoo, MI. Drafted into the Army March 13, 1953. Inducted at Ft. Wayne; processed at Ft. Custer then to basic training with Btry. C, 67th FABN at Ft. Knox, KY. Transferred to Cadre Co. and assigned to teaching M-47 tank driving course for recruits. He enjoyed being part of a great outfit and was selected as Tanker of the Month.

In 1954-55 he served a 11 month tour in Korea with the 24th QM Co. at Hwachon reservoir which we called Yangu Valley. He arrived there the week of Easter and had the pleasure of meeting a real buddy there named Chuck, a 2-year-old Korean born German Shepherd dog. He was given to Csiszar about a month later by a sergeant whose name he recall. Sarge noticed how they made friends in a hurry. When it was time to go to sleep, Chuck would always sleep by Csiszar's cot. When reveille came, Chuck would fall out in formation with me in kneeling position. The company commander walked by and always said, "Good morning, Chuck," and we all chuckled. Also when it came to chow time, he would stand in line with me and waited outside until I got done eating. The cooks always had food for him too. He would always go along with me, rain, snow or shine. There were times I had to go in a jeep or 2-1/2 ton truck and he always went along sitting between the driver and me. He also got showers when everybody else was done. Then the sad day came that all dogs must leave the compound. As I stood there looking at Chuck with tears running down my cheeks,

I thought the world was coming to a end. Our friendship was ending. I told Chuck "Don't worry we will meet again some day and be up there together." I had put a leash around his neck and Jimmy, my laundry boy, led him away to the village to some people he knew. One month later I was rotating to go home. After 44 years my memories still linger for him and me.

Discharged as PFC March 9, 1955. Awards include the National Defense Service Medal, UN Service Medal, Korean Service Medal, Sharpshooters M-1 Carbine,

Docent and security for the Kalamazoo Aviation History Museum (the Air Zoo) member, house committee VFW, Red Arrow Post #1527, member of American Legion Post 54, Battle Creek, MI and Korean War Vet Assoc.

Married Phyllis and one daughter, Paulette Csiszar. Semi-retired working for auto truck parts (Weller's) as driver and salesman.

MICHAEL M. CULLEN joined the service on Oct. 8, 1942, and served with the 24th Cav. Recon Troop. He participated in the Asiatic-Pacific Campaign, New Guinea and the Philippines. He was discharged with the rank of sergeant. Dates served: 1942-45.

JOHN T. (MOE) CURRAN, born Aug. 27, 1931, Jersey City, NJ, enlisted in the Army in May 1949 and took basic training at Ft. Dix, NJ. After basic training went to Ft. Sill, OK into the 2nd Armd. Div. He volunteered to serve in Korea in July 1950. In August 1950 he reported to an army camp in the San Francisco area and was taken to a civilian airport and flown to Japan. After two days in Japan they sailed on a Japanese ferry to Korea. They finally boarded a South Korean train in Pusan and headed towards the front line, where we were set up on a hill.

In 1950-51 he served an eight month tour in Korea with I Co., 3rd Bn., 21st Inf. Regt., 24th Inf. Div. and was wounded on April 16, 1951 after a 120 mm mortar shell hit in front of him injuring both legs and left hand. He walked six miles back to the field hospital, was taken by train en route to board hospital ship to Pusan and train was attacked by the North Koreans. Finally made it to hospital in Japan, where he had a two month stay. He was sent back to Korea and served for approximately two weeks, then rotated back to Japan. Arrived back in San Francisco via the USNS *General John Pope* on Aug. 23, 1951, went to Ft. Monmouth, NJ to finish his term as a PFC on Dec. 23, 1953.

Decorations include The Purple Heart, Combat Infantry Badge, The UN Medal, Korean Service Medal w/5 Bronze Stars, National Defense Medal, Presidential Unit Citation and the ROK PUC. Member of VFW, DAV, Korean War Veterans, and 24th Division.

Married Kathleen Braccio in May 1962 and has three grown children. He retired after 35 years as a plumber.

HAROLD R. CYRUS, born Sept. 10, 1912, drafted February 1942 in infantry and headed an Army flame thrower crew in combat in the South Pacific during WWII.

Discharged Sept. 10, 1945 as master sergeant. Awards include the Bronze Star, Philippine Liberation Ribbon and Asiatic-Pacific Campaign Medal.

Business manager, North Star Clinic, manager finance corp., King Lbr. Co. He was a life member in VFW, DAV, American Legion, 24th Inf. Div. (the Victory Division) and served his church and community.

Married Agnes and had two children, David Cyrus and Mary K. Brennan; four grandchildren: Lynn and John Cyrus, Mark and Ruth Brennan; one great-granddaughter, Rory Alina Anderson.

Married 57 years he was devoted to his wife and family; enjoyed fishing with wife and children with grilled hamburgers on the beach; exchanging visits with war buddy and wife from St. Louis. Harold passed away May 18, 1998.

JAMES W. DANHOFF, born March 9, 1926 and was inducted in US Army at Ft. Sheridan, IL Oct. 31, 1944. Basic training with Btry. D-32 FARTC and was field wireman Nov. 17, 1944 to March 17, 1945. Arrived Leyte, P.I. May 21, 1945 to May 31, 1945 4th Replacement Depot, assigned Service Battery, 13th FABN, Mindanao, P.I. June 2, 1945. Promoted PFC July 16, 1945 and corporal Aug. 15, 1945.

Arrived in Japan, Matsuyama, Shikoku Oct. 21, 1945; participated in occupation of Japan, Shikoku, Honshu, Kyushu Islands; cities of Himeji, Saga, Tokushima and Sasebo.

Promoted to sergeant Dec. 29, 1945; staff sergeant, Feb. 1, 1945; tech sergeant, July 30, 1945 as battalion supply sergeant, Service Battery 13th FABN. Discharged Nov. 14, 1945 Ft. Sheridan, IL.

Decorations include Bronze Battle Star, 3 Good Conduct Medals, Meritorious Service Unit Emblem, Southern Philippines Campaign, Medal of Occupation, Japan, WWII Victory Medal and Asiatic-Pacific Theater Ribbon.

Enlisted US Army Reserve as sergeant 1st class, 1950-1956, as supply sergeant, 41st Military Government Co.

Employed with Michigan Bell Telephone Co. for 38 years as splice repair tech, assistant dept. supervisor and publicity chairman, telephone pioneers of America, retired Nov. 30, 1984.

Married 32 years to Joyce Ann Brandel and has three children: DiAnne Susan Doyle, Jeffrey J. and Leslie Elizabeth; two grandchildren, Jennifer and Heather Doyle. Presently enjoying retirement, golfing, traveling, gardening and VFW Honor Guard.

PAUL F. DARBY, JR., born in Monroe, GA on Aug. 19, 1923. In 1942 was inducted into the Army. Duty stations include Ft. Mac, Atlanta, GA; Ft. McCellan for basic training; Fort Ord, CA for five days then left for the Philippines.

Shipped to Australia for a month. During this time we were all given our rank which was for me was PFC, Co. D, 1st Bn., 24th Div. Left there for New Guinea and fought at Leyte, Luzon, Mindanao and Mindoro.

Left the Philippines four years later and went to Japan where they saw the destruction caused by the atomic bomb. At Japan he became a MP and head cook master. He was one of the lucky ones, being wounded only once and that was minor.

Discharged in January 1946 as PFC. Awards include the Philippine Liberation Ribbon w/2 Bronze Stars, WWII Victory Medal, Good Conduct Medal and Asiatic-Pacific Service Medal w/3 Bronze Stars.

Married Perry Nelle Frost Aug. 1, 1948 and they have one daughter, Donna; two granddaughters, Jeni and Sarah. After 30-1/2 year working with General Motors, he retired.

BOYDEN DAUGHERTY joined the service on Aug. 9, 1946, and served with B Btry., 52nd FA BN, December 1946 to November 1951. Participated in the Korean War and five major battles. Discharged on April 16, 1953, with the rank of sergeant first class. Awards include the Bronze Star, Korean Campaign w/5 Battle Stars, WWII Victory Medal, National Defense Service Medal, UN Service Medal, Army of Occupation (Japan), Good Conduct Medal w/loop, Presidential Citation w/cluster and Korean Presidential Citation. Dates served: December 1946 to November 1951.

LEON DAVENPORT, born Dec. 9, 1926 in Blairsville, GA. He volunteered for immediate induction into the Army in December 1944 and began infantry basic training at Camp Blanding, FL in January 1945. Upon completion of training he shipped to the South Pacific and was assigned to C Btry., 11th FABN on Mindanao, then on to Japan for occupation duty with assignment to A 21st Okayama and later Kumamoto.

He was a member of the championship gimlet football team until departure from the 21st in 1950, upon return to Fecom from a 90 day leave he joined the 555th FABN 5th RCT in Korea.

Upon completion of that tour he returned to the States on leave, and shortly thereafter returned to Japan for assignment to the 1st Cav. Div. in Chitose, Hokkaido. After a few months in Japan he volunteered for return to Korea in 1952 and was assigned to the 3rd Inf. Div., 64th Tank Bn. as a 1st sergeant then acting platoon leader. In June 1953 he was awarded a battlefield commission and promoted to 2nd lieutenant, he resigned from active duty in 1956, and after a five year break in service was recalled to active duty in 1961; after which followed tours in Germany and Vietnam. Stateside assignments during his service included Ft. Carson, Ft. Knox, Ft. Stewart, Ft. Bragg and Ft. Bliss.

Last assignment prior to retirement was assistant inspector general, Ft. Knox, KY. Retirement was in December 1972, after 22 years of service of which 11 years were spent overseas. Military Decorations include three Silver Stars, Bronze Star w/v, Purple Heart, Vietnamese Cross of Gallantry, Combat Infantry Badge and numerous other awards and decorations.

After retirement he returned to Blairsville, GA where he served as chief executive officer of union general hospital until retirement from that facility in 1993.

Married Barbara Twiggs in 1953. They have two children, Cayce Lynn and Ralph Douglas.

LEO R. DAVIGNON, born April 19, 1921 and enlisted in the military April 19, 1942. He served with the 2nd Bn. Medics, 21st Inf. in Hawaii, Australia, Dutch New Guinea and the Philippines.

While in Davao on the island of Mindanao in July

1945, Col. Kelly gave Capt. Mutsiger M.D. permission to go on a photo shoot. Shortly they came upon a stash of ammunition in a two-story house and proceeded up the trail. They soon came out of the brush and found a Japanese cook preparing a meal, cautiously they by-passed him and saw a machine gun in a doorway of another house and realized this was a command post of 11 soldiers. They fired the gun into the building and retreated. The next day they returned to verify their action and found everyone was eliminated and that all the rifles had been demolished. Davignon received a Bronze Star for this action.

Tech 4 Davignon was discharged Nov. 11, 1945. His awards include three Bronze Stars.

He married Vilma Vettor Nov. 28, 1946 and they have two children, Lee and Nancy (Mrs. Mandilakis), and three grandchildren: Eliot and Elise Davignon and Nicholas Mandilakis. Leo is a retired carpenter.

LAURENCE ALBERT DAVIS joined the service on Jan. 27, 1949, and served with A Btry., 11th FA BN. Participated in battles and campaigns from July 3, 1950, to May 31, 1951. Discharged with the rank of private. Dates served: June 1949 to May 1951.

ELMER L. DEAL joined the service on June 9, 1944, and served with Co. K, 21st Inf. Regt., 24th Div. Participated in the Southern Philippines Liberation. Anchored off New Guinea on their way to Leyte, went on to Mindoro, made beachhead landing on Mindanao, to Okayama, Southern Honshu, Japan with occupation forces. He crossed the International Date Line on Dec. 25, 1944, and missed Christmas. Discharged with the rank of technical sergeant. Awards include the Combat Infantryman Badge, Philippine Liberation Ribbon, WWII Victory Ribbon, Good Conduct Medal and Asiatic-Pacific Theater Ribbon. Dates served: June 9, 1944, to May 16, 1946.

SAMUEL GEORGE DEBELLIS joined the service in April 1946 and served with the Med. Det., 34th Inf. Regt. Discharged with the rank of private first class. Awards include the Army of Occupation Medal and WWII Victory Medal. Dates served: August 1946 to August 1947.

SCOTT L. DEFEBAUGH joined the service on Feb. 3, 1943. He was in WWII and recalled in August 1950, with a Reserve unit. He received a direct commission and was sent to the 24th Inf. Div. in Korea. He served with HQ Co., 24th Med. Bn. Served in Korea, August 1951 to February 1953; UN Summer and Fall Offensive; and second Korean winter. Retired from the USAR, with 34 years active Reserve and 40 years of commitment, with the rank of lieutenant colonel. Awards include the Korean Service Medal and Army of Occupation (Japan) Medal.

CHARLES W. DEGREGORIO joined the service on Jan. 6, 1949, and served with HQ Co., 3rd Bn., 21st Regt. Participated in Korea from June 1950 to June 1951. Discharged with the rank of master sergeant. Dates served: 1949-51.

H.A. (DEL) DELAMETER, born Nov. 9, 1922, in Princeton, MO and was raised on a farm. Drafted Feb. 10, 1943, took basic training at Camp Wolters, TX and was assigned to Co. A, 34th Inf. Regt., 24th Div. at Schofield Barracks, HI.

Trained at Rockhampton, Australia, Goodenough Island and was a BARman in 2nd Sqd., 2nd Plt. Participated in the invasion of Holandia, New Guinea and fought on Biak Island. He became the company jeep driver. Also participated in the invasion of Philippines, Leyte, Luzon, battle of Zig Zag Pass, Corregidor. He was at the base of Malinta Hill when the Japanese blew it up from the inside. He then went to Mindoro for R&R and replacements, followed by Mindanao. The Japanese navy and air power were nearly destroyed and many lives were lost on both sides. He was there when the war was over. Del was discharged from Camp Beale, CA.

As a civilian he was a farmer and heavy equipment operator until he retired.

He has been married to Lenora F. Ellis since Feb. 7, 1942.

JOSEPH F. DELUCA joined the service in November 1942 and served with Co. D, 34th Regt. He participated in the Asiatic-Pacific, New Guinea, Biak, Leyte, Mindanao, Mindoro, Central and Western Pacific Theater Operations. He was discharged with the rank of technical sergeant. He served two years, six months and 27 days.

ELMER DEMAREB from Wichita, KS was a machine gunner with Co. C, 21st Inf., 24th Div. and is credited with killing over 500 Japanese on Leyte at Breakneck Ridge and Mindanao. *Submitted by Johnny Rodriguez.*

ALAN D. DEMOSS, born May 27, 1925. He enlisted in the infantry Nov. 6, 1944 and served as a rifleman, infantry replacement on Leyte and Davao, Mindanao, Philippines; then as draftsman in Division Headquarters G-3. Transferred to Division Artillery S-2 in Army of Occupation, Japan at Matsuyama, Shikoko, Himeji, Honshu and Fukuoka Kyushu.

Memorable experience was working as a draftsman and typist in a blacked-out tent with Gen. Woodruff at Davao, Mindanao; also memorable was the barracks fire at Himeji Japan when the 24th Div. Arty. HQ burned.

TSgt. DeMoss was discharged Nov. 25, 1946. His awards include the Philippine Liberation w/Bronze Star, Asiatic Pacific Campaign w/Bronze Star, Commendation Ribbon, WWII Victory Medal and Army of Occupation Medal.

He is a railroad executive with over 50 years service and still does consulting in the railroad, trucking and port industries. Married Mary Ann Carlsen and has two sons, John and Paul, and four grandchildren: Jeffrey, Jason, Alan and Vanessa.

JOHN M. DENNIS, born in Jersey City, NJ. He was drafted Feb. 14, 1951 with basic training at Camp

Chafee, AR and Survey School at Fort Sill, OK. Served with Btry. A, 13th FA from Aug. 3, 1951 through Jan. 17, 1953. He had many duties while with the 13th: driver, F.O. party (always with the 19th), supply sergeant, chief of detail, field first sergeant and battery first sergeant.

Married Kitty Derosa in October 1954 and they have one grown daughter, Paul. He is a life member of the 24th Inf. Div. and also of the VFW.

For the past 21 years he has been a season ticket holder for Army football at West Point and has missed only three games. He also sponsors Cadet Candidates for West Point who are attending the US Military Prep School (USMAPS) at Fort Monmouth, NJ. His greatest accomplishment in life was reporting to Btry. A out of basic training and leaving as first sergeant.

GINO A. DENTE joined the service in June 1942 and served with the 24th Med. Bn., Co. D. He participated in the Pacific from Philippines, New Guinea, Mindanao and Mindoro. Discharged with the rank of captain. Dates served: July 1942 to December 1946.

VINCENT P. DE SANTIS joined the service in July 1941 and served with Co. G, S-4 2nd Bn., Co. F, 19th Inf. Regt. Participated in Southwest Pacific and Hollandia. Discharged with the rank of captain. Dates served: May 1942 to December 1944.

JOHN R. DICK joined the service on Sept. 17, 1946, and served with HQ Co., 19th Inf. Regt. Participated in Beppu, Kyushu, Japan. Discharged with the rank of T/5. Dates served: December 1946 to January 1948.

ERIC DILLER joined the service in June 1943 and served with Co. H, 34th Regt. Participated in New Guinea, Biak, Leyte, Luzon, Mindoro, Mindanao and Hollandia. Discharged with the rank of private first class. Dates served: 1944-45.

FRANK J. DIPINO, born May 1, 1927, New Haven, CT. He was inducted into the Army at Ft. Dix on Aug. 3, 1948 and his training too place at Ft. Jackson, SC and Ft. Riley, KS.

Sent to Seattle, WA for ship transport to Japan in early 1949 and was stationed at Camp Mower, Sasebo, Japan for occupation duty until 1950. He was assigned with the 24th Inf. Div., 34th Inf. Regt., Co. I. On Jul. 2, 1950 he was sent to Pusan, South Korea; they traveled north to Ansong then pushed south through Chonan, Chochiwon, Kum River and to Taejon.

Survived the battle at Taejon, moved to Kochang on July 27. They were surrounded and attacked by the NKPA and DiPino was officially listed as MIA July 29, 1950. He was last seen defending the town of Kochang. His fate is unknown to this day. For his sacrifice, he was awarded the Purple Heart posthumously and promoted to corporal. Other awards include the UN Korean Service, US Korean Service, Good Conduct, WWII Victory Medal, Army of Occupation, National Defense, Combat Infantry Badge, Korean Presidential Unit Citation and Army Presidential Unit Citation.

NORMAN A. DIXON, born May 10, 1932. He enlisted in the Army Oct. 31, 1949. Following infantry basic, he was assigned to HQ Btry., 537th FABN, Camp Carson, CO.

Promoted to staff sergeant and radio section chief in August 1951. He was assigned to Co. G, 21st Regt. as 57 mm recoiless squad leader.

He took part in October 1951 assault on Heights around Kumsong, North Korea, north of Kumhwa was wounded in shoulder by small arms fire and taken to MASH unit for preliminary surgery. He was evacuated to Osaka, Japan and finally to Brook Army Hospital in San Antonio where he was discharged in July 1952 with the rank of staff sergeant.

His awards include the Purple Heart, Korean Service, United Nations, Korean Presidential Citation, Good Conduct, Combat Infantry Badge and National Defense Service.

After the service he went back to school and became a manufacturing and tool engineer. He is now retired. He married Dodie Dixon and has five children: John, Peggy, Pam, Penny and Patience and 14 grandchildren.

THOMAS J. DONAGHY, born Oct. 6, 1929, in Philadelphia, PA. He entered the Army in January 1951 and took basic training at Fort Knox, KY. Went to Korea in October 1951 with B Co., 19th Inf. as a medic. Did not go to Japan with the 24th and was reassigned to Co. A, 23rd Inf., 2nd Inf. Div. as a rifleman.

Returned to the States in July 1952 and was assigned to a basic training outfit in Indiantown Gap, PA. Transferred to Edgewood Arsenal, MD as a driver instructor.

Discharged at Ft. Meade, MD in January 1954. His awards include the Combat Infantry Badge, Combat Medic Badge; Service Medals include National Defense w/3 Bronze Stars, UN and ROK Presidential Unit Citations.

Married Irene "Renee" Fleming in January 1957. They have four children and seven grandchildren. He worked in the power industry for 35 years, 25 in nuclear power as a senior reactor operator shift superintendent and consultant. Retired in 1988.

D.F. DOWNING, born Nov. 4, 1922. As a farmer he was eligible for deferment but waived his right and signified to the draft board his willingness to serve his country. He entered the service July 12, 1944 and served with the 19th Inf., Co. C, 1st Bn.

Stations include Ft. Leavenworth, KS, July 13, 1944; Camp Wolters, TX, July 24, 1944 through Nov. 18, 1944, Co. B, 63rd Inf. Bn., 11th Inf. Regt., Ft. Ord, CA, Co. K, 2nd Regt. Shipped out in December 1944 for the Philippines.

PFC Downing was KIA June 13, 1945 at Mindanao and is buried in Manila. Awards include Rifleman-745, Marksman Badge and Purple Heart.

He was married to Norma Jean Rains and had three children: Meredith A. Downing Mesch, Doris Downing Miller and Wayne Dean Downing. There are five grandchildren and four great-grandchildren. *The family would like more information and would like to hear from anyone who served with D.F. Please contact Doris Downing Miller, 4604 Nicklaus Drive, Lawrence, KS 66047.*

RICHARD F. DRAUS, born March 28, 1928. He was drafted into the Army in January 1951 with basic training at Ft. Leonard Wood, MO. He joined HQ Co., 2nd Bn., 19th Inf. Regt. in July 1951.

Transferred to Reg. HQ, 19th Inf. in April 1952. Cpl. Draus was discharged in January 1953. His awards include the Combat Infantry Badge.

Employed 40 years with Acme Steel Co., Riverdale, IL. Retired as project mechanical engineer in 1988.

Married Mary Jane and they have two children, Richelle Lincoln and Kenneth; and two grandchildren, Richard Wood and Joseph James Lincoln.

JOSEPH J. DROZD (DRUSS), born Nov. 2, 1930. Enlisted in the Army from Lansford, PA, Nov. 18, 1947, taking basic infantry training at Ft. Dix, NJ. Assigned to the 25th Inf. Div. in Japan, May 1948, I Co., 35th Inf. Regt. at Tara Camp, Maizuru, Japan; provided security for a CIC unit interrogating repatriated Japanese POWs from Vladivostok, USSR.

Promoted to corporal in May 1944; completed 25th Inf. Div. NCO course at Shindoyama, near Osaka and graduated in the top three in a class of 65. Became a company instructor in five general military subjects and a squad leader, 2nd Squad, 2nd Plt., Co. A, 35th Inf. Regt., Camp Otso, Japan.

Transferred July 2, 1950 to 24th Inf. Div., 21st Inf. Regt., Co. B, Task Force Smith. Continually in combat, he was wounded Feb. 6, 1951, Chicom machine gunfire, left hand, right foot, south of Seoul near Han River.

Spent nine months at Valley Forge Army Hospital, Phoenixville, PA. Discharged as corporal Nov. 21, 1951. Awards include the Combat Infantry Badge, Purple Heart, Bronze Star, Korean Campaign Ribbon w/4 Battle Stars, Presidential Unit Citation, Good Conduct Medal, UN Medal, Occupation of Japan and ROK Citation.

He and his wife Irene have two sons, two daughters, four grandsons and four granddaughters. Retired in 1995 from Harris Corp. as machinist. He lives in the Pocono Mountains, Eastern Pennsylvania and is a member of the DAV and VFW.

WILLIAM R. DUFFY joined the service in March 1952 and served with the QM Co. Discharged with the rank of corporal. Dates served: March 1952 to June 1953.

WALTER (NMI) DUKE JR., born May 23, 1931 in Owensboro, KY. He enlisted in the military Aug. 2, 1948 and served in Ordnance. Basic training was at Ft. Riley, KS and Ordnance School at Aberdeen, MD.

Other stations include 77th Ord. Base Depot, Guam M.I., heavy equipment operator; Co. E, 188th Abn., Ft. Campbell, KY, refresher training, 1850-51; Co. K, 21st Inf., Korea, rifleman, asst. sq. leader Commo Chief and radio operator, 1951; HQ Co. 3rd Bn., Korea, Japan, Commo Officer/XO, 1951-52; 71st Div., Alaska, army aviator, 1954-56; HQ Armor Center, Ft. Knox, KY, Army Aviator, 1956-60; Bn. HQ, 2/50 4th Armd.

Div. Germany, Bn. S4, 1960-1961; HQ VII Corps, Stuttgart, Germany, Army Aviator, 1961-63; HQ 2nd Avn. Bn. Ft. Benning, GA, Avn. Maint. Officer, 1963-65; 224th Avn. Bn., Vietnam, Bn. Maint. Officer, 1965-66; HQ Avn. School, Ft. Rucker, AL, heli. maint. officer, 1966-68; HQ 7th Army, Korea deputy Army Avn. officer, 1968-69; HQ Armor School, Ft. Knox, KY, chief instructor avn. branch, senior officer preventive maint. course, 1969 to retirement in February 1970.

Released from active duty June 2, 1950; transferred to Reserves as PFC; Oct. 18, 1951 accepted battlefield commission, SFC; Feb. 28, 1970 retired at LT/COL. Awards include Combat Infantry Badge, Army Aviator Wings (1954), Senior Army Aviator Wings (1961), Master Army Aviator (1969), Good Conduct Medal, Bronze Star and Air Medal.

Memorable Experience: ran the helicopter airlift that extracted the *Pueblo* crew from Panmunjom.

At the time of his retirement in 1994 he was an inspector with Kentucky Dept. of Mines & Minerals, Division of Explosives and Blasting.

He and his wife Betty have son, Gregory, and one granddaughter, Tabetha.

DELWYN A. DUNKIN joined the service in 1944 and served with Co. F, Service Co., 19th Regt. Participated in Mindanao, Philippine Islands and Japan. Discharged with the rank of T/5.

JAMES M. DUNLAP joined the service on Nov. 14, 1944, and served with Co. M, 19th Regt. Participated in the Philippine Liberation. Discharged with the rank of sergeant. Dates served: April 1945 to September 1956.

LARRY DEAN DUNN, born Jan. 9, 1931, New Matamoras, OH. He was a member of Co. A, 19th Inf. Regt., 24th Inf. Div. and was killed in action while fighting the enemy along the Kum River in South Korea on July 16, 1950.

WALTER DWORAK, born Oct. 7, 1928. He enlisted in the Army Aug. 28, 1948 and served in Germany, Japan and Korea.

Attended Military Police School and Chemical Defense School while in Germany, 1948-52. Early 1953 he was in Japan and left Korea in August 1954.

Sgt. Dworak was discharged Aug. 18, 1954. His awards include the National Defense Service Medal, UN Service Medal, Korean Service Medal w/Bronze Star, Commendation Ribbon w/Metal Pendant, Occupation of German, Presidential Unit Citation.

He and wife Geraldine have five children: Walter Jr., Kurt, Susie, Paige and Scott, and three grandchildren: Sandy, Johnny and Walter. He is a truck driver.

JOHN S. DYSON joined the service on Sept. 24, 1946, and served with Co. D, 34th Regt. He was stationed at Camp Mower and Sasebo, Japan. Discharged with the rank of private first class. Dates served: January to November 1947.

JOHN EADIE joined the service in July 1940 and served with Co. L, AT CO, Service Co, HQ Co., Med. Co, 19th Inf. Regt. Participated in the Pacific, Pearl Harbor, New Guinea, Philippines and Korea. Discharged with the rank of technical sergeant. Dates served: July 1940 to May 1954.

MILTON EAGER joined the service on Aug. 13, 1943, and served with Co. D, 21st Regt. Participated in New Guinea, Philippines and Occupation of Japan. Discharged with the rank of sergeant. Dates served: 1943-46.

WILLIAM F. EARLEY SR. joined the service in December 1948 and served with the 26th AAA (AW) SP BN, A Btry. Participated in Japan and five major battles in Korea. Discharged in December 1951 with the rank of corporal.

RAYMOND J. ECKARDT SR. joined the service on Sept. 6, 1946, and served with Co. B, 19th Regt., 24th Div. He participated in the Army of Occupation at Japan. Discharged with the rank of sergeant.

CLEON C. ECKLER, born July 14, 1932 in Ithara, NY, enlisted in the Army July 1949. He received basic training at Camp Dix, NJ, July 19, 1949 and was sent to Camp Hood, TX Oct. 12, 1949 and went from Camp Hood to Camp Stoneman, CA.

July 1950 he flew to Japan, Camp Drake to Sasebo, then Korea. Sent to I Co. as a replacement approx. Aug. 10, 1950 and stayed until wounded around Kaesong on April 11, 1951. He went from the field hospital to Pusan on a hospital train. He was flown to Kobe, Japan and was put in 8th Station Hospital. Sent back to Korea May 1951 and rejoined company. He was given a squad and made sergeant. Rotated August 1951 back to Japan and then to Stoneman, CA. After a leave he reported to Camp Gordon, GA and was sent to a basic training company and served as a platoon sergeant until his discharge Sept. 4, 1952.

When he returned home he joined Local 451 Ironworkers and stayed for 36 years. Eckler retired to become active in VFW, MOPH and other organizations.

On Feb. 14, 1953 he married Janet and they have two grown children, Cleon C. Eckler III and Pamela A. Bailey and four grandchildren: Jody A. Eckler, Casey L. Eckler, David C. Bailey and Ryan C. Eckler.

His most honored decoration is his Combat Infantryman's Badge. His other awards include: Purple Heart, Good Conduct, National Defense Korean Service Medal w/five Battle Stars, United Nations Medal, Presidential Unit Citation w/two Bronze Clusters, South Korean Presidential Unit Citation Medal.

From 1997-98 was honored to represent the 24th Div. Assoc. at the Korean War Memorial in Washington, DC and also the Arlington National Cemetery and laying of flowers and presenting the division flag at both locations.

WILLIAM L. EDDY, born Aug. 20, 1926, enlisted in the service Nov. 13, 1944.

He received his training at Camp Roberts and joined H-19th Davao, Mindanao, attached to Rifle Co., May 18, 1945, serving with machine gun section. Assigned August 1946, Fort Rosecrans and discharged at Fort Ord, CA, Sept. 29, 1947 as corporal R.A.

His awards include the Combat Infantry Badge, Bronze Star, Asiatic-Pacific, Philippine Liberation, Unit Citation, Good Conduct, WWII Victory and Japan Occupation.

Eddy's memorable experiences include being assigned to H Co., machine gun squad, May 18, 1945 at Davao, Mindanao. He was bombed and strafed by Marine Corsairs, May 24, 1945. That same day they met guerillas at Bunawan River. He was in the battle for Mad Dog Hill and had machine gun blown up. He was also in the patrol that brought in Col. Clifford.

William is married to Carol and they have nine children: Susan, Jim, Leilani, Bill, Linda, Ralph, Grace, Ernie and Monica. They also have 22 grandchildren and 13 great-grandchildren. He is now a retired building contractor.

ROBERT L. EDSON joined the service on Dec. 26, 1948, and served with A Btry., 13th FA BN. Participated in Korea from July 4, 1950, to Nov. 4, 1950. Was captured on Nov. 4, 1950, and was POW in Pyoktong, North Korea. Discharged with the rank of corporal. Dates served: September 1949 to September 1953.

ROGER V. (IKE) EISENBACHER, born Dec. 12, 1931, Comfrey, MN was drafted into the Army September 1952. He received basic training at Fort Knox, KY. Served with the 34th Regt., 24th Inf. Div. February 1953 to August 1954 in Japan and Korea

From September 1971 until December 1991 was eight years in the National Guard and 12 years in the Army Reserves. Retired a master sergeant.

Retired in 1993 after 38 years with Oscar Mayer Co. He served in the following veterans organizations: life member of VFW, 24th Inf. Div. Assoc. and the US Army Noncommissioned Officer Museum Assoc.

He married Margaret Roush December 1958 and their children include: Michael, David, Katherine, Sally, John and Eric. His grandchildren are: Nichole, Nicholas, Melissa, Ashly, Skylar, Krisdeena, John, Katherine and Jacob.

JOHN S. ELMO joined the service on Feb. 6, 1952, and served with George Co., 21st Inf. Regt. Participated in Japan through Korean mainland, to Koje-Do as a company clerk to the end of the war in 1953. Later he rotated on Koje-Do, a part of the UN Command POW Camp #1. Discharged with the rank of corporal. Dates served: Feb. 6, 1952, to Feb. 10, 1954.

HAROLD A. EMERSON joined the service in September 1946, and served with Co. I, 21st Inf. Regt. Participated in the Pacific Theater, Army of Occupation, Kumumoto, Kyushu, Japan. Discharged with the rank of sergeant. Dates served: December 1946 to January 1948.

RUEBEN A. ENGLE joined the service on July 12, 1944, and served with Co. B, 34th Regt. Participated in the Philippine Islands, Luzon, Mindoro and Mindanao. Discharged with the rank of T/5. Dates served: July 12, 1944, to Jan. 30, 1946.

DANIEL D. ENGLER, born July 17, 1928 in Randolph, MN was drafted November 1950. He received basic training at Fort Riley, KS and medical aidman training in Japan. Served 11 months with the 24th Div. in Korea and Japan. He was in charge of 2nd Btry. Plasma Team, 19th Regt., until wounded in October 1951.

After six weeks in a Swedish Red Cross Hospital, he was assigned as aidman in a heavy mortar company and also served as an aidman in the 13th FA and as VP Control NCO for the 19th Regt.

Engler was awarded the Combat Medical Badge, Commendation Ribbon, Korean Service Medal w/3 Battle Stars, Purple Heart and Japanese Occupation Medal.

He was discharged as a staff sergeant August 1952 and married Mary S. Toews, June 1953. They have three grown daughters and eight grandchildren. Retired in 1987 after 32 years with the IBM Corp. and is now living in Arkansas.

WILLIAM ROBERSON ENGLISH joined the service on Sept. 9, 1949, and served with Co. H, 19th Regt. Participated in Korea from June 19, 1950, to May 15, 1951. Discharged with the rank of corporal. Dates served: Jan. 1, 1950, to May 15, 1951.

NEIL D. ESTES joined the service on Jan. 18, 1951, and served with A Btry., 11th FA. Participated in Japan and Korea. He was discharged with the rank of sergeant. Dates served: June 1951 to September 1954.

ROBERT J. FAIONE joined the service in June 1949 and served with Co. I, 21st Regt. He participated in Korea. He was discharged in July 1952 with the rank of corporal. Dates served: February 1951 to February 1952.

FRANK FANTINO, born May 30, 1925 in Torrington, CT, was drafted July 7, 1943. He received basic training in Camp Croft, SC, and was shipped out February 1944. Assigned to H Co., 2nd Bn., 19th Inf., 24th Div.

Stationed on the following beachheads: April 22, 1944, Hollandia, Dutch New Guinea; Oct. 20, 1944, Leyte; Dec. 15, 1944, Mindoro; side trips to Lubang Island; Jan. 9, 1945, Luzon; April 17, 1945, Mindanao.

He was discharged Jan. 16, 1946 as sergeant first class. His awards include the Combat Infantry Badge, Purple Heart, Presidential Unit Citation, WWII Victory Medal, National Defense, Bronze Star, Good Conduct, American Campaign, Asiatic-Pacific Campaign and the Philippine Independence.

He led a machine gun squad, as a private first class during the Mindanao beachhead landing, two weeks later made sergeant.

Returned to active duty for one year 1950-51, serving in the Panama Canal Zone. Received an Aircraft and Engine Mechanics License and private pilot's license. Worked for McDonnell Douglas Aircraft for 30 years, retiring in 1987 as an electrical engineer manager.

He married Mary G. in 1949 and they had three boys: Chris (deceased), Mike and Frank, the oldest, (born in Panama and served in Vietnam). They also have two grandchildren, Shelley and Stacey.

EDWARD S. (ED) FARMER, born April 19, 1918, enlisted in the Army, April 1936 and was assigned to H Co., 21st Inf. Regt., Schofield Barracks, HI.

Promoted to sergeant, January 1939. Returned to the states, July 1941 (Homesteader) assigned to 210th MP Co., Fort Mason, CA as provost sergeant major. Left for OCS Inf., Fort Benning, GA, Feb. 10, 1942. Graduated May 26, 1942 as second lieutenant. Assigned 44th Inf. Div., Fort Lewis, WA. Promoted to first lieutenant, Aug. 25, 1942 in the 178th Inf.

Returning overseas January 1944, assigned 21st Inf. Regt. with Lt. Col. Jock Clifford who was 1st Bn. CO. He had been one of Jock's platoon sergeants at Schofield. Immediately made a company commander in Hollandia. Was A Co. commander only 10 days in Leyte before being wounded. Upon return to Leyte from General Hospital in Biak, assigned as Bn. S-3, 1st Bn., 21st Inf. Other companies were D and A and 1st Bn. HQ Co. as adjutant; also Bn. S-3. When the war ended, transferred to a regiment where he became Reg. S-4 for occupation in Japan. Left Japan December 1945 because flu shot caused him to develop pneumonia (some shot). In March 1947 was ordered back to Japan and assigned as supply and transportation officer for the Japanese War Crime Trials. Left Japan December 1949.

January 30, 1950 transferred from hospital to 2nd Inf. Div., 23rd Inf. Fort Lewis, WA. March 15, 1950 transferred to Oakland Army Base, CA commanded 6th Army Escort Detachment for the return of the war dead.

March 1953, assigned 1st Inf. Div., 18th Inf. Aschaffenburg, Germany. Transferred to G-4 Section, 5th Corps HQ Frankfurt, Germany. Appointed commander of the Command Maintenance Inspection Team to inspect all 5th Corps units. He says, "Everyone in Corps loved me!" Returned from Germany, July 1956; assigned G-4 California Military District. Retired a major, April 1957 at Presidio of San Francisco, CA.

Enjoyed 13 years overseas service, except New Guinea and Philippines, two years.

After retirement from the Army he was employed in real estate as a broker, insurance, importer and all sales activities.

Received the following citations: Silver Star, two Bronze Stars, two Purple Hearts, Combat Infantry Badge, and numerous ribbons and citations.

Married to Carolyn and they have three children: Mike, Lysa and Sue and a grandchild, Heike. Presently working hard as usual. He was a charter member of #218, 24th Inf. Div. Assoc. (1946-1947).

CHESTER E. FASNACHT joined the service on Nov. 8, 1948, and served with Co. B, 21st Regt. He participated at Osan, July 4, 1950; and served with Task Force Smith, 1st Bn., 1949 to August 1950. He was discharged with the rank of corporal. Dates served: April 1949 to August 1950.

MELVIN J. FAULKNER, born Sept. 10, 1921 in Henderson, TX, joined the US Army December 1939 in Dallas, TX. He was asleep at Schofield Barracks at the time of the Japanese attack on Wheeler and Hickam Fields. Became a charter member of the 24th Inf. Div. when the Hawaiian Div. was split into the 24th and 25th Inf. Divs. in September 1941.

He was promoted to technical sergeant in May 1943. He was a part of the breakout at St. Lo and rushed through France during the champagne days of the war with the 3rd Army.

Married Patty Johnson while at Camp Bowie, TX on March 30, 1944. Returned to Texas and raised two sons, George and John, whom both graduated from Texas A&M University and served in the US Army as officers. Wife Patty passed away in April 1991. Faulkner retired from the Texas Highway Dept. after 30 years of service. He has five grandchildren, four of them Texas Aggies.

His awards include the Asia Pacific w/Battle Star, Good Conduct Medal, ETO w/three Battle Stars, including Normandy, Victory Medal and National Defense.

His memorable experiences include watching his twin sons commissioned second lieutenants out of A&M Core of Cadets, not many bigger events in his life time.

HOWARD FEATHER joined the service on June 11, 1946, and served with Btry. B, 11th FA BN. He participated in the Army of Occupation at Japan. He was discharged with the rank of corporal. Dates served: January 1947 to March 1949.

CHARLES W. (CHARLIE) FEEBACK, born Nov. 15, 1924, drafted into the Army July 28, 1943. Reported to Fort Thomas, KY. Received basic training and advanced training at Camp Croft, SC, then went to Fort Mead, MD and onto New Orleans, LA. From New Orleans, boarded a Cuban mail boat and went through the Panama Canal, on to Milne Bay, New Guinea. Joined the 24th Div. on Goodenough Island and was assigned to Co. C, 1st Bn., 21st Inf. Was in combat at Hollandia, Papuan, Leyte, Mindoro, Lubang and Mindanao, PI.

His position was first scout. Wounded the first time Nov. 15, 1944 by hand grenade on Breakneck Ridge, Leyte, PI. Wounded second time at Mintal, Mindanao May 8, 1945, which resulted in shrapnel in his shoulder. Wounded the third time May 14, 1945 near Mintal Mindanao. His right hand was split by shell explosion in banana tree. Evacuated to Leyte 76 Station Hospital and rejoined company back on Mindanao. Came home on the point system from PI. Discharged at Fort Knox, KY as private first class Dec. 9, 1945.

His awards and medals include the Expert Infantry Medal, Purple Heart w/two Bronze Clusters, and two Bronze Star Medals.

Employed by the Veterans Administration at Lexington, KY for four years. Moved to Tucson, AZ and employed by Sears Roebuck and Co. for 20 years as assistant service manager. Transferred to Yuma, AZ as service manager, and again to Bakersfield, CA as service manager.

After being employed with Sears for 20 years, he decided to go into business for himself in Phoenix, AZ. Opened up his dry cleaning plant in Phoenix, February 1970. It was a very successful business and he was able to retire in 1989 after 20 years.

His accomplishments were that he has owned several businesses and properties and has survived open heart and cartoid artery surgery.

His most memorable experiences were: fighting the Japanese at a young age of 19; conditions they lived in, with very little food that wasn't too tasty; the first time you kill someone that's almost looking you in the eyes, is something that you never forget; buying Tuba wine from the Filipinos and getting dysentery; landing on Lubang Island at night with only 14 soldiers and mounting Filipino horses with grass saddles to carry them over the hills to a Lubang town for the attack on the Japanese garrison; hitching their horses outside of town before entering on foot for the attack with no casualties and was very successful.

Married Janet L. Walker March 17, 1962. They have a son, Ronald Feeback, two daughters, Diane Fleener and Cheryl Lozier. Their children have given them five grandchildren: Heather, Jennifer, Jennelle, Nichole and Charles. They also have one great-grandchild, Arianna.

He is retired, but loves to work, so he enjoys yard sales, flea markets, etc. Buying whatever he likes, taking it home and cleaning it up. He has an antique booth in an antique store, where he takes his treasures and sells them. He loves to travel and collect guns, knives, medals, Scout items, fishing equipment, tools and all old treasures.

KENNETH W. FENTNER joined the service on Aug. 14, 1951, and served with Btry. B, 52nd FA BN. He participated in Japan and Korea. He was discharged with the rank of sergeant. Dates served: February 1952 to July 1953.

DONALD F. FINNEY SR., born in Wilmar, CA, Oct. 29, 1928, enlisted in the Army Aug. 25, 1949.

His assignments included Fort Riley, KS, 10th Mountain Div.; Kokura Japan, 24th Inf.; 3rd Combat Co. C for six months; Korea for a little over a year; 32nd Combat Engr. at Camp McCoy, WI.

He was discharged as sergeant T4, Sept. 17, 1952. His awards include the Distinguished Unit Citation, Presidential Unit Citation, Bronze Star Medal, Korean Service Medal w/5 Bronze Camp Stars.

He has been a Scoutmaster for three years, served on church committees for 20 years and has been a VFW officer for five years.

Donald is married to Dolores Finney and they have four children: Peggy, Donald Jr., Terrie and Shirley. They also have eight grandchildren: Dawn, Donald, Dennis, David, Brandy, Travis, Lisa and Christine. Having worked as a heavy equipment operator he is now retired and they are traveling in their motorhome.

JOSEPH T. FISCHETTI was inducted into the service in October 1950 and served with Co. C, 5th RCT Regt., 724th Ord. Co. He was discharged in July 1952 with the rank of corporal. Awards include the Japan Occupational Medal, Korean Service Medal w/ 4 Bronze Stars, UN Service Medal and CIB.

ALLEN M. FISCHER joined the service on Sept. 30, 1946, and served with Co. D, 21st Regt. He was discharged with the rank of corporal. Dates served: Dec. 30, 1946, to Jan. 4, 1948.

DONALD R. FISHER joined the service on Feb. 1, 1946, and served with Co. G, 2nd Bn., 5th RCT Regt. He participated in Korea, attached to the 24th Div. He was discharged with the rank of sergeant. His awards include five Battle Stars. Dates served: Dec. 27, 1950, to Oct. 15, 1951.

RICHARD R. FISHER, born Jan. 31, 1921 was

drafted Oct. 24, 1945. He went through the 34th Inf. experience from Hawaii to Mindanao. The experiences he relates, however, are of the first three weeks of his service.

He was drafted on Oct. 24, 1942 and went to the induction center at Indiantown Gap, PA. Three days later he was put on a train that finally stopped at Camp Stoneman, CA, POE.

He was there a week, and again was taken by train to San Francisco docks where they were loaded onto the USS *President Johnson*. Five days later, they pulled into Honolulu and were taken to Schofield Barracks. There they got their basic training and he was assigned to the 34th Inf.

His discharge Nov. 13, 1945 as T/5 credits him with two years, 11 months, 20 days overseas service and 26 days Continental service. This type of record is not uncommon with 24th Div. personnel, but he has never seen it recorded before.

Awards and medals include the CBI, Bronze Star, Asiatic-Pacific Theater Ribbon w/Silver Star attachment, Philippine Victory Medal and Victory Medal.

He studied chemistry and worked at it for many years. He was not happy being cooped up in a lab after the active life with 34th. He quit and got involved in construction and has spent a lot of those years cursing architects.

He married the former Betty Guthrie and their son Richard Jr. was born in 1950; daughter Debra born 1952. A granddaughter, Michelle was born in 1986 and grandson, Eric born in 1989.

Fisher is now retired and trying to write his memoirs. He gets to 1942 and 1945 and finds it hard to get through.

CHARLES W. FISKE, born April 5, 1929, Chicago, IL, enlisted Chicago, Sept. 11, 1946. Basic training Fort McClellan, AL. Left US November 1946 and arrived in Japan December 1946, and was assigned to Co. E, 19th Inf., 24th Div., Beppu, Japan.

Co. E was chosen as Imperial Palace guard for a one month tour of duty with an Aussie Co. They had such a good record in Tokyo that when they returned, they became regular MPs. After that he was sent back to Tokyo to Radio Repair School, then back to Beppu. He was promoted to staff sergeant, in charge of regiment radio repair. The next move was to 24th Div. HQ in Kokura to Armed Forces Radio Station WLKH where he remained until it was time to go stateside. His new home was Washington state attached to the 205 Signal Repair Co. He was discharged in September 1949, then went to Dental Tech School under the GI Bill. Upon graduation he took the board test and became a certified dental tech.

His awards include the WWII Victory, Japan Occupation and the Good Conduct. He was discharged Sept. 10, 1949 as a staff sergeant (third grade).

Memorable experiences include finding his wife Nancy, raising two fine sons and being a grandfather.

He married Nancy Southard and has two sons, Charles and Shawn. They have five grandchildren: Steven, Jessica, Michael, Kahlela, Anna and one on the way.

Now retired, he and Nancy live happily in Lakeview, AR. He enjoys woodworking, visiting Civil War sites, going to Corvette shows and traveling the US.

EDWARD D. FITZGERALD joined the service on Sept. 18, 1946, and served with Co. B, 21st RCT Regt., December 1946 to April 1947, corporal; 24th

MP Co., April 1947 to August 1950, sergeant; and 21st RCT HQ Co., 21st RCT Regt., August 1950 to April 1951, sergeant first class. He participated in Korea; received five Battle Stars; was wounded and evacuated to station hospital in Yokahoma in August 1950; went back to Korea in September 1950; and returned to the States in April 1951. He was discharged with the rank of sergeant first class.

LEON E. FLAKE, born Aug. 15, 1930, enlisted June 1948. Attended basic training, Fort Ord, CA; Fort Riley, KS; Leadersship School, stayed to instruct; Co. K, 21st Regt., 24th Inf. Div.

He was discharged Dec. 3, 1951. His awards include the Bronze Star, National Defense Service Medal, two Purple Hearts, Korean Service Medal, Combat Infantry Badge and United Nations Service Medal.

He established Flake Industrial Services, the largest independently owned industrial laundry in Texas.

His most memorable experiences: when Jack Hogue found him after 45 years. He was the tallest man in the US Army when he went to Korea, 6'9" and weighed 220 lbs.; when he came out he was 6'9" and weighted 135 lbs.

His wife is deceased and they had a son, Steve. Leon is presently enjoying life.

CHARLES J. FLANAGAN joined the service in August 1943 and served with the 24th Div., AT Co., 34th Regt. Participated at Good Enough Island, Hollandia, Bataan, Corregidor, Biak Island, Leyte, Mindoro, Luzon and Japan. He was discharged with the rank of staff sergeant. Dates served: January 1944 to January 1946.

KELTON R. FLIEHMAN JR., born July 5, 1929, Noble County, OH was drafted into the Army Jan. 25, 1951. Attended basic training at Fort Knox, KY in B-36 Co. Assigned to Korea July 1, 1951 and served with the 24th Inf. Div. Arty.

In February 1952 the 24th Div. was relieved and they were shipped to Camp Younghans, Japan. Stayed there until June 30. Went to Yokohama, Japan and returned to Pittsburg, CA on USNS *Anderson*.

He went to Fort Knox, KY and was discharged Oct. 24, 1952. His awards include the Korean Service Medal, Japan Occupation Medal and United Nations Medal.

He is a life member of the American Legion, VFW, 40&8.

Kelton married Helen Rauch in November 1952 and they have four children: John, Tom, Susan and Dan and 10 grandchildren. He retired with 38 years of service with IBEW Local 972, Marietta, OH.

JAMES W. FLYNN JR. joined the service on March 5, 1953, and served with H&S Co., 3rd Eng. Comb. Bn. Participated in Korean service from 1953-54. Discharged with the rank of sergeant. Dates served: October 1953 to November 1954.

ROCK FLYNN, born April 15, 1920, enlisted into the Army April 11, 1941, serving with the 19th Inf.

His assignments include: Pearl Harbor, Australia, British New Guinea and Dutch New Guinea.

Discharged as private Aug. 27, 1945. His awards include the Combat Infantry Badge and Bronze Star.

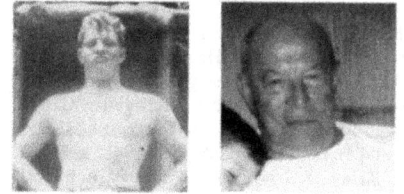

Memorable experience: made a landing in New Guinea and was on inner perimeter where you could use only a machete knife. Dug a foxhole, two men to a hole. One man sleeping, the other on watch. He was on watch, thought everyone else was asleep. He heard a noise coming through the jungle. It sounded like a bowling ball. Nobody in the division was ever as scared as he was. His hair stood straight up on his head. It came in his foxhole and he thought he would die. He grabbed at it, it was hairy. He got a hand full of hair, chopped at it with the machete. It went on down to the beach. Field artillery was on the beach. They caught it. It was a goat. Never ate goat meat.

He married Cpl. Rose Flynn, "sweetest person that ever lived." They have three children: Virginia, Dan and Karry; five grandchildren: Amy, Erin, Rock, Dan and Kyleen; four great-grandchildren: Jake, Brian, Kevin and Megan.

Flynn is presently trying to get over a stroke.

THOMAS E. FLYNN joined the service in September 1949 and served with a heavy mortar company, 21st Regt. Participated at Kumomato, Occupation of Japan, Korean, Osan, Taejon, Chonan, Chonju and Task Force Smith. Discharged with the rank of private. Dates served: 1949-51.

LOUIS A FODOR joined the service on June 13, 1940, and served with Btry. A, 13th FA BN. He participated at Pearl Harbor, Pacific Theater and New Guinea. Discharged with the rank of corporal.

LEONARD FOGEL joined the service on March 22, 1951, and served with the 24th Sig. Co. He participated in the Iron Triangle. Discharged with the rank of corporal. Dates served: Aug. 27, 1951, to March 5, 1953.

KEN FOLDOE joined the service on Jan. 20, 1943, and served with Co. E, 2nd Bn., 34th Regt. Participated in the Philippines, New Guinea and Biak. Discharged on Nov. 14, 1945, with the rank of staff sergeant. Awards include the Purple Heart, Bronze Star and Silver Star.

JAMES R. FONNER joined the service on Oct. 5, 1946, and served with Co. A, 34th Regt. He participated in the Occupation of Japan. Discharged with the rank of private first class. Dates served: January 1947 to January 1948.

C. RUCKER FORD was assigned to the 21st Inf. Regt., in March 1943 as a platoon leader. When the war ended he was sent back to the States, winding up at Walter Reed Hospital, where he left the Army service in March 1947.

Transferred to the USAF as an electronics officer and served one year in Korea. He was forced out of the Reserves in 1955.

He does not recall the dates of all the action of the 21st Inf. Regt., but he was in all of them: training exercises, landings, battles; the good, the ugly and the bad.

HERBERT FORDYCE joined the service in November 1944 and served with Co. E, 2nd Plt., 19th Inf. Regt. He participated at Davao, Mindanao, Shikoku, Kyushu, Leyte, Philippine Islands and Japan. He was discharged with the rank of private first class. Dates served: November 1944 to November 1946.

ROBERT G. FOX, born Dec. 18, 1926 in Lowell, MA, enlisted June 1944. He received infantry training at Camp Rucker, AL. Assigned to Philippines, then Japan G-2 5250 Technical Intelligence GHQ. Discharged November 1946, staff sergeant MI Reserve, FBI employed. Recalled August 1948, sent to OCS, Fort Riley, KS. Qualified for Parachutist and Gliderman Badge.

March 1949, second lieutenant CMP. Assigned 19th Regt., Beppu, Japan. Led the 19th from Pusan to Taegu with six jeeps and 24 MPs. Air evacuated, Osaka General Hospital, Japan. Transferred to USAF, Y-80 WAFB, Germany, forerunner of the U2 program.

Returned to USA. Top-secret SAC security. OIC missile training, Guided Missile Badge, Missile launch officer, Launch Enable System Control officer. Phased out the 556 SMS, Plattsburgh AFB, NY. Retired major, 1966, 22 years. Memorable military experiences: Korea and missile crisis (12 Atlas F-ICBM on the launch pad in the green).

He married Ann Sullivan in 1951 and they have eight children: Sheila, Kathleen, Roberta, Jane, Paula, Erin, Anne and Gregory; and 13 grandchildren. Greatest accomplishment: "did something right as all our children come home to visit."

Raytheon Company, 25-year career, Missile Systems Div. Received degrees from George Washington, Omaha and Northwestern universities. Retired, DAV, and active National Defense Executive Reserve assigned to Federal Emergency Management Agency, Region 1, Boston.

JESSE BERNARD FRANK, born April 29, 1927, enlisted Sept. 11, 1950 in the Army.

His assignments include Fort Jackson, SC. Served in Korea January 1951 to January 1952, 24th Inf. Div., Co. E, 21st Div.

He was discharged June 10, 1952 as sergeant and was awarded the Combat Infantry Badge, Purple Heart, United Nations Service Medal, Korean Service Medal w/four Bronze Stars.

Memorable experiences: Always will remember this kid from Pittsburgh, PA, Pvt. James A. They took basic training together, went overseas and ended up in the same company. They also would pal around together. One day in early April 1951, the Catholic priest came to the front lines. They had Mass and went to communion. A few days later he got killed.

Accomplishments include serving his country with the men he was with in Korea and getting together at Tennessee every year. Talking over old times in Korea.

He is married to Dorothy (Sullivan) Frank and they have six children: Suellen Weese, Cherie Conrad, Bernard, Brian, Scott Frank; 11 grandchildren: Jason, Sean, Brad, Conrad, Kristen, Ashley Weese Brian, Kelley Frank, Nathanel and Candance Frank, Megan Alexis Frank; one great-grandchild, Alyssa.

Now retired, traveling and visiting.

LELON L. FREEMAN joined the service on Nov. 30, 1943, and served with Co. C, 34th Regt. He participated at New Guinea, Southern Philippines and

Luzon. He was discharged with the rank of corporal. Dates served: Oct. 10, 1944, to Feb. 5, 1945.

RONALD A. FRENCH, born Sept. 22, 1922, enlisted in the Army, Oct. 7, 1940.

His assignments included: New Guinea, Biak Southern and Central Philippines, Hawaiian Islands, Australia, North and South Carolina Maneuvers 1940, Louisiana Maneuvers 1940, Infantry Co. F, 34th Regt., platoon sergeant, NCO, Task Force 5602 - Destination Canton Island Feb. 24, 1942, USS *President Taylor*, Camp Caves, Rockhampton, Australia

Discharged Sept. 6, 1945 as staff sergeant. His awards include the Marksman Rifle, Combat Infantry Badge, Good Conduct Medal, Purple Heart, American Defense Service Medal, Philippine Liberation Ribbon w/two Bronze Service Stars, Asiatic-Pacific Theater Campaign Ribbon, Philippine Presidential Unit Citation and Victory Medal.

He was wounded Oct. 21, 1944 in the Philippines and was taken on a hospital ship from Leyte to New Guinea and the hospital ship was bombed but didn't get hit. He saw MacArthur come ashore on the 5th wave liberation of the Philippines.

He married Jennie E. and they have two children, Ronald and Jeffrey, and two grandchildren, Ellen and Emily. Retired after 35 years with the Torrington Company. He is a member of the following Veteran organizations: MOPH, DAV, VFW, AL, lifetime member 24th Div. He participated in Memorial Day parades and firing squad commands.

JOHN W. FREY joined the service in June 1943 and served with Co. H, 21st Regt. He participated in the Southern Pacific, New Guinea, Philippines, Hollandia, Leyte and Breakneck Ridge. Discharged with the rank of private first class. Dates served: 1944-45.

FRANKLIN D. GALLOWAY, born Dec. 28, 1932 enlisted into service March, 2, 1950.

He was with F Co., 19th Inf. in 1951 and was wounded in 1952. He returned to D Co., 3rd Engr. Bn. and stayed until 1954. Remained in the Army for 18-1/2 years.

Galloway was discharged June 6, 1968 as sergeant first class E-7. His awards include the Combat Infantry Badge and Purple Heart 2nd award.

He married Dong Sook and they have a child, Rex. He is retired and 100 percent disabled.

BEDENT B. GALLUP was inducted into the service on March 1, 1943, and served with HQ Co., 21st RCT Regt. He participated in the Asiatic-Pacific, Lubang and Mindanao. He was discharged with the rank of staff sergeant. He served two years, 10 months and six days.

CARL B. GAMEL, born Feb. 18, 1927 in Tampa, FL, was drafted into the Army Sept. 8, 1950, three months after graduation from Villa Madonna College, Covington, KY. Attended basic training at Ft. Knox, KY. Served 11 months in Korea with Dog Co. (Heavy Weapons) 19th Inf. becoming (master sergeant) first sergeant in July 1951. Rotated to the States in December 1951 and assigned as sergeant major (MOS 1812) basic training unit HQ Co. CCR, 3rd Armd. Div. until June 22, 1952.

Awards and decorations include the Combat Infantry Badge, Korean Service Medal w/two Battle

Stars, Good Conduct Medal, Bronze Star (meritorious) and the United Nations Medal.

Married Mary Sue (Meuhlenkamp) June 11, 1955 and they have three daughters: Susan, Joan and Diane; five sons: Jude, Thomas, Carl III, Daniel, Mark and 15 grandchildren: Jude, Edward, Ciara, Thomas, Erin Jo, Samantha, Alison, Mark, Kayla, Olivia, Rachel, Tee, Megan, Ellen and Anna.

PAUL R. GARLAND was inducted into the service on April 19, 1951, and served with Co. H, 5th RCT Regt. Participated in the second Korean winter, and summer and fall 1952. Discharged on March 27, 1957, with the rank of corporal.

THOMAS M. GARRISON, born Nov. 27, 1930 in Georgetown, SC, entered the South Carolina National Guard at age 16, serving as a tank gunner.

Joined the Regular Army Dec. 5, 1948. After basic training in Fort Jackson, SC was assigned to Sasebo, Japan, Co. A, 34th Regt., 24th Div.

When the Korean War started he was shipped to Korea, arriving July 2, 1950 and departing May 1951. He was assigned to Fort Gordon, GA, Fort Ord, CA and at the Army Reserve Center in Asheville, NC.

He participated in numerous assignments overseas, including Japan, Korea, Germany, Taiwan and Turkey.

Served as battalion sergeant major of HQ 3rd Bn., 19th Inf. Regt., 24th Inf. Div. from December 1950 to May 1951. Also as first sergeant of HQ Co., 2nd Bn., 11th Inf. Regt. in Fort Ord, CA in 1955.

During a 22-year Army career had assignments as company clerk, supply sergeant and unit administrator. During service in Taiwan was in charge of supporting the off-shore islands of Matsu and Kinnman and visited both of these island during this period.

During tour in Turkey, worked at various jobs in NATO HQ in Izmir. After leaving the service after 22 years in 1969 he worked 15 years with Lowe's Home Improvement Company, retiring in 1988.

His awards and medals include: Combat Infantryman Badge, Bronze Star Medal (2), Army Commendation Medal, Presidential Unit Emblem, Korean Service Medal, United Nations Service Medal, National Defense Service Medal, Good Conduct Medal, Army Occupation Medal, Armed Forces Expeditionary Medal, Army Commendation Medal, Vietnam Gallantry Cross w/Palm and Unit Citation Badge.

Memorable experience: during assignment in Turkey he had the opportunity to visit, Lebanon, Syria and Jordan on a trip to Holy Land with his family.

He married Betty Ann Williams Dec. 22, 1951. They have three children: Karen G. Russell, Teresa G. Eubanks and Thomas Garrison II; six grandchildren: Paul Russell, Brian Garrison, Julie R. Hodler, Lynne Russell, Matthew Garrison and Andrew Eubanks.

WILLIAM W. GARRY joined the service in March 1946 and served with Co. K, HQ, Hvy. Mortar, 19th Inf. Regt. He participated in the Korean Service.

Was commissioned 2nd lieutenant in 1956 and retired as captain in 1966. Awards include six Battle Stars, Combat Infantryman's Badge and Bronze Star Medal.

WILLIAM CHARLES GAURICH, joined the Army May 5, 1948 in Pittsburgh, PA. He did his basic training at Fort Dix, NJ and was was shipped out of Seattle, WA on the M.M. *Patrick* to Tokyo, Japan.

He served about six months with the 8th Cavalry Div. in Ome, Japan. He volunteered when they were regrouping the 24th Div. and was sent to F Co., 19th Inf. Regt. of the 24th Div. at Beppu, Japan. Later went to Korea with the 24th serving until Feb. 6, 1951 when he was wounded and evacuated to Murphy Army Hospital in Massachusetts. He was discharged from the hospital to HQ and HQ Co., 2nd Student Regt., Fort Benning, GA.

He was discharged from the Army May 14, 1952 with the rank of private first class, RA Inf.

DONALD H. GEORGE joined the service on Dec. 28, 1956, and served with Co. B, 1st Abn. Bn. Gp., 187th Inf. He participated in Beirut, Lebanon in 1958. Discharged with the rank of private first class. Dates served: 1957-63.

CARMELLO FRANK GERACI, born Feb. 24, 1930, was drafted into the Army Jan. 10, 1951. He received basic training at Camp Roberts, CA and was assigned to the 24th Recon Co., 24th Inf. Div. in August 1951. Wounded Nov. 10, 1951. He was taken to M.A.S.H. for preliminary surgery and then to a Army Hospital in Tokyo for additional surgery. Sent to hospital at Camp Cook, CA. Discharged from the Presidio in San Francisco. He was awarded the Purple Heart.

He spent 41 years in title insurance industry. Married Narcisa and they have four children: Lenore, Laura, Lisa and Christopher; five grandchildren: Melissa, David and Tyler Ramirez, Jessica and Matthew Reese.

Now retired and volunteers at USO at the San Jose, CA Airport.

FRANK GIAMBRONE joined the service on Feb. 11, 1958, and served with B Tp., 2nd Recon Sqdn., 9th Cav., 24th Inf. He participated at Augsburg, Germany. Discharged with the rank of private first class. Dates served: 1958-59.

FLOYD S. GIBSON joined the service in April 1943 and served with Companies M and I, 21st Regt. Participated in ETO, Ardennes; Rhineland; Central Europe; Korea, UN Defensive; UN Offensive; CCF Intervention, Vietnam, Vietnam Defense; Vietnam Counter Offensive; Vietnam Counter Offensive, Phase II. Retired with the rank of colonel. Dates served: July 19, 1950, to Jan. 5, 1951.

JOSEPH F. GIBSON joined the service on March 16, 1949, and served with Med. Co., 21st Regt. Par-

ticipated in Korea. Discharged with the rank of sergeant. Dates served: Sept. 1, 1950, to Oct. 4, 1951.

TOMMY E. GILBERT, born April 18, 1934 in Beaumont, TX, enlisted in the Army Sept. 7, 1949. After basic he was sent to Japan to the 24th Div., 34th Regt., K Co. July 1950 was sent to Korea. July 20, 1950 was with Gen. Dean trying to get out. Gen. Dean sent some of them to get ammo. On the way back Gilbert was wounded and captured. He was held in a hut with some other GIs. South Korean civilians killed the guards and they escaped. He made his way back to the lines.

Sent to Japan, 395th Station Hospital in Kobe. Went back to Korea and was wounded two more times. He was then sent home for being too young as he was only 16 years old.

His awards include the Bronze Star, three Purple Hearts, Combat Infantry Badge, Korean Unit Citation, American Unit Citation, Good Conduct, Korean Campaign, UN Medal, Occupation of Japan.

Discharged March 1951. Reenlisted USAF June 7, 1951. Stayed until November 1956.

He married Margie and they had five children: Michele, Tommie Jean, Dianna Lynn, Jewel, Tommy Jr. and nine grandchildren: Chad, Jacob, Bryan, Steven, Jeremmy, Josh, Kasi, Kelly and Destine.

Gilbert is a retired DAV. He coached Little League baseball and football. He worked at a chemical plant until his retirement.

CHARLES L. GIPSON, born April 30, 1932, enlisted in the AAC-Army, August 1947, stationed at Scott Air Force Base, IL. Transferred to 82nd Abn., Fort Benning, GA MOS Military Police. Transferred to Japan December 1948. Transferred to 24th Div., 19th Regt., Co. F, August 1949. Left Korea, April 1951. Discharged December 1952 from San Antonio, TX.

His awards include the Purple Heart and Combat Infantry Badge.

He became a barber in April 1954 and is still following his trade. Barbered in Dallas, TX; Atlanta, GA, Texarkana, TX, now Dardanelle, AR. Ordained a Baptist minister in 1973. Pastored in Arkansas and Texas. His hobbies include genealogy and history.

Married July 24, 1953 to Doris Maxine Womack. They have five children: Stephen, Mava, Heidi, Charles and Allison; 10 grandchildren: Adam, Richard, Stephen, Leah, Anna, Chad, Monica, Tamara, Jonathan and Alex.

LOUIS A. GISONNO joined the service on Aug. 18, 1937, and served with the 74th Ord. Co., on the island of Oahu, HI from Aug. 18, 1937, to Jan. 5, 1940. He was stationed at an ammunition dump located at Red Hill. Also served with the 4th Armd. Div., 98th Ord. Co., HM, later called the 126th Ord. Co., during WWII. He was discharged on Jan. 5, 1940.

RICHARD R. GLENN was inducted into the ser-

vice on Oct. 9, 1942, and served with the 24th Cav. Recon Tp. He participated in the Asiatic-Pacific, Hollandia and Leyte. He was discharged with the rank of T/5. Dates served: January 1943 to January 1945.

BUFORD F. GOFF SR., born Jan. 31, 1931 in Parkin, AR, enlisted in the Army, April 18, 1947.

His assignments include: Camp J.T. Robinson, Little Rock, AR; Fort Jackson, SC; Tokyo, Japan; Beppu, Japan; South Korea; Camp Chaffee, AR; Camp Polk, LA; Fort Hood, TX; Garmisch/Muchnie Germany; Ft. Ord, CA; US Embassy, Tripoli, Lybia; Arkansas Tech University; Russelville, AR.

Retired Aug. 1, 1968 as sergeant first class. His awards include two Purple Hearts, Korean Service Medal w/four Campaign Stars, UN Occupation of Japan and Germany, National Defense w/three Clusters, Good Conduct w/7th Loop, Presidential Unit Citation w/two Clusters, Korean Presidential Unit Citation, Combat Infantry Badge, Glider Badge, Korean Medal of Peace, SKG.

Memorable experiences: US Embassy Hiyba w/attachment, Greece and Malta; Procurement Instructor, ROTC, Arkansas Tech. University, Russellville, AR; Co. F, 19th Inf. Regt., 24th Inf. Div., Beppu, Japan, 1948-50. Good days. Hard to forget July 1950 through December 1950, not so good.

He is a restaurant owner, 32 degree Mason. Serves on the board of directors and EXO of ARVAC, Inc. Life member of VFW, Purple Heart, NCOA, 24th Div. Assoc., DAV, S/off., state commander, TRE Assoc., KWA.

He married Sue A. Sempsion, Oct. 29, 1951 after three weeks of courtship. She died Nov. 6, 1995. Remarried Oct. 28, 1997 to Barbara. He has sons, Buford Jr. and Kenneth W. Goff and grandchildren: Lacey, Lakey K., Peter D., Mary E., Hanaha R. (stepgrandchildren: Jessica and Brooks Harvey).

He enjoys gardening and jewelry craft. At this writing they are expecting their first great-grandchild, a girl, due May 21, 1999, she will be named Mia K. Story.

RICHARD C. GOINY, born in Chicago, IL, July 31, 1919 and drafted into military service June 11, 1941, Camp Grant, IL. Assigned to Scott AFB, IL June 1941 and after basic training was assigned to the 12th School Sqdn. as permanent party. Promoted to corporal October 1941. Was on duty as corporal of the guard Dec. 7, 1941. Later was assigned to supply duty and drill instructor until Aug. 13, 1942 when he was appointed supply sergeant of the 992nd School Sqdn. in the Stevens Hotel, Chicago, IL. Closed the Radio School August 1943. Assigned to Meteorology School at Washington University in St. Louis, MO as acting first sergeant and supply sergeant. Closed the Meteorology School December 1943 and returned to Scott AFB, IL. Supply sergeant in charge of replacement depot for airmen coming into and leaving the base. Closed down the replacement depot and was awaiting reassignment when he was caught in a draft of replacements for Infantry Service. October 1944, arrived at Advanced Inf. NCO School at Camp Howze, TX. Graduated NCO School December 1944, retained the rank of staff sergeant and was assigned to replacement depot at Fort Meade, MD. Shipped to Camp Stoneman, CA to 4th Replacement Depot at Leyte Island, PI. Was then assigned to Co. E, 21st Inf. Mindanao, PI as platoon sergeant while platoon sergeant was hospitalized. Upon his return he was appointed Co. E supply sergeant throughout the windup operations on Mindanao and the occupation of Japan. He left Japan December 20 and arrived in Seattle, WA on Dec. 31, 1945.

Military decorations include the Combat Infantry Badge, Bronze Star Medal, American Defense Medal, Asiatic-Pacific Medal, Philippine Liberation Medal, Philippine Presidential Citation.

NORTON M. GOLDSTEIN, (AKA GOLDY NORTON), born April 11, 1930, enlisted in the Army January 1949.

He received basic and leadership school at Fort Ord, Wire Section of HQ Co., 21st Inf. Regt., June 1949 to June 1951, including 11 months in Korea. Extended involuntarily from two to three years.

Discharged January 1952 as corporal. His awards include the Combat Infantry Badge and Bronze Star.

His accomplishments include being the founding director of US Academic Decathlon; member of Frisbee Hall of Fame; charter member of Southern California Sports Broadcasters Assoc.; author of *The Official Frisbee Handbook* (Bantam, 1972).

Employed as newspaper reporter for the *LA Daily News;* writer producer of radio and TV sports programs, public relations consultant.

He married Judith Marcia Morris October 1955 and they have a daughter, Ann (married to Christopher Williams). Presently he is public relations consultant for Goldy Norton, P.R.

SAMUEL MCC GOODWIN joined the 24th Div. in December 1953 in Korea. He was assigned as assistant chief of staff, G4; served as division G-4 until December 1954 when they were ordered back to Korea. Appointed division chief of staff (rear) then division chief of staff (forward). Departed for the States in March 1955. Discharged with the rank of colonel.

WILLIAM F. GOOLEY JR. joined the service on Oct. 27, 1954, and served with Co. A, 724th Ord. Bn., 2nd Plt. He participated in Korea. Discharged with the rank of SP5. Dates served: April 1955 to August 1956.

THOMAS C. GORE joined the service on Aug. 19, 1943, and served with Co. G, 19th Regt. He participated in New Guinea, Luzon and the Southern Philippines. Discharged on Jan. 18, 1946, with the rank of sergeant. He served 29 months.

ARMOUR L. GOSS, born Dec. 14, 1917, enlisted in the service July 10, 1940, serving with the 34th Regt., 24th Div. He was stationed on the Philippines Islands as tech. sergeant.

He was killed in action May 23, 1945, Mindanao, PI. His awards include Combat Infantry Badge and Bronze Star.

He had been employed as a city fireman and finished high school in Ruston, LA. He had three brothers: R.L. Goss, Wilbur Goss and Billey Goss; four sisters: Lela, Martha, Joyce and Juanita.

R.L. Goss was also in PI Island in 38th Div.

HEINZ GRATZ joined the service in December 1944 and served with Co. G, 21st Regt. He participated in the Philippines. Discharged with the rank of staff sergeant. Dates served: December 1944 to January 1946.

ROBERT O. GRAY joined the service in May 1949, and served with HQ Co., 1st Bn, 19th Regt. Participated in Korea from July 5, 1950, to Sept. 2, 1953; was wounded on July 16, 1950, Sept. 15, 1950, and Nov. 4, 1950; POW from Nov. 4, 1950, to Aug. 30, 1953. Discharged with the rank of corporal. Dates served: May 1949 to October 1953.

EUGENE L. GREENWALT, born Dec. 16, 1928, enlisted March 1950, Fort Leonard Wood, MO, then to Far East commands. Assigned to 24th Inf. Div., C Co., 3rd Engr. Btry. Spent 11 months in Korea from April to January 1951 then went to Japan on rotation. Sent home to Camp Carson, CO. From there to Fort Leonard Wood. He was discharged in December with the rank of corporal and went into the Reserves for five years.

His medals include the Korean Medal and Purple Heart.

After discharge he worked at Boeing Aircraft, Seattle, WA then came back to get married. He married Helen Volkl and they had three daughters: Karen, Janet and Susan; six grandchildren: Jeremy, Michele, Rachel, Brandon Grotzsky and Kelsey and Jordon Ritz.

Started farming and went into the dairy business for 20 years. Farmed for 40 years. Now retired.

Greenwalt belongs to VFW and was commander. He is also a member of the American Legion and Purple Heart Assoc.

ROY GRIAK joined the service in February 1943 and served with Co. E, 21st Regt. He participated in New Guinea, Leyte, Mindanao and Japan. He was discharged with the rank of sergeant.

DON EDWIN GRIFFIN, SR., born July 23, 1933, in Bridgeport, AL, In November 1950 took infantry basic training at Fort Jackson, SC. Went into advance training anti-aircraft AAA, Fort Bliss, TX in December 1950. Sent to Camp Stoneman, CA January 1951, the port of embarkation to Yokohama, Japan.

From Yokohama, Japan went to Korea in spring of 1951 and served 13 months with 24th Div., 21st Inf., Co. D. Went to Korea as private and to NCO School. Left Korea as sergeant first class.

He went to Okinawa, spent five months with 29th Inf. Regt. then rotated back to the states to Fort Jackson, SC. Remainder of time in Army was heavy weapons instructor and Heavy Motor Co. Fire Direction Center instructor. Was on demonstration team for visiting officials.

November 1953 discharged from regular army and joined Tennessee National Guard, 30th Armd. Div. for two years.

His decorations include: Combat Infantry Badge, Bronze Star, Good Conduct, National Defense Ribbon, Presidential Unit Citation from Korean government and United Nations Medal.

Married Sandy and they have six children, 11 grandchildren and two great-grandchildren. Retired after 27 years, driving for McClean Trucking.

J.C. GRIFFIN, born Feb. 14, 1929, Austin, AR was drafted into the Army January 1951. Took basic infantry training at Camp Chaffee, Fort Smith, AR. Arrived in Pusan, Korea in May 1951. Shipped up on line to HQ Co., 2nd Btry., 21st Inf. Regt., 24th Div. Left Korea from Inchon in February 1952. Shipped to Japan where he stayed until August 1952, then shipped back to Camp Chaffee, Fort Smith, AR where he was discharged October 1952.

Married Bobbye K. Busick September 1952. They have two daughters, Nancy J. Marsh and Connie A. Boullie and two grandsons, Clinton G. Boullie and G. Clifton Marsh.

Retired from Southwestern Bell Telephone Co. after 38 years. Most honored military decoration is the Combat Infantry Badge. Retired on a farm near Cabot, AR. He is a member of the Telephone Pioneers of America and Arkansas Bar Association.

CARLTON G. GRODE, born Oct. 4, 1916 and enlisted in the Army Oct. 28, 1942. Left Nov. 11, 1942 for California. Boarded *F. Funston* for Hawaii, Schofield Barracks. Left Hawaii after basic training for Australia, Rockhampton. First combat was Hollandia, New Guinea, Philippines.

Discharged June 29, 1945 as staff sergeant. He was awarded the Silver Star, Good Conduct Ribbon, Asiatic-Pacific Theater Ribbon w/three Bronze Battle Stars, Philippine Liberation Ribbon w/Bronze Battle Star and four Overseas Bars.

Returned to same company he left in 1942. Spent one year in VA hospital. Returned to work total of 37 1/2 years. The company retired him at 59. Last job was as a salesman. Since then he has tried MLM, new products. Some good some not.

Memorable experiences: he recalls the Leyte invasion, particularly Kilay Ridge with Col. Thomas E. Clifford. Ref: pages 244-269 in *Children of Yesterday* by Jan Valtin. Comment on page 136 re: his litter-bearer buddies. Also page 80 in *The Good War* by Studs Terkel.

He married Mary May 26, 1941 and she died in 1945. They had five children: Mary, Stephen, Barbara, Laura and Nicholas; 10 grandchildren: Mary, Paul, Tom, Martie, John, Jennie, Joshua, Jason, Matt and Sara and two great-granddaughters, Amanda and Nika.

Presently he is trying to keep up with addictions: Bible, golf, Rush L, art, paperwork.

NORMAN R. GROETZINGER was inducted into the service on Dec. 30, 1948, and served with Co. E, 19th Inf. Regt. He participated in the Occupation of Japan. He was discharged with the rank of private first class. Dates served: June 1949 to January 1950.

ANDREW (ANDY) GROSS, born May 25, 1929, entered the US Army May 25, 1951. He received basic training at Fort Leonard Wood, MO. Served in Korea with 19th Inf. Regt., 24th Div. He was driver for Col. Riely of the 19th when the 24th Div. was replaced by the 40th Div. Andy, with the 24th, served the rest of his time at Camp Haugen, Japan.

Andy was discharged May 1953 and returned to North Dakota. He farmed all his life at Napoleon, ND.

He married Agnes Weigle and together they had eight children. Andy died in March 1988.

His military awards include the Korean Service w/Bronze Star, Good Conduct, United Nations Service, National Defense Service, Sharpshooter and Meritorious Service.

BENEDICT (BEN) GROSS, born Sept. 1, 1930, enlisted in the Army March 21, 1952. He received basic training at Fort Bliss, TX. Stations include: HQ & HQ Co. at Camp Haugen Japan from August 1952 to July 1953. Moved with 19th to Korea July 1953. September 1953 went to Koju-do, Korea guarding Chinese prisoners. Rotated home from Pusan February 1954.

He was discharged March 5, 1954 at Fort Carson, CO. His medals include Korean Service w/Bronze Service Star, Good Conduct, United Nations Service, National Defense Service and Meritorious Service.

His memorable experiences include entering the Army with only an eighth grade education. Through military and GI Bill he earned a GED, BS degree, MS degree in education in school administration. At age 60 he went back to school evenings and Saturdays for training in ministry. Now ordained deacon of Catholic church. He is a runner and has raced in the Boston Marathon.

He is married to Christina and they have raised eight children: Marie, Eileen, Carol, David, Paul, Joan, Sandra and Gary and eight grandchildren.

He has been a teacher and school administrator for 14 years. Employed as employment and training specialist with Employment and Training Administration of the US Dept. of Labor for 28 years. Retired and very involved doing volunteer work for the church.

Currently enjoying retirement and volunteer work for the church. His hobbies include: finishing basement in new house, running, biking and swimming.

CARL R. GROTH, born May 8, 1928, enlisted in the Army, February 1952. He received basic training at Fort Bliss, TX; August-September 1952, radar operator, 13th FABN, Hokkaido and Mt. Fuji, Japan; October-May 1953, post office specialist, 24th Div. HQ, Sendai and Camp Younghans, Japan; June-January 1954, post office manager, 24th Div., HQ Camp Younghans and Pusan, Korea.

Discharged Feb. 8, 1954 as corporal. His awards include the Korean Service Medal, United Nations Service Medal and the National Defense Service Medal.

He was employed 30 years with Burroughs Corporation (now UNISYS Corp.) as financial administrator and product distribution international manager; life member Livonia, Michigan, VFW Post 3941.

He is a 1950 graduate of the University of Michigan with BBA degree.

He married Stella Maria and they have two children, Karl and Kenneth and four grandchildren: Christopher, Emily, Jonathan and Zachary.

He is now retired and active with VFW Post 3941.

Works the tax season as income tax practitioner and play lots of golf.

CHARLES G. GUIDETTI, born Sept. 20, 1922 in Philadelphia, PA, received his basic training at Fort Stewart. Also stationed at Fort Monmouth and Fort Lewis and served in Korea. Assigned to 358th S/C AA Bn. February 1943. Served with 127th AA in Germany 1945-46.

Recalled to active duty October 1950. Served with D Co., 5th RCT until discharge in November 1954 as corporal. He received the Purple Heart and Combat Infantry Badge. Survived 28 months as POW of Chinese in Korea.

He has been married to Louise Rose for 45 years and they have four children: Frank, Chuck, Cindy and Monica; seven grandchildren: Frank, Chuck, Merissa, Alyassa, Matthew, Megan and Kaitlen. He is now retired and living in Florida. Survived 28 months as POW of Chinese in Korea.

LAWRENCE H. (LARRY) GUMP, born in New Martinsville, WV April 6, 1929, was drafted into service 1951 in Akron, OH.

His basic training was with 3rd Armd. Div. at Fort Knox, KY. He was sent to Korea to the 24th Inf. Div. as rifleman and medic. When the 24th Inf. was replaced in Korea, he served the 24th in Japan.

He was honorably discharged from service in October 1952. Totally disabled and service connected.

He married Alma M. Gump and they three children: Larry, Tim and Kellie. They also have three grandchildren: Adrian, Bryan and Samantha. He received an education as a general machinist certified by the State of California and became a manufacturing planer (industrial engineer).

He has a son who is a lieutenant in the Los Angeles County Sheriff's Dept.; a son who is an airplane pilot and president of the nation's largest aircraft supply company; his daughter was the secretary to the director of Sepulveda VA Medical Center. His wife was secretary to the chief of fiscal at West Los Angeles VA Medical Center for 18 years. He is currently hospitalized for total disability service connected at Sepulveda Medical Center for the rest of his life.

FRANKLIN D. HAAS joined the service on May 9, 1950, and served with Co. L, 5th RCT Regt. He was discharged with the rank of sergeant first class. Awards include the Korean Service Medal and four Bronze Stars. Dates served: September 1950 to August 1951.

KEITH HAGAN, born in Canada in 1930, enlisted in the US Army 1949.

His stations include: Basic H 12th, Leadership School, C, 8th, 4th Inf., Fort Ord; December 1949 - 35th Arty. School, D 87th, 10th Mountain Div., Fort Riley, Camp Funston. Volunteered Korea July 1950; assigned I 21st, 24th August 1950. He served as rifle-

man, runner, wireman, radio operator, HQ platoon sergeant.

He was awarded the Combat Infantry Badge 1950 and Korean War Medals 1991. July 1995, Seoul, Korean Peace Medal. Returned to US September 1951.

Served in the Honor Guard, Oakland Army Base; CBR School, Presidio San Francisco and Division Faculty, Camp Roberts. Discharged September 1952.

He worked as a boilermaker and pipefitter, retiring in 1985. Hagan enjoys home, RVing and other travel with wife, Anita. They attend as many reunions as possible. Have made many new friends; met seven from I 21st.

He corresponds with others, especially Col. Gib who has survived three wars and a deaf RTO. He and Anita have seven children between them: Steven, Gene, Doris, Gilbert, Sydna, Lyn and Vic, and seven grandchildren.

DONALD E. HAHN joined the service Dec. 13, 1948, and served with Co. D, 34th Regt. from March 1949 to September 1950 when he was reassigned to M Co., 19th Regt. until August 1951. From Pusan, South Korea to the Yalu River, North Korea then back to Pyongtaek, South Korea. He was injured Jan. 27, 1951, and returned to the States .

PAUL H. HALE joined the service on March 22, 1967, and served with Co. C, 3rd Eng. Bn., 24th Inf. Div., at Ft. Riley, KS. He participated in Reforger 1. Discharged with the rank of SP4. Awards include the National Defense Service Medal, Vietnam Service Medal, Vietnam Campaign Medal, two Overseas Bars, Army Commendation Medal w/V Device, Army Commendation Medal, Sharpshooter and Rifle Badges. Dates served: Sept. 13, 1968, to March 21, 1969.

EDWARD O. HALL enlisted in the USAC enlisted Reserves on Aug. 3, 1944; was ordered to active duty in the enlisted Reserves on Jan. 18, 1945; and remained on active duty until he retired on June 30, 1972.

Served with the Message Center Plt., 24th Sig. Co. as private first class from September 20 to November 1945; and private first class and T5 from March 1947 to August 1948. His last tour of duty was as a signal operations NCO with the 22nd Div. of the Vietnamese Army in 1971 and 1972.

Received the Pacific Theater of Operations Medal for his first tour of duty, then the Army of Occupation Medal w/Japan clasp.

FRANK B. HALL joined the service on Feb. 25, 1942, and served with B Btry., 63rd FA BN. Discharged with the rank of corporal. Dates served: 1942-43.

JOHN F. HAMILTON joined the service on Dec. 14, 1947, and served with HHC 1-R Plt., 14th Regt. Participated in Korea and all campaigns from June 1950 through May 1951. Remained active for 30 years. Retired in 1972 as an E-9.

DENNIS M. HANRICK joined the service on Jan. 3, 1946, and served with Co. F, 21st Inf. Regt. Participated in four campaigns in Korea; wounded in action on April 11, 1951; took four trips to Vietnam, two fall tours and two short tours; and was wounded in action on Aug. 13, 1963. Retired on Feb. 28, 1970, with the rank of lieutenant colonel. He was awarded the Combat Infantryman's Badge w/star.

MYRON J. HARBAND joined the service on Nov. 9, 1942, and served with HQ Co., 34th Regt. He participated in New Guinea, Hollandia, Biak, Leyte, Luzon and Mindanao. Discharged with the rank of staff sergeant. Dates served: Dec. 26, 1942, to Nov. 10, 1945.

ELMER J. HARRIS joined the service on July 1, 1942, and served with Co. A, 24th Med. Bn. He participated in the Pacific, New Guinea and was wounded at Hollandia on April 23, 1944. Discharged with the rank of major. He was awarded the Purple Heart. Dates served: July 1, 1942, to March 18, 1947.

WILLIAM F. HARRISON joined the service in March 1953, and served with HQ Co., 5th RCT Regt., 1953-54; HQ Co., 19th Inf. Regt., 1954; and 1st Bn. HQ, 34th Inf. Regt., 1954-55. Discharged with the rank of private first class.

PAUL W. HARTLEY joined the service on Feb. 28, 1942, and served with HQ Co., 1st Bn., 21st Inf. Regt., 24th Div. During his three years and three months as a member of the 24th Div., he soldiered in Hawaii, Australia, British New Guinea. He was in the beach landings in Dutch New Guinea, Leyte, Lubang, Mindoro and Mindanao. Discharged with the rank of T-5. Dates served: May 20, 1942, to Aug. 23, 1945.

ROBERT L. HARTLEY, born Dec. 13, 1930 in Mystic, CT and schooled in Mystic and Groton, CT, enlisted in the Army Jan. 6, 1948.

Assignments include basic at Fort Dix, NJ; Fort Sill, OK, April 1948-August 1949, 2nd Inf. Div., 2nd Armd. Div.; Camp Chickamauga, Beppu, Japan with 19th Inf. Regt., Co. B, 24th Inf. Div.; Korea, July 1950-May 1951, Fort Dix, NJ as drill instructor.

Discharged Jan. 6, 1952 as master sergeant. His awards include the Combat Infantry Badge, Bronze Star, Presidential Unit Citation, Korean Presidential Unit Citation, Korean Campaign w/5 Battle Stars and Occupation of Japan.

He started work one week after discharge and retired from Gen. Dynamics Electric Boat Div. in 1994 with 42 years of work.

He married Lila Higbee Sept. 6, 1952. Their children were born between 1953 to 1964: John, William, Linda, Nancy, Donald and James: 12 grandchildren and two great-grandchildren.

Enjoying retirement and grand and great-grandchildren. Wintering in Florida. He also enjoys camping, fishing and attending the 24th Div. Assoc. reunions.

EDWARD S. HARTO joined the service on Sept. 30, 1952, and served with the Tk. Co., 34th Inf. Regt. He was discharged with the rank of sergeant. Dates served: 1953-54.

ARTHUR L. HARVEY, born in Schenectady, NY April 17, 1926, graduated from Scotia High School in 1994. Inducted into service Dec. 13, 1944 in Albany, NY. Processed at Fort Dix, NJ, basic training at Camp Blanding, FL with status of antitank gun crewman.

Shipped out May 8, 1945, arriving in Leyte, PI the end of May. Assigned to the 24th Inf. Div., 34th Inf. Regt., Co. A on June 3, 1945. Sent to Mindanao and participated in the Southern Philippine campaign up the Kibawe Trail to Tamogan. Was saved by Japanese foxhole during the "friendly bombing" of June 24 at the Tamogan bridge crossing which killed five men and wounded 20. Fought past Tamogan toward Kibangay.

Evacuated to the 117th General Hospital, Leyte, diagnosed with hepatitis. Upon release from the hospital was assigned to Co. G, 34th Inf. Regt. in Japan to participate in the Japanese Occupation at Shikoku, Honshu and Kyushu. Discharged November 1946 with the rank of private first class.

His decorations include: Combat Infantry Badge, Asiatic-Pacific Campaign Medal w/Battle Star, Phil-

ippine Liberation Medal w/Battle Star, Philippine Independence Medal, Japanese Occupation Medal, Japanese Occupation Medal, Bronze Star, WWII Victory Medal and New York State Veterans Conspicuous Service Cross.

Harvey is not married, now retired and active in the Scotia Volunteer Fire Dept.

JOHNNY E. HAUGH, born Aug. 26, 1926, was drafted into the service Feb. 10, 1945.

He attended four weeks basic training at Camp Blanding, FL; two weeks of advance jungle training, Fort Ord, CA Went overseas to the Philippine Islands and joined the 24th Div. at Leyte Island. He was assigned to 21st Inf., 3rd Bn., 3rd Plt., Heavy Wpns., 81 mm mortar and 30 cal. water-cooled machine guns, then went to Japan in September 1945 for occupation duty. He was there until 1948. September 1950 he was called back to duty for the Korean Conflict, serving until 1951. Went to Japan again with 298th Engrs and discharged as tech sergeant.

He received the Combat Infantry Badge and other unknown awards.

Haugh worked for Frich Co., making ice machines, saw mills, farm machinery and refrigeration. He worked himself up the ladder to superintendent of the foundry. Now employed at the Borough of Waynesboro, PA as a maintenance man. He was superintendent of Sunday School at Grace Baptist Church. A Christian man, has received Christ as his personal savior.

He has been married to Martha Smiley for 48 years. They have a son, Larry; daughter, Rhonda and six grandchildren: Sherman, Joslyn and Briggs Haugh, Jamie, Tiffany and J.R. Dudick; three great-grandchildren: Natasha, Katrina and Justina.

Enjoys playing the clarinet for the Wayne Band and does woodworking.

RUDOLPH (RUDY) HAUKEBO, born Sept. 14, 1919, on his parent's farm between Battle Lake and Underwood, MN. He was drafted Feb. 3, 1942 and served with the 19th Inf..

He was assigned to Fort Snelling, Camp Wolters, Schofield Barracks, Chickamauga Park, Australia, New Guinea, New Britain, Leyte, Luzon and the Philippines.

He received the Combat Infantry Badge, Good Conduct Medal, Asiatic-Pacific Medal, Philippine Liberation Ribbon w/2 Bronze Stars and one Lapel Button.

Haukebo had two brothers who served in the military in the Philippines. One was wounded in action, losing two fingers and injured his hip. He had completed farm engineer and mamagement course before entering the service. After his time in the service he had a job waiting for him with Ford Tractor and Farm Equipment. He later worked for State Farm Insurance, 1955-88 when he retired.

He is a member of the VFW, American Legion, Lions Club, 4H leader and Red River Valley Council.

His children are Jeff, Craig and Kevin. He has four grandchildren: Angie and Beth (twins), Derek and Josh.

He volunteers everyday for a group who takes care of trees and shrubs for the Minnesota State Highway Dept.

WM. R HAURILAK, born Sept. 1, 1918, enlisted July 2, 1941. Received basic training at Camp Croft and served in the infantry and medical corp. He was a first aid man attached to Co. E, 34th Inf. Served in the Pacific areas as staff sergeant T-3. Ran the aid station, Medical Detachment Co. Dr. D.B. Cameron, MD, Co. E, 34th, CO E. Ross, captain.

Discharged July 14, 1945 as T-3 S/S. His awards include two Bronze Stars, Purple Heart and the usual other Army decorations.

Memorable experiences include rescuing a sick native chief and his niece on Mindanao Island in Jap territory via 16' native catamoran, May 1945. Capt. D.B. Cameron attended the sick chief.

Employed as printer, lithographer, pressman. He was a pressman foreman of a large lithographing corporation. Played some hard-ball baseball and fished, square danced in New England area.

His wife died in 1971. They had one daughter, Lorraine Rowley Danes and one grandchild. Now retired and working with stained glass, attending square dances, antiquing and traveling.

JOHN G. HAVERTY joined the service on Oct. 2, 1946, and served with Co. B, 19th Regt. He participated in Japan. Discharged with the rank of sergeant. Dates served: 1947.

THOMAS F. HAWKINS, born Aug. 23, 1927, enlisted in the Army (FA) Sept. 23, 1948. He served as No. 1 man on 155 howitzer all over Korea. He was discharged May 10, 1952 as private first class.

His awards include the Bronze Star and Purple Heart.

Memorable experiences: General Dean came by Hawkins' battery artillery the night before he was captured by the Koreans. They fired all day and until 5 a.m. the next day. Then the battery commander gave them permission to get some sleep. They were awakened at 8 a.m. that morning and told to go eat breakfast at the chow wagon. It was located below them in an old river bed.

The ROK troops pulled off the front line during the night and let the North Koreans come through.

He picked up his mess kit and headed toward the chow wagon. His mess kit had just been buffed, the sun was reflecting off it as he was walking toward the mess wagon. Suddenly machine gun fire started and was coming right at him. He threw his mess kit down and jumped in a small wash out as the bullets came right over him. He was unharmed but very shaken.

Hawkins is divorced and has three children: Thomas C., Joseph F. and Gary E.; seven grandchildren: Terry, Chad, Brad, Heather, Holley, Renee and Austin. He is now retired.

WILLIAM D. HAZLET JR., born March 17, 1928 in western Pennsylvania, entered the Army October 1950. He attended basic training at Camp Atterbury, IN. Went overseas February 1951 and was discharged July 1952. He was a medic with the 21st Inf., 24th Div. Left Korea February 1952, worked dispensary at Indiantown Gap several months before discharge in July 1952. In 1990 he joined the Moniteau

Ceremonial Squad to perform military funerals. He was with this group while they did over 200 funerals. His health required him to stop.

His special moment in the history of the 24th Div.: Near Thanksgiving 1951 Vice President Barkley visited their area. *Hazlet and another medic were under orders to be with the vice president. They were two aid men, picked out of about 100 men. They both got a new field jacket and a pair of pants. No matter he had not had a shower or changed underclothes for at least four or five months. The outside was new and clean.

*This event is pictured in the *24th Forward Book* which he purchased from Lt. Clifford Rench in 1951. The book was printed by Koyosha Printing Co. 15 Chome Ginzo Higoshi Chou-Ku, Tokyo Japan. He paid $5.00 for this book and would not give it up for any amount of money.

CARL R. HEAD joined the service on July 12, 1948, and served with Co. K, 34th Regt., January 1949 to 1950; and Co. F, 21st Regt., 1950 to August 1953. Was POW from April 1951 to August 1953. Discharged in August 1953 with the rank of sergeant.

WILLIAM P. HEALY, born Chicago, Sept. 27, 1932. Lane tech graduate, 1950. Drafted January 1953. Basic training, Leaders Course Class 100, Camp Roberts, CA. Cadre to escort first "Buddy System" to Korea. Assigned to Co. D, 34th Inf. Regt., 24th Div., 1953-54. 15 months staff sergeant.

Started from Pusan north to escort Chinese prisoners, who elected not return to China, from demilitarized zone to Inchon where they boarded ships to Formosa. Guarded train tracks while Indian troops were transported to Inchon from demilitarized zone. Returned to Pusan, moved north above 38th Parallel to new positions in March 1954 vacated by 40th, 45th Div.

His awards include National Defense Medal, United Nations Medal, Korean Service Ribbon and Republic of Korea Presidenital Unit Citation.

Married Barbara Kuczwara, August 1957 and they have two children, five grandchildren. He has been employed for 42 years as Hi-Rise masonry restorations contractor. He has been a member of Tuckpointers Local 52, for 48 years.

ROBERT J. HEATER joined the service in July 1950, and served the Co. Fox, 19th Regt. He participated in Korea. Discharged with the rank of corporal. He was awarded the Purple Heart w/cluster, but denied the Bronze Star due to loss of records by the government. Dates served: December 1950 to March 1951.

EDWIN C. HECKELSMILLER, born May 31, 1926 was drafted into the Army Jan. 13, 1945.

Inducted June 13, 1945 at Fort Snelling, MN. Took basic training as an infantryman at Fort Hood, TX. Had a five-day furlough and departed overseas Aug.

19, 1945. Landed in White Beach, Leyte, Philippines September 10. Later they moved their 24th Div. to Mindoro and Mindanao and into Japanese occupational troops. The 24th and 1st Cav. Div. were the first ones to land on Japan. He was put into the 52nd FA and later as a provisional MP Co. policing the islands. They were the first out to see the bridge and hole that the Hiroshima A bomb made after it was cleaned of radiation. Departed for US Sept. 16, 1946. Back in US Sept. 27, 1946. Discharged Nov. 15, 1946 as private first class.

His awards include the Victory Medal, Good Conduct Medal, Asiatic-Pacific Service Medal and Army of Occupation Medal (Japan).

Employed as construction worker (heavy equipment), diesel mechanic, carpenter, electrician, truck driver or jack-of-all trades. He built his home, a log house.

He married Donna Mae Heckels Miller and they have two children, Lou Ann Hutchins and Julene Tolle, and four grandchildren: Eric Davis, Chris Davis, Lori and Derick Hutchins.

Heckelsmiller now retired for six years has been traveling, camping, doing crafts and enjoying life.

JAMES HEILES, born Sept. 7, 1928, enlisted Oct. 2, 1952, AMEDS. His assignments include I.G.M.R. basic training (infantry); Camp Fuji, Japan, Medical Bn., 24th Div. from Kojedo Island to Yangu Valley, 24th Medical Bn.; February 1953-August 1954.

Discharged as staff sergeant and received the Bronze Star, Korean Service Medal, UN Medal, Commendation Medal, American Defense Medal and the Good Conduct Medal.

Employed as registered pharmacist and regional sales manager for a pharmaceutical company.

He is past president, Perry Hwy. Lions Club; past Grand Knight, Knights of Columbus 4029; former board member, University of Pittsburgh Pharmacy Alumni Assoc.

He married Anna Mae in 1951 and they have three children: James, Kenneth and David; six grandchildren: Jim, Joe, Jonathan, Katie, Holli and Jared. Now retired and volunteering at a local hospital, he is also a director on two corporate boards.

ROBERT A. HELEBRANDT joined the service on Dec. 3, 1948, and served with the 724th Ord. Co., 21st Inf. Regt. He participated in the Japanese Occupation. Discharged with the rank of sergeant. Awards include the Korean Service Medal w/6 Campaign Stars. Dates served: June 1949 to September 1951.

WALTER D. HELTON joined the service on June 15, 1940, and served with Co. H, 34th Regt., 24th Inf. Div. He participated in the Philippine Liberation, New Guinea, Luzon, Southern Philippines and Asiatic-Pacific Theater. Discharged with the rank of technical sergeant. Dates served: Jan. 14, 1944, to Sept. 15, 1945.

LINDSEY P. HENDERSON JR., born July 14, 1922, enlisted in Troop A, 108th Cav., Georgia National Guard in May 1940. He was working on an appointment, through the Guard, the US Military Academy at West Point, NY.

Called to service in February 1941, his unit was the first American battalion to go into action against the Japanese in the Southwest Pacific Area in Papua, New Guinea in May 1942.

During WWII, he received a battlefield appointment

as a second lieutenant, was wounded and could not pass the physical. He was later disabled out of service.

Just before graduation from the University of Virginia, he passed a physical and received his commission. He was called to active duty in the Pentagon in January 1949 and worked under Gen. Omar Bradley. He was the first "Editor of Officers' Call" and the only second lieutenant on active duty in the Pentagon.

Then on to Fort Benning, to Infantry School and the 30th Inf. Regt. From there to Japan and the 31st Inf. Regt. When the Korean War conflict broke out, he immediately volunteered and was transferred to the 21st Inf. Regt., 24th Inf. Div. which was fighting desperately to stem the N. Korean advance.

He was assigned to Co. L, a truly great, hard fighting unit. Wounded, he was evacuated to Japan and the States. After hospitalization, he was assigned to the 8th Inf. Div. at Fort Jackson, SC, a training division.

From there he was assigned to a Special Operations unit as he excelled in unconventional warfare. Then on to Taiwan, Matsu and Quemoy, Indo China, Vietnam, Cambodia and Laos. After all that, he returned to mundane duties as a sub-sector commander to the US Army Reserves in his hometown of Savannah, GA. There he trained infantry, transportation and medical units. He recruited, organized and trained a fine USAR Special Forces Detachment.

He was then assigned to 513th Military Intelligence Gp. at Camp King and then on to Berlin to command the 513th Military Intelligence Unit there. After a year he was returned to Camp King as deputy group commander. On his return to the States, he was hospitalized and retired on the disability list.

A combat infantryman and paratrooper, his decorations include the Silver Star w/3 OLC, Bronze Star w/V device and OLC, the Army Commendation w/ OLC, the Purple Heart w/3 OLCs, the Presidential Unit Badge, WWII and OLC (Korea), Combat Stars for WWII, Korea and Vietnam. He also received the Freedom's Foundation of Valley Forge, Pennsylvania George Washington Patriots award in 1966. He received additional Freedom Foundation Awards in 1972 and 1978. He received the top "Commendation" from the American Association of State and Local History and is a Fellow and Governor of the Company of Military Historians. He has written for the Combat Forces Journal *Company "L's" Four Days* and *My ROKS Were Good.*

He has been married to the former Eve Whitfield of Savannah for 54 years and they have four children: Daniel, Frank, Elizabeth McDonald and Sarah Fawcett and five grandchildren.

ROBERT L. HENDRIX joined the service in November 1944 and served with Co. A, 34th Regt. He participated in the South Pacific, Southern Philippines, Occupation of Japan (special services). Discharged with the rank of private first class.

JD HENLEY joined the service in October 1943 and was assigned to Co. B, 63rd Tk. Bn., 13th Regt, Camp Fannin, Tyler, TX. He participated in Buna, New Guinea, with Co. B, 19th Inf. from April 1944 until Dec. 31, 1945; New Guinea, Leyte, Romblon, Samar, Mindoro, Mindanao and Kochi City, Japan.

WAYNE J. HICKS, born Sept. 17, 1929, enlisted in the Army Nov. 12, 1950.

Assigned to Fort Jackson, SC for basic training. After basic assigned to cadre, Fort Jackson. On Aug. 1, 1951, volunteered for Korea to join the 24th Div., Co. A, 19th Inf. Regt. as squad leader, first squad. Discharged Nov. 12, 1952 as a corporal.

His awards include the Japan Occupational Medal, Korean Service Medal w/three Bronze Stars, UN Medal and Combat Infantry Badge.

After discharge returned home and worked for Mapes Piano Storage Co. for 39 years, retiring in 1995.

He is married to Ruby Irene and they have children, Diane and Steve and two grandchildren, Jacob and Emily. He is now retired.

DALE E. HIGBEE, born July 9, 1922, enlisted March 1940, serving with the 19th Inf.

His assignments include basic training at Schofield Barracks, Honolulu, TH; Australia, New Guinea, drill instructor, 203 ITB, Camp Blanding, FL.

Discharged at Fort Logan, CO July 1945 as staff sergeant. His awards include Infantry Combat, Bronze Star, American Defense w/Bar, Asiatic-Pacific, WWII, Good Conduct, Pearl Harbor Survivors Ribbon and Medal.

He worked 32 years for Mountain Bell. Married to Dorris Maurine and they have four children: Sandra Pribble, Richard, Vickie, Sallie and grandchildren: David Pribble, Suzann Rickens, Michael Higbee; and four great-great-grandchildren.

Presently he is volunteering at VFW Club and local charities.

GILBERT G. HILKEMEYER, born July 27, 1919, commissioned a second lieutenant infantry USA via: CMTC/ENL, RES. Jan. 16, 1941 WWII active duty; 816 TD Bn. May 24-1942-Sept. 27, 1944; K Co., 19th Inf. Regt., 24th Div. Oct. 4, 1944; Cannon Co., 19th Inf. Regt., March 27, 1945. Regt. S4 19th Inf. Regt. July 1, 1945; D Co. 19th Inf. Regt., Aug. 13, 1945-Oct. 29, 1945.

Attended military schools, Infantry School Jan. 29, 1942; TD School Jan. 12, 1943.

Relieved from active duty March 12, 1946 as captain. His awards include the Combat Infantry Badge, Bronze Star Medal w/OLC. Retired from the Reserves July 27, 1979 as lieutenant colonel. He is married to Emma Lock and they have five children.

JAMES E. HILL joined the service on July 19, 1943, and served with Co. G, 19th Regt. He participated at New Guinea and Leyte. He was killed in action on Leyte, on Nov. 16, 1944.

JAMES F. HILL joined the 24th Div. in July 1949 and was assigned to HQ, 1st Bn., 19th Regt. He participated in the first five campaigns in Korea: UN Defensive, UN Offensive, CCF Intervention, First UN Counter Defense and CCF Spring Offensive. Discharged with the rank of 1st lieutenant. He was awarded

the Combat Infantryman's Badge. Dates served: 1949-51.

RICHARD Y. HIRATA was inducted into the service on April 23, 1941, and served with the 24th Div., 34th Regt. He participated in Leyte, Bataan, Corregidor, Hollandia and Mindanao. Discharged with the rank of T4.

KEITH A. HIRSCH joined the service on Sept. 15, 1946, and served with Co. L, 21st Regt. He was discharged with the rank of sergeant. Dates served: December 1946 to February 1948.

EUGENE E. HITZEMAN joined the service in November 1942 and served with HQ Co., 2nd Bn, 21st Inf. Regt. He participated in Dutch New Guinea and the Philippines. Discharged with the rank of staff sergeant. Dates served: 1942-45.

EARL ROSCOE HOBNET joined the service on Dec. 13, 1941, and served with the 5th Combat Regt., 24th Inf. Div. He participated in WWII and Korea. From March 12, 1958, to Feb. 12, 1959, he served with the Imperial Iranian Armed Forces. He was discharged on Aug. 31, 1966, with the rank of master sergeant. He was awarded the Silver Star, Bronze Star, Meritorious Service Award and several clusters on his campaign ribbons. He passed away on July 11, 1995.

EVERT E. "MOOSE" HOFFMAN, born Nov. 3, 1920, Locust Dale, Columbia County, PA, enlisted in the Army April 1, 1941 for Hawaiian Islands. Assigned to 64th AAA, Fort Shafter, TH. Received recruit training administered by regimental cadre. After Japan attacked Pearl Harbor on Dec. 7, 1941 he served in various operations in Asiatic-Pacific Theater until December 1944 when he rotated to CONUS from Guam and assigned to Fort Dix, NJ.

Hospitalized with malaria and for surgery. Reenlisted for airborne. After completion of airborne training at Fort Benning, GA he was assigned to 82nd Abn. Div., Fort Bragg, NC. Reassigned to 19th Inf., 24th Inf. Div., May 1948.

Korea: July 1950-June 1951, D Co., 19th and HQ 1st Bn., 19th. Received battle field commission July 21, 1950. Reassigned CONUS June 1951, 9th Inf. Div., Fort Dix, NJ. June 1953 assigned to Panama Canal Zone, 33rd Inf. Fort Kobbe. 1955 reassigned HQ Caribbean Command, Quarry Heights, Canal Zone.

1956 returned to CONUS assigned HQ USATC, Fort Dix, NJ. Served in various assignments as company commander, BN EXO, S-3 and G-3.

Attended Infantry Company Officers Course, Fort Benning, GA. 1952 Advanced Infantry Officers Course, Fort Benning, GA 1956-57. In each of both, graduated in top two percent of class. Completed Mountain Climbing Instructor Course, Fort Greely, AK 1959. Wounded in Korea July and September 1950.

His awards include the Silver Star, Bronze Star, Purple Heart, Army Commendation Medal, Combat Infantry Badge. Retired 1963 from Army as major.

Employed at NJ DOT 1963-66; HQ Fort Dix, NJ civilian range officer 1966-83. Fully retired.

Married Beulah R. Johnson "Boots" Dec. 19, 1944. They had two children, Leah Jean (deceased) and Irma R. Brungard and two grandchildren, Evert C. Brungard and Erik Edwin Brungard.

Retired and living in Pennsylvania. He is a life member of the 24th Inf. Div., Pearl Harbor Survivors

Assoc., DAV, VFW, American Legion, M.L. Order Purple Heart, National Order Battlefield Commissions (Mustang), Korean Veterans Assoc.

Fraternal organizations include: Masonic Lodge 414, Shrine, Tall Cedars of Lebanon, National Sojourners.

HAROLD H. HOLBROOK enlisted on Jan. 13, 1948, at Aurora, IL, with the 44th Div., ILNG. Federalized in February 1952; shipped to Japan, November 1952; assigned to the 13th FA BN, December 1952. Served with the 24th Div. as acting motor pool sergeant, December 1952 to September 1953; and served in Korea from late June 1953 to early September 1953 at Camp Yeong Wal. He was discharged on Jan. 13, 1954, with the rank of corporal.

WILBUR L. HOLLAND, born Dec. 25, 1924, grew up a farm boy near King City, MO. He went into the Army in 1944, Inf. 34th Co. C.

Fought in Leyte, Luzon, Mindoro and Mindanao. After the war was in Japan on occupation duty. Discharged Aug. 20, 1946. His awards include the Combat Badge, Good Conduct, Bronze Star, Asiatic-Pacific w/two Bronze Stars, R Badge, Philippine Liberation w/two Bronze Stars, Occupation Medal, Philippine Presidential Medal.

He returned home to the farm and has done many jobs including: billboard poster, bookmobile driver, packing house company, school bus driver and maintenance engineer at a school where he retired in 1986.

Commander American Legion, P.P. Eastern Star, Master Mason, VFW.

He has been married twice and has a daughter Joan Comfort, two sons Kenneth W. and Robert D. Holland, three grandsons, one stepson, two step-grandsons and three step-granddaughters, one foster sister, two step-nieces and their children plus a lot of other relatives.

He has had 38 radiation treatments for prostate cancer, open heart surgery, stroke, hernia operation and still going strong.

ERNEST L. HOLLAR, born March 9, 1912 was inducted into service June 10, 1941 and sent to Camp Wolters, TX until Oct. 3, 1941. Discharged to Enlisted Reserve because of 28-year law. When Pearl Harbor started was called back Feb. 16 until Nov. 3, 1945, Inf., Automotive Maintenance Service on gasoline powered motor vehicles and trucks.

Military education at Detroit Sec. Ord. School, wheel vehicles engine, two week, Cleveland, Sec. Ord., three weeks August 1943. He was at Fort Brady, MI, Sept. 9, 1942-43, Guard Locks at Sault St. Marie, MI, also locks on Canada. Sent to San Francisco, CA Sept. 24, 1944-45 to New Guinea on to Leyte, Mindanao and other islands.

His awards include the American Theater, American Defense Ribbon, Asiatic-Pacific Ribbon w/two Bronze Stars, Philippine Theater Ribbon w/two Bronze Stars, Good Conduct Ribbon and WWII Victory Medal.

Discharged Dec. 3, 1945 and served four years 18 months, 14 days. Worked in the motor pool and made a five star plate out of medal from a Japanese airplane wing for Gen. MacArthur when in area on his jeep. Others didn't know. Also landed on Leyte and a Jap plane flew into boat the next morning.

Honorably discharge technician 4th grade, 24th Inf. Married Marie and they have two sons, Stanley and

Rodney; three grandchildren: Tami, Julie and Mitch; two great-grandchildren. After the Army he resided on a farm with his wife's parents. He died in 1995. His wife and sons still reside on the farm.

JOHN E. HOOVER, born April 28, 1924, Timberville, VA, enlisted in 1942 and took signal basic training at Fort Monmouth, NJ in 1943. Discharged to enter USMA 1944. Commissioned second lieutenant Signal Corps 1947. Joined 24th Signal Co., 24th Div. July 1948, remaining until March 1951, including duty as CO, 21st Inf. Regt. April-June 1949. Ordered to the Signal Training Center, Camp Gordon, GA. Then received an MA from Georgetown University and taught Political Science at USMA. After C&GSC served as S-3 516th Signal Gp., CO 29th Signal Bn., and at USAREUR. After USAWC served in OASD-ISA, at CINCPAC, and then commanded the Regional Communications Gp. in Vietnam. Spent the next three years on the DA Staff in the Office of the Assistant Chief of Staff for Comm-Electronics. After a year as deputy CG of the Army Communications Command became the director of the Defense Joint Tactical Communications Office. Retired as major general April 1, 1978. Decorations include the Distinguished Service Medal, Legion of Merit, Bronze Star Medal, Meritorious Service Medal and Air Medal. Now serving as the Historian Emeritus of the US Army Signal Regt.

Married Mary Jo Cox in 1953. They have two daughters, Kate, a lawyer and artist; and Holly, mother of Maggy and James and married to LTC Stephen Bullock.

JAMES H. HOPKINS joined the service on Sept. 23, 1948. He participated in Korea from July 4, 1950, to July 4, 1951. He was discharged with the rank of sergeant first class. Dates served: Sept. 23, 1948, to May 14, 1952.

WILLIAM C. (BILL) HOSLER, born Dec. 31, 1931, Newsville, PA, joined the Army Jan. 7, 1949. Basic training at Camp Pickett, VA. Joined F Co., 19th Inf. Regt. May 1949 in Beppu, Japa, Co. G, 30th Inf. Regt., Fort Benning, GA, Infantry School.

Went to Korea with the division. The first battle was the Kum River; second battle, Taejon; third battle, Chinyu. Following was the Pusan Perimeter. They traveled twice to P'ohang prior to the offensive north. He was squad point man with BAR, leading the tank column at the time they entered Taejon. Stayed with the unit all the way through North Korea and return. Was wounded on January 3 just north of Seoul. Sent by rail to Swedish hospital in Pusan for surgery, then on to Tokyo Army hospital and to Yokohama hospital. Later to hospital in Fort Devens, MA. September 1951 back to duty at Fort Benning, GA. He served under his old commander in Korea, Gen. Church and Gen. Meloy.

Discharged May 1952 with the rank of sergeant. He was awarded the Combat Infantry Badge, Purple Heart, Bronze Star, Occupation Medal, UN Medal, Korean Service Medal, Good Conduct Medal, National Defense Service Medal and South Korean Presidential Unit Citation.

Memorable experiences: first combat action they lost their chaplain, Capt. Felhoelter on July 16 at Kum River. Hosler was in his jeep shortly before the captain was KIA. He stated that he had to stay with the wounded. They abandoned vehicles and headed for the hills as there was a roadblock ahead.

Employed for Defense Depot, Defense Logistics Agency, Mechanicsburg, PA. Retired after 38 years. Worked 9-1/2 years for book of the month club.

Married to Patricia "Pat" and they have sons, Jeffery and Gregory, and two grandchildren, Nathan and Ashley. Retired and recovering from complete knee replacement.

DAVID E. HOSTERMAN joined the service in September 1942 and served with the 2nd Bn., HQ Co., 21st Inf. Regt. He participated in the South Pacific, New Guinea, Hollandia, Leyte, Mindoro and Mindanao. Discharged with the rank of staff sergeant. Dates served: September 1942 to November 1995.

PHILIP H. HOSTETTER joined the service in 1943 and served with the 1st Bn., Regt. HQ, 19th Regt. Participated in Hollandia, Leyte, Mindoro, Simara, Romblon, Mindanao and Japan. Discharged with the rank of captain. Dates served: 1943-45.

LEWIS R. HOWELL, born July 22, 1928 in Coalinga, CA, enlisted in the Army Sept. 10, 1946 at Bakersfield, CA. After basic training at Fort McClellan, AL, he was assigned to Co. D of the 21st Inf. Regt., 24th Inf. Div at Camp Wood, Kumamoto, Japan, arriving on New Years Day 1947. In September 1947 he was assigned to HQ I Corps G3 Sect. and later to HQ 24th Inf. Div. TI&E Section where he wrote scripts for AFRS station WLKH in Kokura and sports and events columns for *V-Day*, the division newspaper. He was discharged in the summer of 1949 at Fort Lawton, WA. Received the Army of Occupation Medal, Japan. Employed as Army Intelligence and Security Activities 1953-64, school teacher 1965-84, retail sales 1984-94.

He married Suzuko and is now retired.

FREDERICK HOYT joined the service on May 5, 1942, and served with Serv. Btry., 52nd FA BN. Participated in the landing at Tanahmerah and went from the 24th Div. to ATIS-GHQ, USAFE. Discharged on Aug. 9, 1944, with the rank of 1st lieutenant.

ROBERT M. HUBBELL, born Oct. 1, 1938 in Charlotte, VT, enlisted in the Army October 1955, Fort Dix, NJ for basic training; advanced training in Fort Leonard Wood, MO, then went to Fort Carson, CO for fireman duty. He was sent to Camp Hale, CO for cold weather and mountain training. Arrived in Korea in October 1956 and was sent to 34th Regt. K Co., Weap-

ons Plt., 60mm Mortar Sqdn. where he spent a good many cold nights in the field.

He was sent on a 10 mile hike for talking back to first sergeant with full field pack and 60mm mortar, one hell of a day and a lesson to learn to keep your mouth shut. September 1957 sent to 1st Cav. Div., 23rd Transportation on DMZ. Fort Meade, MD in December 1957. Made sergeant in February 1957.

Discharged 1958 October. He has been employed driving a truck for over 40 years. He has one son, Mark, who is 27 years old and a Marine.

GEORGE D. HUDSON, born Dec. 8, 1927, enlisted in the Army Sept. 15, 1946.

His locations and positions included: 19th Inf. Regt., 2nd Bn., 24th Inf. Div., B Co., rifleman, 2nd Tour DI. Basic training, Fort Dix, NJ. He was discharged February 1948 as private first class; February 1952, sergeant first class.

Awarded the WWII Victory Medal, Army of Occupation Medal, Expert Infantryman Badge and the Good Conduct Medal w/Bar.

Memorable experiences include serving first in Cannon Co. (Capt. Longey); after Cannon Co. disbanded served B Co. (Capt. Pierce Reeder). Recalled during Korean Conflict and served as DI until discharged. Served 19th with Sgt. John Haverty, still in contact.

Employed as automotive design engineer, now semi-retired. He is married to Joyce and they have two children: Donald and Beverly. Donald is a Navy vet. They also have six grandchildren: Chris, Donald, Jonathon, Douglas, Alex, Steffane. Still can wear old uniform. He has regimental crest painted on hood of car.

EDWARD E. HULTS joined the service in September 1946 and served with Btry. A, 11th FA BN. He participated in the Japanese Occupation. Discharged with the rank of sergeant. Dates served: December 1946 to December 1947.

BJ HUNT was inducted into the service on March 3, 1943, and served with Co. C, Co. B and Regimental HQ; 19th Inf. Regt. He participated in seven campaigns in Korea.

JUDSON P. HURD joined the service on Feb. 3, 1941, and served with HQ Btry., 13th FA BN. Participated in the Pacific and Pearl Harbor. Discharged with the rank of technical sergeant. Dates served: Feb. 3, 1941, to March 1943. He was killed in action on Oct. 3, 1951, in Korea.

BOYCE HUSON joined the service on June 16, 1939, and served with HQ and MP Co., Hawaiian Div., 1939-41; and HQ and MP Co., 24th Div. Discharged with the rank of sergeant. Awards include the Asiatic-Pacific w/Battle Star, ETO and two Battle Stars.

MATT M. HUSS entered the service on Feb. 6, 1942; attended basic in Camp Walters, TX; and assigned to Co. H, 21st Regt. He was shipped over to Hawaii on June 6, 1942; then to Australia, July 1943; and Good Enough Island, March 1944. Landed in New Guinea on April 20, 1944, at Humbold Bay; then went to the Philippines in October 1944, on to Leyte, to Mindoro. He wound up in Mindanao and was wounded in August. Discharged on Nov. 6, 1945, with the rank of staff sergeant.

CHARLES HUTTINGER, born Feb. 22, 1929, enlisted in the Army January 1951. His assignments include Korea and Japan. Discharged October 1952 as private first class.

He received the Combat Infantryman Badge and Purple Heart.

He is a retired airline pilot. Married to Fern and they have three children: Mike, Denise and Ben.

JAMES H. HYATT joined the service on Nov. 28, 1948, and served with Co. D, 6th Tk. Bn. Participated in Korea from July 1950 to July 1951. Discharged with the rank of sergeant. Dates served: May 1949 to July 10, 1951.

NIILO MATT HYYTINEN joined the service on June 5, 1944, and served with HQ Btry., 11th FA BN. Participated in Leyte, Mindoro and Mindanao. Discharged with the rank of T-4. June 5, 1944, to May 11, 1946.

LESLIE A. INGELSON, born Jan. 5, 1910 in Moline, SC enlisted Oct. 21, 1942 and served with the 24th Medical Bn.

Assignments include basic training at Camp Stoneman, HI; maneuvers in Rockhampton, Queensland, Australia; fought in Hollandia, New Guinea battle; Goodenough Island battle; Leyte invasion and Romblon and Mindoro battles, South Philippines.

Discharged Dec. 3, 1945 as corporal technician fifth grade. His awards include the Victory Medal, Asiatic-Pacific Theater Ribbon w/two Bronze Battle Stars, Philippine Liberation Ribbon w/two Bronze Battle Stars, six Overseas Service Bars, Service Stripe, Good Conduct Medal, Meritorious Unit Award, Bronze Arrowhead, WWII Victory, American Campaign, Asiatic-Pacific Campaign.

Memorable experiences: As a surgical technician, he set up a medical aid station in Japanese-captured Romblon Island. It is here he delivered medicine to a Filipino family which developed into a lifelong friendship.

He married Verna Johnson Nov. 2, 1947 and had two daughters. Retired from Farmall Works. Belongs to American Legion, VFW and Masons.

FREDERICK A. IRVING entered USMA from Massachusetts and graduated in Class of April 1917. Served with 5th Infantry Division AEF in World War I. Commandant of Cadets USMA 1941-42. In World War II, as Major General, commanded the 24th Division during the Hollandia and Leyte campaigns and the 38th Division on Luzon. Deputy Commanding General Sixth Army 1950-51, Superintendent USMA 1951 until retirement as Major General in 1954.

FRANK E. ISBRECHT enlisted in the service on June 8, 1946, and entered active duty in 1947. He served with A Co., 19th Regt. He was discharged in 1950 from the USAR with the rank of technical sergeant. Awards include the WWII Victory Medal, Occupation Medal of Japan, UN Service Medal, Bronze Star Medal, Korean Service Medal w/4 Bronze Service Stars, Combat Infantryman's Badge and Good Conduct Medal.

JAMES N. JACK joined the service on Feb. 14, 1948, and served with HQ & HQ, 19th Regt. He participated in the UN Defensive, UN Offensive, CCF Intervention, 1st UN Counter Offensive, CCF Spring Offensive and authority DAGO 80-54. He was discharged with the rank of sergeant first class. Dates served: June 1948 to June 1951.

EDWARD V. (ED) JACKSON, born March 26, 1939, enlisted Feb. 3, 1959, Army.

In July 1959, after basic training at Fort Jackson, SC, he was assigned to Fort Benning, GA with the Infantry School. They wore the "Follow Me" patch. January 1, 1960 he arrived in Germany and was assigned to 1st Bomb Gp., 21st Inf., 24th Div.

Discharged March 28, 1962 Spec. E4. His awards include the National Defense Service, Good Conduct and Combat Infantry Badge.

Employed 1962-73 National Cash Register; 1976-72, self-employed Allied Business Systems; 1994-present, Lowes Home Improvement.

Self-employed 17 years. Volunteer fireman and fire chief. As a result of Army training, now serving with fire department. He has over the past 25 years saved two lives in two separate car wrecks. Went back to Germany in 1980 for vacation. Went to Fort Stewart, GA to welcome 24th back from Desert Storm.

Married Kathleen Marquette April 26, 1986, his birthday he has two children: Edward Jr., currently USCG, Dawn and three stepchildren. They also have 10 grandchildren, including step. One of his daughters died at age four. He would like to go to Germany to visit Berlin in early year 2000.

JULIUS JANZ joined the service on Feb. 4, 1941, and served with Co. A, 19th Regt. He was stationed in the Southwest Pacific, New Guinea and the Philippines. He was discharged with the rank of technical sergeant.

EDWARD J. JARMUSZKA joined the service in 1952 and served with C Co., 6th Tk. Bn., 24th Div. He was stationed in Korea. He was discharged with the rank of corporal. Dates served: 1953-54.

JEFF JEFFREY joined the service on May 30, 1969, and served with Btry. A, 5th Bn., 521st ADA Regt., 1976-78; and the 1st Bn., 5th Air Attack Arty., 1988-90. He achieved the rank of lieutenant colonel.

SPENCER S. JENKINS, born Nov. 18, 1926, in Wildwood, GA was drafted in the Army on Jan. 23, 1945. Took infantry basic training in 1945 at Camp Blanding, FL. Departed overseas July 21, 1945 and arrived on the Island of Luzon near Manila in the Philippines Aug. 19, 1945. Transferred later to the Island of Mindanao. Left the Philippines to go to the Island of Shikoku for the Occupation of Japan near the town of Matsuyama. Transferred to other camps with the 63rd FABN, 24th Inf. Div. near towns such as Niihama, Himeji, Mitsuhama and Tokushima.

Discharged Nov. 18, 1946 at Fort Sam Houston, TX with the rank of corporal. His awards include the Asiatic-Pacific Campaign Ribbon, WWII Victory Ribbon, Army of Occupation of Japan, Rifle Marksman, two Overseas Bars.

Retired from the Tennessee Valley Authority Power Co. after 34 years of service.

CHARLES W. JEREMIAH joined the service on June 30, 1945, and served with Co. C, 21st Regt.

He participated in the UN Defensive and Task Force Smith. He was discharged with the rank of sergeant. Dates served: April 1949 to September 1950.

CHARLES W. JOHNSON, born March 13, 1931, in Camden, OH, was inducted into the Army Jan. 8, 1948. Assigned to Fort Jackson, SC for basic training. Arrived in Japan August, 1948, served nine months at GHQ in Tokyo as an honor guard. Transferred to Co. A, 34th Inf. Regt., 24th Inf. Div., Sasebo, Japan, April 1949. Served as BAR man, later as a rifleman in Korea. Wounded at Taejon July 1950. After two months in a Tokyo hospital, sent to Kobe. Returned home November 1951. Assigned Induction Center, Camp Crowder, MO January 1952. Discharged from Camp Atterbury, IN March 6, 1954 as a staff sergeant. Most honored possession is the Combat Infantry Badge.

Retired 1993 from Belden Corporation, Richmond, IN after 38 years as mechanic and inspector. He and his wife, Irene live in Cincinnati. They have eight children and 17 grandchildren. Activities include corresponding via computer with family and friends. The 34th still lives.

EDWARD F. JOHNSON joined the service on June 24, 1940, and served with the 24th QM Co., 24th Inf. Div. He was stationed at Schofield Barracks, Australia, Pearl Harbor, New Guinea, Philippines and Leyte. He was discharged with the rank of staff sergeant. Dates served: June 24, 1940, to May 18, 1945.

GLEN A. JOHNSON joined the service in April 1945 and served with HQ Co., HQ Regt. He participated in the Occupation of Japan. He was discharged with the rank of T-4. Dates served: October 1945 to October 1946.

RODNEY W. JOHNSON, born Aug. 29, 1927 Luck, WI, enlisted in the Army Oct. 4, 1946 in St. Paul, MN. Received basic training at Fort Knox, KY. Arrived in Japan, Jan. 5, 1947. Served with L Co., 34th Inf. Regt. at Camp Ainoura at Sasebo, Kyushu until April 1947. Transferred to the 24th Div. School Center at Kokura as a student and later as an instructor in the Armorer Section. August 1947, transferred back to the 34th Regt. Service Co. in Sasebo as a regimental armorer where he served until being discharged in April 1948.

After discharge, he attended college at Waldorf Lutheran College and University of Wisconsin at River Falls.

He and his wife Carol live in Santa Rosa, CA. He was previously married to the late Lynn Herbert Johnson. He has four children: Steve, Vicky, Deborah and Matthew and three stepchildren: Kathy, Donald and Nikki. He also has five grandchildren: Abigail, Christiana, Alexandria, Carolanne and Treyton.

He has been involved in egg production farming, equipment rental and property management. He is now semi-retired and loves to RV when possible and enjoys visiting his family.

ALFRED J. JONES, born March 10, 1917 in Liverpool England, came to the US in 1925 and lived in New Jersey. He was living in California when war broke out and was drafted into the Army November 1942, Sacramento, CA. Shipped out to Hawaiian Islands, received basic training at Schofield Barracks and was assigned to Co. C, 34th Inf. Regt. Shipped out to Australia for jungle training. Met his brother whom he hadn't seen in 10 years. He was in the Seabees, attached to the 1st Marines.

He was shipped out to Goodenough Island to prepare for the invasion of Hollandia in Dutch New Guinea. After Hollandia was secured he was promoted to staff sergeant. They were sent to the Island of Biak fighting Jap marines.

After Biak he went back to Hollandia to prepare for the invasion of the Philippines. After fighting on Leyte for a couple of weeks he was wounded and shipped back to Hollandia, and then back to US. After spending time in William Beaumont Hospital in El Paso, TX and then Camp Pickett, VA, he was discharged in August 1945.

IVINS E. JONES, born June 30, 1931 in St. George, UT, enlisted in Army January 1949 at Fort Douglas, UT. Received basic training with 22nd Regt., 4th Div., Fort Ord, CA. Assigned to several different 3rd Army units at Fort Jackson, SC and Fort Bragg, NC, including 11th Regt., 5th Div. and 14th QM Bn., 18th Abn. Corps. Participated with the 82nd Abn. Div. in three major field training maneuvers; operations "Tar Heel" and "Swarmer" in North Carolina and Operation Portrex in the Caribbean.

Was retained at Fort Bragg during the first year of the Korean War as cadre to train incoming personnel and activating new units. Was sent to Korea August 1951 and assigned to 5th RCT. After contracting malaria was reassigned to 24th QM Co. as sergeant in charge of P.O.L. Supply. Returned to Japan in February 1952 along with other support units and the 21st Regt. was stationed at Camp Schlimmelpfennig, Northern Honshu for occupation duty, rebuilding of units and training.

Discharged at Camp Stoneman, CA July 17, 1952 with the rank of sergeant first class. Service with the 24th Div. was 11 months, August 1951-June 1952.

Married Thirza Hardy October 1953. They have four children and 11 grandchildren. Retired as purchasing manager from Titanium Metals Corp., "Timet", after 37 years. He is a life member of VFW and long term member of American Legion.

JACK JORGENSEN, born March 24, 1924 enlisted in the infantry June 18, 1943.

He received training at Camp Roberts, CA Infantry Replacement Training Center, then was assigned as cadre at the IRTC School, Camp Roberts. He then went overseas in August 1944. Assigned to 34th Regt. in October 1944 and pulled out day before the regiment left for Leyte. Assigned to 24th Div. HQ where he re-

mained until returning to the states in January 1946 as tech sergeant. Discharged Jan. 31, 1946

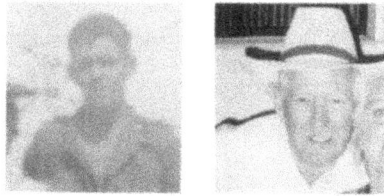

He received the usual campaign ribbons, Bronze Arrowhead for Leyte, Good Conduct Ribbon, etc. Recalled into service October 1950 and to Chemical Corp., Camp Atterbury, IN until released August 1951.

Employed in the construction business and retail lumber business. Owned his own business in Eau Claire, WI until retiring in 1989. Started Jorgensen Construction and Design Company. Presently still working.

Memorable experiences: nothing spectacular. September 1944 he was lost in jungle at Buna, New Guinea for 18 hours along with two others at the replacement depot. They found an Australian outpost and returned to replacement depot.

He is married to Christel and has four children and two stepchildren: Kathy, John, Barbara, Kari, Boyd and Marla; nine grandchildren: Corey, Shannon, Erin, Brook, Eric, Charesse, Kayla, Keish and Bret; one great-granddaughter, Mackenzie.

He is still in the construction and design business, but limited. He also works part-time at a lumber company as an estimator.

JAMES O. JOYAL, born Nov. 22, 1922, enlisted in the Army April 6, 1943.

His assignments included HQ Co. 264th Inf., 66th Inf. Div., Camp Blanding, FL. Promoted in grade to staff sergeant as message center chief. Sent as replacement to New Guinea. Assigned to G Co., 34th Inf. September 1944. After Leyte was transferred to HQ Co., 2nd Bn., 34th Inf. Message Center Section for remainder of Philippine Operation. After recuperation on Mindoro took part in Mindanao campaign, then occupation duty in Matsuyama, Japan. Returned to US December 10 and was discharged at Camp Devens, MA on Dec. 24, 1945. He has many good memories and does not dwell on the bad.

Discharged as T/5 Dec. 24, 1945. His awards include the Purple Heart, Combat Infantry Badge, Bronze Star, Good Conduct, American Theatre, Asiatic-Pacific Theatre, Philippine Liberation and Japanese Occupation.

Employed as service technician for Tecnifax Corp. installing and servicing Diazo printing machines and micro film processing equipment for the area east of the Mississippi and Eastern Canada.

Memorable experiences: Will always remember the overall experiences of day-to-day living in the Leyte, Bataan, Mindoro, Mindanao, combat, and his short occupation duty in Matsuyama Japan. Wounded in Zig Zag Pass Feb. 4 and 5, 1945, probably worst episode of the war.

His wife, Rose, died May 9, 1997 and they have four children: Rosemary, Sandra, James, Jeanne and Theresa and eight grandchildren: Andrew, Jeffery, Shannon, Kelly, Kevin, John, Brian and Jennifer; four great-grandchildren: Kiersten, Siobhan, Connor and Collin.

Retired, his hobbies include woodworking and crafts.

ALBERT P. JUNGBLUT JR. joined the Regular Army on Sept. 16, 1940, and served with the 24th Div. Arty. He was stationed at Pearl Harbor, Hollandia, Leyte and Mindoro. He was discharged with the rank of master sergeant. He received a Bronze Star w/OLC in Leyte.

MELVIN F. KAHLE joined the service on Oct. 22, 1942, and served with Co. G, 19th Inf. Regt. He was stationed at Hollandia, Dutch New Guinea, Leyte, Mindoro, Luzon, Mindanao and Leyte Lost Battalion. He was discharged on Nov. 28, 1945, with the rank of sergeant.

ROBERT E. KAISEN joined the service in September 1952 and served with the 6th Tk. Bn. He was stationed in Korea and Japan. He was discharged with the rank of sergeant. Dates served: 1952-55.

STANLEY J. KALICH joined the service on Dec. 10, 1950, and served with the 24th Recon Co. He participated in the spring and summer Defensive and Fall and Winter Offensive. He was discharged with the rank of staff sergeant. Dates served: August 1951 to November 1952.

ARTHUR L. KEMP, born Nov. 10, 1920, joined the service August 1943 and served with Co. C, 21st Regt. He participated at Goodenough Island, Hollandia, Dutch New Guinea, Philippine Islands, Leyte, Pasoan, Mindoro, Mindanao, Japan and Okayama.

He was discharged with the rank of staff sergeant.

Awards include the Rifle and Sharpshooter Badge, Good Conduct Medal, Asiatic-Pacific Medal, Combat Infantryman's Badge, Purple Heart, Bronze Star, Philippine Liberation Medal and WWII Victory Medal. He is a charter member of the 24th Div. Assoc. Served 1943-46.

HAROLD J. KENNEDY joined the service on June 12, 1941, and served with HQ Btry., 13th FA BN. He participated at Leyte, Philippine Islands, Mindoro, Hollandia, New Guinea, Tanahmerah Bay. He was discharged with the rank of private. Dates served: June 12, 1941, to May 5, 1945.

LAWRENCE KENT enlisted in the Regular Army on May 16, 1956. He arrived in Korea on Nov. 11, 1956. He served with the Finance Corps, 24th Inf. Div. through Oct. 14, 1957; Div. HQ, Ponqilichoni Korea. Departed Korea on Feb. 20, 1958, and arrived in California on March 5, 1958. He received a honorable discharge on Sept. 30, 1962, with the rank of E-5.

HERB KENZ, born Jul. 1, 1928 and enlisted in the Army in June 1946. Kentz was recruited by the ROTC, receiving a deferment and finished his college while serving as a reserve officer.

He served 19 months in Korea with the 8th Army Arty. and in occupied Japan towards the end of WWII in the Military Police. It was rather chaotic with Japanese nationals coming out of tunnels not yet convinced of the war's end. During his active tenur, Kenz met several key figures including Gen. Dwight D. Eisenhower, Gen. MacArthur and Japanese Emperor Hirohito.

In 1950 Kenz was recalled Stateside and enrolled at Western Michigan where he would later earn a degree in secondary education. He became the executive officer for the ROTC training company at Fort Lee, VA. In 1956 he resigned his regular army commission and re-entered the active reserves until his retirment in 1988.

In his final five years of military service Kenz served

at Ft. Meade and retired as chief warrant officer. He earned his master's degree in education and served as a high school teacher and as associate director for student financial aid at his alma mater, Western Michigan. He also taught adult education for 11 years in the Kalamazoo School System. Recently he was inducted into the Western Michigan University ROTC Wall of Fame and proudly says, "I can still get in my uniform."

He and his wife, Jean, enjoy the many aspects of retired life in the Glade plus a thriving acting/modeling career. Both have appeared in area TV and print ads and Herb made his national TV debut in 1997 with a part in *Unsolved Mysteries*.

FREDERICK L. KEPKE joined the service on Nov. 25, 1942, and served with HQ Co., 63rd FA BN. He participated in the Korean Conflict. He was discharged with the rank of 1st lieutenant. Dates served: August 1951 to October 1953.

JOHN A. KEPPEL joined the service on June 17, 1944, and served with Co. B, 1st Bn., 34th Regt. He participated in the Southern Philippines Liberation, Co. B, 1st Bn., 34th Regt. from June 11, 1945, to Aug. 2, 1946. He was discharged with the rank of corporal.

THOMAS F. KILFOYLE, born June 6, 1931, enlisted in the Armd. Cav., Nov. 12, 1947.

He received basic training and Leadership School at Fort Ord, CA. Shipped to Japan on the *Edmund B. Alexander* assigned to the 24th Mechanized Cav. Recon. Troop June 1948 (later changed to 24th Recon Co.). He was with the company until he rotated home as a sergeant in June 1951. Note: He was in Leadership School at Eta Jima, Japan when the war started.

Discharged Nov. 14, 1951 as sergeant (P). His awards include the Bronze Star, Good Conduct, Occupation Medal w/Japan clasp, National Defense Medal, Korean Service Medal, w/five Battle Stars, UN Service Medal, US and South Korean Presidential Unit Citations.

Appointed to the New York City Police Dept. Feb. 1, 1955, retired June 25, 1976. Moved to Arizona in August 1976 and joined the Arizona State Capitol Police Nov. 14, 1976. Retired Oct. 28, 1992.

He married his wife, Genevieve Ann, Aug. 6, 1955. They have five children: Carol Anne, Thomas, Kathleen, Mary Anne and Nancy; four grandchildren: Brandon, Brianna, Andrew and Cole.

Presently he is on call to help his children when they have house problems such as plumbing, electrical, painting, etc.

He was also known as Joseph W. Doyle Jr. while he was with the 24th Recon. Co.

JOSEPH KINDYA, born Feb. 8, 1915, enlisted in the service July 7, 1941. Inducted at Camp Upton, NY. Received basic training, Camp Croft, SC, July 17-Oct. 28, 1941; Co. C, and HQ 1st Bn., 34th Inf. 1941-45.

Discharged Oct. 8, 1945 as tech. sergeant. His awards include the Bronze Star w/OLC, Combat Infantryman Badge. 1st Bn., 34th received the Presidential Unit Citation (Kilay Ridge), American Defense, Good Conduct, Asiatic-Pacific and WWII Victory Medal.

He worked for the IRS from December 1945-October 1974. He is a retired IRS agent. After retiring he worked 5-1/2 years for New York State as auditor.

Memorable experiences: serving as battalion sergeant major under Col. Thomas E. Jack Clifford when

battalion received Presidential Unit Citation. Left battalion on June 23, 1945 at Talomo, Mindanao on furlough to the US. The war ended and he was honorably discharged at Fort Dix, NJ.

He is married to Angela and they have a son, Joseph, and three grandchildren: Joseph, Amy and Emily. Presently enjoying retirement.

GEORGE P. KING enlisted into the service on Feb. 25, 1942, and was assigned to Btry. A, 198th FA BN. In April 1943 he transferred to Btry. B, 11th FA BN. He was stationed in New Guinea, Leyte, Bataan and Mindanao. He was discharged with the rank of T/4. Dates served: April 1943 to July 1945.

HERBERT R. KINGSBURY joined the service on July 20, 1943, and served with Co. C, 34th Inf. Regt. He was stationed in New Guinea, Southern Philippines, Biak and Leyte. He was discharged with the rank of private.

DEAN L. KLEFFMAN joined the service in November 1959 and served with Co. A, 24th Med. Bn. He was stationed in Germany. He was discharged with the rank of SP4. Dates served: May 1960 to February 1962.

JOHN KOCHER joined the service on Jan. 29, 1954, and served with Co. I, 34th Regt. He was stationed in Korea. He was discharged with the rank of private first class. Dates served: 1954-55.

MELVIN FREDERICK KOHLE, born March 27, 1922 in Blackwell, OK. He was inducted into the service in Tulsa, OK October 1942. Received his basic training at Schofield Barracks or Tent City in Hawaii. In January 1943 he was placed in G Co. of 19th Inf. on July 27, 1943 they sailed for Australia and were stationed at Rockhampton for about six months then to Hollandia, Dutch New Guinea. From there they landed at Leyte, PI, Oct. 20, 1944.

It was the second battalion to take hill and they were to block the road to stop the Japs. The morning they were to leave, the Japs made a (Banzai) attack, but they held the hill and came back to their own lines.

They then went to Luzon to keep the roads clear for movement of troops, then on to Mindoro and the large island of Mindanao. They encountered ack-ack guns in the mountains. They were sick and exhausted from all the fighting.

He was in the service for three years without a leave or R&R, only a few days once a month. He was in Communications of Co. G, carrying a radio. He also a Jap zero hit the smoke stack of an American cruiser so it had you back to state for repairs.

Discharged November 1945 with the rank of sergeant. After his discharge he came back to the family farm and continued farming and was also an oil well pumper.

He married his wife, Naomi, June 8, 1947 and has been married for 52 years. They had two daughters, Donna Page and Ruth Brown; four grandchildren: Lori (Page) and Brian Page, Barry and Mark Brown; one great-grandson, Tyler Lane Voegle.

After having a heart attack he had to give up his farming, so he is semi-retired from pumping wells also.

HOWARD J. KONING, born May 26, 1929 in Kalamazoo, MI. Drafted into the Army Nov. 7, 1950. Basic training at Camp McCoy, WI, 114th Engr. Bn.

Served in Korea, arriving in the spring 1951. Served with the 24th Inf. Div., 19th Regt., 3rd Bn. L Co. Was a rifleman in the machine gun squad.

He remembers the spring offensive, April 1951, and the counteroffensive that took back some of the same ground months later. Left Korea at the time the 24th Inf. moved to Japan. Returned to the states and served at Fort Hood, TX, Co. B, 47th Armd. Medical Bn. He was discharged Aug. 14, 1952. He was awarded the Combat Infantry Badge and Korean Service Medal w/four Bronze Service Stars.

Married Wilma Schipper in 1955. They have three children: James, Jenny Scheffers and Catherine Meeuwse and eight grandchildren. Retired from the US Post Office in 1989 after 31 years of service. Retired and enjoying garden work and hunting.

CHARLES V. KOWALSKI joined the service on Jan. 24, 1940, and served with Co. C, 21st Inf. Regt., staff sergeant, March 1940 to 1944; and HQ Co., 3rd Bn., 21st Inf. Regt., 1st lieutenant; August 1950 to 1951. He was discharged with the rank of 1st lieutenant.

BRUNO A. KRAMARZ, born Jan. 7, 1931, enlisted in the Army Oct. 1, 1952. Took basic training at Breckenridge, KY. Sent to Japan for advanced training, then sent to Kobe Island in Korea to guard Korean prisoners. Established a base at mainland Korea at Yangu Valley, Korea.

Discharged Sept. 23, 1954 as corporal. His awards include the Korean Service Medal w/ Bronze Star, United Nations Service Medal and the Presidential Unit Citation. Rock DA Co. 28 March 31, 1954.

Worked for M.H. Fishman Co. for 20 years, then worked for Nestle Foods Co. for 25 years. Retired in 1990. Belongs to the VFW Post 569, also belongs to color guard and performs military funerals and parades.

Memorable experiences: had a rank of corporal and was a squad leader. We did a lot of night patrol, looking for enemy, gathering information about heavy equipment and position the enemy had.

Married for 43 years to Betty and they have two children: Sandra and Joann; seven grandchildren: Chad and Melissa, Jeremy, Justin, Joshaua, James and Jessica.

He volunteers at Mischard Nursing Home, grandparents in Volney Elementary School for kindergarten and first grade children.

KARL A. KRASSLER joined the service on June 9, 1966, and served with Co. A, 2nd Bn., 21st Regt. He was discharged with the rank of 2nd lieutenant. Dates served: 1967-69.

ERWIN J. KRAUSE, born Sept. 26, 1921, enlisted in the Army June 1944 and served as medical tech. Served as combat medic to Co. K, (3rd Plt.), 3rd Bn., 34th Regt., 24th Inf. Div. in Philippine Islands (assault and battles).

Discharged in 1946 as medic, combat tech 406. His awards include the Combat Medic Badge, Bronze Star, etc.

Self-employed as engineer, mechanical/electrical design of machinery.

Memorable experiences: the awesome destructive

power of enemy and friendly (short rounds) of mortars and artillery, the smell of dead, rotting bodies; the suddenness of death in combat; the closeness of the Japanese soldiers (5 to 15 feet away); knowing he survived.

He is married to Violet E. and they have children: Erwin J. Krause Jr., Ann Louise Perrault, Martha G. Hein; and eight grandchildren: Donald, Stephen and Jennifer Perrault; Jessica and Bethany Hein, John Erwin, Paul and Christopher Krause.

He is now retired and lives and works on a tree farm.

OSCAR HENRY KRIESEL, born July 14, 1931, Cole Camp, MO, enlisted in the Army Nov. 16, 1950 in Iowa. He attended basic training at Fort Leonard Wood, MO. Assigned to the 5th Regimental Combat Team, Co. A, in April 1951 as a 4th Plt. light 30 cal. machine gun squad leader. April 1952 assigned to 10th Recon., 10th Inf., Fort Riley, KS. Discharged Nov. 15, 1953 as sergeant first class.

Married Oct. 18, 1953, to Barbara Sparrow. They are the parents of two daughters, Lori Heiple and Linda Riley and grandparents of Lauren and Robert Heiple, Andrew, Jacob and Broden Riley.

Employed as route salesman and sales manager for Butternut Bread, 16 years. Sales manager with Snyders Potato Chip Co. until retirement. His career locations: Colorado, Missouri, Indiana and Pennsylvania.

Retired September 1987, returned to Cole Camp, MO and now have a register Salers cow/calf operation.

WALTER W. KROECK, born Feb. 3, 1932, New Jersey and graduated high school in 1950 and enlisted in the Army Sept. 15, 1950. He took basic training for one month in Fort Knox, KY and was shipped out of Seattle, WA over to Korea and assigned to the 19th Regt. (B Co.), 24th Div. Inf. with a 57 recoilless rifle squad. After about 10 days there he was hit with a mortar and was evacuated to a schoolhouse hospital in Pusan. Patched up (still have some of the metal in him to this day), volunteered to go back to his company, instead of going stateside, and then was machine gunned three days later. Shipped home in a body cast and was in Murphy Army Hospital, Waltham, MA for 3-1/2 years. They tried to save his leg; after 57 operations and many procedures, it was amputated. Sent to Walter Reed Army Hospital in Washington, DC for 1-1/2 years of rehab and in 1954, he was medically discharged.

His memories are many during that time, but he especially enjoyed working with the Special Services fund raisers in Murphy Hospital for the Children's Hospital in Massachusetts. He met many singers and movie actors of the 50s and Patti Page presented him with a puppy which she used while singing her popular recording of "Doggie in the Window". As he couldn't keep the pup in the hospital, three days later he presented it to the poster girl for the Muscular Dystrophy Assoc.

General Dean came to visit four of them at Walter Reed, after his release from being captured. He pinned the Good Conduct Medal on Kroeck. What an honor!

At the Korean War Monument dedication activities, he was presented a Korean flag at the Arlington Cemetery by their cabinet members. He also was in a documentary done by Dan Rather and a feature story on the evening TV news.

He was discharged Sept. 30, 1954 and received the Combat Infantry Badge, UN Ribbon, Good Conduct Ribbon, Purple Heart w/OLC and Korean Service Medal.

Married Lois Oct. 12, 1958 and they have three children: Dawn, Roger and Donna; and three grandchildren: Ryan, Brandon and Amanda. Now retired because of an ongoing breakdown of stump at age 61. He now is on crutches most of the time.

KARL E. KUNKEL, born July 18, 1926, enlisted in the service Nov. 21, 1944, 19th Inf., 24th Div.

Inducted into the Army at Camp Joe T. Robinson, AR, where he took basic training. Sailed from San Francisco on the USS *General E.T.Collins* for the Pacific. Landed on Leyte, Philippine Islands as a BAR man with the 19th Inf., 24th Div. Went on to serve on Mindanao where he was transferred to the medics and served as company aid man. Left the Philippines at the close of the war and sailed to Kyushu, Japan, where he served as part of the occupation force at several bases in Japan. Later returned to the US and was discharged at Fort Sam Houston, TX. Returned home to Newport, AR.

Discharged as technical sergeant Nov. 23, 1946. His awards include the Asiatic-Pacific Theatre Campaign Ribbon w/Bronze Star, Good Conduct Medal, Philippine Liberation Ribbon w/Bronze Star, Army Occupation (Japan) Victory Ribbon, two Overseas Service Bars, Distinguished Unit Badge, SO #40 HQ 8th Army April 27, 1946 Army Commendation Ribbon, Lt. Maj. Gen. Lester 24th Inf. Div. Aug. 16, 1946, Combat Infantry Badge and Combat Medic Badge Oct. 31, 1945.

Entered and graduated from the Indiana College of Mortuary Science. Worked as a mortician and funeral director. He then started to work as a tool and die maker for a local industry.

Married Mary Frances Leach and they have three children: Charles F., Mary Elizabeth and Linda Jo; five grandchildren: Shelley, Jennifer, Stephanie, Felicia, Meghan; three great-grandchildren: Deshea, Madelyn and Jackson.

He is now retired and involved with the Civil War re-enacting.

CHARLES E. LACROIX, born Oct. 8, 1934, enlisted in the Army in 1953. He served with the MP Training Regt., Camp Gordon, GA. Assigned Armed Forces Police, Boston 1953-54, then went to Korea with the 24th Div., MP Co., 1954-1956. Discharged Aug. 31, 1961 as SP5.

His awards include the Good Conduct Medal and National Defense Service Medal.

He is a member of the DAV, American Legion and VFW. His memorable experience is the Non-commissioned Officers Academy, Korea.

LaCroix married Marie Rose and they have a daughter, Diane. Retired after 30 years with Massachusetts Department of Correction.

CLYDE S. LAFITTE joined the service in 1942 and joined the 24th Div. in New Guinea. He served with Co. A Btry., 11th FA BN. He was stationed in New Guinea, Leyte, Mindoro and Luzon. He was discharged with the rank of 1st sergeant. Dates served: 1942-45.

CHARLES E. LAKE, born Feb. 19, 1931, enlisted in the service June 1948, serving in the infantry.

His assignments: Fort Dix, basic training; shipped to Japan November 1948; assigned to Camp Wood, 1st Bn., when 3rd Bn. was formed; assigned to Co. K and went to Korea July 3, 1950.

Discharged Dec. 31, 1950 as corporal. His awards include the Combat Infantry Badge, Purple Heart and all that was given. Wounded Oct. 19, 1950 in South Pyongyang. Lost left eye with 135 shrapnel wounds, now rated 100 percent disabled.

Employed as heavy equipment operator for 20 years and 20 years in water department, city of Ogdensburg.

Memorable experiences: being surrounded at Chochiwon where his battalion was nearly wiped out. There were only a few who got away. Lost some very good friends there. Lost more friends on Hill #99. Went from the Pusan Perimeter to south of Pyongyang.

He married Theresa Dec. 6, 1952 and they have three daughters: Debra, Kim and Linda and five grandchildren: Brandi, Kris, Tim, Jen and Branna. Currently just growing old.

ROBERT E. LAKIE, born Aug. 22, 1930, enlisted in the service June 1948.

His assignments included: 1st Cav., 8th Regt., Tokyo; 24th Inf. Div., 21st Inf. Regt., K Co., Kumamoto, Kyushu, Japan; 45th Inf. Div., 179th Regt., Co. G, Korea.

Discharged Aug. 22, 1990 EO7, sergeant first class after 36 years.

His awards include the Purple Heart, Bronze Star, United Nations Medal, Korean War w/2 Battle Stars, Combat Infantry Badge, Japan Occupation, 101st Abn. Camp Breckinridge, KY.

Memorable experiences: as he lay in an aid station after being wounded by sniper fire and run over by their own company jeep, Lakie was then taken to an aid station shed, when a runner came in and told the doctor to leave the wounded that they were ____.

He married Jennie J. and they have four children: Robert Jr., Daniel, Sandra J. and Mark W. and eight grandchildren: Lindsey, Matt, twins Dan and Bill, Nicole, Allison, Katlyn and Liam. Retired as tractor trailer driver.

GEORGE F. LANCE, born Oct. 20, 1931 in Reading, PA was drafted into the Army November 25, 1952 at Harrisburg, PA. Took 16 weeks infantry training at Camp Breckinridge, KY, followed by eight weeks Leadership School. Served 11 months in Korea attached to Personnel Section of Service Co., 21st Inf. Regt. First located on Koje Island and later moved north near the 38th Parallel. Separated from service Sept. 8, 1954 as private first class.

His awards include the Korean Service Medal, United Nations Service Medal, National Defense Service Medal and Good Conduct Medal.

Married Janice A. Brehm Aug. 1, 1953. They have four grown children: Sharon Jean, Michael George, Diane Marie and Linda Louise and three grandchildren: Benjamin George Lance and Larry Chad and Megan Sara Swick. He had been a self-employed farmer 1948-52, and resumed part-time farming operations upon separation. Took a full-time job as mechanic on farm equipment for local dealer until late 1956, then joined Towmotor Corp. as full-time field service mechanic, covering 26 counties of Pennsylvania. Joined Forklifts, Inc. in 1964 as general parts and service manager, retiring after 32 years of service. Now retired and doing some traveling. He likes to "tinker" in his work shop, work outside on their 18 acres and also does consulting.

TROY LANDRUM, born June 17, 1921, enlisted in the service Nov. 30, 1942, serving in Inf., 24th Div. as technical sergeant.

Discharged Jan. 11, 1946 as technical sergeant and received the WWII Victory Medal and American Service Medal.

His awards include the Good Conduct Medal, Philippine Liberation Ribbon w/two Bronze Stars, Asiatic-Pacific Service Medal w/two Bronze Stars.

He was employed for the city of Atlanta, GA. Retired 1981.

Memorable experiences include seeing action while stationed in the Philippines most of his service time.

He married Ruth and they have one son, Danny and three grandchildren: Derrick, David and Carra Landrum. Troy died in 1988.

HAROLD J. LAREW, born May 31, 1926, enlisted in the Army infantry November 1944. Inducted at Jefferson Barracks, MO and received basic training, Camp Wolters, TX. Departed from Fort Ord, CA, arrived at Leyte and joined 24th Div. on Mindanao. Moved to Japan with 34th Regt. at Matsuyama, Himeji, and Nagasaki. Left from Yokohama via Seattle to Fort Sheridan, IL.

Discharged November 1946 as technical sergeant. His awards include the Combat Infantry Badge, Asiatic-Pacific Theater Ribbon w/Bronze Battle Star, Philippine Liberation Ribbon w/Bronze Battle Star, Good Conduct Medal, Army of Occupation Medal, Japan and Sharpshooter w/M1 Rifle.

Memorable experience: sergeant major, 3rd Bn., 34th Regt., 24th Inf. Div.

He has been a farmer since 1947. Also employed with Amana Refrigeration 5-1/2 years; Sears Roebuck 26 years, National Computer System, one season; American College Testing 1989-present.

He married Lue Hruby June 11, 1949 and they have five children: Stephen, Edgar, Mark, Eric and Neal;

seven grandchildren: Dawn, Tiffany, Joshua, Claire, Rebecca, Corinne and Craig.

Presently farming, employed at American College Testing. Lives on a farm near Oxford, IA.

EARL E. LAWRENCE, born Sept. 25, 1926 in Greenwood County, KS. Enlisted March 10, 1947 and took basic training in Fort Jackson, SC. Attended two cook schools. Served with the Heavy Mortar Co. in Korea in 1950 and 1951. Served two tours each in Germany and Korea, one in Hawaii and six months in Goose Bay, Labrador.

Attended Mess Stewards and Food Service Supervisor Schools, then after about 15 years attended Special Weapons School and served the rest of his 26-year career in the Army.

Discharged June 30, 1973 as master sergeant E-8, and received National Defense Service Medal w/OLC, Army Commendation, UN Defensive, UN Offensive, CCF Intervention, 1st UN Counteroffensive, Korea, CCF Spring Offensive and Korea and Presidential Unit Citation.

In 1948 met and married Lillian King. They have two daughters born in California, Patricia and Peggy and three sons born in Virginia, Roy, Carl and Richard.

Since retiring in 1973 they have mostly traveled in their recreation vehicle. They have 12 grandchildren: Michael, Timothy, Suzanne, Geni, Luke, Phillip, Rachel, Jessica, David, Alex, Andrew and Hannah. They have been married for over 50 years. Three of their children live in Colorado, one in Texas and one in Georgia. Besides visiting with our kids, we belong to membership campgrounds.

BURT LAWSON JR., born April 28, 1929 was drafted into the Army Oct. 31, 1950. Trained at Camp Chaffee, Arty. Sent to Korea, 1951-52, rifleman, assigned to the 21st Inf., Co. I, Rifle Plt.

Went into first major battle May 1. Can't recall all the hills and villages, but where the 3rd Bn. went he was there. First as a rifleman, squad leader, radioman and truck driver in that order.

He was wounded July 13, 1951. Went back to Japan to the 128th Station Hospital. Back to Korea after recovery and drove company truck.

Left Korea in 1952 with the 24th Div. to Japan. Returned to the states and was discharged in 1952.

His awards include the Good Conduct Ribbon, Presidential Citation, Korean Ribbon, Campaign Ribbon w/four Bronze Stars, Purple Heart and Combat Infantry Badge.

His memorable experiences: Spring offense May 1951, does not remember the names of the areas but wherever the 21st was, he was there in a rifle platoon. Wounded July 13, 1951 and hospitalized in Japan. Returned to the company after recovery and drove the company truck.

Retired from the city of Detroit as body repair foreman. He is married to Saundra and they have a child,

Arlester and two grandchildren, Dwayne and Janeane. Enjoys traveling, playing golf, bowling and reading; belongs to six veteran organizations.

DONALD K. LE GAY joined the service on April 21, 1947, and served with Co. C, 19th Regt. He was POW from Nov. 4, 1950, until April 1953. He was discharged with the rank of private first class. Dates served: July 1950 to April 1953.

JAMES W. LEMON, born Feb. 7, 1926, enlisted in Army Nov. 10, 1944.

His assignments included the Philippine Island and Occupation of Japan. Served as assistant BAR man, rifleman, scout, squad leader and platoon sergeant.

Discharged Nov. 10, 1946 as staff sergeant and received the Combat Infantry Badge.

Employed 50 years with the Friendship State Bank.

He is married to Patricia and they have three children: Evelyn Israel, James William and Tracy; seven grandchildren and one great-grandchild.

Semi-retired from bank and farming own farm and raising beef cattle.

GERALD W. LEVESQUE joined the service on Sept. 24, 1946, and served with A and C Btrys., 13th FA BN. He participated in the Occupation of Japan. He was discharged with the rank of private first class. Dates served: Dec. 12, 1946, to Dec. 23, 1947.

JERRY LEVINE joined the service in June 1944 and served with Co. E, 34th Inf. Regt. He participated at Luzon, Mindanao, Philippine Islands and Japan. He was discharged in July 1946 with the rank of corporal.

CHARLES R. LEWIN, born Sept. 25, 1918. Pleasantville, NJ, graduated from the University of Illinois, 1940. Married high school sweetheart, Jane Dunbar, January 1941. Moved to California where he worked four years in an aircraft factory before entering the Army September 1944. Basic training Camp Roberts, CA. Received commission Infantry Officers Candidate School, Fort Benning, GA, July 1945. Platoon leader, Fort McClellan, AL prior to assignment to Japan September 1945. Platoon leader, then assigned information and education officer, 126th Regt., 32nd Inf. Div., Kokura. When 32nd was deactivated he was assigned to 24th Inf. Div., G-2, as division historian and public relations officer, Okayama, 1946, then on to Kokura. One of his major duties was to prepare, under direction of Commanding Gen. James A. Lester, a history of the 24th through first year of occupation. The book was ready for publication when Lewin received orders to return to US, September 1946.

Left active duty October 1946 as first lieutenant. Served first years in Active Reserve, Logistics Div., Fort MacArthur, CA, followed by two years Inactive Reserve. Service ribbons: American Theater, Asiatic-Pacific, WWII Victory, Occupation of Japan and Army Officer's Reserve.

He received an MA degree from the University Southern California in 1947 and Doctor's degree in education, USC in 1963. Taught in private military academy, then served as public school teacher, counselor, building administrator, and district associate superintendent. Lectured part-time, Graduate School of Education, California State Polytechnic University.

Lewin is retired. He and Jane have three adult children: Jeff, Debbie and Heather and three grandsons: Jason, Joshua and Brett.

EARL L. LEWIS joined the service on Oct. 15, 1942, and served with HQ Co., 1st Bn., 34th Inf. Regt. He participated at Hollandia, Biak, Leyte, Luzon and

Mindanao. He served from 1942 to 1945. Discharged with the rank of sergeant.

FRANK E. LEWIS (PAT) joined the service on Jan. 22, 1943, and served with HQ Co., 3rd Bn., 34th Regt. He participated in the Asiatic-Pacific, New Guinea, Philippines, Corregidor, Leyte and Luzon. He was discharged with the rank of technical sergeant. Dates served: June 1943 to November 1945.

RICHARD F. LEWIS joined the service in June 1941 and served with Co. B, 11th FA BN. He participated at Good Enough Island, Hollandia, Leyte, Luzon, Mindoro and Mindanao. Discharged in December 1945 with the rank of corporal.

He was recalled in September 1950 to serve in the first five campaigns in Korea. He participated in the Shikoku Occupation. He was discharged in July 1951 with the rank of sergeant first class.

FRED R. LIBERMAN joined the service in October 1950 and served with Co. A, 1st Bn., 19th Inf. Regt., 4th Plt. He participated in the Korean War. He was discharged with the rank of sergeant first class. Dates served: May 1951 to February 1952.

LARRY LICHTENBERGER joined the service on July 28, 1966, and served with Co. A, 21st Regt., 2nd Bn. He was stationed in Germany, Munich and Ft. Riley. He was discharged with the rank of sergeant.

FLOYD J. LINN joined the service in November 1944 and served with Co. A., 21st Regt. He participated in the Philippines and Mindanao. He was discharged with the rank of sergeant. Dates served: 1945-46.

WILLIAM T. LLEWELLYN, born July 15, 1925 in Chicago, IL, and died Oct. 23, 1984 Baguio City, Philippines.

He was inducted into the Army in 1943 at age 18 and was discharged after the war before his 21st birthday.

During WWII he was an intelligence observer with the 2nd Bn., 34th Inf. Regt., 24th Inf. Div. During combat, he would be assigned with other members of his section to make reconnaissance patrols, with rifle company members to make contact with the enemy, determine their location, withdraw and report the location on the situation map so that combat patrols or artillery fire could be directed against them. His outfit made three major landings in the Philippines, Leyte, the second Luzon landing, and Mindanao as well as several smaller ones.

Leyte was the largest amphibious operation in the Pacific up to that time with over 600 ships and four Army divisions participating in the landing. On October 20, he went with the 9th Wave on Red Beach, loaded down with M-1 rifle, pack, helmet and two extra bandoleers of ammunition to use or pass forward to the troops ahead until more could be unloaded.

Bill received the Bronze Star, Combat Infantry Badge, Conduct Medal and Victory Medal. On Oct. 19, 1984 he received the Award of the Philippines, Republic Presidential Unit Citation Badge for acts and services of gallantry and heroism rendered by its officers and men during the Leyte campaign for the liberation of the Philippines from Oct. 17, 1944 to Sept. 3, 1945, thus contributing to the success of one of the decisive battles of WWII and earning the lasting admiration of the Filipinos.

He married his college sweetheart in May 1950. Worked at Ryerson Steel Co. for 34 years before the Lord took him in the Philippines on Oct. 23, 1984. He wanted to go back after 40 years to see his beloved country and people.

Bill loved his family: wife, son, daughter and granddaughter (one year old) on Oct. 11, 1984.

DONALD J. LLOYD, born Aug. 5, 1931 in Denver, CO, enlisted in the Army, Sept. 2, 1949 and took basic training at Fort Riley, KS. Assigned to the 3rd Engrs., 24th Inf. Div. at Kokura, Japan. Served in Korea, 1950-51. Stationed at Camp Carson until discharged on Oct. 19, 1952.

During his time in the Army he was awarded the Bronze Star, Distinguished Unit Medal, Korean Presidential Unit Citation, Army of Occupation Badge w/ Japan Clasp, Korean Service Medal w/Silver and Bronze Service Star.

He moved to Washington State and worked construction, logged timber, commercial fished in Alaska, owned a service station and restaurant, and was a tune-up mechanic.

He married Dorothy on Dec. 17, 1958 and they had three children and six grandchildren.

May 2, 1962 he took a job with the Wenatchee Fire Dept. Worked there until 1980 when he had to retired due to injuries received on a fire. Don rose to the rank of assistant chief in charge of training and personnel.

FRANCIS A. LOCKWOOD entered active duty on Feb. 4, 1943, trained at Camp Roberts, CA, and was assigned to Co. F, 34th Regt. on June 15, 1943. He participated in four campaigns in the Asiatic-Pacific and during the Philippine Liberation. He was discharged with the rank of staff sergeant. Awards include the Bronze Star w/OLC and V device, Purple Heart w/ cluster, Good Conduct Medal, Asiatic-Pacific Medal, Philippine Liberation Medal and Combat Infantryman's Badge. Dates served: Feb. 4, 1943, to Nov. 15, 1945.

CARL A. LONKART, conscripted into the US Army at Lemoyne, PA, March 10, 1953. Completed infantry and engineer training at Fort Belvoir, VA and assigned to Co. D, 3rd Engr. Bn., 24th Inf. Div. at Camp P.W. 9 near Pusan, Korea. Moved north to Camp George, located across the Hwach'on Reservoir from the ruins of Yanggu, Korea. Transferred to the 65th Engr. Bn., 25th Inf. Div. at Schofield Barracks on Oahu Island, US Territory of Hawaii.

Awarded the National Defense, Korean Campaign, United Nations, and Army Good Conduct Medals then mustered out at Fort Meade, MD, as a corporal, Feb. 25, 1955.

Commander of Lemoyne VFW, Post 7530 1970-71, president of Citizens Fire Company in Lemoyne, PA 1976 and 1977, retired as an iron worker in 1998, and now resides in Jamaica, Queens, New York City.

GEORGE P. LOSIO, born April 2, 1922 in Northern Italy of American citizens. Drafted into the Army January 1944. Took basic training at Fort Eustis, VA AAA and Fort Ord, CA Inf. Served in British New Guinea where he was assigned to the 19th Inf. and told by their indoctrinating officer that 75% of them would either be dead, wounded or missing within 90 days. Quite an eye opener for the 22-year old GI. Lost several buddies in a head on collision at Oro Bay, plus suffering from dysentery and jungle rot. Reported to the 19th at Hollandia, Dutch New Guinea.

Made the initial landing at Red Beach after his landing barge, LCVPA 7/9, was sunk and they were rescued by LCVP PA 7/18 and finally landed after being under heavy shore battery fire. Received Combat Infantry Badge, Asiatic-Pacific Ribbon w/2 Stars and Arrowhead plus other awards. Discharged from Camp Upton, LI March 1945.

Had hand, head and leg injuries plus several bouts of dysentery and jungle rot.

Just before Leyte landings noticed that wrong ammo had been issued and supervised the issuance of the proper M1 ammo.

Married to Dorothy and they have a daughter, Donna Marie and grandson, Andrew. Spent 40 years with Remington Rand and his own business until retirement. He is member of VFW, DAV and 24th Inf. Assoc.

JOHN I. LOWGREN, arrived at Goodenough Island, New Guinea as a replacement sometime in March 1944. He was assigned to K Co., 19th Regt.

He landed at Tanahmerah Bay, New Guinea and also Leyte, Mindoro, Luzon, and Mindanao, all islands in the Philippines. From there he went to Shikuko, Japan as part of the Army of Occupation. He left for the States on December 6. The reason he knows this is they were advised, while aboard ship, that their barracks in Japan had burned down on December 7. Accident, he hopes.

During his time with the 24th Div. he was awarded the following medals: Silver Star, Bronze Star, Good Conduct, Asiatic-Pacific Campaign w/three Battle Stars, WWII Victory, WWII Occupation, Philippine Liberation, Pacific Campaign, WWII Commemoration, Philippine Presidential Unit Citation, Bronze Arrow Head and Combat Infantry Badge.

CLARENCE G. LUEDY, born in 1920 and was drafted in the Army in November 1944. Trained at J.T. Robinson, Little Rock, AR and Ft. Ord, CA. Assigned to Co. G, 21st Inf., 24th Inf. Div. In 1945 he participated in action at Red Beach, Leyte, Philippines, Tacloban, Mindanao.

After being wounded, was sent to 118th Hospital then air-lifted to the States. After hospital stay he was given medical discharge in May 1946 as PFC. Awards include the Combat Infantry Badge, Purple Heart, Asiatic-Pacific and Bronze Stars.

He is retired.

THOMAS A. LYKE, born Oct. 5, 1932, enlisted in the Army Jan. 17, 1949. Assignments included basic at Fort Knox, KY; advanced armor training at Camp Hood, TX. Shipped to Korea with 6th Medical Tank Bn., July 1950. Assigned to 24th Div. Wounded Oct. 26, 1950. Sent to Japan to hospital. Returned to active duty December 1950. Continued serving with 6th Tank Bn. until captured April 29, 1951. Released from POW camp Aug. 28, 1953. Discharged Oct. 24, 1953.

His awards include the Bronze Star, Purple Heart w/two OLC, POW Medal, Korean Service Medal w/ four Bronze Stars, Good Conduct Medal, UN Service Medal, Distinguished Unit Service and National Defense Presidential Unit Citation and Korean Presidential Unit Citation.

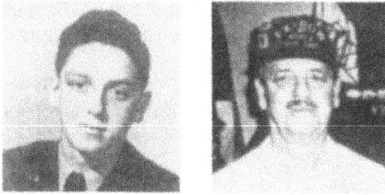

Memorable experiences: National president of Korean War Ex-POW Assoc. for three years, on board of directors for 13 years. Worked to raise funds for Korean War Memorial in Washington, DC. Photo taken with President Bush at ground breaking ceremony. Minted the eighth coin of the Korean War Memorial coin in Philadelphia, PA.

He owned Lyke Construction Co. (home building) 1983-86. Worked for another building construction company in Arlington, TX until forced to 100% service connected disability retirement. Married to Charlotte A. and they have two children, Thomas J. and Charlene K.; one grandson, Connor Scott Floyd.

FRANKLIN R. LYON JR., born Oct. 9, 1927, enlisted in the Army June 11, 1945.

His assignments included 64th AGF Band, Heidelberg, Germany Bandsman 1946-47; 8111 Sv. Det. (11th Signal Service Bn.), Okinawa, Personnel Adm. 1949-50; 24th Signal Co., 24th Inf. Div., Korea, Message Center Operations 1950-51.

Discharged as private first class March 26, 1947; corporal, Feb. 2, 1952.

His awards include the Victory Medal, Army of Occupation Medal (Germany), Meritorious Unit Commendation, Occupation Medal (Japan), Good Conduct Medal, Republic of Korea Presidential Unit Citation, Korean Service Medal w/five Campaign Stars.

Memorable experiences: graduate of the University of Missouri Columbia, MO School of Business and Public Administration, January 1955; Signal School, Fort Monmouth, NJ, 1948; Adjutant General School, FE, Eta Jima, Japan, 1949.

Employed in general farming, accounting offices in Columbia, MO; Kansas City, KS; Mission, KS; Oakbrook, IL. Engineering tester of earth moving equipment near Huntsville, MO. Storekeeper with Missouri Dept. of Corrections, Moberly, MO Corrections Center.

He married Lois Maxine Howard and they have four children: Frank Lelin, Philip Lowell Lyon, David Scott and Sara Beth Frank; five grandchildren: Anita and Amy Lyon, Dustin, Elizabeth and Joseph Frank. Now retired, but keeps busy with many activities.

GEORGE E. LYON, born April 28, 1924 in Florence, AL, served with the 3rd Marine Div. in WWII in the operation of Guam and the taking of Iwo Jima. Joined 104th AAA Bn., 31st Army Div. in 1949. Federalized with 31st Dixie Div. Jan. 16, 1951, and joined the pipeline to Korea Aug. 22, 1951. Assigned to HQ Btry., 13th FA as first sergeant when they were near Kumsong, Korea. Around Jan. 17, 1952 they were relieved by the 45th Div. and assumed their quarters at Camp Haugen, Japan. Rotated back to US and discharged Aug. 26, 1952.

Members of the 13th FA, officers and men were some of the finest he has served with.

Married Lois E. Gladney Jan. 30, 1942 and is the father of two sons, Michael Duane and James Edwin. Retired as an electrical maintenance supervisor from

Reynolds Metals Sheet and Plate Plant at Listerhill, AL in 1982.

WILLIAM F. MACINTIRE enlisted in the service on Oct. 24, 1942, and was assigned to Co. C., 34th Inf. on Jan. 17, 1943. He was stationed in Hollandia, Biak and Leyte. Transferred to the 724th Ord. on Jan. 10, 1945, and participated at Mindoro, Luzon and Mindanao. He was discharged on Dec. 10, 1945, with the rank of T/4.

ALFRED K. MACK JR. joined the service on July 3, 1952, and served with Co. C, 3rd Eng. Bn., 34th Regt. He was stationed in Korea. Discharged with the rank of sergeant.

RODERICK A. MACKENZIE III, (AKA: WARD ALEXANDER), born Dec. 22, 1934, enlisted in the Army March 3, 1952. Joined Co. G, 21st Inf. Regt. straight from Hawaiian Inf. Training Center, Schofield Barracks, TH. Assigned 57mm Recoiless Rifle Squad. The regiment was at Camp Schimmelfenning, Sendai, Japan, training exercises, great and glorious battles at O-Jo-Ja-Hara Range, Amphibious Training, Matsushima, a mock raid on Masaua, AFB (via air) and some snow training in Hokkaido. 1953 found them in Song-Wan, Korea and Koje-do, Korea.

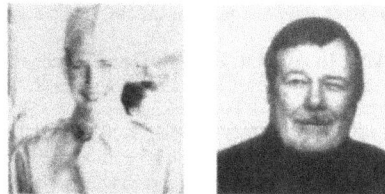

He was TDY to UNPFIK and 187th ARCT before leaving Far East. In Fort Devens, MA he was in the 74th RRCT before discharge. Reenlisted went Abn./Ranger, saw Vietnam as advisor, 2nd discharge Fort Bragg, NC, March 4, 1955, E-6.

His awards include the Combat Infantry Badge, Korean Service Medal w/1 Bronze Star, United Nations Service Medal, National Defense Service Medal, Good Conduct Medal, Purple Heart, Senior Parachute Badge.

His memorable experiences: stayed alive/manipulated the system and living in great health, expecting a very long life.

Went into family business of aerial acts for circuses. Later owned a circus carnival and now trains flying trapeze acts human cannon balls, stunt persons and builds props, paint shows in their winter quarters in Newberry, FL.

He has been married six times and has no children.

DONALD E. MAGGIO, born in Champaign, IL, Nov. 23, 1945, enlisted in the Army November 1965, did basic training at Fort Knox, KY and Finance School at Fort Benjamin Harrison, IN. He was commissioned a second lieutenant at Fort Benning, GA, in January 1967. After Adjutant General School, Fort Benjamin Harrison, IN, he was assigned to the 24th Administration Co., Augsburg, Germany. Returning to Fort Riley, KS, with the division under Operation Reforger he worked on manpower planning to insure NATO defense commitments could be met. He left the Army in January 1969.

He earned a BS degree from the University of Illinois in Business Administration and an MBA from Butler University, Indianpolis. Married to Shirley Cauble they have two grown sons. After 20 years with Gerber Products Company, he now works for Langham

Logistics Services in operations and strategic planning. He has been active in the Boy Scouts.

RONALD E. MAHAN enlisted in the service on Aug. 10, 1942, and joined Co. M, 3rd Bn., 19th RCT at Schofield Barracks in January 1943. He was stationed in Hawaii, Australia, Good Enough Island, New Guinea, Tanahmerah Bay, Hollandia, Philippines, Leyte, Mindoro, Luzon, Mindanao and Samal. He was discharged with the rank of staff sergeant. Dates served: Aug. 10, 1942, to Dec. 1, 1945.

ROBERT K. MAKAIWI, born April 23, 1922, enlisted April 18, 1942, US Army.

His assignments included rifleman, Co. B, 298th Regt., Hawaiian Islands; Guadalcanal, Solomon Islands. Discharged in Honolulu, Jan. 6, 1946. Enlisted April 25, 1946 FOA (Hawaiian Islands); corporal, assigned 5th RCT, July 23, 1950 (HHC); assigned HITC (HI), 1951-54; Co. A, 69th Inf. Div. 1954-55 (Tng.), Fort Dix, NJ; Germany, 1955-58; California, 1958-63; MAG-TM 22, VNF April 1963-64; Fort Ord, CA, 1964-67; Fort Richardson, AK (1967-70); Korea, 1970-71.

Discharged Sept. 30, 1972 as master sergeant E-8 at Fort Ord, CA. His awards include the Combat Infantry Badge w/2 stars.

Memorable experiences: attending 5th RCT reunion in 1956 at Garmiesh Rec. Center, West Germany and Chinese Recreation Center in 1957.

He married Eva Leilani Davis Makaiwi and they have children: LaVerne Makaiwi Cutolo; Luita, Harvey, Douglas and Nelson Makaiwi. Presently enjoying retirement and attending reunions when possible. Civilian activities: PC, VFW 1629, Monterey, CA.

EDWARD M. MANDERVILLE joined the service on March 14, 1961, and served with Co. B, 24th Sig. Bn. He was discharged with the rank of corporal. Awards include the Good Conduct Medal, Unit Citation, National Defense Service Medal, Germany Occupation Medal, UN Service Medal and Armed Forces Expeditionary Medal. Dates served: June 1961 to February 1964.

DAVID B. MANN, enlisted March 1943 and was assigned to the Artillery Center, Fort Bragg, NC, for basic training. Six months ASTP Mississippi State College, then Scout Corporal Battery A 869th FABN, 65th Div., Camp Shelby, MS.

He graduated OCS Class #363 November 1944, Fort Benning, GA, and joined G Co., 34th Inf., January 1945, aboard ship in Tacloban Harbor bound for Zambales Operation. Participated in ZigZag Pass, week-long operation on Mindoro, throughout Mindanao campaign and occupation duty in Japan. Discharged as first lieutenant in July 1946. He received a Bronze Star.

JOHN R. MANNERING, born Nov. 9, 1927 and

enlisted in the Army Sept. 9, 1946. His assignments included serving as rifleman and marksman, Co. A, 21st Inf., Japan, post finance officer, Baumholder, Germany.

Discharged March 1947 as private first class; October 1953 as first lieutenant.

His awards include the Army of Occupation, Japan, Germany and WWII Victory.

Employed as a surety bond broker and is married to Janet. They have four children: John, Elizabeth, Thomas and Maureen; 11 grandchildren: John, Christina, Melissa, Jeffrey, Emily, Russell, Lynn, Stephen, Eric, Rachael and Rebecca.

ROBERT MANSELIAN, born Dec. 11, 1920 was drafted September 1942 and received basic training at Camp Roberts. Sent to Hawaii into 24th Div. MP, then to Australia and onto the ship *Bontico* (Indian ship) where everybody on ship was sick from Atabri to New Guinea. Their job as MP was to direct traffic and keep it going.

He contracted Japanese liver flu. Took treatment on New Guinea. He then went to the States to Van Nuys Vets Hospital where he got a malaria attack.

He was discharged September 1945 and is married to Jackie; he has one stepson, Ara. Retired he enjoys gardening, attending church and visiting friends.

ANGELO J. MANTINI joined the service in 1942 and served with Co. A, 19th Inf. Regt. He was stationed in the Pacific, Hollandia, Leyte, Mindoro and Mindanao. He was discharged with the rank of staff sergeant. Dates served: 1942-45.

ROLAND W. MAPES joined the service on Feb. 15, 1943, and served with the HQ Co., 3rd Bn., 21st Inf. Regt. He was stationed in New Guinea, Southern Philippines, Leyte, Mindanao, Mindoro and Japan. He was discharged on with the rank of staff sergeant. Dates served: Oct. 16, 1944, to Jan. 3, 1946.

NICHOLAS L. MARASCO, born Jan. 13, 1919 in Honeoye Falls, NY, 1919, inducted at Buffalo, NY for one-year basic training at Camp Croft, SC. Assigned to 34th Inf. at Fort Jackson, SC where newly equipped, they entrained to San Francisco to sail to the Philippines Dec. 9, 1941. Pearl Harbor bombing delayed sailing until Dec. 16, 1941 to Oahu. With the 24th Div. they sailed to Australia, staged in Goodenough Island, made beach landings at Hollandia, Dutch New Guinea; Biak, Schouten Islands; Philippines at Leyte, Luzon, Mariveles. First troops back to Bataan. Made the beach landings to recapture Corregidor. After four years he rotated from Mindoro for his first furlough home. Thanks to President Truman's atomic bomb, Japan capitulated Aug. 14, 1945 and he was discharged Aug. 15, 1945, making it through the war from start to finish.

Discharged as staff sergeant, he was awarded the Silver Star, Bronze Star, Combat Infantry Badge, Good

Conduct Medal, American Defense Medal, Asiatic-Pacific Medal w/4 Bronze Stars and Bronze Arrowhead, Philippine Liberation Medal w/2 Bronze Stars, Victory Medal and the Presidential Unit Citation.

STEPHEN T. MARKS joined the service on Nov. 2, 1961, and served with HQ & HQ Co., 34th Inf. Regt. He was discharged with the rank of private first class. Dates served: April 1962 to October 1963.

LEEVON H. MARSHALL, born Nov. 24, 1932 in Richwood, WV, quit high school to join the Army, Feb. 2, 1951. Served two terms in Korea, the first term was with the 24th Inf., 19th Regt., Co. B and earned the Combat Infantry Badge on the front line. The second term was served with a trucking company. He met his brother, Forrest "Bud," (shown in the picture), while serving the second term in Korea. It was a great reunion meeting with a brother, who was drafted, so far away from home.

He was discharged Feb. 2, 1954 and returned home to complete his education on the GI Bill. He is married to Jo Ann Cottrell and they have two children, Terry and Kelly; six grandchildren: Julie, Tara, Abby, Alexa, Karli, Kyle and one great-grandchild, Tyler. He now lives in Okron, OH where he is retired and enjoying traveling.

DAVID W. MARTIN, born Dec. 29, 1936, enlisted in the Army November 1955. Attended basic training at Fort Dix, NJ; Advanced Infantry Training (AIT) at Fort Dix, then he went to Korea and was assigned to 24th Div., 21st Regt. Service Co. as a truck driver.

Discharged August 1957 and was awarded the Good Conduct Medal.

Memorable experiences (some good some bad), while in Korea he volunteered for special operations group (Able - Alpha - Azimuth, under Col. A, from Osaka, Japan). He considers his best accomplishment to be his three children and wife.

He married Carol and they have three children: Clifford, David and Barbara. After the service he was a printer for 20 years and later changed vocations and became a police officer. He will retire December 2001.

JULIO MARTINEZ, born Sept. 5, 1915, Albuquerque, NM. He was inducted in the service Feb. 2, 1945 as chief steward. Discharged Oct. 24, 1946 as staff sergeant. Awards include the Asiatic-Pacific Campaign Medal, Good Conduct Medal, WWII Victory Medal and Army of Occupation Medal.

PERRY MASCHINO, joined the regular Army in February 1951. Had basic at Fort Jackson, SC in the Dixie Div. and shipped to Japan in 1952 and in HQ Co. of the 24th Div. The 24th Div. had just come off the front lines to make replacements of men killed and brought to guard prisoners. They were back to strength and ready to proceed to the front lines. Ships were waiting in the Yellow Sea to get them back to the front lines. At this time there was talk of an armistice and

slept under the stars for three days. They then helped send the prisoners home. This was done with the help of the Navy and Marines. Had his time in the service at this time and shipped home to civilian life. Glad to have served his country and now retired with 23 years service with the Indianapolis Fire Dept.

EARL J. MASON joined the service in 1944 and served with Co. F, 2nd Bn., 21st Regt. He participated in the Southern Philippines Liberation. He was discharged with the rank of private first class. Dates served: 1945-46.

SIDNEY A. MATHES, born Oct. 19, 1927, Pardeeville, WI, enlisted in the US Army, Oct. 22, 1946. Assignments: Fort Sheridan, IL; Fort Jackson, SC; MOS (745) rifleman (infantry basic training); Camp Stoneman, CA; overseas Yokohama, Sasebo, Kokura, Japan; 34th Regt., Co. K, 24th Inf. Div. plus file clerk, AG Record Section, Div. HQ under Maj. Gen. James Lester, 1947.

Discharged March 30, 1948 in California as private first class. His awards include the Blue Presidential Unit Citation, WWII Victory Medal, Army of Occupation Medal, Japan, Asiatic-Pacific Theater Ribbon.

Memorable experiences: traveled through Hiroshima, Nagasaki, Tokyo, Emperor's palace grounds (bridge). Volunteered to Pusan, Korea as repatriation guard, MP Co., January 1948.

Employed with A&P Food Co., Kiechaefer Mercury Outboard Motors, Green Giant and Speed Queen Washers. He has been employed with the Division of Correction's Wisconsin Youth Counselor III State School for boys for 29-1/2 years.

He married Mary Jean Lehman, now a retired teacher, and they have a son, Mark A., Protestant minister in Minnesota.

Now retired and working for the Milwaukee Brewer's Baseball Team part-time (parking cashier). Commander VFW, American Legion, MOC.

JAMES E. MATHIS, born April 18, 1924, enlisted in the Army Jan. 3, 1943. Trained in Australia, South Pacific, Leyte, Corregidor, Jaro and Japan, serving as first cook. Discharged Dec. 30, 1945 as technical sergeant and received the normal ribbons.

He was employed with heavy equipment and as mechanic. Always self-employed. A member of Elks 1929, lifetime VFW 10726; lifetime 24th Div. and AOPA and EAA. He has been a private pilot for 52 years.

Married Jackie Jensen in 1985 and between them they have four daughters, eight grandchildren and two great-grandchildren. They have been well blessed with good health and they still fly their 1951 Cessna 170 all over the USA. They also take trips in their RV and live on the Colorado River where they have their boat in front of their home. They went to the Philippines in 1984 for their 40th reunion. Lots of memories for sure.

NICHOLAS MATVIYA (MICKEY) joined the service on Feb. 24, 1942, and served with Btry. A, 11th FA BN. He participated in the Central Pacific, Oahu, Southwest Pacific, Dutch New Guinea, Leyte, Luzon and Mindanao. He was discharged on Sept. 15, 1945, with the rank of corporal. He received three arrowheads. Dates served: May 28, 1942, to Aug. 8, 1945.

BARRY R. McCAFFREY, United States Military Academy, 1963. Served four combat tours: Dominican Republic, Vietnam (twice) and Iraq. Twice received the Distinguished Service Cross and awarded three Purple Heart Medals for wounds sustained in combat.

During Operation Desert Storm, he commanded the 24th Inf. Div. and led the 370-kilometer "left hook" attack into the Euphrates River Valley. General McCaffrey served as the JCS assistant to Gen. Colin Powell and supported the chairman as the staff advisor to the Secretary of State and the US Ambassador to the UN. At retirement from active duty, he was the most highly decorated and youngest four star general in the US Army. Was confirmed by unanimous vote of the US Senate as the director of the White House Office of National Drug Control Policy on Feb. 29, 1996.

CLOYD R. MCCANDLISH was inducted into the service in September 1950 and served with Co. D, 21st Regt. He was stationed in Korea. He was discharged in May 1952 with the rank of corporal. Dates served: March 1951 to April 1952.

WILLIAM C. MCCLURE, born Aug. 1, 1928, enlisted in the Army Nov. 24, 1950.

Assignments include: basic 101st Abn. Div., Camp Breckinridge, KY; Mechanic School, 724th Ord., 24th Inf., APO 24, April 27-May 18, 1950; Mechanic 24th Div. 21st Regt., 2nd Bn., HQ Co., Korea, A Btry., 200th Armd. Camp Campbell, KY.

Discharged from the regular Army Aug. 28, 1952 and the Reserve Aug. 29, 1956 with the rank of corporal.

His awards include the Combat Infantry Badge, Korean Service Medal w/Bronze Service Star, United Nations Service Medal, Good Conduct Medal and National Defense Service Medal.

He worked as a truck driver and mechanic on farm equipment from 1952 until 1968; heavy equipment 1973; garage foreman for Peabody Coal Co. when retired in 1989.

Memorable experiences: He will always remember Bernard Poazig, the best friend he had when he was in Korea. Poazig passed away in 1998. They met at Camp Breckinridge and were together when they returned there in 1952.

He is married to Sue and he states that he is presently "not doing a thing."

WARREN ASHTON MCCRARY joined the Reserves on Nov. 19, 1942. He entered active duty in December 1943 until March 1946; returned to the Reserves until October 1950; then two years of active duty. He joined the 24th Div. in Korea on Jan. 4, 1951. He served with the 724th Med. Bn. and HQ Med. Det. He completed 41 years of service on March 1, 1984, with the rank of brigadier general.

WILLIAM I. MCKENNA joined the service in June 1944, and served with Co. A, HQ Co., 1st Bn., 34th Regt. He participated in Leyte, Luzon, Corregidor, Min-danao and Japan. He was discharged with the rank of corporal. Dates served: December 1944 to March 1946.

DAVID R. MCLELLAN joined the service on March 7, 1957, and served with Co. A, 24th Sig. Bn. He participated at Flak Kassern, Augsburg, Germany. He was discharged with the rank of private first class. Dates served: July 1, 1958, to Feb. 12, 1959.

FRANCIS W. (FRANK) MCMANUS, born in New York City, Oct. 25, 1930. Enlisted Aug. 17, 1948. Received basic training at Camp Breckinridge, KY; Signal School at Fort Monmouth, NJ until November 1949. Arrived in Kokura, Japan in January 1950, assigned to 24th Signal Co. Went to Korea in July 1950. Attached to 21st Regt. until November of 1950, then transferred to 19th Regt., HQ Co., I & R Plt. Wounded in March 1951, spent some time in a MASH hospital then returned to his unit. Rotated home in August 1951.

Assigned to 278th Inf. RCT at Camp Drum, NY. Discharged in May 1952. After discharge worked as a NYC police officer, retired after 20 years as a detective. After retiring went into the field of nursing and worked as an RN for 22 years. He has BA and MS degrees in health management.

Married in 1951, has five grown children and 12 grandchildren. He resides in Warwick, NY, and works as a part-time police dispatcher in Washingtonville, NY.

His decorations include the Combat Infantry Badge, Purple Heart, Korean Service Medal w/5 Bronze Service Stars.

DANIEL (DAN) MECCA, born Dec. 11, 1926, New Brunswick, NJ, enlisted in the service Sept. 22, 1950, serving in the artillery and infantry.

Discharged Aug. 29, 1952 and received the Good Conduct Medal, Army Occupation, National Defense, Korean Service, UN, and Korean Presidential Unit Citation.

Memorable experiences: Forward observer during operation NOMAD in October 1951 and beyond. Promoted to corporal for this action with G Co., 19th Regt.

He is married to Diane and they have four children and one grandchild.

CARL H. MEDLIN, born March 26, 1929 in Jackson County, TN, was drafted into the Army in 1951. He took his basic training at Indiantown Gap, PA and had medic training in Japan. Served as a front line medic from 1951-53. He was stationed at West Point, NY until his discharge in late 1953. Served with many units as he was needed and with the 5th RCT.

Married Ruth in 1949 and they have two daughters, Judith and Janet and one treasured granddaugh-

ter, Laura. He worked as an instructor and supervisor in California for 32 years. His most honored medals are his Medic Badge and Combat Infantry Badge.

JERRY H. MEGEE joined the service on Feb. 17, 1942, and served with HQ Co., 3rd Eng. He was stationed in New Guinea and the Philippine Islands. He was discharged with the rank of technical sergeant.

JACOB MEIER joined the service on Oct. 1, 1942, and served with the 3rd Bn. Meds., 19th Inf. Regt. He participated in the Asiatic-Pacific, New Guinea, Leyte and Luzon; in the Hollandia Landing at Tanahmerah Bay, April 22, 1944; Beach Assault Landing Palo Area, third wave, Palo, Pastrana and across the Island to Carugara, Oct. 20, 1944; assault landing at San Jose, Mindoro Island, Dec. 15, 1944; saw action at Ft. McKinley on Luzon Island near Manila, February 1945; and the assault landing at Parang, and across the island on foot to the city of Davao, April 17, 1945. He was discharged with the rank of T-3. He served two years, six months and 29 days.

RALPH W. MELCHER, born Oct. 20, 1927, Ottawa, KS, was drafted into the service May 2, 1946. He graduated from OCS, Fort Sill, OK. From 1946 to 1949 he served in 63rd FABN, 19th Inf. Regt., and 8th Army Special Services in Japan. In 1950-51 did a 14-month combat tour in Korea with 8th FABN, 25th Inf. Div. Upon return from Korea was assigned to staff and faculty a the FA School, Fort Sill, OK for two years and then went to Germany to 2nd Armd. Div., serving in 14th AFA Bn., 1954-57. Returned to Fort Sill, OK serving as an instructor in Gunnery Dept., 1958-59. In 1960 attended USA Cmd. & Gen. Staff College at Fort Leavenworth, KS and then was assigned General Staff duty in HQ 7th Army in Stuttgart, Germany for three years. Returned to US in 1963 and served in OACSI (Pentagon), as general staff officer until 1966. Went to Korea in 1967 to command 1st Bn., 17th FA for 14 months. Returned to Fort Sill, OK in 1968 and served as deputy brigade commander, Officer Candidate Bde., CO of 9th Missile Gp., and executive officer of III Corps Arty. until 1971. Served as team chief, battle staff, airborne command post, USEUCOM in England 1972-73. Returned CONUS in 1974 to position of post commander, Selfridge ANGB at Mt. Clemens, MI until retirement.

Retired Sept. 1, 1974 as colonel and received the Silver Star, Legion of Merit, Meritorious Service Medal, ARCOM, WWII Victory Medal, AOM (Japan), AOM (Germany), NBSM, KSM w/five Campaign Stars, AFEM, AFRM, UNSM, AGS Ident. Badge, Perm Acft. Crmn. Badge.

Inducted into FA Officer Candidate School Hall of Fame at Fort Sill, OK.

He received a BGS from University of Nebraska at Omaha, NE; MA in Public Administration from University of Colorado at Colorado Springs, CO.

Melcher is a member of VFW, American Legion, TROA, National Sojourners, 24th Inf. Assoc. and 25th Inf. Assoc.

He married Anita Nov. 8, 1946 and they have children, Mark and Laura and four grandchildren: Brian, Kaitlin, Raychal and Josh.

JOE MELLON (SLIM) joined the service on Jan. 16, 1951, and served with Co. C, 19th Regt.; Co. E, 223rd Regt., 40th Div., January 1951 to August 1951; and the 24th Div., September 1951 to January 1953. He participated in the fall and winter, 1951-52, MLR

Iron Triangle, back to Japan with the division in January 1952 to Camp Haugen. Discharged on Jan. 19, 1953, with the rank of private first class.

EDWARD MENNONA joined the service on July 26, 1950, and served with Btrys. B and C, 13th FA BN. He was stationed in Korea. He was discharged with the rank of 1st lieutenant. Dates served: May 1955 to September 1956.

RICHARD J. MERCY - ROBERT W. MERCY, born Oct. 15, 1930, enlisted in the service Oct. 24, 1947.

Assignments: Basic training, Fort Ord, CA; from there their assignment was with the 11th Abn. Div., Camp Schimmelfenning, Sendai, Japan, where they both attended parachute school, and received their airborne qualification. Transferred to the 7th Inf. Div., 17th Regt., when 11th Abn. Div. was rotated back to the ZI, in 1948. June 29, 1950; assigned to Co. G, 19th Inf., 24th Inf. Div., Korea. Rotated back to the ZI in July 1951; assigned to the 9th Inf. Div., Fort Dix, NJ. Assigned to 1242 ASU as Army advisors, assigned to the New York National Guard. To Ft. Benning, GA Infantry School, where they served with the Hand-to-Hand Combat Committee. They were discharged from the regular Army in November 1955, with the rank of SFC.

Richard J. Mercy enlisted in the New York National Guard, 42nd Inf. Div. and remained in the guard and reserve components, where he was commissioned as a second lieutenant in 1958 and was assigned to various units, which included the 19th Special Forces Group, (Abn.). Retired as major, 1980.

Richard received the Combat Infantry Badge, three Purple Hearts, Bronze Star and Korean Campaign Ribbon w/6 clusters.

Robert received the Combat Infantry Badge, Silver Star, Purple Heart and Korean Campaign Ribbon w/6 clusters.

Richard joined the New York City Police Dept. as a patrolman, June 1957. Retired as lieutenant in 1978.

Robert pursued an acting career and appeared in numerous motion pictures.

Accomplishments/memorable experiences: In August 1950, Co. G was assigned a contingent of ROK soldiers. Unlike other units in the US Army, their ROK soldiers were not integrated into the other platoons of the company. Rather, they had been organized into a separate platoon and placed under the command of Lt. George Buckley. Robert and Richard and several other sergeants, including Richard Robertson, were assigned to leadership positions in the platoon. Because of battlefield attrition, and after Lt. George Buckley had been killed sometime in December 1950, the command structure of the platoon was reduced to three noncoms, which included Richard, Robert and Richard Robertson. Their platoon fought valiantly and received recognition from the highest levels in the 8th Army. Their unit was involved in some of the more memorable ground operations of the war, such as Operations Ripper and Killer. It is believed that Co. G, 19th Inf. Regt. was the only

company in the war which had successfully executed a company-sized bayonet attack against Chinese forces. This attack had been made against an entrenched enemy who had formed a "reverse slope" defense. The attack had been gallantly led by Capt. Anthony Denucci, who survived that action only to be killed later in another attack he had been leading, sometime in February 1951. Their platoon was literally decimated after a pitched battle on Hill 584, during which the platoon made a frontal assault against an entrenched fortified enemy position, which resulted in over half of the platoon being either killed or seriously wounded. However, they continued to function until the date of March 6, 1951, which was the first day of a UN offensive, during which the platoon sustained heavy casualties, including the entire command element of the platoon; Richard Robertson, Robert W. Mercy, and Richard J. Mercy, all were wounded during hand-to-hand fighting repelling a nighttime Chinese counterattack.

Richard married Joan T. Hanold in 1956. They have six children: Richard, Steven, Donna, Mark, Robert and Kimberly, a Vietnamese war orphan whom they adopted in 1975, and who was under one year of age, at the time. They also have the following grandchildren: Jonathan, Eric, Michael, Richard and Elizabeth.

Robert is a bachelor and is a private investigator.

MELVIN MERKEN joined the service on Jan. 19, 1944, and served with the Med. Det., 21st Regt. He participated in the Asiatic-Pacific Campaign. He was discharged with the rank of T-3. Dates served: 1945-46.

CLARENCE W. MERKLEY joined the service on Nov. 10, 1943, and served with Btry. B, 52nd FA BN, 24th Div. He was stationed in Leyte, Mindoro, Mindanao, Sarrgania Bay and Japan. He was discharged with the rank of T-4. Dates served: Nov. 10, 1943, to Feb. 11, 1946.

CHARLES MILLARD, born Feb. 8, 1929, enlisted January 1949. Had artillery basic training at Fort Lewis, WA, 2nd Div.

Assigned to Japan, Camp Chitose, November 1949. Shipped to Korea, July 7, 1950. July 10, 1950, assigned to 11th FA, C Btry.; July 17, 1950, assigned to 11th FABN.

Kept in for extra year by President Truman. Shipped to the states, September 1951.

Discharged as corporal June 1952, Camp McCoy, WI. He was awarded the Bronze Star, Korean Service Medal w/five Bronze Campaign Stars, Korean Presidential Unit Citation, Distinguished Unit Emblem, two Overseas Bars and Occupation Medal (Japan).

He married Joanne in 1953 and they have three daughters: Robin (Millard) Kohlhamer, husband Richard; twins, Tina (Millard) Lohry, husband, Mike; two grandsons, Keith and Steven; Terry (Millard) Rosenall, husband Dan; grandson, Seth; granddaughter, Cozette.

Employed for the Dept. of Corrections in Wisconsin for 32 years as sergeant. Retired Feb. 8, 1991 and is enjoying going to 24th Army reunions and seeing old comrades.

JOHN ALEXANDER MILLER, born Nov. 26, 1923 and enlisted in the Army, Dec. 11, 1942. Received basic training, Camp Wolters, TX; ASTP University of Michigan, 1943; Camp McCoy, WI, 76th Inf. Div., Fort Benning, GA - Officer Candidate. Graduated second lieutenant November 1944. Assigned 24th Inf. Div., 1/45 Leyte, PI. Platoon leader 34th Regt. through Luzon, Corregidor, Mindoro, Mindanao, Occupation Army, Japan 1945-46.

Discharged September 1946 as captain. Joined Army Reserve, 89th Div. Inf. as Co. CO, Bn. CO., S-

1, S-3, S-4, Brigade Exec. Off. Retired lieutenant colonel December 1960.

His awards include the Combat Infantry Badge, Purple Heart and Army Commendation Medal.

Graduated U of Colorado 1949. Employed as insurance broker until 1955. Opened his own insurance agency, and sold to James S. Kemper Co. 1973; president of JSK Colorado then through mergers became president of Rollins Burdick Hunter of Colorado. Retired 1985 and once again opened another independent insurance office, J.A. Miller and Co. Retired again 1996.

Accomplishments: president, Colorado Insurers Assoc.; State National Director National Assoc. of Insurance Agents; Board of Governors of Colorado Golf Assoc.

He married Judy A. Miller and they have children: Judith Ann, Christine, Clay and Todd and eight grandchildren: Jason, Adam, Sarah, Stephanie, Jeremy, Renee, Ian and Colin.

Currently he is traveling, playing golf and officiating golf tournaments.

JOHN R. MILLS SR. joined the service on June 14, 1938, and served with the 24th Div., MP Regt. He was stationed at Pearl Harbor, Central Pacific, Leyte and the Philippine Islands. He was discharged on Dec. 7, 1941, with the rank of private.

JAMES W. MIMS, born Oct. 18, 1923. He was a freshman at Texas A&M Dec. 7, 1941, in FA ROTC. Took voluntary draft, Jan. 7, 1943, Fort Bliss, TX. Engineer basic at Fort Leonard Wood, MO; then in lieu of OCS, six months ASTP at Boston College, MA. He next went to the Military Intelligence Training Center at Camp Ritchie, MD, studying Photo Interpretation. Overseas to Dobadura, New Guinea, 5th Replacement Depot July 1944; joined the 24th Div. G-2 Section as member of 114th Photo Interpretation team at Hollandia Oct. 9, 1944. Left for invasion of Leyte the following Friday, October 13. Made that landing, and was later on Mindoro, Lubang and Mindanao, PI. Flew home on emergency furlough last of June 1945. Discharged Oct. 25, 1945, Camp Lee, VA with rank of staff sergeant.

Married to Mary Alice Bell in 1947 and they have one son, two daughters, five grandchildren and one great-granddaughter. Retired May 1998 after 52 years in family insurance agency.

JULIUS MINKOFF joined the service on Sept. 14, 1942, and served with Co. B, 19th Regt. He was stationed in Hollandia, Leyte, Mindoro, Simara, Romblon and Mindanao. He was discharged with the rank of sergeant. Dates served: 1943-45.

ROBERT I. MONCUR, born Dec. 22, 1929, enlisted in the Army, June 1948.

Assignments: Fort Meade, MD, assigned to 3rd Armd. Cav. Div. under one year enlistment act. Recalled in October 1950 and sent to Fort Campbell, KY for refresher training and eventually ended up assigned to Fox Co., 19th Regt., 24th Div. in Korea.

Discharged 1952 after a year in active reserve with rank of sergeant first class.

He was awarded the Combat Infantry Badge and Korean Service Medal w/three Service Stars. His greatest accomplishment was to serve his country in time of need, to the best of his ability, and to return home uninjured to his wife.

Employed as printer (Gravure) for 20 years and then fork lift operator until retirement in 1996.

He married Ann before going to Korea and they have a son, Bobby; daughter, Michelle and granddaughter, Dominique.

Currently enjoying Dominique, retirement and his Harley Davidson.

THOMAS W. MONROE joined the service on Jan. 11, 1949, and served with Co. K, 34th Regt.; Co. F, 21st Regt.; and Security Co., 24th Div. He was stationed in Korea. He was discharged with the rank of sergeant first class. Dates served: 1949-51.

RUSSELL D. MONTCALM joined the service on Dec. 31, 1948, and served with Co. F, 19th Regt. He participated in the Korean War. He was discharged with the rank of corporal. Dates served: 1949-51.

DONALD E. MONTGOMERY, born Jan. 3, 1934, Minneapolis, MN. Stationed at Camp Roberts, CA for basic; 19th Inf. Regt., 24th Inf. Div., Korea, 1953-54; Item Co. Heavy Wpns. Plt.; HQ & HQ Co., as chaplain's assistant; S-1 Regt. records administrator. Discharged as corporal, age 20, with the usual medals.

Attended University of Nebraska and received B.Sc. 1957; MA, 1958; extracurricular: debate, forensics, theater, radio-TV. Market research, 1958-59, Michigan State University. Taught high school, 1959-62, Lansing, MI; coached debate; directed forensics. Awarded Indiana University National Defense Education Act (NDEA) Russian Institute Fellowship, graduated May 1963. Engineering administrator, Honeywell Aero, 1963-65; various other industries and management assignments 1965-97.

In 1968, assisted state department in freeing captured USS *Pueblo* crew from North Korea. Wrote study reports, articles and novel, *The Krasnodar Affair.*

Married Donna Lagorio and they have eight children: Timothy, Michael, Amy, Laurie, Patrick, Katie, Anthony and Molly; two granddaughters, Ada and Madison. He owns Twin Cities Mortgage Company, Edina, MN, specializing in home financing.

RAYMOND C. MONTGOMERY joined the service on Oct. 23, 1942, and served with Co. L, 21st Regt. He participated in the Southwest Pacific, New Guinea, Leyte, Mindoro, Mindanao Islands, Philippine battle of Breakneck Ridge, Cslinan and Talomo. He was discharged with the rank of private first class. 1943-45.

ROBERT S. (RED) MONTGOMERY, born

March 10, 1928, enlisted in the service Sept. 9, 1946. Attended basic training at Camp Polk, LA, September-October-November 1946. Delay in route to Camp Stoneman, CA. Shipped to Japan via Korea aboard transport, *Gen. Black*, November-December 1946. Arrived 19th Inf. Regt. Camp Chickamauga, Beppu, Kyushu, Japan, Dec. 23, 1946; served in M Co., 3rd Btry., Mortar Plt. as a jeep driver until December 1947. Discharged at Camp Stoneman, CA, Dec. 27, 1947 with the rank of corporal.

He was awarded the WWII Victory Medal, Army of Occupation Medal and Presidential Unit Citation while in the 24th Div.

Attended Baldwin-Wallace College in Berea, OH on GI Bill 1948-52. Was involved in own business (material handling equip.) 1961-89. Retired Jan. 1, 1990. Married Kathryn Hastings in July 1952 and they have two children, Leslie E. Zola and Robert E. Montgomery. They also have four grandchildren: Maureen and Robert Montgomery; Sara and Joseph Dietz.

Most memorable service experience was serving as a member of a three-man patrol in the town of Takada, Kyushu, Japan during the month of April 1947. Supervising the first free elections held in Japan for local, prefectural and national government officials.

He has several antique and collector cars (Buicks), plays the bagpipes with three bands and solo. Plays golf, travels and maintains homes in Ohio and Sarasota, FL.

DAN C. MOORE joined the service on Feb. 10, 1942, and served with Co. H, 21st Regt. He participated in Hawaii, Australia, Good Enough, New Guinea, Hollandia, Philippines, Leyte, Mindoro and Mindanao. He was discharged with the rank of captain. Dates served: 1942 to Oct. 20, 1945.

CHARLES L. MORGAN joined the service on June 12, 1944, and served with Co. E, 21st Regt.; Cannon Co., 21st Regt. He participated in the Asiatic-Pacific until Oct. 15, 1945; Mindanao, Philippine Islands, April 14, 1945; and Okayama, Japan, April 19, 1946. He was discharged with the rank of corporal.

MARVIN J. MORIN, born Nov. 30, 1928, Minneapolis, MN, was drafted Dec. 1, 1950. Attended basic training, Fort Riley, KS. Served in Korea, May 1951-April 1952, 24th Signal, 5th RCT, 3rd Bn., radioman, sergeant.

Discharged September 1957 as sergeant and received the Combat Infantry Badge.

Memorable experiences: Minnesota Electric apprenticeship, journeyman electrician license. Located Bob Kadrlik after 45 years, the unknown GI that carried Jim McCabe, wounded, back to their lines.

He has been a member of the IBEW for 46 years.

Married Marlene and they have four children: Michael, Matana, Marcella and Maria; four grandchildren: Corey, Brandon, Kathryn and Emily.

Now retired from the IBEW, Marvin is a VFW

member, dancer and volunteer for seven organizations. He also travels and enjoys the outdoors.

GEORGE P. MORRIS joined the service on Aug. 1, 1938, and served with Co. H, 21st Regt. Was stationed in Europe with the 26th Div. and Korea with the 187th ARCT. He retired in 1966.

From 1940-66 he served with the 1302nd Svc. Unit, Ft. Meade, MD; Co. D, 101st Inf., 26th Div., Europe; Camp Pickett, VA; Armor Training Center, Ft. Knox; 511th Air, 11th Abn. Div.; 187th Abn. Regt. Combat Korea Team; parachute maintenance, Jeffersonville and Memphis General Depot; 744th QM Det., parachute maintenance, Verona, Italy; and Parachute Maintenance Det. Presidio, San Francisco, CA. Dates served: 1938-66.

He has two sons, George P. Morris Jr., served as captain in Vietnam and lieutenant colonel in Special Forces USAR; Richard D. Morris, served as sergeant, Ord. Co., Europe; and granddaughter, Stacy N. Morris.

CHARLES H. MORRISON III joined the service on Feb. 12, 1982, and served with HHC, 24th Inf. Div. He participated in operations Desert Storm and Shield, DISCOM and DIVARTY and served as assistant division chaplain. He was discharged in with the rank of major. Dates served: June 1990 to June 1991.

WALTER MORRISON JR., born Feb. 17, 1931, enlisted in the Army March 28, 1948.

Assignments include: 1st Cav. Japan, 24th Inf. Div., Japan and Korea June 25, 1950-Aug. 14, 1951, 1st Army, NYC, 40th CID, 1240 MP Unit, Germany.

Discharged Aug. 17, 1957 as sergeant. Awarded Korean and US Presidential Citation, Bronze Star Medal w/V, Combat Infantry Badge, Army Occupation, Japan and Korea, ETAL.

Memorable experiences: Gen. Ridgeway bodyguard in Korea. Obtained law degree and J.D.; acquired commercial pilot's license after discharge from service.

Employed as insurance investigator, real estate broker and appraiser, air line pilot, part-time master guide and lawyer. His wife has died and they had two daughters, Linda and Pamela and seven grandchildren. He is presently doing real estate appraisals.

ALAN H. MOSER joined the service in September 1949 and served with Co. A, 724th Ord. Bn. He participated in Korea, Vietnam, South Camp Fuji and Pusan. He was discharged in September 1974 with the rank of 2nd lieutenant. Dates served: January to October 1953.

NIELS ELDON MORTENSEN joined the service on Dec. 16, 1944, and served with Med. Det., 19th Inf. Regt. He participated in the Southern Philippines and the Occupation of Japan. He was discharged on Nov. 17, 1946, with the rank of T-3.

WILLIAM AARON MULLENS joined the service on Sept. 12, 1949, and served with Co. B, 21st Regt. He was stationed in Korea from July 5, 1950, until August 1951, and was a member of Task Force Smith. He participated in the UN Defensive, UN Offensive, CCF Intervention, 1st UN Counter Offensive, CCF Spring Offensive and UN Summer and Fall Offensive. He was discharged on Oct. 13, 1952, with the rank of private.

Joined the USAF on March 20, 1955, and served until Feb. 1, 1980. He was stationed in Vietnam from June 1967 until August 1968. He achieved 78 combat flying hours and TET in January 1968.

He retired on Feb. 1, 1980, with the rank of E-8.

WILLIAM L. MULLINS, born Nov. 24, 1923, enlisted in the Army Feb. 12, 1942. He received basic training at Camp Lee, VA; Artillery training, Fort Bragg, NC. Joined 24th Inf. Div. May 1942, Schofield Barracks, Btry. C, 13th FA, Australia Goodenough Island, New Guinea, Hollandia. Wounded at the invasion of Red Beach, Leyte, Philippine Islands, Oct. 20, 1944. Hospitalized 27th General Hospital, New Guinea and Littleman General Hospital, San Francisco, CA; William Beaumont General Hospital, Fort Bliss, TX.

Discharged Sept. 21, 1945 with the rank of staff sergeant. Held 60% disability with loss of limb. He received the Asiatic-Pacific Campaign Medal, two Battle Stars, two Arrowheads, WWII Medal, American Campaign Medal, WWII Victory Medal, Good Conduct Medal, Philippine Liberation Medal, w/Battle Star and Arrowhead, Purple Heart. Philippine Medals: Philippine Liberation Medal, Philippine Republic Presidential Unit Citation Badge, Philippine Independence Medal, Asiatic-Pacific Campaign Medal and WWII Victory Medal.

Served in the CCC before the war; 26 years American Standard; six years CCS; 13 years security, retired captain.

Memorable experiences: Forward observer, three infantry regiments, received exceptional emergency care from Pvt. Cochran, including his personal sulfa niliomide. He should have received the Medal of Honor.

Married Lois and they have four children: William, Dale, Susan, Jaynie and three granddaughters, Deborah, Rachel and Rebecca.

Retired and member of VFW, AL, Ruptured Duck. He is also active in MOPH, DAV.

FRANK L. MUNDSCHENK JR., born in Albion, NE, April 5, 1926 and drafted in the Army Sept. 20, 1944. He received training at Camp Hood, TX. After a seven-day furlough Jan. 15, 1945 he returned to Fort Ord, and left San Francisco Feb. 9, 1945. Arrived Replacement Center in Leyte March 11, 1945. Some how seems strange to him it was April 1, 1945. Easter, April Fools and Sunday. Whoever was in charge came through rows of tent. Everybody out at 4 a.m. Guys were saying April Fools back at him. He said "No April Fools, this means go." He called off the roster, Frank was one. They loaded on LST in afternoon, which took them to Mindoro where he was assigned to Co. D, 21st Inf., 24th Div. A couple days later they were loading ships to make a landing on Mindanao. He was on LST going toward Mindanao and heard news of President Roosevelt's death. Japan surrendered. Went to Okayama Japan old Army camp. Later went to Camp Wood, Kumansoto Japan. Left Japan Sept. 7, 1946 and arrived back in States Sept. 18, 1946.

Discharged Nov. 22, 1946 and went back to the farm and lived there until Sept. 26, 1996. He then moved to Grand Island, NE.

JESSE A. MURGA joined the service in March 1944 and served with Companies A and C, 21st Regt. He was stationed in Korea from July 9, 1950, to May 1951. He was discharged with the rank of 1st lieutenant.

JAMES F. MURPHY, born Sept. 22, 1919, enlisted Sept. 30, 1940, serving in the Army infantry.

His stations include: Fort McClellan, AL; Infantry School, Fort Benning, GA; Maui, TH Schofield Barracks; Australia; Goodenough Island; New Guinea and Philippine Islands.

His awards include the Combat Infantry Badge, Bronze Star, Purple Heart, American Campaign, Asiatic-Pacific Campaign Ribbon w/Arrowhead, Philippine Liberation Ribbon w/two Stars and the Victory Medal.

Memorable experiences include moving a gun platoon to Breakneck during night time. Removing 2nd Bn. wounded from Break Neck Ridge after dark.

Married for 53 years to Ara Nell and they have three children: Sharon Alessi, Terence Murphy and Jan Murphy; five grandchildren and four great-grandchildren. He worked as a tool and die maker. Now retired and plays golf in the summer and shovels snow in the winter.

JOHN MURPHY, born in New York City, was inducted into the Army March 1953. Received basic training at Fort Campbell, KY with 11th Abn. Div. Sent to Korea and assigned to 24th Inf. Div., 19th Inf. Regt.

After Korean service he was stationed at Schofield Barracks, HI with the 25th Inf. Div. Discharged in 1955.

He has never complained of the cold after surviving a winter in Korea. He is happy that there is a Korean War Memorial in Washington, DC, even though it took over 40 years.

Married with one son, John and one granddaughter Aileen. Enjoys exercising at local gym. Active member in American Legion, also a member of the 24th Inf. Div. Assoc. He served 33 years in the New York City Police Dept., retiring as sergeant.

THOMAS C. MURPHY joined the service on Jan. 14, 1953, and served with the Med. Co., 19th Regt. He was stationed in Korea from 1954-55. He was discharged with the rank of corporal. Joined the Reserves and retired with the rank of sergeant first class. Dates served: 1954-55.

DAVID MURRAY joined the service in January 1951 and served with Co. D, 3rd Eng. He was stationed in Korea. He was discharged with the rank of private first class. Dates served: 1951-52.

BOBBY L. MYERS joined the service on Feb. 13, 1943, and served with Cannon Co., 34th Inf. Regt. He participated in New Guinea, South Philippines, Luzon, Hawaii, Australia, Hollandia, Biak, Leyte, Mindanao, Corregidor and Japan. He was discharged with the rank of sergeant. Awards include the Combat Infantryman's Badge, Purple Heart, Bronze Arrowhead, Asiatic-Pacific Campaign Medal, Philippine Liberation Ribbon w/2 Bronze Stars, Good Conduct Medal, WWII Victory Medal, Philippine Defense Medal, Philippine Independence Medal and Philippine Republic Presidential Unit Citation Badge. Dates served: Feb. 13, 1943, to Dec. 16, 1945.

PHILIP H. NAST, born Dec. 15, 1923, enlisted in the service March 18, 1942. His stations include: IRTC (cadre), Fort Stewart, Camp Croft, Camp Robinson, OCS, Fort Benning.

Discharged April 26, 1946 as first lieutenant. His awards include the Combat Infantry Badge, Bronze Star, Purple Heart, Asiatic-Pacific Theater w/two Bronze Stars, one Arrowhead.

His memorable experiences: Met some great guys and came home alive.

Married to Hilja J. Nast. Employed as high school principal. He enjoys skiing, snowshoeing, carving, reading and most importantly, breathing.

JOSEPH P. NEGRELLI joined the service on Sept. 9, 1946, and entered active duty in December 1946. He served with Co. L, 19th Inf. Regt., December 1946 to December 1947; Svc. Co., HQ & HQ Co., 19th Inf. Regt., January 1949 to July 1951. He was discharged in December 1947.

Recalled on Oct. 26, 1948, and was discharged in July 1951. Awards include the WWII Victory Medal, Occupation of Japan Medal, Korean Service Medal w/ Silver Star, Distinguished Unit Citation, ROK Distinguished Unit Citation, Combat Infantryman's Badge and Bronze Star Medal.

RANDALL P. NEHR joined the service on Nov. 23, 1953, and served with Co. C, 6th Tk. Bn., He was discharged with the rank of E-3. Dates served: April 1954 to October 1955.

ELLSWORTH (DUTCH) NELSEN, born in Omaha in 1925 and drafted into the Army in 1946. Served with the 34th Inf. Regt., Sasebo, Japan 1946-47 as private, private first class, corporal. OCS at Fort Riley, KS. 13th FABN, Fukuoka, Japan, then with first troops into Korea July 5, 1950.

His first six campaigns: 471 days in combat, 2nd lieutenant, 1st lieutenant. Again with 24th in Germany, 19th Inf., 13th Field, Division Trains, captain and major. Retired as lieutenant colonel, chief of staff, Fort Carson, 24 years service.

His awards include the Purple Heart, Bronze Star w/V twice, two Legion of Merit, two Army Commendation Medal, enlisted Good Conduct Medal, Korean Service w/six Battle Stars, Vietnam Service w/four Battle Stars.

He married Margo in Germany in 1954. They have three children and four grandchildren. His family hobbies include rock hounding, gold prospecting and model railroad.

JAMES D. NELSON, born June 2, 1931, enlisted Sept. 17, 1952. He received basic training, Fort Knox, KY. Attended Armored School, for Torret Arty. mechanic. C Btry., 63rd FABN, 24th Div., South Camp Fuji, Japan; Korea; one year, three months, 21 days overseas.

Discharged Sept. 10, 1954 as corporal. His awards include the Korean Service Ribbon w/Bronze Service Star, Good Conduct Medal, United Nations Service Medal, National Defense Service Medal, Republic of Korea Presidential Unit Citation.

Memorable experiences: Computer and plotter for Fire Direction Center. July 1953, their unit went forward to support the 1st Rox north of Seoul. Near Impl. Gang River where they fired on the enemy. Three days later they moved to the Chorwon Valley in support of 27th Regt., 25th Inf. where again they fired on the enemy. They were also fierce around both positions. C Btry. were the only ones to fire on the enemy.

Graduated from University of Minnesota School of Agriculture. He is a member of VFW and American Legion.

James married Ruth May 26, 1956 and they have four children: Dale, Jeffrey, Thomas and Mark; six grandchildren: Dareth, Dylan, Daniel, Chelsey, Shawna, Tanner. He is a retired farmer.

PETE NEPOTE joined the service on Nov. 18, 1938, and served with Co. C, 3rd Eng. He participated in the Korean War. He was discharged with the rank of 1st sergeant. Dates served: July 1950 to July 1951.

DONALD NESS, born Aug. 26, 1925 in Portage, WI, enlisted in the Army Nov. 25, 1944.

His assignments: 24th Div., 21st Regt., Co. I, Mintal, Mindanao, PI; Okayama, Japan for occupation. Attended basic training at Camp (now Fort) Hood, TX.

Discharged Nov. 15, 1946 as corporal T5. His awards include the Presidential Unit Citation, Combat Badge and Battle Star.

Memorable experiences: An eight-man patrol into a deep ravine between Mintal and Ula villages, Mindanao. Ambushed on way back to perimeter. A platoon sergeant was killed, one other man shot in shoulder. Squad leader was Sgt. Campbell. Donald's best buddy, James Namath, from Detroit was killed by mortar fire. Donald saw Hiroshima a few months after the atom bomb was dropped there.

He married Reiko Oka and they have a daughter, Sarah Ness Vining.

LINWOOD (JOHN) NEWELL, born June 23, 1932, enlisted into the Army July 13, 1950. He received basic training at Fort Ord, NJ, July 1950-September 1950; Engineer School, Fort Belvoir, VA, September 1950-December 1950; Korea February 1951-July 1951 with Co. C, 19th Inf., 24th Div.; February 1953 to July 1953, Fort Rucker, AL.

Discharged July 15, 1953 as sergeant. His awards include the Combat Infantry Badge, Purple Heart w/ OLC, Korean Service Medal w/two Battle Stars and UN Service Medal.

Memorable experiences: The men he served with in the 24th Inf. Div. These were the truest friends he ever met, although he has not had any contact since military service. He has presumed that most perished or have since passed away.

Employed with the state of Maine, Employment Security Comm. for 24 years and took early retirement as an office manager. He was also employed with the US Postal Service from 1981 to 1995.

He was married in 1961 to Tamarra and they have two children, Barbara and Tamerica. He has three children from a previous marriage: Eddy, Teddy, Tanya and also has six grandchildren and one great-grandchild.

Retired and maintaining a home on a 25-acre plot. Enjoys hunting big game, fishing and snowmobiling.

ROBERT A. NEWKIRK joined the service on Jan. 3, 1941, and served with Co. H, 21st Inf. Regt. He participated at Pearl Harbor, Leyte and the Philippine Islands. He was discharged with the rank of staff sergeant. Dates served: 1941-45.

JOHN ROSS NOGENT joined the service on Nov. 22, 1940, and served with QMC Det. He transferred to the 325th QM BN, 25th Inf. Div. on Oct. 1, 1941. He was discharged with the rank of private first class.

JACK NOONEY, born Dec. 15, 1927, enlisted in the Army August 1946.

Inducted at Fort MacPherson, GA. Received basic training at Fort Bragg, NC. Assigned to 24th Div. Arty.,

Camp Hakata, Japan. Appointed acting sergeant January 1947. Promoted to sergeant mid-1947.

Discharged January 1948. His awards include the Victory Medal, Good Conduct, Occupation of Japan. Served as chief of detail, B Btry., 63rd Bn., (105 howitzers).

Returned to college in fall 1948. Graduated with a BS degree June 1951 from Florida State University. He was hired by State Farm Insurance Co. in 1953 as a management trainee. He served in various management positions for 40 years and retired in 1993.

Memorable experiences: appointment to county school board in 1975. Reelected four times and retired in October 1992 after serving 17 years.

He and Patsy K. have been married since 1956 and they have two children, Patrick and Scott and five grandchildren: Shannon, Heather, Jeffery, Caroline and Hank.

He is presently working half days as office administrator for son, Scott, who is a practicing attorney. He is also member of County Civil Service Board.

JAMES D. NUGENT, born Nov. 27, 1919, enlisted in the service March 12, 1940. His assignments include the 35th Inf. Regt., H Co., Schofield Barracks, HI; 19th Inf. Regt., H Co., 1943 Schofield Barracks, HI. Campaigns: Pearl Harbor, New Guinea.

Discharged June 6, 1945 as sergeant and received the Combat Infantry Badge.

He is married to Corabell and they have two children, Beverley and Linda and four grandchildren: Cody Clawson, Chelsie Clawson, Lori Scivally, Terra Tanant. He is a retired building contractor.

STANLEY OBREMSKI joined the service on July 12, 1948, and served with Co. A, 6th Tk. Bn. He participated in the North Korean Defensive, North Korean Offensive, Chinese Intervention, Naktong River and Taejon. He was discharged with the rank of corporal. Dates served: July 1950 to June 1951.

JOSEPH P. O'CONNELL, born June 22, 1930 in Cambridge, PA, attended schools in Randolph and Stoughton, MA. He enlisted in the service February 1951 and attended basic training with Co. M, 136th Inf., 47th Div., Camp Rucker, AL. In August 1951 he was assigned to Co. H, 19th Inf., 24th Div. in Korea as a machine gunner. He was with H Co. until August 1953 and then returned to US and discharged as sergeant January 1954.

After discharge he served three years in the Army Reserve as first sergeant of artillery battery while attending Boston University on the GI Bill. He graduated in 1956 After graduation worked for Shawmut Bank of Boston. In 1967 relocated to Warminster, Bucks County, PA, where he still resided.

He married Jean Mazeika of Walpole, MA and she died in 1991. They had one son and two grandchildren. He retired in 1995 as vice president of Trust

Investments. In Pennsylvania he was employed by Girard, Mellon and Bucks County Banks respectively. During his career he was active in a number of professional, civic and charitable organizations. Of all his awards, civilian or military, he is most proud of his Combat Infantry Badge.

DANIEL E. O'CONNOR joined the service on Sept. 9, 1949, and served with Co. L, 21st Regt. He was discharged with the rank of private first class. Dates served: 1950.

JOSEPH R. ODE, born March 23, 1932 in Buffalo, NY, enlisted in the US Army Sept. 30, 1950. He was sent to Fort Sill, OK where he trained on the 105s.

He was going home for Christmas, but they cancelled it and said they were to be shipped out as soon as possible. They did not tell them where, but they had a good idea. They made him a corporal while he was there. Soon after, some of them were placed with an artillery outfit. He went to the 13th FA Baker Btry. He was there only a short time and was ranked as staff sergeant. He was then in charge of one of the 105s. They moved around often. Most of the guys names he can't remember.

They set up in one place and unloaded the ammo truck. As he left he attempted to turn around and ran over a mine. They weren't hurt too bad, the area was checked and more mines were found and the area was taped off.

They went up to or near the front lines for direct fire and moved out real fast both day and night. It was just about time for them to be taken over by another outfit, the artillery section of the 40th Div. They fired their last round in the Kumsong Valley.

He was shipped to Japan for a while then went home. After a leave he returned and was assigned to Btry. D, 738 AAA Gun Bn., FA which was from Fort Dix, NJ, and stationed in Philly. He was there a short time and ended up in Valley Forge Army Hospital.

It didn't take long for him to go from a boy to a man. They had a lot of fire missions day and night. He knows that those who belonged to these outfits did a lot of North Koreans in.

Discharged Dec. 31, 1953 as staff sergeant. His awards include the National Defense Service Medal, United Nations Service Medal, Good Conduct Medal, Korean Service Medal, Bronze Service Star.

He is married to Bonnie M. Ode and they have three children: Cheryl, Jackie and Kim; four grandchildren: Melissa, Ricky, Joey and Kimberly and a great-granddaughter, Kaitlyn. He worked at a dairy before entering service and has also been employed as an auto mechanic.

He has had many surgeries. He lost a leg and kidney during service and had a heart valve replaced in 1982. He now has a tumor in his abdomen and one growing on his spine, both of which are unoperable. He says that he can live with it as long as he has the Lord.

EDWARD J. O'HARA, born Aug. 21, 1933, enlisted in the New York National Guard in March 1950 in the Flushing Armory serving with HQ, 3rd Bn., 69th Inf. Regt. staying there until September 1952. He then went into the US Army for three years. His National Guard 21945093 then went to RA, he was then sent to Camp Killman, NJ then to Camp Breckinridge, KY with the 101st Abn. Div. (training).

After 16 weeks of heavy weapons training he was sent to Japan, serving with the 24th Inf. Div., 21st Inf. Regt., A Co. as a 60mm mortarman, the Division after reorganization was sent back to Korea for the second time.

He rose in the ranks from mortarman to motor sergeant to P&A platoon sergeant in charge of the Bn. ammo dump. He served in Korea for 21 months returning to the US a SFC. He went to the 19th Combat Engrs., 2nd Army HQ, Fort Meade, MD, until his honorable discharge in September 1955.

After his discharge he joined the New York National Guard, again this time to HQ 3rd Bn., 71st Inf. Regt. at 3rd Bn., 71st Inf. Regt. at 33rd St. and Park Ave. serving as a communication chief from battalion to battle group, to 1st Bde. He then went to Jamaica, after the reorganization of the 3rd Bde. which became the 1st Bde. He became first sergeant of HQ Co. and then to 1st Bde. CSM until Oct. 1, 1981, at that time he was transferred to 2nd Bde. CSM until Aug. 1, 1983.

His awards include the Good Conduct Medal, United Nations, National Defense, Korean Service, Armed Forces Service, Army National Guard, New York State Military Commendation, NY Faithful Service (30 years) Medal, NY State Service in aids of civil authorities, 71 Faithful service, Senior NCO (ESMA).

Married Mary O'Hara and they have three children: John, William Jones and Debbie; two grandchildren: William Jr. and Natalie Roberta. He is now retired.

LLOYD E. OLER SR., born in West Lima, WI March 20, 1929, took basic training at Fort Ord, CA. In September 1948 he was picked by Gen. MacArthur's aids to serve as guard at Sugamo prison Tokyo, Japan. In July 1950 while serving as jailor at Sugamo he was put on orders with 150 fellow Sugamonites to be a POW escort guard in Korea. When arriving in Korea he was assigned to the 2nd Bn., F Co., 19th Inf. Regt., 24th Inf. Div. Reassigned to the 339th Replacement Depot, Pusan, Korea, January 1951 because of frozen hands and feet. Left Korea August 1951. He originally had enlisted for three years, Feb. 18, 1948 and that was extended for one year by President Truman. Discharged Feb. 18, 1952 as corporal.

He received Japan Occupational Medal, Combat Infantry Badge, Korean Service Ribbon w/five Campaign Stars and the Meritorious Unit Commendation.

Memorable experiences: Sugamo prison was the home of Tojo, Tokyo Rose and all of the Japanese war criminals. He was at Sugamo Dec. 23, 1948 when Tojo was hung for war crimes that were committed.

He was a heavy equipment operator. Retired in 1988 from Local 150 Operating Engineers Countryside, IL.

His wife of 37 years died of cancer. He raised four boys. Roger is a retired Air Force fighter pilot. Gordon owns Silo Construction Company. Robert is a

quality control specialist, Mercury Industries, Richland Center, WI. Lloyd Jr. is computer programmer in the Air Force serving at Fort Meade, MA National Security Agency.

LOUIS OLIVER, born in Oxnard, CA, Nov. 16, 1940, enlisted in the US Army at the age of 17. In 1958, he took infantry basic training at Fort Ord, CA. After basic training he attended Wheel Vehicle Mechanic School. In March 1959, he went overseas and was stationed in the 24th Signal Bn., 24th Inf. Div., Flak Kaserne, Augsberg, Germany. He served 25 months in the 24th Inf. Div., Flak Kaserne, Augsberg, Germany. He served 25 months in the motor pool and was rotated back to the US in 1961, as a specialist fourth class. He was then stationed at the Presidio, San Francisco. A month later he was transferred to HQ Detachment 4th MSL Bn., 67th Arty. in Berkeley, CA, motor pool. He was selected by Col. R.C. Britt to be his driver. He was due for discharge in October 1961, but that was extended until February 1962. At that time he received an honorable discharge.

His medals include the Good Conduct Medal, Expert Shooting Medals for submachine gun and carbine rifle and Marksman Medal for M-1 Rifle.

He married Patricia A. Stahl in August 1962. They have four sons, two granddaughters and two grandsons; with a great-grandchild due any time. Currently, he is employed by G&S Acoustics as vice president. He plans to retire in 2002 and travel the country with his wife in their 1930 Model A Ford Coupe.

JERRY OLIVO joined the service on Sept. 26, 1941, and served with Co. K, 21st Regt. He participated at Pearl Harbor, New Guinea, Central Pacific and the Philippine Islands campaigns. He was discharged with the rank of technical sergeant. Dates served: Sept. 26, 1941, to May 23, 1945.

ROBERT A. OLSON joined the service on Aug. 3, 1942, and served with Co. M, 34th Regt. He participated in the South Pacific, Hollandia, Biak and Leyte. He was discharged with the rank of private first class. Dates served: 1942-45.

THOMAS O'MEARA, born Nov. 21, 1930 in Dry Branch, WV, son of Mr. and Mrs. Jane O'Meara, enlisted in the service Jan. 20, 1949. He was assigned to Fort Knox, KY for basic training and then assigned to I Co., 34th Inf. Regt., 24th Div. at Camp Mower near Sasebo, Japan April 1949. Went to Korea July 2, 1950. Served with I Co. from April 1949 to September 1950. Served in various battles, the worse being Taejon, July 19 and 20, 1950. Wounded in action at Battle of Kuchong, September 1950. Returned to duty November 1950. Discharged June 5, 1952 as sergeant at Fort George G. Meade, MD.

Memorable experiences: Returned to the US on *General M.C. Meigs.* Five days out of Japan, while standing in one of the chow lines, he was with a friend

from home. He pointed out that he thought he knew the soldier standing in the second chow line. He replied "I guess you should, he's your brother." They had not seen each other since joining the Army, three years earlier. They had fought very close to each other in Korea.

Memories of the war include many battles such as Taejon and Kuchong, the heat, rain, snow, and bitter, bitter cold of the winters of 1950 and 1951, which he is sure none of them will ever forget. Rotated out of Korea May 1951.

He was the recipient of the Purple Heart and Combat Infantry Badge among others.

Retired from Libby Owens Ford Glass Co. in 1984. Member VFW 4299, member 3/34 and 2/21 Inf. Battalions Assoc.

Married June 28, 1952 to Margaret Howard. They have one son, Thomas. He and his wife, Debbie, have their three grandchildren: Philip Scott, Matthew Louis and Stephenie Lee.

He has been involved in Clifton Forge and Alleghany County, VA School Sports Club for 35 years. The clubs support all sports and try to supply equipment when requested.

FRANK R. ORLOSKI joined the service on Sept. 30, 1950, and served with H&S Co., 3rd Eng. He was discharged with the rank of E-7. Dates served: March 1951 to February 1952.

CRESENCIO V. ORTIZ, born June 15, 1925, enlisted in the Army Nov. 12, 1943.

His assignments include basic training at Camp Fannin in Tyler, TX. Shipped to Oro Bay, New Guinea. Joined 24th in Hollandia, Co. D, 21st, water-cooled machine gunner.

Discharged Jan. 23, 1946 as staff sergeant, Fort Sam Houston, San Antonio, TX.

His awards include the Asiatic-Pacific, two Bronze Stars, Philippine Liberation Ribbon w/two Bronze Stars, Good Conduct Medal, three Overseas Bars and the Victory Ribbon.

There were many memorable experiences but his happiest memory occurred when he went on a three-day pass to see his brother in Osaka, Japan. Cresencio was stationed in Okayama, Japan.

He was employed in aircraft work. Retired from Justin Boot Co. after 30 years as factory supervisor. He also served as master sergeant from the Texas National Guard 1953-1962.

He married Anna M. Duarte, April 27, 1947 and they two have daughters: Yolanda and Laura Ann and five grandchildren: Ernie, Monica, Michelle, Todd and Desere and two great-grandsons, Jordan and Noel.

Presently employed as security and runner for the Dent Law Firm, Fort Worth, TX.

GLENN L. OSBORN joined the service on Feb. 27, 1942, and served with the Svc. Co., 34th Regt. He participated at New Guinea, Hollandia, Biak and the Philippines. He was discharged with the rank of staff sergeant.

WILLIAM H. OSLIN joined the service on March 8, 1943, and served with Cannon Co., 2nd Bn., 19th Regt. He participated in the Pacific, Leyte, Mindoro, Lubang, Mindanao, North and South Philippines campaigns and Shikoku, Japan. He was discharged with the rank of private first class. Dates served: October 1944 to January 1946.

ROBERT JEREMIAH OSWALD joined the service on April 20, 1966, and served with Co. B, 2nd Bn., 21st Inf. Regt. He was discharged with the rank of SP4. Dates served: 1968.

ROBERT F. OTTE SR. joined the service on Jan. 3, 1951, and served with HQ Co., 3rd Bn., 5th RCT Regt. He was stationed in Korea from August 1951 to May 1952; Hills 1073, 663 and 770; Kumsong; and Punch Bowl. He was discharged in October 1952 with the rank of staff sergeant.

CURTIS VINING PACKARD, born Dec. 19, 1910, in Mansfield, AR, grew up in Fort Smith, AR and died Sept. 15, 1993, in Little Rock, AR, where he had resided since 1959.

His Army career began with study at the University of Chicago ASTP program to be in an Army intelligence unit going to Germany. Instead he was sent to the Pacific as a member of a seven-man photo interpreter unit with the rank of master sergeant. This unit made maps from aerial photographs. By studying the plant life in the photographs, Botanist Packard determined the terrain and whether it was suitable for a beach landing. He was with the Army Occupation of Japan after the war.

Because he had malaria and some unknown South Sea fever, he left teaching, studied law on the GI program and obtained a law degree at the age of 40. He retired as chief attorney for real estate at the Corps of Engineers office in Little Rock. In 1948 he married Dorothy Ruwe Barton. They had three children and four grandchildren.

DORWIN C. PACKARD joined the service on Feb. 14, 1942, and served with Co. H, 21st Inf. Regt. He participated in New Guinea and the Southern Philippines. He was discharged with the rank of 1st sergeant. Dates served: Feb. 14, 1942, to Nov. 7, 1945.

ROBERT GENE (BOB) PALLESEN, born Dec. 16, 1933, enlisted in the service January 1949, serving as a medic.

His assignments included: Medical Detachment 24th Div. Arty., Camp Hakata, Japan; 118 Hospital, 26th AAA in May 1950.

He was captured July 14, 1950 and died a POW October 1950.

DOMENICK J. PANTALONE, entered service May 1951, Philadelphia, PA.

Served foreign service one year and 16 days. Trained at Indiantown Gap, PA from May to July then assigned to Fort Bliss, TX until October 1951. Left for overseas from California sometime in October 1951 and was assigned to 24th Div., 19th Inf., E Co.

He was with the 24th Div. until February 1952. The 24th Div. moved to Japan and he stayed as a replacement and was assigned to 40th Div., 160th Regt., as he did not have enough points to rotate with the 24th Div. Their first hill with 24th Div. Outpost 747, they were located in Kumwha and the Kumsong area.

Left Korea September 1952 and was released from Fort Meade, MD.

His decorations include the Combat Infantry Badge and the United Nations Service Medal.

RICHARD PARMERTER, born Feb. 22, 1932, enlisted in the Army December 1950. Received basic at Fort Devens, MA; advanced training with Tank Co., 278th RC, Fort Devens and Fort Drum; Korea, 6th Tank Bn., 1951. Went to Japan with 24th in February 1952.

Returned home 1953 and was discharged in 1954 as corporal E-4. His awards include the Korean Service w/2 Bronze Stars, UN Service Medal, Good Conduct, Occupation Japan and the American Defense.

Employed as retail store manager for 35 years. Stopped work after 50 years with same company. He had started with that company in 1946 at age 14.

He married Gloria in 1955 and they have no children. He is now retired.

JOSEPH PARISI, born in Brooklyn, NY, Nov. 28, 1926 was drafted into the Army Jan. 4, 1945. He received basic training at Camp Robinson, AR.

Sent overseas in September 1945 and landed in Leyte, going to Mindanao, where he was assigned to HQ Co., 2nd Btry., 34th Inf. Moved to Matsuyama, Japan. He lived in Jap barracks where they were infested with lice. They were then moved into tents and from there to Kobe to live in quonset huts. Sent to Etajima, where their job was to check all caves and burn all ammo on the island. They found a glider in a cave, which several of them put together. They tried flying it by towing it with a 3/4 ton weapons carrier, but could only get it up about 10 feet. They then were sent to Sasebo where he became the 2nd Btry. motor sergeant. They would go to the town of Anora and drink green beer.

After spending 13 months in Japan he was sent home and discharged in 1946 as sergeant.

As a civilian he was employed as a machinist at Brooklyn, NY Navy Yard; auto mechanic and grader operator engineer for New York City Highway Dept., retiring in 1989.

He is married to Marion and they have two children, Lynn and Diane; and seven grandchildren: Michael, Victoria, Joseph, Laura, Crista, Gary Nicholas.

Now retired and living in Florida for four months in the winter and in New York State for eight months. His hobby is playing golf.

JACKIE R. PARKS joined the service on Aug. 6, 1953, and served with HQ & HQ Co., 34th Regt. He was stationed in Korea, DMZ. He was discharged with the rank of private first class. Dates served: May 25, 1954, to Sept. 25, 1955.

RICHARD PARMERTER joined the service on Jan. 15, 1951, and served with H&S Co., 6th Tk. Bn. and Co. C., 24th Inf. Regt. He participated in the summer and winter offensives. He was discharged with the rank of E-4. Dates served: May 1951 to August 1954.

LOUIS J. PASCAL joined the service on March 1, 1940, at Schofield Barracks. He served with Co. H, 21st Inf. Regt. He was discharged on July 12, 1945, with the rank of sergeant.

KENNETH E. (KENNY) PATE, born Feb. 19, 1920, Mediapolis, IA, was drafted into the Army Feb. 2, 1942.

His assignments included: Camp Wolters, Hawaiian Islands, New Guinea, Philippines, Mindoro, Mindanao, Goodenough, Australia, Leyte in lost battalion.

He was awarded the WWII Victory Medal, Battle Star Pin (one for Leyte, two for Mindoro, three for Mindanao), Hawaiian Badge, Arrowhead Badge, Good Conduct Medal, Riflemans Pin, Medallion used for decoration, Eagle pin for decoration, US flag pin for decoration, sign of 24th Inf., Toro Leaf.

Served with the 19th Inf., E Co., 24th Div. Discharged Sept. 5, 1945.

Employed at grocery warehouse for 33 years and the city parks for six years. Retired because of poor health.

He married "Brownie" Oct. 6, 1946 and they have two daughters, Vickie Renee and Jerri Kay; and two granddaughters, Lisa Marie and Kori Kay. Presently resides in Burlington, IA and is a life member of the 24th Div. Assoc., American Legion and VFW.

LUTHER C. PATTERSON joined the service on Aug. 22, 1949, and served with Co. G, 19th Regt. He was stationed in Korea. He was discharged on July 2, 1953, with the rank of private first class. Dates served: Feb. 1951 to November 1951.

DAVID R. PAYNE joined the service on July 2, 1943, and served the HQ Btry., 11th FA BN. He participated at New Guinea, Philippines and Japan. He was discharged with the rank of master sergeant. Dates served: May 1944 to December 1945.

BERNARD EDWARD PEARSALL enlisted in the service on Oct. 10, 1946, and attended the 24th Inf. Div. School. He served with Co. K, 34th Inf. Regt. He participated in the Far East, Camp Mower and Japan. He was discharged with the rank of private first class. Awards include the WWII Victory Medal and Army of Occupation Medal (Japan). Dates served: October 1946 to June 4, 1948.

DONALD B. PERRIN, born May 21, 1931, enlisted in the Army Jan. 15, 1949. Assignments: Basic, Fort Jackson, SC; medical training, Fort Benning, GA base hospital. Sent to Japan and from there he was reassigned to Inf. Co. C, 1st Bn., 19th Regt., 24th Div. Task Force Smith July 1950.

He was wounded and reassigned as medic to C Co. Spent 13 months underfire with 24th Div. After being wounded the second time he was reassigned to A Co. November 1951 and assigned to Fort Sam Houston, TX teaching battlefield conditions. In 1953 he was reassigned to Fort Stewart, GA in charge of physical examinations.

Discharged as sergeant June 15, 1954. His awards

include the Purple Heart w/two Clusters, five Silver and six Bronze Battle Stars, two US Presidential Citations, two Korean Presidential Citations and other miscellaneous campaign medals.

Self-employed plumber most of his life. Worked as a life insurance salesman until stroke in 1976. Self-employed in sales after that. Married had five children and divorced and remarried in 1978. Started "Stand up for America" parade as commander of Amvets in February 1980 in the Keys, Marathon, FL. Very active at the time in Elks and Veterans Organizations in the Keys. Traveled US in motor home for several years and then settled in the Sebastian area in 1988. Joined the VFW while there and joined MOPH in 1996 which he is now active in.

His activities have been curtailed quite a bit because of problems with his feet, a result of frost bite; arthritis in his back from being wounded and finally the bypass heart surgery in January 1990. He likes to go fishing and tries to travel as much as he can in his motor home. He also enjoys going to reunions. There are not many of the "Task Force Smith" survivors left.

MILLER G. PERRY served as commanding officer of the 52nd FA BN, from Sept. 13, 1949, until Sept. 13, 1950. He then served as executive officer of Div. Arty. from Sept. 13, 1950, until July 1, 1951. He participated in five Korean War campaigns.

ARLO L. PETERSON joined the service on May 23, 1955, and served with the 24th Med. Bn., 24th Div. He was discharged on Feb. 28, 1957, with the rank of SP3.

AUBREY H. PETERSON was inducted into the service on Dec. 12, 1944, and served with the 19th Inf. Regt., 2nd Bn. He was discharged on Oct. 30, 1946, with the rank of Tec 5. Awards include the Combat Infantryman's Badge, Army of Occupation Medal, Asiatic-Pacific Campaign Medal, Philippine Liberation w/Bronze Star, Good Conduct Medal and WWII Victory Medal. He also served two years in the US Merchant Marines during WWII.

FRANK H. PETERSON, born June 26, 1929, enlisted in the Army Nov. 24, 1950. Received basic training at Fort Knox. Served in Korea April 1951-52 with the 21st Inf. Regt.

Discharged September 1952 and received the Combat Infantry Badge, two Bronze Stars w/ OLC, Korean Service Medal and the United Nation Service Medal.

His memorable experiences: chairman, local farm service agency for 15 years. Lifetime member of VFW, member of and helped organize Honor Guard.

Self-employed as landowner and operator. He is married to Betty Lanham Peterson and they have four surviving children: Phyllis, John, Lorraine and Daniel and two deceased children, Pamela and Scott; and 13 grandchildren. He is presently overseeing and operating a diverse farming operation.

CHESTER P. PETTEY joined the service on Feb. 3, 1943, and served with Co. D, HHC, 3rd Eng. He participated in five campaigns in Korea. He was discharged on July 1, 1943, with the rank of captain. Dates served: 1950-51 and 1959-62.

HUGH PHARAOH (KENT) joined the service on July 19, 1966, and served with HQ & HQ Co. He served with the 24th Div. in Germany and made first Reforger to Ft. Riley, KS. He was discharged with the rank of SP5. Dates served: 1968-69.

CHARLES FRANCIS PHILLIPS, born Oct. 16, 1928, enlisted in the Army August 1949. Assignments

include basic training, Fort Riley, KS. Transferred to Co. A, 25th Inf. Div., Sasebo, Japan. Transferred to Co. C, 21st Inf., 24th Div. Task Force Smith, first into Korea.

He was KIA, July 12, 1950. His awards include the Purple Heart, Bronze Star, National Korean, United Nations Medal and Combat Badge.

He was escorted home June 12, 1952 by his brother Donald C. Phillips as his brothers escort for a full military funeral.

DONALD C. PHILLIPS, born Dec. 2, 1933, enlisted in the Army December 1951. Attended basic training Schofield Barracks, HI then returned to the USA. Discharged Dec. 12, 1955 with the rank of corporal.

His awards include the Good Conduct, Bronze Stars, National Korean w/Star, United Nations Defense Medal, Combat Infantry and numerous certificates.

Memorable experiences: Escorted his brother's body home for military funeral June 12, 1950. His brother was killed in action in Korea. He was first in with Task Force Smith.

Divorced and has six children: Donald C., Timothy, Brian E., Russell W., Marsha J., Pamela J. and eight grandchildren and one great-granddaughter. He is now retired.

ROBERT L. PHILLIPS, born Sept. 23, 1927, enlisted in the Army Jan. 25, 1946. Assignments: Fort Belvoir, VA (basic training); Oliver General Hospital (OT tech); Ambulance Co., 24th Medical Bn., 24th Inf. Div. (company clerk); platoon sergeant, first sergeant, Kokura, Japan and Korea (July 1949-May 1951). Received battlefield commission, May 1951. Assigned to Clearing Co., 24th Med. Bn. as platoon leader.

Returned to USA July 1951 assigned to Med. Repl. Tng. Ctr. (MRTC) at Camp Pickett, VA and Fort Sam Houston, TX; 4th Armd. Div., Fort Hood, TX and rotated to Germany with 4th Armd. Div. as medical supply officer; Fort Meade, MD, 128th Station Hospital, medical supply officer until discharged June 18, 1963 as captain MSC

His awards include the Bronze Star, NDSM, Korean Service Medal, United Nations Service Medal, Presidential Unit Citation (ROK), O/S Service Medal, Good Conduct Medal, Presidential Unit Citation and Combat Medical Badge.

Employed as manager of Quality Inns, Holiday Inns, Baltimore, Cumberland and Eastern Shore of Maryland. Condominium manager, Ocean City, MD. Given "Pride" Award by Holiday Inn University in May 1974.

Married Geraldine F. Hart, January 1946 and they have five children: Robert L. Jr., Steven W., Beverly S. Heinmueller, Donald E. and Joseph A.; seven grandchildren: Stephanie, John, Kelly, Sarah, Andrew, Evan and Leah and two great-grandchildren.

Semi-retired and doing some work as locksmith (hobby). In 1989 had vocal cords removed (larygectomy) due to cancer on vocal cords.

DONALD N. PIERCE joined the service in June 1943, at Ft. Leavenworth, KS, and attended basic train-

ing at Camp Abbott, OR. He served with Co. B, 3rd Combat Eng. Bn. He joined the 24th Div. in September 1944 and participated in the Philippines and the Occupation of Japan until June 1947. He was discharged with the rank of captain.

DONALD R. PIERCE joined the service on July 11, 1950, and served with Co. B, 21st Regt. He was stationed in Korea. He was discharged with the rank of sergeant. Awards include four Bronze Service Stars. Dates served: February to October 1951.

HARRY L. PINKHAM joined the service in October 1950 and served with HQ Co., 5th RCT Regt. He participated in the Occupation of Korea. He was discharged in July 1952 with the rank of staff sergeant.

PETER A. PISCITELLI, born in New York City, Aug. 8, 1917. On March 7, 1941, he took basic training at Fort Jackson, SC, and was discharged on May 18, 1945 from Fort Dix. During this period, he was the 1st Bn. supply sergeant. He served in Hawaii and the Philippines.

He was awarded the Bronze Star for saving his battalion when they were attacked on the island of Leyte in the Philippines.

He married Sylvia Faluotico on April 6, 1947. They have three grown children and six grandchildren. After working over 60 years as a butcher, he retired in 1995.

ALFRED N. POIRIER joined the service on April 1, 1941, and served with Btry. E, 13th FA as a private, April 26 to Sept. 30, 1941; and Btry. B, 63rd FA BN, Oct. 1, 1941, to March 20, 1945. He participated at Pearl Harbor, Hollandia, Tanahmerah Bay, New Guinea, Leyte and Luzon. He was discharged with the rank of private.

JOSEPH POLITO joined the service in October 1944 and served with Co. H, 19th Inf. Regt. He participated in the Asiatic-Pacific Campaign and Philippines Liberation. He was discharged in November 1946 with the rank of private first class.

JOHN R. PORTER joined the service in February 1942 and served with HQ Co., 2nd Bn., 21st Inf. Regt. He participated in Hawaii, Australia, New Guinea, Mindoro, Leyte and Mindanao. He was discharged with the rank of 1st sergeant. Dates served: February 1942 to November 1945.

JAMES LEA POSTMA, born Osage City, KS, Feb. 2, 1916, entered the Army at Ft. Leavenworth, KS, March 14, 1942. He volunteered for duty with the Counter-intelligence Corps. Transferred to US Inf. and volunteered for officers training at Fort Benning, GA.

Commissioned second lieutenant of infantry and arrived at Pearl Harbor, March 7, 1943, assigned to 24th Inf. Div., 21st Regt., Co. K, leader, 3rd Plt. Other assignments included Goodenough Island, Hollandia, Panoan Island (Leyte Operation). Wounded at Breakneck Ridge, Leyte, Philippines, Nov. 6, 1944. Endured three days of kamikaze attacks. 1945 Camp Carson, CO and Camp Rucker, AL hospitals (malaria). Assigned to Judge Advocate General. 1946 discharged from active duty, transferred to active reserves. Training with 89th Div. in Wisconsin (1951) and Fort Carson, CO (1952). Discharged from active reserves, 1953 and received the Purple Heart and Philippine Liberation Medal.

He was a graduate of University of Kansas and KU School of Law and practiced in Lawrence, KS from 1941 to 1997. He married Sally Fitzpatrick in December 1954 and they had a daughter, Rosalea and two granddaughters, Sally and Magdalene (Postma Carttar). He died April 18, 1998.

JAMES D. POTEAT, born 1935, Spindale, NC, was commissioned second lieutenant, The Citadel, 1957. Infantry officer basic course. Platoon leader, 11th Abn. Div. and 19th Inf., 24th Inf. Div. 1958 reactivation, Augsburg, Germany. 24th Inf. Div. Trains, 1959-60.

Parachutist and Master Army Aviator, masters degree, Kansas State University. Graduate Army C&GSC and Army War College. Commanded four companies, one in Vietnam and a battalion, and held various staff positions.

His decorations include a Bronze Star Medal, five Meritorious Service Medals, three Air Medal, three Army Commendation Medals w/V, National Defense Service Medal, Armed Forces Expeditionary Medal, Vietnam Service Medal (three Battle Stars), Vietnam Cross of Gallantry w/Palm; Vietnam Campaign Medal and Meritorious Unit Device.

Retired 1983 in Conyers, GA. Served as Consecrated, Diaconal minister, United Methodist Church, 1990. Inducted as Distinguished member, Transportation Corps Regt., 1997.

He married Clara Yelton Poteat and they have four children and 10 grandchildren.

LLOYD T. POTTERTON joined the service on May 13, 1943, and served with Co. E, 19th Regt. He participated in the Southern Philippines of the first wave into Leyte. He was wounded on Oct. 25, 1944. He was discharged from Camp Carson on Oct. 31, 1945.

ERNEST POWELL, born April 17, 1931, enlisted in the service on Jan. 15, 1951.

Assignments included basic training at Fort Knox, Item Co., Korea, 19th Inf. Regt., B Co., 21st Regt. Wounded October 1951. Attended Leadership School near Sendai Japan. Rotated October 1953 from Koji Do.

Discharged January 1954 as sergeant first class. His awards include the Combat Infantry Badge, Korean Service Badge, Purple Heart and the Good Conduct Medal.

Memorable experiences: being able to serve as platoon sergeant, under the best platoon leader, Lt. Selby. Serving as scout for platoon size patrol the first day on the front line, which was real scary to say the least.

He is a member of VFW and 4th degree Knights of Columbus. Powell has attended 21st RCT, 19th and 34th reunions. Ernest, now retired, is married to Flossie and is presently trying to staying active.

WILBERT M. PRAY, born Nov. 23, 1916, enlisted in the Army September 1943. He attended basic training at Camp Blanding, FL and then was assigned to C Co., 21st RCT, 24th Inf. Div., Goodenough Island. Participated in the following action: Hollandia invasion, Panaon, Leyte, Battle of Breakneck Ridge, Mindoro, Lubang, Mindanao, Battle for Mintal. He was severely wounded at the Talomo River Crossing May 8, 1945.

Returned to the US July 6, 1945 and was discharged Oct. 31, 1945 from Percy Jones Hospital, MI with the rank of sergeant. His awards include the Good Conduct, Combat Infantry Badge, Bronze Star, two Purple Hearts, Unit Citation, Asiatic-Pacific and Philippine Liberation.

Wilbert married Vivian Lockwood, Nov. 19, 1940 and they had a son, Gary and a granddaughter, Arielle. He was in and out of Midwest VA hospitals, 1945-66. Employed as timekeeper at Roper Appliance, Kankakee, IL, retiring in 1980. He enjoyed fishing and vacations throughout US and Canada and volunterring at St. Mary's Hospital, Kankakee.

He was a member of the Kankakee American Legion, Moose Lodge, St. Martin's Catholic Church and also served as a Boy Scout leader. Wilbert died Sept. 6, 1990.

BRUCE W. PRICE SR. joined the service on Sept. 17, 1940, and served with Companies B and C, 19th Inf. Regt. He participated in the Asiatic-Pacific Campaign, Hollandia, Tanahmerah Bay, Papuan, New Guinea, Philippine Leyte Campaign, Hawaii, Australia, Good Enough Island, New Guinea and the Philippine Islands. He was discharged with the rank of 1st lieutenant. Dates served: March 24, 1943, to Sept. 19, 1945.

NELON K. PRINCE joined the service on June 5, 1943, and served with Co. L, 34th Regt. He participated in the Pacific Theater, Hollandia, Biak, Leyte, Luzon, Corregidor and Mindanao. He was discharged on Jan. 2, 1946, with the rank of staff sergeant.

ALFREDO A. PRINCIPE joined the service on Sept. 12, 1949, and served with Co. A, 19th Regt. He participated in Korea, Taejon, Kum River and others. He was discharged with the rank of corporal. Dates served: February 1950 to April 1951.

RALPH D. (DALE) PULIS, born May 22, 1928 in Mexico, MO was drafted into the Army, Nov. 30, 1950. He received basic training at Fort Leonard Wood, MO. Served five months in Korea, from May to October 1951, with the 24th Inf. He was wounded and carried off a hill to be taken to a MASH unit where initial surgery was performed, then air evacuated to the 279th General Hospital in Japan for further surgery. After spending approximately five months in the hospital in Japan he was taken to Walter Reed Hospital in Washington, DC and honorably discharged Aug. 30, 1952, after spending approximately a month hospitalized at Walter Reed.

He earned the Purple Heart, two Silver Stars and a Combat Badge, along with various ribbons.

He married Grace Guffey in October 1956 and they have two grown children and five grandchildren. He retired recently after working as a machinist, farmer and small business owner.

FREDRICK PUTZ joined the service on June 14, 1944, and served with Co. G, 21st Inf. Regt. He participated in the Philippines, Mindoro, Leyte, Mindanao and the Occupation of Japan after the war until May 10, 1946. He was discharged with the rank of T5. Dates served: Dec. 12, 1944, to April 26, 1946.

PAGE L. QUINN joined the service on Oct. 13, 1944, and served with Co. H, 21st Regt. He participated in the Southern Philippines, Kumamoto, Yonago, Japan. Discharged with the rank of corporal. Awards include the Combat Infantryman's Badge, Bronze Star, Good Conduct Medal, Asiatic-Pacific Campaign Ribbon w/star, Presidential Unit Citation and Philippine Liberation Medal w/star.

HILLMAN PAUL RABALAIS joined the service on Oct. 11, 1948, and served with Co. K, 19th Regt. He participated in the Korean War and 10 major battles; was wounded three times; and was a POW of the Chinese for 28 months. Discharged with the rank of sergeant. Dates served: 1950-53.

LAWRENCE O. RAFFERTY joined the service on March 4, 1941, and served with Co. K, 21st Regt. Served at Schofield Barracks during the Japanese attack on the island of Oahu, Dec. 7, 1941; New Guinea; and Philippine Liberation Campaign. He was discharged with the rank of private first class. Awards include the American Defense Service Medal and the Asiatic-Pacific Theater Campaign Ribbon w/3 Bronze Stars. Dates served: March 4, 1941, to May 29, 1945.

DAVID E. RAMSEY, born June 3, 1920, Morrison, TN was drafted into service July 23, 1945 and entered active service Aug. 6, 1942 at Fort Oglethorpe, GA.

He took basic training at Camp Roberts, CA from July until November 1942. Sailed for Honolulu, HI in January 1943 and was assigned to HQ Co., 3rd Bn., 21st Inf., 24th Div. at Oahu, HI. He was part of the 8th Army under Gen. Douglas MacArthur. Took special training for jungle warfare at Camp Caves, Australia. From Australia went to Goodenough Island, Panaon Island, Hollandia, Dutch New Guinea, the Philippines on the islands of Leyte, Mindoro, and Mindanao. Advanced to sergeant at Mindanao and was jeep driver for the following commanders: Colonel Chester A. Dahlen, Maj. Tom W. Suber, Col. Francis R. Dice and Col. Eric P. Ramee.

Sailed for Kure Naval Base in Japan. After the bombing, spent one day at Hiroshima. Departed Japan Nov. 7, 1945. Landed in San Francisco, Nov. 21, 1945. He recived an honorable discharge Nov. 30, 1945, Camp Chaffee, AR.

His awards and medals include the AP Theater Ribbon w/teo Bronze Stars, Good Conduct Medal, WWII Victory Ribbon, American Theater Ribbon, Lapel button issued Sept. 2, 1945, Southern Philippines GO 67, WD 45, New Guinea GO58 WD.

Following discharge David returned to Vogt Knitting Mill where he had been employed since 1939. In April 1955 he accepted employment with the US Postal Service. While on his rural route April 1966, he discovered a lady having a heart attack and got medical aid for her. For this he received a Post Office Award.

In December 1968 he saved the lives of three children by rescuing them from a burning house and was again rewarded by the postal service. In 1982 he received a Safe Driving Award, an honor given by the Fraternal Order of Police. He is active in the Church of Christ and a member of the American Legion.

He married a local teacher, Ruth Boyd February 1951. Their son David Boyd Ramsey was born in 1965. He and his wife, Angela Davenport Ramsey will make David E. a grandfather in the spring of 1999.

HANFORD RANTS, born in Yakima, WA, May 16, 1923. In early 1943, after basic training at Camp Wolters, TX he joined the 34th Regt. in Hawaii as the unit (34) moved on to Australia in August. From the staging area on Goodenough Island (February-March 1944) he went on to beach heads and combat at Hollandia, Biak, Luzon, Mindoro, and Mindanao. He was a 2nd Btry. lineman reaching the rank of sergeant and being awarded the Soldiers Medal and Bronze Star.

Soon after being discharged Nov. 7, 1945 he married Shirley Viken on Jan. 20, 1946. He returned to Washington State University to complete two bachelors and a masters degree. During his 31 years as a high school principal he completed a doctoral degree at the University of Southern California. The highlight of Shirley and Hanford's 53 year marriage is a family of three sons, five grandchildren and three great-grandchildren.

MICHAEL RASIAK, born June 2, 1926, enlisted in the Army Oct. 6, 1950.

His assignments included: Camp Edward, MA, basic training; Indiantown Gap, PA, cadre. Left for Korea and assigned to Co. A, 19th Regt., TDY Regt. HQ, Special Service move to Japan.

Memorable experiences: When he was drafted he was told that after six months service he would receive his citizenship papers. After six months he was told that it had changed to 18 months. After 18 months he was told 36 months. After spending five years in the service he finally received his citizenship papers.

Discharged May 22, 1958 as corporal. His award include the Combat Infantry Medal, Korean Service Medal, two Bronze Star Campaign Stars, Occupation Japan, UN Service Medal, National Defense Service Medal and Occupation of Germany.

He is married to Rosa and they have two children, Jerry and Thomas and three grandchildren: Nicole, Brian and Kateline. Enjoys bowling.

JEROME E. RASMUSSEN, born July 20, 1930, enlisted in the Army April 1948. He was shot or blown up by a mortar in Korea July 20, 1950.

Stationed in Japan and Korea. He went to New Jersey and parachuted from somewhere.

Discharged as corporal 1950-52. His awards include the Purple Heart and others.

He went to graduate school at the University of Oklahoma - Phillips University. From the time he retired from the Army he was a student, drug detailer, salesman for Fox and Jacobs in Texas, Pemtom, Orrin Thompson, New Horizon and Geodesic Domes, all new construction homes. He was also a broker.

Jerome married Jean (Sheehan, Phillips) Nov. 15, 1974. He has three children by his first wife, Mary Lou Wilson: Susan, Jerome Jr. and Julie. He also has three stepchildren, Jean's children from her first husband: Dale, Wade and Shelly. Together they raised 25 children. These children were appointed to them by the courts because their parents didn't want them. He also has 22 grandchildren and five great-grandchildren.

He retired in 1981. From 1985 to 1992 he took care of his parents. He was an artist, did his own photography, played the Ensonique organ and worked on the computer.

The first part of January 1997 he was working on computers with fractuals and was going to put fractuals with the organ and make music with fractuals. January 20, 1997 Jerome had a stroke that left him paralyzed on his left side and in a wheelchair for life. He has chronic osteolyomitis in his right leg, is a diabetic and has had a lung embolism and angina attack.

He and Jean now resides in Waverly, MN. He is a life member of the DAV, Purple Heart and 24th Div.

JOHN W. RAY, born June 14, 1925, left school to join the Army and did basic training in Camp Fannin, TX. From there he went overseas to New Guinea and joined the 24th Inf. Div., 34th Regt. He was fresh out of basic training and met an older soldier with army experience and they became friends. He taught John plenty. When they landed on Leyte Island, Philippine Island, they were on the outer perimeter the first night in their foxhole when they were fiercely attacked by the enemy. It lasted most all night. The enemy were all around their foxholes. When the few remaining men started to withdraw, Moon and John remained in their foxhole to give cover.

Private Harold Moon threw a grenade and was cut down by a machine gun and fell dead back over John. John called for a buddy, Pvt. Casey to help him and he got in the foxhole with John to help with Pvt. Moon.

Harold Moon put up a good fight. It is not known how many he killed that night. Private Harold Moon was awarded the Medal of Honor and John received the Distinguished Service Cross.

John took Moon's tommy gun the next morning and kept it and served as First Scout the rest of the war. He misses his friend Harold Moon, he was a good soldier.

John married Nell Rose Nelson and they have three children: Rose N., John L. and Sheila A.; six grandchildren: Shawn, Felicia, Wendy, April, Jake and Ashley.

He was employed in the air conditioning and refrigeration business and is a member of DAV, American Legion, life member VFW and the Purple Heart.

Now retired he enjoys fishing, traveling, sports and doing things with his children and grandchildren.

ROY R. RAY, born Feb. 8, 1919 and enlisted in the service in 1937; discharged in 1939 and re-enlisted 1939 to 1943. He was stationed at Schofield Barracks, HI and served with 1st Inf. Div., 76th Inf. Div., 24th Div. as first sergeant trained in chemical warfare. Also served detached service with USN. Awards include several Fire Arms Expert.

He is a life member of 24th Div., 1st Inf. Div., 76th Inf. Div., DAV, American Legion and NRA.

HAROLD C. RECK joined the service on Feb. 5, 1945, and served with Co. C, 3rd Combat Eng. Bn. He was discharged with the rank of T/5. Dates served: Aug. 10, 1945, to Oct. 7, 1946.

ROBERT W. REDMOND JR. joined the service on Sept. 11, 1946, and served with Co. E, 19th Regt. He participated in Gen. MacArthur's honor guard. He was discharged with the rank of private first class. Dates served: Sept. 11, 1946, to March 29, 1948.

DOUGLAS E. REED joined the service on Jan. 4, 1949, and attended basic training at Camp Pickett, VA. He was assigned to HQ & HQ Co., 34th Inf. Regt. He was discharged with the rank of private first class. Dates served: May 10, 1949, to Dec. 1, 1949.

MARVIN O. REICHMAN, born Nov. 15, 1926, enlisted in the Army September 1944. He was assigned as rifleman, SW Pacific Regimental Bugler, 21st Inf., Japan.

Discharged November 1946 as private first class. His awards include the Combat Infantry Badge, Bronze Star, Purple Heart, Good Conduct, Occupation Medal, Japan, WWII Victory, Asiatic-Pacific Campaign w/ Bronze Battle Star, Philippine Liberation w/Bronze Battle Star and Philippine Independence.

Memorable experiences: The day one of their artillery shells hit a Japanese warehouse, (the warehouse was filled with condoms and the condoms started raining down on them), they thought it had started to snow in the Philippines. It is his guess that the Japanese army was into safe sex even in those days.

He is married to Inez and they had two children, a son, Ken, who is deceased and Minda; and two grandchildren, Zoe and Isabel. Presently he is employed as an insurance salesman.

JOHN J. REILLY, born July 19, 1944, enlisted in the Army Feb. 5, 1965.

Assignments include the US Army, Europe; Munich Germany/Berlin Germany. Served as sergeant, S&T Plt. Spec. 5, TDY with the 1st Inf. 1/18th.

Discharged February 1971. His memorable experiences include working the Berlin Wall for six months. He served with some of the best in the 1/21st, 24th Inf. Div. Worked Check Point Charlie and ran the frontier in the winter in open top jeeps. They had no heaters.

He is employed as a police detective with the Summit, NJ Police Dept. and has been with this department since he was discharged from the service. He plans to work for another five years. He married Ginger April 18, 1970 and they have no children.

FREEMAN S. REVELS, born May 20, 1921, in Tampa, FL, served USN, July 1941 to February 1942, US Merchant Marines, March 1942-September 1942; US Army October 1942-October 1953. Wounded Aug. 14, 1950 in Ch'ongon, serving with B Co., 19th Regt., 24th Div.

Discharged as master sergeant and awarded Combat Infantry Badge w/star, Bronze Star Medal w/2 OLCs, V Device, Purple Heart, Good Conduct Medal, American Defense, American Campaign, Asiatic-Pacific Campaign w/star, WWII Victory, Army of Occupation, National Defense, Korean Campaign w/star, Philippine Liberation, UN Service Medal, Presidential Unit Citation, Philippine Republic Presidio Citation and Republic of Korea Presidential Citation.

He married Rose Lane Mitchell, October 1949 and they have six children: Rose-Lane, Paul, Francis, David, Freeman Jr. and Sidney and 11 grandchildren. After service he was employed as a chemical engineer and self-employed seafood importer. He is now retired and living in Wesley Chapley, FL. Member of MOPH Chapter 87.

CLARENCE H. RHODES joined the service in December 1947 and served with Hvy. Mortar Co.; Co. D, 21st Regt.; Hvy. Motor Co., 34th Inf. Regt. In November 1949 he transferred to GHQ, Gen. MacArthur's honor guard; February 1950 transferred to 21st Inf.; to Japan, Hvy. Mtr. Co.; Co. D, 21st Regt., 2nd Plt. He participated in all five major campaigns in Korea. He was discharged with the rank of corporal. Dates served: February 1950 to June 1951.

OLAN M. RICE joined the service in 1943 and served with Co. L, 21st Regt. He participated at New Guinea and the Southern Philippines Liberation. He was discharged with the rank of sergeant. Awards include the Philippine Liberation Ribbon w/2 Bronze Stars, Asiatic-Pacific Theater Ribbon w/2 Bronze Stars, Good Conduct Medal, WWII Victory Medal, Purple Heart, Combat Infantryman's Badge and Rifleman's Badge. Dates served: 1943-45.

DAN RICKERT joined the service on Jan. 14, 1951, and served with Co. D, 3rd Cbt. Eng. He was stationed in Korea from 1951-52. He was discharged with the rank of corporal.

NORMAN J. RIEGLER joined the service on Feb. 9, 1951, and served with Co. C, 19th Regt. He was stationed in Korea and participated in the Fall Offensive and 2nd Winter Offensive. He was discharged with the rank of 1st lieutenant. Dates served: September 1951 to February 1952.

GORDON W. RITER, born Oct. 29, 1921 at Willow Lake, SD, enlisted in Army Oct. 15, 1942. He attended Radio Code Signal Corp School in Aberdeen, SD for six months, then in Des Moines, IA for nine weeks. Entered active service Aug. 23, 1943 at Fort Snelling, MN. Basic training was at Camp Kohler, CA, followed by Radio Operator School at Camp Davis, CA. He was shipped overseas to the Pacific Theater May 15, 1944. Campaigns were in New Guinea and Southern Philippines, landing in Leyte in October

1944. Carrying hand operated transmitter and receiver with another soldier on their backs making this the initial landing in Leyte. Following this campaign he completed campaigns in Mindoro and Mindanao prior to going to Japan. He was discharged in January 1946 as a staff sergeant.

He attended South Dakota State University and received a BS in electrical engineering and was a T/4 in the National Guard until his discharge June 1, 1948.

Gordon received the Presidential Unit Medal, Meritorious Unit Medal, American Campaign Medal, Asiatic-Pacific Campaign Medal w/two Bronze Stars, one Arrowhead, WWII Victory Medal, Philippine Liberation Medal w/two Bronze Stars and the Honorable Service Lapel WWII.

Married Margaret Hamilton in 1952 and they had five sons, one deceased and five grandchildren. He retired from Texas Instruments in Dallas, TX, 1987.

He is spending retirement building houses with Habitat for Humanity, volunteering at Stew Pot, delivering food stuffs to local shelters. He and his wife are enjoying traveling, watching their grandchildren grow up and remaining busy with church activities.

DAVID R. RIVES joined the service on Aug. 23, 1948, and was assigned to Co. I, 21st Regt. He served with the 24th Sig. Bn. from July 3 to Aug. 10, 1950. He was discharged with the rank of corporal. He was awarded five Battle Stars. Dates served: July 3, 1950, to April 15, 1951.

RAYMOND H. ROBERTS joined the service in September 1946 and served with Co. E, 34th Regt. He was stationed in the Pacific and Japan. He was discharged with the rank of private first class. Dates served: 1946-48.

JAMES W. ROBINSON, was in the 24th Div. and served as a battalion adjunct and company commander. He participated in Leyte, Hollandia, New Guinea, Biak and Bataan, under Gen. Kruegar, Gen. Irving, and Lt. Col. Robert Spraggins.

"I have heard many of the stories that I now read in Volume I of the 24th Div. A general on TV stated some of the fiercest fighting in all WWII, was in this area. I believe that." states his wife, Janice Robinson.

On Leyte after two days of bombing they were still pinned down by enemy fire and could not get off the beach.

One of the stories: Jim stepped out of the foxhole to give an order and the next shell exploded in it. Three soldiers were killed and his sergeant (radio man) Kirkpatrick from Carolina, died in his arms.

Jim saw trucks full of dead soldiers; banzai attacks; and was behind enemy lines with air drops of food.

One close friend, Joe Malloy, had been killed. His mother was invited to the first reunion in New York. How brave he had to be to join them as her son did not return.

Jim returned ill and Capt. Edward Croxdale tended to him. Jack Clifford, the CO that took Jim's place was killed the next landing.

A close friend had an appendectomy on the beach. Can you believe all this was happening. Jim relived much of it before his death 2-1/2 years ago.

"I would like to hear from anyone that was with Jim. He loved the 24th Div." *Submitted by Janice Robinson, wife of James W. Robinson*

ROLAND DEE ROBINSON, born Jan. 19, 1931, enlisted into the service Sept. 24, 1954.

His assignments included Co. H, mail clerk, DMZ above Imjin River and between the Libby and Freedom bridges, Korea, 1955-56; TI&E NCO.

Discharged July 26, 1956 with the rank of Sp third class. He received a Letter of Commendation from the 2nd Bn. commander for graduating from the I Corp NCO Academy, with distinction of being in the top of the class. All other former candidates from their battalion had been sent back, failing to graduate with their respective classes. He was "Soldier-of-the-Month", many times (Co. H and 2nd Bn.)

He received a BA degree in Office Administration from BYU; MA degree in Business Education from Arizona State University. He has taught Business Education in high school and college before owning and operating seven music stores in the state of Arizona for 10 years, a music store in Utah for eight years and currently a music store in Sugar City, ID for three years.

He is now divorced and has six children: Tricia Mae, Helen Jane, Rodney William, Leona Shirley, Roland Scott and Steve A. One daughter, Alice Bunting died at three months of age. He also has nine grandchildren: Nichole, Bradley, Blake, Craig, Ericka, Jared, Natasha, Kyle and Ryan. He is semi-retired and presently associated in a partnership with Ruth Adamson, a dear friend.

ALVIS L. ROCK served with the 24th Div., 21st Inf., Co. B, from 1944-46. He participated in Leyte, Mindoro and Mindanao. He left Japan on Christmas day in 1945.

ELMER O. RODES JR. joined the service on April 6, 1943, and served with Div. HQ. He participated in the American Theater, Army of Occupation (Japan) and the Philippine Liberation. He was discharged with the rank of 1st lieutenant. Dates served: Sept. 13, 1945, to July 1946.

ALFREDO RODRIGUEZ joined the service in September 1960 and served with Combat Support Co., 19th Inf. Regt., 1st Battle Group. He was ordered into West Berlin, Germany, when the wall went up in August 1961. He was discharged with the rank of E-4. Dates served: September 1960 to September 1962.

JOHNNY M. (ROD) RODRIGUEZ, joined the 24th Div. at Hollandia from Goodenough, Panoan, Tacloban, Dulag, Carigara, Valencia, Mindoro, Lubang and Mintal Mindanao. He became first scout and gunner on the flame thrower.

He received basic training at Camp Fannin, TX and was sent to Goodenough Island. He performed musically with Eddie Longorio and Frank Castelan. Ed was from New York and played accordion. Frank was from Phoenix and he was a ventriloquist. Both were members of the 5th Special Services. Johnny and Frank presented a program to all the ships that were in the Tacloban, Leyte area from one of the large ships over the radio room.

Frank and Rod performed at Goodenough, Leyte and Mindoro, (San Jose).

He received awards for Asiatic-Pacific w/two Bronze Stars, WWII Victory, Philippine Liberation Ribbon and Medal w/Bronze Arrowhead and two stars, Good Conduct and Purple Heart.

He and Eddie performed at Goodenough only after the war. Rod studied music and became a professional musician. When he was sent to Fitzsimmons General Hospital in Denver, he performed in an Army program that was presented to all the Armed Forces radio, two different times. He now lives in the Kansas City area, where three of his daughters reside. His son, Jon and daughter, Kim reside in Wichita, KS.

At the present time he is still playing music and donating 15 to 20 hours of music to Rehab Centers.

SERGIO RODRIGUEZ, born in San Antonio, TX, Dec. 7, 1928 was drafted into Army on Dec. 7, 1950; some happy birthday.

Took basic training at Camp Chaffee, AR and combat engineer training at Fort Belvoir, VA.

He went to Korea in May 1951, serving with HQ & HQ Co., 3rd TMRS. Transferred to Btry. C, 52nd FABN, 24th Inf. Div. for duty as a recon. sergeant with the Colombian Inf. Bn. from South America. In January 1952 he was transferred to Btry. C, 57th FABN, 7th Inf. Div. along with the Colombian Bn.

Returned to the US in May 1952. Served with HQ & HQ Btry., 73rd AFA Bn., 1st Armd. Div. at Fort Hood, TX. Separated from active duty on Sept. 19, 1952.

Joined the Texas National Guard in August 1953, starting as a section of leader of 60mm mortars in Co. A, 141st Inf. Regt., 36th Inf. Div. He then served as rifle platoon sergeant, weapons platoon sergeant, and first sergeant of Co. A. He was discharged in May 1967.

He worked for the city of San Antonio, TX from Sept. 29, 1952 until his retirement Sept. 28, 1990. He spent 14 years with the Planning Dept. and 24 years with the Dept. of Public Works.

He has been married to Janie V. Rodriguez 46 years and they have one daughter, Mary P. Zepeda; two grandsons, Steven and Michael. One son, Mario A. Rodriquez, two boys, Tiger and Cougar and one granddaughter, Lexxus.

VERLA L. ROLL JR. joined the service on July 12, 1943, and served with Co. H, 21st Regt. He participated in New Guinea and the Southern Philippines. He was discharged with the rank of technical sergeant. Dates served: 1944-45.

JOHN P. ROONEY joined the service on Sept. 27, 1948, and served with Co. F, 19th Regt. He participated in the Chinese Intervention and UN Offensive, and two campaigns in Korea. He was discharged on May 31, 1952, with the rank of corporal. Dates served: 1951.

ARNOLD ROSE joined the service on Jan. 5, 1951, and served with Co. L, 19th Regt. He was discharged with the rank of sergeant first class.

DONALD E. ROSENBLUM, born June 3, 1929 was commissioned June 15, 1951. His assignments included: Korea 1952-53, lieutenant, platoon leader; Co. commander, 82nd Abn. Div., 1957-59; Co. Cdr. 6th Inf., Berlin 1960-62; Bn. Cdr., 1st Bde., 101st Abn. Div. (Vietnam) 1966-67; DISCOM Cdr. 101st Abn. (Vietnam) 1970-71, Cdr. 24th Div., 1975-77; Cdr. 1st Army 1981-84. Three assignments in the Pentagon, two with the Dept. of the Army and one with Joint Chiefs of Staff.

Retired Aug. 1, 1984 as lieutenant general. His awards include the Combat Infantry Badge, (two awards), Distinguished Service Medal, Legion of Merit (two awards), Bronze Star w/V Device (two awards), Meritorious Service Medal, Air Medal w/V, Army Commendation Medal w/V and Joint Service Commendation Medal.

He is president of Rosenblum & Associates, a consulting firm. Director of a local bank as well as a director of The Citadel Development Foundation; life member of the 24th Div. Assoc., life member of The Citadel Alumni Assoc., member of Savannah Rotary, former chairman of Savannah Metropolitan Planning Commission, former vice chairman Savannah Vietnam Memorial Committee.

Memorable experiences: January 1975 he reported to Fort Stewart, GA and assumed command of the 1st Bde. (Separate) 24th Div. In fact it consisted of about 300 officers and enlisted. In September 1975 he assumed command of the newly activated 24th Div. and commanded it as its first CG until September 1977.

He is married to Laura and they have five daughters and two sons. One son served in the 24th as a Co. CO. They also have two granddaughters and 10 grandsons. He is presently employed in consulting.

ROBERT J. RUANE, born Sept. 29, 1929 in Scranton, PA was drafted into the Army, January 1951. He attended basic training at Fort Dix, NJ. Served in Korea from May 1951 until February 1952 with the Heavy Mortar Co., *Gimlet* 21st Regt., 24th Div. Made rank of corporal in September 1951. Served four months occupation duty in Hokkaido, Japan after the 24th was relieved of combat in Korea. Discharged October 1952.

His decorations include the Korean Service Medal w/Bronze Service Star, UN Service Medal, AOM (Japan), Combat Infantry Badge and Bronze Star.

Married Catherine O'Malley in May 1953. They have five children and six grandchildren. Retired after 37 years as a draftsman with Mayflower Showcase Co.

He is a member of the following Veterans organizations: Korean War Vets of Kingston, PA; Korean Service Vets Assoc., Johnstown, PA; Veterans of Foreign Wars and the American Legion.

JAMES L. RUSSELL joined the service in 1956 and served with Cbt. Support Co., 2nd Battle Group, 28th Inf. He was discharged with the rank of colonel. Dates served: 1961-62.

NICHOLAS A. RUSSIELLO, born March 29, 1919, drafted into the service March 7, 1941.

It all began March 7, 1941 when a group of New York and New Jersey "selecties" (as draftees were referred to at that time) were shipped to Fort Jackson, SC. They were to begin basic training under a cadre of the 34th Inf. Regt. of the 8th Div. After basic training they became part of the 34th Regt. (regular army) and promptly became involved in the Carolina Maneuvers. Half way through the maneuvers the 34th (about 300 men) were the only ones that were withdrawn and told to pack up for a trip to the West Coast. There were rumors that they were going to be shipped overseas. They all could hardly believe it, because they only had six more months to go before they would have been civilians again and out of the army for good. But this was not to be. They took a troop train (including a Pullman sleeper) through Chicago and the Southwest.

The trip last for 10 days until the end of November and finally arrived at the Presidio of San Francisco. Soon after they were ordered to leave for Clark Field, Luzon, Philippines on Dec. 7, 1941 at 8 pm.

Nickolas and six of his buddies managed to obtain and pass for December 7 to go into San Francisco and have a last fling in the USA. While they were in town, about 11 a.m, the radios were blasting about an attack on Pearl Harbor. They asked, "Where the heck is Pearl Harbor?"

A civilian told them that it was in Hawaii. They knew where Hawaii was, but never heard of Pearl Harbor being Army infantry. They delayed going back to the Presidio even though the radios blased "All military personnel report to you units immediately." They were not going to let something like a war ruin what may be their last chance to enjoy themselves.

They finally got back to the Presidio about 7 p.m. Their unit was packed and ready to board ship. There was chaos everywhere. They lined up and started boarding the SS *Monterey* which was still in civilian service, staterooms, waiters, and the frills of a cruise ship. The first sergeant checking the roster barked "Russiello", he answered Nicholas A. private 320 110 81. It was raining like hell. They were arguing with one another, "How could they get us to the Philippines, when they have no Navy left." About 2 a.m., Dec. 8, 1941 in the pouring rain after a "cruise supper" they were told to disembark. One battalion went to San Luis Obispo, one to Monterey, and his battalion, the third, stayed to guard San Francico and assigned to a MP unit.

He was a browning automatic man and usually had at least 200 rounds of ammunition, but only had about five rounds. They put him on sentry duty on a pier near Fisherman's Wharf where a real old California National Guardsman challenged him in broad daylight when their post met one another.

He finally reached Hawaii, Dec. 16, 1941, where they became part of the 24th Inf. (Victory) Div. of Desert Storm fame. From there they went to Australia, New Guinea, Dutch East Indies and the Philippines. His battalion was selected to recapture the island of Corregidor, which they did in February 1945, with the help of the 503rd Paratroopers. They almost got to Clark Field, Philippines, the regiment was only about 20 miles away. Being infantry 20 miles was a snap and they would have finally gotten to Clark field after 4 1/2 years. Thirty-five years later, (1976) he visited San Francisco, and there in the harbor was the SS *Monterey*. After asking, he found out it was a sister ship. He had outlasted the original SS *Monterey* and Dec. 7, 1941.

Discharged June 7, 1945 and received the Silver Star, Bronze Star, two Presidential Citations, four Battle Stars w/ Spearhead, Combat Infantry Badge and other medals.

He is married to Alice and they have two children, Richard, a psychologist and William, an attorney. At this time they have no grandchildren.

He was employed as meat cutter for 45 years and is presently a paralegal for his son William, who is an attorney.

HERBERT F. RYAN joined the service on July 20, 1952, and served with Co. C, 19th Regt. He was stationed in Korea. He was discharged with the rank of colonel.

MICHAEL J. SACCHITELLA joined the service on July 21, 1948, and served with HQ & HQ Co., 21st Regt. He was stationed in Korea, June 1950 to April 1951; and Japan, November 1948 to April 1951. He was discharged with the rank of corporal.

KENNETH LEE SARTIN joined the service on Nov. 15, 1945, and was assigned to the 24th Sig. Co., HQ Special Troops, March 1947 to Nov. 14, 1948. He then served with HQ Btry., 26th AAA AW, from September 1953 to March 28, 1955. He was awarded the

Japanese Occupation Medal, WWII Victory Medal, Good Conduct Medal (3rd award), National Defense Service Medal, Korean Service Medal, UN Service Medal, Master Parachutist Badge and Air Assault Badge.

CARL W. SCHAAD was commissioned 2nd lieutenant, USAR, May 26, 1939. He was called to active duty on Sept. 16, 1940, and received Regular Army commission on July 1, 1942. Served with the 24th Inf. Div.; 63rd FA BN and 13th FA Regt., July 1941 to June 1944; 52nd FA BN, June 1944 to May 1945; and 63rd FA BN, May 1945 to February 1946. He participated in the Asiatic-Pacific Theater from Dec. 7, 1941, to February 1946. He was also stationed in the Central Pacific, New Guinea, Western Pacific, Leyte, Southern Philippines and the Occupation of Japan. He retired on Jan. 31, 1972, with the rank of colonel.

ROBERT B. SCHAFER, born April 18, 1928, enlisted in the service Sept. 13, 1946.

His assignments: September-November 1946 Infantry basic at Fort Bragg, NC; December 1946-December 1947, 19th Inf. Regt., Cos. M & D, Heavy Machine Gun Squad; Leader at Camp Chickamauga, Beppu, Kyushu, Japan.

Discharged Dec. 29, 1947 as sergeant and awarded the WWII Victory Medal, Occupation (Japan), Army, National Defense, Korean Service Air Force, Armed Service Reserve and Meritorious Service.

His memorable experiences include unforgettable service in the 19th. They were continually training. In camp, in the hills around Beppu, 15 mile hikes, bivouacs in the hills, inspection and parades every Saturday morning. He had many good buddies and values his Army experience very much.

He received a BS in Architectural Engineering and a Air Force Reserves Commission from Kansas State University in 1951. Served on active duty at Goodfellow AFB, TX as civil engineering officer until April 1953. Remained active in Air Force Reserve, retiring June 1981 as a colonel.

Became a licensed professional engineer as a structural engineer and construction management. Retired in 1988 as assistant chief engineer at the VA Medical Center in Topeka, KS.

Married Oleta Patterson Dec. 22, 1950 and they have children: Deborah, Annette and Mark; four grandchildren: Alexandra and Kathleen Schafer; Danielle and Matthew Cavanaugh.

Presently he and Oleta are retired and enjoy traveling in their trailer. He has been in 48 states and also traveled to Europe four times.

VALENTINE SCHAAF joined the service on April 17, 1941, and served with Co. H, 21st Inf. Regt. He was stationed in Pearl Harbor, South Pacific, New Guinea, Leyte and Mindoro. He was discharged on May 27, 1945, with the rank of technical sergeant.

FRANCIS C. (FRANK) SCHMILLEN, born June 6, 1919 in Fairbank, IA was inducted into the Army Oct. 9, 1942. He was sent to Hawaii for basic training and served with Co. F, 34th Inf. Regt., 24th Inf. Div. in New Guinea, Hollandia, Biak, the Battles for Leyte and Luzon and Philippine Islands.

After induction, he never returned home. His sister is writing this from information given to her by the members of the 24th Div. with whom she has been communicating. This information is correct to the best of her knowledge.

Frank was leader of the First Mortar Squad and promoted to staff sergeant shortly before his death Feb. 4, 1945. He was killed by a shrapnel wound to the head in the Battle of Zig Zag Pass.

In addition to the Campaign Ribbons, he was awarded the Purple Heart and Bronze Star. He is buried at Manila American National Cemetery. *This bio has been submitted by his sister, Francis Schmillen who was only 23 years old when he left for the service, so she is not well informed about her brother's years in the Army. She knows he would feel honored to be remembered along with the other brave men who served in the 24th Div.*

GEORGE J. SCHNEIDER joined the service on Jan. 27, 1951, and served with Co. M, 19th Inf. Regt. He participated in the Fall Offensive and in Korea. He was discharged in January 1953 with the rank of staff sergeant.

DONALD LEROY SCHONLAU, born Feb. 8, 1932, enlisted Army November 1949. He received basic training at Fort Riley, KS. Arrived A Co., 3rd Engr. Combat Bn., April 1950, 2nd Plt., 2nd Sqdn.

Entered Korea June 1950 and left Korea August 1951. His awards include six Bronze Stars, six Presidential Unit Citations, six Korean Presidential Citations, six Campaign Clusters, Korean Service, UN Medal and Japan Occupation Medal.

He arrived in Japan as private. Promoted to sergeant first class by January 1951 and discharged as sergeant first class November 1952 from Camp Polk, LA.

He became general house building contractor. Retired to Arizona and ranching 1974-94. He is a life member of the DAV, VFW, KWVA and 24th Inf. Div.

LEROY V. (CORKY) SCHRUMPF, born June 15, 1928 was raised in the village of Ridgefield Park, NY. He graduated 1945 and enlisted in the Army July 1946. Took basic training at Fort Dix, NJ. After basic transferred to Camp Stoneman, CA. After arrival they were moved to Fort Lawton, WA and on November 8, he left Seattle heading for PTO. Arrived Japan port of Yokohama, November 22, 1946. Within days they were moved to the Island of Kyushu, city of Kokura and assigned to Div. HQ I&E Section, answering to Lt. Col. Milton Skelly. He served 11 months at Div. HQ. then headed back to the States Oct. 15, 1947 and arrived Fort Lawton, WA Oct. 27, 1947.

Discharged December 1947 with the rank of T/5 Spec. He received the WWII Victory Medal and the Japan Army of Occupation Medal.

He went to college after discharge and earned a BS degree. Retired from *Bergen Record* newspaper Hackensack, NJ after 40 years service.

He is a member of Ford Nelson VFW Post 277, Ridgefield Park, NJ. A retired commissioner, Village of Ridgefield Park, NJ. He retired after 28 years of active duty as a volunteer fireman. He is also a retired member of the Advertising Media Executive Assoc.

Married Ann February 1951 and they have celebrated their 48th anniversary. They have three children: Roy, Robert and Ann Marie.

HARRY M. SCHULTZ was drafted into the service on Oct. 1, 1950, as a combat photographer. He covered the 19th and overlapped the MLR of the 5th RCT. He was assigned to the 24th Sig. Co. He participated in the UN Summer and Fall Offensive, 2nd Korean Winter, Korean Summer and Fall 1952. He was discharged in 1952 with the rank of corporal.

ALVIN L. SEBRING, born Nov. 23, 1929, enlisted in the Army March 12, 1947. Assignments: cadre Co. A, 12th Inf. Fort Ord, CA, 1947-48; Post Finance, Camp Chaffee, AR; sergeant major 1st Guided Missile Bde., 1951-53.

Discharged as master sergeant February 1953. His awards include two Bronze Stars and the Combat Infantry Badge.

His memorable experiences: in 1950 went to HQ Co., 24th Inf. Div. Finance. Volunteered Co. I, 21st Inf., July 1950 as squad leader, then transferred to HQ Co., 3rd Bn., 21st as sergeant major until August 1951, then rotated.

He married Genelle in June 1946 and they have three children: Michael, Harold and Tony and two grandchildren: Jason and Bobby. Alvin is now retired. Employed as salesman and business owner.

LEON SELONKE joined the service on April 30, 1949, and served with Co. E, 21st Regt.; and Co. I, 34th Regt. He was stationed in Korea and fought from Pusan to the Yalu. He was discharged with the rank of sergeant first class. Dates served: Aug. 26, 1950, to September 1951.

C.V. KOWALSKI SGM participated in the Central Pacific Campaign. He was awarded the Bronze Star Medal, Purple Heart, Korean Service Medal w/6 Bronze Service Stars, Combat Infantryman's Badge w/stars and Vietnam Service Medal.

CARL G. (BUD) SHAFFER, born in Stoystown, PA March 10, 1928, joined the Army in June 1946 and took basic training at Fort McCellan, AL and wa shipped to Japan November 1946. Assigned to the Ord Bn. north of Tokyo was returned home and released November 1947. Called to active duty from the Inactive Reserves October 1950. He took a three weeks refresher basic at Fort Campbell, KY and shipped to Korea in December 1950. Assigned to I&R HQ Co., 1st Bn., 19th Regt. through August 1951 and discharged October 1951 as a staff sergeant at Indiantown Gap, PA.

He married Alice Baltzer September 1948 and they live in Canton, OH. They have a son, two daughters and five grandsons. He retired from the Timken Co. in 1985 after 33 years of service.

His most honored military decorations are the Combat Infantry Badge and Bronze Star for valor.

EARL E. SHANNON, born March 13, 1932, enlisted in the Army April 21, 1950. He reported to Fort Riley, KS for 13 weeks infantry basic training, then received a 13-day leave home. He traveled by bus to Kansas City, MO, then by airplane to Fort Lawton, WA. After 14 days at Fort Lawton he flew to Tokyo, Japan. Traveled by train to Sasebo, Japan, then by boat to Pusan, Korea. Joined up with 24th Div., 21st Regt. Co. E, Heavy Wpns. Plt. He was a gunner for 57 Recoilless rifle until he was wounded and then a gunner on 3.5. Arrived in Korea Sept. 2, 1950. They waited two weeks in some apple orchard for more replacements, then started the big push north. He was hit by shell fragments from a T34 tank shell Sept. 25, 1950 and sent to a hospital in Yokohama, Japan for about 1 1/2 months.

He returned to his unit and went through some bad times. He was hit again on April 12, 1951, and sent back to Japan for two months. Returned to Korea and put in the Alabama National Guard engineer unit. Rotated back to the United States in late 1951 and reported to Fort Sheridan, IL. He was assigned to the Pennsylvania National Guards Btry. A, 86th AAA Gun Bn. and stationed in Chicago, IL. They joined the Civil Defense. He was the elevation sitter on a 120mm anti-aircraft artillery gun and operated two generators to supply electricity to the ant-iaircraft guns.

Discharged on April 20, 1953. His awards include the Purple Heart, Combat Infantry Badge, Korean Service Medal, Distinguished Emblem, one Overseas Service Bar, three Bronze Stars and United Nations Service Medal.

Employed as a grocery clerk for 10 years, built helicopters for Brantley Helicopter Co. for five years, Dallas Air Motive for two years, Weber Aircraft for 20 1/2 years as general inspector and NDT, Non Destruction Testing inspector.

His memorable experiences: being in the 24th with the men in Korea and raising two of the best looking, smartest and best sons in the US. They gave him three grandsons and one granddaughter.

He is married to Elsie Lavon Burden and has two sons, Earl Dean Shannon and Kenneth Shannon; and four grandchildren: Ritchie Lynn, Amber Dawn, Stewart Overton and Jeffery Kinneth.

He will be going back to Weber after the first of 1999 and work for another two years and retire again.

GARY R. SHERMAN, born June 16, 1933, enlisted in the Army Nov. 30, 1953. Assignments: first eight weeks Fort Dix, NJ; second eight weeks, Camp Pickett, VA for training as a medic. Shipped to Korea April 1954. Assigned to 5th RCT attached to 555 FABN in Pusan. In June 1954 he transferred to the 24th Inf. Div.; July 1954, 19th Inf. Regt. until he rotated October the same year and eventually was discharged. Attained the rank of staff sergeant and discharged as an SP-2.

His awards include the Korean Service Medal, Good Conduct Medal, UN Service Medal, National Defense Service Medal. Spent the majority of the time on the DMZ town of Pajori.

Attended Northeastern University, Boston, MA. He has spent the last 39 years working in the corrugated packaging industry in the Boston, MA area in sales.

Gary found his experiences during his enlistment helped to better prepare him during his working years. He had the opportunity to experience being a medic and to interact (even though he saw no combat) with fellow GIs in life and death situations.

He is divorced and has two daughters, Adriane Sherman, single and Karen Davidson, who is married to Jonathan Davidson. There is one grandchild on the way.

He is currently employed in outside sales for Abbott Avon Packaging, Canton, MA.

ALAN JOHN SHIELDS, born June 24, 1923, Philadelphia, PA, served in maritime service 1941-42. Drafted Feb. 4, 1943. Assigned 86th Inf. Camp Howze, TX for basic. April 1944, POE San Francisco. Joined E. Co., 21st Inf., 24th Div. as first scout, first squad, first platoon in Hollandia, New Guinea. Fought with the 24th in the Philippines at Breakneck Ridge, Leyte, Mindoro and Mindanao. He had a brief hospital stay because of jungle rot and malaria. Remained with the unit until rotated home from occupation duty in Japan. Discharged January 1946 and received two Bronze Stars and Combat Infantry Badge.

Entered North Texas on the GI Bill and received a BA and a MA in history. Married Dec. 30, 1947 to Clydene and they have three children: Susan, Christopher and Stephen. After additional graduate work at Texas University he joined the Sociology Dept., Auburn University 1956, retiring in 1989 as Associate Professor Emeritus of Sociology and Criminology.

He has been a volunteer counselor for many years at the Julia Tutwiler Prison for Women. Established the Edwina Mitchell Society to assist ex-offenders. Director of service unit of Salvation Army and a member of Auburn Lions Club.

EDWARD L. SHIELDS, born Dec. 31, 1924, Auburn, NY, was drafted into the Army in 1943 during high school. He received basic training at Camp Croft, SC and was shipped via New Orleans and the old Jackson Barracks to the Pacific Theater aboard the USAT *Shawnee* during WWII. Stationed with the 34th Inf., 24th Div., HQ Co. Went to Hollandia, Biak, Tacloban and Leyte and was in the Philippines when MacArthur landed to state "I have returned." Honorably discharged in 1945 while technician fifth grade.

Happily married to Olean B. Shields since July 10, 1948. They have three children: David (Nancy) Shields, Nancy (Arne) Lindquist, and Patty (Don) Pfister; and five grandchildren: Michael and Suzanne Shields, Anika and Erik Lindquist, Amelia Pfister. Retired from Rochester Gas and Electric Co. after 38 years. Now enjoys boating and fishing on the St. Lawrence River and traveling. Member of Charlotte

Corinthian Masonic Lodge and a life member of DAV, Combat Infantry Assoc. and the 24th Inf. Assoc.

JAMES CHARLES SHIELDS JR., born Sept. 4, 1918, enlisted February 1944. His assignments include Jan. 29, 1945 landing at San Antonio, Luzon, PI. March to Olongapo. First action at Lighthouse Point. Moved into Zig Zag Pass and was killed by short round of American 105s on Feb. 5, 1945.

He was ranked as private at the time of his death. His awards include the Purple Heart, Bronze Star, Asiatic-Pacific Campaign Medal, WWII Victory Medal, Philippine Liberation Ribbon and the Good Conduct Medal.

He was married to Sadie W. and they had two children: R. Gary Shields (Lake City, FL) and Jim Shields III (Raleigh, NC); three grandchildren: April Shields Williams, Robb Shields and Emily Shields. His sons, Gary and Jim, would like to hear from anyone who knew their dad.

ROBERT E. SHILHARVEY, born Feb. 11, 1925, enlisted in the Army June 11, 1944.

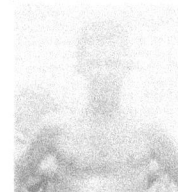

His assignments and stations include: C Co., 21st Regt., 24th Div., Leyte, January 1945, 60mm mortar squad. Served on Mindoro, Lubang, Mindanao. Went to Japan September 1945.

Memorable experiences: Ran across Japanese payroll office and picked up enough yen to fill his waterproof bag. After the war they were told they could use the yen. He thought he was rich. Loaned most of it to his buddies. Some payed him back, some didn't. It seemed good to have money when they got to Japan.

Discharged May 31, 1946 as staff sergeant. His awards include the Asiatic-Pacific Theater Ribbon w/ two Bronze Stars, Philippine Liberation Ribbon, WWII Victory Medal, Good Conduct and Combat Infantry Badge.

Employed in the trucking business. In 1955 started carpentry and was a carpenter for 35 years until he retired.

Married Anna Marie Pietzman April 20, 1950 and they have children: Michael, Gail, Ann, Danial and Joseph; four grandchildren: Erica, Audry, Megan and Charlie.

Retired and now restores old farm tractors and machinery. President and member Warren County Old Threshers.

WINFORD A. SHILLING joined the service in December 1948 and served with Co. K, 21st Regt. He participated in all campaigns of the Korean War campaigns the first year that the 24th Div. was involved in July 1950 to June 1951. He was discharged with the rank of corporal. Dates served: May 1949 to June 1951.

GLEN E. SIMMONS, born May 23, 1923, enlisted in the service Feb. 11, 1943. Stationed at Camp Howze, TX; Fort Ord; New Guinea; Philippines.

Discharged as staff sergeant, Jan. 11, 1946. His

awards include two Purple Hearts, three Bronze Stars, Combat Infantry Badge and several others.

He was a farmer, rural mail carrier, real estate broker, jack-of-all-trades, master of none.

Memorable experiences: He was just one of several million good men and through their efforts and with Divine help from God they won the damned war. Lost a lot of good men and women. He was not brave, scared most of the time, but kept going forward. A big hello to anybody that was in Co. B, 1st Bn., 19th Inf., 24th Div.

He married B. Nadine and has a son, Michael E. and one grandson, Anthony Kraig. Today he is doing the least possible.

EDWARD J. SHIRLEY joined the service in October 1942 and served in the 24th Sig. Co. He was stationed in Hollandia. He was discharged with the rank of T/5. Dates served: November 1942 to October 1944.

DONALD C. SHRADER joined the service on July 9, 1942, and served with the 21st Reg. HQ, 21st Inf. Regt. He participated in New Guinea, Battle of Leyte, Mindoro and Mindanao. He was discharged with the rank of Tec 4. Dates served: July 9, 1942, to Jan. 9, 1946.

OLIVER C. SIMMERS JR. joined the service in January 1952 and served with Co. G, 21st Regt. He was stationed in Korea. He was discharged with the rank of private first class. Dates served: June 1952 to December 1953.

GLEN E. SIMMONS joined the service on Feb. 11, 1943, and served with Co. B, 19th Regt. He participated at New Guinea, Leyte, Mindoro, Southern Luzon, Samara, Romblon and Mindanao. He was discharged on Jan. 22, 1946, with the rank of staff sergeant.

ROBERT J. SIMPSON joined the service in June 1950 and served with Co. D, 5th RCT Regt. He was discharged on Oct. 31, 1951.

STEWART EDWARD SIZEMORE joined the service on June 10, 1948, and served with Co. L; Co. D; HQ 1st Bn.; 34th Regt.; and 19th Regt. He participated in all campaigns in Korea. He was discharged with the rank of corporal. Dates served: 1948-51.

WILLIAM M. SLATAPER joined the TXNG on Nov. 18, 1940. He served with the Troop Service, 124th Cav., 342nd Regt. He participated in the Pacific, Subic, Corregidor and Mindanao. He was discharged with the rank of 2nd lieutenant.

EDWARD N. SLATER, born May 16, 1930, enlisted in the Army Feb. 2, 1948. First assignment was Korea after basic training. After spending a year in Korea on occupation duty he was transferred to Japan for occupation duty. When the Reds invaded Korea, he was sent back for combat duty.

His unit was overrun by enemy troops and he was caught behind enemy lines by himself for 19 days before being captured by the North Koreans. He spent about four months on a death march and survived the Sunchon Tunnel Massacre, ending the march with 380 American troops dead, Oct. 2, 1950.

He was sent back to a hospital in Japan where he stayed a week or so, then sent home in time for Christmas.

Ed received quite a few medals, including the Purple Heart w/cluster, Combat Infantry Badge, Prisoner of War Medal, Ambassador to Peace Medal and others.

He has spent the last 30 years living in Missouri with wife, Phyllis, a son, Terry, daughter, Melinda; six grandchildren and two great-granddaughters.

Retired from the sales field, he spends most of his time volunteering at the VA Medical Center in Kansas City fighting for veterans benefits and helping those that can't help themselves.

DONALD P. SLETTEN, born March 10, 1921, enlisted in the Army April 9, 1941.

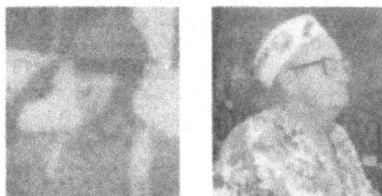

His stations include: Australia, Hollandia and Tanathmera Bay, New Guinea; Luzon, Bataan, Corregidor and Leyte, Philippines. Served with 1st Plt., A Btry., 11th FA, 24th Div.

He served as artillery front line forward observer and staff sergeant. (the enlisted man who went up on the front lines with an officer, first lieutenant or second lieutenant) The officer was the go-between from their observation point and the infantry command on that front.

In his case, in all his battles he remained on the front as the actual observer calling in the missions and calling for fire for effect.

The total number of OPs he can't remember, but in his case, that is exactly how it was done. He had a lineman and a radioman with him and as the case developed, the officer, at times.

Discharged May 15, 1945 and received the WWII Medal, Asiatic-Pacific w/four Battle Stars, two Arrowheads, American Campaign, American Defense, Philippine Campaign, Philippine Presidential and Good Conduct Medal.

His memorable experiences include many Red Cross rescues over the years and many writings of history.

Employed as carpenter superintendent. He married Eloise L. and has three children: Constance L. Myers, Darwin Norman and Terry D. Toepfer; four grandchildren: Shandon, Erik, Michael and Jason. He is now retired, service connected, DAV.

RONALD S. SLOAT (BUCK) joined the service on March 5, 1941, and served with HQ Co., 34th Regt. In 1944 he transferred to cadre to form the 71st Inf. Div. and then went on to France, Germany and Austria. He was discharged with the rank of technical sergeant.

ARTHUR D. SMITH joined the service on June 12, 1944, and served with Co. K, 34th Regt. He participated in Luzon and Corregidor. He was discharged on Nov. 3, 1945, with the rank of private.

DONALD T. SMITH joined the service in January 1948 and served with Btry. A, 11th FA BN. He participated in Japan, five campaigns in Korea from July 1950 to August 1951, and ETO in Germany from 1951-54. He was discharged with the rank of staff sergeant. Dates served: 1949-51.

ROBIN SVEN SMITH joined the service on Oct. 3, 1983, and served with Companies A and B, 124th MI BN. He participated in Operations Desert Storm and Shield. He was discharged on Feb. 1, 1984, with the rank of sergeant. Dates served: Aug. 23, 1990, to March 31, 1991.

FRANK L. SMOLINSKI, born in Boston, NY, July 23, 1929, enlisted the Army Sept. 15, 1947.

Attended basic training at Fort Dix. Assigned to the 24th Signal Co. in April 1948 and stayed there until discharge, Aug. 15, 1951 as sergeant first class (E-7).

His awards include the Bronze Star, Korean Service Medal w/three Bronze Stars, Distinguished Unit Emblem, Merit Unit Commendation, Army of Occupation (Japan), Good Conduct Medal, ROK Presidential Citation and Combat Infantry Badge.

His memorable experiences: attended NCO School, Glider School, Kelo School Command, Ordnance School A.B. Maryland. Through all his schooling and ended up as division command chief.

He works for the VFW and had worked as an electrician until his retirement Dec. 30, 1988 after 35 years from General Motors. He now resides in St. Petersburg, FL.

He is married to Jane and they have three children: Lawrence, Nancy and Michael; and five grandchildren: Marc, Pamala, Christopher, Kyle and Brian.

LYMAN SNODDERLEY joined the service on Feb. 2, 1942, and served with Co. F, 21st Regt. He participated in New Guinea and the Southern Philippines. He was discharged on Aug. 17, 1945, with the rank of sergeant.

JAMES P. SNOW joined the service on Oct. 3, 1942, and served with Co. L, 24th Div., 19th Inf. Regt. He participated at Biak, New Guinea, Philippines, Luzon and Mindoro. He was discharged with the rank of private first class. Dates served: 1944-45.

MARVIN L. SNOW, born May 28, 1932, enlisted Army June 18, 1950.

His assignments included basic training, Fort Knox, KY. Discharged June 19, 1952 as corporal. His awards include the Combat Infantry Badge, Purple Heart and Silver Star.

Memorable experiences: Wounded Dec. 15, 1950 and shipped to Tokyo General Hospital. Enjoyed first Christmas away from home there.

He worked for the VA Center 16 years and transferred to IRS and worked there for 17 years.

He is married to Betty Jean and they have a daughter, Debra Kay Snow Hensell and grandson, Jason Walter Hensell. Marvin is now retired.

EVAN S. LEON SNYDER joined the service on Feb. 26, 1952, and served with the 24th Inf. Regt., 26th AAA. He was discharged with the rank of corporal.

RICHARD SOLAT, born Sept. 27, 1928, enlisted in the Army December 1950. Assignments: 26th AAA Bn., S-2 Intelligence Section, Chief of an Observation Post in Korea 1951; Battalion Draftsman in Camp Younghans, Japan 1952.

Discharged Dec. 17, 1952 as corporal. His awards include the Korean Service Medal w/two Bronze Stars, Good Conduct Medal, United Nations Service Medal, Army Presidential Unit Citation and Korean Presidential Unit Citation.

Employed as an art teacher and chairman of art department, West Valley, NY; Bethpage, NY and North Babylon, New York High Schools.

He married Arline Benz August 1954 and they have two children, Nancy Solat Lemble and Sally Solat Switzer and a grandson, Alexander Lemble.

Retired from teaching in 1985. Painting is his hobby. He is a member of American Legion Post No. 49 and Metro Masters Swim Club of New York 1981.

PETER A. SOLTYSIAK joined the service in December 1948 and served with Serv. Co., 34th Regt. and Co. L, 19th Regt. He participated in the Japanese Occupation, Taejon and the Pusan Perimeter. He was wounded on August 26, 1950, and returned to ZI. He was discharged in September 1950 with the rank of private first class.

ROBERT A. SPAULDING joined the service on Nov. 17, 1952, and served with HQ Co., 63rd FA BN. He was stationed in Korea. He was discharged with the rank of private first class. Dates served: 1952-54.

ROBERT A. SPAULDING, born June 25, 1932, enlisted in the Army Nov. 17, 1952.

Assignments: Fort Bliss, TX, basic training, eight weeks; 90mm AAA, eight weeks, counter mortar radar maint., nine months, Korea on Christmas Ridge, then to 63rd FABN, HQ.

Discharged Oct. 28, 1954 at Ft. Sheridan, IL, as private first class. His awards include the Good Conduct, National Defense Service Medal, UN Service Medal, Korean Service Medal w/four Bronze Stars, Sharpshooter Badge w/Rifle Bar and Marksman Badge w/Carbine Bar.

Memorable experiences: He built the relays that put the men on the moon.

Married Doyne Ann Personnette and they have three children: Robert, Valerie and Vickie; four grandchildren: Mike, David, Christi and Joshua. He built and adjusted industrial relays. He was also in the Reserves and worked for United Technologies for 38 years. Now retired and doing little. He belongs to the VFW and American Legion.

MICHAEL F. SPIGELMIRE joined the service on June 6, 1960, and served with the 2nd Battle Group, 2nd Inf. He was platoon leader in 1961 and assistant division CG from September 1985 to June 1987; and CG from July 1987 to September 1988. He was discharged in September 1988 with the rank of 2nd lieutenant.

ROBERT B. STARNER JR., born March 18, 1937, enlisted into the Army Jan. 2, 1956. He received basic at Fort Graham, SC, B Co. 502nd Inf., 101st; 1956-57, HQ Co., 3rd Engr. Bn., 24th Div., squad operator, 1959-61, B Co., 83rd Engr. Bn., France; 1962-64, platoon sergeant, 11th Engr. Bn., Korea, 1967-68 Vietnam; 1970-71, Sr. advisor to Vietnam Army.

Discharged Aug. 13, 1976 as master sergeant. He

received the Bronze Star, Meritorious Service Medal, Good Conduct and the Vietnam Honor Medal.

His memorable experiences include serving as first sergeant in a combat engineer battalion, 11th Engr. in Korea when President Kennedy was assassinated.

He is married to Jana Kay and has three children: Billy Ray, Paul Francis and Robert B. III and seven grandchildren. Employed as mail carrier from Feb. 17, 1977 to present.

CARNELL STACY joined the service on March 11, 1943, and served with the 1st Plt., Co. C, 3rd Eng. Bn. He participated in six battles. He was discharged with the rank of 1st sergeant. Dates served: August 1950 to September 1951.

ARTHUR A. STAMLER joined the service in March 1943 and served with Med. Co., 21st Regt. He was stationed in Korea from July 1950 to February 1951. He was discharged in June 1952 with the rank of captain.

JACK S. STARR, born Jan. 4, 1921, enlisted in the Army, Aug. 3, 1938, stationed at Schofield Barracks, TH.

When he got back to the States he was assigned to Co. C, 32nd Inf., Fort Ord, CA. The second day he was there he was called in to meet the company commander. He checked his record and said that's all Sgt. Starr. Starr said that he was a private, and the CO said, "You're a sergeant now" and the platoon sergeant of the 3rd Plt. They had some platoon tests and they were one of the ones who had it the hardest. They were down on the King ranch in Southern California. They had to go 50 miles across a section of the ranch and come out within a certain area and not be discovered. He had an Arizona Indian named Ochoa. He could track a rattlesnake across a rock. They had to wade the San Jauquin River and three guys were bitten by rattlesnakes. They rested all day and hid out. At night they traveled. They used as little of their food and water as they possibly could, but they made it ahead of time. They later heard (after the judging) that they won first place. They got five days of leave and a trophy. When Starr received the trophy he turned and gave it to Ochoa, and said he was the one who got them through at night.

He was employed for 26 years for the USAF, retiring in 1970.

Memorable experiences include attending Deep Sea Diving School, Washington, DC.

Married to Dora and they have a son, John Starr and a grandson, Scott. He is now retired and residing in Naples, FL.

LLOYD STEINGASS joined the service on Feb. 5, 1945, and served with Co. D, 21st Regt. He participated in the Philippines and the Occupation of Japan. He was discharged with the rank of private first class. Dates served: September 1945 to November 1946.

KIM STENSON joined the service on Oct. 13, 1975, and served with HQ Co., 24th Inf. Div. He participated in the Defense of Saudi Arabia, Liberation of Kuwait and Southwest Asia. He was discharged with the rank of major.

THOMAS F. STEWART joined the service on May 13, 1972, and served as battalion commander of the 1-24 Attack Bn. He participated in Operations Desert Storm and Shield. He was discharged with the rank of lieutenant colonel. Dates served: May 1990 to May 1992.

RODNEY F. (ROD) STOCK, born Feb. 15, 1931, Detroit, MI, attended Grandview Heights High School,

Ohio, 1949. Football ride Washington and Lee University, ended by the draft 1951. Attended basic, Camp Breckinridge, KY, 101st Abn., July 10, 1951. Korea, December 1951. Wireman/wire chief, 811th Engrs. December 1952. 505th Signal Gp. Dispatcher, Camp San Luis Obispo, January-April 1953. Staff sergeant, instructor, 331st Inf., Ohio Reserve, 1953-54. Ohio State student, GI Bill. Active duty December 1954, Fort Hood, platoon sergeant, 702nd AIB, reupped Bonus March 1955. 24th Inf. Div., 34th Tank, platoon sergeant, DMZ Korea, Ammo sergeant/Field 1st Sergeant. On 1955 Div. Football Team. Camp Irwin, CA October 1956. Commo chief, 16th Armd. Gp. July 1958 released to 331st Inf., Fort Hayes, OH, was acting sergeant major prior to 1960 discharge.

Retired police commander. Married 41 years to Carol Anne Stock and they have one son and two granddaughters. He is a life member #702, 24th Inf. Div. Assoc. and has been a charter life member of VFW for 45 years.

OSCAR W. STOEBENER, born Dec. 5, 1916 and inducted into the Army at Leavenworth, KS, Feb. 15, 1942 and basic training at Camp Wolters, TX. From there they went to Angel Island in San Francisco which was an embarkation station. From there they went to Oahu, HI, and assigned to the 2nd Bn., HQ Co., 19th Regt., 24th Div. They were there about 13 months then went to Brisbane, Australia for some more training. For three months they were at Rockhampton before going to Goodenough Island.

They made their first landing in New Guinea near Hollandia, the most uncivilized place he had ever seen. From there they went to the first landing of Leyte, the Philippines. This island is where they gained the name of the Lost Battalion. They then made a landing on Mindoro. They did guard duty there and then went to a small unnamed island. He started his journey home, suffering from too much combat. He went through three hospitals and went home on a hospital ship. They landed in San Francisco in May 1945 and he was discharged as private first class, May 17, 1945.

He received the Good Conduct, Asiatic Pacific Theater, Rifleman Badge, Bronze Star (Combat duty) and Discharge Button.

He was employed as a maintenance carpenter at Kansas University for 22 years. He has served on the church council and enjoys gardening and reading.

He married Pearl R. Brohammer July 31, 1949 and she is now deceased. They had two children, Barbara Johnson and Paul Bowlin; four grandchildren: Tamara and Melissa Johnson; Sara and Matthew Bowlin. He is now retired.

DOUGLAS L. STOKES joined the service on April 30, 1945, and served with Co. G, 21st Regt. He was discharged with the rank of corporal. He was awarded the Asiatic-Pacific Campaign Ribbon, Army of Occupation Ribbon (Japan), WWII Victory Ribbon and Overseas Bar. Dates served: October 1945 to October 1946.

ALLEN B. STONE joined the service in 1949 and served with Co. A, 19th Regt. He was stationed in Korea and Japan. He was discharged with the rank of sergeant. Dates served: 1949-52.

RICHARD A. STUBEN joined the service on March 17, 1948, and served with Co. C, H&S Co., 3rd Eng. Bn., June 1949 to September 1950; and Co. C, HQ Co., 1st Bn., 19th Inf. Regt., 24th Div., September 1950 to May 1951. He was stationed in Korea. He was discharged on March 19, 1952, with the rank of corporal.

HOWARD W. STRUECKER joined the service on Nov. 20, 1944, and served with Co. E, 19th Regt. He participated in the Southern Philippines and Asiatic-Pacific Campaigns. He was discharged with the rank of corporal. He was awarded the WWII Victory Medal, Good Conduct Medal, Army of Occupation Ribbon (Japan), Combat Infantryman's Badge and Unit Award. Dates served: May 6, 1944, to Nov. 14, 1946.

LLOYD L. SUMMERS joined the service on Nov. 15, 1950, and served with Co. L, 19th Regt. He was stationed in Korea and Japan. He was discharged with the rank of private first class. Dates served: June 13, 1951, to June 15, 1952.

MYRON JOHN SWANSON joined the service on Nov. 27, 1944, and served with Co. E, 19th Regt. He participated in the Southwest Pacific, Mindanao Campaign, May through August 1945 and the Japanese Occupation on Shikoku, Kyushu and Honshu. He left Japan on Sept. 13, 1946, and was discharged on Nov. 29, 1946, with the rank of staff sergeant.

WILLIAM J. SWANSON joined the service on Dec. 23, 1949, and served with the Med. Det, HQ Co., 24th Inf. Div. He was discharged with the rank of sergeant. He was awarded the Korean Service Medal w/6 Bronze Service Stars. Dates served: 1950-51.

VICENTE H. SYDIONGCO joined the service on Oct. 26, 1944, and served with Co. I, R Plt., HQ Co., 34th Regt. He participated at Leyte, Luzon and Mindanao. He was discharged with the rank of sergeant. Dates served: Oct. 26, 1944, to Sept. 15, 1945.

CHESTER H. SZURLEY was inducted into the service on Sept. 13, 1949, and served with Co. M, 34th Regt. and Co. H, 21st Regt. He was discharged on Oct. 7, 1952, with the rank of private first class. He was awarded five Battle Bronze Stars, Korean Campaign Ribbon, UN Service Medal, Presidential Unit Citation, Purple Heart, Korean Presidential Unit Citation and Combat Infantryman's Badge. Dates served: July 27, 1950, to Oct. 16, 1951.

WILL HILL TANKERSLEY joined the service on June 2, 1950, and served with Co. I, Hvy. Mtr., HQ, 19th Regt. He participated in six campaigns of the Korean War. He was discharged with the rank of 1st lieutenant. Dates served: August 1950 to December 1951.

WILLIAM E. TANKERSLEY joined the service on Dec. 8, 1952, and served with the Med. Co., 19th Regt. He participated in Korea, Corregidor Island, Kajodo Island, Yang-gu Valley and Pusan. He was discharged with the rank of corporal. Dates served: November 1955 to February 1957.

DAWAYNE TAYLOR served with the 24th Div., Svc. Btry., 11th FA BN, from 1951 to July 1953, at Camp Young Hans, Japan Sendi. *Submitted by Marvin Taylor*

MARVIN TAYLOR joined the service on May 27, 1955, and served with D Btry., 26th AAA BN. He was stationed in Korea. He was discharged with the rank of SP4. Dates served: November 1955 to February 1957.

DAVID E. TEICH SR., born in Brooklyn, NY, Sept. 23, 1925, enlisted in the US Army at age 16 on July 7, 1942. He received basic training as a tank crewman at Fort Knox, KY. Assigned as a medical aid man to the 744th Light Tank Bn. at Camp Hood, TX but during the European Campaign he transferred to the recon. platoon as a scout. The battalion fought in five major campaigns supporting eight different infantry divisions. He was awarded the British Military Medal by King George for actions as a scout during the Holland campaign. After WWII reenlisted in USAAC spent a tour in Alaska with the Aviation Engineers. Returned stateside and was assigned as an infantry platoon sergeant. Attended Officers Candidate School at Fort Riley, KS, graduating in 1949 as a second lieutenant, Armor Cav. Assigned platoon leader, Co. B, 44th Tank Bn., 82nd Armd. Div. In September 1950 was sent to Korea as a replacement. Joined the 6th Tank Bn. November 1950 and was assigned to Co. C as 3rd Plt. leader. It was while supporting the 1st ROK Inf. Div. near the Yalu River in November that he earned his Purple Heart while attempting to return a Chinese hand grenade. The 3rd Tank Plt. usually supported the 3rd Bn., 19th and 21st Inf. Regts., and the 8th Ranger Co. In September 1950 he was evacuated to Japan with Hepatitis A. Returning stateside he was again assigned to Fort Knox, first as a tank gunnery instructor, then as CO, Co. B, 84th Tank Bn., 3rd Armd. Div.

Next tour was to the 2nd Armd. Cav. in Europe, where he commanded A Troop, 1st Sqdn. until 1956. Assigned as Army advisor to the Ohio National Guard's 1st Sqdn., 107th Armd. Cav. Regt. until 1959 when he was again assigned to the 24th Inf. Div., Munich Germany. There he commanded both D & E Tank Cos., 34th Armor until June 1962 when he received a compassionate transfer to the Military District of Washington because his wife was hospitalized at Walter Reed Army Hospital.

His last duty assignment was Plans and Operations officer for Logistics for all ceremonies in Washington, DC. He retired September 1963 after 20 years of service with the rank of major.

His awards include the Commendation Medal, Purple Heart, Good Conduct, American Campaign, European Theater (five stars), Victory Medal, Army of Occupation (Germany), National Defense, Korean Service w/four stars, British Military Medal and the United Nations Medal.

Employed as deputy sheriff (inspector), chief of police, private investigator, security manager for Security Pacific Bank's Data Processing Center, Denver, CO.

Memorable experiences: Awarded British Military Medal by King George during WWII. Rescue of 8th Ranger Co. Abn. from Hill 628 April 1951, Korea. After retirement going back to school and earning associate, bachelors and double masters degrees while working full time. Was also Cub Master, Scout Master and Explorer advisor while raising three sons.

He is married to Cora G. (Trudy) and they have children: David Jr., Terry Lee and Thomas Edward; one grandson, Tristan Edward, USN.

Retired and travels with Denver Unit Airstream Club, builds and flies radio controlled model airplanes.

Loves fishing, boating (has 25.5 Bayliner, cabin cruiser) and wood working.

DONALD E. TENCH, born June 5, 1929, enlisted in the Army Nov. 23, 1950. He served with the 24th Signal Co. Construction, Korea. He was a truck driver and later team sergeant.

Discharged July 23, 1952 and received the Korean Service Medal, Bronze Star and three OLCs.

Memorable experiences include 38 years in the National Guard and Army Reserves.

Married Bonnell C. Tench and they have children, Cranford Milton and Charles Steven; three grandchildren: Adam Eugene, Carin Mackenzie and Meredith Ryan T. He is now retired from Georgia State Corrections Dept.

ERNEST P. TERRELL JR. joined the service on July 28, 1948, and served with Btry. A, 11th FA BN. He was discharged with the rank of 1st lieutenant. He received seven Battle Stars. Dates served: January 1950 to August 1951.

JOHN L. TESTER, born Sept. 29, 1930, enlisted in the Army Jan. 19, 1949. He served in Btry. A, 26th AAAA WBN, 24th Div. in Japan and Korea.

His assignments include: A Btry., 13th FABN, Camp Hakata Japan, April 1949-July 1950; Korea July 1950-June 1951, gunner of Section Number 3.

Discharged June 9, 1952 as sergeant. He received the Bronze Star Medal, Good Conduct Medal, Presidential Unit Emblem, Army of Occupation Medal w/Japan Clasp, National Defense Service Medal, Korean Service Medal w/five stars, United Nations Service Medal and Korean Presidential Unit Citation Badge.

He was employed for 30 years as a railroad conductor and brakeman.

Married Billie Jean Lawson Oct. 24, 1952 and they had four children: John, Dorothy, Constance and Martin and 11 grandchildren. He is now retired and living in Florida.

MARION THACKER, born March 2, 1928, enlisted in the Army Dec. 14, 1948.

Dischargd Oct. 31, 1951 as corporal. His awards include the Bronze Star, Purple Heart w/OLC, Good Conduct Medal, National Defense Occupation, Korean Service w/star and United Nations.

Memorable experiences included being badly wounded Aug. 10, 1950. Al Lewchuck came from a place of safety and got him out of the line of fire.

He is married to Donna Mae and they have two children, Craig and Kathryn and two grandchildren: Samantha and Daniel.

Employed as engineer, Bureau of Reclamation Planning Office. Now retired and serving as finance officer for MOPH, service officer NARFE and searching for Army buddies.

SANFORD U. THATCHER, born May 4, 1932, enlisted in the Army Sept. 12, 1949.

Assignments include Dog Co., 21st Inf., Regt., 24th Div., Machine Gun Plt.; Indiantown Gap, basic training instructor.

Discharged as private first class in 1952. His awards include the Bronze Star, Combat Infantry Badge, five Battle Stars, Korean Service Medal and UN Service Medal.

His memorable experiences include crossing the Naktong River in assault boats, paddling very fast to get to the far side. In the middle of the river automatic weapons started firing at them. Bullets came up to the front of the boat and Thatcher stopped paddling. He froze and the bullets stopped too. Took deep breath and finished crossing and pushed on to Seoul.

He is married to Shirley M. and they have a daughter, Dianne (Thatcher) Becker and three grandchildren: John, Dan and Keri Becker. He is now a retired railroad engineer.

WILBUR THIEL (MIKE) joined the service in August 1950 and served with Co. L, 21st Regt. He participated in the first six campaigns in Korea. He was discharged in September 1951 with the rank of master sergeant.

JOHN C. THOMAS served with the Svc. Co., 19th Regt. He was discharged with the rank of corporal.

DONALD E. THOMPSON joined the service on Nov. 28, 1941, and served the 724th Ord. Co. He participated in the Asiatic-Pacific Campaign and received one Battle Star and in Korea, receiving six Battle Stars. He was discharged with the rank of sergeant first class. Dates served: July 1950 to February 1951.

WILLIAM F. THOMPSON, born Oct. 1, 1929, enlisted in the Army Jan. 26, 1951. He was inducted at Canton, OH Jan. 26, 1951. Attended basic training at Fort Knox, KY. There was a 21-day delay enroute to Feacom. Debarked Camp Drake and processed to Sasebo, Japan. Landed Puson and trained to Yong Dong Po to 24th Replacement Co. assigned to 724th Ord Co. January 1952 transferred with division to Japan Camp Fuji, rotated back to States July 1952 and processed for discharge Indiantown Gap with the rank of corporal.

His awards include the UN Medal, Japan Occupation Medal and Korean Service Medal w/Bronze Star.

Married Marjorie A. Thompson and they have three children: Rebecca, John and Andrew; six grandchildren: Scott, Nikki, Chris, Jessica, Britta and Brett.

Employed with Shelby S&L as teller and progressed through the ranks to executive vice president and M/O, Dirc. He served as director, Peoples Savings Bank. Elected Mayor, City of Shelby, served two terms and retired. He is a life member of American Legion and VFW. Now retired, his hobbies are enjoying his grandchildren, traveling and golf.

WILLIAM H. THORNTON joined the service in February 1944 and served with Co. B, 21st Inf., 1st Bn., 24th Div., from February 1948 until 1951; and with Co. A, 19th Inf., 1st Bn., 24th Div. from March 1968 until 1970. He participated in WWII, the Korean War and the Vietnam War. He was discharged with the rank of sergeant first class.

URBAN L. THROM joined the service on July 1, 1943, and served with the Med. Bn., 3rd Eng., Div. Arty, Div. HQ. He participated at Leyte, Mindoro, Luzon and Mindanao. Dates served: October 1944 to July 1946.

THOMAS J. TOLAN, born March 23, 1925, enlisted Nov. 2, 1944, serving in the 1st Bn., C Co., 21st Inf. Ret.

Assignments include: Camp Blanding, FL, basic training; Philippine Islands, Luzon, Mindanao, Army of Occupation, Japan, Okayama and Kumamoto, landed at Yokohama.

Discharged November 1946 as private first class. His awards include the Army of Occupation, Asiatic-Pacific Campaign Medal, Philippines Liberation Medal, WWII Victory Medal, Good Conduct Medal, Combat Infantry Badge, New York State Conspicuous Service Cross.

Memorable experiences: guarding commanding general of the 24th Inf. Div. When word was received by him that the war was over he supplied them with a pit barbecue prepared by his personal chef. To this day it is the best meat he has ever eaten.

Employed at Seneca Army Depot, January 1947-November 1970. Last job at SEAD fire chief. Transferred to GSA New York City as strategic materiels inspector. Retired April 1980. Founding member of local fire department, West Lake Rd., Geneva, NY, serving as assistant chief.

Married Sara Johnson and their family includes: Joseph and Von Tolan, Thomas and Amy Tolan, John and Mary Vadenmoortel; six grandchildren: David and Daniel Tolan, Jacqueline and Jay Tolan, Kate and John Vandemoortel. He is very active in American Legion Post #396 with over 1,000 members and VFW Post 2670.

BARTOW D. TOMBLIN joined the service on Aug. 11, 1943, and served with HQ Div., G-2 Section. He participated at Hollandia, Leyte, Mindanao and the Occupation of Japan. He was discharged with the rank of master sergeant. Dates served: February 1944 to December 1945.

LOUIS R. TORRES, born Oct. 15, 1928. Before entering the Army on Feb. 6, 1951 he was an unskilled laborer, fruit picker, migratory worker and high school drop out. He went from the agricultural fields of California through basic training at Camp Roberts and to Korea. After his return from Korea he entered the University of California at Santa Barbara where he earned a BA in Zoology, a masters degree in Biology and a California teaching credential.

Memorable experiences: first weeks in the front lines; being wounded near Kumsong North Korea, Oct. 19, 1951; being sent to the rear in search of the battalion aid station; a hairy ride to the regimental medical station and another exciting ride in a crowded ambulance, packed with wounded, including a Chinese infantryman, who much to his relief, was given

water, food and a cigarette; his eyes literally shone with surprise and gratitude. Arriving at a Mash unit they were treated with love and kindness by the medical personnel. They treated each one of them as very special patients. After recovering in Japan, going back to his unit L Co. in a very white Korea. The most unforgettable sight, the fully illuminated Golden Gate Bridge. He gave thanks to God for allowing him to return.

Discharged Feb. 7, 1953 as private first class and received the Combat Infantry Badge, Purple Heart, United Nations Medal, Korean Campaign w/two Battle Zone Stars and Army of Occupation.

He married Sheridan Force and they have children: Louis, Aislinn, Tenley and two children from previous marriage Carol and Marina; four grandchildren: Brian, Meghan, Erin and Mark.

He is teaching Science (Biology-Life Science) at Santa Barbara High School, Santa Barbara, CA.

ENOS TORSCH joined the service in August 1941 and served with Co. L, 34th Regt. He participated at Hollandia, New Guinea, Philippines, Corrigedor. He was discharged with the rank of sergeant. Dates served: August 1941 to June 1946.

NORMAN E. (LUCKY) TREDWAY, enlisted in the service at 17 and completed basic training with D Co., 364th Inf. Regt., 69th Inf. Div. at Fort Dix, NJ in 1954. After completing MP School at Camp Gordon, GA, he was assigned to the 2nd Traffic Plt., 24th MP Co., at Yong Ju Gol, Korea. Duties included road, train and walking patrol, civilian control lines (check points) and Special Operations details. An additional duty included assignment to the 24th Div., HQ MP Plt., providing security to the division commanding general. He later transferred to E Co., 21st "Gimlet" Inf. Regt. He served 16 months in Korea and upon returning home, was stationed at Fort Campbell, KY with the 2nd Abn. Battle Gp., 187th "Rakkasan" Inf. Regt., 101st Abn. Div. and Fort Sill, OK with the 522nd Inf. Bn. (Sep.), which was later reflagged as the 2nd Battle Gp., 30th Inf. Regt. He attained the rank of corporal.

In August 1961, he married Patricia Caley. He was a police officer in New Jersey until disabled on the job. He received a BA in psychology from Rutgers University and a masters in project management from George Washington University. He has been employed as a marketing manager with AT&T for over 20 years and is a member of VFW.

ROBERT E. TREADWAY joined the service on May 21, 1941, and served with Co. G, 21st Inf. He participated in the Central Pacific, Southern Philippines and New Guinea. He was discharged on May 31, 1945, with the rank of sergeant. Awards include the Philippine Liberation Ribbon, American Defense Service Ribbon, Asiatic-Pacific Service Ribbon,

Combat Infantryman's Badge and Sharpshooter Rifle Badge.

JOHN G. TRINCA joined the service on Oct. 11, 1944, and served with Co. C, 21st Inf. Regt. He participated in the Philippines and Mindanao. He was discharged with the rank of staff sergeant. Dates served: May 1945 to November 1946.

DAVID B. TUCKER joined the service on Oct. 2, 1946, and served with Co. C, 34th Inf. Regt. and HQ, 24th Div., T.I.&E WLKH. He participated in the Occupation forces in Japan. He was discharged with the rank of T/5.

JOHN L. TUCKER enlisted September 13, 1949 and had 16 weeks of Infantry basic at Ft. Knox, KY. He was assigned 24/34/D Co., Sasebo, Japan as a driver for 81mm Mortar Squad. He deployed Korea June 1950 and lost a vehicle and crew served gun during battle of Taejon. He was later reassigned to 24/19/M Co. as a Radio Operator (SCR300) for 81 mm Mortar Forward Observer Team.

Tucker was discharged Ft. Meade, MD during October 1952. Spent eight years with the Maryland national Guard, 29/115/Heavy Mortar Co Forward Observer/Aerial, M/Sgt.

He received the Combat Infantry Badge, Purple Heart, Presidential Unit Citation, Korean Unit citation, Korean Service medal with four clusters.

Married Elizabeth Houston during August 1952. They have four children and six grandchildren. Tucker has been a cabinet maker for 40 years and enjoys amateur radio. His call sign is K3NNI.

THOMAS A. TUCKER joined the service in 1950 and served with Co. C, 21st Regt. He was discharged with the rank of private. Dates served: 1950-51.

RICHARD W. TURNER joined the service in June 1949 and served with Co. I, 1st Plt., 21st Regt. He was discharged with the rank of sergeant. Dates served: June 1950 to December 1951.

TED D. TURNER was inducted into the service on Oct. 14, 1953, and served with Co. E, 34th Regt. He participated in Korea, DMZ. He was discharged with the rank of private first class. Dates served: Oct. 14, 1953, to October 1955.

ERNEST E. VALENZUELA, born Oct. 5, 1931, enlisted in the Army July 21, 1948. Received basic training, Fort Ord, CA. Later participated in Joint Puerto Rico exercise called "Operation Portrex" with 3rd Inf. Div. in 1950.

Arriving at Fort Benning, GA after the exercise was the turning point of his infantry training, for it was the aggression of North Korea that took him to Korea. Arrived there after the defeat of Taejon on Aug. 1, 1950

and assigned to "Baker" Co. of 21st Inf. Regt. He was a gunner for 3.5 bazooka, and later 57 Recoilless Rifle. He doesn't remember incidents, as they were always on the go, heading north on the west coast of Korea, to the Yalu River, not knowing anything about Chinese intervention, which was about to happen. Those days were mixed emotions as the Chinese were building up over 200,000 men with a ratio of 50 to 1. "If you can't take it, burn it" was their motto.

In 1951, after several months of bitter fighting, freezing, hardships and everything that goes with war, he was ordered to return to the States to train draftees with the 1st Inf. Regt., 6th Inf. Div., at Fort Ord, CA. He was glad that he had the experience to change civilians to US Infantrymen.

Walk proudly, as you are part of the finest army in the world "The Infantry".

His awards include the Korean Service Medal w/ three Bronze Service Stars, Distinguished Unit Emblem, Combat Infantry Badge (was his most honored decoration).

Married Diana Rodarte in November 1953 and they have three grown sons: Ernest Jr., James and Tim; three granddaughters and one grandson. Retired after 34 years with major grocery stores. Served as post commander of the VFW, 1985-86.

DANIEL VALLES was inducted into the service in January 1942. He joined the 24th Div. in Hawaii, and was assigned to Co. K, 34th Regt. He participated in Southwest Pacific, New Guinea, Biak, Leyte, Luzon and Corregidor. He was injured in Corregidor. He was discharged with the rank of staff sergeant. Dates served: May 1942 to December 1945.

HERB VANDERHORST joined the service on Sept. 22, 1950, and served with Co. I, 5th RCT Regt. He was stationed in Korea. He was discharged with the rank of sergeant. Awards include the Silver Star. Dates served: April 1, 1951, to March 1, 1952.

WILBUR VANDERVORST, born June 4, 1917, enlisted in the service Feb. 2, 1942, served with the 21st Inf., 3rd Bn., 3rd Bn. HQ.

His locations and stations included: Hawaii; Goodenough Island; Australia, New Guinea, Leyte, Philippines, Mindoro, Mindanao and Mussenburg.

Discharged Aug. 25, 1945 as staff sergeant. His awards include the Purple Heart, Good Conduct Medal, Asiatic-Pacific Service Medal and Philippine Liberation Medal w/Bronze Star.

Memorable experiences: Went to Russia on an agriculture study mission in 1974, also included were Holland, Belgium, France and Germany. Great experience.

He married Dorothy, June 1947 and she died in 1968. Remarried Yvonne 1975. He has three children: James, Gary and Timothy and six grandchildren: Shannon, Holly, Dustin, Corissa, Malissa and Jeremy.

He was a farmer; state legislator 18 years; State Soil Conservation Committee, six years; State Association board member eight years. Served on several county boards and employed 40 years as county supervisor Soil Conservation Board.

Presently recuperating from cancer. He has been active in community affairs and doing some grain farming.

JOEL STEVEN VARGO SR. joined the service on March 12, 1953, and served with the Tk. Co., 5th

RCT Regt. He was stationed in Korea. He was discharged with the rank of corporal. Dates served: 1953-54.

DOMINGO VASQUEZ, born Dec. 20, 1920 in Logan, UT, entered the Army Inf., Sept. 13, 1942. Assigned rifle squad leader. Wounded Nov. 8, 1944, while serving with the 21st Inf., L Co., 24th Div.

Discharged as sergeant Dec. 15, 1945. Awarded Victory Medal, Asiatic-Pacific Campaign Medal, Philippine Liberation Ribbon w/two Bronze Stars, Good Conduct Medal, Purple Heart, Philippine Presidential Unit Citation, Combat Infantryman Badge and WWII Victory Medal.

Married to Angelina Vasquez, Jan. 5, 1952 and they have three children: Lorraine, Arthur and Amanda. After service he was employed in construction. Now retired and life member of AMVETS, American Legion and VFW.

ALFRED G. VAUGHN JR., born May 14, 1911, enlisted in the service Oct. 23, 1942.

His assignments include: Wpns. Plt., Co. F, 2nd Bn., US 19th Inf. Regt.

Discharged as sergeant Aug. 30, 1945. His awards include the Combat Infantry Badge, Good Conduct Medal, three Bronze Stars, Pacific Theatre Ribbon w/three Overseas Bars and the Philippine Liberation w/two Bronze Stars.

His memorable experiences: when he landed on New Guinea he almost drowned when the landing craft dropped him too far from shore and the weight of the machine gun ammunition he was carrying dragged him under. Fortunately, somebody grabbed him in time and saved him.

Employed as bricklayer in his hometown of St. Louis. He married Ann Budzik and they had no children. He died Sept. 12, 1998 at the age of 87.

JOHN M. VELETTO joined the service in March 1952 and served with Hvy. Mtr. Co., 21st Regt. He served guard duty on Koje Island from 1953-54. He was discharged with the rank of private first class. Dates served: 1953-54.

VINCENT VELLA joined the service on Nov. 22, 1944, and served with Co. K, 21st Regt. He participated in the Pacific, Philippines and Mindanao. He was discharged with the rank of private first class. Dates served: Nov. 22, 1944, to Nov. 22, 1946.

WILLIAM E. VICKERS JR., born June 9, 1923, Los Angeles, CA, enlisted from Teachers College into Army November 1942. Attended asic training at Camp Roberts, CA and was sent to Hawaii June 7, 1943. Served in Australia with the 24th Inf. Div., 34th Regt., 3rd Bn., HQ Co. Served following campaigns: Biak Island, Hollandia, New Guinea, Leyte, Corregidor, Luzon, South Philippines and Japan. During most of the campaigns he was Col. Postlethwait's radio operator.

His most memorable action was an eight day march behind enemy lines to recover wounded men from K or L Co. Half of the rescue party was shot up.

He received the Service Strip, five Overseas Service Bars, Asiatic-Pacific Theater Ribbon w/Bronze

Star, Philippine Liberation Ribbon w/two Bronze Star, WWII Victory Medal and Good Conduct Medal.

He was returned to the US in time for Christmas 1945 as a staff sergeant.

With the GI Bill of Rights he finished Teachers College in 1949 and received an MA degree from Northwestern University 1952 and an advanced degree in 1965. He taught in Alabama, Chicago and retired in 1988 as director for special education in Waukegan, IL, after 40 years of teaching/administration to our children.

ERNEST L. VIENNEAU joined the service on Oct. 2, 1941, and served with Companies I, K and M, 21st Inf. Regt. He participated in the Asiatic-Pacific Theater, New Guinea Campaign, Philippines, Hollandia, Leyte, Mindoro, Marinduque and Mindanao. He was discharged with the rank of lieutenant colonel. Dates served: May 1942 to June 1945.

WILLIAM F. VOGL joined the service on Feb. 24, 1954, and served with Co. C, 6th Tk. Bn. He was stationed in Korea, DMZ. He was discharged with the rank of SP3. Dates served: 1954-55.

EDWARD J. VOSO joined the service on March 29, 1939, and served with Co. D, 21st Regt. He participated during the Japanese attack on Oahu and then went to Europe. He was discharged with the rank of sergeant. Dates served: April 1939 to May 1942.

CARL S. WAGENFUEHRER joined the service on Dec. 26, 1942, and served with H&S Co., 3rd Eng. Bn. He participated at New Guinea and the Philippines. He was discharged with the rank of T-5. Dates served: May 1943 to December 1945.

BEN WAHLE joined the service in 1941 and served with Co. E and G, 34th Regt. He participated in Hawaii, Australia, New Guinea, Biak, and the Philippines. He was discharged with the rank of captain. Dates served: 1491-45.

ROBERT WANDERSEE, born June 15, 1934 joined the Minnesota National Guard, March 1953.

Took basic training at Fort Riley, KS June 1953 and Artillery Training at Camp Carson, CO, September 1953. He was assigned to 7th Div. Arty., HQ Btry. in Korea spring of 1954. Reassigned to 24th Div. HQ Btry., 11th Field, summer of 1954. The division was sent to Japan in the fall of 1954. Their battery went to Camp OTSU. They were sent back to Korea in the winter of 1954-55. He ended up with a good assignment; Showing the nightly movies to all the troops of 11th Field. He had a tent with equipment, private sleeping quarters and a movie schedule on front.

Discharged as sergeant in 1961. His awards include the Korean Service Medal, National Defense, Good Conduct and United Nations Service Medal.

Married Arlene and they have six children: Jackie, Stacy, Mike, David, Lynn, Arlinda and 10 grandchildren.

He was employed as a building contractor in Minneapolis, MN. For the last 15 years he has owned an antique store and repair shop. He is a life member of Canby, MN VFW #117.

BILLIE H. WASSMAN, born May 10, 1929, enlisted in the Army June 1952.

He received basic training at Fort Dix, NJ and attended Radio School there too. Assigned to HQ Co., 2nd Bn., 19th Inf. Regt. and served 11 months in Korea.

Discharged June 1954 as corporal E-4. His awards include the Good Conduct, National Defense, Korean Campaign and UN Medal.

Memorable experiences: After truce was signed he ran a post exchange. He has served for six years as commander of his VFW Post.

Married Muriel Taft Wright in 1954 and they have two children, Patrice and Clifford and two grandchildren, Peter and Matthew.

Served as advertising director for major book publishers. Freelanced as advertising consultant and graphic artist. Now retired. Teaches adult classes in photography, publishes greeting cards, sells antiques and serves as recycling coordinator for town, and trustee of two historical societies.

GARY WATERKAMP, born May 12, 1931 in Elkhorn, WI, graduated from Creston High School, Grand Rapids, MI, in June 1949 and joined the regular army in July 1949. Basic training at Fort Riley, KS (Camp Funston) with Co. D, 85th Inf. Regt., 10th Div. Completed Leaders School and was assigned to the 14th Regimental Combat Team at Camp Carson, CO. On assignment at Camp McCoy, WI when alerted for overseas duty in July 1950. Assigned to I Co., 24th Div., 21st Regt. in August 1950. Returned to US in October 1951. Assigned to 4th Army HQ in San Antonio, TX. Discharged Sept. 15, 1952 and married his wife, Betty Jo Henricksen, who was in the service at Fort Sam Houston at this time also.

He served on the Kalamazoo City Police Dept. while earning a BS degree from Western Michigan University. Taught high school for five years while earning a MA in School Administration. Served as a high school principal for two years and a superintendent of schools for over 25 years, retiring in 1992. They have one daughter, Susan, who is married to Col. Michael Quinlan, USMC, and have two sons, Joseph and William, who is a police officer in St. Paul, MN. He and his wife April, have two children, Quentin and Kendel.

JAMES EDWARD WATKINS, born in Scranton, PA, Aug. 12, 1964attended BCT at Fort Jackson and was trained as a motor transport operator at Fort Dix, NJ. He served in the 1003rd General Supply Co., USAR, in Scranton, PA. After reentering active duty he was assigned to the 416th Transportation Co., 260th Quartermaster Bn., 24th Inf. Div. (Mechanized), Hunter Army Airfield, GA. Participated in Hurricane Hugo disaster relief and Operations Desert

Shield and Desert Storm, October 1990 through April 1991.

SPC Watkins returned to the 1003rd General Supply Co. and later enlisted in HHC 2nd Bn., 103rd Armor, PA Army National Guard. He returned to active duty and was assigned to HHC, 1st Bn., 8th Inf., 4th Inf. Div., Fort Carson County. While assigned to the 4th Inf. Div. he participated in exercises with the Canadian Armed Forces and Intrinsic Action with the 3rd Bde. Combat Team in Kuwait.

As of this writing he is assigned to HHC 2nd Bn., 103rd Armor, PA Army National Guard.

Decorations include the Army Commendation Medal, the Army Achievement Medal w/seven OLCs, Armed Forces Expeditionary Medal, Southwest Asia Service Medal w/three Bronze Stars, Kuwait Liberation Medals (Saudi Arabia and Kuwait), Army Good Conduct Medal (2nd Award), various USAR and Pennsylvania State Awards.

WILLIAM L. WATKINS joined the service on May 25, 1942, and served with the HQ Co., 24th Div. Arty. He participated in the Philippine Liberation. He was discharged with the rank of major.

RICHARD C. WATSON, born Aug. 10, 1922, enlisted in the Army Oct. 29, 1942.

His assignments included basic training December 1942, Oahu Hawaii, Australia, Goodenough Island, New Guinea, Leyte, Mindoro, Ambalong, Luzon and Mindanao.

Discharged Nov. 28, 1945 as T-4. His awards include the Silver Star, three Bronze Stars, Combat Medical Badge, President Unit Citation USA and Philippines and other ribbons.

Memorable experiences: basic in Hawaii; survivor of the lost battalion in the Ormoc Valley, Philippines.

Married Phyllis E. Watson, Nov. 28, 1948. Retired from General Motors with 39 years. Traveling and enjoying retirement. He is past president of the 24th Inf. Div. Assoc., Life #74; life member American Legion; life member VFW, 32 degree Mason, Shriner, Eastern Star, Eagle, Elks, UAW #662, Kentucky Colonel.

DALE A. WELCH joined the service on July 13, 1955, and served with Co. K, 21st Inf. Regt. He was discharged with the rank of SP3. Dates served: Dec. 23, 1955, to March 12, 1957.

FRANCIS H. WELCH, born in Montgomery, WV, May 13, 1924, inducted into Army July 27, 1943. Reported to Fort Thomas, KY and then to Camp Fannin, TX for infantry basic training. After basic, sent to Fort Ord, CA for amphib training and onto the Pacific.

Arrived Milne Bay, New Guinea February 1944. Assigned to Co. L, 21st Regt., 24th Div. on Goodenough Island. Served with the weapons platoon, Co. L in the Hollandia, Dutch New Guinea invasion, D-Day Oct. 20, 1944, Leyte, Philippine invasion and the Mindoro and Mindanao operations.

Wounded in action outside Davao, Mindanao, May 4, 1945. Hospitalized in field units on Mindanao and in Army General Hospital on Leyte. Left by hospital plane on June 9, 1945 for US and surgery at Fletcher General Hospital, Cambridge, OH, then transferred to

Newton D. Baker Hospital, Martinsburg, WV. Discharged May 10, 1946 from Newton D. Baker Hospital with the rank of sergeant.

His decorations include the Combat Infantryman Badge, Bronze Star, Purple Heart, Victory Medal and the Philippine Liberation Medal.

Attended college under the GI Bill, graduating from West Virginia Institute of Technology, Montgomery, WV in 1950 with a BS degree in Printing Management.

Married Dolores Jane Smith March 1949. Following college he worked nine years at Kentucky Printing Co., Louisville, KY. In 1959, joined Westvaco Paper Co. in New York City as technical service representative. In 1989, retired from Westvaco as the fine papers manager with 30 years service.

Fran and Dolores (Dee) reside in Old Bridge, NJ. They have three daughters: Frances Evanto, West Virginia; Susan Graziano, Florida; Robin L. Welch, New Jersey; and son, Roger H. Welch, North Carolina; a grandson, Erik Evanto, West Virginia and granddaughter, Jessica Welch.

He is a member of the American Legion and DAV.

ROY H. WELLS, born March 2, 1930 in Henryetta, OK entered the Army July 10, 1947. After basic training at Fort Jackson, SC served as a clerk in GHQ, Tokyo, Japan (General MacArthur's HQ).

Reenlisted Nov. 4, 1949, commissioned second lieutenant May 5, 1951 upon graduation from OCS, Fort Riley, KS. March 1952 was assigned to Btry. A, 26 AAA AW Bn (SP), 24th Inf. Div. Btry. A was attached to 19th Inf. Regt. at Camp Haugen in Northern Japan May 1953 as first lieutenant. Assigned as executive officer to Btry. B, which was attached to 21st Inf. Regt. at Camp Schimmelpfennig, Japan.

July 1953 the 24th Inf. Div. returned to Korea. After the cease-fire, B Btry. was attached to the 1st Bn., 19th Inf. Regt. guarding PW Camp No. 6, near Taejon. After Camp 6 prisoners were transported to Panmunjom, B Btry. was returned to the 26th AAA near Masan. Released Oct. 22, 1953, remained in the Reserves until retirement as lieutenant colonel in June 1979.

Married Betty Patterson in July 1954 and they have three children and four grandchildren.

WEIFORD RUFUS WELLS, born Sept. 24, 1924 in Grandcrossing, Chicago, IL. Inducted into the Army March 1, 1943. After seven days reservist reported for duty March 8, 1943. Shipped to Camp Wallace, TX, for AAA replacement training in infantry basic and radio operation CW code school. Joined the HQ Btry., 68th AAA Bde. in New Caledonia after leaving Angel Island. Was stationed on Guadalcanal and Bougainville. Transferred to 736th AAA Gun Bn., Btry. B in the Treasury Islands in September 1944. Stationed with the 736th there, Finschhafen, New Guinea and Vigan, Northern Luzon until September 1945 when transferred to HQ Btry., 104th AAA (AW) Bn. Moved with the 104th up to airfield outside Matsuyama, Shikoku Island, Japan with the 24th Inf. Div. aboard the LST No. 986 with an evacuation medical unit from the European theatre. The 104th was stationed on the airfield that was rumored to be where the Japanese suicide pilots were trained.

He received the Asiatic-Pacific Medal w/Bronze Star (Northern Solomons), Philippine Liberation Medal, Good Conduct Medal, WWII Victory Medal, four Overseas Bars and a Ruptured Duck Lapel Pin.

With 60 points, he shipped home through the 11th redeployment depot in Nagoya, Japan on the APA USS *Adm. E.W. Eberle* to Seattle, WA in December 1945. He was discharged Jan. 10, 1946 at Camp Grant, IL. Served in communications as radio operator, teletype operator, telephone lineman.

He has been married to Leona Emma Thuro since June 25, 1966. She is a St. Louis, MO native. They have no children.

He is a retired professional mechanical engineer with BSME from Purdue University (1951) and registered in Indiana and Illinois. He retired with 25 years and four months federal service from Puget Sound Naval Shipyard (PSNS) on Jan. 3, 1985. He is a life member of VFW, Amvets, American Legion PUFL, DAV, ASME and ASHRAE and PU Alumni Assoc.

He has many hobbies including: Amateur radio (KA7LBG), drawing, painting, woodcarving, gardening, reading, traveling and enjoying life.

EUGENE (GENE) M. WELSH, born May 9, 1925, enlisted in the Army, Aug. 10, 1943. He spent 19 months overseas in the Asiatic-Pacific Theater with the 19th Inf., Co. C, 24th Inf. Div. Also served in New Guinea, Leyte, Mindoro, Luzon, Romblom and Mindanao.

Discharged Jan. 31, 1946 as staff sergeant and received the Purple Heart w/Bronze OLC, Philippine Liberation Ribbon w/2 stars, Good Conduct Medal and Combat Infantry Badge. He was wounded seven times.

He is a life member of the American Legion, VFW, active in community service. He has been a square dance caller for 40 years. Citizen of the year in Ceres, 1988. Rotarian of the Year 1986. Active in Vets Day function in Ceres, CA.

He owned and operated Ceres Body Shop and Towing until his retirement. Towing is now operated by his two sons.

He is married to Bettye. She was his pen pal all during the war. He returned to marry her June 14, 1946 and they have been married 50 years. Their sons are Ron and Mike Welsh. They also have eight grandchildren: Shelly, Jeff, Krista, Morgan, Kim, Mike and Nicolas; great-grandchildren: Myles, Amanda and Zarcary.

Now retired and enjoying grandchildren, traveling and fishing.

LESTER L. WHEELER joined the Regular Army on June 12, 1935, and served with Co. G, 21st Inf. Regt.; 19th Regt.; and 34th Regt. He retired with the rank of brigadier general.

RODNEY A. WHITE joined the service on April 11, 1951, and served with Co. K, 34th Regt. He was stationed at Camp Fuji, Japan. He was discharged with the rank of sergeant. Dates served: November 1951 to March 1953.

JAMES E. WHITFIELD joined the service on

March 18, 1951, and served with Co. L, 21st Regt. He was stationed in Korea and Japan. He was discharged with the rank of private first class.

GEORGE R. WHITNEY joined the service on Oct. 9, 1941, and served with Co. G, 19th Inf. Regt. He participated in Australia, Buna, New Guinea, Hollandia, Philippines, Leyte, Mindoro, Luzon and Mindanao. He was discharged with the rank of 1st lieutenant. Dates served: January 1944 to July 1945.

FRANK H. (GODY) WIEGAND, born Dec. 17, 1910 in Appleton, WI, was drafted in June 1944 with infantry training at Camp Wolters, TX, serving with Co. D, 54th Bn. He went to the Philippines in the fall of 1944 while with the 34th Inf., 24th Div., Co. B.

On May 9, while hauling ammunition and rations to his company area 1,000 yards north of the city of Bancal, Mindanao, a barrage of mortar fire was landing in the vicinity of his jeep. He ran to the side of the road to seek protection, then was shot in the back by a Japanese sniper, instantly killing him. His final resting place is in the Manila American Cemetery in the Philippines.

He leaves behind his wife, Evelyn, three children, 10 grandchildren and four great-grandchildren. He is in their hearts forever.

His daughter, Dianne belongs to an organization called AWON, or, (WWW.AWO.ORG) American War Orphans Network. A great support group for the children left behind by WWII.

She would be interested in finding anyone who knew her dad during that time. (OMADI@AOL.COM) *Submitted by Dianne Wiegand Baczynski.*

GEORGE C. WILD joined the service on Dec. 11, 1941, and served with HQ Co., 1st Bn., 19th Regt. He participated in the Southwest Pacific, Japan, Korea and Germany. He was discharged with the rank of sergeant first class. Dates served: July 1948-54

GERALD AMOS WILLEY joined the ROTC at Ohio State University, 1947-49; USAR, March 7, 1950, as private first class in the 83rd Div.; and volunteered for active duty on June 27, 1951. He was assigned to HQ Co., 3rd Inf., 65th Inf. Regt. He participated in Alaska, Korea and Japan; battles at Kelly Hill, Old Baldy, White Horse Mountain; served in Iron Triangle, in and around Chorwan. He was an official US Army correspondent for the 3rd Inf. Div. and Stars and Stripes Korea Edition and, as such, was among many units and divisions and foreign units.

He was discharged with the rank of corporal. Awards include the Commendation Medal for Meritorious Service, Korean Service Medal, UN Service Medal, National Defense Service Medal, Presidential Press Citation Letter and the EUSAK Commendation for Meritorious Service Letter. Dates served: July 2, 1952, to Feb. 13, 1953.

EDWARD D. WILLIAMS joined the service on Oct. 18, 1948, and served with Co. G, 19th Regt. He was discharged on May 7, 1952, with the rank of sergeant first class. Awards include the Combat Infantryman's Badge, Purple Heart w/2 clusters, Bronze Star w/V device and Silver Star w/cluster.

MARION M. WILLIAMS, born Mar. 4, 1920 in Wishek, ND. He enlisted in January 1940 and arrived at Schofield Barracks in March 1940. Assigned to Co. I, 21st Inf. He writes this not as a member who fought with the 21st but as one with it when the big boom started December 7.

Co. I had the weapons carrier with a machine gun mounted on it and it was parked in front of Co. I when they went in for breakfast. Williams was the first gunner, but he was on the boxing team and did not pull guard. The section leader was Guston Pugh and others in the squad were Sides, Liptrop, Crompton, Bridges and others. They all heard the loud noise as Williams started down the stairs for breakfast. He could see planes dropping bombs on Wheeler Field and his first thought was to get his steel helmet. He fired the first machine gun at the Japanese that came over the 21st Regt.

A lieutenant yelled "Cease fire." Robberts yelled back, "Cease fire, hell, we're being attacked. Hogg (the supply sergeant) bring out more ammo."

In 1942 was sent to Fanning Isl. and from there to D Co., 136th Inf., 33rd Div., Finchhafen, New Guinea, loading and off loading ships plus jungle training. He was put in 18 man battalion assult group, was shot through right leg in training and was hospitalized for 21 days.

Joined his outfit on Morotai. The firefight was over, but they were bombed every night (called Piss Call Charley). Also at Lingayen Gulf and Luzon. Wounded on May 1, 1945 and went by plane to Leyte, 18 days hospital ship, San Francisco by train to Barnes Hospital, Van Couver Barracks.

Discharged Dec. 18, 1945 at Ft. Lewis, WA. After three years apprenticeship, he was a meat cutter until he retired in 1975. Oregon has approximately 1200 lakes, streams, river and the Pacific Ocean. He can't fish them all, but he does have his favorites.

Married Jane Marie Fowler July 18, 1952, Ashland, OR. They have one daughter, Patricia; three sons: Sam, Warren and Marcus; and seven grandchildren.

JOSEPH M. (MIKE) WILLIAMSON, born in Morocco, IN, graduated with highest honors from Purdue University and eceived a direct appointment into the regular US Army. He reported as a lieutenant to the 46th FABN in 1940 and advanced rapidly to the rank of lieutenant colonel, commanding the 412th Armd. FABN in Germany when hostilities ended in the EAME Theater in 1945.

His unit was redeployed for the invasion of Japan. Following WWII, he was assigned to the 13th FABN, 24th Div. until return to the USA in 1949. He occupied command and staff positions in many countries including the 5th Div., 20th Armd. Div., 2nd Armd. Div., 24th Div., Abn. Command, HQ Berlin Command, HQ I Corps (Korea), HQ III Corps, HQ 1st Army, Southern Command (Panama). Retired in 1971 after 31 years of service.

Always active in military and civilian communities, he received many awards. Military decorations and medals include the Legion of Merit (twice), Bronze Star, Army Commendation, American Campaign, EAME Campaign, WWII Victory, Army of Occupation (Germany and Japan) and National Service Medals and the American Defense Service Medal.

The National Council Boy Scouts, presented him the Silver Beaver in 1964 for distinguished service to boyhood. In 1990, Purdue University presented him

the Alumni Citizenship Award for strong commitment to community service. In 1996, inducted into the Purdue Army ROTC Hall of Fame for his contribution and leadership to society during his career.

He not only devoted his time to community service during his lifetime but financial support as well.

BILLY JOE WILLIS, born Oct. 11, 1928, enlisted in the service Dec. 4, 1950 and Sept. 4, 1952 he was assigned to the 19th Regt., 2nd Bn., Fox Co. He received basic training at Camp Chaffee, Fort Smith, AR; Korean Campaign March 1951 through March 1952. Discharged Sept. 4, 1952 at Camp Chaffee as a sergeant.

Married to Faye Willis and they have a daughter, Sandy Jo Willis Green and two grandchildren, Kyle Green and Kelly Green.

He retired from Arkla Gas Co. 1985, Hot Springs, AR after 30 years and is now enjoying retirement. He is a member of Oaklawn Baptist Church, Oaklawn Lions Club, Hot Springs, AR; past president of Oaklawn Lions Club. Now serving as secretary of Hot Springs Lions, Oaklawn for several years. Serving on Salvation Army advisory board.

EDWARD M. WILSON joined the service in December 1947 and served with the MP Co., Co. M, 21st Regt. He participated at Kumamoto, Japan, Pusan and Korea. He was discharged with the rank of corporal. Dates served: March 1948 to July 1950.

GRANTON E. WILSON joined the service on Oct. 7, 1940, and served with Co. E, 19th Inf. Regt. He participated at Pearl Harbor and New Guinea. He was discharged with the rank of sergeant. Dates served: Oct. 7, 1940, to Sept. 22, 1945.

ROBERT A. WILSON joined the service on Sept. 26, 1942, and served with Co. A, 24th Med. Bn., 21st, 19th and 34th Regt. He participated in New Guinea, Hollandia, Philippines, Japan, Panoan Island, Leyte, Mindoro and Mindanao. He was discharged with the rank of staff sergeant. Dates served: June 13, 1943, to Dec. 7, 1945.

KEITH L. WINCHENBACH, born July 13, 1923, inducted into the Army Nov. 4, 1943, Fort Devens, MA. He received basic training at Fort Knox, KY; tanks, Fort Ord, CA. Shipped to New Guinea and joined 24th Div., 21st Inf. Regt., 1st Bn. HQ Co. He was at the Philippine Islands on D-Day until the end of war. Served in the Japan Occupation and wounded May 8, 1945, Mintal Philippines.

Discharged Jan. 13, 1946 as staff sergeant. His awards include the Purple Heart, Asian Medal, five Combat Stars, Combat Rifle Badge and the Good Conduct Medal.

His memorable experiences: while in Mindanao, PI, Jack Tait, driver of jeep and Keith were in convoy moving up 35 miles to front. Their jeep stuck in third

gear. They had to go through a gulley where the bridge was gone. Lost the front and rear of convoy.

He is married and has five children, 11 grandchildren, four step-grandchildren and one great-granddaughter.

He operated a poultry farm for 13 years and took over his father's retail feed business four years. Opened a hardware and lumber store and was also a contractor for 26 years. He built about 50 homes. Now retired and residing in Florida. He is a volunteer on the Council For Aging.

EMERSON WINSTEAD, born Sept. 12, 1932, enlisted into the Army, Sept. 12, 1949. He received basic training at Fort Knox, KY and was assigned to 3rd Inf. at Fort Benning, GA. He went to Korea August 1950-51 with the 24th Inf., Co. B, 21st Regt. Discharged in 1952 and enlisted again in 1955. He served three assignments in Germany. Attended school at Fort Eustis for aircraft maintenance, and became an aircraft maintenance supervisor. Served two tours in Vietnam 1967-68 and 1970-71. Retired in 1973 after 20 years. His awards include the Combat Infantry Badge, Air Medal, Bronze Star and Army Commendation Medal.

His most memorable experiences: the people he met while in service and getting in touch with a lot of them in later years, such as Col. William Daris, his platoon leader, 1950-51 and a dear friend, Charles B. Tiller, squad leader.

He is married to Geraldine Winstead and they have four children: Emerson Jr., Donna Sue, Gwendolyn and Robert Wayne and ten grandchildren. He went to college after retiring and received a degree in Business Administration. Worked until 1994 building homes and apartments. He is now retired.

HURDIS EARL WISE, born on Easter Sunday, April 12, 1925, was raised in the country, with its farm life in Northwest Florida, north of Pensacola. His dad died when he was six years old. He joined the Army at 18 years of age, June 1943. After 17 weeks of infantry training he was sent overseas and joined the 24th Inf. Div. in Goodenough Island in New Guinea. He fought as rifleman, scout and later platoon sergeant in New Guinea, all over the Philippines and was among the first troops in Japan.

He was discharged Dec. 20, 1945 and received two Purple Hearts, Service awards in New Guinea, Pacific area, Philippine Islands and Japan.

After the war he became a mechanical engineer for DuPont, Brooklie AFB; Alcoa Aluminum Company of America; University of Arkansas at Little Rock. Construction engineer in Suriname, South America. Construction manager for Alcoa in Perth, Australia and Pittsburgh, PA.

His memorable experiences include his early experience as a Boy Scout and Sea Scout. Infantry fighting for two years during WWII in New Guinea, Philippines and Occupation of Japan. He has recently written a book, *Think Man Think,* about WWII and hopes to live in peace.

He is married to Virginia Sue Wise and they have three children: Karen Sue Wise, Kathryn Lynn Ellickson, Douglas Barron Wise; four grandchildren: Emily and David Wescott, Terry and Luke Ellickson.

He is now retired and selling his recently published book, *Think Man Think.* It is a book about his experiences with the 24th Inf. Div. during WWII.

JAMES A. WITTKOWER, born in Dallas, TX,

Jan. 25, 1926. From May to September 1994, took infantry basic training, South Camp Hood, TX. Attended Infantry OCS, Fort Benning, GA. Graduated second lieutenant, Inf., Jan. 26, 1945. Joined Co. K, 34th Inf. Regt., 24th Div., April 9, 1945 on Mindoro. Wounded in action on Mindanao, May 15, 1945. Released from the 44th General Hospital, Leyte, July 26, 1945.

Assigned to HQ, AFWESPAC, AG Radio/Cable, Manila, Aug. 11, 1945. Released from active duty, Nov. 15, 1946 at Fort Sam Houston, TX and assigned to Officers' Reserve Corps. Completed 20 years active and reserve duty. Retired Major-AUS Jan. 25, 1986.

His decorations include the Bronze Star, Purple Heart, Combat Infantryman Badge, Asiatic-Pacific Campaign Medal and Philippine Liberation Medal.

He received an AA degree, North Texas Agricultural College, January 1944; BBA, accounting, Southern Methodist University May 1948; MBA, management, Michigan State University June 1968.

He married Jeannette Bridges June 28, 1952 and they have three grown daughters and four grandchildren. Retired August 1987 from E-Systems and Predecessor Companies after 39 years. He is currently a volunteer tutor in math and language arts at local schools and a volunteer tax preparer for IRS Vita Program.

HARRY L. WITTMAN JR., born Oct. 9, 1927, Grafton, WV. Graduated from Victory High School, Clarksburg, WV 1946. After graduation went to work for B&O Railroad. He was drafted into the Army October 1950, trained at Camp Atterbury, IN. Landed in Korea April 1951, and left February 1952. Assigned to Co. G, 21st Regt. In Korea awarded the Combat Infantry Badge, Bronze Star, Purple Heart, Korean Service Ribbon, four Battle Stars, UN Ribbon and Good Conduct Medal.

October 15 he was wounded in action pushing into Iron Triangle, Co. G, 21st Regt. and was awarded the Presidential Unit Citation.

He returned to the B&O Railroad and retired after 39 years. Married Frances February 1952 and they have been married 47 years. At present he is the Quartermaster for the 24th Div. Assoc. and works hard getting new members.

ANTHONY J. WOJTAS, born March 15, 1924, Batavia, NY. Enlisted in the Army, July 13, 1943 serving with 24th Branch II.

He reported for basic training Aug. 2, 1943, Camp

Fannin, TX and was shipped to New Guinea, Dec. 12, 1943. Shipped to Goodenough Island Jan. 4, 1944 and joined his outfit Co. M, 3rd Bn., Heavy Mortar 81 Heavy 21st Inf., Regt, 24th Div., March 15, 1944.

His first campaign was Dutch New Guinea, April 20, 1944, took Hollandia Airport; Oct. 17, 1944, Philippine Islands; Leyte, southeastern of Leyte and Panaon Island next move was to Breakneck Ridge to relieve the 34th Regt., Nov. 5, 1944. Then they were relieved by the 32nd Inf. Div., Dec. 8, 1944 when Japan lost Leyte they lost the war. They landed on Mindoro Dec. 30, 1944 in the northeast corner and secured the island. Mindanao April 17,1945. Landed on Bonin Island and the 24th Div. moved to take the island and it was secured by Aug. 15, 1945. Landed in Okayama, Japan, Oct. 15, 1945. December 25, 1945 he was shipped out to the US and was discharged Feb. 2, 1946 from Camp Atterbury, IN with the rank of staff sergeant. He received the Pacific Theater, Philippine Liberation and Victory Medal.

When he was discharged and returned home to Batavia, NY, he found it very hard to adjust to civilian life, as all of you know. His war experiences were always in his mind and he still can relive his life in that period. He wanted to go to college so under the GI Bill he started, but after several months he quit because of malaria and was in the veterans hospital in Batavia, NY for two months. Got a job and worked until the shop closed.

On May 6, 1950 he married Audrey Domser and they moved to Oneida, NY where he got a job with Oneida Silverware Co. In 1953 a little girl named Linda was born. In 1960 they opened a pizza shop which they named Pepi's Pizza and he found it was something he really enjoyed. In 1993 he started franchising his Pepi's Pizza with the help of his oldest grandson, Chip and they now have six shops. His son-in-law, Cyrus Noble, runs the original and his four children, Chip, Chad, Leanna and Craig, all help, so it is a family business. The pizza shop has been a source of great joy by creating a well-known quality pizza and meeting and gaining a wealth of friends. Audrey and their daughter, Linda, have been in business together for 25 years, running Pepi's Bridal Boutique in Oneida.

BOBBY LEE WOLFE, born April 2, 1930, enlisted in the Army July 24, 1948 and was sent to Fort Ord, CA. Assigned duty with 24th Inf. Div. as clerk typist May 1949. Volunteered assignment to Co. E, 21st Regt., 24th Inf. Div. July 1950. Discharged April 23, 1952.

His awards include the Bronze Star Medal for duty in Korea July 2 - Nov. 2, 1950.

Reenlisted into the Army 1955 and made it a career. Returned to Korea 1962, also assigned duty in Germany and Vietnam where he was awarded the Silver Star in 1968. Retired as sergeant major in 1972.

He received a MBA in Management, Eastern Michigan University; BS, Business Administration, Eastern Illinois University; private pilot's license. Returned to Korea in 1983 in the Revisit Korea Program and was treated royally.

He married Emma Lou Easton Wolfe and they had four children: Laura, Robert, Alan and David; four grandchildren: Robyn, Phillip, Brannon and Nathan Wolfe. Bobby died Aug. 17, 1997.

DONALD M. WONG joined the service on March 24, 1941, and served with H&S Co., 3rd Eng. He participated at Hollandia and Leyte. He was discharged

with the rank of technical sergeant. Dates served: March 24, 1941, to June 8, 1945.

RICHARD A. WOODLAND, born Jan. 26, 1929, was drafted into the Army Jan. 9, 1951. He received basic training Fort Knox, KY, Inf. January 1951-April 1951. Arrived Inchon June 1, 1951 and assigned to M Co. (machine gun), 3rd Bn., 19th Inf., 24th Div. Transferred to HQ Co., 3rd Bn., 19th Inf. August 1951, I&R Plt. March 1951, 19th Inf. transferred to Camp Haugen Japan. Returned to the states July 1952 and finished out at Camp Atterbury, IN. September 1951 made corporal. April 1952 promoted to sergeant. Separated from service October 1952. Honorably discharged October 1956.

He married Shirley Temple Sept. 6, 1957 and they have two children, Drenda L. and Richard Bradley. They also have six grandchildren: Ryan and Alex Lunka and Megan, Alicia, Andrew and Kendra Woodland.

His awards include the Combat Infantry Badge, Army of Occupation Medal, Japan, Korean Service Medal w/three Battle Stars, UN Service Medal and National Defense Service Medal.

He worked 33 years for Western Electric Co. installing telephone equipment for Bell Telephone System and also worked for Bell Labs, AT&T Technologies. Retired July 1985.

His memorable experiences include raising a family and coaching Little League baseball.

Presently he is not doing much of anything. Enjoying his grandchildren. They like to go fishing, to the zoo and science museum.

KEVIN M. WOODS, born March 17, 1961, San Jose CA. Entered the Army after graduating from Auburn University (ROTC Scholorship) in 1983. After commissioning attended the Transportation Officers Basic Course at Ft Eustis VA. After graduation attended Initial Entry Rotary Wing Training (Flight School) at Ft Rucker AL. Graduated from flight school as an Aeroscout in March 1985 and reported to the 4th Squadron, 2nd Armored Cavalry Regiment. Served as an Aeroscout Platoon and Support Platoon Leader from March 1985 until Feb 1988. Attended the Infantry Officers Advance Course, Airborne School and Pathfinder School from March of 1988 until Sep 1988. Reported to the 24th Infantry Division (Aviation Brigade) in Savannah GA in Sep 1988. Served in various positions on the Aviation Brigade and 1st Battalion, 24th Aviation Regiment (Attack) staff from Sep 1988 until Aug 1990. Deployed with the 24th Infantry Division HQ to Saudi Arabia as the Assistant Division Aviation Officer in Aug 1990. On 7 Dec 1990 took command of B Company, 1st Battalion, 24th Aviation Regiment (Attack) (AH-64) and served as the commander for the remainder of Desert Shield / Desert Storm and redeployment. Departed command and the 24th ID(M) in May 1992 and reported to the National Training Center, FT Irwin, CA as an Attack Helicopter Company Trainer. Next assignment in July 1994 was to the Pentagon as a Joint Chiefs of Staff Intern assigned to the J1 and J33 Directorates followed by a tour as the Chief of Special Operations Aviation Branch at PERSCOM. Reported to the Naval War College (College of Naval Command and Staff) in July 1996 and graduated with honors in July 1997. Reported to Ft Bragg, NC in Aug 1997 to serve as the Executive Officer of the 3rd Battalion, 229th Aviation Regiment. Became the Operations officer (S3) of the 3rd Battalion, 229th Aviation Regiment in July 1998 and subsequently deployed with the battalion to Bosnia. Currently serving as the 3-229th Battalion S3 at Camp Comanche, Bosnia (SFOR).

His awards include the Bronze Star, Air Medal, MSM, ARCOM, AAM, Joint Commendation Medal, Joint Achievement Medal.

Woods is very active in church and scouting.

Commanding in combat (Persian Gulf) and bringing everyone home in one piece is his most memorable experience.

Married to the former Michelle Rene Collins and has three children Ian, Colin, and Emma.

He is currently serving on active duty (Major) with the 229th Aviation Regiment, XVIII Airborne Corps.

STANLEY M. WRIGHT, born Jan. 16, 1927 and was drafted into the Army Jan. 20, 1954. His assignments include: basic training, Fort Knox, KY; Tank, Ft, Knox; LVT, Camp Delmar, CA; 56th Amph. Tank Bn., Camp McGill, Japan; Co. C, 6th Tank Co., Camp Fuji, Japan; 6th Tank Korea, March-December 1955, served in communications. Discharged Dec. 22, 1955, Spec. 2.

He received his Marksman Medal.

Stanley has been a full-time farmer from January 1956-present. Dairy for 10 years; beef cattle and hogs, plus crops in partnership with son. Active in Morning Sun Presbyterian Church; Farm Bureau; County Historical Society; Friendship Force, traveling for home stays and hosting people from other countries.

His memorable experiences: on their Friendship Force exchange to Japan and Korea in 1987 he was privileged to again see Mt. Fuji Army Base and Panmunjum check point.

He married Helen Hall Wright April 1956 and have children: Diane (Michael Grycz), Anita (Tom Melton), John (Melissa); grandchildren: Claire, Bonnie, Seth Wright and Anna Grycz.

WILLIAM A. (BILL) WRIGHTSON, born Jan. 20, 1930, enlisted in the service Jan. 12, 1951, 19th Inf. Regt., 3rd Bn., Co. L and HQ Co.

His assignments include: Camp Roberts, CA, basic training; Korea: June 1951-January 1952, combat the "Iron Triangle" Bar Man in Co. L, I&R Section, Advancing to rank of sergeant and section leader. Camp Haugen, Japan, January 1952-June 1952. Brooklyn Army base: August 1952-January 1954; Honor escort of military deceased, promoted to SFC May 1953. Received commendation letter from commanding officer for superior service as an honor escort and an honorable discharge Jan. 12, 1954 as sergeant first class.

His awards include the Combat Infantry Badge, Korean Service w/three Bronze Service Stars, National Defense, United Nations, Army of Occupation (Japan) Medals.

After discharge in January 1954 he commenced his professional career in the business world. The major-

ity of his experience included 28 year in cost accounting and seven years in customer support. Included in his career is experience in aerospace and electronic industries, a hospital and telecommunications manufacturing at Rolm in Santa Clara from which he retired in March 1992.

Memorable experiences: in the service as an RA enlistee, he performed multiple assigned responsibilities and was rewarded for his dedication and skills eventually being promoted to SFC. In his professional career: In aerospace he was the administrative accountant assigned to the Titan 3C booster program in Sunnyvale, CA for United Technology Center. At Rolm, his contribution was to provide management with accurate, timely data in cost accounting and customer support.

Married April 1956 to Kathleen A. Moroney though divorced in April 1983 they remain friends and devoted parents to their son, Bill, his wife and their two children.

Current companion of 11 years is Penelope Spangler. They also have grandchildren: Lindsay and Michael.

Currently employed as an accounting assistant part-time for Ceitronic, an electronic contracting corporation in San Jose, CA. He is enjoying his work and contribution to the "team effort" in finance and working with project managers and a variety of customers they service. Attended Los Altos United Methodist Church serving as an usher.

PAUL WURZER joined the service on June 6, 1948, and served with Btry. A, 13th FA BN. He was discharged with the rank of corporal. Dates served: July 1950 to May 1951.

JACK G. YOUNG joined the service on July 8, 1944, and served with Co. I, 34th Regt. He participated in the Zig Zag Pass, Corregidor, Mindanao and the Philippines. He was discharged with the rank of technical sergeant.

CARL D. YOUNGBLOOD joined the USN in August 1944; and the US Army in June 1949. He served with H&S Co., 6th Tk. Bn. from October 1953 until March 1955; and HQ Co., 24th Inf. Div., from November 1956 until October 1957. He was stationed in Japan and Korea. He was discharged with the rank of sergeant first class.

RAYMOND YOUNGBLOOD, born May 10, 1915. enlisted April 5, 1941. He was assigned to the 21st Inf. Regt. at Schofield Barracks for two years, four months in Hawaii. Also served in Australia, Philippines, New Guinea and Good Enough Islands.

Awards include the Combat Infantry Badge, Bronze Star, Good Conduct Medal and the Pacific Combat Medal. He was discharged Aug. 31, 1945 at Fort Levenworth, KS.

He has been a sheet rock finisher and taper since his discharge. He currently lives in Kansas City, KS.

CARTER E. YOST, born Jan. 1, 1922, drafted into the Army Sept. 16, 1942.

Assignments include: Camp Butner, NC, basic training. HQ and Service Co., 339th Engr. Bn. Shipped out April 14, 1943, returned Nov. 26, 1945. Served two years, seven months and 28 days.

Discharged Dec. 23, 1945 as sergeant T4. His awards include the Asiatic-Pacific Theater Ribbon w/three Bronze Stars, Philippine Ribbon w/two Bronze Stars, Good Conduct Ribbon, Meritorious Unit Award, Bronze Arrowhead and the Victory Medal.

He is married to June and they have children: Terry Yost, Sierra Secaur, Ron Anderson, Bruce Anderson and Millie Reed. He is a retired farmer.

ROBERT S. ZARGER, born Oct. 23, 1923, enlisted in the service March 5, 1953. His assignments include: New Guinea, Southern Philippines (Leyte), Mindoro, Romblon and Mindanao.

Discharged Feb. 12, 1946 as sergeant. His awards include the Good Conduct Medal, Philippines Liberation Ribbon, American Theatre Service Medal, Asiatic-Pacific Theater Service Medal w/2 Bronze Stars, one Arrowhead and the Victory Medal.

Married Joanne Applegate Oct. 4, 1952. Graduated from the University of Pennsylvania June 1948. Spent 11 years personnel field, 17 years as insurance agent. His severe hearing loss in both ears put him in disability retirement 1976.

He married Joanne and they have children Lee Anne, Amy Emily and six grandchildren: Alyssa, Amanda, Trista, Jessica, Tara, Melanie. He is now a retired investor.

JOSEPH G. ZEKAS, drafted into the Army, June 1945, in Wilkes-Barre, PA. Spent 12 weeks of medical basic training at Camp Crowder, MO and 12 weeks of surgical tech courses at Fitzsimmons Army Hospital in Denver, CO. Spent one year at Beaumont Army Hospital, El Paso, TX. Discharged December 1946. Reenlisted January 1949, attended Quartermaster School at Fort Lee, VA.

Sent to Japan and assigned to the 24th Medical Bn., 24th Inf. Div. at Kitakyushu, Kyushu. Left Japan July 2, 1950 aboard ship for Pusan, Korean. Was in the battle for Taejon, Masan, Pusan Perimeter and the race for the 38th Parallel. Went up the west coast to within 35 miles of the Yalu River. Received a promotion to sergeant (E5). As admission clerk, recorded Gen. Walker's death by jeep accident.

Returned to Japan on April 21, 1951, to be processed for the first rotation back to the US. Assigned to Fort Meade, MD to train medical recruits.

He received a Purple Heart, Bronze Star, Combat Medical Badge, Occupation Medal, (Japan), Korean Service Medal, four Combat Stars and Distinguished Unit Emblem and one Overseas Service Bar.

Returned home to Fernbrook, PA, married Dolores Ruk and they have three daughters, two sons and six grandchildren. Retired from Lockheed Electronics Co. after 33-1/2 years.

Life member of the Korean War Veterans Assoc. and DAV and member of the American Legion and 24th Inf. Div. Assoc.

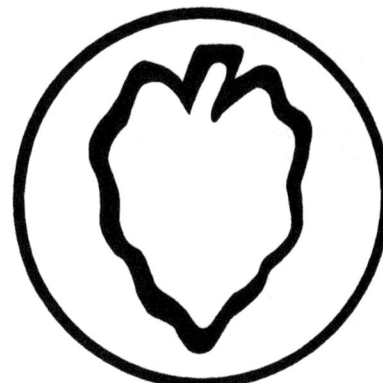

INDEX

Editor's Note: This index contains only the names and places listed in the history and special stories. It does not include the biography section since those names listed already appear in alphabetical order.

24TH DIVISION CASUALTIES

CAMPAIGN	KIA	WIA	TOTAL
World War II			
Pearl Harbor	3	8	11
Hollandia	76	528	604
Biak	19	83	102
Leyte*	558	1,784	2,342
Mindoro	18	81	99
Luzon			
ZigZag Pass	66	268	334
Corregidor	38	153	191
Nasugbu			
Visayas			
Verde	0	6	6
Lubang	10	20	30
Simara	10	20	30
Romblon	15	35	50
Mindanao**	540	1,885	2,425
Total World War II	**1,353**	**4,871**	**6,224**
Korea***	3,735	8,154	11,889
Korea (POWs)	496 (Died)		496
Total Korea	**4,231**	**8,154**	**12,385**

Sources:
*M. Hamlin Cannon, Leyte: The Return to the Philippines
**Robert Ross Smith, Triumph in the Philippines
***Michael Clodfelter, A Statistical History of the Korean War

24th Medical
Battalion

24th Aviation
Company

3rd Engineer
(Combat) Battalion

24th Reconnaisance
Company

24TH INFANTRY DIVISION

5th RCT

19th Infantry
Regiment

"Duty"
21st Infantry
Regiment

"Toujours In Evant"
34th Infantry
Regiment

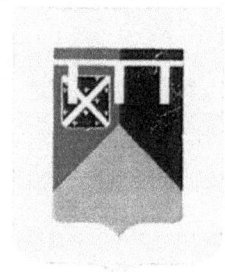

Sixth Tank Battalion

VALOR AWARDS

Medal
of Honor

Distinguished
Service Cross

Silver Star

Bronze Star

Presidential Unit
Citation

Republic of Korea
Présidential Unit Citation

Philippine
Liberation Ribbon

United Nations
(Korea)